The Europa Directory of
LITERARY AWARDS AND PRIZES

The Europa Directory of
LITERARY AWARDS AND PRIZES

FIRST EDITION

Europa Publications
Taylor & Francis Group

LONDON AND NEW YORK

First Edition 2002

© **Europa Publications Limited 2002**
11 New Fetter Lane, London EC4P 4EE, United Kingdom
(A member of the Taylor & Francis Group)

ISBN 1 85743 146 4

Development Editor: Cathy Hartley
Editor: Susan Leckey
Proof-reader: Jane Carroll

Typeset by Bibliocraft Ltd, Dundee
Printed and bound by TJ International Ltd, Trecerus Industrial Estate, Padstow, Cornwall

FOREWORD

This is the first edition of *The Europa Directory of Literary Awards and Prizes*, a unique compilation of information on literary awards from around the world. It brings together for the first time a comparable listing of more than 1,000 awards from some 70 countries.

The awards included range from official state prizes to popular awards where the winners are selected by vote among ordinary readers. While the listing includes some very well-known and long-established prizes, many of the awards included are newly established, and some are so new that they have not yet made their inaugural award. The directory aims to include awards which are international in scope or which are of major importance to writers and publishers in the awarding country. For the purposes of inclusion in the directory, no lower limit has been set on the prize money awarded, as there are awards with little financial recompense that are of great significance to prize-winners in terms of prestige and future book sales.

Not all kinds of literary award have been included; the main exclusions are small local prizes or awards where the eligibility is severely restricted; awards which are very specialized or academic by nature; and awards which are mainly for journalism (although there are some major literary awards, such as the Pulitzer Prizes, which include categories for journalism, and these are included). One-off prizes are also not listed. The directory does not include bursaries or scholarships at academic establishments.

Information for each award includes, where available, details of the sponsoring organization, the history of the award, eligibility, how to apply, and a listing of recent winners.

It should be noted that the information included for the prizes is intended as a guide-line; details of full rules for entry and entry fees to the awards, for example, and of precise deadlines (many of which change each year) should be checked directly with the relevant sponsoring organizations, for which contact details are supplied. The value of cash prizes may also change from year to year, and this book provides the latest information available at the time of compilation. In European countries belonging to the eurozone, the value of cash prizes is stated in the new currency wherever possible, although many organizations continue to express the value of prizes in the traditional currency; an approximate conversion to the euro value is included where possible.

Within the main body of the directory awards are listed alphabetically by name, but each entry is indexed, enabling the reader to find particular entries by country, by sponsoring organization, or by subject (fiction, non-fiction, children's literature, illustration, history, biography, etc.).

In terms of research methodology, the directory has been compiled using a comprehensive programme of desk research. As a starting point over 1,000 organizations were mailed in order to collect as much material as possible direct from the sponsoring bodies; in addition numerous specialist associations in different countries were contacted for advice on the leading awards in each country; subsequently, extensive research was carried out in order to fill any gaps and supplement the initial information.

Every care has been taken in the compilation of this volume, but it is possible that there may be some errors or omissions, for which Europa Publications may not be held responsible. Comments, and suggestions of additional prizes for inclusion are welcomed, in order that future editions of *The Europa Directory of Literary Awards and Prizes* may be able to build on the success of this first edition.

October 2002

ACKNOWLEDGEMENTS

The editors wish to thank all those organizations and individuals who responded to our requests for information. We are grateful for the interest the project has generated in individuals and sponsoring organizations.

The publishers also gratefully acknowledge Susan Leckey for her hard work and perseverance in making sure that *The Europa Directory of Literary Awards and Prizes* is as accurate and up-to-date as possible, and for her interest and enthusiasm at all stages of the development of the project.

CONTENTS

Abbreviations	ix	Israel	443
Currencies and		Italy	443
Exchange Rates	xi	Japan	444
		Jordan	445
Literary Awards and Prizes	1	Kazakhstan	445
		Korea (Republic)	445
Index of Awards	385	Malaysia	445
Index of Awarding		Malta	445
Organizations	417	Mexico	445
Index of Awards by Country	431	Monaco	446
Australia	431	Mongolia	446
Austria	432	Myanmar	446
Argentina	432	Nepal	446
Belgium	433	Netherlands	447
Brazil	433	New Zealand	447
Bulgaria	434	Nigeria	448
Burkina Faso	434	Norway	448
Canada	434	Pakistan	449
Chile	436	Philippines	449
China (People's Republic)	436	Poland	449
Colombia	436	Portugal	450
Costa Rica	436	Romania	450
Cuba	436	Russia	450
Czech Republic	436	Saudi Arabia	450
Denmark	437	Singapore	450
Dominican Republic	437	Slovakia	450
Egypt	437	Slovenia	451
Estonia	437	South Africa	451
Finland	437	Spain	451
France	438	Sri Lanka	452
Germany	440	Sweden	452
Ghana	442	Switzerland	453
Greece	442	Thailand	453
Haiti	442	Turkey	453
Hungary	442	United Arab Emirates	453
Iceland	442	Ukraine	453
India	442	United Kingdom	454
Indonesia	443	United States of America	459
Iran	443	Uruguay	465
Ireland	443	Venezuela	466

CONTENTS

Zimbabwe	466	History	490
Index of Awards by Subject	467	Illustration	493
Adult Fiction	467	Lifetime Achievement	495
Biography	480	Non-fiction	499
Children's Literature	482	Poetry	508
Drama	487	Translation	516

ABBREVIATIONS

AB	Alberta	Dir	Director
AD	Anno Domini	DN	Distrito Nacional
ACT	Australian Capital Territory	Dr	Doctor
		Dr.	Drive
Admin	Administration	E	East(ern)
Admin.	Administrator, Administrative	Ed.	Editor
		Edif.	Edificio (Building)
AG	Aktiengesellschaft (Joint Stock Company)	edn	edition
		e.g.	exempli gratia (for example)
AIDS	acquired immunodeficiency syndrome	esq.	esquina (corner)
AK	Alaska	etc.	et cetera
AL	Alabama	e.V.	eingetragener Verein
Apdo	Apartado (Post Box)	Exec.	Executive
approx.	approximately	fax	facsimile
Apt	Apartment	FL	Florida
AR	Arkansas	GA	Georgia
Asscn	Association	Gdn(s)	Garden(s)
Assoc.	Associate	Gen.	General
Asst	Assistant	GmbH	Gesellschaft mit beschränkter Haftung
Avda	Avenida (Avenue)		
Ave	Avenue	GPO	General Post Office
AZ	Arizona	HI	Hawaii
BBC	British Broadcasting Corporation	HIV	human immunodeficiency virus
BC	British Columbia	HM	His (or Her) Majesty
Bldg	Building	Hon.	Honorary; Honourable
Blvd	Boulevard	HRH	His (or Her) Royal Highness
BP	Boîte postale (Post Box)	Hwy	Highway
bul.	bulvar (boulevard)	IA	Iowa
c.	circa	ID	Idaho
CA	California	i.e.	id est (that is to say)
CEO	Chief Executive Officer	IL	Illinois
Chair.	Chairman, Chairwoman	IN	Indiana
c/o	care of	Inc	Incorporated
Co.	Company; County	Izq.	Izquierda (left, Spanish)
CO	Colorado	Jr	Junior
Col.	Colonia, Colima	km	kilometre(s)
Commr	Commissioner	KS	Kansas
Corpn	Corporation	KY	Kentucky
CP	Case Postale; Caixa Postal; Casella Postale (Post Box)	LA	Louisiana
		Ltd	Limited
Cres.	Crescent	m.	million
Ct	Court	M.	Monsieur
CT	Connecticut	MA	Massachusetts
Cttee	Committee	Man.	Manager; Managing
DC	District of Columbia; Distrito Central	MB	Manitoba
		MD	Maryland
DE	Delaware	ME	Maine
Dept	Department	mem.	member
devt	development	MI	Michigan

ABBREVIATIONS

MN	Minnesota	retd	retired
MO	Missouri	Rm	Room
MS	Mississippi	RI	Rhode Island
Mt	Mount	S	South(ern)
MT	Montana	SA	Société Anonyme, Sociedad
N	North(ern)		Anónima (Limited
NB	New Brunswick		Company); South Australia
NC	North Carolina	SC	South Carolina
ND	North Dakota	SD	South Dakota
NE	Nebraska; North-east(ern)	SE	South-east(ern)
NF	Newfoundland	Sec.	Secretary
NH	New Hampshire	Sec.-Gen.	Secretary-General
NJ	New Jersey	SK	Saskatchewan
NM	New Mexico	SL	Sociedad Limitada
no(.)	Numero; number	Sq.	Square
nr	near	Sr	Senior
NS	Nova Scotia	St	Street; Saint
NSW	New South Wales	Sta	Santa
NT	Northwest Territories;	Ste	Sainte
	Northern Territory	Str.	Strasse (street, German)
NU	Nunavut Territory	SW	South-west(ern)
NV	Nevada; Naamloze	TN	Tennessee
	Vennootschap	trans.	translated; translation;
NW	North-west(ern)		translator
NY	New York	Treas.	Treasurer
Of.	Oficina (Office, Spanish)	TV	television
OH	Ohio	TX	Texas
OK	Oklahoma	u.	utca (street, Hungarian)
ON	Ontario	UK	United Kingdom
OR	Oregon	ul.	ulitsa (street, Polish,
p.	page		Russian)
PA	Pennsylvania	UN	United Nations
PE	Prince Edward Island	UNESCO	United Nations
PEN	Poets, Playwrights,		Educational, Scientific and
	Essayists, Editors and		Cultural Organization
	Novelists (Club)	UNICEF	United Nations Children's
per.	pereulok (lane, alley,		Fund
	Russian)	Urb.	Urbanización (urban
Pkwy	Parkway		district)
Pl.	Place	US(A)	United States (of America)
PLC	Public Limited Company	USSR	Union of Soviet Socialist
PMB	Private Mail Bag		Republics
POB	Post Office Box	UT	Utah
PO Box	Post Office Box	VA	Virginia
PR(O)	Public Relations (Officer)	Vic	Victoria
Pres.	President	VT	Vermont
Prof.	Professor	vul. (vulitsa)	Street (Ukrainian)
Pty	Proprietary	W	West(ern)
Publ.(s)	Publication(s)	WA	Western Australia;
QC	Québec		Washington (state)
Qld	Queensland	WI	Wisconsin
qv	quod vide (to which refer)	WV	West Virginia
Rd	Road	WY	Wyoming
Rep.	Republic	YT	Yukon Territory

CURRENCIES AND EXCHANGE RATES

(as at 31 May 2002, unless otherwise stated)

Country	Currency	£ sterling 1,000 = £	US $ 1,000 = $	€ 1,000 = €
Argentina	new peso	192.057095	281.690141	300.085374
Australia	$A	386.854844	567.400000	604.452967
Austria	euro (previously Schilling – Sch)	640.008182	938.700000	1,000.000000
Belgium	euro (previously Belgian franc)	640.008182	938.700000	1,000.000000
Brazil	real	270.342064	396.510706	422.404076
Bulgaria	lev	327.230987	479.949689	511.291881
Burkina Faso	CFA franc	0.975686	1.431039	1.524490
Canada	C $	446.352004	654.664484	697.416091
Chile	peso	1.041811	1.528024	1.627809
China, People's Republic	yuan	82.378141	120.824020	128.714200
Colombia	peso	0.293734	0.430819	0.458953
Costa Rica	colón	1.912329	2.804813	2.987976
Cuba	peso	681.802686	1,000.000000	1,065.303079
Czech Republic	koruna	21.035502	30.852771	32.867551
Denmark	krone (DKK)	86.111205	126.299304	134.547037
Dominican Republic	peso	38.173774	55.989474	59.645759
Egypt	Egyptian pound (LE)	151.511708	222.222222	236.734017
Estonia	kroon (EEK)	40.860763	59.930481	63.844126
Finland	euro (previously Markka)	640.008182	938.700000	1,000.000000
France	euro (previously French franc)	640.008182	938.700000	1,000.000000
Germany	euro (previously Deutsche Mark – DM)	640.008182	938.700000	1,000.000000
Ghana	new cedi	0.087118	0.127776	0.136120
Greece	euro (previously Drachma)	640.008182	938.700000	1,000.000000
Haiti	gourde	25.279947	37.078098	39.499412
Hungary	forint (FT)	2.627776	3.854159	4.105847
Iceland	króna (IKR)	7.483291	10.975744	11.692493
India	Indian rupee (R)	13.905827	20.395676	21.727577
Indonesia	rupiah (Rp)	0.077610	0.113830	0.121264
Iran	rial	0.086032	0.126183	0.134423
Ireland	euro (previously Irish pound – IR£)	640.008182	938.700000	1,000.000000
Israel	new shekel	138.690538	203.417413	216.701196
Italy	euro (previously Italian lira)	640.008182	938.700000	1,000.000000
Japan	yen	5.480729	8.038585	8.563530
Jordan	dinar (JD)	961.639896	1,410.437236	1,502.543129
Kazakhstan	tenge	4.459141	6.540222	6.967319

CURRENCIES AND EXCHANGE RATES

Country	Currency	£ sterling 1,000 = £	US $ 1,000 = $	€ 1,000 = €
Korea, Republic	won	0.555984	0.815461	0.868713
Malaysia	ringgit (RM)	179.421760	263.157895	280.342915
Malta	Maltese lira (Lm)	1,556.214631	2,282.500000	2,431.554277
Mexico	new peso	70.922118	104.021470	110.814392
Monaco	euro (previously French franc)	640.008182	938.700000	1,000.000000
Mongolia	tögrög (tugrik)	0.618135	0.906618	0.965823
Myanmar	kyat	102.335898	150.096061	159.897796
Nepal	Nepalese rupee	8.707569	12.771392	13.605403
Netherlands	euro (previously Guilder – DFL)	640.008182	938.700000	1,000.000000
New Zealand	$NZ	324.060817	475.300000	506.338553
Nigeria	naira (N)	5.862448	8.598452	9.159958
Norway	krone (NOK)	85.585866	125.528790	133.726206
Pakistan	Pakistani rupee	11.331894	16.620489	17.705859
Philippines	peso (P)	13.680378	20.065011	21.375318
Poland (28/3/02)	new zloty	170.036525	241.995983	277.391085
Portugal	euro (previously escudo)	640.008182	938.700000	1,000.000000
Romania	leu	0.020332	0.029821	0.031769
Russian Federation	new rouble	21.777893	31.941636	34.027523
Saudi Arabia	Saudi riyal (SR)	182.056792	267.022697	284.460101
Singapore	S $	381.855327	560.067208	596.641321
Slovakia (28/2/02)	koruna	14.596545	20.680385	23.905196
Slovenia	tolar (SIT)	2.829785	4.150445	4.421482
South Africa	rand (R)	69.632098	102.129398	108.798762
Spain	euro (previously peseta – pta)	640.008182	938.700000	1,000.000000
Sri Lanka	Sri Lanka rupee	7.087346	10.395010	11.073837
Sweden	krona (SEK)	69.200983	101.497082	108.125154
Switzerland	Swiss franc (SFr)	437.024990	640.984552	682.842817
Thailand	baht	16.089815	23.598931	25.140014
Turkey	Turkish lira	0.00047299	0.00069373	0.00073904
Ukraine	hryvnya	127.934754	187.641904	199.895498
United Arab Emirates	UAE dirham (AED)	185.650834	272.294078	290.075719
United Kingdom	pound sterling (£)	1,000.000000	1,466.700000	1,562.480026
United States of America	US dollar ($)	681.802686	1,000.000000	1,065.303079
Uruguay	peso uruguayo	41.146813	60.350030	64.291073
Venezuela	bolívar (B)	0.620526	0.910125	0.969559
Zimbabwe (30/4/02)	Z.$	12.472543	18.170000	20.170959

AAAS/Orbis Books Prize for Polish Studies

The prize, inaugurated in 1996, is awarded annually for the best book in any discipline, on any aspect of Polish affairs. The winner is selected by a committee, and receives a cash award.

Eligibility and Restrictions: Open to English-language books published outside Poland during the previous year. Textbooks, translations, bibliographies and reference works are not eligible. Preference is given to works by younger scholars.

How to Apply: Publishers, editors and authors should send copies of eligible works to each committee member by mid-May.

Recent Winners: 2001: Karin Friedrich, *The Other Prussia: Royal Prussia, Poland and Liberty 1569–1772* and Johannes Remy, *Higher Education and National Identity: Polish Student Activism in Russia 1832–1862* (joint winners); 2000: Grzegorz Ekiert and Jan Kubik, *Rebellious Civil Society: Popular Protest and Democratic Consolidation in Poland 1989–1993*; 1999: Daniel H. Cole, *Instituting Environmental Protection: From Red to Green in Poland*; 1998: Padraic Kenney, *Rebuilding Poland: Workers and Communists 1945–1950*; 1997: Kathleen M. Cioffi, *Alternative Theatre in Poland*.

Sponsoring Organization: American Association for the Advancement of Slavic Studies/Orbis Books Ltd.

Address: American Association for the Advancement of Slavic Studies, 8 Story St, Cambridge, MA 02138, USA. **Telephone:** (617) 495-0677. **Fax:** (617) 495-0680. **E-mail:** aaass@hcs.harvard.edu.

Kjeld Abell Prisen

The prize, named after Danish dramatist Kjeld Abell (1901–1961), was awarded for the first time in 1976, and is traditionally awarded every second or third year for a contribution within theatre or film. The members of the Danish Academy select the prizewinner by a simple majority. The prize stands at DKK 50,000.

Eligibility and Restrictions: Open only to Danish-language authors.

How to Apply: No direct applications are accepted.

Recent Winners: 2000: Peter Asmussen; 1997: Morti Vizki; 1995: Jens Kistrup; 1993: Lars von Trier and Niels Vørsel (joint winners).

Sponsoring Organization: Kjeld Abellfondet/Danish Academy.

Contact: Administrator Dr Allan Philip.

Address: Det Danske Akademi, Rungstedlund, Rungsted Strandvej 111, 2960 Rungsted Kyst, Denmark. **Telephone:** 33 13 11 12. **Fax:** 33 32 80 45. **Internet:** www.danskeakademi.dk. **E-mail:** lawoffice@philip.dk.

Academia Brasileira de Letras Children's Literature Prize

Established in 1998 by the Academia Brasileira de Letras (ABL), the prize is awarded every July for an outstanding contribution to children's literature. Three nominations are made by a committee of three ABL members, and the final winner is chosen by a vote among all ABL members. The winner receives 12,000 reais and a diploma.

Eligibility and Restrictions: Only open to Brazilian writers.

How to Apply: No applications are accepted.

Recent Winners: 2001: Ruth Rocha, *Odisséia*; 2000: Manoel de Barros, *Exercício de ser criança*; 1999: Maurício de Souza, *A turma da Mônica*.

Sponsoring Organization: Academia Brasileira de Letras.

Contact: Cultural Asst Leila Longo.

Address: Academia Brasileira de Letras, Av. Presidente Wilson 203, 20030–0221 Rio de Janeiro, RJ, Brazil. **Telephone:** (21) 2533-8800. **Fax:** (21) 2220-6095. **Internet:** www.academia.org.br. **E-mail:** llongo@academia.org.br.

Academia Brasileira de Letras Essay Prize

The Prize was established in 1998 when the ABL replaced its former programme of awards with a set of new ones to honour Brazilian writers whose work is distinguished by its originality and creative language. Three nominations are made by a committee of three ABL members, and the final winner is chosen by a vote among all ABL members. The winner receives 12,000 reais and a diploma.

Eligibility and Restrictions: Open only to Brazilian writers for work in the field of literary history and criticism.

How to Apply: No applications are accepted.

Recent Winners: 2001: Octavio Ianni, *Enigmas da modernidade – mundo*; 2000: Nelson Mello e Souza, *Modernidade: estratégia do abismo*; 1999: Cláudio Veiga, *Um brasilianista francês – Philéas Lebesgue*.

Sponsoring Organization: Academia Brasileira de Letras.

Contact: Cultural Asst Leila Longo.

Address: Academia Brasileira de Letras, Av. Presidente Wilson 203, 20030–0221 Rio de Janeiro, RJ, Brazil. **Telephone:** (21) 2533-8800. **Fax:** (21) 2220-6095. **Internet:** www.academia.org.br. **E-mail:** llongo@academia.org.br.

Academia Brasileira de Letras Fiction Prize

The Prize was established in 1998 when the ABL replaced its former programme of awards with a set of new ones to honour Brazilian writers whose work is distinguished by its originality and creative language. Three nominations are made by a committee of three ABL members, and the final winner is chosen by a vote among all ABL members. The winner receives 12,000 reais and a diploma.

Eligibility and Restrictions: Open to Brazilian writers only in the field of novel, drama or short stories.

How to Apply: No applications are accepted.

Recent Winners: 2001: Marcos Santarrita, *Mares do sul*; 2000: Clair de Mattos, *Masaico em branco e preto*; 1999: Sergio Faraco, *Dançar tango em Buenos Aires*.

Sponsoring Organization: Academia Brasileira de Letras.

Contact: Cultural Asst Leila Longo.

Address: Academia Brasileira de Letras, Av. Presidente Wilson 203, 20030–0221 Rio de Janeiro, RJ, Brazil. **Telephone:** (21) 2533-8800. **Fax:** (21) 2220-6095. **Internet:** www.academia.org.br. **E-mail:** llongo@academia.org.br.

Academy of American Poets Fellowship

Since 1946 the Academy of American Poets has regularly awarded Fellowships to American poets for distinguished poetic achievement. The Fellowship was the first award of its kind in the USA and remains one of the most distinguished. Fellows are elected each summer by majority vote of the Academy's Board of Chancellors. The Fellowship is awarded to one poet each year, each of whom receives a stipend of $35,000.

How to Apply: No applications are accepted.

Recent Winners: 2001: Ellen Bryant Voigt; 2000: Lyn Hejinian; 1999: Gwendolyn Brooks; 1998: Charles Simic; 1997: John Haines.

Sponsoring Organization: Academy of American Poets.

Address: Academy of American Poets, 588 Broadway, Suite 1208, New York, NY 10012, USA. **Telephone:** (212) 274-0343. **Fax:** (212) 274-9427. **Internet:** www.poets.org/academy. **E-mail:** academy@poets.org.

J. R. Ackerley Prize for Autobiography

An annual award for literary autobiography. The winner is chosen from a short-list drawn up by the Literary Executors of J. R. Ackerley, and receives a prize of £1,000.

Eligibility and Restrictions: Entries should be written in English and published in the year preceding the award.

How to Apply: Nominations are not accepted.

Recent Winners: 1999: Margaret Forster, *Precious Lives*; 1998: Kathryn Fitzherbert, *True to Both My Selves*; 1997: Tim Lott, *The Scent of Dried Roses*.

Sponsoring Organization: English Centre of International PEN.

Address: 7 Dilke St, London SW3 4JE, UK.

Adamji Prize

A long-established award for a novel, often described as Pakistan's most prestigious literary award.

Recent Winners: Former winners include Abdullah Hussein, *Udaas Nasal*; Shaukat Siddiqi, *Khuda ki Basti*; Zahir Raihan, *Hazar Bochor Dhore*; Mushtaq Ahmad Yousufi, *Khakum Badehn*; and Muhammad Khalid Akhtar, *Chakiwara mein Wisal*.

Sponsoring Organization: Pakistan Writers Guild.

Address: 11 Abok Road, Anarkali, Lahore, Pakistan.

Jane Addams Children's Book Award

An annual award established in 1953 and named after the first woman to win the Nobel Peace Prize. It is presented to a book that best combines literary merit with themes stressing peace, social justice, world community and the equality of the sexes and all races. The winner, chosen by a national committee of experts in the field of children's books, receives a hand-illuminated scroll.

Eligibility and Restrictions: Open to books for pre-school through to high school age, including translations or titles published in English in other countries.

How to Apply: Books may be submitted by the publishers or requested by the committee.

Recent Winners: Longer Book: 2001: Pam Muñoz Ryan, *Esperanza Rising*; 2000: Ruby Bridges, *Through My Eyes*; 1999: Virginia Euwer Wolff, *Bat 6*
Picture Book: 2001: Antonio Skármeta (author) and Alfonso Ruano (illustrator), *The Composition*; 2000: Alice McGill (author) and Chris K. Soentpiet (illlustrator), *Molly Bannaky*; 1999: Aliki, *Painted Words, Spoken Memories: Marianthe's Story*.

Sponsoring Organization: Jane Addams Peace Association/Women's International League for Peace and Freedom.
Address: 777 United Nations Plaza, 6th Floor, New York, NY 10017, USA.
Telephone: (212) 682-8830. **Fax:** (212) 286-8211. **Internet:** www.soemadison.wisc.edu/ccbc/public/jaddams.htm. **E-mail:** apa@igc.apc.org.

Adikarya Book Awards

A series of annual book awards presented by the Indonesian Book Publishers Association; categories include books for children and adolescents, as well as illustration and book design.

Recent Winners: Children's: 2001: Mansur Samin,*Ucok dan Si Pelor (Ucok and Si Pelor)*
Adolescents: 2001: S. Pd. Darsan, *Milenium Target*
Illustration for Children: 2001: Yoyok, *Istana Baru*
Illustration for Adolescents: 2001: Asma Nadia, *Dewa T-Rex.*

Sponsoring Organization: Ikatan Penerbit Indonesia (IKAPI—Indonesian Book Publishers Association).

Address: Ikatan Penerbit Indonesia (IKAPI), Jl. Kalipasir No. 32, Jakarta, Pusat 10330, Indonesia. **Telephone:** (21) 314 1907. **Fax:** (21) 314 6050. **Internet:** www.ikapi.or.id. **E-mail:** sekretariat@ikapi.or.id.

Aesop Prize

An annual award presented by the Children's Folklore Section of the American Folklore Society for English language books for children and young adults, both fiction and non-fiction.

Eligibility and Restrictions: Folklore should be central to the book's content. The reader's understanding of folklore should be enhanced by the book, which should reflect the high artistic standards of the best of children's literature and should have strong appeal to the child reader.

Recent Winners: 2000: Howard Schwartz (author) and Monique Passicot (illustrator), *The Day the Rabbi Disappeared: Jewish Holiday Tales of Magic*; 1999: Elie Wiesel (author) and Mark Podwal (illustrator), *King Solomon and His Magic Ring* and Howard Norman (author) and Tom Pohrt (illustrator), *Trickster and the Fainting Birds* (joint winners); 1998: Chief Lelooska, *Echoes of the Elders: The Stories and Paintings of Chief Lelooska.*

Sponsoring Organization: Children's Folklore Section of the American Folklore Society.

Address: American Folklore Society, 4350 North Fairfax Dr, Suite 640, Arlington, VA 22203, USA. **Internet:** http://afsnet.org.

Africa's 100 Best Books of the Twentieth Century

An ongoing project to select the 100 best African books of the 20th century. The project was founded by the celebrated author Ali Mazrui at the Zimbabwe International Book Fair (ZIBF) in 1998. The project aims to highlight the achievements of African writers and stimulate future writing, reading and publishing of African literature. For the first round 1,521 nominations were received, which were reduced to a shortlist, with the final winners selected by a 15-member jury. Twelve winners were selected in 2002, with the awards ceremony due to take place at ZIBF later in the year.

Eligibility and Restrictions: Only books written by Africans are eligible. ZIBF defines an African as "someone either born in Africa or who became a citizen of an African country". This includes African writers who live on other continents. Any non-African authors who have contributed to African writing and publishing will be assessed individually. Three categories are considered: children's writing, non-fiction/scholarship and creative writing, which further divides into short stories, novels, poetry and drama. Open to works in Afrikaans, Arabic, English, French, Kikuyu, Portuguese, Sesotho, Shona, Swahili, IsiXhosa, Yoruba and IsiZulu.

Recent Winners: 2002: Chinua Achebe, *Things Fall Apart*; Meshack Asare, *Sosu's Call*; Mariama Bâ, *Une si longue lettre (So Long a Letter)*; Mia Couto, *Terra Sonambula*; Tsitsi Dangarembga, *Nervous Conditions*; Cheikh Anta Diop, *Antériorité des Civilisations Nègres (The African Origins of Civilization: Myth or Reality)*; Assia Djebar, *L'Amour, La fantasia*; Naguib Mahfouz, *The Cairo Trilogy*; Thomas Mofolo, *Chaka*; Wole Soyinka, *Ake: The Years of Childhood*; Ngugi wa Thiongo, *A Grain of Wheat*; Léopold Sédar Senghor, *Oeuvre Poétique*.

Sponsoring Organization: Zimbabwe International Book Fair (ZIBF)/Kingdom Securities Holdings Ltd.

Address: Zimbabwe International Book Fair, PO Box CY 1179, Causeway, Harare, Zimbabwe. **Telephone:** (4) 702104/8. **Fax:** (4) 702129. **Internet:** www.zibf.org. **E-mail:** execdir@zibf.org.zw.

Aftonbladets litteraturpris

An annual prize established in 1957 by the newspaper *Aftonbladet* to encourage a Swedish writer who is still at an early stage of their creative development. The winner receives a prize of SEK 50,000.

Recent Winners: 2001: Lotta Lotass; 2000: Lars Jakobson; 1999: Malin Lindroth; 1998: Kristian Lundberg; 1997: Elisabeth Rynell.

Sponsoring Organization: Aftonbladet.

Address: Aftonbladet, Stockholm, Sweden. **Internet:** www.aftonbladet.se/.

Agatha Awards

A series of annual awards established in 1988 for the best publications in the field of mystery writing. Prizes are presented in five categories: novel, first mystery novel, non-fiction, short story and children's/young adult mystery novel. The winners are chosen by vote at the annual Malice Domestic international mystery convention, and receive an Agatha Award Teapot.

Eligibility and Restrictions: Entries must be written by a living author, and first published in the USA during the previous calendar year.

How to Apply: There is no application; works are nominated by fans and authors.

Recent Winners: Novel: 2000: Margaret Maron, *Storm Track*; 1999: Earlene Fowler, *Marine's Compass*; 1998: Laura Lippman, *Butcher's Hill*
First Novel: 2000: Rosemary Stevens, *Death on a Silver Tray*; 1999: Donna Andrews, *Murder, With Peacocks*; 1998: Sujat Massey, *The Salaryman's Wife*
Non-Fiction: 2000: Jim Huang (Editor), *100 Favorite Mysteries of the Century*; 1999: Daniel Stashower, *Teller of Tales: The Life of Arthur Conan Doyle*; 1998: Alzina Stone Dale, *Mystery Reader's Walking Guide to Washington DC*
Short Story: 2000: Jan Burke, *The Man in the Civil Suit*; 1999: Nancy Pickard, *Out of Africa*; 1998: Barbara D'Amato, *Of Course You Know that Chocolate is a Vegetable*.

Sponsoring Organization: Malice Domestic international mystery convention.
Address: Malice Domestic, POB 31137, Bethesda, MD 20824–1137, USA.
Internet: www.malicedomestic.org. **E-mail:** malice@erols.com.

AIP Science Writing Awards in Physics and Astronomy

Set up by the American Institute of Physics (AIP) to improve the general public's appreciation and understanding of physics and astronomy by recognizing effective science communication in print and broadcast media sources. The award takes the form of a $3,000 prize, an engraved Windsor chair and a certificate of recognition. Entries are judged by a committee of distinguished scientists and journalists.

Eligibility and Restrictions: Entries must have been published in English during the previous calendar year. Categories judged are journalists (books written by professional journalists or feature writers), scientists (books written by physicists, astronomers or members of the AIP), children's (books intended for children from pre-school age up to 15), and broadcast media (scripted radio and television programmes).

How to Apply: Authors should submit an entry form, along with nine original copies of their work, by the beginning of March.

Recent Winners: Recent winners include Tyson, Lin and Irion, *One Universe*; Cynthia Pratt Nicolson, *Exploring Space*; Marcia Bartusiak, *Einstein's Unfinished Symphony*; and Jon Palfreman, *What's Up With the Weather?*.

Sponsoring Organization: American Institute of Physics.

Contact: Co-ordinator Fiory Gonzalez.

Address: American Institute of Physics, 1 Physics Ellipse College Park, MD 20740, USA. **Telephone:** (301) 209-3090. **Fax:** (301) 209-0846. **Internet:** www.aip.org/aip/writing. **E-mail:** pubinfo@aip.org.

Akademieprys vir Vertaalde Werk (Academy Prize for Translated Work)

An annual award for translated literary works in the genres prose, poetry or drama. The prize is presented for a translation into Afrikaans of a literary work from any other language.

Recent Winners: 2002: Janie Oosthuysen, for her translation of J. K. Rowling's *Harry Potter* books.

Sponsoring Organization: Suid-Afrikaanse Akademie vir Wetenskap en Kuns (South African Academy for Science and Arts).

Address: Die Suid-Afrikaanse Akademie vir Wetenskap en Kuns (the South African Academy for Science and Arts), PO Box 538, Pretoria, 0001, South Africa. **Telephone:** (12) 328 5082. **Fax:** (12) 328 5091. **Internet:** www.akademie.co.za. **E-mail:** akademie@mweb.co.za.

Akademiets Oversætterpris (Translation Prize of the Danish Academy)

Established by the Uno-X Foundation in 1988, this prize is normally awarded every other year for a high-quality translation of literary works from foreign languages into Danish. The prize can be awarded for a single outstanding translation or for a contribution by a translator of a number of works. The winner, who is selected by members of the Danish Academy, receives a prize of DKK50,000.

Eligibility and Restrictions: Preference is given to women nominees.

How to Apply: No direct applications are accepted.

Recent Winners: 2000: Karsten Sand Iversen; 1997: Per Øhrgaard; 1995: Jørgen Sonne; 1993: Else Henneberg Pedersen.

Sponsoring Organization: Danish Academy.

Contact: Administrator Dr Allan Philip.

Address: Det Danske Akademi, Rungstedlund, Rungsted Strandvej 111, 2960 Rungsted Kyst, Denmark. **Telephone:** 33 13 11 12. **Fax:** 33 32 80 45. **Internet:** www.danskeakademi.dk. **E-mail:** lawoffice@philip.dk.

Akron Poetry Prize

The Akron Poetry Prize was founded in 1995, with the aim of bringing to the public writers who speak in original and compelling voices. The final selection is made by a nationally prominent poet; the winning poet receives $1,000 and publication of his or her book.

Eligibility and Restrictions: Open to all poets writing in English. Books accepted for the Akron Series in Poetry must exhibit three essential qualities: mastery of language, maturity of feeling, and complexity of thought.

How to Apply: Manuscripts should be submitted to the address given between 15 May and 30 June. An entry fee of $25 is required for each manuscript submission. Manuscripts must include a cover page (with author's name, address, phone number, and manuscript title), a title page (with no biographical information), and an acknowledgements page listing poems previously published in periodicals.

Recent Winners: 2001: George Bilgere, *The Good Kiss*; 2000: John Minczeski, *Circle Routes*; 1999: Dennis Hinrichsen, *Detail from the Garden of Earthly Delight*; 1998; Beckian Fritz Goldberg, *Never Be the Horse*; 1997: Jeanne E. Clark, *Ohio Blue Tips*.

Sponsoring Organization: University of Akron Press.

Contact: Poetry Editor Elton Glaser.

Address: The University of Akron Press, University of Akron, 374B Bierce Library, Akron, OH 44325–1703, USA. **Telephone:** (330) 972-6953. **Fax:** (330) 972-8364. **Internet:** www.uakron.edu/uapress. **E-mail:** uapress@uakron.edu.

Akutagawa Ryûnosuke Shô (Akutagawa Prize)

Japan's top literary award for young writers. Established in 1935 by Kikuchi Kan, the editor of *Bungei Shunjû* magazine, in memory of novelist Akutagawa Ryûnosuke. Awarded twice a year in January and July to the best literary short story published in a newspaper or magazine by a new author. The winner receives a pocket watch and a cash prize of 1 million yen; the award also attracts considerable media attention.

Recent Winners: 126th Akutagawa Prize (for works published in the second half of 2001): Nagashima Yû, *Môsupiido de haha wa (Mother at Hyperspeed)*; 125th Akutagawa Prizes: Gen'yû Sôkyû, *Chûin no hana (Flowers in Limbo)*; 124th Akutagawa Prize: Seirai Yûichi, *Seisui (Holy Water)*, and Horie Toshiyuki, *Kuma no shikiishi (The Bear and the Paving Stone)*; 1998: Keiichiro Hirano, *Nisshoku (Solar Eclipse)*.

Sponsoring Organization: Association for the Promotion of Japanese Literature (Nihon Bungaku Shinkô Kai).

Address: Association for the Promotion of Japanese Literature, Bungei-Shunju Bldg, 3 Kioi-cho, Chiyoda-ku, Tokyo, 102, Japan.

Al-Uweis Literary Award

Awarded by the Abu Dhabi Cultural Foundation for outstanding works of Arab poetry.

Recent Winners: 1997: Ibrahim Nasrallah.

Sponsoring Organization: Cultural Foundation.

Address: Cultural Foundation, Corner of Airport Road and Zayed First Street, Abu Dhabi, UAE. **E-mail:** info@ns1.cultural.org.ae.

Alberta Book Awards

The Alberta Book Awards recognize excellence in writing and publishing within the province of Alberta. The awards are presented annually in two sections: publishing awards by the Book Publishers Association of Alberta, and writing awards by the Writers Guild of Alberta; among the most prestigious is the Grant MacEwan Author's Award, which carries a prize of C$25,000.

Recent Winners: Alberta Children's Book of the Year: 2002: Teresa Toten, *The Game*

R. Ross Annett Award for Children's Literature: 2002: Katherine Holubitsky, *Last Summer in Agatha*

Henry Kreisel Award for Best First Book: 2002: Gloria Sawai, *A Song For Nettie Johnson*

Wilfred Eggleston Award for Non-Fiction: 2002: A.K. Hellum, *A Painter's Year in the Forests of Bhutan*

Howard O'Hagan Award for Short Fiction: 2002: Gloria Sawai, *A Song for Nettie Johnson*

Georges Bugnet Award for Novel: 2002: Thomas Wharton, *Salamander*

Gwen Pharis Ringwood Award for Drama: 2002: Chris Craddock, *Naked at School*

Stephan G. Stephansson Award for Poetry: 2002: Marilyn Dumont, *Green girl dreams mountains*

Jon Whyte Essay Competition: 2002: Caterina Edwards, *All that Remains*

Grant MacEwan Author's Award: 2002: Ken McGoogan, *Fatal Passage: The Untold Story of John Rae, the Arctic Adventurer Who Discovered the Fate of Franklin* and Aritha van Herk, *Mavericks: An Incorrigible History of Alberta* (joint winners).

Sponsoring Organization: Book Publishers Association of Alberta/Writers Guild of Alberta.

Contact: Heather Marshall.

Address: Writers Guild of Alberta, Percy Page Centre, 11759 Groat Rd, Edmonton, AB T5M 3K6, Canada. **Telephone:** (780) 422-8174. **Internet:** www.writersguild.ab.ca/eventframe.htm.

Aldeburgh Poetry Festival First Collection Prize

An annual prize established in 1989 by the Aldeburgh Poetry Trust in recognition of the year's best first collection of poetry. The prize carries both a cash award (£500, plus fee, currently £200, for reading at the Festival) and an automatic invitation to read at the subsequent year's Aldeburgh Poetry Festival. The winner is chosen by a small panel of judges – readers of contemporary poetry and professional poets.

Eligibility and Restrictions: Must be first full collection (minimum 40 pages) and published in UK or Eire within the previous year.

How to Apply: Submissions are accepted from publishers or individual poets. Three copies of the collection must be submitted to the Aldeburgh Poetry Trust at the address given, together with a note of publication date, by 30 September.

Recent Winners: 2001: Esther Morgan, *Beyond Calling Distance*; 2000: Colette Bryce, *The Heel of Bernadette*; 1999: Cliff Yates, *Henry's Clock*; 1998: Tamar Yoseloff, *Sweetheart*; 1997: Robin Robertson, *A Painted Field*.

Sponsoring Organization: Aldeburgh Poetry Trust.

Contact: Dir Naomi Jaffa.

Address: Aldeburgh Poetry Festival, Goldings, Goldings Lane, Leiston IP16 4EB, UK. **Telephone:** (1379) 668345. **Internet:** www.aldeburghpoetryfestival.org. **E-mail:** njaffa@aldeburghpoetryfestival.org.

Alex Awards

The Alex Awards have been awarded each year since 1998, to 10 adult books that will be enjoyed by young adults (aged 12 to 18). The titles are selected by the YALSA Adult Books for Young Adults Task Force. The Project is funded by the Margaret Alexander Edwards Trust.

Eligibility and Restrictions: Open to works of both fiction and non-fiction, from genres with special appeal to young adults. Entries must have been published in the previous calendar year.

Recent Winners: 2002 winners: Geraldine Brooks, *Year of Wonders: A Novel of the Plague*; William Doyle, *An American Insurrection: The Battle of Oxford, Mississippi*; David Anthony Durham, *Gabriel's Story*; Barbara Ehrenreich, *Nickel and Dimed: On (Not) Getting by in Boom-Time America*; Leif Enger, *Peace like a River*; Kobie Kruger, *The Wilderness Family: At Home with Africa's Wildlife*; Donna Morrissey, *Kit's Law*; Mel Odom, *The Rover*; Vineeta Vijayaraghavan, *Motherland*; Rebecca Walker, *Black, White, and Jewish: Autobiography of a Shifting Self*.

Sponsoring Organization: Young Adult Library Services Association (YALSA).

Address: YALSA, American Library Association, 50 East Huron, Chicago, IL 60611–2795, USA. **Telephone:** (800) 545-2433. **Fax:** (312) 944-7671. **Internet:** www.ala.org/yalsa/booklists/alex. **E-mail:** yalsa@ala.org.

Alexander Prize

The Alexander Prize is offered for a paper based on original historical research, and the winner is awarded £250 or a silver medal.

Eligibility and Restrictions: Candidates must either be under 35 years of age or be registered for a higher degree (or have been registered for such a degree within the last three years). The paper must not exceed 8,000 words and can relate to any historical subject.

How to Apply: Closing date for submissions is 1 November.

Sponsoring Organization: Royal Historical Society.

Contact: Exec. Sec. Joy McCarthy.

Address: Royal Historical Society, University College London, Gower St, London WC1E 6BT, UK. **Telephone:** (20) 7387 7532. **Fax:** (20) 7387 7532. **Internet:** www.rhs.ac.uk. **E-mail:** royalhistsoc@ucl.ac.uk.

Mast Tauq Ali Award

The Pakistan Academy of Letters administers a series of annual prizes established in 1980 under the Hijra National Literary Awards Scheme. The aim of the awards is to promote literary activities and recognize outstanding contributions. The Mast Tauq Ali Award is an annual prize of Rs 50,000 for works written in Balochi language.

Recent Winners: 2000: Manzoor Bismal, *Aaprang*; 1999: Saba Dashtiari, *Angreen Wahag*; 1998: Ghani Parwaz, *Mausum Unt Wadarani*.

Sponsoring Organization: Pakistan Academy of Letters.

Contact: Deputy Dir Naseem Mahmood.

Address: Pitras Bokhari Road, Sector H-8/1, Islamabad, Pakistan. **Telephone:** 9257164. **Fax:** 9257159. **E-mail:** academy@apollo.net.pk.

Amazon.com/Books in Canada First Novel Award

The Amazon.com/Books in Canada First Novel Award, established in 1977 by Books in Canada, is given annually to the best first novel in English published the previous year by a citizen or resident of Canada.

Recent Winners: 2001: Eva Stachniak, *Necessary Lies*; 2000: David Macfarlane, *Summer Gone* and Alan R. Wilson, *Before the Flood* (joint winners) ; 1999: André Alexis, *Childhood*; 1998: Margaret Gibson, *Opium Dreams*; 1997: Anne Michaels, *Fugitive Pieces*.

Address: Toronto, Canada.

Ambassador Book Awards

An annual award which recognizes books that have made 'an exceptional contribution to the interpretation of life and culture in the United States'. Books are judged in four categories: fiction; American studies; poetry; and biography. A committee of writers, editors and former publishers, chaired by J.D. McClatchy, selects the winning books, copies of which are sent to English Speaking Union (ESU) libraries around the world.

How to Apply: There is no application process.

Recent Winners: Fiction: 2000: Russell Banks, *Angel on the Roof*
American Studies: 2000: Nathaniel Philbrick, *In the Heart of the Sea: The Tragedy of the Whaleship Essex*
Biography: 2000: David Nasaw, *The Chief: The Life of William Randolph Hearst*
Poetry: 2000: Hass, Hollander, Kizer, Mackey, Perloff (Editors), *American Poetry: The 20th Century*.

Sponsoring Organization: English-Speaking Union of the United States (ESU).

Address: The English-Speaking Union, 144 East 39th Street, New York, NY 10016, USA. **Telephone:** (212) 818-1200. **Fax:** (212) 867-4177. **Internet:** www.english-speakingunion.org/programs.htm.

American Academy of Arts and Letters Annual Awards

A series of annual awards which honour writers of exceptional talent. Categories include the $5,000 Award of Merit Medal for a complete body of work; the $5,000 Morton Dauwen Zabel Award for writers of 'progressive and experimental tendencies'; the $5,000 Addison Metcalf Award for Literature, given to a young writer of great promise; the $5,000 Richard and Hinda Rosenthal Foundation Award, given to a young writer for a novel published during the previous year, which, though not a commercial success, is a considerable literary accomplishment; the $5,000 Harold D. Vursell Memorial Award, given to a writer for the quality of his or her prose; the $2,500 Sue Kaufman Prize for First Fiction, given for the best first novel or collection of short stories of the preceding year; and the $2,500 Witter Bynner Prize, given to an emerging poet.

How to Apply: The awards are given by members of the Academy; there is no application process.

Recent Winners: Morton Dauwen Zabel Award: 2001: Paul Violi; 2000: Edward Said
Addison Metcalf Award: 2001: Dave Eggers; 2000: Jhumpa Lahiri
Richard and Hinda Rosenthal Foundation Award: 2000: Mathew Stadler
Harold D. Vursell Memorial Award: 2000: Richard Powers, *Plowing the Dark*; 1998: Howard Bahr, *The Black Flower*; 1995: Dava Sobell, *Longitude*
Sue Kaufman Prize for First Fiction: 2000: Nathan Englander, *For the Relief of Unbearable Urges*; 1998: Charles Frazier, *Cold Mountain*
Witter Bynner Prize: 2000: Dana Levin; 1998: Elizabeth Spires
Award of Merit Medal: 1998: Thom Gunn.

Sponsoring Organization: American Academy of Arts and Letters.

Address: American Academy of Arts and Letters, 633 West 155th Street, New York, NY 10032, USA. **Telephone:** (212) 368-5900.

American Academy of Arts and Letters Gold Medal

A series of prestigious awards which rotate between literary and artistic disciplines. Each discipline is represented once every six years; categories include poetry, belles-lettres and criticism, history, drama, fiction, essays, music and architecture.

Recent Winners: Belles-lettres and Criticism: 1999: Harold I. Bloom
Poetry: 1985: Robert Penn Warren.

Sponsoring Organization: American Academy of Arts and Letters.

Address: 633 West 155 St, New York, NY 10032–5699, USA. **Telephone:** (212) 368-5900.

Hans Christian Andersen Awards

The awards were established in 1956 in memory of Hans Christian Andersen, and aim to honour a children's writer and illustrator for their life's work. The awards are presented biennially, and consist of a gold medal and a diploma. The nominees are selected by the National Sections of the International Board on Books for Young People (IBBY), and the final winners are chosen by an international jury of experts.

Eligibility and Restrictions: Two awards are made every two years, to a writer and an illustrator whose complete works have made a lasting contribution to children's literature. Awards are open to living candidates from any country.

How to Apply: Nominations are made by National Sections of IBBY.

Recent Winners: Writing: 2002: Aidan Chambers (UK); 2000: Ana Maria Machado (Brazil); 1998: Katherine Paterson (USA); 1996: Uri Orlev (Israel); 1994: Michio Mado (Japan)
Illustration: 2002: Quentin Blake (UK); 2000: Anthony Browne (UK); 1998: Tomi Ungerer (France); 1996: Klaus Ensikat (Germany); 1994: Jörg Müller (Switzerland).

Sponsoring Organization: International Board on Books for Young People (IBBY).

Contact: Exec. Dir Leena Maissen.

Address: Nonnenweg 12, Postfach, 4003 Basel, Switzerland. **Telephone:** (61) 272 29 17. **Fax:** (61) 272 27 57. **Internet:** www.ibby.org. **E-mail:** ibby@eye.ch.

H. C. Andersen Prize

An annual prize of €50,000, presented by the Danish Minister of Culture.

Recent Winners: 2002: Jackie Wullschlager, *The Life of a Storyteller*; 2001: Bodil Udsen; 1999 Kirsten Dreyer, *H.C. Andersens brevveksling med Lucie & B.S. Ingemann*; 1997: Tove Barfoed Møller; 1994: Bent Mejding and Susse Wold; 1993: Villy Sørensen; 1991: Flemming Hovmann.

Sponsoring Organization: Ministry of Culture/Media and Grants Secretariat.

Address: Ministry of Culture, Media and Grants Secretariat, Nybrogade 10, 1203 Copenhagen, K, Denmark. **Telephone:** 33 92 30 40. **Fax:** 33 14 64 28.

Aniara Priset (Aniara Prize)

An annual award for fiction written in Swedish, sponsored by the Swedish Library Association. The award was first presented in 1974.

Recent Winners: 2001: Agneta Pleijel; 2000: Jesper Svenbro; 1999: Birgitta Stenberg; 1998: Lennart Sjögren; 1997: Willy Kyrklund.

Sponsoring Organization: Svensk biblioteksförening (Swedish Library Association).

Address: Svensk biblioteksförening (Swedish Library Association), PO Box 3127, 103 62 Stockholm, Sweden. **Internet:** www.biblioteksforeningen.org/.

Anisfield-Wolf Book Awards

These annual awards were created by Edith Anisfield-Wolf, a poet and philanthropist from Cleveland, OH, to recognize books which address the issue of racism or promote appreciation of human diversity. The awards, which are endowed by a fund from the Cleveland Foundation, are presented in fiction and non-fiction categories, as well as a lifetime achievement award. Each winner receives $10,000.

Eligibility and Restrictions: Entries must be written in English and published during the preceding year. Plays and screenplays are excluded.

How to Apply: There are no application forms or fees. Entries should be sent to each member of the jury by 31 January; see website for details of jury.

Recent Winners: Fiction: 2002: Colson Whitehead, *John Henry Days*
Non-Fiction:2002: Quincy Jones, *Q: The Autobiography of Quincy Jones* and Vernon Jordan, *Vernon Can Read* (joint winners)
Lifetime Achievement Award: 2002: Jay Wright.

Sponsoring Organization: Cleveland Foundation.

Address: Cleveland Foundation, 1401 Euclid Ave, Suite 1400, Cleveland, OH 44115, USA. **Telephone:** (216) 861-3810. **Fax:** (216) 861-1729. **Internet:** www.clevelandfoundation.org. **E-mail:** asktcf@caclevefdn.org.

Anthony Awards

The Anthony Awards, named after Anthony Boucher, have been given annually since Bouchercon XVII (an international mystery convention) to recognize outstanding achievement in the field of mystery writing. The members of each Bouchercon convention make the nominations for the awards and also vote for their choice in each category (novel, first novel, paperback original, short story and criticism/biography).

Recent Winners: Best Novel: 2001: Val McDermid, *A Place of Execution*
Best First Mystery: 2001: Qu Xiaolong, *Death of a Red Heroine*
Best Paperback Original: 2001: Kate Grilley, *Death Dances to a Reggae Beat*
Best Short Story: 2001: Edward D. Hoch, *The Problem of the Potting Shed*
Best Anthology/Short Story Collection: 2001: Lawrence Block (Editor), *Master's Choice II*
Best Non-Fiction/Critical Work: 2001: Jim Huang (Editor), *100 Favorite Mysteries of the Century*.

Sponsoring Organization: Bouchercon—the World Mystery Convention.

Address: Bouchercon, POB 11700, Washington, DC 20008, USA. **Internet:** www.bouchercon2001.com/.

Anti-Booker Prize

Founded in opposition to the semi-official Russian Booker Prize (now the Booker/Open Russia Prize, qv). The prize money is around $12,501 – i.e. the amount of the Russian Booker Prize, plus one dollar. It is awarded to the most 'scandalous and unexpected' writers in all genres (prose, poetry, drama, criticism, non-fiction).

Recent Winners: 1998: Andrei Volos, *Khurramabad.*

Address: Anti-Booker Prize, Moscow, Russia.

Anugerah Persuratan (Bidang Esei Sastera)

The leading literary award for literary essays, awarded by the Singapore Malay Language Council.

Recent Winners: 1995: Masuri S.N.

Sponsoring Organization: Singapore Malay Language Council.

Address: Singapore Malay Language Council, Singapore, Singapore.

Arar Literary Award

The Arar award is given in recognition of a body of work. The general committee for literature awards the prize in memory of Suleiman Arar, a politician and an intellectual who served in several important positions. He was chairman of the board of director of the Jordan Press Foundation and editor-in-chief for *Al Rai* newspaper.

The committee of judges comprises distinguished scholars and experts.

Eligibility and Restrictions: Open to works by Jordanian and other Arab poets.

13

Recent Winners: 2001: Laila Abdul Majeed; 1991: Ibrahim Nasrallah.

Sponsoring Organization: Al Hussein Cultural Centre.

Address: Al Hussein Cultural Centre, Amman, Jordan.

Arts Council Bursaries and Commissions

The awards take two forms: Theatre Writing Bursaries are intended to provide experienced playwrights with an opportunity to research and develop their work for the theatre; the bursaries are of £5,500 each. Commission Awards allow theatre companies and groups to apply for grants of up to half the cost of paying a writer a commission or fee to write a new play.

Eligibility and Restrictions: For Theatre Writing Bursaries, applicants must be resident in England and have had two professional stage productions of their work within the past 10 years. Commission Awards are open to any theatre or group based in England. For both awards applications can only be made with regard to plays for the stage, not radio, screen, TV, opera, etc.

How to Apply: For Theatre Writing Bursaries, applicants should telephone the Theatre Writing Section on the number given to discuss the application. For Commission Awards an application form is available upon request.

Sponsoring Organization: Arts Council of England.

Contact: Asst Drama Officer Jemima Lee.

Address: Drama Dept, Arts Council of England, 14 Great Peter St, London SW1P 3NQ, UK. **Telephone:** (20) 7973 6431. **Fax:** (20) 7973 6983. **Internet:** www. artscouncil.org.uk. **E-mail:** info.drama@artscouncil.org.uk.

Arts Council of England Children's Award

The award was founded in 2000 by the Arts Council of England to celebrate the accomplishments of and raise the profile of playwrights who write for children. The award is given to a play in which the writing is of special quality, which stimulates the imagination, and demonstrates innovation in the use of language or form. The value of the award is £6,000.

Eligibility and Restrictions: Open to plays suitable for children up to the age of 12, lasting at least 45 minutes. The playwright must be resident in England. No writer who has previously won the award may reapply, and plays that have previously been submitted are excluded.

How to Apply: Applications are invited from writers or their representatives. Three copies of the script should be submitted, accompanied by an application form and biographical details, by early July.

Recent Winners: 2001: Brendan Murray, *Eliza's House*; 2000: Mike Kenny, *Stepping Stones*.

Sponsoring Organization: Arts Council of England.

Contact: Asst Drama Officer Jemima Lee.

Address: Drama Dept, Arts Council of England, 14 Great Peter St, London SW1P 3NQ, UK. **Telephone:** (20) 7973 6431. **Fax:** (20) 7973 6983. **Internet:** www. artscouncil.org.uk. **E-mail:** info.drama@artscouncil.org.uk.

Arts Council of England Writers' Awards

The Arts Council of England Writers' Awards are intended to enable 15 writers to finish a work in progress. Each winner receives a cheque for £7,000. Many well-known writers have been recipients of these awards in the past, including A.S. Byatt, Ted Hughes, Salman Rushdie and Carol Ann Duffy.

Eligibility and Restrictions: The Arts Council Writers' Awards are open to residents in England, who have had at least one book previously published, and who have embarked on a new work. Entries can be poetry, fiction (including short stories), autobiography, biography, literature for young people, drama, and other literary works.

How to Apply: Application forms are available from the address given; deadline is September.

Recent Winners: Poetry: 2000: Elizabeth Barrett, Bernadine Evaristo, Paul Farley, Adele Geras, Mick Imlah
Literature for Young People: 2000: Chris Firth
Biography: 2000: Jackie Wullschlager
Fiction: 2000: Francesca Clementis, Andrew Crumey, Jane Harris, Reuben Lane, Jim Poyser, Leone Ross, Henry Shukman, Atima Srivastava.

Sponsoring Organization: Arts Council of England.

Address: Arts Council of England, 14 Great Peter St, London SW1P 3NQ, UK.
Internet: www.artscouncil.org.uk. **E-mail:** info.literature@artscouncil.org.uk.

Arts Council of Wales Book of the Year Awards

An annual competition, established in 1992 to celebrate the best of Welsh writing in both Welsh and English. Two awards of £3,000 are made (one for works in English, one in Welsh), plus four runners-up prizes of £1,000. Winners are selected by two panels of judges.

Eligibility and Restrictions: All creative work by writers born in or living in Wales is eligible.

How to Apply: Three copies should be submitted to the address given.

Recent Winners: English language: 2001: Stephen Knight, *Mr Schnitzel*; 2000: Sheenagh Pugh, *Stonelight*; 1999: Mike Jenkins, *Wanting to Belong*; 1998: Sian James; 1997: Nigel Jenkins
Welsh language: 2001: Owen Martell, *Cadw dy Ffydd, Brawd*; 2000: Gwyneth Lewis, *Y Llofrudd Iaith*; 1999: R. M. Jones, *Ysbryd y Cwlwm: Delwedd y Genedl yn ein Llenyddiaeth*.

Sponsoring Organization: Arts Council of Wales.

Contact: Literature Officer.

Address: 9 Museum Place, Cardiff CF11 3NX, UK. **Telephone:** (2920) 376500.
Fax: (2920) 221447. **Internet:** www.ccc-acw.org.uk. **E-mail:** info@ccc-acw.org.uk.

Arvon Poetry Competition

Biennial poetry competition sponsored by the *Daily Telegraph*, for poems of any length written in English, not previously published or broadcast. There is a first prize of £5,000 with at least 15 other prizes.

Recent Winners: 1999: B. A. Humar, *Technical Assistance*; 1997: (no award given); 1995: Paul Farley, *Laws of Gravity*; 1993: Don Paterson, *Private Bottling*.

Sponsoring Organization: Daily Telegraph.
Address: 11 Westbourne Crescent, London W2 3DB, UK.

Aschehougprisen (Aschehoug Prize)

An annual prize sponsored by the publisher H. Aschehoug & Co. The prize was first awarded in 1973, and is worth NOK 100,000. Since 1998 a separate prize for a debut novel, the Aschehougs debutantpris, worth NOK 50,000, has also been presented.

Recent Winners: Aschehougprisen: 2001: Ole Robert Sunde; 2000: Laila Stien; 1999: Øyvind Berg; 1998: Gro Dahle; 1997: Jon Fosse
Aschehougs debutantpris: 2000: Eli Sol Vallersnes; 1999: Kurt Aust; 1998: Bjarte Breiteig; 2001: Carl Frode Tiller.

Sponsoring Organization: H. Aschehoug & Co.

Address: H. Aschehoug & Co, PB 363, Sentrum, 0102 Oslo, Norway. **Telephone:** (22) 400 400. **Internet:** www.aschehoug.no.

ASF Translation Prize

The ASF Translation Prize and the Leif and Inger Sjöberg Prize are the only prizes regularly awarded for English translation of Nordic literature. The ASF Translation Prize is an annual prize for the best translation of poetry, fiction or literary prose written by a Scandinavian author after 1800. The award includes a prize of $2,000, publication of an excerpt in an issue of *Scandinavian Review*, and a commemorative bronze medallion. The Leif and Inger Sjöberg Prize of $1,000 is also awarded each year alongside the main prize.

Eligibility and Restrictions: The prize is awarded for an outstanding English translation of poetry, fiction, drama or literary prose originally written in Danish, Finnish, Icelandic, Norwegian or Swedish. Prose entries must be at least 50 pages long; poetry entries should be at least 25 pages long; however these limits should not be exceeded by more than a few pages. Translations must be from the writing of one author, although not necessarily from a single work.

How to Apply: Send four copies of the translation, including a title page and a table of contents; this should be accompanied by one copy of the work(s) in the original language, a separate sheet containing details of the translator and the title and author of the manuscript with the original language specified, and a letter or other document signed by the author, the author's agent or the author's estate granting permission for the translation to be entered in the competition and published in *Scandinavian Review*. Deadline for submissions is 1 June.

Recent Winners: ASF Translation Prize: 2001: Philip Roughton, *Iceland's Bell* by Halldór Laxness; 2000: Lotta M. Löfgren, *Selected Poems by August Strindberg*; 1999: Pétur Knútsson, *Selected Poems by Árni Ibsen*; 1998: Thom Satterlee, *Selected Poems of Henrik Nordbrandt*; 1997: Rose-Marie Oster, *The Knifethrower's Woman, a poem by Kerstin Ekman*
Leif and Inger Sjöberg Prize: 2001: Patrick Phillips, *Selected Poems by Paul la Cour*; 2000: Jon Stewart, *Philosophical Texts by Johan Ludvig Heiberg*; 1999: Anastazia Little, *Selected Autobiographical Writings of Hans Christian Andersen*; 1998: Joel Tompkins, *Selected Short Stories by Per Olof Sundman*; 1997: Verne Moberg, *Aunt Blossom, a play by Kristina Lugn*.

Sponsoring Organization: American-Scandinavian Foundation.

Address: 58 Park Avenue, New York, NY 10016, USA. **Telephone:** (212) 879-9779. **Internet:** www.amscan.org. **E-mail:** info@amscan.org.

Asham Award for Women

The prize was established in 1996 to support and encourage new writing by women. It is named after Asham House in East Sussex where Virginia Woolf lived. The award is given every two years and carries a total prize of £3,000 (sponsored by Waterstone's); of this, £1,000 goes to the winning entry, with smaller prizes for up to 12 runners-up. The winning stories are also included in an anthology published by Serpent's Tail alongside specially commissioned stories by established women writers.

Eligibility and Restrictions: Open to women aged over 18, resident in the UK, who have not yet had a novel or collection of short stories published. The competition, which is for a short story (up to 4,000 words), is judged by the publisher (Serpent's Tail) and two leading novelists. The work must be in English, and must be previously unpublished.

How to Apply: Details available from the Administrator in October; deadline for entry is late January. An entry fee of £5 is payable.

Recent Winners: 2001: Frances Childs (plus 11 runners-up); 1999: Ann Jolly (plus 9 runners-up); 1996: Erica Wagner, Ann Jolly (plus 11 others).

Sponsoring Organization: Asham Literary Endowment Trust/Waterstone's.

Contact: Administrator Carole Buchan.

Address: The Asham Award, the Administrator, Asham Literary Endowment Trust c/o Lewes House, 32 High St, Lewes BN7 2LX, UK. **Telephone:** (1273) 484400. **Fax:** (1273) 484373. **E-mail:** arts@lewes.gov.uk.

Aspekte-Literatur-Preis

The Aspekte-Literatur-Preis is awarded for a first novel, or for the second or third book by a relatively unknown author. It is sponsored by the German national television station Zweites Deutsches Fernsehen (ZDF). A prizewinner is nominated on an annual basis and introduced on the ZDF programme, Aspekte. The prize has been awarded since 1979.

Recent Winners: 2000: Andreas Maier, *Wäldchestag*; 1999: Christoph Peters, *Stadt Land Fluss*; 1998: John von Düffel, *Vom Wasser*; 1997: Zoë Jenny, *Das Blütenstaubzimmer*; 1996: Felicitas Hoppe, *Picknick der Friseure*; 1995: Ingo Schulze, *33 Augenblicke des Glücks*.

Sponsoring Organization: Zweites Deutsches Fernsehen (ZDF).

Address: ZDF, Postfach 40 40, 55 100 Mainz, Germany. **Internet:** www.zdf.de/wissen/aspekte.

Associated Writing Programs (AWP) Award Series in Poetry, Fiction and Creative Non-fiction

A series of annual awards for poetry (established in 1975), fiction (established in 1978) and creative non-fiction (established in 1984). Winners in all genres receive a $2,000 cash honorarium from AWP, and their entries are published by a participating press, with subsequent royalties also going to the writers. Winners are chosen by a panel of judges and screeners who are published professionals in the relevant genre.

Eligibility and Restrictions: Open to authors writing in English regardless of their nationality or place of residence. Works of poetry are accepted up to 48 pages in length; fiction and non-fiction manuscripts should be between 150 and 300 pages. Creative non-fiction is defined as factual and literary writing that has the narrative, dramatic, meditative, and lyrical elements of novels, plays, poetry and memoirs. Poems and stories previously published in periodicals are eligible for inclusion in submissions, but manuscripts previously published in their entirety, including self-published, are excluded.

How to Apply: Detailed guidelines available on website; entries should be accompanied by a handling fee of $20, and must be postmarked between 1 January and 28 February.

Recent Winners: Poetry: 2001: Gray Jacobik, *Brave Disguises*; 2000: Joanie Macowski; 1999: Connie Voisine; 1998: Edward K. Mayes; 1997: Josie Rawson
Fiction: 2001: Christie Hodgen, *A Jeweler's Eye for Flaw*; 2000: Michelle Richmond; 1999: C. J. Rhibal; 1998: Bonnie Jo Campbell; 1997: Toni Graham
Non-fiction: 2001: Jill Christman, *Darkroom: An Autobiography*; 2000: Brian Lennon; 1999: Lia Purpura; 1998: Michael Martone; 1997: Peter Chilson.

Sponsoring Organization: Associated Writing Program.

Contact: Man. Supriya Bhatnagar.

Address: Associated Writing Program, Mail Stop 1E3, George Mason University, Fairfax, VA 22030, USA. **Telephone:** (703) 993-4308. **Fax:** (703) 993-4302. **Internet:** www.awpwriter.org. **E-mail:** awpchron@mason.gmu.edu.

Association of Nigerian Authors Literature Prizes

These prizes, first presented in 1983, are awarded in seven categories: two poetry awards (ANA Poetry Prize and ANA/Cadbury Prize); two prose awards (ANA Prose Prize and ANA/Spectrum Prize); ANA Drama Prize; ANA/Chevron Prize; and the prestigious Christopher Okigbo Prize (prize money of $1,000). The prize money ranges from 10,000 naira to 50,000 naira.

Recent Winners: 1999: Maik Nwosu, *Invisible Chapters* and Femi Ojo-Ade, *One Little Girl's Dreams* (joint winners); 1998: Ike Okonta,*The Expert Hunger of Rats*; 1997: Remi Raji, *A Harvest of Laughters*; 1996: Akinwumi Adesokan, *Roots in the Sky*
ANA/Cadbury Prize: 1997: Dr Ezenwa-Ohaeto, *The Voice of the Night Masquerade*; 1996: Obi Nwakanma, *The Roped Urn*
Christopher Okigbo Prize: 1997: Mobolaji Adenubi; 1996: Festus Iyayi, *Awaiting Court Martial*
Spectrum Prize: 2001: Akachi Adimora-Ezeigbo, *House of Symbols*.

Sponsoring Organization: Association of Nigerian Authors (ANA).

Address: Association of Nigerian Authors, ANA House, 26, Ladipo Labinjo Street, Off Bode Thomas Street, Surulere, Lagos, Nigeria.

Atlanta Review Poetry Competition

An annual competition run by *Atlanta Review*, a leading US literary journal. All entries are considered for publication in a special autumn issue. Prizes include Gold ($2,000), Silver ($500) and Bronze ($250) prizes, plus 50 International Merit awards.

Eligibility and Restrictions: Poems must not have appeared in a national print publication.

How to Apply: Entries should be submitted by 6 May, accompanied by a stamped, self-addressed envelope and entry fee of $5 for the first poem and $2 for each additional poem.

Sponsoring Organization: Atlanta Review.

Address: POB 8248, Atlanta, GA 31106, USA.

Atlantic History Prize

The Prize in Atlantic History was created in 1998 by a gift from James A. Rawley, Carl Adolph Happold Professor of History Emeritus at the University of Nebraska at Lincoln. It is offered annually to recognize outstanding historical writing in the field of integration of Atlantic worlds before the 20th century.

Recent Winners: 2001: Jorge Cañizares-Esguerra, *How to Write the History of the New World*; 2000: Karen Ordahl Kupperman, *Indians and English: Facing Off in Early America*; 1999: Jeremy Adelman, *Republic of Capital: Buenos Aires and the Legal Transformation of Atlantic World*.

Sponsoring Organization: American Historical Association.

Contact: Lynn Hunt.

Address: American Historical Asscn, 400 A St, SE, Washington, DC 20003-3889, USA. **Telephone:** (202) 544-2422. **Fax:** (202) 544-8307. **Internet:** www.theaha.org/prizes. **E-mail:** press@theaha.org.

Atlantic Poetry Prize

Established in 1997 by the Writers' Federation of Nova Scotia, the prize honours the best collection of poetry written by an Atlantic Canadian in the previous calendar year. The prize, of C$1,000, is awarded at the end of May each year, to a collection of poetry judged the best by a peer jury.

Eligibility and Restrictions: Entries must have been published in the previous calendar year, and written by an author who was born in and has spent a considerable proportion of their working life in Atlantic Canada (Nova Scotia, New Brunswick, PEI, Newfoundland), or a writer who has lived there for 24 months prior to the deadline.

How to Apply: Four copies of eligible titles should reach the Writers' Federation of Nova Scotia by the first Friday in December.

Recent Winners: 2001: Anne Simpson, *Light Fall*; 2000: Ken Babstock, *Mean*; 1999: John Steffler, *That Night We Were Ravenous*; 1998: Carmelita McGrath, *To the New World*.

Sponsoring Organization: Writers' Federation of Nova Scotia.

Contact: Exec. Dir Jane Buss.

Address: Writers' Federation of Nova Scotia, 1113 Marginal Rd, Halifax, NS B3H 4P7, Canada. **Telephone:** (902) 423-8116. **Fax:** (902) 422-0881. **Internet:** www.writers.ns.ca. **E-mail:** talk@writers.ns.ca.

József Attila Prize

This prize, named after a Hungarian poet, ranks among the leading Hungarian awards. It is presented annually by the Ministry of Culture and Education.

Recent Winners: 1991: Ottó Tolnai; 1985 and 1973: Otto Orbán; 1983: Árpád Göncz; 1982: Laszlo Bertok; former winners include Janos Marno and Stojan Vujicic.

Sponsoring Organization: Ministry of Culture and Education.

Address: Ministry of Culture and Education, Szalay ut 10/14, 1055 Budapest, Hungary.

Augustpriset (August Prize)

The Swedish Publishers' Association established the annual August Prize in 1989, originally launched as an award for the year's best book by a Swedish writer. Since its inception, it has grown to become the most prestigious Swedish literary award. In 1992, two additional categories were introduced. Awards are now made in three categories: fiction, non-fiction and children's and young adult books. The winners receive a prize of SEK 100,000 as well as a bronze statuette by Mikael Fare.

How to Apply: Any Swedish publishing house may nominate books for the award.

Recent Winners: Fiction: 2001: Torbjörn Flygt, *Underdog*; 2000: Mikael Niemi, *Populärmusik från Vittula*; 1999: Per Olov Enquist, *Livläkarens besök*; 1998: Göran Tunström, *Berömda män som varit i Sunne*; 1997: Majgull Axelsson, *Aprilhäxan*
Non-fiction: 2001: Hans Hammarskiöld, Anita Theorell and Per Wästberg, *Minnets stigar*; 2000: Dick Harrison, *Stora döden*; 1999: Jan Svartvik, *Engelska – öspråk, världsspråk, trendspråk*; 1998: Bengt Jangfeldt, *Svenska vägar till St Petersburg*; 1997: Sven-Eric Liedman, *I skuggan av framtiden*
Children's and Young People's: 2001: Sara Kadefors, *Sandor slash Ida*; 2000: Pija Lindenbaum, *Gittan och gråvargarna*; 1999: Stefan Casta, *Spelar död*; 1998: Henning Mankell, *Resan till världens ände*; 1997: Annika Thor, *Sanning eller konsekvens*.

Sponsoring Organization: Svenska Förläggareföreningen (Swedish Publishers' Association).

Address: Svenska Förläggareföreningen, Drottninggatan 97, 2 tr, 113 60 Stockholm, Sweden. **Telephone:** (8) 736 19 40. **Fax:** (8) 736 19 44. **Internet:** www.forlagskansli.se/Augustpriset/2001/index.html.

Aurealis Awards

The Aurealis Awards for Excellence in Australian Speculative Fiction were established in 1995 by the publishers of Aurealis magazine to recognize the achievements of Australian science fiction, fantasy and horror writers. A separate prize is awarded for children's fiction (aged 8–12 years).

Eligibility and Restrictions: To be eligible, works must have been written by an Australian and first published in the relevant calendar year.

Recent Winners: Best Science Fiction Novel: 2002: Sean Williams and Shane Dix, *The Dark Imbalance*
Best Science Fiction Short Story: 2002: Adam Browne, *The Weatherboard Spaceship*
Best Fantasy Novel: 2002: Sara Douglass, *The Wounded Hawk*
Best Fantasy Short Story: 2002: Sue Isle, *The Woman of Endor*
Best Horror Novel: 2002: Kim Wilkins, *Angel of Ruin*
Best Horror Short Story: 2002: Simon Haynes, *Sleight of Hand*
Best Young Adult Novel: 2002: Louise Katz, *The Other Face of Janus*

Best Young Adult Short Story: 2002: Isobelle Carmody and Steven Wollman (illustrator), *Dreamwalker*
Best Children's Long Fiction: 2002: Sally Odgers, *Candle Iron*
Best Children's Short Fiction: 2002: Jackie French, *Cafe on Callisto*
Peter McNamara Convenors' Award for Excellence: 2002: Emily Rodda and Mark McBride, *The Deltora Quest* series and *The Deltora Book of Monsters*; and Peter McNamara for his outstanding contribution to speculative fiction (joint winners).

Sponsoring Organization: Aurealis magazine.

Address: PO Box 2164, Mt Waverley, VIC 3149, Australia. **Telephone:** (3) 9504 1516. **Fax:** (3) 9504 1517. **Internet:** www.sf.org.au/aurealis/intro.html.

Auschwitz Foundation Prize

An annual prize of €2,500, established in 1990, for an original and unpublished text which makes an important contribution to the political, economic, social or historical analysis of the world of the Nazi concentration camps and the processes leading to its creation. The winner is selected by a special jury.

Eligibility and Restrictions: Open to works in all genres; entries must be unpublished.

How to Apply: Three copies of entries should be submitted to the address given.

Recent Winners: 2001: Sara Valentina di Palma, *Bambini e adolescenti nella Shoah* and Caroline Brugvin, *Témoigner sur Ravensbrück* (joint winners); 1999: Markus Meckl, *Helden und Märtyrer*; 1997: Régine Waintrater, *La valeur de travail psychique du témoignage dans la transmission de la Shoah*; 1995: Dirk Luyten, *De vervolging van de economische collaboratie na de Tweede Wereldoorlog in België* and Maud Strosberg, *Le poids du secret* (joint winners); 1992: Didier Pollefeyt, *De Holocaust*.

Sponsoring Organization: Auschwitz Foundation.

Contact: Dir Yanis Thanassekos.

Address: 65 rue des Tanneurs, 1000 Brussels, Belgium. **Telephone:** (2) 512-79-98. **Fax:** (2) 512-58-84. **Internet:** www.auschwitz.be. **E-mail:** auschwitz@cafondation.be.

Australia Council Literature Board Emeritus Awards

Annual awards of up to A$40,000 administered by the Australia Council Literature Board. The purpose of the awards is to acknowledge the achievements of eminent literary writers over the age of 65 who have made outstanding and lifelong contributions to Australian literature.

How to Apply: Nominations are accepted up to mid-May; writers may not nominate themselves.

Sponsoring Organization: Australia Council Literature Board.

Address: Australia Council Literature Board, POB 788, Strawberry Hills, NSW 2012, Australia. **Internet:** www.ozco.gov.au/literature/weaward.html.

Australian Christian Book of the Year

An award made annually for original Christian books, written by Australians and published by Australian publishing houses. A separate prize is offered for best Christian children's book of the year. The winner is selected by a panel of judges, based on the original nature of the work, its literary style, design and Christian contribution. The prize for the Australian Christian Book of the Year is A$2,000 and a framed certificate for both author and publisher. For the children's book category the prize is A$500.

Eligibility and Restrictions: Must have been published during the previous calendar year (April–March).

How to Apply: Publishers should send four copies of entries, with an entry fee of A$30 per title; closing date is early April.

Recent Winners: 2001: John J. Taylor, *Between Devotion and Design: The architecture of John Cyril Hawes 1876–1956*; 2000: Tim Costello, *Tips from a Travelling Soul-Searcher* and John Dickson, *Simply Christianity: Beyond Religion* (joint winners); 1999: Michael Frost, *Eyes Wide Open: Seeing God in the Ordinary*; 1998: John Hannaford, *Saints & Bushrangers* and Janet West, *Daughters of Freedom* (joint winners); 1997: Lance Shilton, *Speaking Out: A Life in Urban Mission*
Children's Book of the Year: 1999–2001: no award; 1998: John Emmett (Editor), *Get More New Life*; 1997: no award.

Sponsoring Organization: Australian Christian Literature Society.

Address: Australian Christian Literature Society, Box 190, Rundle Mall Post Office, Adelaide, SA 5000, Australia. **Fax:** (8) 8364 4647. **Internet:** www. spcka.org.au. **E-mail:** acls@.spcka.org.au.

Australian Literature Society Gold Medal

Awarded for an outstanding literary work published in the preceding calendar year. The award was inaugurated by the Australian Literature Society which was incorporated into the ASAL in 1982. The winner receives a gold medal.

How to Apply: No direct application is accepted. No nominations are required; instead ASAL members are invited to propose potential winners to the judging panel.

Recent Winners: 2001: Rodney Hall, *THDWHHHome*; 2000: Drusilla Modjeska, *Stravinsky's Lunch*; 1999: Murray Bail, *Eucalyptus*; 1998: James Cowan, *A Mapmaker's Dream*; 1997: Robert Dessaix, *Night Letters*.

Sponsoring Organization: Association for the Study of Australian Literature (ASAL) Ltd.

Address: Dept of English, University College, ADFA, Campbell, ACT 2600, Australia. **Telephone:** (3) 9244 3909. **Fax:** (3) 9244 6755. **Internet:** idun.itsc.adfa.edu.au:16080/asal/winnersals.html.

Australian Science Fiction Achievement Awards—Ditmars

These were set up in 1969 by Martin James (Ditmar) Jenssen, a founding member of the Melbourne Science Fiction Club, who financially supported the award until about 1975. The Ditmars are awarded at the Australian National Science Fiction Convention. Nominations are drawn from the broad Australian science fiction community. The winners are selected by popular vote of members of the Australian National Science Fiction Convention, and receive a trophy.

Eligibility and Restrictions: Open to works by an Australian citizen or permanent resident of Australia, which were published for the first time in the preceding calendar year or were first generally available in Australia during that year. Definitions for the different categories are: Best Australian Novel: more than 40,000 words; Best Australian Short Fiction: less than 40,000 words; Best Australian Collected Work: collection or anthology, magazine or journal which includes works by different contributors. At least one edition of a collected work must have been issued in the eligible calendar year. Other categories include best artwork, and professional achievement.

How to Apply: There is no direct application process; entries must be nominated.

Recent Winners: Best Novel: 2001: Sean Williams and Shane Dix, *Evergence 2: The Dying Light*
Best Short Fiction: 2001: Stephen Dedman, *The Devotee* and Terry Dowling, *The Saltimbanques* (joint winners)
Best Collected Work: 2001: Terry Dowling, *Blackwater Days*.

Address: GPO Box 1212K, Melbourne, Vic 3001, Australia.

The Australian/Vogel Literary Award

The Australian/Vogel Literary Award is Australia's richest and most prestigious award for an unpublished manuscript, and aims to provide an opportunity for young writers. The Award was founded in 1980 when Niels Stevns, the owner of Vogels Bread, established the prize in collaboration with *The Australian* newspaper. The award is administered each year by Allen & Unwin Publishers. The prize money has increased over the years, and in 2002 stood at A$20,000. In addition Allen & Unwin guarantee to publish the winning manuscript.

Eligibility and Restrictions: Open to original unpublished manuscripts of fiction or Australian history or biography. Entrants must normally be residents of Australia aged under 35. Manuscripts must be between 30,000 and 125,000 words and must not be under offer to any other publisher at the time of submission to the Award.

How to Apply: Details and entry forms are available on the Allen & Unwin website. Closing date for applications is the end of May.

Recent Winners: 2001: Sarah Hay, *Skins*; 2000: Stephen Gray, *The Artist is a Thief*; 1999: Hsu Ming Teo, *Love and Vertigo*; 1998: Jennifer Kremmer, *Pegasus in the Suburbs*; 1997: Eva Sallis, *Hiam*.

Sponsoring Organization: Allen & Unwin Publishers.

Contact: Publisher's Asst Emma Sorensen.

Address: POB 8500, St Leonards, NSW 1590, Australia. **Telephone:** (2) 8425 0100. **Fax:** (2) 9906 2218. **Internet:** www.allanandunwin.com.

Austrian Award of Merit for Children's Literature

This prize, established in 1980, is given every two years for the complete works of an author, illustrator or translator. The winner receives €11,000.

Eligibility and Restrictions: Only open to Austrian authors, illustrators or translators.

Recent Winners: 2000: Monika Pelz (author); 1998: Lisbeth Zwerger (illustrator); 1996: Wolf Harranth (translator); 1995: Lene Mayer-Skumanz (author); 1992: Renate Welsh (author).

Sponsoring Organization: Austrian Federal Culture Dept.

Contact: Anna Doppler.

Address: Bundeskanzleramt – Kunstsektion, Abt II/15, Schottengasse 1, 1014 Vienna, Austria. **Telephone:** (1) 53115 7612. **Fax:** (1) 53115 7561. **E-mail:** anna.doppler@bka.gv.at.

Austrian National Award for Poetry for Children

This prize, established in 1993, is awarded every two years for the complete works of an author, in the field of poetry for children written in German. The winner receives a prize of €7,300.

Eligibility and Restrictions: Works of poetry for children in the German language are eligible.

Recent Winners: 2001: Georg Bydlinski (Austria), Gerald Jatzek (Austria); 1999: Friedl Hofbauer (Austria); 1997: Josef Guggenmos (Germany); 1995: Frantz Wittkamp (Germany); 1993: Hans Manz (Switzerland).

Sponsoring Organization: Austrian Federal Culture Dept.

Contact: Anna Doppler.

Address: Bundeskanzleramt – Kunstsektion, Abt II/15, Schottengasse 1, 1014 Vienna, Austria. **Telephone:** (1) 53115 7612. **Fax:** (1) 53115 756. **E-mail:** anna.doppler@bka.gv.at.

Austrian National Children's and Juvenile Book Awards

The Austrian National Children's and Juvenile Book Awards, which were established in 1955, are awarded annually for the publication of outstanding books for children and young people. Categories fall into three Children's Book Awards, one Juvenile Book Award, one Award for Translation, one Award for Non-fiction, and one Award for Illustration. The winners receive a cash prize of €18,200, plus books to the value of €10,200.

Eligibility and Restrictions: Open to books published in Austria as well as books from Austrian authors, illustrators or translators published abroad.

Sponsoring Organization: Austrian Federal Culture Dept.

Contact: Anna Doppler.

Address: Bundeskanzleramt – Kunstsektkion, Abt II/15, Schottengasse 1, 1014 Vienna, Austria. **Telephone:** (1) 53115 7612. **Fax:** (1) 53115 756. **E-mail:** anna.doppler@bka.gv.at.

Authors' Club Best First Novel Award

The award was established in 1954 by Lawrence Meynell to encourage new novelists. An annual prize of £1,000 is presented at a dinner held in the Club to the author of the most promising first novel published in the UK during each year.

Eligibility and Restrictions: Open to first works of fiction by a British author. Entries are accepted during October and November and must be full-length novels; short stories are not eligible.

How to Apply: Publishers should apply to the Club Secretary, by sending three copies of each entry.

Recent Winners: 2002: Carl Tighe, *Burning Worm*; 2000: Brian Clarke, *The Stream*; 1999: Ann Harries, *Manly Pursuits*; 1998: Jackie Kay, *Trumpet*; 1997: Mick Jackson, *The Underground Man*; 1996: Rhidian Brook, *The Testimony of Taliesin Jones* and Diran Adebayo, *Some Kind of Black* (joint winners).

Sponsoring Organization: Marsh Christian Trust.

Contact: Club Sec. Ann de la Grange.

Address: Authors' Club, 40 Dover St, London W1X 3RB, UK. **Telephone:** (20) 7499 8581. **Fax:** (20) 7409 0913. **Internet:** www.theartsclub.co.uk.

Aventis Prize

Originally established in 1988 by COPUS – the Committee on the Public Understanding of Science of the Royal Society, the Royal Institution and the British Association for the Advancement of Science – and the Science Museum. Rhône-Poulenc, now renamed Aventis, became involved as sponsor in 1990. Awarded to authors of popular non-fiction, science or technology books, written in English, which are judged to contribute most to the public understanding of science. Prizes are awarded in two categories: £10,000 for the best scientific book, and £10,000 for the best children's science book.

Recent Winners: Scientific Book: 2002: Stephen Hawking, *The Universe in a Nutshell*; 2001: Robert Kunzig, *Mapping the Deep: The Extraordinary Story of Ocean Science*; 2000: Brian Greene, *The Elegant Universe*; 1999: Paul Hoffman, *The Man Who Loved Only Numbers*
Children's Science Book: 2002: Richard Walker, *The DK Guide to the Human Body*; 2001: Michael Allaby, *The DK Guide to Weather*; 2000: Peter Bond, *The DK Guide to Space*.

Sponsoring Organization: Aventis and Institut de France.

Address: Royal Society, 6 Carlton House Terrace, London SW1Y 5AG, UK. **Telephone:** (20) 7839 5561. **Fax:** (20) 7930 2170. **Internet:** www.royalsoc.ac.uk. **E-mail:** info@royalsoc.ac.uk.

Awgie Awards

Presented annually since 1967, the AWGIE awards were established to recognize excellence in writing for stage, screen, television and radio. The AWGIEs have a special position as they are the only writers' awards judged solely by professional writers; the judging is based on the written script (ie the writers' intention) rather than the finished product. Awards are presented in 24 categories, mainly film, stage and TV scripts.

Recent Winners: Major Award: 2001: John Romeril, *One Night the Moon*.

Sponsoring Organization: Australian Writers' Guild.

Address: Australian Writers' Guild, 197 Blues Point Rd, North Sydney, NSW 2060, Australia. **Internet:** www.awg.com.au.

BA/Book Data Author of the Year

This annual award of £1,000, plus a trophy, is judged by members of the Booksellers Association (3,200 bookshops) in a postal ballot. The award, which was founded in 1993, is given to the author judged to have had the most impact for booksellers in the year.

Eligibility and Restrictions: Any living British or Irish published writer in any category is eligible.

How to Apply: No applications are made, since the shortlist is drawn up from postal votes by booksellers.

Recent Winners: 2000: Philip Pullman; 1999: J. K. Rowling; 1998: J. K. Rowling; 1997: Louis de Bernières; 1996: Kate Atkinson; 1995: Pat Barker.

Sponsoring Organization: Booksellers Association of the UK and Ireland Ltd.

Contact: Asst to the Manager, Denise Bayat.

Address: 272 Vauxhall Bridge Road, London SW1V 1BA, UK. **Telephone:** (20) 7834 5477. **Fax:** (20) 7834 8812. **Internet:** www.booksellers.org.uk. **E-mail:** denise.bayat@booksellers.org.uk.

Ingeborg Bachmann Preis

Established in 1977 by the City of Klagenfurt, the Bachmann Prize of 250,000 Sch (around €18,175) is awarded following a series of public debates and readings, with all decisions taken in public. The Ernst Willner Prize is awarded at the same time, with a prize of 160,000 Sch (around €11,600).

Eligibility and Restrictions: Only unpublished texts are eligible.

How to Apply: Nominations are made by a jury.

Recent Winners: 1999: Terézia Mora, *Der Fall Ophelia*; previous winners include Gert Jonke, Ulrich Plenzdorf, Sten Nadolny, Urs Jaeggi, Jürg Amann, Friederike Roth, Erica Pedretti, Katja Lange-Müller, Reto Hänny, Franzobel.

Sponsoring Organization: City of Klagenfurt.

Contact: Frau Salbrechter.

Address: ORF Kärnten, Sponheimer Str. 13, 9020 Klagenfurt, Austria. **Telephone:** (463) 5330 228.

Bad Sex in Fiction Awards

Established by the Literary Review in 1993, and awarded for the 'worst, most redundant or embarrassing description of physical joining in a novel'.

Recent Winners: 2001: Christopher Hart, *Rescue Me*; 2000: Sean Thomas, *Kissing England*; 1999: A. A. Gill, *Starcrossed*; 1998: Sebastian Faulks, *Charlotte Gray*; 1997: Nicholas Royle, *The Matter of the Heart*.

Sponsoring Organization: Literary Review, London, UK.

Balzan Prize for Culture

The International Balzan Foundation makes a series of annual awards in the fields of science, culture, humanities and humanitarian causes. The Foundation chooses different subjects each year within these fields. Each prize is worth 1 million Swiss francs, of which winners are asked to set aside half to support new projects from young scholars. The winners are chosen by the 18-member General Prize Committee.

Eligibility and Restrictions: Subjects for forthcoming awards are announced on the website. The award is open to applicants from any country.

How to Apply: Nominations are submitted by universities and learned societies at the Foundation's request.

Recent Winners: 2001: Literary History and Criticism (post-1500): Prof. Marc Fumaroli (France).

Sponsoring Organization: International Balzan Foundation.

Address: International Balzan Foundation, Piazzetta U. Giordano 4, 20122 Milan, Italy. **Telephone:** (2) 7600 2212. **Fax:** (2) 7600 9457. **Internet:** www.balzan.it. **E-mail:** balzan@balzan.it.

Bancroft Prizes

The Bancroft Prizes were established following a bequest from Fredric Bancroft, whereby provision was made for two annual prizes of equal rank and of the value of $4,000 each to be awarded to the authors of distinguished works in either or both of the following categories: American History (including biography) and Diplomacy.

Eligibility and Restrictions: Entries must have been published during the previous year. The awards are open to anybody in any country. Works must have been originally written in English or translated into English. Volumes of papers, letters, and speeches, unless edited by the author, are not eligible. Autobiography is eligible, but books reporting on recent personal experiences of Americans, within a limited area both in time and geographically, are excluded.

How to Apply: Four copies of entries should be submitted by 1 November.

Recent Winners: 2001: Michael Bellesiles, *Arming America: The Origins of a National Gun Culture*, Susan Lee Johnson, *Roaring Camp: The Social World of the California Gold Rush* and David Nasaw, *The Chief: The Life of William Randolph Hearst*; 2000: John Dower, *Embracing Defeat*, Linda Gordon, *The Great Arizona Orphan Abduction* and James Merrell, *Into the American Woods*; 1999: Ira Berlin, *Many Thousands Gone*, Jill Lepore, *The Name of War* and Philip Morgan, *Slave Counterpoint*; 1998: Christine Leigh Heyrman, *Southern Cross*, Walter Lafeber, *The Clash* and Thomas Sugrue, *The Origins of the Urban Crisis*.

Sponsoring Organization: Columbia University Trustees.

Address: Columbia University, Office of Public Affairs, 202A Low Library, MC 4310, 535 West 116th St, New York, NY 10027, USA. **Telephone:** (212) 854-6581. **Fax:** (212) 678-4817. **E-mail:** jrb60@columbia.edu.

Bank of New Zealand Essay Award

A biennial award which forms part of the Katherine Mansfield Memorial Award series (qv). This category is for an essay on a topic of the writer's choice, sponsored by the Bank of New Zealand. The winner receives a prize of $NZ1,000.

Eligibility and Restrictions: Entries should not exceed 2,500 words.

Recent Winners: 2001: Karen Butterworth, *Parochialism and Identity*.

Sponsoring Organization: Bank of New Zealand.

Contact: Lyndal McMeeking.

Address: Level 5, BNZ Tower, 125 Queen Street, Auckland, New Zealand. **Telephone:** (3) 3532004. **Internet:** www.bnz.co.nz. **E-mail:** lyndal_mcmeeking@ bnz.co.nz.

Bank of New Zealand Katherine Mansfield Memorial Awards

A set of biennial awards which have been sponsored by the Bank of New Zealand since 1958, and have become New Zealand's premier short story awards. The awards commemorate Katherine Mansfield's contribution to New Zealand literature and aim to assist New Zealand writers to achieve recognition in their own country. The winners are selected by a process of 'double blind judging', whereby each section is judged individually, by respected writers and academics, who remain anonymous until judging is completed. All entries are anonymous, written under a pen-name, and there is no pre-selection of entries. The awards are in four categories: the Bank of New Zealand Essay Award; The Bank of New Zealand Novice Writer's Award; The Bank of New Zealand Young Writer's Award (see separate entry for each of these three); and the Bank of New Zealand Katherine Mansfield Award, which is the main award category. For this latter award, the winner receives $NZ5,000 plus a special framed picture of Katherine Mansfield; one runner-up receives $NZ1,500.

Eligibility and Restrictions: Unpublished works only are accepted, with a maximum length of 3,000 words.

Recent Winners: 2001: Janis Freegard, *Mill*; earlier winners include Maurice Shadbolt (1963, 1967 and 1995), Frank Sargeson (1965), Keri Hulme (1975), Vincent O'Sullivan (1979) and Daphne de Jong (1981).

Sponsoring Organization: Bank of New Zealand.

Address: Level 5, BNZ Tower, 125 Queen Street, Auckland, New Zealand. **Telephone:** (3) 3532004. **Internet:** www.bnz.co.nz. **E-mail:** lyndal_mcmeeking@bnz.co.nz.

Bank of New Zealand Novice Writer's Award

A biennial award which forms part of the Katherine Mansfield Memorial Award series (qv). This category is for a writer who has not previously had fiction published or broadcast for payment, sponsored by the Bank of New Zealand. The winner receives a prize of $NZ1,500.

Eligibility and Restrictions: Entries must not exceed 3,000 words.

Recent Winners: 2001: Tracey Slaughter, *Her First*.

Sponsoring Organization: Bank of New Zealand.

Address: Level 5, BNZ Tower, 125 Queen Street, Auckland, New Zealand. **Telephone:** (3) 3532004. **Internet:** www.bnz.co.nz. **E-mail:** lyndal_mcmeeking@bnz.co.nz.

Bank of New Zealand Young Writer's Award

A biennial award which forms part of the Katherine Mansfield Memorial Award series (qv). This category is for a young secondary school writer, sponsored by the Bank of New Zealand. The winner receives a prize of $NZ1,000, while their school receives $NZ500.

Eligibility and Restrictions: Entries should be between 750 and 2,000 words in length.

Recent Winners: 2001: Susan Johnston, *True Colours*.

Sponsoring Organization: Bank of New Zealand.

Address: Level 5, BNZ Tower, 125 Queen Street, Auckland, New Zealand. **Telephone:** (3) 3532004. **Internet:** www.bnz.co.nz. **E-mail:** lyndal_mcmeeking@bnz.co.nz.

Verity Bargate Award

A biennial award, established in honour of the Soho Theatre Company's co-founder and made to the writer of a new and previously unperformed full-length play. The prize of £1,500 represents an option for the theatre to produce the play.

Eligibility and Restrictions: The award is open to any writer resident in the British Isles and Republic of Ireland for an original stage play written in English. Plays should be full-length (not less than 70 minutes), unperformed, suitable for theatre production and unencumbered by any third-party rights. Writers with three or more professional productions to their credit are ineligible.

How to Apply: Entries should be sent by 31 July to the address given, with two stamped self-addressed envelopes (one for acknowledgement and one for return of the script) and a title page giving writer's contact details.

Recent Winners: 2000: Shan Khan, *Office*.

Sponsoring Organization: Soho Theatre and Writers Centre.

Address: 21 Dean Street, London W1D 3NE, UK. **Telephone:** (20) 7287 5060. **Internet:** www.sohotheatre.com.

Herb Barrett Award

An annual prize for poetry in the haiku tradition, with the winner chosen for its originality, haiku style, content, and technical mastery. There is a first prize of US $200, with a second prize of $150 and third prize of $100. All winning entries are published in a special anthology.

Eligibility and Restrictions: Poems may be published or unpublished, and must be in English or accompanied by an English translation. Poems must be no more than 4 lines long. They do not have to follow the traditional 17-syllable form, but should be in the haiku tradition. Up to 10 poems may be submitted per entry.

How to Apply: Entries should be submitted by 30 November, accompanied by an entry fee of $12 per entry; author's identity should not appear on the entry, but on a separate sheet of paper.

Recent Winners: 1999: Sandra Fuhringer; 1998: Timothy Russell; 1997: Giovanni Malito.

Sponsoring Organization: Hamilton Haiku Press.

Address: Hamilton Haiku Press, 237 Prospect St South, Hamilton, ON L8M 2Z6, Canada. **Telephone:** (905) 312-1779. **Internet:** www.meklerdeahl.com/contests.

Bastian Prize

An annual prize sponsored by the Norwegian Association of Literary Translators for the outstanding translation of the year.

Recent Winners: Merete Alfsen, *Orlando* by Virginia Woolf.

Sponsoring Organization: Norwegian Association of Literary Translators.

Address: Postboks 579, Sentrum 0105, Oslo, Norway. **Internet:** www.boknett.no.

Mildred L. Batchelder Award

This award, established in honour of the former director of the Association for Library Service to Children (ALSC) in 1966, is presented to an American publisher for a children's book considered to be the most outstanding work originally published in a foreign language in a foreign country, and subsequently translated into English and published in the USA. The aim of the award is to encourage American publishers to seek out superior children's books abroad and to promote communication among the peoples of the world.

How to Apply: One copy of the book should be sent to the ALSC office and one copy to the Chair of the Award Committee, by 31 December of the year of publication.

Recent Winners: 2002: Karin Gündisch, *How I Became an American* (translated by James Skofield); 2001: Daniella Carmi, *Samir and Yonatan* (translated by Yael Lotan); 2000: Anton Quintana, *The Baboon King* (translated by John Nieuwenhuizen); 1999: Schoschana Rabinovici, *Thanks to My Mother* (translated by James Skofield); 1998: Josef Holub, *The Robber and Me* (translated by Elizabeth D. Crawford).

Sponsoring Organization: Association for Library Service to Children (American Library Association).

Address: Association for Library Service to Children, American Library Association, 50 East Huron, Chicago, IL 60611-2795, USA. **Fax:** (312) 944-7671. **Internet:** www.ala.org/alsc. **E-mail:** alsc@ala.org.

Herbert Baxter Adams Prize

Named after one of the Association's founding members and its first secretary, this prize was established in 1903 for works in the history of the Eastern hemisphere. It is offered annually for an author's first substantial book, and the chronological coverage alternates between the early European period one year and the modern period the next.

Recent Winners: 2001: Malachi Haim Hacohen, *Karl Popper: The Formative Years, 1902–1945. Politics and Philosophy in Interwar Vienna*; 2000: Daniel Lord Smail, *Imaginary Cartographies*; 1999: Gabrielle Hecht, *The Radiance of France: Nuclear Power and National Identity after World War II*; 1998: David Nirenberg, *Communities of Violence: Persecution of Minorities in the Middle Ages*; 1997: Pieter M. Judson, *Exclusive Revolutionaries: Liberal Politics, Social Experience, and National Identity in the Austrian Empire, 1848–1914*.

Sponsoring Organization: American Historical Association.

Contact: Lynn Hunt.

Address: American Historical Asscn, 400 A St, SE, Washington, DC 20003–3889, USA. **Telephone:** (202) 544-2422. **Fax:** (202) 544-8307. **Internet:** www.theaha.org/prizes. **E-mail:** press@theaha.org.

BBC Wildlife Magazine Literary Awards

Awards are given in three categories: the Bradt Travel Writing Award, the Poet of the Year Award and the Nature Writing Award. Prizes vary from holidays (travel writing) to cash prizes and publication in *BBC Wildlife Magazine*.

Eligibility and Restrictions: Bradt Travel Award: open to travel essays which are a true account of an encounter with wildlife, either local or exotic, no more than 800 words in length. Poet of the Year: open to poems on the subject of the natural world, in any format or style but no longer than 50 lines in length. Nature Writing Award: open to new and established writers, for an essay about nature; main exclusions are that it should not be pure fiction, a poem, or written from an animal's point of view, and should not exceed 800 words.

How to Apply: Entry forms for each category are published in separate issues of *BBC Wildlife Magazine*.

Sponsoring Organization: BBC Wildlife Magazine/BBC Worldwide.

Contact: Asst to the Editor Sarah Heymans.

Address: Broadcasting House, Whiteladies Rd, Bristol BS8 2LR, UK. **Telephone:** (117) 973 8402. **Fax:** (117) 946 7075. **E-mail:** wildlife.magazine@bbc.co.uk.

Beatriceprisen

The prize was founded in 1983 by Beatrice and Paul L.C. Beckett, and is given annually to a writer of either prose fiction or lyric poetry. The winner, selected by members of the Danish Academy, receives a prize of DKK50,000.

Eligibility and Restrictions: Open to Danish-language authors.

How to Apply: No direct applications are accepted.

Recent Winners: 2001: Jens Martin Eriksen; 2000: Pia Juul; 1999: Janina Katz; 1997: F. P. Jac; 1996: Knud Holten.

Sponsoring Organization: Danish Academy.

Contact: Administrator Dr Allan Philip.

Address: Det Danske Akademi, Rungstedlund, Rungsted Strandvej 111, 2960 Rungsted Kyst, Denmark. **Telephone:** 33 13 11 12. **Fax:** 33 32 80 45. **Internet:** www.danskeakademi.dk. **E-mail:** lawoffice@philip.dk.

Henriëtte de Beaufort-prijs

Established by the Maatschappij der Nederlandse Letterkunde (MNL) in 1985 following a gift from Henriëtte de Beaufort. The prize takes place every three years, and recognizes authors of a biographical work; the winner is selected by a committee of experts. A prize of €2,500 is awarded, alternately, to a Dutch and a Flemish author.

Eligibility and Restrictions: The work must have been published within the preceding six years; the prize alternates between Dutch and Flemish language works.

How to Apply: Application is open to anybody.

Recent Winners: 2001: Joris van Parys; 1998: Hans Goedkop; 1995: Hedwig Speliers; 1992: Helene Nolthenius; 1989: Christine D'haen.

Sponsoring Organization: Maatschappij der Nederlandse Letterkunde (MNL) (Dutch Literature Association).

Address: Maatschappij der Nederlandse Letterkunde, Postbus 9501, 2300 RA Leiden, Netherlands. **Telephone:** (71) 5144962. **Fax:** (71) 5272836. **Internet:** www.leidenuniv.nl/host/mnl. **E-mail:** mnl@library.leidenuniv.nl.

George Louis Beer Prize

Established in 1918 by a bequest from Professor Beer, a historian of the British colonial system before 1765, this prize is offered annually in recognition of outstanding historical writing in European international history since 1895.

Recent Winners: 2001: John Connelly, *Captive University: The Sovietization of East German, Czech and Polish Higher Education, 1945–1956.*

Sponsoring Organization: American Historical Association.

Contact: Lynn Hunt.

Address: American Historical Asscn, 400 A St, SE, Washington, DC 20003–3889, USA. **Telephone:** (202) 544-2422. **Fax:** (202) 544-8307. **Internet:** www. theaha.org/prizes. **E-mail:** press@theaha.org.

Bellmanpriset (Bellman Prize)

Established in 1920 by the painter Anders Zorn and his wife, to honour a 'truly outstanding Swedish poet'. The award is of SEK 200,000.

How to Apply: Direct applications are not accepted.

Recent Winners: 2001: Olle Adolphson; 2000: Jesper Svenbro; 1999: Bruno K. Öijer; 1998: Björner Torsson; 1997: Eva Runefelt.

Sponsoring Organization: Swedish Academy.

Contact: Sec. Bo Svensen.

Address: Swedish Academy, POB 2118, 103 13 Stockholm, Sweden.

Pura Belpré Award

The Pura Belpré Award, established in 1996, is presented every two years to a Latino/Latina writer and illustrator whose work best portrays and celebrates the Latino cultural experience in an outstanding work of literature for children and youth. The award is named after the first Latina librarian from the New York Public Library.

How to Apply: One copy of the book should be sent to the Association for Library Service to Children (ALSC) office, and one copy to the Chair of the Award Committee, by 31 December of the year of publication.

Recent Winners: Narrative: 2002: Pam Munoz Ryan, *Esperanza Rising*; 2000: Alma Flor Ada, *Under the Royal Palms: A Childhood in Cuba*; 1998: Victor Martinez, *Parrot in the Oven: mi vida*
Illustration: 2002: Susan Guevara (illustrator), Gary Soto (author), *Chato and the Party Animals*; 2000: Carmen Lomas Garza, *Magic Windows*; 1998: Stephanie Garcia (illustrator), Gary Soto (author), *Snapshots from the Wedding*.

Sponsoring Organization: Association for Library Service to Children (American Library Association).

Address: Association for Library Service to Children, American Library Association, 50 East Huron, Chicago, IL 60611–2795, USA. **Fax:** (312) 944-7671. **Internet:** www.ala.org/alsc. **E-mail:** alsc@ala.org.

Benson Medal

Founded in 1916 by A. C. Benson to recognize 'praiseworthy works of poetry, fiction, biography or belles-lettres'. It is awarded irregularly by the Council of the Royal Society of Literature, and is regarded as marking a lifetime of achievement. The award comprises a solid silver medal.

Eligibility and Restrictions: Open to writers with a substantial body of work written in English.

How to Apply: The medal cannot be applied for, as it is awarded by nomination only.

Recent Winners: 2000: Christopher Fry; 1995: Naguib Mahfouz and Shusaku Endo; 1993: Julien Green; 1990 Wole Soyinka.

Sponsoring Organization: Royal Society of Literature.

Address: Royal Society of Literature, c/o Royal Literary Fund, off Fleet St, London EC4A 3EA, UK. **Telephone:** (20) 7845 4676. **Fax:** (20) 7845 4679. **Internet:** www.rslit.org. **E-mail:** info@rslit.org.

Berliner Preis für deutschsprachige Gegenwartsliteratur
(Berlin Prize for Contemporary German Literature)

The Berliner Preis für deutschsprachige Gegenwartsliteratur recognizes substantial contributions to the development of contemporary literature (both poetry and prose) written in German. It is sponsored by the Preussische Seehandlung in Berlin and has been awarded every two years since 1989. The prize consists of seven awards for collected works and two additional awards, the 'Johannes-Bobrowski-Medaille', for unpublished texts. The authors and the judges spend three days together at the Literarische Colloquium in Berlin.

Recent Winners: In the last few years awards have gone to Marcel Beyer, Wilhelm Genazino, Angela Krauss, Katja Lange-Müller, Ulrich Peltzer, Raoul Schrott, Josef Winkler, Anne Duden, Bodo Hell, Reinhard Jirgl, Gert Friedrich Jonke, Irina Liebmann, Ingo Schulze and Jörg Steiner.

Sponsoring Organization: Preussische Seehandlung.

Address: Preussische Seehandlung, 1000 Berlin, Germany.

Mordechai Bernstein Literary Prizes

A series of literary awards presented every two years by the Mordechai Bernstein Literary Prizes Association. Prizes include: 50,000 NS for an original Hebrew novel; 25,000 NS for poetry; 10,000 NS for literary criticism in the daily Hebrew press; 20,000 NS for the first book in prose by a new immigrant; 10,000 NS for the first book in poetry by a new immigrant; and 10,000 NS for a Hebrew play.

Sponsoring Organization: Mordechai Bernstein Literary Prizes Association.

Address: Book Publishers of Israel, 29 Carlebach St, 67132 Tel Aviv, Israel. **Telephone:** (3) 5614121. **Fax:** (3) 5611996. **Internet:** www.tbpai.co.il/abouteng. htm. **E-mail:** hamol@tbpai.co.il.

David Berry Prize

The David Berry Prize was set up by a legacy from David Anderson-Berry in memory of his father, the Reverend David Berry. The prize is administered by the Royal Historical Society on behalf of the David Berry Trust, and carries a prize of £250 awarded annually for the best essay on a subject dealing with Scottish history.

Eligibility and Restrictions: The essay should be between 6,000 and 10,000 words. Previous winners may not reapply.

How to Apply: Candidates are invited to send their essays to the Royal Historical Society by 31 October.

Sponsoring Organization: David Berry Trust/Royal Historical Society.

Contact: Exec. Sec. Joy McCarthy.

Address: Royal Historical Society, University College London, Gower St, London WC1E 6BT, UK. **Telephone:** (20) 7387 7532. **Fax:** (20) 7387 7532. **Internet:** www.rhs.ac.uk. **E-mail:** royalhistsoc@ucl.ac.uk.

Besterman/McColvin Medals

Two Besterman/McColvin Medals are awarded for outstanding works of reference published in the UK – one for print and one for electronic formats. The Awards are sponsored by Whitaker and judged by panels of reference librarians and members of the Society of Indexers. The winners receive a golden medal, a certificate and a prize of £500.

Eligibility and Restrictions: Works must have been published in the 18 months between the preceding January and July.

How to Apply: Nominations are invited from Members, publishers and others.

Recent Winners: Printed category: 2001: Maurice Rickards and Michael Twyman (Editor), *The Encyclopedia of Ephemera*; 1999: Victoria and Albert Museum, *A Bibliography and Exhibition Chronology, 1852–1996*; 1998: *Handbook for British and Irish Archaeology Sources and Resources*; 1994: *Bibliography of Printed Works on London History to 1939*; 1993: *Africa – A Guide to Reference Material*
Electronic format: 2001: James L. Harner, *The World Shakespeare Bibliography Online*; 1997: *The World Shakespeare Bibliography on CD-ROM*.
Sponsoring Organization: Chartered Institute of Library and Information Professionals (CILIP)/Whitaker.
Contact: Reference Awards Administrator Mary Casteleyn.
Address: Chartered Institute of Library and Information Professionals, 7 Ridgmount St, London WC1E 7AE, UK. **Telephone:** (20) 7255 0500. **Fax:** (20) 7255 0501. **Internet:** www.cilip.org.uk. **E-mail:** info@cilip.org.uk.

Albert J. Beveridge Award

This award was established in 1928 in memory of Senator Beveridge of Indiana, former secretary and long-time member of the Association, through a gift from his wife, Catherine Beveridge and donations from AHA members from his home state. It is awarded annually for the best English-language book on American history (USA, Canada, or Latin America) from 1492 to the present.
Recent Winners: 2001: Alexander Keyssar, *The Right to Vote: the Contested History of Democracy in the United States.*
Sponsoring Organization: American Historical Association.
Contact: Lynn Hunt.
Address: American Historical Asscn, 400 A St, SE, Washington, DC 20003–3889, USA. **Telephone:** (202) 544-2422. **Fax:** (202) 544-8307. **Internet:** www.theaha. org/prizes. **E-mail:** press@theaha.org.

Bhanu Bhakta Memorial Award

An annual award presented by the Nepal Sikshya Parisad (Nepal Education Council), a private society dedicated to the advancement of Nepali language and literature. The award is in memory of the Nepali poet Bhanu Bhakta, and is presented for an outstanding contribution to the development of Nepali literature.
Recent Winners: 2000: Madan Mani Dixit.
Sponsoring Organization: Nepal Sikshya Parisad (Nepal Education Council).
Address: Nepal Sikshya Parisad (Nepal Education Council), Kathmandu, Nepal.

Shah Abdul Latif Bhitaee Award

The Pakistan Academy of Letters administers a series of annual prizes established in 1980 under the Hijra National Literary Awards Scheme. The aim of the awards is to promote literary activities and recognize outstanding contributions. The Shah Abdul Latif Bhitaee Award is an annual prize of Rs 50,000 for works written in Sindhi language.
Recent Winners: 2000: Dr Shah Nawaz Sodhar, *Ojage Ujaria*; 1999: Dr Badar Uja, *Sindhi Adab Main Tanqeed Nigari*; 1998: Jamal Abro, *Disee Doah Akhyun Seen.*
Sponsoring Organization: Pakistan Academy of Letters.

Contact: Deputy Dir Naseem Mahmood.

Address: Pitras Bokhari Road, Sector H-8/1, Islamabad, Pakistan. **Telephone:** 9257164. **Fax:** 9257159. **E-mail:** academy@apollo.net.pk.

Bialik Prize for Literature

An annual prize established by the city of Tel Aviv in memory of Chaim Nachman Bialik (1873–1934), the figurehead of modern Hebrew poetry. The Bialik Prize has grown in reputation to become one of Israel's top literary awards. Devora Baron was the first recipient of the prize. The prize is awarded in recognition of a lifetime's contribution to Hebrew literature.

Recent Winners: Previous winners include Nurit Govrin, Aharon Megged, Moshe Dor, Aharon Appelfeld, Yehoshua Kenaz, Meir Wieseltier and Yehuda Amichai.

Sponsoring Organization: Tel-Aviv -Yafo Municipality.

Address: Tel-Aviv Yafo Municipality, Dept of Municipal Prizes, Tel Aviv, Israel.

Horst Bienek Preis für Lyrik (Horst Bienek Award for Poetry)

A biennial award for poetry, administered by the Bavarian Academy of Fine Arts, with a prize of €10,000. The award was first presented in 1991, to John Ashbery. A separate Horst Bienek Encouragement Prize (Horst-Bienek-Förderpreis) is also presented to an emerging young talent.

Recent Winners: 2001: Michael Hamburger; 2000: Philippe Jaccottet; 1999: Wulf Kirsten; 1998: Inger Christensen; 1997: Oskar Pastior.

Sponsoring Organization: Horst Bienek Stiftung.

Address: Bayerische Akademie der Schönen Künste, Max-Joseph-Platz 3, 80539 Munich, Germany. **Telephone:** (89) 290077-0. **Fax:** (89) 290077-23. **Internet:** www.badsk.de. **E-mail:** info@badsk.de.

Biennial of Illustrations Bratislava (BIB)

An international competition for children's book illustrations, established in 1967. It was founded with the support of UNESCO and the International Board on Books for Young People (IBBY), and remains the only big non-commercial event of its kind in the world. The award, which takes place alongside the Biennial festival, represents an opportunity to present the best works from countries with a rich book culture in the area of illustration for children, as well as to give illustrators from other countries a chance to present their work. An international jury awards the following prizes: Grand Prix BIB, five Golden Apples, and five Plaques.

Eligibility and Restrictions: Entrants may submit up to 10 illustrations from one or two different books. No more than 20 artists may enter from any country. Artists who are taking part in BIB for the first time may submit illustrations from the previous five years, while others can only enter works from the two previous years.

How to Apply: Applications must be submitted by 31 May.

Sponsoring Organization: Ministry of Culture/Slovak Commission for UNESCO/BIBIANA International House of Art for Children.

Address: BIBIANA, the BIB Secretariate, Panská ul. 41, 815 39 Bratislava, Slovakia. **Telephone:** (2) 5443 3550. **Fax:** (2) 5443 3550. **Internet:** www. bibiana.sk/bib_infe.htm. **E-mail:** bib@bibiana.sk.

BILBY—Books I Love Best Yearly—Award

The Bilby Awards are the Queensland part of a series of Australian Children's Choice awards at both national and state level. They are run by the Children's Book Council of Australia (Queensland Branch) in association with Education Queensland. Their aim is to foster participation in reading while increasing enjoyment of literature.

Recent Winners: Early Readers: 2001: Martin Handford, *Where's Wally?*; 2000: Rod Clement, *Grandad's Teeth*; 1999: Terry Denton, *Gasp!*
Younger Readers: 2001: J. K. Rowling, *Harry Potter* series; 2000: Andy Griffiths, *Just Stupid*; 1999: Bruce Whatley and R. Smith, *Detective Donut and the Wild Goose Chase*
Older Readers: 2001: J. K. Rowling, *Harry Potter* series; 2000: Melina Marchetta, *Looking for Alibrandi*; 1999: Morris Gleitzman, *Bumface*.

Sponsoring Organization: Children's Book Council of Australia (Queensland Branch).

Address: Children's Book Council of Australia, POB 828, Spring Hill, Qld 4004, Australia. **Internet:** www.home.gil.com.au/~cbcqld/bilby.htm.

Geoffrey Bilson Award for Historical Fiction for Young People

The Geoffrey Bilson Award was established in 1988 in memory of Geoffrey Bilson, a respected historian and children's author who died in 1987. The C$1,000 prize is awarded annually to the Canadian author of an outstanding work of historical fiction for young people.

Eligibility and Restrictions: Open to Canadian historical novels for children published between 1 January and 31 December of the previous year.

Recent Winners: 2002: Virginia Frances Schwartz, *If I Just Had Two Wings*; 1999: Iain Lawrence, *The Wreckers*.

Sponsoring Organization: Canadian Children's Book Centre.

Address: Canadian Children's Book Centre, 40 Orchard View Blvd, Suite 101, Toronto, ON M4R 1B9, Canada. **Telephone:** (416) 975-0010. **Fax:** (416) 975-8970. **Internet:** www.bookcentre.ca/. **E-mail:** info@bookcentre.

Binkley–Stephenson Award

The Binkley–Stephenson Award, first given in 1967, is an annual award of $500 and a certificate for the best scholarly article published in the *Journal of American History* during the preceding calendar year (March, June, September, December issues). It is named after two former presidents of the Organization of American Historians (OAH), William C. Binkley and Wendell H. Stephenson.

Recent Winners: 2001: Elizabeth A. Fenn, *Biological Warfare in Eighteenth-Century North America: Beyond Jeffrey Amherst*; 2000: Mary Hershberger, *Mobilizing Women, Anticipating Abolition: The Struggle Against Indian Removal in the 1830s*; 1999: Charles Capper, *A Little Beyond: The Problem of the Transcendentalist Movement in American History*; 1998: Glenn C. Altschuler, Jean Harvey Baker, Norma Basch, Stuart M. Blumin, Harry L. Watson, *Political Engagement and Disengagement in Antebellum America*; 1997: Michael Bellesiles, *The Origins of Gun Culture in the United States, 1760–1865*.

Sponsoring Organization: Organization of American Historians.

Address: Organization of American Historians, 112 North Bryan St, Blooming-ton, IN 47408–4199, USA. **Telephone:** (812) 855-9852. **Fax:** (812) 855-0696. **Internet:** www.oah.org. **E-mail:** awards@oah.org.

Biographers' Club Prize

This annual prize was established in 1999 by Andrew Lownie, and is awarded for an uncommissioned proposal for a biography by a previously unpublished writer. The winner is chosen by a panel of three judges made up of distinguished writers from the field of biography, and receives £1,000.

Eligibility and Restrictions: Open to writers who have not had previous works published. Entries should comprise a proposal of 15–20 pages, broken down by chapter synopsis with a note of the author's credentials, the market for the book, sources and competing/comparable books.

How to Apply: Proposals for entry should be submitted to the Secretary by the beginning of September.

Recent Winners: 2001: Adnan Fort; 2000: Adrienne Gavin; 1999: Lucy Jago.

Sponsoring Organization: Daily Mail/Biographers' Club.

Contact: Sec. Andrew Lownie.

Address: Biographers' Club, 17 Sutherland St, London SW1V 4JU, UK. **Telephone:** (20) 7828 1274. **Fax:** (20) 7828 7608. **Internet:** www.booktrust. org.uk. **E-mail:** lownie@globalnet.co.uk.

Paul Birdsall Prize in European Military and Strategic History

The Birdsall Prize, administered by the American Historical Association (AHA), was established in 1985 after a gift from Professor Hans Gatzke. The prize, named after an eminent historian, is awarded biennially for the most important work on European military or strategic history since 1870 by a citizen of the USA or Canada.

Recent Winners: 2000: Marc Trachtenberg, *A Constructed Peace: The Making of the European Settlement, 1945–63*; 1998: John F. Beeler, *British Naval Policy in the Gladstone-Disraeli Era, 1866–1880*; 1996: David G. Hermann, *The Arming of Europe and the Making of the First World War*; 1994: Leondard V. Smith, *Between Mutiny and Obedience*; 1992: Dennis E. Showalter, *Tannenberg: Clash of Empires*.

Sponsoring Organization: American Historical Association.

Contact: Lynn Hunt.

Address: American Historical Asscn, 400 A St, SE, Washington, DC 20003–3889, USA. **Telephone:** (202) 544-2422. **Fax:** (202) 544-8307. **Internet:** www. theaha.org/prizes. **E-mail:** press@theaha.org.

James Tait Black Memorial Prizes

The prize was founded in 1918 by Mrs Janet Coats Black in memory of her late husband, and is now part-funded by the Scottish Arts Council. The winner is chosen by the Professor of English Literature at the University of Edinburgh. Two winners are chosen each year, in the categories of biography and fiction. Each winner receives a prize of £3,000.

Eligibility and Restrictions: Entries must have been published in English in the UK during the previous year.

How to Apply: Publishers only may apply; one copy should be submitted to the Dept of English Literature by 30 September.

Recent Winners: Fiction: 2001: Sid Smith, *Something Like a House*; 2000: Zadie Smith, *White Teeth*; 1999: Timothy Mo, *Renegade, or Halo2*; 1998: Beryl Bainbridge, *Master Georgie*; 1997: Andrew Miller, *Ingenious Pain*; 1996: Graham Swift, *Last Orders*
Biography: 2001: Robert Skidelsky, *John Maynard Keynes: Vol. 3, Fighting For Britain 1937–46*; 2000: Martin Amis, *Experience*; 1999: Kathryn Hughes, *George Eliot: The Last Victorian*.

Sponsoring Organization: Scottish Arts Council/University of Edinburgh.

Contact: Prof. John Fron.

Address: Dept of English Literature, University of Edinburgh, Edinburgh EH8 9JX, UK. **Telephone:** (131) 650 3619. **Internet:** www.ed.ac.uk/englit/jtbint.htm. **E-mail:** s.strathdee@ed.ac.uk.

Blagovist Prize (Church Bells Prize)

Awarded in five categories: for poetry, prose, critical and literary articles, folklore, and author's first book.

Sponsoring Organization: National Writers Union of Ukraine (NSPU).

Contact: V. Yavorivsky.

Address: Blvd Bankova 2, 01024 Kiev, Ukraine. **Fax:** (44) 293-45-86. **Internet:** www.nspu.kiev.ua. **E-mail:** nspu@I.kiev.ua.

Karen Blixen Medaljen

The medal, which was first awarded in 1985, is presented to a foreign author at irregular intervals. The winner, selected by members of the Danish Academy by a simple majority, receives the Karen Blixen Medal.

How to Apply: No direct applications are accepted.

Recent Winners: 1999: Einar Mar Gudmondsson and Thor Vilhjalmsson (joint winners); 1996: Václav Havel; 1985: Astrid Lindgren and William Heinesen (joint winners).

Sponsoring Organization: Danish Academy.

Contact: Administrator Dr Allan Philip.

Address: Det Danske Akademi, Rungstedlund, Rungsted Strandvej 111, 2960 Rungsted Kyst, Denmark. **Telephone:** 33 13 11 12. **Fax:** 33 32 80 45. **Internet:** www.danskeakademi.dk. **E-mail:** lawoffice@philip.dk.

Blue Peter Children's Book Awards

The Blue Peter Book Awards are administered by the Scottish Book Trust and supported by BBC Education and The Chartered Institute of Library and Information Professionals. Three categories of winner are chosen, one of which is also designated overall Blue Peter Book of the Year. The winners are decided by a panel of celebrity judges and the Blue Peter young judges, a panel of children selected from viewers who have sent in reviews.

Recent Winners: The Book I Couldn't Put Down: 2001: William Nicholson, *The Wind Singer*; 2000: Alan Gibbons, *The Shadow of the Minotaur*
The Best Book to Read Aloud: 2001: Alan Ahlberg, *The Bravest Ever Bear*; 2000: Julia Donaldson, *The Gruffalo*
The Best Book to Keep Forever: 2001: Geraldine McCaughrean, *Kite*
2000: Geraldine McCaughrean, *The Pilgrim's Progress*
Blue Peter Book of the Year: 2001: William Nicholson, *The Wind Singer*.

Sponsoring Organization: Scottish Book Trust.

Address: Scottish Book Trust, Scottish Book Centre, 137 Dundee St, Edinburgh EH11 1BG, UK. **Internet:** www.bbc.co.uk/cbbc/bluepeter/bookawards.

R. H. Blyth Award

A new award created in 2002 by the World Haiku Club, which aims to become one of the most prestigious and important haiku-related awards in the world.

Eligibility and Restrictions: Open to entrants in any country. Works must be new, original, unpublished and not being considered for awards elsewhere. Entries may be Haiku poems in any form, style, subject or convention, written in English (haiku written in any other languages must be translated).

How to Apply: Each entrant may submit up to three haiku. Entries should be accompanied by brief biographical details and an entry fee of £5/US$10/ Yen 1,000 per entry regardless of the number of works submitted. Deadline for submissions is end of May.

Sponsoring Organization: World Haiku Club.

Address: Leys Farm, Rousham, Bicester OX25 4R, UK. **Telephone:** (1869) 340261. **Fax:** (1869) 340619. **Internet:** www.worldhaikuclub.org. **E-mail:** whc.susumu@virgin.net.

BMA (British Medical Association) Medical Book Competition

The British Medical Association established its annual BMA Medical Book Competition in 1996. The competition aims to encourage and to reward excellence in medical publishing. The competition is administered by the BMA Library for the BMA's Board of Science and Education. The main objective is to encourage the production of high-quality medical books. All entries are individually reviewed and appraised by doctors and educators who are interested in medical publishing. The final judging panel of BMA president and secretary, Board of Science and Education chairman and BMA librarian meets to review the specialist panels' recommendations and to select the BMA Medical Book of the Year. Prizes are awarded in nine categories, with an overall BMA Medical Book of the Year award made from the category winners. There are no cash prizes, but the winners receive a glass trophy.

Eligibility and Restrictions: There are nine categories covering basic sciences, mental health, popular medicine, primary health care, surgery and anaesthesia, etc. Nursing and dentistry are excluded. All titles must be in English and have been published in the previous year.

How to Apply: Applications are usually made by publishers. Two copies of the work and a completed entry form for each title should reach the BMA Library by no later than 28 February.

Recent Winners: BMA Medical Book of the Year: 2001: Michael H. Crawford and John P. Di Marco, *Cardiology*; 2000: Amit Gupta, Simon P. J. Kay and Luis R. Scheker,*The growing hand: diagnosis and management of the upper extremity in children*; 1999: Christina Faull, Yvonne Carter and Richard Woof, *Handbook of palliative care*; 1998: Jan A. Rozendaal, *Vector control: methods for use by individuals and communities*; 1997: John C. Pickup and Gareth Williams, *Textbook of Diabetes*.

Sponsoring Organization: British Medical Association/Board of Science.

Contact: Competition Director, Richard M Jones.

Address: BMA Library, BMA House, Tavistock Sq., London WC1H 9JP, UK. **Telephone:** (20) 7383 6614. **Fax:** (20) 7388 2544. **E-mail:** rjones@bma.org.uk.

Boardman Tasker Award

The prize was established in 1983 to commemorate the lives and writing of climbers Peter Boardman and Joe Tasker who were lost attempting to climb the unclimbed North-East ridge of Everest in 1982. The annual award of £2,000 is given to a work which has made an outstanding contribution to mountain literature.

Eligibility and Restrictions: The award is judged by a panel of independent experts. Entries must be in book format, in the English language, published or distributed in the UK.

How to Apply: Publishers should submit four copies of the work.

Recent Winners: 2001: Roger Hubank, *Hazard's Way*; 2000: Peter and Leni Gillman, *The Wildest Dream*; 1999: Paul Pritchard, *The Totem Pole*; 1998: Peter Steele, *Eric Shipton*;1997: Paul Pritchard, *Deep Play*.

Sponsoring Organization: Boardman Tasker Charitable Trust.

Contact: Hon. Sec. Maggie Body.

Address: Pound House, Llangennith, Swansea SA3 1JQ, UK. **Telephone:** (1792) 386 215. **Fax:** (1792) 386 215. **Internet:** www.boardmantasker.com. **E-mail:** margaretbody@lineone.net.

George Bogin Memorial Award

The George Bogin Memorial Award, which is administered by the Poetry Society of America (PSA), was established by the family and friends of George Bogin for a selection of four or five poems that 'use language in an original way to reflect the encounter of the ordinary and the extraordinary and to take a stand against oppression in any of its forms'. The winner receives $500.

Eligibility and Restrictions: Open to anyone; there is no limit on the length of poems entered.

How to Apply: Two copies of submissions should be sent accompanied by a cover sheet and entry fee (non-members) between 1 October and 21 December.

Recent Winners: 2002: Kevin Prufer.

Sponsoring Organization: Poetry Society of America.

Address: Poetry Society of America, 15 Gramercy Park, New York, NY 10003, USA. **Telephone:** (212) 254-9628. **Internet:** www.poetrysociety.org.

Bokhandlerprisen

An annual prize administered by the Norwegian book trade to recognize outstanding works of general literature or children's literature. The prize was first presented in 1948. The winner receives a bronze statuette.

Recent Winners: 2001: Lars Saabye Christensen, *Halvbroren*; 2000: Jo Nesbø; 1999: Erlend Loe; 1998: Erik Fosnes Hansen; 1997: Karin Fossum.

Sponsoring Organization: Den Norske Bokhandlerforening (Association of Norwegian Bookdealers).

Address: Den Norske Bokhandlerforening, Ovre Vollgate 15, 0153 Oslo, Norway. **Telephone:** (22) 396 800. **Fax:** (22) 396 810. **Internet:** www.bokhandlerfor.no/info/arrange1.htm.

Heinrich-Böll-Preis der Stadt Köln

The Heinrich-Böll-Preis der Stadt Köln, named after the Nobel-prize winning author, is awarded for outstanding works of literature written in German, and its winners may include previously unknown authors. Sponsored by the city of Cologne, it was introduced in 1980 and is normally awarded annually, although since 1995 the prize has only been awarded every two years.

Recent Winners: 1999: Gerhard Meier; 1997: W.G. Sebald; 1995: Jürgen Becker.

Sponsoring Organization: City of Cologne.

Address: Cologne, Germany.

Bollingen Prize in Poetry

Biennial award for the best book of poetry by an American during the preceding two years. The winner receives a prize of $50,000.

How to Apply: No applications accepted.

Recent Winners: 2001: Louise Glück; 1999: Robert White Creeley; 1997: Gary Snyder; 1995: Kenneth Koch.

Address: Beinecke Rare Book and Manuscript Library, Yale University Library, PO Box 208240, New Haven, CT 06520, USA.

Bologna New Media Prize (BNMP)

Established in 1996 to reward excellence in the field of interactive media products for children up to the age of 15. The winners are chosen by an international panel of experts (editors, authors, journalists, teachers, IT experts, etc) and receive a plaque and promotion at the annual Bologna Children's Book Fair in April. A new category was introduced in 2002, for the Children's eBook Award, inaugurated by the International E-Book Award Foundation to recognize excellence in the field of electronic book publishing for children.

Eligibility and Restrictions: New media (interactive media) products are eligible, from any country and from any size publisher. Eligible products include CD-ROMs, Internet sites, smart toys, web-enabled CDs and eBooks. Entries must have been released between 1 January and 31 December of the preceding year.

How to Apply: Applicants should send two copies of each title to the prize co-ordinator, accompanied by a completed entry form.

Recent Winners: 2002: *Bioscopia* (Germany), *Findus bei den Mucklas* (Sweden) and *Zoo Tycoon* (USA)

Children's eBook Award: 2002: *My First Internet Manual* (Italy).

Sponsoring Organization: Children's Software Revue and The Bologna Children's Book Fair.

Contact: Warren Buckleitner.

Address: 44 Main St, Flemington, NJ, New York, NY, USA. **Telephone:** (908) 284-0404. **Fax:** (908) 284-0405. **Internet:** www.bookfair.bolognafiere.it. **E-mail:** bnmp@childrenssoftware.com.

Bologna Ragazzi Award (Bologna Children's Award)

Awarded at the Bologna Children's Book Fair, held each April, to a work of fiction or non-fiction. The prizes are awarded by an international jury to the best children's titles, based on graphic design, educational, artistic and technical qualities, with particular emphasis on the overall publishing project. Winners are displayed at the Book Fair and in travelling shows staged around the world by the Book Fair.

Eligibility and Restrictions: Entry is open only to exhibitors at the Bologna Book Fair. Titles must have been published between January and December of the previous year. Categories are fiction, 0–16 years, and non-fiction, 0–16 years.

How to Apply: Publishers may submit one or more titles; three copies of each entry should be sent to the Award Secretariat by the end of January.

Recent Winners: 2002: Fiction: Sandy Turner, *Silent Night* and Oliveiro Dumas (illustrator), *El Senor Korbes y Otros Cuentos de Grimm* (joint winners); Non-fiction: Iluïsot, *Una Temporada en Calcuta*.

Sponsoring Organization: Bologna Book Fair.

Contact: Marisa del Todesco.

Address: Fiera del Libro per Ragazzi, Bologna Book Fair, Viale della Fiera 20, 40128 Bologna, Italy. **Telephone:** (51) 282 213/282 111. **Fax:** (51) 282 328. **Internet:** www.bookfair.bolognafiere.it. **E-mail:** marisa.deltodesco@bolognafiere.it.

Gerard Bonniers Pris (Gerard Bonnier Prize)

Established in 1988, and awarded to writers active in a variety of literary fields. The prize is of SEK 125,000.

Recent Winners: 2001: Stig Larsson; 2000: Agneta Pleijel; 1999: Torgny Lindgren; 1998: Bengt Emil Johnson; 1997: Göran Sonnevi.

Sponsoring Organization: Swedish Academy.

Contact: Sec. Bo Svensen.

Address: Swedish Academy, POB 2118, 103 13 Stockholm, Sweden. **Internet:** www.svenskaakademien.se/ENG/index.html.

Book Sense Book of the Year Award

This prize, established in 1991, was known as the American Booksellers Book of the Year Award (ABBY) until its name was changed in 2000. The prize is given by the American Booksellers Association for the book its members most enjoyed selling.

Eligibility and Restrictions: ABA members may nominate any work published in any year for the annual award; members elect the winner from the five titles that receive the most nominations.

How to Apply: There is no application process.

Recent Winners: Adult fiction: 2002: Leif Enger, *Peace Like a River*; 2001: Anita Diamant, *The Red Tent*; 2000: Barbara Kingsolver, *The Poisonwood Bible*; 1999: Rebecca Wells, *Divine Secrets of the Ya-Ya Sisterhood*; 1998: Charles Frazier, *Cold Mountain*
Adult non-fiction: 2002: Laura Hillenbrand, *Seabiscuit: An American Legend*; 2001: Ross King, *Brunelleschi's Dome*
Children's literature: 2002: Ann Brashares, *The Sisterhood of the Traveling Pants*
Children's illustrated: 2002: Ian Falconer, *Olivia Saves the Circus*
Rediscovery Winner: 2002: Ruth Stiles Gannett, Ruth Chrisman Gannett (illustrator), *My Father's Dragon*.
Sponsoring Organization: American Booksellers Association.
Address: American Booksellers Association, 828 South Broadway, Tarrytown, NY 10591, USA. **Telephone:** (914) 591-2665. **Internet:** www.bookweb.org/news/awards/3433.html.

Booker/Open Russia Prize

The Russian Booker prize was founded in 1991 as the first independent literary prize in Russia, with the support of the British Booker Prize. From 1997 the financing of the Russian Booker was underwritten by United Distillers & Vintners, the owners of Smirnoff vodka, but in 2002 general sponsorship of the prize was taken over by the regional charitable organization Open Russia. The Prize was renamed accordingly the 'Booker/Open Russia' Prize.

The prize is awarded each year for the best novel written in the Russian language, and aims to encourage the creativity of authors writing in Russian, to arouse interest in contemporary Russian literature, and to assist the renaissance of the publishing industry and of translations from Russian into other languages. The finalists receive $1,000 each while the winner is awarded $12,500.

Eligibility and Restrictions: Works considered for the prize are put forward by Russian and foreign nominators appointed by the Russian Booker Committee as well as by Russian publishing houses. After screening for conformity with the rules of the competition, these works comprise the Long List which is then judged by a jury consisting of professional literary critics, authors and other leading cultural figures. The jury delivers its Short List of six finalists, before finally choosing the winner.

How to Apply: To be nominated a work must have been published for the first time either as a separate book or in a periodical publication within the previous 12-month period.
Works presented in printers' galleys (or electronic equivalent) should be submitted later in final published form. Only novels in the Russian language can be considered for the prize. Works translated into Russian, other than authors' translations, cannot be accepted. Only works written by a living author are eligible. Each publisher may nominate up to two works. The jury's decision is final.

Recent Winners: 2001: Lyudmila Ulitskaya, *The Kukotsky Case*; 2000: Alexander Shishkin, *The Storming of Izmail*; 1999: Mikhail Butov, *Freedom*; 1998: Alexander Morozov, *Someone Else's Letters*; 1997: Anatolii Azol'skii, *The Cage*.

Sponsoring Organization: Russian Booker Foundation/Open Russia.

Contact: Gilbert Doctorow – Chair., Russian Booker Committee.

Address: Booker/Open Russia Prize, Khoshlovski Per. 13, Str. 1, 109028 Moscow, Russia. **Telephone:** (95) 789 3173. **Fax:** (95) 789 3177. **Internet:** www.russianbooker.ru.

F. Bordewijkprijs

Annual prize of 10,000 DFL, for a novel.

Recent Winners: 2000: Peter Verhelst, *Tongkat. Een verhalenbordeel.*

Sponsoring Organization: Jan Campertstichting (Jan Campert Foundation).

Address: PO Box 12654, 2500 DP The Hague, Netherlands. **Telephone:** (353) 36 37. **Fax:** (353) 30 58.

Boston Globe–Horn Book Award

An annual award established in 1967 by *The Boston Globe* and *The Horn Book Magazine* for books published within the previous year in the categories of fiction, non-fiction and picture book. The winners each receive a prize of $500.

Eligibility and Restrictions: Books must be published in the USA.

Sponsoring Organization: *The Boston Globe.*

Address: Boston Globe, 135 William T. Morrissey Blvd, Boston, MA 02125, USA.

Louise Louis/Emily F. Bourne Student Poetry Award

The Louise Louis/Emily F. Bourne Student Poetry Award , which is administered by the Poetry Society of America (PSA), is endowed by the wills of Louise Louis Whitbread and Ruth M. Bourne. The award, of $150, is given for the best poem by a poet of high-school age from the USA.

Eligibility and Restrictions: Open to poems by US students in high school grades 9 to 12. There is no limit on the length of the poem.

How to Apply: Two copies of submissions should be sent accompanied by a cover sheet and entry fee (non-members) between 1 October and 21 December.

Recent Winners: 2002: Julia Friedlander.

Sponsoring Organization: Poetry Society of America.

Address: Poetry Society of America, 15 Gramercy Park, New York, NY 10003, USA. **Telephone:** (212) 254-9628. **Internet:** www.poetrysociety.org.

Alba Bouwerprys vir Kinderliteratuur
(Alba Bouwer Prize for Children's Literature)

First presented in 1989, this award is given by the South African Academy of Science and Arts for children's (8–12 years) literature in Afrikaans. The prize is given every three years.

Eligibility and Restrictions: Open to works published during the preceding three calendar years. Entries must be written in Afrikaans, but translations are eligible; however preference is given to original works. An author may receive the award more than once.

Recent Winners: 2001: Martie Preller, *Die Balkieboek.*

Sponsoring Organization: Suid-Afrikaanse Akademie vir Wetenskap en Kuns (South African Academy for Science and Arts).

Address: Die Suid-Afrikaanse Akademie vir Wetenskap en Kuns (South African Academy for Science and Arts), PO Box 538, Pretoria, 0001, South Africa. **Telephone:** (12) 328 5082. **Fax:** (12) 328 5091. **Internet:** www.akademie.co.za. **E-mail:** akademie@mweb.co.za.

BP Natural World Book Prize

The prize is an amalgamation of two awards: the BP Conservation Book Prize, established in memory of Sir Peter Kent, and the Wildlife Trusts' Natural World Book of the Year Award. It is the UK's best-known award for environmental literature. An award of £5,000 is made to the winner, and, at the discretion of the judges, a runner-up prize of £1,000 may also be awarded.

Eligibility and Restrictions: Awarded to the book that 'most imaginatively promotes the understanding and conservation of the natural environment'.

How to Apply: Publishers only may submit entries.

Recent Winners: 2000: Brian Clarke, *The Stream*; 1999: Steve Jones, *Almost Like a Whale*; 1998: David Attenborough, *Life of Birds*; 1997: Grahame Harvey, *The Killing of the Countryside*.

Sponsoring Organization: BP Amoco, in association with the Wildlife Trusts, administered by the Book Trust.

Address: Book Trust, 45 East Hill, London SW18 2QZ, UK. **Telephone:** (20) 8516 2972. **Internet:** www.booktrust.org.uk/prizes/bp.htm.

Helmut M. Braem Preis

Established in 1978 to recognize literary translation of prose pieces into German. A prize of DM20,000 is awarded every other year, alternating with the Christoph-Martin-Wieland-Preis (qv), with the winner chosen by a panel of experts.

Eligibility and Restrictions: The translation must have been published by a German publisher and be widely available.

How to Apply: Two copies of the translation plus a copy of the original work should be submitted, accompanied by biographical details of the nominee.

Recent Winners: 2001: Marcus Ingendaag.

Sponsoring Organization: Freundeskreis zur internationalen Förderung literarischer und wissenschaftlicher Übersetzungen.

Contact: Pres. Ragni Maria Gschwend.

Address: Freundeskreis zur internationalen Förderung literarischer und wissenschaftlicher Übersetzungen, Ragni Maria Gschwend, Runzstr. 56, 79102 Freiburg im Breisgau, Germany. **Telephone:** (76) 12 61 98. **Internet:** www.literaturuebersetzer.de.

Brageprisen

A major award for outstanding works of literature, awarded annually since 1992 by the Norwegian Publishers Association. Categories include adult fiction, books for children and young people, non-fiction, poetry, and the Hedersprisen (Honorary Prize) for lifetime achievement. Each year there is an additional open category, which varies between categories such as crime, biography, and others. The winners receive a statuette.

How to Apply: Publishers are invited to submit entries by the deadline in early September.

Recent Winners: Adult Fiction: 2001: Lars Saabye Christensen, *Halvbroren*; 2000: Per Petterson, *I kjølvannet*; 1999: Frode Grytten, *Bikubesong*
Books for Children and Young People: 2001: Anne B. Ragde, *Biografien om Sigrid Undset. Ogsaa en ung Pige*; 2000: Rune Belsvik, *Ein naken gut*; 1999: Erna Osland, *Salamanderryttaren*

Non-fiction: 2001: Atle Næss, *Da jorden stod stille – Galileo Galilei og hans tid*; 2000: Johan Galtung, *Johan uten land. På fredsveien gjennom verden*; 1999: Torbjørn Færøvik, *India – Stevnemøte med skjebnen*
Poetry: 2001: Annie Riis, *Himmel av stål*
Honorary Prize: 2001: Dr Jon Bing; 2000: Eldrid Lunden; 1999: Kjell Aukrust
Open category: 2000 (Crime): Karin Fossum, *Elskede Poona*; 1999 (Biography): Anders Heger, *Mykle. Et diktet liv.*

Sponsoring Organization: Den norske forleggerforeningen (Norwegian Publishers Association).

Address: Den Norske Forleggerforeningen, Ovre Vollgt 15, 0158 Oslo, Norway. **Telephone:** (22) 00 75 80. **Fax:** (22) 33 38 30. **Internet:** www.brageprisen.no/.

Branford Boase Award

This annual award was established in 2000 (and first presented in 2001) in memory of two important figures in the children's book world, Henrietta Branford and Wendy Boase. The award is supported by several publishers, and aims to identify and celebrate the work of the most promising new children's writer in the previous year. The winner, selected by a panel of five judges, receives £1,000 plus a specially engraved box. The editor of the winning book also receives recognition (and a specially engraved box) for encouraging new talent.

Eligibility and Restrictions: Awarded to an outstanding first-time novel for children. The book must be in English, by a UK-based writer.

How to Apply: Publishers apply on behalf of writers, submitting six copies of the book accompanied by an application form giving biographical and editorial details. The deadline is around 25 March.

Recent Winners: 2001: Marcus Sedgwick (writer), Fiona Kennedy (editor); 2000: Katherine Roberts (writer), Barry Cunningham (editor).

Contact: Administrator, Lois Beeson.

Address: 18 Grosvenor Rd, Portswood, Southampton SO17 1RT, UK. **Telephone:** (23) 8055 5057. **Fax:** (23) 8055 5057. **Internet:** www. henriettabranford.co.uk. **E-mail:** locol@csi.com.

James H. Breasted Prize

Established in 1985, this prize, named after James Henry Breasted, a pioneer in ancient Egyptian and Near Eastern history and president of the American Historical Association in 1928, is offered for the best book in English in any field of history prior to 1000 AD. The prize is endowed by Joseph O. Losos, a longtime member of the Association.

Recent Winners: 2001: Barry Cunliffe, *Facing the Ocean: The Atlantic and Its Peoples 8000 BC–AD 1500.*

Sponsoring Organization: American Historical Association.

Contact: Lynn Hunt.

Address: American Historical Asscn, 400 A St, SE, Washington, DC 20003–3889, USA. **Telephone:** (202) 544-2422. **Fax:** (202) 544-8307. **Internet:** www. theaha.org/prizes. **E-mail:** press@theaha.org.

Bremen Literatur Förderungspreis (City of Bremen Literary Encouragement Prize)

The prize was established in 1952 in honour of Rudolf Alexander Schröder, at first under the name Literaturpreis der Freien Hansestadt Bremen. It was later renamed the Literaturpreis der Rudolf Alexander Schröder-Stiftung, before finally becoming known as the Bremen Literaturpreis. The annual prize is presented to a German-speaking writer for a single outstanding work, and consists of DM30,000.

Recent Winners: 2001: Alexander Kluge; 2000: Adolf Endler; 1999: Dieter Forte; 1998: Einar Schleef; 1997: Michael Roes.

Sponsoring Organization: City of Bremen.

Address: Bremen City Council, Herdentorsteinweg 7, 28195 Bremen, Germany.

Bridport Prize

Established in 1973 by Peggy Chapman-Andrews, this is an annual award for short stories and poems, with a cash prize of £3,000 for the winning work, £1,000 for the runner-up, and 11 smaller prizes. In addition an anthology of the winning works is published each year. The selection is made by two judges, usually professional authors or poets.

Eligibility and Restrictions: Open to previously unpublished work which has not been entered in any other current competitions. Short stories should be up to 5,000 words, poems up to 42 lines.

How to Apply: Official entry forms are available from the address or website given.

Recent Winners: Story: 2001: Chris Hill; 1990: Helen Dunmore and Kate Atkinson
Poetry: 2001: Rowland Malony; 1996: Tobias Hill; 1989: Glynn Maxwell.

Sponsoring Organization: Bridport Arts Centre.

Contact: Administrator Frances Everitt.

Address: Bridport Arts Centre, South St, Bridport DT6 3NR, UK. **Telephone:** (1398) 459444. **Fax:** (1308) 459166. **Internet:** www.bridportprize.org.uk. **E-mail:** frances@bridport-arts.com.

Katharine Briggs Folklore Award

An annual book prize established by the Folklore Society to encourage the study of folklore and to commemorate the life and work of the distinguished scholar Katharine Mary Briggs (1898–1980). The prize is awarded to a book that has made the most distinguished contribution to folklore studies. The winner is chosen by three judges, and receives an engraved goblet and a cheque for £50.

Eligibility and Restrictions: Entries must have been originally published in English in the UK or Ireland between 1 June and 31 May in the year in which the prize is awarded. Translations and folktales retold to children are not eligible; reprints and second editions are also excluded.

How to Apply: Submissions are invited from publishers and authors. Four copies of each book submitted for the award must reach the Society's office by 31 May.

Recent Winners: 2001: Adam Fox, *Oral and Literate Culture in England, 1500–1700*; 2000: Diarmuid O'Giollain, *Locating Irish Folklore: Tradition, Modernity, Identity*; 1999: Marina Warner, *No Go the Bogeyman*; 1998: Joseph Falaky Nagy, *Conversing with Angels and Ancients*; 1997 Neil Jarman, *Parading Culture: Parades and Visual Displays in Northern Ireland*.

Sponsoring Organization: Folklore Society.

Address: The Folklore Society, The Warburg Institute, Woburn Square, London WC1H 0AB, UK. **Telephone:** (20) 7387 5894. **Internet:** www.folklore-society. com.

British Academy Book Prize

An annual award established in 2001 to recognize the best book published in social sciences and the humanities in the preceding year. The first award, of £2,500, was presented in December 2001. The longlist is drawn up by around 700 Fellows of the British Academy, then a shortlist and winner are decided by a panel of five judges.

Eligibility and Restrictions: Awarded to books published in English in the UK during the previous year. Entries must be outstanding works of scholarship that are accessible to the general reader.

How to Apply: Nominations from publishers are accepted; deadline is late February.

Recent Winners: 2001: Ian Kershaw, *Hitler: 1936–45* and Rees Davies, *The First English Empire: Power and Identities in the British Isles 1093–1343* (joint winners).

Sponsoring Organization: British Academy.

Contact: Asst Sec. Jonathan Breckon.

Address: British Academy, 10 Carlton House Terrace, London SW1Y 5AH, UK. **Telephone:** (20) 7969 5263. **Fax:** (20) 969 5414. **E-mail:** secretary@britac.ac.uk.

British Book Awards

Established in 1989 to reward the book and publishing industry. There are 21 awards, known as Nibbies, in a range of categories, with various awards sponsored by different companies. Literary awards include the Securicor Omega Express Author of the Year, Butler & Tanner Book of the Year, Publishing News Trophy for Lifetime Achievement, the Virgin Books Newcomer of the Year Award, W H Smith Children's Book of the Year, the BCA Illustrated Book of the Year and The Bookseller Services to Bookselling Award. There are no cash prizes. Other awards are given for exporting, marketing, bookselling, design and so on.

Eligibility and Restrictions: Books must have been published in English in the calendar year prior to the awards. Criteria for various categories include: Book of the Year: for a book that has made an outstanding impact, a bestseller which has brought people into bookshops and created wide media attention; Author of the Year: outstanding literary achievement, combining readability with strong sales; Illustrated Book of the Year: for an adult book with high-quality illustrations and production; Children's Book of the Year: for a book with wide appeal, which has made a significant impact within the trade and among the public; Newcomer of the Year: a new author, start-up publisher or new bookselling venture.

How to Apply: Nomination forms are published in the book trade press in October.

Recent Winners: Securicor Omega Express Author of the Year: 2001: Philip Pullman; 2000: Nigella Lawson; 1999: Beryl Bainbridge; 1998: Louis de Bernières; 1997: Bill Bryson
Butler & Tanner Book of the Year: 2001: Pamela Stephenson, *Billy*; 2000: Tony Parsons, *Man and Boy*; 1999: Ted Hughes, *Birthday Letters*; 1998: Helen Fielding, *Bridget Jones's Diary*; 1997: Dava Sobel, *Longitude*
Publishing News Trophy for Lifetime Achievement: 2001: Mark Barty-King; 2000: Ernest Hecht; 1999: Spike Milligan; 1998: Maeve Binchy; 1997: Jilly Cooper
Virgin Books Newcomer of the Year Award: 2001: Pete McCarthy, *McCarthy's Bar*; 2000: Zadie Smith, *White Teeth*; 1999: Chris Stewart, *Driving Over Lemons*; 1998: Borders UK; 1997: Daisy & Tom
W H Smith Children's Book of the Year: 2001: Eoin Colfer, *Artemis Fowl*; 2000: Philip Pullman, *The Amber Spyglass*; 1999: Jacqueline Wilson, *The Illustrated Mum*; 1998: J. K. Rowling, *Harry Potter and the Chamber of Secrets*; 1997: J. K. Rowling, *Harry Potter and the Philosopher's Stone*
BCA Illustrated Book of the Year: 2001: BBC Books, *The Blue Planet*; 2000: *The Beatles Anthology*; 1999: Bruce Bernard, *Century*; 1998: Raymond Briggs, *Ethel and Ernest*; 1997: Tim Smit, *The Lost Gardens of Heligan*
The Bookseller Services to Bookselling Award: 2001: Martyn Goff; 2000: Terry Pratchett; 1999: Tim Godfray; 1998: Willie Anderson; 1997: Dick Francis.

Sponsoring Organization: Publishing News.

Contact: Administrator Merric Davidson.

Address: Publishing News, 39 Store St, London WC1E 7DB, UK. **Telephone:** (20) 7692 2900. **Fax:** (20) 7419 2111. **Internet:** www.publishingnews.co.uk. **E-mail:** nibbies@mdla.co.uk.

British Columbia Book Prizes

The BC Book Prizes, established in 1985, celebrate the achievements of British Columbia writers and publishers. The prizes are administered and awarded by members of the West Coast Book Prize Society, a non-profit society, who represent all facets of the publishing and writing community. Awards are presented in six categories including fiction, non-fiction, poetry and regional prizes. In 2001 a new awards category, the Christie Harris award for illustrated children's literature, was announced.

Eligibility and Restrictions: The prizes are awarded each spring for books published during the preceding calendar year; residency conditions for authors vary according to the category; check website for details.

How to Apply: The submission deadline each year is 23 December.

Recent Winners: Ethel Wilson Fiction Prize: 2002: Madeleine Thien, *Simple Recipes*; 2001: Eden Robinson, *Monkey Beach*
Haig-Brown Regional Prize: 2002: Keith Thor Carlson, Colin Duffield, Albert (Sonny) McHalsie, Jan Perrier, Leeanna Lynn Rhodes, David M. Schaepe and David Smith, *A Stó:lo–Coast Salish Historical Atlas*; 2001: Dan Francis, *The Encyclopedia of British Columbia*
Hubert Evans Non-Fiction Prize: 2002: Susan Crean, *The Laughing One: A Journey to Emily Carr*; 2001: Terry Glavin, *The Last Great Sea*
Bill Duthie Booksellers' Choice: 2002: Terry Reksten, *Illustrated History of British Columbia*; 2001: Dan Francis, *The Encyclopedia of British Columbia*

Dorothy Livesay Poetry Prize: 2002: Karen Solie, *Short Haul Engine*; 2001: Don McKay, *Another Gravity*

Sheila Egoff Children's Prize: 2002: Polly Horvath, *Everything on a Waffle*; 2001: James Heneghan, *The Grave*.

Sponsoring Organization: West Coast Book Prize Society.

Address: West Coast Book Prize Society, #902207 West Hastings St, Vancouver, BC V6B 1H7, Canada. **Telephone:** (604) 687-2405. **Fax:** (604) 669-3701. **Internet:** www.harbour.sfu.ca/bcbook/. **E-mail:** info@rebuscreative.net.

British Comparative Literature Association Translation Prize

Awarded annually for the best unpublished literary translation from any language into English. The winner receives £350, with £200 and £100 for second- and third-placed entries respectively. Winning entries are published in the annual journal *Comparative Criticism*.

Eligibility and Restrictions: Open to poetry, fiction or prose from any period; entries may be up to 25 pages in length. There are no restrictions on entrants with respect to age, nationality, place of residence or professional status.

How to Apply: Contact Mary Fox at the address given for an entry form. The entry fee is £5 per entry, and a maximum of three entries may be submitted per entrant. The closing date is 31 January.

Recent Winners: 2001: Sylvester Mazarella, *Lord Nevermore* by Agneta Pleijel.

Sponsoring Organization: British Comparative Literature Association/British Centre for Literary Translation.

Contact: Dr Jean Boase-Beier.

Address: School of Language, Linguistics and Translation Studies, University of East Anglia, Norwich NR4 7TJ, UK. **Telephone:** (1603) 592143. **Internet:** www.bcla.org. **E-mail:** transcomp@uea.ac.uk.

British Fantasy Awards

A set of awards presented by the British Fantasy Society (BFS) at its annual conference in categories including best novel (the August Derleth Award), best short story, and best anthology. The winners are selected by BFS members, and receive a statuette.

Recent Winners: August Derleth Award (Novel): 2001: China Mieville, *Perdido Street Station*; 2000: Graham Joyce, *Indigo*

Short Fiction: 2001: Tim Lebbon, *Naming of Parts*; 2000: Tim Lebbon, *White*

Best Anthology: 2001: Brian Willis (Editor), *Hideous Progeny*; 2000: Stephen Jones (Editor), *The Mammoth Book of Best New Horror*

Collection: 2001: Kim Newman, *Where the Bodies are Buried*; 2000: Peter Crowther, *Lonesome Roads*.

Sponsoring Organization: British Fantasy Society.

Address: 201 Reddish Road, South Reddish, Stockport SK5 7HR, UK. **Internet:** www.britishfantasysociety.org.uk/bfsindex.htm. **E-mail:** info@ britishfantasysociety.org.uk.

British Science Fiction Association Awards

The awards were established in 1966 to promote the best British (and other) science fiction novel, story, artwork, etc. The awards are announced annually at Easter; the prize for the winner of each category is an original artwork trophy.

Eligibility and Restrictions: Categories are best novel; best short fiction; best non-fiction; and best artwork. Entries must have been first published in the UK in the current calendar year.

How to Apply: No applications are permitted; nominations are made by British Science Fiction Association (BSFA) members, and the shortlist is decided by the Awards Administrator based on nominations. The final winners are voted by ballot. The closing date for nominations is the end of January.

Recent Winners: Best Novel: 2000: Mary Gentle, *Ash: A Secret History*; 1999: Ken MacLeod, *The Sky Road*; 1998: Christopher Priest, *The Extremes*; 1997: Mary Doria Russell, *The Sparrow*; 1996: Iain M. Banks, *Excession*
Best Short Fiction: 2000: Peter F. Hamilton, *The Suspect Genome*; 1999: Eric Brown, *Hunting the Slarque*; 1998: Gwyneth Jones, *La Cenerentola*; 1997: Stephen Baxter, *War Birds*; 1996: Barrington J. Bayley, *A Crab Must Try*
Artwork: 2000: Dominic Harman, *Hideaway*; 1999: Robert Charles Wilson, *Darwinia*; 1998: Jim Burns, *Lord Prestimion*; 1997: SMS, *The Black Blood of the Dead*; 1996: Jim Burns, *Ancient Shores*.

Sponsoring Organization: British Science Fiction Association.

Contact: Administrator Tanya Brown.

Address: British Science Fiction Association, 8 Century House, Armoury Rd, London SE8 4LH, UK. **Telephone:** (20) 8469 3354. **Internet:** www.bsfa.co.uk. **E-mail:** awards@amaranth.aviators.net.

Broumovska literarni cena (Broumov Literary Prize)

The award was established in 2001 and is focused on literary works connected with Broumovsko region in the Czech Republic and the neighbouring area of Poland. The Broumov Literary Prize has three national sections, where literary works in three languages are honoured: Marie Stryjova Prize (Cena Marie Stryjove), for works in the Czech language, Hugo Scholz Prize (Cena Huga Scholze), German language and Joseph Wittig Prize (Cena Josepha Wittiga), Polish language. These three prizes are decided by the national committees in each of the countries, while an international board decides on the main Broumov Literary Prize in Broumov. The amount of the prize money varies according to sponsors.

Eligibility and Restrictions: There are several categories by age and type of literary works, but these are variable. The only fixed rule is that the work or the author must have links with the Broumovsko region.

How to Apply: Deadline for applications is mid-June.

Recent Winners: Marie Stryjova Prize: 2001: Josef Skvorecky (writer)
Hugo Scholz Prize: 2001: Rainhard Meissner (journalist)
Joseph Wittig Prize: 2001: Karol Maliszewski (poet)
Broumov Literary Prize: 2001: Josef Skvorecky (writer).

Sponsoring Organization: Centrum Broumov.

Address: Centrum Broumov, Pivovarska St, Broumov, Czech Republic. **Telephone:** 447 521357. **Internet:** www.centrumbroumov.cz. **E-mail:** info@ centrumbroumov.cz.

Bucharest Writers' Association Prizes

A series of annual awards presented by the Bucharest Writers' Association for outstanding books in the following categories: poetry, prose, essay, memoir, translation, drama, criticism and debut work.

Recent Winners: Poetry: 2000: Mircea Bârsila, *O linie aproape neagra*; Rodica Draghincescu, *Eu-genia*; Ion Draganoiu, *Alice în tara notiunilor*; Liviu Ioan Stoiciu, *Copacul animal*
Prose: 2000: Iolanda Malamen, *Felipe si Margarita*; Constantin Stan, *Provizoriu*; Dan Stanca, *Domnul clipei*
Essay: 2000: Gabriel Dimisianu, *Lumea criticului*; Octavian Soviany, *Textualism, postmodernism, apocaliptic*
Memoir: 2000: Radu F. Alexandru, *Gimnastica de dimineata*; Constantin Toiu, *Ravase din Kamceatca*
Translation: 2000: Antoaneta Ralian, *Sexus* by Henry Miller; Mariana Stefanescu, *Peisaj pictat în ceai de Milorad Pavic*
Translation from Romanian: 2000: Geo Vasile, Bilingual Italian-Romanian edition of *Eminescu poeme alese*
Drama: 2000: Stefan Agopian, *Republica pe esafod*; Lucia Verona, *Grand Hotel Europa*
Criticism: 2000: Nicolae Gheran, *Opere-Rebreanu, vol. 20*
Debut: 2000: Constantin Virgil Banescu, *Câinele, femeia si ocheada*; Gabriela Vrânceanu-Firea, *O alta lume*; Vera Ion, *Copilul cafea*; Grasiel Popescu, *Domnisoara Popescu, amoruri fictive.*

Sponsoring Organization: Asociatiei Scriitorilor din Bucuresti.

Address: Asociatiei Scriitorilor din Bucuresti, Str. Nicolae Golescu 15, Sectorul 1, Bucharest, Romania. **Telephone:** (1) 2128208. **Fax:** (1) 128208. **Internet:** asbucuresti.tripod.com/indexen.htm.

Georg-Büchner-Preis (Georg Büchner Prize)

First presented 1951, the Georg Büchner Prize has grown to be recognized as Germany's foremost literary award. It carries a prize of €40,000, and is awarded in recognition of the winner's special status and contribution to contemporary German culture. (From 1951 to 1923, it was awarded under a different arrangement by the State of Hesse, and was presented for a wider range of artistic achievements.)

Eligibility and Restrictions: Awarded to a novelist or poet writing in German.

Recent Winners: 2002: Wolfgang Hilbig; 2001: Friederike Mayröcker; 2000: Volker Braun; 1999: Arnold Stadler; 1998: Elfriede Jellinek; the list of earlier winners includes the most eminent German-language writers of the 20th century, including Günter Grass, Heinrich Böll, Peter Handke, Paul Celan, Elias Canetti, Christa Wolf, etc.

Sponsoring Organization: Deutsche Akademie für Sprache und Dichtung.

Contact: Pres., Deutsche Akademie für Sprache und Dichtung, Darmstadt Prof. Dr Christian Meier.

Address: Deutsche Akademie für Sprache und Dichtung, Alexandraweg 23, 64287 Darmstadt, Germany. **Telephone:** (6151) 40920. **Fax:** (6151) 409299. **Internet:** www.deutscheakademie.de.

Pitras Bukhari Award

The Pakistan Academy of Letters administers a series of annual prizes established in 1980 under the Hijra National Literary Awards Scheme. The aim of the awards is to promote literary activities and recognize outstanding contributions. The Pitras Bukhari Award, named after a prominent Pakistani writer, is an annual prize of Rs 50,000 for works written in English.

Recent Winners: 2000: Abdul Basit Haqqani, *Papio*; 1999: Ikram Chaghtai, *Goethe, Iqbal and Orient*; 1998: Safdar Mir, *Modern Urdu Poets*.

Sponsoring Organization: Pakistan Academy of Letters.

Contact: Deputy Dir Naseem Mahmood.

Address: Pitras Bokhari Road, Sector H-8/1, Islamabad, Pakistan. **Telephone:** 9257164. **Fax:** 9257159. **E-mail:** academy@apollo.net.pk.

Bulwer-Lytton Fiction Contest

The Bulwer-Lytton Fiction Contest was established in 1982 by the English Department at San José State University. It takes the form of a whimsical literary competition that challenges entrants to compose the opening sentence to an imaginary badly written novel. The contest was founded by Professor Scott Rice, and is named after the originator of the line *It was a dark and stormy night*, the Victorian novelist Edward George Earle Bulwer-Lytton. Winners are selected in numerous categories, and their entries are published on the website.

Eligibility and Restrictions: Sentences may be of any length, and entrants may submit more than one, but all entries must be original and previously unpublished. Entries are judged by categories, from 'general' to detective, western, science fiction, romance, and so on. There are overall winners as well as category winners.

How to Apply: Entries should be submitted on index cards, the sentence on one side and the entrant's name, address, and phone number on the other. Deadline is late June.

Recent Winners: Fiction: 2001: Sera Kirk
Detective: 2001: Rephah Berg
Fantasy: 2001: Nicolas Juzda
Purple Prose: 2001: Shauna Banta
Science Fiction: 2001: Mike Rottmann
Western: 2001: Jeff Riopelle
Romance: 2001: Carol E. Scott
Adventure: 2001: Bob Wakulich
Children's: 2001: Delano Lopez

Sponsoring Organization: San José State University English Department.

Address: Dept of English, San José State University, San José, CA 95192–0090, USA. **Internet:** www.bulwer-lytton.com.

Bungakukai Shinjin Shô (Bungakukai Prize for New Writers)

Established in 1955 by the Bungei Shunjû publishing company for the purpose of recognizing promising new writers. Previously unpublished manuscripts are solicited twice a year for the award, with the winning entry appearing in *Bungakukai* magazine. The winner receives a commemorative gift and a cash prize of 500,000 yen.

Recent Winners: 1983: Yasuo Tanaka, *Nantonaku kurisutaru (Somehow Crystal)*.

Sponsoring Organization: Bungakukai magazine.

Address: Bungakukai magazine, Tokyo, Japan.

Buxtehuder Bulle

The Buxtehuder Bulle was established by Winfried Ziemann in 1971, and is sponsored by the City of Buxtehude. The prize is named after a bull from the 1937 book *The Story of Ferdinand* by US writer Munro Leaf. It is awarded annually for the best new book for young readers published in Germany in the previous year. The winner is selected by a jury consisting of 11 teenagers and 11 adults who change each year. The prize consists of €5,000 and a steel sculpture of Ferdinand the bull.

Eligibility and Restrictions: Entries must have been published in German during the previous year, and be aimed at readers aged between 14 and 17.

How to Apply: Entry is by international nomination only.

Recent Winners: 2000: Sherryl Jordan, *Junipers Spiel*; 1999: John Marsden, *Gegen jede Chance*; 1998: Andreas Steinhöfel, *Die Mitte der Welt*; 1997: Ralf Isau, *Das Museum der gestohlenen Erinnerungen*; 1996: Jostein Gaarder, *Durch einen Spiegel, in einem dunklen Wort*.

Sponsoring Organization: City of Buxtehude.

Contact: Frau Bruns-Decker.

Address: Stadt Buxtehude, Fachgruppe für Kultur, Stavenort 5, 21614 Buxtehude, Germany. **Telephone:** (4161) 501 344/454. **Fax:** (4161) 501 423.

CAA Air Canada Award

The CAA Air Canada Award, which has been given since 1979, is presented to the Canadian (or landed immigrant) writer under 30 deemed to show most promise in the field of literary creation. A trustee appointed by the Canadian Authors Association (CAA) Awards Chair reviews the entries and selects a winner. The prize consists of two tickets to any destination on Air Canada's routes.

Eligibility and Restrictions: There are no restrictions on genre and a winner may be chosen for work in a variety of forms. Previous winners are ineligible but there is no limit on the number of times a writer may be nominated before the age limit (under 30 at 30 April in the year of the competition) is reached.

How to Apply: Nominations are made through CAA branches, other writing organizations, agents or publishers. Self-nominations are not accepted. Nomination can be in any form but the recommended approach is to submit a biography of the writer accompanied by an introductory letter and samples of the writer's work. The deadline is 31 March.

Recent Winners: Recent winners include Richard van Camp, Lynn Coady, Rob McLennan, Treena Kortje and Madeleine Thien.

Sponsoring Organization: Canadian Authors Association (CAA)/Air Canada.

Address: 320 South Shores Road, POB 419, Campbellford, ON K0L 1L0, Canada. **Telephone:** (705) 653-0323. **Fax:** (705) 653-0593. **E-mail:** canauth@redden. on.ca.

Caine Prize for African Writing

The Caine Prize for African Writing was established in 2000 in memory of the late Sir Michael Caine, former Chairman of Booker plc and Chairman of Africa 95. The first prize was awarded in 2000, and in its first year the prize attracted entries from 20 African countries. The award is made in July each year, with a special focus on short stories. There is a cash prize of $15,000 for the winning author and a travel award for each of the short-listed candidates (up to five in all). The prize was won in 2002 by a short story which had appeared in an internet magazine rather than as a conventional hard-copy publication.

Eligibility and Restrictions: Open to short stories of between 3,000 and 10,000 words, by an African writer published in English, whether in Africa or elsewhere. An 'African writer' is defined as someone who was born in Africa, or who is a national of an African country, or whose parents are African, and whose work has reflected African sensibilities. Work must have been originally published in the 30 months preceding the submissions deadline (changing to 5 years from the 2003 prize) and not previously considered for a Caine Prize. Unpublished work and work in languages other than English is not eligible. However, works translated into English from other languages are not excluded, provided they have been published in translation. If such a work wins, a proportion of the prize would be awarded to the translator.

How to Apply: Submissions should be made by publishers and should be accompanied by 12 original published copies of the work for consideration, sent to the address given. The deadline for submissions is 31 January. There is no application form.

Recent Winners: 2002: Binyavanga Wainaina (Kenya), *Discovering Home*; 2001: Helon Habila (Nigeria); 2000: Leila Aboulela (Sudan), *The Museum*.

Sponsoring Organization: Africa Centre.

Contact: Administrator, Nick Elam.

Address: Caine Prize for African Writing, 2 Drayson Mews, London W8 4LY, UK. **Telephone:** (20) 7376 0440. **Fax:** (20) 7938 3728. **Internet:** www. caineprize.com/. **E-mail:** caineprize@jftaylor.com.

Randolph Caldecott Medal

Established in 1937 and named after Randolph Caldecott, a 19th-century British illustrator; this medal, alongside the John Newbery Medal, represents the most prestigious US award in children's literature. It is awarded annually to the illustrator of the 'most distinguished American picture book for children'.

Eligibility and Restrictions: Illustrations must be original work by artists who are citizens or residents of the USA and must have been published in the USA during the previous year. The work must not have been published originally outside the USA. The award may be made posthumously.

How to Apply: One copy of the book should be sent to the Association for Library Service to Children (ALSC) office, and one copy to the Chair of the Award Committee, by 31 December of the year of publication.

Recent Winners: 2002: David Wiesner, *The Three Pigs*; 2001: David Small, *So You Want To Be President?*; 2000: Simms Taback, *Joseph Had a Little Overcoat*; 1999: Mary Azarian, *Snowflake Bentley*; 1998: Paul O. Zelinsky, *Rapunzel*; 1997: David Wisniewski, *Golem*.

Sponsoring Organization: Association for Library Service to Children, a division of the American Library Association.

Address: Association for Library Service to Children, American Library Association, 50 East Huron, Chicago, IL 60611–2795, USA. **Fax:** (312) 944-7671. **Internet:** www.ala.org/alsc. **E-mail:** alsc@ala.org.

California Young Reader Medal

An award established in 1974 with the aim of introducing young readers to the enjoyment of reading purely for pleasure. Under the scheme, young people suggest the names of favourite books for nomination, or teachers and librarians note repeatedly read or requested titles, and these are submitted to the California Young Reader Medal Committee. Members of the committee then draw up a list of nominees, and the winners are selected by vote among the young readers. Prizes are awarded in four categories: Primary, Intermediate, Middle School/Junior High, and Young Adult (9–12 years).

Eligibility and Restrictions: Entries must be an original work of fiction published within the last five years by a living author.

How to Apply: Recommendations for nomination are due each year by 1 April for consideration as a nominee the following year.

Recent Winners: Primary: 2002: Helen Lester, *Hooway for Wodney Wat!*
Intermediate: 2002: Dan Gutman, *The Million Dollar Shot*
Middle School/Junior High: 2002: Jack Gantos, *Joey Pigza Swallowed the Key*
Young Adult: 2002: Jean Ferris, *Bad*
Picture Books for Older Readers: 2002: Paul Fleischman, *Weslandia*.

Sponsoring Organization: California Library Association.

Address: California Library Association, 717 20th Street, Suite 200, Sacramento, CA 95814, USA. **Telephone:** (916) 447-8541. **Fax:** (916) 447-8394. **Internet:** www.cla-net.org/. **E-mail:** info@cla-net.org.

Calwer Hermann-Hesse-Preis

Established in 1987, the Hermann Hesse Literature Prize is awarded every two years on the birthday of the eminent German author Hermann Hesse. There are two categories: the Calwer Hermann Hesse Encouragement Prize (€15,000) for German-language literary magazines which publish the work of young authors or those who are not yet established, and the Calwer Hermann Hesse Translators Prize (€15,000) for the translation of works by Hermann Hesse into another language, or the translation of outstanding foreign literary works into German. The winners are selected by a specially appointed jury.

Eligibility and Restrictions: The Encouragement prize is open to German language literary magazines which publish significant works by new authors. The Translators prize alternates between translation of works by Hermann Hesse into another language, and translation of foreign literary works into German. Entries must be already published.

Recent Winners: 2001: Marlene Streeruwitz, *Nachwelt*.

Sponsoring Organization: Hermann-Hesse-Stiftung (Hermann Hesse Foundation).

Address: Hermann-Hesse-Stiftung, Calw, Germany. **Internet:** www.kskcalw.de/hesse.

John W. Campbell Memorial Award for the Best New Writer

The John W. Campbell Memorial Award for the Best New Writer in the field of science fiction is administered by the World Science Fiction Society (WSFS) Worldcon Committee along similar lines to the Hugo Award (qv). The winner is chosen by nominations from, and a popular vote of, the membership of WSFS.

Sponsoring Organization: World Science Fiction Society (WSFS)/ Davis Publications/ Dell Publications.

Address: World Science Fiction Society, POB 426159, Kendall Square Station, Cambridge, MA 02142, USA. **Internet:** worldcon.org.

Jan Campert Prize

An annual prize of 10,000 DFL, for poetry.

Recent Winners: 2000: K. Michel, *Waterstudies*.

Sponsoring Organization: Jan Campertstichting (Jan Campert Foundation).

Address: PO Box 12654, 2500 DP The Hague, Netherlands. **Telephone:** (353) 36 37. **Fax:** (353) 30 58.

Canada-Switzerland Literary Prize

An annual award presented in alternate years to a Canadian or Swiss writer for a work of poetry, fiction, drama or non-fiction. The prize may also be awarded for the French translation of a work written originally in English by a Canadian writer or in German, Italian or Romansch by a Swiss writer. The winner receives C$2,500.

Eligibility and Restrictions: Entries must have been published in French during the preceding eight years.

Sponsoring Organization: Canada Council.

Address: Canada Council, 350 Albert St, POB 1047, Ottawa, ON K1P 5V4, Canada.

Canadian Authors Association Literary Awards

A series of annual awards including fiction (The CAA MOSAID Technology, Inc. Award for Fiction), poetry (The CAA Jack Chalmers Poetry Award), short story (The CAA Jubilee Award for Short Stories), biography (The CAA Birks Family Foundation Award for Biography), Canadian history (The CAA Lela Common Award for Canadian History), drama (The CAA Carol Bolt Drama Award, new in 2002), children's (CAA Children's Short Story Award, new in 2002) as well as a special award for a complete body of work. Winners in each category receive $2,500 and a silver medal.

Eligibility and Restrictions: Awards are for full-length English-language literature by authors who are Canadians or landed immigrants. All entries must have been first published during the preceding year. Publication may have taken place outside Canada. Previous winners are not eligible for awards they have won, but may be entered in the other categories. Reprints, translations and posthumous entries are not eligible.

How to Apply: Five copies of the entries, plus a competed entry form and fee of $20 per title, should be submitted by mid-December.

Recent Winners: CAA MOSAID Technology, Inc. Award for Fiction: 2002: Will Ferguson, *Generica*

CAA Lela Common Award for Canadian History: 2002: Ken McGoogan, *Fatal Passage: The Untold Story of John Rae, the Arctic Adventurer Who Discovered the Fate of Franklin*; 2001: Will Ferguson

CAA Jack Chalmers Poetry Award: 2002: Tim Bowling, *Darkness and Silence*; 2001: Carmine Starnoi, *Credo*; 2000: Helen Humphreys, *Anthem*; 1999: Janice Kulyk Feeper, *Marrying the Sea*

CAA Carol Bolt Drama Award: 2002: Kent Stetson, *The Harps of God*

CAA Jubilee Award for Short Stories: 2002: Melissa Hardy, *Uncharted Heart*

CAA Birks Family Foundation Award for Biography: 2002: Julian Sher, *Until You are Dead*

CAA Children's Short Story Award: 2002: Irene Morck, *Riches This Christmas*.

Sponsoring Organization: Canadian Authors Association (CAA)/Canada Council for the Arts.

Contact: Alec McEachern.

Address: 27 Doxsee Ave North, POB 419, Campbellford, ON K0L 1L0, Canada. **Telephone:** (705) 653-0323. **Fax:** (705) 653-0593. **Internet:** www.CanAuthors. org. **E-mail:** canauth@redden.on.ca.

Canadian Library Association Book of the Year for Children Award

First presented in 1947, this prize is awarded to an outstanding contribution to Canadian children's literature, in any genre of creative writing.

Eligibility and Restrictions: To merit consideration a book must have been published in Canada during the past year and its author must be a Canadian citizen or a permanent resident of Canada. Any work that is an act of creative writing (i.e. fiction, poetry, retelling of traditional literature) is eligible regardless of published format, including anthologies and collections.

How to Apply: Nominations should be sent by 1 January each year to: Ottawa Public Library, Carlingwood Branch, 281 Woodroffe Avenue, Ottawa, ON K2A 3W4.

Recent Winners: 2001: Nan Gregory, *Wild Girl & Gran*; 2000: Kenneth Oppel, *Sunwing*; 1999: Tim Wynne-Jones, *Stephen Fair*; 1998: Kenneth Oppel, *Silverwing*; 1997: Brian Doyle, *Uncle Ronald*.

Sponsoring Organization: National Book Service.

Address: Canadian Library Association, 328 Frank St, Ottawa, ON K2P 0X8, Canada. **Telephone:** (613) 232-9625. **Fax:** (613) 563-9895. **Internet:** www. cla.ca.

Canadian Library Association Young Adult Book Award

Established in 1980 by the Young Adult Caucus of the Saskatchewan Library Association, the Young Adult Canadian Book Award is administered by the Young Adult Services Interest Group of the Canadian Library Association. The award recognizes an author of an outstanding English-language Canadian book which appeals to young adults between the ages of 13 and 18. The award is given annually, when merited, at the Canadian Library Association's (CLA's) annual conference. The winner receives a leather-bound book with the title, author and award seal embossed on the cover in gold.

Eligibility and Restrictions: To be eligible for consideration, the following must apply: it must be a work of fiction (novel or collection of short stories) published in the previous year, the title must be a Canadian publication in either hardcover or paperback, and the author must be a Canadian citizen or landed immigrant.

How to Apply: Eligible titles should be sent to: Jennifer Johnson, Rosemount Branch, Ottawa Public Library, 18 Rosemount Avenue, Ottawa, ON K1Y 1P4. Deadline is 1 January each year.

Recent Winners: 2001: Beth Goobie, *Before Wings*; 2000: Katherine Holubitsky, *Alone at Ninety Foot*; 1999: Gayle Friesen, *Janey's Girl*; 1998: Martha Brooks, *Bone Dance*; 1997: R. P. MacIntyre, *Takes: Stories for Young Adults*.

Sponsoring Organization: Canadian Library Association.

Address: Canadian Library Association, 328 Frank St, Ottawa, ON K2P 0X8, Canada. **Telephone:** (613) 232-9625. **Fax:** (613) 563-9895. **Internet:** www.cla.ca.

Canadian Literary Awards

Three annual prizes of C$10,000 each are awarded for poetry, short story, and essay/memoirs. The awards are intended to encourage excellence and variety in these genres, and others (radio drama, children's story) for which awards have in the past been presented. The awards were formerly known as the Tilden Canadian Literary Awards (1995–96), the CBC/Saturday Night Literary Awards and, from 1979–94, the CBC Radio Literary Competition.

Sponsoring Organization: Canadian Broadcasting Corporation/Saturday Night Magazine/The Canada Council.

Address: CBC, 250 Lanark Ave, POB 3220, Station C, Ottawa, ON K1Y 1E4, Canada.

Cao Yu Drama Literature Prize

Named after Cao Yu (1910–1996), China's top playwright and founding father of the country's modern dramas, the award is sponsored by the Chinese Dramatists' Association. The prize is China's leading award in the field of dramatic literature. In 2000 awards were granted to 10 outstanding drama and opera literature works.

Recent Winners: 2000: Li Baoqun, *Father*, plus four other drama literary works and Feng Zhi, *Rural Policeman*, plus four other opera literary works; former winners have included dramas such as *Mayor Chen Yi, Warm Currents Outside the Room, Duet Romance, Weddings and Funerals, Tang Poet Li Bai*, and *A Crouching Tiger on Mount Zhong*.

Sponsoring Organization: Chinese Dramatists' Association, China.

Karel Čapek Award for Literary Achievement

Named after a Czech novelist, short-story writer, playwright, and essayist, the prize was instituted by the Czech branch of the International PEN Club and the Association of Czech PEN Friends in 1994. The prize is awarded every other year for prose, drama and essay work. A lifetime achievement prize is also awarded, with preference given to a Czech author.

Recent Winners: Lifetime achievement: 1996: Arnost Lustig.

Sponsoring Organization: Czech PEN Centre.

Address: Czech PEN Centre, 28 října 9, 110 00 Prague, Czech Republic. **E-mail:** centrum@pen.cz.

Cappelen-prisen

An annual prize presented by the publisher Cappelens. The award was first presented in 1979, and the winner receives a prize of 50,000 NOK.

Eligibility and Restrictions: Open only to writers and employees at Cappelen.

Recent Winners: 2001: Anne Holt; 2000: Gro Dahle; 1999: Georg Johannesen; 1998: (no award given); 1997: Erlend Loe.

Sponsoring Organization: J. W. Cappelens Forlag AS.

Address: J. W. Cappelens Forlag AS, Mariboesgt 13, Postboks 350, Sentrum, 0101 Oslo, Norway. **Telephone:** (22) 36 50 00. **Fax:** (22) 36 50 40. **Internet:** www.cappelen.no/main/kanal.asp. **E-mail:** web@cappelen.no.

Carnegie Medal

The Carnegie Medal is awarded annually for an outstanding book for children while its sister award, the Kate Greenaway Medal, is for an outstanding illustrated book for children. The awards are open for nominations from members during February each year and are judged by a panel of 12 children's librarians from the Youth Libraries Group. A shortlist for the medal is announced at the beginning of May and the winner is announced in July. The winner receives a gold medal and £1,000-worth of books to donate.

Eligibility and Restrictions: Open to books for children written in English and receiving their first publication in the UK during the preceding year.

Recent Winners: 2001: Terry Pratchett, *The Amazing Maurice and his Educated Rodents*; 2000: Beverley Naidoo, *The Other Side of Truth*; 1999: Aidan Chambers, *Postcards from No Man's Land*; 1998: David Almond, *Skellig*; 1997: Tim Bowler, *Riverboy*.

Sponsoring Organization: Youth Libraries Group.

Contact: Louisa Myatt.

Address: Chartered Institute of Library and Information Professionals, 7 Ridgmount St, London WC1E 7AE, UK. **Telephone:** (20) 7255 0650. **Fax:** (20) 7255 0501. **Internet:** www.cilip.org.uk. **E-mail:** marketing@cilip.org.uk.

Lar Cassidy Award

A new award established by the Irish Arts Council in 2002 to commemorate the life and work of the late Lar Cassidy, pioneering arts administrator and former Arts Council Literature and Community Arts Officer. The aim of the award is to support an individual writer working on a new or experimental fiction project. (In alternate years, the award will be offered to an arts practitioner working in the field of combined arts.) The prize is €15,000.

How to Apply: Application form from website; deadline for applications is mid-May.

Sponsoring Organization: Arts Council/An Chomhairle Ealaion.

Address: The Arts Council, 70 Merrion Square, Dublin, 2, Ireland. **Telephone:** (1) 618 0200. **Fax:** (1) 676 1302. **Internet:** www.artscouncil.ie. **E-mail:** info@ artscouncil.ie.

Alice Fay di Castagnola Award

The Alice Fay di Castagnola Award, which is administered by the Poetry Society of America (PSA), is offered in memory of a benefactor and friend of the PSA for a manuscript in progress. This award, which totals $1,000, is partially endowed by the estate of Rachel Dalven.

Eligibility and Restrictions: Open to PSA members only. Entries should be a manuscript-in-progress of poetry or verse-drama. Previously published work may be included. There is a line limit of 300 lines of verse, or one sample scene, 20 pages or less, if verse-drama.

How to Apply: Two copies of submissions should be sent accompanied by a cover sheet with a one-paragraph description of the project, between 1 October and 21 December.

Recent Winners: 2002: Andrew Zawacki.

Sponsoring Organization: Poetry Society of America.

Address: Poetry Society of America, 15 Gramercy Park, New York, NY 10003, USA. **Telephone:** (212) 254-9628. **Internet:** www.poetrysociety.org.

Paul-Celan-Preis

Annual prize of DM20,000 given for literary translation into German of a work from the field of belles-lettres. It is twinned with the Prix Gérard de Nerval (qv) which recognizes a translation from German into French.

Eligibility and Restrictions: Works must be recently published in a German edition and be widely available.

How to Apply: It is not possible to apply directly for the prize.

Sponsoring Organization: Deutscher Literaturfonds eV.

Address: Deutscher Literaturfonds eV, Alexandraweg 23, 64287 Darmstadt, Germany. **Telephone:** (6151) 40930. **Fax:** (6151) 40930.

Chalmers Awards for Creativity and Excellence in the Arts

The awards were established in 1972 following an endowment given by the Chalmers family, and are administered by the Ontario Arts Council Foundation. The complete series of awards honours achievements in dance, crafts, music, visual arts, film and video and arts administration. In the field of literature, the Floyd S. Chalmers Canadian Play Awards honour Canadian playwrights whose work is produced in metropolitan Toronto by a professional theatre company, while a separate award recognizes plays for young people.

Recent Winners: Floyd S. Chalmers Canadian Play Awards: 2001: Florence Gibson, *Belle*; Chris Earle, *Radio:30*; Michael Redhill, *Building Jerusalem*; George F. Walker, *Heaven*; 2000: Linda Griffiths, *Alien Creatures: A Visitation from Gwendolyn MacEwan*; Michel Tremblay, *Encore une fois, si vous permettez*; Ronnie Burkett, *Street of Blood*; Michael Healey, *The Drawer Boy*; 1999: Michel Marc Bouchard, *The Orphan Muses*; Leah Cherniak, Oliver Dennis, Maggie Huculak, Robert Morgan, Martha Ross and Michael Simpson, *The Betrayal*; Jason Sherman, *Patience*; George F. Walker, *The End of Civilization*; 1998: George F. Walker, *Problem Child*; Djanet Sears, *Harlem Duet*; Carole Frechette, *The Four Lives of Marie*; David Rubinoff, *Stuck*
Theatre For Young Audiences: 1990: The Great Unwashed Fish Collective, *i.d.*; Jim Betts, *The Groundworld Adventure*; Shirley Barrie, *Straight Stitching*; 1989: Carol Bolt, *Ice Time*; Marvin Ishmael, *Forever Free*; 1988: Beverley Cooper and

Banuta Rubess, *Thin Ice*; Frank Etherington, *The Snake Lady*; Robert Morgan, *Not As Hard as it Seems*; 1987: Dennis Foon, *Skin*; Robert Morgan and David Craig, *Morgan's Journey*.

Sponsoring Organization: Ontario Arts Council Foundation.

Address: Ontario Arts Council Foundation, 151 Bloor St West, 5th Floor, Toronto, ON M5S 1T6, Canada. **Telephone:** (416) 969-7413. **Fax:** (416) 921-8763. **Internet:** www.arts.on.ca/english/foundation/awards.

Adelbert-von-Chamisso-Preis der Robert-Bosch-Stiftung

The Chamisso Prize has been awarded annually since 1986 with the aim of recognizing contributions to German literature from authors who are not native German speakers. The prize may be presented for lifetime work as well as for single outstanding publications. It is sponsored by Robert-Bosch-Stiftung, Stuttgart, and the Bayerische Akademie der Schönen Künste, in partnership with the Deutsch als Fremdsprache (German as a Foreign Language) Institute, University of Munich. The winner receives a prize of €15,000, with two runner-up prizes of €7,000.

Recent Winners: 2002: Said; 2001: Zehra Çirak; 2000: Ilija Trojanow; 1999: Emine Sevgi Özdamar; 1998: Natascha Wodin.

Sponsoring Organization: Bayerische Akademie der Schönen Künste/Robert-Bosch-Stiftung.

Contact: Dr Karl Esselborn.

Address: Bayerische Akademie der Schönen Künste, Max-Joseph-Platz 3, 80539 Munich, Germany. **Telephone:** (89) 290077-0. **Fax:** (89) 290077-23. **Internet:** www.badsk.de. **E-mail:** info@badsk.de.

Raymond Chandler Society's 'Marlowe' Award for Best International Crime Novel

An annual award, established in 1991, for the best English-language crime novel. Separate awards are also offered for best German-language crime novel and best German-language crime story.

Sponsoring Organization: Raymond Chandler Society.

Address: Heidenheimer Str. 106, 89075 Ulm, Germany. **Telephone:** (114) 255 6302. **E-mail:** william.adamson@zsp.uni-ulm.de.

Chapters/Books in Canada Award

An annual prize of C$5,000, presented to the best debut novel by a Canadian author.

Recent Winners: 2001: Eva Stachniak, *Necessary Lies*; 2000: David MacFarlane, *Summer Gone* and Alan R. Wilson, *Before the Flood* (joint winners); 1999: André Alexis, *Childhood*; 1998: Margaret Gibson, *Opium Dreams*.

Sponsoring Organization: National Library of Canada.

Address: National Library of Canada, 395 rue Wellington, Ottawa, ON K1A 0N4, Canada. **Telephone:** (613) 995-9481. **Fax:** (613) 943-1112. **Internet:** www.nlc-bnc.ca. **E-mail:** reference@nlc-bnc.ca.

Chicano/Latino Literary Prize

An annual contest established in 1974 by the Spanish and Portuguese Department of the University of California at Irvine. The genre rotates each year between drama (2002), novel (2003), short story collection (2004), and poetry collection (2005). The first prize is of $1,000, plus publication of the work if not under previous contract, and free travel to Irvine to receive the award. Second and third prizes are $500 and $250. Winners are announced in October.

Eligibility and Restrictions: Only one entry per author will be accepted; author must be a citizen or permanent resident of the USA. For drama, the work must be an unpublished full-length play in Spanish or English, of at least 90 typed pages (minimum number of pages changes according to genre).

How to Apply: Three bound copies must be submitted by 1 June.

Recent Winners: 1999–2000 (short story): Ramon Betancourt; 1998–1999 (novel): Patricia Santana; 1997–1998 (drama): Angelo Parra; 1996–1997 (poetry): Andres Montoya; 1995–1996 (short story): Mike Padilla.

Sponsoring Organization: University of California.

Contact: Prize Co-ordinator Barbara Caldwell.

Address: University of California, Irvine, Dept. of Spanish and Portuguese, 322 Humanities Hall, Irvine, CA 92697–5275, USA. **Telephone:** (949) 824-5443. **Internet:** www.hnet.uci.edu/spanishandportuguese/contest.html. **E-mail:** cllp@uci.edu.

Children's Book Award

Annual award judged by children. The shortlist is announced at the annual conference of the Federation of Children's Book Groups. The three categories are picture books, shorter novels and longer novels, all of which are then considered for the Best Book of the Year award. Prizes: Shortlisted authors and illustrators receive a portfolio of children's letters inspired by their work; category winners receive a silver bowl; the overall winner is awarded a silver and oak tree sculpture.

Recent Winners: Best Book of the Year: 2001: Kes Gray, *Eat Your Peas*; 2000: Michael Morpurgo, *Kensuke's Kingdom*; 1999: J. K. Rowling, *Harry Potter and the Chamber of Secrets*.

Sponsoring Organization: Federation of Children's Book Groups.

Address: 2 Bridge Wood View, Horsforth, Leeds LS18 5PE, UK. **Telephone:** (113) 2588910. **Fax:** (113) 2588920. **Internet:** www.fcbg.mcmail.com/pick.htm. **E-mail:** fcbg@cwcom.net.

Children's Book Awards

An annual award offered for an author's first or second published book in the field of children's literature. Open to works of both fiction and non-fiction in two categories: Younger Readers Primary (aged 4–10 years) and Older Readers (10–17 years). The winner in each category receives $500.

Eligibility and Restrictions: Books from any country and in any language will be considered; entries in a language other than English must be accompanied by a one-page abstract in English and a translation into English of one chapter. Entries must have been published during the previous year.

How to Apply: Entries must be received by 1 November.

Recent Winners: Fiction – Younger Readers: 2001: Carl R. Sams II and Jean Stoick, *Stranger in the Woods*
Non-fiction – Younger Readers: 2001: Sophie Webb, *My Season with Penguins*
Fiction – Older Readers: 2001: Peggy Brookes, *Jake's Orphan*
Non-fiction – Older Readers: 2001: Catherine Thimmesh, *Girls Think of Everything.*

Sponsoring Organization: International Reading Association.

Address: PO Box 8139, Newark, DE, New York, NY, USA. **Telephone:** (302) 731-1600. **Fax:** (303) 731-1051. **Internet:** www.reading.org. **E-mail:** jbutler@ reading.org.

Children's Book Guild Award for Non-fiction

An annual award established in 1977 by the Children's Book Guild to honour 'an author or author-illustrator whose total work has contributed significantly to the quality of non-fiction for children'. The *Washington Post* became a joint sponsor in 1982. The winner receives a cash prize and an inscribed paperweight.

Eligibility and Restrictions: Any living American author or author/illustrator is eligible. Non-fiction is defined as written or illustrated work in the following fields: science, technology, social science, history, biography, and the arts.

How to Apply: Recommendations are accepted by the Award Committee.

Recent Winners: 2000: Diane Stanley; 1999: Laurence Pringle; 1998: Jean Craighead George; 1997: Rhoda Blumberg; 1996: James Cross Giblin.

Sponsoring Organization: Children's Book Guild/*Washington Post.*

Address: Children's Book Guild, Washington, DC, USA. **E-mail:** theguild@ childrensbookguild.org.

Children's Book of the Year Awards

Established in 1946, these annual awards are presented for children's books of outstanding literary merit. There was originally just one Book of the Year category, but subsequently new sections have been added: Picture Books (1952), Younger Readers (1982), the Eve Pownall Award for Non-fiction (1993), and Early Childhood (2001).

How to Apply: Entries must be submitted to the Awards Co-ordinator (Book Distribution) by 31 December. Entry forms and guidelines available from website.

Recent Winners: Book of the Year: Older Readers: 2001: Judith Clarke, *Wolf on the Fold*; 2000: Nick Earls, *48 Shades of Brown*; 1999: Phillip Gwynne, *Deadly, Unna?*
Younger Readers: 2001: Diana Kidd, *Two Hands Together*; 2000: Jackie French, *Hitler's Daughter*; 1999: Meme McDonald and Boori Pryor, *My Girragundji*
Picture Book of the Year: 2001: Ron Brooks and Margaret Wild, *Fox*; 2000: Anne Spudvilas and Margaret Wild, *Jenny Angel*; 1999: Shaun Tan and John Marsden, *The Rabbits*
Eve Pownall Award for Non-fiction: 2001: David Kennett and Dyan Blacklock, *Olympia: Warrior Athletes of Ancient Greece*; 2000: John Nicholson, *Fishing for Islands: Traditional Boats and Seafarers of the Pacific*; 1999: Yvonne Edwards and Brenda Day, *Going for Kalta: Hunting for Sleepy Lizards at Yalata*.

Sponsoring Organization: Children's Book Council of Australia.

Address: Children's Book Council of Australia, POB 470, Mount Lawley, WA 6929, Australia. **Internet:** www.cbc.org.au/awards.htm.

Children's Laureate

A biennial award of £10,000, plus a Children's Laureate Medal, founded in 1999 by the author Michael Morpurgo and poet Ted Hughes to honour a writer or illustrator of children's books for a lifetime's achievement. The award is administered by the International Board of Books for Young People (IBBY) with support from the Department of Culture, Media and Sport along with Waterstone's and several children's publishers.

Eligibility and Restrictions: Award is made to a writer or illustrator of children's books who is UK-based; nominees must have a significant body of work and have attracted critical and popular success.

How to Apply: Publishers and members of IBBY submit nominations. A new Laureate is appointed every two years: the winner is chosen by a panel of experts from children's publishing and by votes from children.

Recent Winners: 2001–2003: Anne Fine; 1999–2001: Quentin Blake.

Sponsoring Organization: International Board of Books for Young People (IBBY).

Contact: Administrator Lois Beeson.

Address: The Administrator, 18 Grosvenor Rd, Portswood, Southampton SO17 1RT, UK. **Telephone:** (23) 8055 5057. **Fax:** (23) 8055 5057. **Internet:** www.childrenslaureate.org. **E-mail:** locol@csi.com.

Children's Literature Association Book Awards

Awarded annually by the Children's Literature Association to recognize outstanding book-length contributions to the history, scholarship, and criticism of children's literature.

Eligibility and Restrictions: Eligible titles must be published, book-length works on the history of and/or scholarship or criticism on children's literature, written in English exclusively by the author(s) whose name(s) appear on the title page, and bearing an original copyright date of the year under consideration. Anthologies, reference works, textbooks, reprints or new editions of previously published books are not eligible.

Recent Winners: 1999: Mary Farquar, *Children's Literature in China*; 1998: Donna Rae MacCann, *White Supremacy in Children's Literature: Characterizations of African-Americans 1830–1900*; 1997: Ann Romines, *Constructing the Little House: Gender, Culture, and Laura Ingalls Wilder*.

Sponsoring Organization: Children's Literature Association.

Address: Children's Literature Association, POB 138, Battle Creek, MI 49016–0138, USA. **Internet:** ebbs.english.vt.edu/chla/.

China Literature Foundation Awards

The foundation awards several literary prizes, including the C. W. Chuang Literary Prize, presented once a year since 1988 to outstanding young writers, literary periodicals, and literary works; the Writer's Prize for Contributing to International Understanding and Friendship, a prize given to foreign writers who have made outstanding contributions to making China and its culture better known throughout the world by their literary writings; and the Sino-American Literary Exchange Prize. The foundation is also planning to launch the World Chinese Literature Prize, which will give a substantial award to outstanding writers both at home and abroad who write in Chinese.

Sponsoring Organization: China Literature Foundation.

Address: China Literature Foundation, #67 Di An Men Si Dajie, Xicheng District, Beijing, 100009, China. **Telephone:** 10-66181846. **Fax:** 10-66181948.

Chôkû Shô (Chôkû Prize)

Established in 1967 by the Kadokawa Shoten publishing company in memory of waka poet Orikuchi Nobuo (who used the pen-name Shaku Chôkû). It is considered the most prestigious prize awarded in the field of waka poetry. Since 1976, the prize has been sponsored by the Kadokawa Foundation for the Promotion of Culture (Kadokawa Bunka Shinkô Zaidan). In addition to a certificate and memorial prize, the winner receives a cash award of 500,000 yen.

Recent Winners: 2001 (35th Chôkû Prize): Takano Kimihiko, *Suien (Water Garden)*.

Sponsoring Organization: Kadokawa Foundation for the Promotion of Culture (Kadokawa Bunka Shinkô Zaidan).

Address: Kadokawa Foundation for the Promotion of Culture (Kadokawa Bunka Shinkô Zaidan), Tokyo, Japan.

Cholmondeley Awards

The Cholmondeley Awards for poets were endowed by the late Dowager Marchioness of Cholmondeley in 1966. The annual non-competitive award is for a whole body of poetic work, rather than for a specific book. The prize of £8,000 is shared equally between four winners.

How to Apply: Submissions are not accepted.

Recent Winners: 2002: Moniza Alvi, David Constantine, Liz Lochhead, Brian Patten; 2001: Ian Duhig, Paul Durcan, Kathleen Jamie, Grace Nichols; 2000: Alistair Elliot, Michael Hamburger, Adrian Henri, Carole Satyamurti; 1999: Vicki Feaver, Geoffrey Hill, Elma Mitchell, Sheenagh Pugh.

Sponsoring Organization: Society of Authors.

Address: Society of Authors, 84 Drayton Gdns, London SW10 9SB, UK. **Telephone:** (20) 7373 6642. **Fax:** (20) 7373 5768. **Internet:** www.societyofauthors.org. **E-mail:** info@societyofauthors.org.

Chrichton Award for Book Illustration

The prize was established from a bequest by W. Crichton, aimed at recognizing new talent in the field of children's book illustrations in Australia. The Award is judged by a panel of three – the Convenor, an established illustrator and a children's literature expert – and comprises a framed certificate and A$1,500.

Eligibility and Restrictions: Awarded to an illustrator for their first picture book where the illustrations form a significant part of the narrative. Applicants must be residents of Australia.

How to Apply: Four copies of the book accompanied by a completed entry form should be sent to the Convenor by the end of February in the year following publication.

Recent Winners: 2001: Caroline Magerl (illustrator), Libby Hathorn (writer), *Grandma's Shoes*; 2000: Loretta Broekstra, *Baby Bear Goes to the Zoo*; 1998: Shaun Tan (illustrator), Gary Crew (writer), *The Viewer*; 1997: Anne Spudvilas (illustrator), Christobel Mattingley (writer), *The Race*.

Sponsoring Organization: Children's Book Council of Australia (Victoria Branch).

Contact: Convenor Dr Virginia Lowe.

Address: Children's Book Council of Australia (Victoria Branch), POB 275, Carlton South, Vic 3053, Australia. **Telephone:** (3) 9349 3111. **Fax:** (3) 9349 3111. **Internet:** www.cbc.org.au. **E-mail:** crichton@cbc.org.au.

Mr Christie's Book Awards

The awards were established in 1990 to encourage the development and publishing of high quality Canadian children's books and to stimulate children's desire to read. There are three categories in both English and French for children's books (ages 7 and under, 8 to 11, and 12 to 16).

Eligibility and Restrictions: Books must be created by a Canadian author and/or illustrator.

Recent Winners: Age 7 and under (English): 2000: Maxine Trottier and Rajka Kupesic, *Claire's Gift*
Age 7 and under (French): 2000: Marie-Louise Gay, *Stella étoile de la mer*; 1998: Robert Soulières and Anne Villeneuve, *Une gardienne pour Étienne*; 1997: Daniel Marcotte and Stéphane Poulin, *Poil de serpent, dent d'araignée*; 1996: Pierrette Dubé, *Au lit, princesse Émilie!*
Age 8 to 11 (English): 2000: Kenneth Oppel, *Sunwing*
Age 8 to 11 (French): 2000: Gilles Tibo and Jean Berneche, *Les yeux noirs*; 1998: Gilles Tibo, *Rouge timide*; 1997: Robert Davidts and Richard Bach, *Jean-Baptiste Coureur des bois*; 1996: Christiane Duchesne, *La bergère de chevaux*
Age 12 to 16 (English): 2000: Martha Brooks, *Being with Henry*
Age 12 to 16 (French): 2000: Stanley Pean, *Le temps s'enfuit*;1998: Jean-Michel Schembré, *Les citadelles du vertige*; 1997: Jacques Lazure, *Rêve couleur d'orange*; 1996: Jean Lemieux, *Le trésor de Brion*.

Sponsoring Organization: Christie Brown & Co. (a division of Nabisco).

Address: Christie Brown & Co., 2150 Lakeshore Blvd, Toronto, ON M8V 1A3, Canada.

Christopher Awards

Established in 1949, the Christopher Awards are presented in the fields of feature films, broadcast TV and cable programmes and books for adults and young people. They are presented in recognition of 'the highest values of the human spirit'. The book awards are divided into Books for Adults and Books for Young People (subdivided by age). Six winners in each category were chosen in 2001.

Eligibility and Restrictions: To be eligible for a Christopher Award during their year of release books must exhibit exceptional artistic proficiency, be significantly positioned to have an impact on the widest possible audience and, above all, must affirm the highest values of the human spirit.

How to Apply: Potential winners are nominated and reviewed throughout the year by panels of media professionals, members of The Christophers' staff with expertise in publishing, and by specially supervised children's reading groups.

Recent Winners: Books for Adults: 2001: Barbara Ehrenreich, *Nickel and Dimed*; Jimmy Carter, *An Hour Before Daylight*; Lynne Olson, *Freedom's Daughters*; Antoinette Bosco, *Choosing Mercy*; David Snowdon, *Aging with Grace*; and David McCullough, *John Adams*
Books for Young People: 2001: Amy Hest and Anita Jeram (illustrator), *Kiss Good Night*; Page McBrier and Lori Lohstoeter (illustrator), *Beatrice's Goat*; Sharon Creech, *Love That Dog*; Ralph Fletcher, *Uncle Daddy*; Don Wulffson, *Soldier X*; and Karen Hesse, *Witness*.

Sponsoring Organization: The Christophers.

Address: 12 East 48th St, New York, NY 10017, USA. **Telephone:** (212) 759-4050. **Internet:** www.christophers.org.

Christy Awards

The Christy Awards were created in 1999 and named in honour of Catherine Marshall, a pioneer in Christian fiction and the author of *Christy*. The awards, which are annual, were developed to recognize Christian novels of exceptional quality and impact. Prizes are awarded in several categories: Contemporary/General; Futuristic; International historical; North American historical; Romance; Suspense; and First Novel.

Eligibility and Restrictions: Open to full-length works of fiction. All entries must be in English and published in the USA either for the first time during the calendar year preceding the awards presentation, or republished by a new publisher during the calendar year preceding the awards presentation. Translations into English of works originally published in another language are eligible if they are first published during the qualifying period.

How to Apply: Publishers are invited to enter as many titles in each category as they wish. There is a $150 entry fee for each title submitted. Ten copies of each entry, accompanied by an entry form, should be submitted by 8 December.

Recent Winners: Contemporary/General: 2001: Philip Gulley, *Home to Harmony* and Robert Whitlow, *The Trial* (joint winners)
Futuristic: 2001: Randall Ingermanson, *Transgression*
International historical: 2001: Francine Rivers, *Unashamed*
North American historical: 2001: Gilbert Morris, *Edge of Honor* and Rosey Dow, *Reaping the Whirlwind* (joint winners)
Romance: 2001: Catherine Palmer, *A Touch of Betrayal*
Suspense: 2001: T. Davis Bunn, *The Great Divide*
First Novel: 2001: Sharon Ewell Foster, *Passing by Samaria*.

Address: The Christy Award LLC, 1571 Glastonbury Rd, Ann Arbor, MI, 48103, USA. **Telephone:** (734) 663-7931. **Fax:** (734) 663-7931. **Internet:** www. christyawards.com/home.htm. **E-mail:** CA2000DK@aol.com.

City of Vancouver Book Award

An annual prize administered by the City of Vancouver Office of Cultural Affairs which aims to recognize and support the contribution of the book community to Vancouver, and to heighten awareness and appreciation of the city of Vancouver. A prize of C$2,000 is awarded to the author of a book that contributes significantly to the appreciation and understanding of Vancouver's history, unique character, and/or the achievements of its residents. The winner is decided by an independent panel of three judges.

Eligibility and Restrictions: Entries may be fiction, non-fiction, poetry, or drama written for adults or children, which deals with any aspect of Vancouver (city, history, geography, current affairs, or the arts). Open to books written and/or published anywhere in the world, but they must have been published in the previous year.

How to Apply: Publishers are invited to submit three copies of eligible titles by mid-June, accompanied by an entry fee (C$15 per title in 2002) and an application form.

Recent Winners: 2001: Madeleine Thien, *Simple Recipes*; 2000: Lilia D'Acres and Donald Luxton, *Lions Gate*; 1999: Bud Osborn, *Keys to Kingdoms*; 1998: Chuck Davis, *The Greater Vancouver Book: An Urban Encyclopaedia*; 1997: Rhodri Windsor Liscombe, *The New Spirit: Modern Architecture in Vancouver, 1938–1963*.

Sponsoring Organization: City of Vancouver Office of Cultural Affairs.

Address: City of Vancouver Office of Cultural Affairs, 453 West 12th Ave, Vancouver, BC V5Y 1V4, Canada. **Telephone:** (604) 873-7487. **Fax:** (604) 871-6048. **Internet:** www.city.vancouver.bc.ca/oca. **E-mail:** oca@city.vancouver.bc.ca.

Russell Clark Award

This annual award was established in 1975 to recognize the most distinguished contribution to illustration for children published in the preceding year. The winner is chosen by a panel of judges, and receives an inscribed medal and a sum of money which is decided each year by the Library and Information Association of New Zealand Aotearoa (LIANZA) Council ($NZ1,000 in 2002). The winner is chosen by a panel of three judges. LIANZA suspended its awards from 1999–2000 but reinstituted them in 2001.

Eligibility and Restrictions: Open to illustrated books for children, with or without text, which have been published in the preceding year by a citizen or resident of New Zealand. The illustrations must be original work and must convey the spirit of the book. The book must be still in print and available for public purchase. Reprints or new editions are not eligible.

How to Apply: Publishers may send in nominations, and are requested to provide three copies of each entry.

Recent Winners: 2001: Bob Kerr, *After the War*; 1998: Sue Hitchcock-Pratt, *Emily's Wonderful Pie*; 1997: Amanda Jackson (author), Murray Grimsdale (illustrator), *George's Monster*; 1996: Joy Cowley (author), Linda McClelland (illustrator), *The Cheese Trap*; 1995: Philip Temple (author), Chris Gaskin (illustrator), *Kotuku: The Flight of the White Heron*; 1994: Patricia Grace (author), Kerry Gemmill (illustrator), *The Trolley*.

Sponsoring Organization: Library and Information Association of New Zealand Aotearoa (LIANZA).

Contact: Office Man. Steve Williams.

Address: LIANZA, POB 12–212, Wellington, 6001, New Zealand. **Telephone:** (4) 4735834. **Fax:** (4) 4991480. **Internet:** www.lianza.org.nz. **E-mail:** office@lianza.org.nz.

Arthur C. Clarke Award for Science Fiction

Established in 1987 by Arthur C. Clarke to encourage science fiction in the UK. The award was of £2,002 in 2002 (the amount paid rises by £1 each year), accompanied by an engraved bookend. The winner is chosen by a jury.

Eligibility and Restrictions: Open to science fiction novels receiving their first UK publication in the previous calendar year.

How to Apply: Publishers should supply copies of the work to each juror and the Administrator.

Recent Winners: 2001: China Mieville, *Perdido Street Station*; 2000: Bruce Sterling, *Distraction*; 1999: Tricia Sullivan, *Dreaming in Smoke*; 1998: Mary Doria Russell, *The Sparrow*; 1997: Amijav Ghosh, *The Calcutta Chromosome*.

Sponsoring Organization: Rocket Publishing.

Contact: Administrator Paul Kincaid.

Address: 60 Bournemouth Rd, Folkestone CT19 5AZ, UK. **Telephone:** (1303) 252939. **Fax:** (1303) 252939. **Internet:** www.clarkeaward.com. **E-mail:** clarke@ appomattox.demon.co.uk.

CNA Letterkkunde Toekenning (CNA Literary Award)

This annual literary award, the highest honour for South African literature, was established in 1961. Books by South African residents or citizens may be submitted in any of the following categories: novel, poetry, biography, drama, history and travel.

Recent Winners: Former winners include J. M. Coetzee, *Waiting for the Barbarians*, Sarah Ruden, *Other Places*, Christopher Hope, *White Boy Running* and A. H. M. Scholtz, *A Place Called Vatmaar*; earlier recipients include Ivan Vladislavic, Justin Cartwright, Ellen Kuzwayo, Nadine Gordimer (1974, 1979, 1981, 1991), Etienne van Heerden and André Brink.

Sponsoring Organization: Central News Agency.

Address: Central News Agency Ltd, POB 9380, Johannesburg, South Africa.

Jacinto Prado Coelho Award

An annual prize promoted and developed by the Centro Português da Associação International de Críticos Literários.

Sponsoring Organization: Centro Português da Associação International de Críticos Literários.

Contact: Pres. Prof. Fernando Martinho.

Address: Centro Português da Associação International de Críticos Literários, Rua Prof. Mark Athias, Edif. A4 – 7°B, 1600 – 646 Lisbon, Portugal. **E-mail:** dace@iplb.pt.

Morton N. Cohen Award for a Distinguished Edition of Letters

Established in 1989 by a gift from Morton N. Cohen, professor emeritus of English at City University of New York, the prize is awarded each odd-numbered year to an outstanding edition of letters published in the previous two years. The winner is selected by a committee made up of members of the Modern Language Association of America (MLA), and receives $1,000 and a certificate.

Eligibility and Restrictions: Eligible entries are important collections of letters published during the two years preceding the prize. Collections of letters in any field may be entered, and membership of the MLA is not required.

How to Apply: Publishers or editors may apply. Four copies of entries should be sent to the address shown by 1 May.

Recent Winners: 2000–01: Albert J. Devlin and Nancy Marie Patterson Tischler, *The Selected Letters of Tennessee Williams: Volume 1, 1920–1945*; 1997–98: Ignas Kestutis Skrupskelis, *The Correspondence of William James*; 1995–96: Clyde de L. Ryals, *The Collected Letters of Thomas and Jane Welsh Carlyle*; 1993–94: Paul Mattheisen, *The Collected Letters of George Gissing*; 1991–92: Georges Lubin, *Correspondance de George Sand*.

Sponsoring Organization: Modern Language Association of America (MLA).

Contact: Co-ordinator of Book Prizes and Special Projects.

Address: Modern Language Asscn of America, 26 Broadway, 3rd Floor, New York, NY 10004–1789, USA. **Telephone:** (646) 576-5141. **Fax:** (646) 458-0033. **Internet:** www.mla.org. **E-mail:** awards@mla.org.

David Cohen British Literature Prize

The prize is awarded every two years by a private trust fund formed by David and Veronica Cohen in 1980, which supports music and the arts. The David Cohen prize is awarded to a writer in recognition of a lifetime's literary distinction. The jury includes the Chair of the Arts Council of England's Literary Advisory Panel plus nominees from the Arts Councils of Northern Ireland, Scotland and Wales. The prize totals £30,000.

Eligibility and Restrictions: Entries must be in English.

How to Apply: No direct applications are permitted, as the winner is chosen from a shortlist compiled by the jury.

Recent Winners: 2001: Doris Lessing; 1999: William Trevor; 1997: Muriel Spark; 1995: Harold Pinter; 1993: V. S. Naipaul.

Sponsoring Organization: David Cohen Family Charitable Trust/Arts Council of England.

Contact: Literature Asst Pippa Shoubridge.

Address: Arts Council of England, 14 Great Peter St, London SW1P 3NQ, UK. **Telephone:** (20) 7973 6442. **Fax:** (20) 7973 6520. **Internet:** www.artscouncil. org.uk. **E-mail:** pippa.shoubridge@artscouncil.org.uk.

Colorado Prize

An annual prize of $2,000 presented for a book-length collection of poems. The winning collection is also published by the Center for Literary Publishing and distributed by the University Press of Colorado.

Recent Winners: 2002: Robyn Ewing, *Matter*.

Sponsoring Organization: Colorado Review.

Contact: Dir David Milofsky.

Address: Colorado Review, Dept of English, Colorado State University, Fort Collins, CO 80523, USA. **Telephone:** (970) 491-5449. **Internet:** www. coloradoreview.com.

Commonwealth Writers Prize

The Commonwealth Writers Prize was established in 1987 to reward excellence in Commonwealth literature; it is sponsored by the Commonwealth Foundation and administered by Book Trust. For the purposes of the award the Commonwealth is divided into four regions, Africa, the Caribbean and Canada, Eurasia (which includes the United Kingdom), and Southeast Asia and the South Pacific. A shortlist is drawn up with a best book and a best first book for each region. The regional winners each receive a prize of £1,000; the winner of the book of the year receives £ 10,000, and the winner of the best first book receives £3,000. Each year the award ceremony is held in a different Commonwealth country.

Eligibility and Restrictions: Open to any work of prose fiction; drama and poetry are excluded. The work must have been written by a living citizen of the Commonwealth, must be of a reasonable length and be in English. It must have been first published during the previous calendar year. To be eligible for the 'best first published book' category the entry must be the first work of fiction (i.e. a novel or collection of short stories) which the author has published.

How to Apply: Entries must be made by the publisher. Publishers are restricted to four entries per region: two for the best book prize and two for the best first published book. The same book may not be entered in both categories. Entries should be submitted to the region of the writer's Commonwealth citizenship. Three copies of each entry accompanied by the entry form should be sent to the Chairperson of the appropriate regional panel of judges by mid-November each year. In addition, one copy of each book should be sent to the Administrator at Book Trust. Entry forms are available from Book Trust.

Recent Winners: 2002: Richard Flanagan, *Goud's Book of Fish*; 2001: Peter Carey, *True History of the Kelly Gang*; 2000: J. M. Coetzee, *Disgrace*; 1999: Murray Bail, *Eucalyptus*; 1998 Peter Carey, *Jack Maggs*
First Book: 2002: Manu Herbstein, *Ama*; 2001: Zadie Smith, *White Teeth*; 2000: Jeffrey Moore, *Prisoner in a Rose-Red Chain*; 1999: Kerri Sakamoto, *The Electrical Field*; 1998: Tim Wynveen, *Angel Falls*.

Sponsoring Organization: Commonwealth Foundation.

Address: The Commonwealth Writers Prize Administrator, Book Trust, Book House, 45 East Hill, London SW18 2QZ, UK. **Telephone:** (20) 8516 2972. **Fax:** (20) 8516 2978. **Internet:** www.booktrust.org.uk. **E-mail:** tarryn@ booktrust.org.uk.

Concurso Annual de Literatura (Annual Literature Competition)

A set of annual awards which aim to recognize the authors of both published and unpublished works. These official awards are organized by the Ministry of Education and Culture, and are presented in the categories poetry, narrative, children's literature, drama and essay. Separate prizes are awarded for published and unpublished works in each category. The winners receive a cash prize, the level of which is determined by the Ministry.

Eligibility and Restrictions: For the published category, entries must have appeared during the preceding year. Authors must be citizens of Uruguay; works by authors who have died before the period of judging are excluded.

How to Apply: The Biblioteca Nacional (National Library) draws up a shortlist of nominations; however, authors themselves may apply by sending five copies of eligible works to the address given by 31 January.

Recent Winners: Poetry: 2000: Jorge Arbeleche, *Para hacer una pradera*; Washinton Benavides, *El mirlo y la misa* and Marosa Di Giorgio, *Diamelas a Clementina Medici*
Narrative: 2000: Tomás de Mattos, *Bernabé, Bernabé* and Omar Prego Gadea, *Cuentos Completos*
Children's Literature: 2000: Elena Pesce, *Instantáneas de voces y risas*

Drama: 2000: Mauricio Rosencof, *Y nuestros cabalos eran blancos*
Essay: 2000: Felipe Arocena, *De Quilmes a Hyde Park: Las fronteras culturales en la vida y la obra de W. H. Hudson.*
Sponsoring Organization: Dirección de Cultura/ Departamento de Letras.
Address: Dirección de Cultura, Departamento de Letras, Ministerio de Educación y Cultura, San José 1116 esq. Paraguay, Montevideo, Uruguay. **Telephone:** 9013833. **Fax:** 9021572. **Internet:** www.mec.gub.uy/culture/.

Concurso de Prosa y Poesía Timón de Oro ('Golden Helm' Prose and Poetry Competion)

An annual literary award for prose and poetry sponsored by the national naval military college and the Institute of Culture. The winner receives a prize of $15,000 plus a gold medal in the form of a ship's helm.

Eligibility and Restrictions: Open to works on any theme, though preference is given to entries with a maritime or naval theme. Works must be unpublished; there is no limit on length of entries.

How to Apply: Entries should be submitted by the end of September.

Sponsoring Organization: Asociación de la Heroica Escuela Naval Militar A.C/ Instituto de Cultura de la Ciudad de México.

Address: Asociación de la Heroica Escuela Naval Militar, A.C, Eje 2 Ote. Tramo H.E.N.M. 861, edif. B, tercer piso, Col. Los Cipreses, CP 04830, Coyoacán, Mexico City, DF, Mexico. **Telephone:** (55) 56 24 65 00. **Internet:** www.semar.gob.mx/ timon.htm.

Concurso Literario Premio Emecé

The prize was established in 1954 by publisher Emecé Editores, and was the first Argentinian award of its type. It is awarded each year for works of fiction by new writers. The winner receives a prize of $5,000, and the winning work is usually published by the company.

Eligibility and Restrictions: Entry is limited to works of prose fiction, written in Spanish, and between 40,000 and 120,000 words in length. Works are only accepted from unpublished writers.

How to Apply: Three copies of entries should be submitted by 31 August.

Recent Winners: 2001: Sergio Bizzio, *En esa época.*

Sponsoring Organization: Emecé Editores SA.

Address: Emecé Editores SA, Alsina 2048, piso 2, 1090AAF Buenos Aires, Argentina. **Telephone:** 4954-0105. **Fax:** 4953-4200. **Internet:** www.emece. com.ar/concursos/concursos.htm. **E-mail:** edicion@emece.com.ar.

Concurso Nacional de Cuento Juan José Arreola

A competition for unpublished short stories by Mexican writers aged between 18 and 35. The winner receives a prize of $20,000 plus publication of the winning entry.

Eligibility and Restrictions: Entrants must be residents of Mexico; works must be written in Spanish and be between 80 and 120 pages in length.

How to Apply: Entries should be submitted between November and March.

Sponsoring Organization: University of Guadalajara.

Address: Centro Universitario del Sur de la UdG, Prol. Colón s/n, Carr. Libre a Cd. Guzmán-Guadalajara, Edif. S, aula S1CP 49000, Ciudad Guzmán, Mexico. **Telephone:** (341) 412 40 44. **Internet:** www.cusur.udg.mx.

Concurso Nacional de Dramaturgia Teatro Nuevo
(National Competition for Modern Works of Drama)

A $60,000 award for new works of drama, jointly organized by the Department of Culture, the Mexican Writers' Society and the National Polytechnic Institute. The award was established to encourage new trends in dramatic writing. The winning entries are published in a special anthology.

Eligibility and Restrictions: Open to all writers resident in Mexico, for an unpublished work of drama on any theme, between 30 and 70 pages in length.

Sponsoring Organization: Secretaría de Cultura/Sociedad General de Escritores de México/Instituto Politécnico Nacional.

Address: Subdirección de Artes Escénicas de la Secretaría de Cultura, Av. de la Paz 26, tercer piso, Col. Chimalistac, CP 01070, Álvaro Obregón, Mexico City, DF, Mexico. **Telephone:** (55) 56 62 78 09. **Internet:** www.cultura.df.gob.mx.

Cool Awards

The COOL (Canberra's Own Outstanding List) awards are the Canberra part of a series of Australian Children's Choice awards at both national and state level. They began in 1991 and are administered by a committee comprising representatives from the Australian Capital Territory (ACT) Government, Catholic and Independent Schools, the Children's Book Council, the Australian Reading Association and the Association for Teachers of English.

Recent Winners: Picture Book: 2000: David Legg, *Bamboozled*; 1999: Rod Clement, *Grandad's Teeth*
Primary: 2000: Emily Rodda, *Bob the Builder and the Elves*; 1999: Morris Gleitzman, *Bum Face*
Secondary: 2000: John Marsden, *Night is for Hunting*; 1999: John Marsden, *The Third Day the Frost*.

Sponsoring Organization: Administered by Australian Capital Territory (ACT) Public Library.

Address: ACT Public Library, Canberra, ACT, Australia. **Internet:** www.act. gov.au/publiclibrary/coolawards.

Duff Cooper Prize

Annual award to a literary work in the field of history, biography, politics or poetry, published in the previous year. The winner receives a prize of £3,000 and a presentation copy of Duff Cooper's autobiography *Old Men Forget*.

Recent Winners: 2000: Robert Skidelsky, *John Maynard Keynes*; 1999: Adam Hochschild, *King Leopold's Ghost*; 1998: Richard Holmes, *Coleridge: Darker Reflections*.

Address: 54 St Maur Rd, London SW6 4DP, UK. **Telephone:** (20) 7736 3729. **Fax:** (20) 7731 7638.

County of Cardiff International Poetry Competition

An annual poetry competition for eight prizes totalling £5,000. Prizes are awarded for unpublished poetry written in English (first prize of £3,000, second prize £700, third prize £300, plus five runners-up prizes of £200).

Eligibility and Restrictions: Entries should be unpublished poems of up to 50 lines, written in English.

How to Apply: Closing date is 1 November.

Sponsoring Organization: Academi, Cardiff/ Welsh Academy.

Address: Welsh Academy, Third Floor, Mount Stuart House, Mount Stuart Sq., Cardiff CF1 6DQ, UK.

Rose Mary Crawshay Prize

Two annual prizes for women, established by the British Academy in 1888, for outstanding scholarly work on any subject concerned with English literature. The prizes are of £500 each, and carry considable academic prestige.

Eligibility and Restrictions: Open to women of any nationality. Entries must have been published in the preceding three years; entries may be on any literary subject, but preference is given where possible to studies of the poets Byron, Shelley or Keats.

Recent Winners: 2000: Marina Warner, *No Go the Bogeyman: Scaring, Lulling and Making Mock* and Joanne Wilkes, *Lord Byron and Madame de Staël: Born for Opposition* (joint winners); 1999: Elizabeth Wright, *Psychoanalytic Criticism: A Reappraisal* and Karen O'Brien, *Narratives of Enlightenment: Cosmopolitan History from Voltaire to Gibbon* (joint winners).

Sponsoring Organization: British Academy.

Address: British Academy, 10 Carlton House Terrace, London SW1Y 5AH, UK. **Telephone:** (20) 7969 5264. **Fax:** (20) 7969 5414. **Internet:** www.britac.ac.uk.

Cultural Center of the Philippines Literary Awards

The Cultural Center of the Philippines (CCP) was created in 1966 with the purpose of promoting and preserving Filipino arts and culture. As part of this aim the CCP presents a number of prestigious awards in recognition of achievements in all areas of the arts, including literature.

Sponsoring Organization: Cultural Center of the Philippines (CCP).

Address: Cultural Center of the Philippines, CCP Bldg, CCP Complex, Roxas Boulevard, Pasay City, 1300, Philippines. **Telephone:** (2) 832-1125. **Internet:** www.culturalcenter.gov.ph/ccpourhome_right.htm. **E-mail:** ccp@culturalcenter. gov.ph.

C. H. Currey Memorial Fellowship

The award, established after a bequest from the well-known Australian historian Dr Charles Herbert Currey, aims to promote the writing of Australian history from original sources of information, preferably making use of the resources of the State Library of New South Wales (NSW). The amount of the Fellowship is A$20,000. The money may be used to supplement a writer's income during work on his/her project or to meet the necessary research and travel costs, within the aim of the Fellowship. The award is paid in two amounts, the first on presentation of the Fellowship and the second on satisfactory progress of the research, as evidenced in programmes, publications and presentations.

Sponsoring Organization: State Library of NSW Press.

Address: State Library of NSW Press, Macquarie St, Sydney, NSW 2000, Australia. **Internet:** www.slnsw.gov.au/awards/.

Ernst-Robert-Curtius-Preise für Essayistik

The Ernst-Robert-Curtius-Preise für Essayistik aim to promote essay-writing as an independent literary form. Prizewinners must be under the age of 40, and prizes may be awarded for lifetime achievement or for an individual text. A main prize and a commendation prize, sponsored by the bookshop Universitätsbuchhandlung Bouvier in Bonn, have been awarded annually since 1984. The winner is selected by a jury of eminent judges.

Recent Winners: 2000: Günter de Bruyn; 1999: Hans-Peter Schwarz; 1998: Rüdiger Safranski; 1997: Hans Magnus Enzensberger; 1996: Odo Marquard.

Sponsoring Organization: Universitätsbuchhandlung Bouvier.

Address: Universitätsbuchhandlung Bouvier, Am Hof 28, 53113 Bonn, Germany.

CWA Awards

The Crime Writers Association (CWA), in conjunction with sponsor The Macallan, makes a series of 10 annual awards for outstanding works in the field of crime literature. Categories include: The Cartier Diamond Dagger, The John Creasey Memorial Dagger, The Macallan Gold Dagger and Silver Dagger for Fiction, The Macallan Gold Dagger for Non-fiction, the Macallan Short Story Dagger, The Ellis Peters Historical Dagger, The Debut Dagger, the Dagger in the Library and the Ian Fleming Steel Dagger. Most awards carry a prize of an ornamental dagger plus a cash prize ranging from £1,000 to £3,000. The awards are administered by the CWA, and most are sponsored by The Macallan; however the Fleming Steel Dagger, launched in 2002, is sponsored by the estate of James Bond creator Ian Fleming.

Eligibility and Restrictions: Different prizes awarded for both fiction and non-fiction, short stories, debut works and lifetime achievement.

How to Apply: Applications are invited from publishers; see website for details.

Recent Winners: Gold Dagger for Fiction 2001: Henning Mankell, *Sidetracked*
Silver Dagger for Fiction: 2001: Giles Blunt, *Forty Words for Sorrow*
Macallan Short Story Dagger: 2001: Marion Arnott, *Prussian Snowdrops*
Gold Dagger for Non-fiction: 2001: Philip Etienne, Martin Maynard and Tony Thompson, *The Infiltrators*
John Creasey Memorial Dagger: 2001: Susanna Jones, *The Earthquake Bird*
Cartier Diamond Dagger: 2002: Sara Paretsky
Ellis Peters Historical Dagger: 2001: Andrew Taylor, *The Office of the Dead*
Debut Dagger: 2001: Edward Wright, *Clea's Moon*.

Sponsoring Organization: Crime Writers Association/The Macallan.

Address: Crime Writers Association, Meadow View, The Street, Bossingham CT4 6DX, UK. **Telephone:** (1227) 709 782. **Fax:** (1227) 709 782. **Internet:** www. thecwa.co.uk. **E-mail:** judith.curler@virgin.net.

CYBER—Children's Yearly Best-Ever Reads—Award

The CYBER awards, inaugurated in 1999, are the Tasmanian part of a series of Australian Children's Choice awards at both national and state level. CYBER stands for Children's Yearly Best-Ever Reads. The winners, in three categories, are selected when students in primary and secondary schools around Tasmania vote for their favourite book. Voting is conducted through schools, public libraries and bookshops.

Recent Winners: Older Readers: 2000: John Marsden, *Tomorrow When The War Began*
Younger Readers: 2000: Andy Griffiths, *Just Crazy!*
Picture Book: 2000: Bob Graham, *Buffy: An Adventure Story*.

Address: POB 216, Claremont, Tas 7011, Australia. **Internet:** www.neat. tas.edu.au/CYBER.TAS.

Danish Ministry of Culture Children's Book Prize

Established in 1954 by the Ministry of Education. The award is presented annually, and celebrates a writer who has contributed to Danish children's literature. The winner is selected by a panel of experts, and receives a prize of DKK 30,000.

Eligibility and Restrictions: Open to high-quality children's literature books, which must be written in Danish.

How to Apply: Direct applications are not accepted.

Recent Winners: 2001: Janne Teller, *Intet*; 2000: Kåre Bluitgen, *Niels Klims Underjurdiske Rejse 1–4*; 1999: Martin Petersen, *Med Ilden i Ryggen*; 1998: Wivi Leth, *Engle Græder Ikke*; 1997: Cecilie Eken, *Sikkas Fortælling*.

Sponsoring Organization: Ministry of Culture/Media and Grants Secretariat.

Contact: Consultant Eva Jensen.

Address: Ministry of Culture, Media and Grants Secretariat, Nybrogade 10, 1203 Copenhagen, K, Denmark. **Telephone:** 33 92 30 40. **Fax:** 33 14 64 28. **Internet:** www.kulturtilskud.min.dk. **E-mail:** tips@kutlturtilskud.dk.

Dartmouth Medal

An annual medal presented to a reference work of outstanding quality and significance. The award, which is administered by the American Library Association's (ALA's) Reference and User Services Association (RUSA), may be given for writing, compiling, editing, or publishing books or electronic information. Dartmouth College has sponsored the award since 1974, when it commissioned a specially designed bronze medal. The winner is selected by a committee of ALA members.

Eligibility and Restrictions: Open to works that have been published during the previous calendar year. A publisher of reference works can be nominated according to the following criteria: writing, editing, compiling, or publishing books or the provision of information in other forms for reference use, e.g. a data bank.

Recent Winners: 2002: *The Oxford Encyclopedia of Ancient Egypt*; 2001: *Women in World History*; 2000: *Scribner's Encyclopedia of the Renaissance*; 1999: John A. Garraty and Mark C. Carnes (Editors), *American National Biography*; 1998: *Jewish Women in America: An Historical Encyclopedia*.

Sponsoring Organization: American Library Association/Dartmouth College.

Address: Reference and User Services Asscn, American Library Asscn, 50 East Huron, Chicago, IL 60611, USA. **Telephone:** (707) 826-3441. **Fax:** (707) 826-3440. **Internet:** www.ala.org.

Harvey Darton Award

A biennial award established in 1990 by the Children's Books History Society (CBHS) and named after F. J. Harvey Darton (1879–1936), chiefly noted for his 1932 publication *Children's Books in England*. The award is presented to books that have made a significant contribution to the understanding of the history, bibliogaphy and literary content of British children's literature of the past. The prize is £100 and three years' membership to the Society. Entries are nominated by members of the Society, and books reviewed in the Society's Newsletter can also be considered.

Eligibility and Restrictions: Open to books published in English during the previous two years. Foreign-language books, if available in English, are also eligible.

How to Apply: Nominations should be forwarded to the Secretary of the Society by the last day of November.

Recent Winners: 2002: Nigel Tattersfield, *John Bewick: Engraver on Wood 1760–1795*; 2000: (no award given); 1998: John Goldthwaite, *The Natural History of Make-Believe: A Guide to the Principal Works of Britain, Europe and America* and Peter Newbolt, *G. A. Henty 1832–1902: a bibliographical study* (joint winners); 1996: Marina Warner, *From the Beast to the Blonde*; 1994: Colin Campbell, *William Nicholson: the graphic work*.

Sponsoring Organization: Children's Books History Society (CBHS).

Contact: Pat Garrett.

Address: Children's Books History Society, 25 Field Way, Hoddesdon EN11 0QN, UK. **Telephone:** (1992) 464 885. **Fax:** (1992) 464 885. **E-mail:** cbhs@abcgarrett.demon.co.uk.

Dazai Osamu Shô (Dazai Osamu Prize)

Established in 1965 by the Chikuma Shobô publishing company. The prize is awarded annually to an outstanding, previously unpublished short story by an unrecognized author. The prize was supsended for a period after its 14th presentation in 1978, due to financial difficulties, but it was revived in 1999 after the city of Mitaka offered to co-sponsor it. The winner receives a commemorative gift and a cash prize of 1 million yen.

Recent Winners: 2001: 17th Dazai Osamu Prize: Kojima Koriku, *Itteki no arashi (A One-Drop Storm)*.

Sponsoring Organization: City of Mitaka.

Address: Dazai Osamu Prize (Dazai Osamu Shô), Mitaka, Japan.

Tibor-Déry-Preis

Awarded every year for literary translation from Hungarian into other languages. The prize is of 250,000 FT.

How to Apply: It is not possible to apply directly for the prize. **Address:** Jászai Mari tér 4/a, 1137 Budapest, Hungary. **Telephone:** (1) 112 36 39.

Deutscher Jugendliteraturpreis (German Youth Literature Prize)

The Deutscher Jugendliteraturpreis was founded 1956 to support the development of outstanding literature for children and young people in Germany. It is awarded annually to German or foreign authors of children's and teenage literature for outstanding individual works or lifetime achievement. The prize is sponsored by the Bundesministerium für Familie, Senioren, Frauen und Jugend. The winners are selected by an elected jury of 13 people (experts and young readers), and receive €8,000 and a sculpture of Michael Ende's Momo. The award is shared jointly by the author and the translator if the winner is a non-German speaker.

Eligibility and Restrictions: Open to German or non-German authors of children's or young people's literature. Entries must have been published in German during the previous year. Eligible types of work are: picture books, children's fiction, teenage fiction, and children's non-fiction.

How to Apply: In general publishers apply on behalf of writers. However, anyone is able to suggest a book to the Arbeitskreis für Jugendliteratur. Two copies of entries should be submitted to the address given.

Recent Winners: Picture book: 2001: Jutta Bauer, *Schreimutter*; 2000: Nadia Budde, *Eins zwei drei Tier*; 1999: Karl Friedrich Waechter, *Der rote Wolf*; 1998: Jack Gleich (illustrator), Amelie Fried (author), *Hat Opa einen Anzug an?*; 1997: Grégoire Solotareff (author), Erika Klewer (translator), Karl A. Klewer (illustrator), *Du groß, und ich klein*
Children's book: 2001: Jutta Richter, *Der Tag, als ich lernte die Spinnen zu zähmen*; 2000: Bjarne Reuter (author), Peter Urban-Halle (translator), *Hodder der Nachtschwärmer*; 1999: Annika Thor (author), Angelika Kutsch (translator), *Eine Insel im Meer*; 1998: Irene Dische (author), Reinhard Kaiser (translator), *Zwischen zwei Scheiben Glück*; 1997: Sheila Och (author), Miroslav Novák (translator), *Karel, Jarda und das wahre Leben*
Juvenile book: 2001: Richard Van Camp (author), Ulrich Plenzdorf (translator), *Die ohne Segen sind*; 2000: Charlotte Kerner, *Blueprint – Blaupause*; 1999: Ted van Lieshout (author), Mirjam Pressler (translator), *Bruder*; 1998: Bart Moeyaert (author), Mirjam Pressler (translator), *Rotraut* and Susanne Berner (illustrator), *Bloße Hände*; 1997: Per Nilsson (author), Birgitta Kicherer (translator), *So lonely*
Non-fiction book: 2001: Susanne Paulsen, *Sonnenfresser. Wie Pflanzen leben*; 2000: Antje von Stemm, *Fräulerin Pop und Mrs Up und ihre große Reise durchs Papierland*; 1999: Peter Sis (author), Michael Krüger (translator), *Tibet*; 1998: Susanna Partsch, *Das Haus der Kunst*; 1997: Reinhard Kaiser, *Königskinder*.

Sponsoring Organization: Bundesministerium für Familie, Senioren, Frauen und Jugend/Arbeitskreis für Jugendliteratur e.V.

Contact: Bettina Stelzner.

Address: Arbeitskreis für Jugendliteratur e.V., Metzstr. 14C, 81667 Munich, Germany. **Telephone:** (89) 45 80 80 6. **Fax:** (89) 45 80 80 6. **Internet:** www.jugendliteratur.org. **E-mail:** info@jugendliteratur.org.

Deutscher Jugendliteraturpreis Sonderpreis (Special Prize of the German Youth Literature Prize)

The Sonderpreis was founded in 1990 by the Bundesministerium für Familie, Senioren, Frauen und Jugend to honour a German author, translator or illustrator for her/his complete works.The prize is awarded every year at the Leipzig Book Fair and is part of the Deutsche Jugendliteraturpreis. The winners are selected by an elected jury of three experts, and receive €10,000 and a sculpture of Michael Ende's Momo.

Eligibility and Restrictions: The prize is awarded in yearly rotation to a living German author, translator or illustrator for her/his complete works in the field of children's literature.

How to Apply: In general publishers nominate authors, translators or illustrators to the Arbeitskreis für Jugendliteratur. However, nominations may be made by anyone.

Recent Winners: 2001: Peter Härtling (author); 2000: Nikolaus Heidelbach (illustrator); 1999: Brigitta Kicherer (translator); 1998: Peter Hacks (author); 1997: Binette Schroeder (illustrator).

Sponsoring Organization: Bundesministerium für Familie, Senioren, Frauen und Jugend/Arbeitskreis für Jugendliteratur e.V.

Address: Arbeitskreis für Jugendliteratur e.V, Metzstr. 14C, 81667 Munich, Germany. **Telephone:** (89) 45 80 80 6. **Fax:** (89) 45 80 80 6. **Internet:** www.jugendliteratur.org. **E-mail:** info@jugendliteratur.org.

Deutscher Kinder- und Jugendtheaterpreis (German Youth Theatre Prize)

Supported by the Ministry of the Family, Women and Youth, the annual prize is Germany's most valuable prize for drama for young people, with a total prize fund of €35,000. Two main prizes of €10,000 are awarded in the categories Youth Theatre or Children's Theatre. Winners are chosen by a specially selected jury.

Eligibility and Restrictions: All German-language theatre companies and publishers of drama are invited to send nominations; however, authors themselves may not apply.

How to Apply: Six copies of works entered should be submitted by 1 March.

Sponsoring Organization: Kinder- und Jugendtheaterzentrum in der Bundesrepublik Deutschland.

Contact: Dir Dr Gerd Taube.

Address: Kinder- und Jugendtheaterzentrum in der Bundesrepublik Deutschland, Schützenstr. 12, 60311 Frankfurt/Main, Germany. **Telephone:** (69) 296661. **Fax:** (69) 292354. **Internet:** www.kjtz.de. **E-mail:** zentrum@kjtz.de.

Deutscher-Krimi-Preis

The Deutscher-Krimi-Preis, sponsored by the Bochumer Krimi Archiv and various German publishing houses, is awarded for the best crime novels published during the previous year. Three prizes are awarded annually for both original editions in German and for first-time translations into German. The prize was first awarded in 1985.

Eligibility and Restrictions: All entries must have been newly published in the previous year.

Recent Winners: National (German) category: 2001: Ulrich Ritzel, *Schwemmholz*; 2000: Thea Dorn, *Die Hirnkönigin*; 1999: Wolf Haas, *Komm, süsser Tod*; 1998: Robert Hültner, *Die Godin*; 1997: Alexander Heimann, *Dezemberföhn*
International category: 2001: Jean-Claude Izzo, *Chourmo*; 2000: Garry Disher, *Gier*; 1999: Jerry Oster, *Sturz in Dunkel*; 1998: Patricia Melo, *O Matador*; 1997: Philip Kerr, *Game Over*.

Sponsoring Organization: Bochumer Krimi Archiv.

Contact: Reinhard Jahn.

Address: Bochumer Krimi Archiv, Dorneburger Str. 38, 44652 Herne, Germany. **Telephone:** (23) 25 910 900. **Internet:** www.kaliber38.de/preise/dkp.htm.

Isaac and Tamara Deutscher Memorial Prize

The Deutscher Memorial Prize, established in 1969, is presented for the best book of the year in history and the social sciences, which 'exemplifies the best and most innovative new writing in or about the Marxist tradition'. There is a prize of £250, the winning title is announced in the press, and the author is invited to deliver the following year's Deutscher Memorial Lecture. The award is named after the distinguished Polish-born socialist historian Isaac Deutscher, and his wife, Tamara, a gifted writer and intellectual in her own right.

Eligibility and Restrictions: Open to works of English-language scholarship which have benn published from the previous May through to July of the year of award.

How to Apply: Anyone can nominate a candidate; nomination form available on website. Closing date for nominations is 1 May.

Recent Winners: 2001: James Holstun, *Ehud's Dagger*; 2000: P. Gowan, *The Global Gamble*; 1999: F. Wheen, *Karl Marx*; 1998: (no award given); 1997: R. Blackburn, *The Making of New World Slavery*.

Sponsoring Organization: Isaac Deutscher Memorial Foundation.

Contact: Elizabeth Dore.

Address: School of Modern Languages, University of Southampton, Highfield, Southampton SO17 1BJ, UK. **Internet:** www.deutscherprize.org.uk. **E-mail:** ed2@soton.ac.uk.

Denis Devlin Memorial Award for Poetry

An award held every three years for English-language poetry. The winner receives a prize of €2,500.

Eligibility and Restrictions: Open to new books of English-language poetry published in the last three years.

How to Apply: There is no direct application; nominations are drawn up by the Arts Council.

Recent Winners: 2001: Paula Meehan.

Sponsoring Organization: Arts Council/ An Chomhairle Ealaion.

Address: The Arts Council, 70 Merrion Square, Dublin, 2, Ireland. **Telephone:** (1) 618 0200. **Fax:** (1) 676 1302. **Internet:** www.artscouncil.ie. **E-mail:** info@artscouncil.ie.

Dewan Bahasa dan Pustaka Prize

An annual prize sponsored by Dewan Bahasa dan Pustaka (DBP), the national literary agency. The winner receives a cash prize of RM3,000, plus a trophy, a plaque, and a certificate; in addition the winning books are published by DBP.

Recent Winners: Yuslizal b. Monek Nurkalbi.

Sponsoring Organization: Dewan Bahasa dan Pustaka.

Contact: Rohanl Rustam, Chief Librarian.

Address: Government of Malaysia, Language and Literacy Agency, 50926 Kuala Lumpur, Malaysia. **Internet:** www.dbp.gov.my.

Diagram Group Prize

Awarded to the oddest title of the year as nominated by readers of *The Bookseller* magazine. The winner receives a bottle of vintage champagne.

How to Apply: Entries are not required, although nominations are encouraged.

Recent Winners: 2001: *Butterworths Corporate Manslaughter Service*; 2000: *High Performance Stiffened Structures*.

Address: The Bookseller, 12 Dyott St, London WC1A 1DF, UK.

Discovery/The Nation Joan Leiman Jacobson Poetry Prizes

Established in 1974, the Discovery/The Nation contest, co-sponsored by The 92nd Street Y Unterberg Poetry Center and *The Nation* magazine, is designed to attract large audiences to poets who have not yet published a book of poems. Each of the four winners is awarded $300, a reading at the Poetry Center and publication in *The Nation*. Grace Schulman, Poetry Editor at *The Nation*, founded the contest and co-ordinates the award. Each year three different leading poets are invited to be judges.

Eligibility and Restrictions: Open to poets who have not published a book of poems. All poems must be original and in English (translations are excluded).

How to Apply: Four identical sets of a typed 10-page manuscript should be submitted; no personal identification should appear on any of the poems. Entries should be accompanied by a covering letter, a list of submitted poems, and a $5 entry fee.

Recent Winners: 2001: Linda Jenkins, Gregory McDonald, Andrew Varnon and Stefi Weisburd; former winners include Mary Jo Bang, Nick Flynn, Debora Greger, Garrett Hongo, Katha Pollitt, Mary Jo Salter, Sherod Santos, Gary Soto, David St. John, Ellen Bryant Voigt and Rosanna Warren.

Sponsoring Organization: 92nd Street Y Unterberg Poetry Center/The Nation.

Contact: Editor Grace Shulman.

Address: Discovery/The Nation, Unterberg Poetry Center, 92nd St Y, 1395 Lexington Ave, New York, NY 10128, USA. **Telephone:** (212) 415-5759. **Internet:** www.92ndsty.org..

Alfred-Döblin-Preis

The Alfred-Döblin-Preis, jointly sponsored by the eminent German author Günter Grass and the Stiftung Alfred-Döblin-Preis, has been awarded every two years since 1978 for epic works not yet published. Entrants are invited to read their work before an audience at an authors' conference held in Berlin. The winner receives a grant to spend time writing at Villa Grassimo, while there is also a runner-up commendation prize.

Recent Winners: Recent winners include Katja Lange-Müller, *Verfrühte Tierliebe*; Ingomar von Kieseritzky, *Unter Tanten und andere Stilleben*; Michael Wildenhain, *Erste Liebe, deutscher Herbst*; and Norbert Gstrein, *Die englischen Jahre*.

Sponsoring Organization: Stiftung Alfred-Döblin-Preis/Günter Grass.

Address: Akademie der Künste, Hanseatenweg 10, 10557 Berlin, Germany.

Dobloug Priset (Dobloug Prize)

This prize is given annually for outstanding works of Swedish or Norwegian literature or history of literature. It was established following a bequest in 1955 from Birger Dobloug, and now carries a prize value of SEK 60,000.

Recent Winners: 2002: Anne-Marie Berglund, Claes Hylinger, Erling Kittelsen and Hanne Ørstavik; 2001: Birgitta Lillpers, Magnus Florin, Svein Jarvoll and Thorvald Steen; 2000: Louise Ekelund, Per Odensten, Jan Kjærstad and Einar Økland; 1999: Kristina Lugn and Ole Söderström; 1998: Klas Östergren, Ulf Eriksson, Ola Bauer and Karsten Alnäs;.

Sponsoring Organization: Swedish Academy.

Address: Borshuset, Kallargrand 4, 111 29 Stockholm, Sweden.

Donner Prize

Established in 1998 to recognize the year's best book on Canadian public policy. The winner receives C$25,000, while two runners-up each receive C$10,000. The purpose of the prize is to acknowledge, encourage and reward excellence in public policy writing in Canada. The winner is selected by a jury made up of five members who bring varied backgrounds and areas of expertise to the task.

Eligibility and Restrictions: Public policy is defined to include public finance, the environment, regulatory reform, economic policy, urban affairs, health care, educational reform, and social issues. All entries must have been published in English or French between 1 January and 31 December of the prize year.

How to Apply: Applications are accepted from publishers only. Six copies of each title should be delivered to the Prize Manager by 30 November.

Recent Winners: 2001: Marie McAndrew, *Immigration et diversité à l'école: le débat québécois dans une perspective comparative*; 2000: Tom Flanagan, *First Nations? Second Thoughts*; 1999: David Gratzer, *Code Blue: Reviving Canada's Health Care System*; 1998: Thomas Courchene and Colin Telmer, *From Heartland to North American Region State: The Social, Fiscal and Federal Evolution of Ontario*.

Sponsoring Organization: Donner Canadian Foundation.

Address: 8 Prince Arthur Ave, 3rd Floor, Toronto, ON M5R 1A9, Canada. **Telephone:** (416) 920-6460. **Internet:** www.donnerfoundation.org.

An duais don bhfilíocht as Gaeilge (Prize for Poetry in Irish)

A prize of €4,000 awarded every three years for a new book of Irish language poetry published in the last three years. The winner is chosen by an independent panel of assessors.

How to Apply: There is no direct application; nominations are drawn up by the Arts Council.

Sponsoring Organization: Arts Council/ An Chomhairle Ealaion.

Address: The Arts Council, 70 Merrion Square, Dublin, 2, Ireland. **Telephone:** (1) 618 0200. **Fax:** (1) 676 1302. **Internet:** www.artscouncil.ie. **E-mail:** info@ artscouncil.ie.

Dundee Book Prize

A biennial prize established in 1996 and first presented in 1999, as a joint venture between the City of Discovery Campaign and the University of Dundee; the prize has the backing of leading Scottish publisher Polygon. The prize is awarded for an unpublished novel. The winner receives a prize of £6,000 and a trophy, plus the chance of publication by Polygon.

Eligibility and Restrictions: Open to unpublished works of fiction. Manuscripts must be in English. The theme for the second Dundee Book Prize (2002) was 'discovery'.

How to Apply: Application forms are available from the address given; deadline for 2004 competition is 31 August 2003.

Recent Winners: 1999: Andrew Murray Scott, *Tumulus*.

Sponsoring Organization: City of Discovery Campaign/Dundee University.

Contact: Co-ordinator Deborah Kennedy.

Address: Dundee City Council, Economic Development, 3 City Square, Dundee DD1 3BA, UK. **Telephone:** (1382) 434275. **Fax:** (1382) 434096. **Internet:** www.dundeecity.gov.uk. **E-mail:** deborahkennedy@dundeecity.gov.uk.

Thomas Dunne Books Award for the Novel

An annual award established in 1975 to foster the presentation of new literary talent to important publishing houses. The winner, chosen by a panel of judges and screeners who are published professionals, receives advance earnings of $10,000 ($5,000 on signing and $5,000 on publication) and publication of the novel by Thomas Dunne Books.

Eligibility and Restrictions: Open to authors writing in English regardless of their nationality or place of residence. Manuscripts should be at least 60,000 words in length.

How to Apply: There is no direct application process; Associated Writing Program (AWP) submits 10 eligible entries, which it considers to be the best, to Thomas Dunne Books.

Recent Winners: 2001: (no award given); 2000: Alexandra Parsons; 1999: Aaron Roy Even; 1997 and 1998: (no award given); 1996: (no competition held).

Sponsoring Organization: Associated Writing Program (AWP).

Contact: Man. Supriya Bhatnaga.

Address: Associated Writing Program, Mail Stop 1E3, George Mason University, Fairfax, VA 22030, USA. **Telephone:** (703) 993-4308. **Fax:** (703) 993-4302. **Internet:** www.awpwriter.org. **E-mail:** awpchron@mason.gmu.edu.

John H. Dunning Prize

Established by a bequest from Mathilde Dunning in 1927 in memory of her father, John Dunning, and her brother, William A. Dunning, a former president of the association, both historians of the South, this prize is awarded to a young scholar for an outstanding monograph in manuscript or in print on any subject relating to US history. This prize is offered biennially in odd-numbered years.

Recent Winners: 2001: Ernest Freeberg, *The Education of Laura Bridgman: First Deaf and Blind Person to Learn Language.*

Sponsoring Organization: American Historical Association.

Contact: Lynn Hunt.

Address: American Historical Asscn, 400 A St, SE, Washington, DC 20003–3889, USA. **Telephone:** (202) 544-2422. **Fax:** (202) 544-8307. **Internet:** www. theaha.org/prizes. **E-mail:** press@theaha.org.

DV Cultural Award

The newpaper *DV* presents an annual award to artists, authors and others for outstanding work in various cultural fields, including literature.

Sponsoring Organization: *DV.*

Address: Menningarverdlaun, Thverholt 11, IS-105 Reykjavík, Iceland. **Telephone:** 5505000. **Fax:** 5505020. **Internet:** www.strik.is/dv/. **E-mail:** dvrits@ff.is.

Dymocks Children's Choice Awards

Annual awards organized by Dymocks bookshop. The winners are selected by popular vote from children across Australia, with prizes awarded in five categories: favourite author, picture book, younger readers, older readers, and teenage.

Eligibility and Restrictions: Entries must have been published during the preceding year.

Recent Winners: Favourite Australian Author: 2000: Paul Jennings
Picture Book: 2000: Jeannie Baker, *The Hidden Forest*
Younger Reader Category: 2000: Various authors, *Aussie Bites* series
Older Reader Category: 2000: Morris Gleitzman, *Toad Rage*
Teenage Category: 2000: John Marsden, *Tomorrow* series.

Sponsoring Organization: Dymocks Pty Ltd.

Address: Dymocks Pty Ltd, 428 George St, 6th Floor, Sydney, NSW, Australia. **Telephone:** (2) 9224 0411. **Fax:** (2) 9224 9401. **Internet:** www.dymocks.com.au/asp/awards/childrens%20choice.asp. **E-mail:** feedback@dymocks.com.au.

Dymocks Singapore Literature Prize

The National Book Development Council of Singapore (NBDCS) launched the Dymocks Singapore Literature Prize in 1999, as a resurrection of the former Singapore Literature Prize (SLP), to promote English-language fiction writing. It is presented to the best published work of fiction by a Singaporean or permanent resident author, whether published in Singapore or overseas. The prize is modelled on the British Booker Prize; however, it consists of a trophy but no cash incentives.

How to Apply: Entries should be submitted through publishers to the address given by the beginning of May.

Recent Winners: 2000: Shelley Rex, *A River of Roses*; 1999: Alfian Sa'at, *Corridor: 12 stories*, Daren V. L. Shiau, *Heartland*, Colin Cheong, *The Man in the Cupboard* and Rosemary Lim, *The Seed from the Tree* (joint winners).

Sponsoring Organization: National Book Development Council of Singapore.

Address: National Library, 91 Stamford Road, Singapore, 178896, Singapore.

Margaret A. Edwards Award

The Margaret A. Edwards Award, established in 1988, honours an author's lifetime achievement for writing books that have been popular with teenagers over a period of time. The annual award is administered by the Young Adult Library Services Association (YALSA) of the American Library Association (ALA) and sponsored by *School Library Journal* magazine. It recognizes an author's work in helping adolescents become aware of themselves and addressing questions about their role and importance in relationships, society, and in the world. The award is named after the late Margaret A. Edwards, an administrator of young adult programmes at Enoch Pratt Fee Library in Baltimore, Md., for more than 30 years.

Winners are announced at the ALA Midwinter Meeting, usually in January, and receive $2,000 along with a citation at the Annual Conference in June.

Eligibility and Restrictions: Criteria include literary quality, popularity with young adults and how well the books satisfy the curiosity of young adults and help them develop a philosophy of life. The author must be living at the time of nomination. In the case of co-authors, one must be living. The book or books honoured must have been published in the USA no less than five years prior to nomination.

How to Apply: Nominations may be submitted by young adult librarians and teenagers. A judging committee is responsible for the final selection.

Recent Winners: 2001: Robert Lipsyte, *The Contender, The Brave, The Chief, One Fat Summer*; 2000: Chris Crutcher, *Staying Fat for Sarah Byrnes, Athletic Shorts, Chinese Handcuffs, The Crazy Horse Electric Game, Stotan!* and *Running Loose*; 1999: Anne McCaffrey, *Dragonflight, Dragonquest, The White Dragon, The Ship Who Sang, Dragonsong, Dragonsinger* and *Dragondrums*; 1998: Madeleine L'Engle, *Meet the Austins, Ring of Endless Light, A Wrinkle in Time* and *A Swiftly Tilting Planet*; 1997: Gary Paulsen, *Hatchet, Woodsong, Winter Room, The Crossing, Canyon* and *Dancing Carl*; 1996: Judy Blume, *Forever*; 1995: Cynthia Voigt, *Homecoming, Dicey's Song, A Solitary Blue, Building Blocks, The Runner, Jackaroo, Izzy* and *Willy-Nilly*.

Sponsoring Organization: American Library Association/*School Library Journal*.

Address: American Library Association, 50 East Huron, Chicago, IL 60611–2795, USA. **Fax:** (312) 944-7671. **Internet:** www.ala.org/alsc. **E-mail:** alsc@ala.org.

Eesti Kirjanduse Aastapreemia

Two annual prizes of 12,500 EEK each, awarded for literary translation into and from Estonian.

Eligibility and Restrictions: There are no restrictions on genre, but the translation must have appeared in the year of the award.

How to Apply: It is not possible to apply directly for the prize.

Sponsoring Organization: Eesti Kultuurkapital.

Address: Eesti Kultuurkapital, Kirjanduse sihtkapital, Suur-Karja 23, 10148 Tallinn, Estonia. **Telephone:** 644 69 22. **Fax:** 631 40 85. **Internet:** www.ee/kulka. **E-mail:** kulka@www.ee.

Egyptian Literary Award

The Egyptian Literary Award was launched in 1997, with the aim of becoming a highly esteemed new Arab literary award to parallel the international Nobel award. The prize is awarded by a jury made up of renowned scholars and intellectuals, comprising seven members from Egypt and other Arab countries. The LE 50,000 award (US $15,000) is given to the winner for his or her body of work, with special emphasis on a recent novel.

Sponsoring Organization: Ministry of Culture.

Address: Ministry of Culture, 2 Sharia Shagaret ed-Dor, Cairo (Zamalek), Egypt. **Telephone:** (2) 3320761. **Fax:** (2) 3406449. **E-mail:** mculture@idsc.gov.eg.

Ehrenpreis des Österreichischen Buchhandels für Toleranz in Denken und Handeln (Austrian Book Trade Honorary Award for Tolerance in Thought and Action)

Presented annually since 1990, the award recognizes the contribution of an author's work to tolerance towards other cultures, with the aim of promoting peaceful European coexistence. The award, of 100,000 Sch (€7,270), is presented during Austrian Book Week.

Recent Winners: 2001: Karl-Markus Gauss; previous winners include Milo Dor, Viktor Frankl, Inge Merkel, Franz Kardinal König, Gerhard Roth, Simon Wiesenthal, Hugo Portisch, H. C. Artmann, Christine Nöstlinger, Sir Peter Ustinov and Josef Haslinger.

Sponsoring Organization: Hauptverband des Österreichischen Buchhandels.

Contact: Ernst Grabovszki.

Address: Hauptverband des Österreichischen Buchhandels, Grünangergasse 5, 1010 Vienna, Austria. **Telephone:** (1) 53115 7612. **Fax:** (1) 53115 756. **Internet:** www.buecher.at/Presse/Pressemeldungen/Presse.htm. **E-mail:** grabovszki.anzeiger@hvb.at.

T. S. Eliot Prize

Founded in 1993 by the Poetry Book Society, and sponsored in 2000–2002 by bol.com. The annual £10,000 prize, awarded to the author of the best collection of new poetry, is funded by Mrs Valerie Eliot, widow of T. S. Eliot. The winner is chosen by a changing panel of three poets.

Eligibility and Restrictions: Open to collections of new poetry published in the UK and Ireland. Self-published work is not eligible.

How to Apply: Publishers apply on behalf of poets; guidelines are available from the address given.

Recent Winners: 2001: Anne Carson, *The Beauty of the Husband*; 2000: Michael Longley, *The Weather in Japan*; 1999: Hugo Williams, *Billy's Rain*; 1998: Ted Hughes, *Birthday Letters*; 1997: Don Paterson, *God's Gift to Women*.

Sponsoring Organization: Poetry Book Society.

Contact: Dir Clare Brown.

Address: Poetry Book Society, Book House, 45 East Hill, London SW18 2QZ, UK. **Telephone:** (20) 8870 8403. **Fax:** (20) 8877 1615. **Internet:** www.poetrybooks. co.uk. **E-mail:** info@poetrybooks.co.uk.

T. S. Eliot Prize for Poetry

An annual award for the best unpublished book-length collection of poetry in English. The purpose of the prize is to publish and promote contemporary English-language poetry, regardless of a poet's nationality, reputation, stage in career, or publication history. The winner receives $2,000 and publication of the winning collection.

Eligibility and Restrictions: Manuscripts should be between 60 and 100 typed pages of original poetry in English.

How to Apply: Entries should be sent by 31 October, accompanied by contact details and a $25 reading fee. Author's name should not appear in the manuscript, but on a separate title page.

Recent Winners: 2002: James Gurle, *Human Cartography*; 2001: Christopher Bakken, *After Greece*; 2000: H. L. Hix, *Rational Numbers*; 1999: David Keplinger, *The Rose Inside*; 1998: Rhina Espaillat, *Where Horizons Go*.

Sponsoring Organization: Truman State University Press.

Address: 100 East Normal St, Kirksville, MO 63501, USA. **Telephone:** (800) 916-6802. **Fax:** (660) 785-4480. **Internet:** tsup.truman.edu. **E-mail:** tsup@ truman.edu.

Arthur Ellis Awards

Established in 1984 and named after the pseudonym of Canada's official hangman, the Arthur Ellis Awards are awarded annually by the Crime Writers of Canada. Includes a category for best juvenile mystery.

Eligibility and Restrictions: Entries must be published within the preceding year by a Canadian resident, regardless of nationality, or a Canadian writer living abroad.

Recent Winners: 1999: Norah McClintock, *Sins of the Father*; 1998: Norah McClintock, *The Body in the Basement*; 1997: Linda Bailey, *How Can A Frozen Detective Stay Hot On The Trail?*; 1996: Norah McClintock, *Mistaken Identity*; 1995: James Heneghan, *Torn Away*.

Sponsoring Organization: Crime Writers of Canada.

Address: Crime Writers of Canada, 3007 Kingston Rd, Box 113, Scarborough, Ontario, M1M 1P1, Canada. **Telephone:** (416) 466-9826. **Fax:** (416) 461-4489.

Emerson-Thoreau Medal

Established in 1958 to give broad recognition in the field of literature, the medal is awarded for a body of work rather than a specific title. The medal is awarded at the discretion of the Council of the American Academy of Arts and Sciences (AAAS).

How to Apply: Nominations are made by a committee.

Recent Winners: 1989: Norman Mailer; 1979: James T. Farrell; 1977: Saul Bellow; 1975: Robert Penn Warren; 1970: I. A. Richards.

Sponsoring Organization: American Academy of Arts and Sciences.
Address: 136 Irving Street, Cambridge, MA 02138, USA. **Telephone:** (617) 576-5000. **Fax:** (617) 576-5050. **Internet:** www.amacad.org/.

Encore Award

An annual award established in 1990 to recognize an outstanding second published novel. The prize, sponsored by Miss Lucy Astor, is of £10,000, which may be shared between several winners.

Eligibility and Restrictions: Open to books first published in the UK during the previous year.

How to Apply: Publishers are invited to submit entries by 30 November.

Recent Winners: 2001: Anne Enright, *What Are You Like?*; 2000: John Burnside, *The Mercy Boys*, Claire Messud, *The Last Life* , Matt Thorne, *Eight Minutes Idle* and Phil Whitaker, *Triangulation* (joint winners); 1999: Christina Koning, *Undiscovered Country*; 1998: Timothy O'Grady, *I Could Read The Sky* and Alan Warner, *These Demented Lands* (joint winners).

Sponsoring Organization: Society of Authors.

Address: Society of Authors, 84 Drayton Gdns, London SW10 9SB, UK. **Telephone:** (20) 7373 6642. **Fax:** (20) 7373 5768. **Internet:** www.societyofauthors.org. **E-mail:** info@societyofauthors.org.

Marian Engel Award

Presented by the Writers' Development Trust to a Canadian woman author for outstanding prose writing. The winner receives a prize of $10,000.

Recent Winners: 2000: Anita Rau Badami; 1999: Janice Kulyk Keefer; 1998: Sharon Butala; 1997: Katherine Govier; 1996: Barbara Gowdy.

Sponsoring Organization: Writers' Development Trust.

Address: Writers' Development Trust, 24 Ryerson Ave, Suite 201, Toronto, ON M5T 2P3, Canada.

European Jewish Publication Society Grant to Publishers

Founded in 1995 to enable the publication of works of Jewish interest (history, religion, philosophy, politics and culture) that would otherwise not be published. Awards of up to £3,000 are given to publishers for works of fiction or non-fiction and up to £1,000 for poetry.

Eligibility and Restrictions: Translations from other languages are considered, but the work must be published in Europe. Children's work and educational manuscripts are excluded.

How to Apply: Manuscripts should be submitted to the address given.

Sponsoring Organization: European Jewish Publication Society.

Contact: Editorial Dir Dr Colin Schindler.

Address: European Jewish Publication Society, PO Box 19948, London N3 3ZJ, UK. **Telephone:** (20) 8346 1668. **Fax:** (20)8 346 1776. **Internet:** www.ejps.org.uk. **E-mail:** cs@ejps.org.uk.

European Online Journalism (EOJ) Award

The European Online Journalism (EOJ) Award, which aims to reward excellence in web journalism, is the only pan-European award of its kind. The awards were set up in 1998 in recognition of the huge changes online publishing is making to journalism and were the first awards to honour the work of online journalists. The judges are drawn from leading media houses across the continent. The EOJ Awards are administered by a supervisory board consisting of leading European journalism educators.

Eligibility and Restrictions: The competition is open to all European journalists; practising journalists as well as students in journalism schools may compete. Awards are offered in 21 categories.

How to Apply: All entries must be submitted via the entry form on the website Deadline for submission of entries is 31 May.

Recent Winners: Past winners of EOJ Awards include BBC Online, *Dagens Nyheter*, *Times Europe*, *Helsingin Sanomat*, Enredando, NRH Radio, *The Guardian*, *New Scientist*, Oslopuls, *Central Europe Review*, Transitions On Line, OutThereNews, and Reuters AlertNet.

Address: London, UK. **Telephone:** (20) 7637 790. **Fax:** (20) 7636 4888. **Internet:** www.net-media.co.uk.

Evens Foundation European Prize for Literature

The Evens Foundation established this prize in 2002 to reward an essay on the subject of a person or community that contributed to the unification of Europe. The winner is selected for the high quality of both its ethical content and its style.

Sponsoring Organization: Evens Foundation.

Address: Evens Foundation, Van Breestraat 14, 2018 Antwerp, Belgium. **Telephone:** (3) 231 39 70. **Fax:** (3) 233 94 32. **Internet:** www. evensfoundation.be/Eng/literature.htm. **E-mail:** ef@evensfoundation.be.

Christopher Ewart-Biggs Memorial Prize

Awarded in memory of the British Ambassador to Ireland who was assassinated in Dublin in 1976. The prize was established in 1977 and aims to create greater understanding between the peoples of Britain and Ireland, or co-operation between the partners of the European Community. It is awarded to a book, a play or a piece of journalism that best fulfils this aim.

Eligibility and Restrictions: Entries must have been published during the two-year period up to 31 December.

Recent Winners: 1996: Sebastian Barry, *Steward of Christendom*, Norman Porter, *Rethinking Unionism – An Alternative Vision for Northern Ireland* and A. T. Q. Stewart, *Summer Soldiers – 1798 Rebellion in Antrim and Down*.

Address: Secretary to the Judges' Committee, Flat 3, 149 Hamilton Terrace, London NW8 9QS, UK.

Geoffrey Faber Memorial Prize

Founded in 1963 in memory of the founder of the publishing firm Faber & Faber, the prize is awarded annually, alternating between verse and fiction. The winner is chosen by a panel of three judges, and receives a prize of £1,000.

Eligibility and Restrictions: Entrants must be under 40 years of age and a citizen of the UK and dependencies, the Commonwealth, or the Republic of Ireland. Entries must have been published in the two years preceding the year in which the award is given.

Recent Winners: 2001: Trezza Azzopardi, *The Hiding Place*; 2000: Kathleen Jamie; 1999: Gavin Kramer; 1998: Don Paterson; 1997: Emily Perkins; 1996: Kathleen Jamie.

Sponsoring Organization: Faber and Faber Ltd.

Address: 3 Queen Square, London WC1N 3AU, UK. **Telephone:** (20) 7465 0045. **Fax:** (20) 7465 0043. **Internet:** www.faber.co.uk.

John E. Fagg Prize

This prize was established in 2001 for the best publication on the history of Spain and Latin America, in honour of Professor John E. Fagg, who taught Latin American history at New York University from 1945 to 1981.

Recent Winners: 2001: Jorge Cañizares-Esguerra, *How to Write the History of the New World*.

Sponsoring Organization: American Historical Association.

Contact: Lynn Hunt.

Address: American Historical Asscn, 400 A St, SE, Washington, DC 20003–3889, USA. **Telephone:** (202) 544-2422. **Fax:** (202) 544-8307. **Internet:** www. theaha.org/prizes. **E-mail:** press@theaha.org.

Alfred Fagon Award

An annual award of £2,500 for the best new play for the theatre by writers from the Caribbean. Established in memory of Alfred Fagon, a Jamaican playwright and actor, and first presented in 1997. The award is supported by the Peggy Ramsay Foundation, and the winner is chosen by a selection committee with two permanent members plus three or four new members who take part each year.

Eligibility and Restrictions: Open to new works of drama written in English by writers from the Caribbean or with Caribbean antecedents. Television and radio plays and film scripts are not eligible.

How to Apply: Applicants should send two copies of the script plus a CV and details of Caribbean connections to the Royal Court Theatre, Sloane Square, London SW1W 8AS, by the end of August.

Recent Winners: 2000: Adeshegun Ikoli; 1999: Sheila White and Grant Buchanan-Marshall (joint winners); 1998: Shenagh Cameron; 1997: Roy Williams.

Contact: Chair Harriet Cruickshank.

Address: c/o Cruickshank Cazenove Ltd, 97 Old South Lambeth Rd, London SW8 1XU, UK. **Telephone:** (20) 7735 2933. **Fax:** (20) 7820 1081.

John K. Fairbank Prize

Established in 1968 by friends of John K. Fairbank, an eminent historian of China and a president of the American Historical Association (AHA) in 1967, the prize is an annual award offered for an outstanding book on the history of China proper, Vietnam, Chinese Central Asia, Mongolia, Korea, or Japan since the year 1800.

Recent Winners: 2001: Peter Zinoman, *The Colonial Bastille: A History of Imprisonment in Vietnam, 1862–1940*.

Sponsoring Organization: American Historical Association.

Contact: Lynn Hunt.

Address: American Historical Asscn, 400 A St, SE, Washington, DC 20003–3889, USA. **Telephone:** (202) 544-2422. **Fax:** (202) 544-8307. **Internet:** www. theaha.org/prizes. **E-mail:** press@theaha.org.

Fairlight Talking Book Award of New South Wales

Annual awards for audio books, administered by the Royal Blind Society of New South Wales with sponsorship from California-based Fairlight Inc. The awards are presented during the Sydney Writers' Festival.

Recent Winners: Young Adult: 2000: Melina Marchetta, *Looking for Alibrandi* (narrated by Sher Guhl)
Adult: 2000: Christopher Koch, *Highways to a War* (narrated by David Baldwin).

Sponsoring Organization: Fairlight Inc.

Address: Royal Blind Society of New South Wales, POB 176, Burwood, NSW 2134, Australia.

King Faisal International Prize for Arabic Literature

The award was established in 1977 and first presented in 1979. It is administered by the King Faisal Foundation and stands alongside similar prizes for services to Islam, Islamic Studies and Medicine. The Literature prize (like the other categories) comprises a cash award of SR750,000 (US$200,000); the winner also receives a gold medallion and a certificate outlining the work for which the prize has been awarded.

Eligibility and Restrictions: Nominations are not acceptable from political institutes.

How to Apply: Institutions and organizations around the world nominate candidates for the prizes.

Recent Winners: 2002: Prof. Houssam Al-Din Amin Al-Khateeb and Prof. Husni Mahmoud Hussein, *Studies on Modern Palestinian Literature.*

Sponsoring Organization: King Faisal Foundation.

Address: P.O.Box 353, Riyadh, 11411, Saudi Arabia. **Telephone:** (1) 465 2255. **Fax:** (1) 465 6524. **Internet:** www.kff.com/prize/winners/2002/2002winners.htm. **E-mail:** info@kff.com.

Norma Farber First Book Award

The Norma Farber First Book Award, which is administered by the Poetry Society of America (PSA), was established by the family and friends of Norma Farber, poet and author of children's books, for a first book of original poetry written by an American. The winner receives $500.

Eligibility and Restrictions: Entries must have been published in either a hard or soft cover in a standard edition during the previous calendar year.

How to Apply: Submissions can only be entered by publishers; two copies should be sent accompanied by a cover sheet and entry fee (non-members) between 1 October and 21 December.

Recent Winners: 2002: Jennifer Michael Hecht, *The Next Ancient World.*

Sponsoring Organization: Poetry Society of America.

Address: Poetry Society of America, 15 Gramercy Park, New York, NY 10003, USA. **Telephone:** (212) 254-9628. **Internet:** www.poetrysociety.org.

Khwaja Ghulam Farid Award

The Pakistan Academy of Letters administers a series of annual prizes established in 1980 under the Hijra National Literary Awards Scheme. The aim of the awards is to promote literary activities and recognize outstanding contributions. The Khwaja Ghulam Farid Award is an annual prize of Rs 50,000 for works written in Siraiki language.

Recent Winners: 2000: Saeed Akhtar, *Wasakh*; 1999: Zubair Ahmad, *Chandi Marrhe Taak*; 1998: Allama Azam Saeedi, *Ramz Fareedi*.

Sponsoring Organization: Pakistan Academy of Letters.

Contact: Deputy Dir Naseem Mahmood.

Address: Pitras Bokhari Road, Sector H-8/1, Islamabad, Pakistan. **Telephone:** 9257164. **Fax:** 9257159. **E-mail:** academy@apollo.net.pk.

Eleanor Farjeon Award

Award for distinguished service to children's books both in the UK and overseas. Recipients include librarians, publishers, booksellers and authors, and are chosen from nominations from members of the Children's Book Circle. The prize is of £500.

Recent Winners: 2000: Julia Eccleshare; 1999: Klaus Flugge; 1998: Gina Pollinger.

Sponsoring Organization: Children's Book Circle.

Address: Hampshire Co Library, 81 North Walls, Winchester SO23 8BY, UK.

Herbert Feis Prize

Established in 1982, this annual prize is named after Herbert Feis (1893–1972), public servant and historian of modern American foreign policy. It recognizes the outstanding work of public historians or independent scholars.

Recent Winners: 2001: Benjamin Filene, *Romancing the Folk: Public Memory and American Roots Music*.

Sponsoring Organization: American Historical Association.

Contact: Lynn Hunt.

Address: American Historical Asscn, 400 A St, SE, Washington, DC 20003–3889, USA. **Telephone:** (202) 544-2422. **Fax:** (202) 544-8307. **Internet:** www. theaha.org/prizes. **E-mail:** press@theaha.org.

Fellowship of Australian Writers Literature Awards

The Fellowship of Australian Writers presents a series of literary awards, at either a national or state level. Book awards include the Melbourne University Literature Award, of A$1,000 for a work with an Australian theme; the Christina Stead Award of A$500 for biography, autobiography or memoir; the Christopher Brennan Award for poetry; the Tom Collins Poetry Prize (A$1,000); and the Ann Elder Poetry Award of A$1,000 for a first book of poetry. In addition there are a number of awards for manuscripts, including the Jennifer Burbidge Short Story

Award (A$250), the Mary Grant Bruce Short Story Award for Children's Literature (A$600), the John Shaw Neilson Poetry Award (A$500), the Jim Hamilton Award (novel or short stories, A$1,000) and the Angelo B. Natali Short Story Award (A$600).

Eligibility and Restrictions: Entry is open to any Australian resident.

How to Apply: Authors or publishers may submit entries. Entries must be accompanied by an entry form (available on website) and the appropriate entry fee. Closing date for submissions is 31 October.

Sponsoring Organization: Fellowship of Australian Writers.

Address: Fellowship of Australian Writers (Vic) Inc, 33 Windsor Cres, Camberwell, Vic 3127, Australia. **Internet:** www.writers.asn.au/documents/ 2001_Awards_Entry_Form.PDF.

Kathleen Fidler Award

Annual award of £1,000 for an unpublished children's novel. The winning entry is published by Hodder Children's Books, and the author also receives a rosewood and silver trophy to be held for one year.

Eligibility and Restrictions: Open to unpublished manuscripts in the field of children's novels; entries should be not less than 25,000–28,000 words, for children aged 8–12. The author must not have had a novel for this age group published previously.

Recent Winners: 2001: Patricia Elliot, *The Ice Boy*; 2000: Gill Vickery, *The Ivy Crown*.

Sponsoring Organization: Book Trust Scotland.

Address: Book Trust Scotland, Scottish Book Centre, Fountainbridge Library, 137 Dundee St, Edinburgh EH11 1BG, UK. **Internet:** www.scottishbooktrust. com.

Finlandia Award

Considered to be Finland's leading literary award, this is presented by the Suomen kirjasäätiö (Finland Book Foundation) with a prize of 150,000 markka; a separate Finlandia Junior award is also presented for the best work of literature for children.

Recent Winners: 2001: Hannu Raittila, *Canal Grande*; 2000: Johanna Sinisalo, *Ennen päivänlaskua ei voi*; 1999: Kristina Carlson, *Maan ääreen*; 1998: Pentti Holappa, *Ystävän muotokuva*; 1997: Antti Tuuri, *Lakeuden kutsu*

Finlandia Junior: 2001: Kira Poutanen, *Ihana meri*; 2000: Tomi Kontio, *Keväällä isä sai siivet*; 1999: Kari Levola, *Tahdon*; 1998: Leena Laulajainen, *Kultamarja ja metsän salaisuudet*; 1997: Alexis Kouros, *Gondwanan lapset*.

Sponsoring Organization: Suomen kirjasäätiö (Finland Book Foundation).

Address: Suomen Kirjasäätiö, Lonnrotinkatu 11A, 00120 Helsinki, Finland. **Telephone:** (9) 228 77 250. **Fax:** (9) 612 1226. **E-mail:** veikko.sonninen@ skyry.net.

Firecracker Alternative Book Awards

A set of awards established in 1996 by a group of book industry professionals to celebrate and publicize the best in alternative publishing. Prizes are awarded during the annual BookExpo America Convention in Chicago.

Recent Winners: Fiction: 2002: Beth Lisick, *This Too Can Be Yours*
Non-fiction: 2002: Eric Schlosser, *Fast Food Nation*
Poetry: 2002: Dodie Bellamy, *Cunt-Ups*
Politics: 2002: Noam Chomsky, *9–11*
Sex: 2002: Annie Sprinkle and Gabrielle Cody, *Hardcore from the Heart*
Drugs: 2002: Phil Shoenfelt, *Junkie Love*
Music: 2002: Punk Planet, *We Owe You Nothing*
Art/Photo: 2002: Chris Cooper, *Devil's Advocate: The Art of Coop*
Graphic Novel: 2002: Joe Sacco, *Palestine*
Children's: 2002: Art Spiegelman and Francoise Mouly (Editors), *Little Lit: Strange Stories for Strange Kids*
Wildcard/Special Recognition: 2002: Daphne Gottlieb, *Why Things Burn*.

Sponsoring Organization: BookExpo America Convention.

Contact: Martin Quinn.

Address: BookExpo America Convention, Reed Exhibitions, 383 Main Ave, Norwalk, CT 06851, USA. **Internet:** www.firecrackerbooks.org/fihome.html. **E-mail:** qmartin@hotmail.com.

Percy Fitzpatrick Medal

This prize of R1,000 is for an original literary work aimed at children aged between 10 and 14 years. The English Academy of Southern Africa took over the administration of the prize in 2000.

Eligibility and Restrictions: Must be written in English by a person resident in Southern Africa at the time of publication, and published in Southern Africa.

Recent Winners: Elana Bregin.

Sponsoring Organization: Media Tenor South Africa/Institute for Media Analysis.

Contact: Admin. Officer C. James.

Address: POB 124, Witwatersrand, 2050, South Africa. **Telephone:** (11) 717 9339. **Fax:** (11) 717 9339.

Norma Fleck Award for Children's Non-Fiction

The annual Norma Fleck Award was established in 1999 to recognize an author, or author and illustrator, of Canadian non-fiction for children. The recipient is chosen by a jury made up of professionals within the field of children's literature. The winner receives a C$10,000 prize, the largest of its kind in Canadian children's literature; in addition in 2002 $5,000 in matching funding was made available for promotional purposes to the publishers of the five books on the shortlist.

Eligibility and Restrictions: Entries must be published between 1 May and 30 April in the year of the award.

How to Apply: Entry forms available from the address given.

Recent Winners: 2000: Simon Tookoome and Sheldon Oberman, *The Shaman's Nephew: A Life in the Far North*; 1999: Andy Turnbull and Debora Pearson, *By Truck to the North: My Arctic Adventure*.

Sponsoring Organization: Canadian Children's Book Centre.

Contact: Rebecca Sjonger.

Address: Canadian Children's Book Centre, 40 Orchard View Blvd, Suite 101, Toronto, ON M4R 1B9, Canada. **Telephone:** (416) 975-0010. **Fax:** (416) 975-8970. **E-mail:** brenda@bookcentre.ca.

Sir Banister Fletcher Prize of the Authors' Club

Named after the late Sir Banister Fletcher, a former President of both the Authors' Club and the Royal Institute of British Architects (RIBA), this prize is awarded 'for the most deserving book on architecture or the arts'. Established in 1954, the prize of £1,000 is awarded annually, alternating between titles on architecture and on fine arts. The award is made on the recommendation of the Professional Literature Committee of RIBA.

How to Apply: Publishers only are invited to apply to the Club Secretary; nominations for eligible titles should be submitted by the end of May of the year after publication.

Recent Winners: 2001: Mark Wilson Jones, *Principles of Roman Architecture*; 2000: Tanya Harrod, *The Crafts in Britain in the 20th Century* and David Alan Brown, *Leonardo da Vinci – Origins of a Genius* (joint winners).

Sponsoring Organization: Authors' Club.

Contact: Club Sec. Ann de la Grange.

Address: Authors' Club, 40 Dover St, London W1X 3RB, UK. **Telephone:** (20) 7499 8581. **Fax:** (20) 7409 0913. **Internet:** www.theartsclub.co.uk.

John Florio Prize

Awarded to the best English translation of a full-length Italian work of literary merit and general interest, published by a British publisher. The winner receives £1,000.

Eligibility and Restrictions: Entries for the each award must have been published during the two years preceding the competition, and the original must have been published this century.

How to Apply: Applications are accepted from publishers only.

Recent Winners: 2000: Martin McLoughlin, *Why Read the Classics?* by Italo Calvino.

Sponsoring Organization: Translators Association.

Address: European Literary Translation Prizes, Translators Association, 84 Drayton Gdns, London SW10 9SB, UK.

FNB VITA Poetry Award

A new award established in 2000 by First National Bank. The award is presented in recognition of the best volume of South African poetry published during the previous year. The award aims to honour new talent and contribute to the inspiration and recognition of South African poetry. It is presented during the annual Poetry Africa festival in Durban.

Recent Winners: 2000: Antjie Krog, *Down to my Last Skin*.

Sponsoring Organization: First National Bank.

Address: c/o University of Natal Centre for Creative Arts, Durban, 4041, South Africa. **Telephone:** (31) 260 2506. **Fax:** (31) 260 3074.

Förderungspreis für Literatur (Literary Encouragement Prize)

This prize, established in 1996, is given every two years for outstanding contributions to children's literature by an author, illustrator or translator. The winner receives a prize of €7,300.

Eligibility and Restrictions: Open to Austrian authors, illustrators or translators for achievements in the field of children's literature.

Recent Winners: 2000: Linda Wolfsgruber (illustrator); 1998: Heinz Janisch (author); 1996: Martin Auer (author).

Sponsoring Organization: Austrian Federal Culture Dept.

Contact: Anna Doppler.

Address: Bundeskanzleramt – Kunstsektion, Abt II/15, Schottengasse 1, 1014 Vienna, Austria. **Telephone:** (1) 53115 7612. **Fax:** (1) 53115 756. **E-mail:** anna.doppler@bka.gv.at.

Morris D. Forkosch Prize

This biennial prize, established in honour of Morris D. Forkosch, an intellectual and legal historian, recognizes the best book in the fields of British, British imperial, or British Commonwealth history since 1485. It replaces the Robert Livingston Schuyler Prize covering the same fields.

Recent Winners: 2001: Richard Drayton, *Nature's Government: Science, Imperial Britain and the 'Improvement' of the World*.

Sponsoring Organization: American Historical Association.

Contact: Lynn Hunt.

Address: American Historical Asscn, 400 A St, SE, Washington, DC 20003–3889, USA. **Telephone:** (202) 544-2422. **Fax:** (202) 544-8307. **Internet:** www.theaha.org/prizes. **E-mail:** press@theaha.org.

Forward Prizes for Poetry

Established in 1992 by William Sieghart to bring new poets and poetry to the attention of the public and to develop an appreciation of the quality and diversity of contemporary poetry. The prizes are awarded annually on the eve of National Poetry Day in October, and represent the UK's most valuable annual awards for poetry. There are three categories: Forward Prize for Best Collection (prize money of £10,000); Waterstone's Prize for the Best First Collection (£5,000); and Tolman Cunard Prize for Best Single Poem (£1,000).

Eligibility and Restrictions: Open to work published in the UK and Ireland during the previous year. The panel of judges, which changes each year, is made up of poets, critics and journalists.

How to Apply: Entry forms are sent out to publishers and literary editors of journals and newspapers.

Recent Winners: Forward Prize for Best Collection: 2001: Sean O'Brien, *Downriver*; 2000: Micheal Donaghy, *Conjure*; 1999: Jo Shapcott, *My Life Asleep*; 1998: Ted Hughes, *Birthday Letters*; 1997: Jamie McKendrick, *The Marble Fly* Waterstone's Prize for the Best First Collection: 2001: John Stammers, *The Panoramic Lounge-bar*; 2000: Andrew Waterhouse, *IN*; 1999: Nick Drake, *The Man in the White Suit*; 1998: Paul Farley, *The Boy from the Chemist is Here to See You*; 1997: Robin Robertson, *A Painted Field*

Tolman Cunard Prize for Best Single Poem: 2001: Ian Duhig, *The Lammas Hireling*; 2000: Tessa Biddington, *The Death of Descartes*; 1999: Robert Minhinnick, *Twenty-Five Laments for Iraq*; 1998: Sheenagh Pugh; 1997: Lavinia Greenlaw.

Sponsoring Organization: Forward Arts Foundation.

Contact: Administrator Truda Spruyt.

Address: Forward Arts Foundation, 17–18 Margaret St, London W1W 8RP, UK. **Telephone:** (20) 7631 2666. **Fax:** (20) 7631 2699. **Internet:** www.forwardartsfoundation.com. **E-mail:** pr@cdmangeltypr.co.uk.

Dixon Ryan Fox Manuscript Prize

Originally known as the New York State Historical Association Manuscript Award (from 1973), the award was renamed in 1997 to commemorate a former president of the Association. The prize, which consists of a $3,000 award and assistance in publication for the winning entry, is presented each year to the best unpublished, book-length monograph dealing with some aspect of the history of New York State.

Eligibility and Restrictions: Open to works dealing with any aspect of New York State history. Biographies are eligible, as are manuscripts dealing with literature and the arts, provided that in such cases the methodology is historical. Works of fiction and works of article length are not eligible.

How to Apply: Two unbound copies and a covering letter should be submitted by 20 January (there are no application forms).

Recent Winners: 2001: Elizabeth Clement, *Trick or Treat: Prostitution and Working-Class Women's Sexuality in New York City, 1900–1932*; 2000: Sara Sidstone Gronim, *Ambiguous Empire: The Knowledge of the Natural World in British Colonial New York*; 1999: Reeve Huston, *Land and Freedom: Rural Society, Popular Protest, and Party Politics in Antebellum New York*; 1998: Timothy Shannon, *The Crossroads of Empire: Indians, Colonists, and the Albany Congress of 1754*; 1997: Evan William Cornog, *The Birth of Empire: DeWitt Clinton and the American Experience, 1769–1828*.

Sponsoring Organization: New York State Historical Association.

Contact: Editor Daniel H. Goodwin.

Address: New York State Historical Asscn, Lake Rd, POB 800, Cooperstown, NY 13326–0800, USA. **Telephone:** (617) 547-1481. **Fax:** (617) 547-1404. **Internet:** www.nysha.org/publications/Fox_Prize_winners__list_of.htm. **E-mail:** goodwind @nysha.org.

Fraenkel Prize in Contemporary History

The award was established in 1989 by Ernst Fraenkel to provide an incentive and encouragement to young writers of history. The prize is awarded for an out-standing work in the field of contemporary history covering one of the traditional areas of interest to the Wiener Library, such as Central European and Jewish history in the 20th century, the Second World War, fascism and totalitarianism, political violence, racism, etc. There is a prize of US $6,000 for one section (open to all entrants) and of US $4,000 for the other section (entrants who have yet to publish a major work).

Eligibility and Restrictions: Two separate awards are made: one open to all entrants (entries between 50,000 and 150,000 words), and one open to entrants who have yet to publish a major work (entries between 25,000 and 100,000 words).

Selection is made by a committee in consultation with other experts. The work must be written in English, French or German and be unpublished at the deadline for submissions.

How to Apply: Manuscripts should reach the Administrative Co-ordinator by early May of each year. Two copies should be submitted, one in manuscript form and one on floppy disc or CD, accompanied by a short curriculum vitae.

Recent Winners: Section A (open to all): 2001: Dr Karel C. Berkhoff, *Hitler's Clean Slate: Soviet Ukraine under Nazi Rule 1941–44*; 2000: Dr Mark Roseman, *The Past in Hiding* and Prof. John Horne and Dr Alan Kramer, *German Atrocities in 1914: Meanings and Memories of War* (joint winners); 1999: Prof. Robert Moeller, *War Stories: The Search for a Usable Past in the Federal Republic of Germany*; 1998: Dr Joanna Bourke, *An Intimate History of Killing*; 1997: Prof. Vicki Caron, *Uneasy Asylum: France and the Jewish Refugee Crisis 1932–1942* Section B (for those who have yet to publish a major work): 2001: Dr Alon Rachamimov, *Austro-Hungarian POWs in Russia 1914–1918* and Dr Nikolaus Wachsmann, *Reform and Repression: Prisons and Penal Policy in Germany 1918–39* (joint winners); 2000: Dr Maureen Healy, *Vienna Falling: Total War and Everyday Life 1914–1918*; 1999: Dr des Till van Rahden, *Juden und andere Breslauer*; 1998: Dr Gunnar S. Paulsson, *Hiding in Warsaw*; 1997: Dr Nicholas Doumanis, *Myth and Memory in the Mediterranean*; 1996: Dr Neil Gregor, *Rationalisation Policy at Daimler-Benz AG 1939–45* and Dr Rainer Liedte, *Jewish Welfare in Hamburg and Manchester c. 1850–1914* (joint winners).

Sponsoring Organization: Institute of Contemporary History/ Wiener Library.

Contact: Administrative Co-ordinator Marion Koebner.

Address: The Wiener Library, 4 Devonshire St, London W1W 5BH, UK. **Telephone:** (20) 7636 7247. **Fax:** (20) 7436 6428. **Internet:** www.wiener library.co.uk. **E-mail:** info@wienerlibrary.co.uk.

Dr Wijnaendts Francken-prijs

Founded in 1934 by the Maatschappij der Nederlandse Letterkunde (MNL) following a gift from Dr Wijnaendts Francken. The prize is awarded in recognition of a literary work in the field of either essays and literary criticism, or cultural history. The prize, of €2,500, is awarded every three years, in each of the two categories alternately.

Eligibility and Restrictions: The work must have been published in Dutch during the preceding six years.

How to Apply: Application is open to anybody.

Recent Winners: 2000: Remieg Aerts; 1997: Hugo Brems; 1994: Willem Otterspeer; 1991: Jaap van Heerden; 1988: Frits van Oostrom.

Sponsoring Organization: Maatschappij der Nederlandse Letterkunde (MNL— Dutch Literature Association).

Contact: Sec. Dr Leo L van Maris.

Address: Maatschappij der Nederlandse Letterkunde, Postbus 9501, 2300 RA Leiden, Netherlands. **Telephone:** (71) 5144962. **Fax:** (71) 5272836. **Internet:** www.leidenuniv.nl/host/mnl. **E-mail:** mnl@library.leidenuniv.nl.

Miles Franklin Award

Established by the will of Miles Franklin for a published novel or play, to encourage and assist the advancement of Australian literature. There is an annual award of A$28,000.

Eligibility and Restrictions: Open to novels or plays first published in the year preceding the award, which present Australian life in any of its phases. Biographies, collections of short stories or children's books are not eligible.

How to Apply: One copy of the work must be submitted to each of the five judges.

Recent Winners: 2001: Frank Moorhouse, *Dark Palace*; 2000: Thea Astley, *Drylands* and Kim Scott, *Benang* (joint winners); 1999: Murray Bail, *Eucalyptus*; 1998: Peter Carey, *Jack Maggs*; 1997: David Foster, *The Glade Within the Grove*.

Address: Permanent Trustee Company Ltd, 35 Clarence St, Sydney, NSW 2000, Australia. **Telephone:** (2) 8295 8100. **Fax:** (2) 8295 8659. **Internet:** www. permanentgroupcom.au. **E-mail:** linda.ingaldo@permanentgroupcom.au.

Ivan Franko Prize

An international prize awarded for translating and popularizing Ukrainian literature abroad, named after a famous Ukrainian writer.

Recent Winners: 1997: Vera Rich; 1989: Baotsian; Yuriy Lukanov.

Sponsoring Organization: National Writers Union of Ukraine (NSPU).

Contact: V. Yavorivsky.

Address: Blvd Bankova 2, 01024 Kiev, Ukraine. **Fax:** (44) 293-45-86. **Internet:** www.nspu.kiev.ua. **E-mail:** nspu@.kiev.ua.

Sigmund-Freud-Preis für wissenschaftliche Prosa
(Sigmund Freud Prize for Scientific Prose)

The prize was established in 1964 to promote the development of scholarly prose, named in honour of the pioneering psychiatrist Sigmund Freud. The award carries a prize of €12,500.

Recent Winners: 2002: Klaus Heinrich (philosopher); 2001: Horst Bredekamp (art historian); 2000: Kurt Flasch (philosopher); 1999: Reinhart Koselleck (historian); 1998: Ilse Grubrich-Simitis (psychoanalyst).

Sponsoring Organization: Deutsche Akademie für Sprache und Dichtung.

Address: Deutsche Akademie für Sprache und Dichtung, Alexandraweg 23, 64287 Darmstadt, Germany. **Telephone:** (6151) 40920. **Fax:** (6151) 409299. **Internet:** www.deutscheakademie.de.

Erich-Fried-Preis

Awarded for outstanding works in the field of German language and literature. It has been presented annually since 1990 by the Internationale Erich-Fried-Gesellschaft in Vienna. The winner is selected by an independent jury, and receives a prize of 200,000 Sch (€14,540).

Recent Winners: 2000: Klaus Schlesinger; 1999: Elfriede Gerstl; 1998: Bert Papenfuss; 1997: Gert Jonke; 1996: Paul Nizon; 1995: Elke Erb.

Sponsoring Organization: Internationale Erich-Fried-Gesellschaft.

Address: Internationale Erich-Fried-Gesellschaft, Vienna, Austria.

Friedenspreis des Deutschen Buchhandels (German Book Trade Peace Prize)

The prize was established in 1950 and is sponsored by the Börsenverein des Deutschen Buchhandels (German Book Trade Association). The prize of €15,000 is awarded annually at the Frankfurt Book Fair in October for an exceptional contribution to the promotion of peace, primarily through activity in literature, science or art.

Recent Winners: 2002: Chinua Achebe; 2001: Jürgen Habermas; 2000: Assia Djerba; 1999: Fritz Stern; 1998: Martin Walser.

Sponsoring Organization: Börsenverein des deutschen Buchhandels eV.

Address: Börsenverein des deutschen Buchhandels eV, Grosser Hirschgraben 17–21, 60311 Frankfurt/Main, Germany. **Internet:** www.boersenverein.de.

Frogmore Poetry Prize

An annual poetry prize established in 1987 by Andre Avans, with the aim of promoting good poetry. The winner receives a prize of 200 guineas and a lifetime subscription to *The Frogmore Papers*; there are also runners-up prizes of 50 and 25 guineas, each with a lifetime subscription to *The Frogmore Papers*; 10 shortlisted poems are published in the September issue.

Eligibility and Restrictions: Awarded for unpublished poems of no more than 40 lines, written in English.

How to Apply: Poems should be submitted to the Frogmore Press by 30 June, accompanied by the appropriate entry fee.

Recent Winners: 2001: Gerald Watts; 2000: Ann Alexander; 1999: Joan Benner.

Sponsoring Organization: Frogmore Foundation.

Contact: Managing Editor Jeremy Page.

Address: Frogmore Press, 42 Morehall Ave, Folkestone CT19 4EF, UK. **Internet:** www.frogmorepress.co.uk.

Frost Medal

The Frost Medal, which is administered by the Poetry Society of America (PSA), was established in 1930 and is awarded annually for distinguished lifetime service to American poetry. The winner receives $2,500.

How to Apply: There is no public application process; entry is by nomination only.

Recent Winners: 2002: Galway Kinnell; 2001: Sonia Sanchez; 2000: Anthony Hecht; 1999: Barbara Guest; 1998: Stanley Kunitz.

Sponsoring Organization: Poetry Society of America.

Address: Poetry Society of America, 15 Gramercy Park, New York, NY 10003, USA. **Telephone:** (212) 254-9628. **Internet:** www.poetrysociety.org.

Fujin Kôron Literary Prize

Established in 1961 under the name Women's Literary Prize to encourage the production of literary works by women, and sponsored by the Chûô Kôronsha publishing company. The pirze is awarded annually to the best work of fiction by a woman. The winner receives a commemorative plaque and a cash prize of 1 million yen.

Recent Winners: 2001: Taguchi Randi, *Dekireba mukatsukazu ni ikitai (Life Would Be Nice If I Didn't Have to Get So Angry)*.

Sponsoring Organization: Chûô Kôronsha Publishing Company.

Address: Chûô Kôronsha Publishing Company, Tokyo, Japan.

Milán Füst Literary Prize

The Füst Milan Literary Prize, given by the Hungarian Academy of Sciences, is among the most prestigious literary prizes in Hungary. The prize is given in memory of Milán Füst (1888–1967), a Jewish-Hungarian poet, novelist, essayist and playwright, whose work is considered particularly difficult to translate. The bi-annual prize has been presented since the early 1990s to outstanding foreign translators of Hungarian poetry and prose. There is a modest cash prize, supported by the proceeds of Milán Füst's estate.

Recent Winners: 1995: Zsuzsanna Ozsvath, *Foamy Sky: The Major Poems of Miklós Radnóti*.

Sponsoring Organization: Hungarian National Academy of Science.

Address: Hungarian National Academy of Science, 9 Roosevelt tér, 1051 Budapest, Hungary. **Telephone:** (1) 411 6100. **Internet:** www.mta.hu/. **E-mail:** hernadi@office.mta.hu.

Gay, Lesbian, Bisexual and Transgendered Book Awards

The American Library Association Gay, Lesbian, Bisexual and Transgendered Book Awards were established in 1971, and are awarded to authors who demonstrate exceptional merit in examining the lesbian, gay and/or bisexual experience. Prizes are awarded each year in the categories non-fiction and literature.

Recent Winners: Non-fiction: 2002: *The Scarlet Professor: Newton Arvin, a literary life shattered by scandal*; 2001: William Eskridge, *Gaylaw: Challenging the apartheid of the closet*; 2000: Barrie Jean Borich, *My lesbian husband: landscapes of a marriage*; 1999: Sarah Schulman, *Stagestruck: Theatre, AIDS, and the marketing of gay America*; 1998: Adam Mastoon, *The shared heart: portraits and stories celebrating lesbian, gay and bisexual young people*
Literature: 2002: Moses Kaufman and the Tectonic Theatre Project, *The Laramie Project*; 2001: Sarah Waters, *Affinity*; 2000: Marci Blackman, *Po Man's Child*; 1999: Michael Cunningham, *The Hours*; 1998: Lucy Jane Bledsoe, *Working Parts: A Novel*.

Sponsoring Organization: American Library Association.

Address: American Library Association, 50 East Huron, Chicago, IL 60611–2795, USA. **Fax:** (312) 944-7671. **Internet:** www.ala.org/alsc. **E-mail:** alsc@ala.org.

Otto Gelstedprisen

The foundation which sponsors the prize was established in 1969 and the first award was made in the same year. The prize is awarded annually to a poet, journalist or young writer for his or her second or third book. The members of the Danish Academy select the winner by a simple majority, and the winner receives DKK 65,000.

Eligibility and Restrictions: Open only to Danish-language authors.

How to Apply: No direct applications are accepted.

Recent Winners: 2001: Inge Eriksen; 2000: Thomas Boberg; 1999: Niels Frank; 1998: Bo Green Jensen; 1997: Carsten Jensen.

Sponsoring Organization: Otto Gelsteds Mindefond/Danish Academy.

Contact: Administrator Dr Allan Philip.

Address: Det Danske Akademi, Rungstedlund, Rungsted Strandvej 111, 2960 Rungsted Kyst, Denmark. **Telephone:** 33 13 11 12. **Fax:** 33 32 80 45. **Internet:** www.danskeakademi.dk. **E-mail:** lawoffice@philip.dk.

David Gemmell Cup Short Story Competition

The annual David Gemmel Cup Short Story Competition, organized by Hastings Writers Group and sponsored by best-selling fantasy author David Gemmell, was founded in 1988 to encourage aspiring writers. It is now a well-established and prestigious competition. There are six cash prizes, with the winner receiving the largest prize of £250.

Eligibility and Restrictions: Open to writers living in East Sussex, West Sussex, Kent, Surrey, London and the London Boroughs. The word limit is 1,500 and stories may be in any genre except children's stories.

How to Apply: Entries should be submitted by 31 August, accompanied by an entry form and a stamped self-addressed envelope. Entry fees are £3.50 for one entry and £3 each for two or more entries.

Sponsoring Organization: Hastings Writers Group.

Address: 39 Emmanuel Road, Hastings TN34 3LB, UK. **Internet:** www.bohemia20.freeserve.co.uk/gemmel.htm.

Leo Gershoy Prize

Established in 1975 by a gift from Mrs Ida Gershoy in memory of her late husband, the eminent French historian and faculty member of New York University, this annual prize is awarded to the author of the most outstanding work in English on any aspect of 17th- and 18th-century European history.

Recent Winners: 2001: Jonathan Israel, *The Radical Enlightenment: Philosophy and the Making of Modernity, 1650–1750*; 2000: Ruth MacKay, *The Limits of Royal Authority: Resistance and Obedience in Seventeenth-Century Castile*; 1999: Adrian Johns, *The Nature of the Book: Print and Knowledge in the Making*; 1998: Carla Rahn Phillips and William D. Phillips, *Spain's Golden Fleece: Wool Production and the Wool Trade from the Middle Ages to the Nineteenth Century*; 1997: Timothy Tackett, *Becoming a Revolutionary: The Deputies of the French National Assembly and the Emergence of a Revolutionary Culture, 1789–1790*.

Sponsoring Organization: American Historical Association.

Contact: Lynn Hunt.

Address: American Historical Asscn, 400 A St, SE, Washington, DC 20003–3889, USA. **Telephone:** (202) 544-2422. **Fax:** (202) 544-8307. **Internet:** www. theaha.org/prizes. **E-mail:** press@theaha.org.

Geschwister-Scholl-Preis

This annual prize is awarded to a book which is considered to demonstrate spiritual independence and to promote moral, intellectual and aesthetic freedom.

Recent Winners: 2001: Arno Gruen, *Der Fremde in uns*; 2000: Helene Holzman, *Dies Kind soll leben*; 1999: Peter Gay, *Meine deutsche Frage. Jugend in Berlin 1933–1939*; 1998: Saul Friedländer, *Das Dritte Reich und die Juden*; 1997: Ernst Klee, *Auschwitz, die NS-Medizin und ihre Opfer*.

Sponsoring Organization: Landeshauptstadt München/ Verband Bayerischer Verlage und Buchhandlungen.

Address: Verband Bayerischer Verlage und Buchhandlungen, Munich, Germany.

André-Gide-Preis für deutsch-französische Literaturübersetzungen (André Gide Prize for German-French Literary Translation)

A prize awarded every two years for works of translation between French and German in the field of poetry or narrative prose. A translator for each language receives a prize of DM20,000. The prize is aimed at young translators who have already published some successful work.

Eligibility and Restrictions: Open both to works already published and works not yet completed.

How to Apply: Entries should be submitted accompanied by brief biographical details and a description of the work submitted.

Address: DVA-Stiftung, Neckarstr. 121, 70190 Stuttgart, Germany.

Giller Award

An annual award of C$25,000, presented to the author of the best novel or collection of short stories published in English.

Recent Winners: 2001: Richard B. Wright, *Clara Callan*; 2000: Michael Ondaatje, *Anil's Ghost* and David Adams Richards, *Mercy Among The Children* (joint winners); 1999: Bonnie Burnard, *A Good House*; 1998: Alice Munro, *The Love of a Good Woman*.

Sponsoring Organization: National Library of Canada.

Address: National Library of Canada, 395 rue Wellington, Ottawa, ON K1A 0N4, Canada. **Telephone:** (613) 995-9481. **Fax:** (613) 943-1112. **Internet:** www.nlc-bnc.ca. **E-mail:** reference@nlc-bnc.ca.

Mary Gilmore Award

Awarded for a first book of poetry published in the preceding two calendar years (until 1998 it was for a first book published in the preceding calendar year).

How to Apply: No direct applications are accepted.

Recent Winners: 2000: Lucy Dougan, *Memory Shell*; 1998: Emma Lew, *The Wild Reply*; 1997: Morgan Yasbincek, *Night Reversing*; 1996: Jordie Albiston, *Nervous Arcs*; 1995: Aileen Kelly, *Coming Up for Light*.

Sponsoring Organization: Association for the Study of Australian Literature Ltd.

Address: Dept of English, University College, ADFA, Macarthur Campus, Campbelltown, ACT 2560, Australia. **Internet:** http://idun.itsc.adfa.edu.au:16080/asal/wingilmore.html.

Gladstone History Book Prize

Administered by the Royal Historical Society and awarded to an original and scholarly work of historical research published in the English language. The prize, of £1,000, is awarded annually.

Eligibility and Restrictions: The book must be on any historical subject not primarily related to British history and be its author's first solely written history book. The author must normally be resident in the UK. The book must have been published in English in the previous calendar year.

Sponsoring Organization: Royal Historical Society.

Contact: Exec. Sec. Joy McCarthy.

Address: Royal Historical Society, University College London, Gower St, London WC1E 6BT, UK. **Telephone:** (20) 7387 7532. **Fax:** (20) 7387 7532. **Internet:** www.rhs.ac.uk. **E-mail:** royalhistsoc@ucl.ac.uk.

John Glassco Prize for Literary Translation/Prix de Traduction John-Glassco

Created in 1981 by the Literary Translators' Association of Canada, in memory of John Glassco, poet and translator, to encourage beginners in literary translation. The winner is selected by a jury made up of three specialists in literary translation; the members of the jury change each year. The prize of C$1,000 is awarded each autumn.

Eligibility and Restrictions: Eligible entries are translations in book form, published in the preceding year, which for the translator constitutes a first literary translation. It must be a translation into either French or English, of a work written in any language. Translations may be in any of the following genres: fiction, poetry, essays or young adult literature. Entrants must be Canadian citizens or have landed immigrant status.

How to Apply: Four copies of entries should be mailed to 272 Heneker, Sherbrooke, Quebec J1J 3G4, by 30 June.

Recent Winners: 2001: Agnès Guitard, *Les Hauturiers* (Original: Farley Mowat, *The Farfarers*); 2000: Chava Rosenfarb (for translation of two novels originally written by herself in Yiddish), *Bociany* and *Of Lodz and Love*; 1999: Jill Cairns, *The Indiscernible Movement* (Original: collection by Aude, *Ce mouvement imperceptible*); 1998: Diego Bastianutti, *A Major Selection of the Poetry of Giuseppe Ungaretti*; 1997: Don Coles, *For the Living and the Dead* (Original: Tomas Tranströmer, *För Levande och Döda*).

Sponsoring Organization: Literary Translators' Association of Canada.

Contact: Prof. Patricia Godbout.

Address: Literary Translators' Association of Canada, Concordia University – SB 335, 1455 blvd de Maisonneuve ouest, Montreal, PQ H3G 1M8, Canada. **Telephone:** (819) 820-1244. **Fax:** (514) 848-4514. **E-mail:** patricia.godbout@courrier.usherb.ca.

Friedrich-Glauser-Preis—Krimipreis der Autoren

Established in 1986 by Syndikat, a group of German-language authors in the field of crime literature. Yearly prizes of €5,000 for the best novel and (since 2002) €1,500 for the best debut work are presented, as well as an honorary mention ('Ehrenglauser') in recognition of a lifetime's achievement. The winner is selected by a six-member jury.

Eligibility and Restrictions: Open to authors in the field of crime novels from German-speaking countries only.

How to Apply: Publishers should send six copies of the work to the members of the jury.

Recent Winners: Best novel: 2002: Thomas Glavinic, *Der Kameramörder*; 2001: Horst Eckert, *Die Zwillingsfalle*; 2000: Uta-Maria Heim, *Engelchens Ende*; 1999: Alfred Komarek, *Polt muß weinen*; 1998: Robert Hültner, *Die Godin*
Lifetime Achievement: 2002: Gerhard Neumann; 2001: Fred Breinersdorfer; 2000: Doris Gercke; 1999: Felix Huby; 1998: Michael Molsner
Debut Work: 2002: Christoph Spielberg, *Die russische Spende*.

Contact: Thomas Przybilka.

Address: c/o Thomas Przybilka, Buschstr. 14, 53113 Bonn, Germany. **Telephone:** (228) 213410. **Fax:** (228) 242385. **Internet:** www.das-syndikat.com.

Esther Glen Award

This annual award was established in 1944 to recognize the most distinguished contribution to literature for children published in the preceding year. The winner is chosen by a panel of judges, and receives an inscribed medal and a sum of money which is decided each year by the Library and Information Association of New Zealand Aotearoa (LIANZA) Council ($NZ1,000 in 2002). LIANZA suspended its awards from 1999–2000 but reinstituted them in 2001.

Eligibility and Restrictions: Open to works of children's literature which have been published in the preceding year and written by a citizen or resident of New Zealand. Books must be an original work and longer than 14 pages. They must be still in print and available for public purchase.

How to Apply: Judges may nominate books for consideration, or books may be submitted to the judges or the Executive Director of LIANZA; publishers are requested to provide three copies of each entry.

Recent Winners: 2001: Margaret Mahy, *24 Hours*; 1998: David Hill, *Fata, Four-eyed and Useless*; 1997: Kate de Goldi, *Sanctuary*; 1996: Janice Marriott, *Crossroads*; 1995: Maurice Gee, *The Fat Man*; 1994: Paula Boock, *Sasscat to Win*.

Sponsoring Organization: Library and Information Association of New Zealand Aotearoa (LIANZA).

Contact: Office Manager Steve Williams.

Address: LIANZA, POB 12–212, Wellington, 6001, New Zealand. **Telephone:** (4) 4735834. **Fax:** (4) 4991480. **Internet:** www.lianza.org.nz. **E-mail:** office@lianza.org.nz.

Glenfiddich Food & Drink Awards

The Glenfiddith Food & Drink Awards, established in 1970, recognize excellence in writing, publishing and broadcasting on the subjects of food and drink, and represent the food and drink industry's most prestigious media awards. Categories include best food book, best drinks book, best newspaper cookery writer, restaurant critic of the year and best drinks writer.

How to Apply: Entries are accepted from publishers only.

Recent Winners: Food: 2002: Hugh Fearnley-Whittingstall, *The River Cottage Cookbook*; 2001: Donna Hay, *Marie Claire Flavours*; 2000: Sally Clarke, *Sally Clarke's Book*

Drink: 2002: Susy Atkins and Dave Broom, *Drink!... Never mind the peanuts*; 2001: Michael Schuster, *Essential Winetasting: The Complete Wine Tasting Course*; 2000: Stephen Brook, *The Wines of California*.

Sponsoring Organization: Glenfiddich.

Contact: Lindsay Stewart.

Address: Glenfiddich Food and Drink Awards, 4 Bedford Sq., London WC1B 3RA, UK. **Telephone:** (20) 7255 1100. **Fax:** (20) 7436 4164. **Internet:** www. graylinggroup.com.

Glimmer Train Literary Awards

The publisher Glimmer Train Press Inc offers a series of awards to encourage different genres of writing. The Fiction Open Award, for example, was founded in 1999 to encourage the longer short story form. The winner receives $1,000 and publication in the short story journal *Glimmer Train Series*. Other awards include the Poetry Open (held each April and October, first prize of $500), the Short Story Award For New Writers (first prize of $1,200), and the Very Short Fiction Award (first prize of $1,200).

Eligibility and Restrictions: For the Fiction Open short stories of up to 12,000 words in length are eligible. Novels and children's literature are excluded. For the Poetry Open, poems by all writers, on all themes, and of all lengths are eligible. The Short Story Award For New Writers is open only to writers whose fiction has not appeared in any publication (printed or online) with a circulation over 5,000. Stories must not exceed 8,000 words. The Very Short Fiction Award is open to all writers; entries must not exceed 2,000 words.

How to Apply: Entrants are encouraged to submit work via the website, accompanied by relevant reading fee. Closing dates vary according to category – check details on website.

Recent Winners: Fiction Open: 2001: H. G. Carroll, *Leche*; 2000: David Koon, *The Bone Divers*; 1999: Karen Outen
Poetry Open: October 2001: Jenny A. Burkholder, *A Poem about Hesitation and Adrenalin*; April 2001: Matthew Doherty, *Texas*; October 2000: Rita D. Costello, *Shadow Trees*; April 2000: Ron Egatz, *Post-Eisenhower Nourishment*
Short Story Award For New Writers: Autumn 2001: Aaron Tillman, *The Great Salt Lake Desert*; Spring 2001: R. Clifton Spargo, *A History of Minor Trespasses*; Autumn 2000: Gerard Varni, *Death's Noisy Herald*; Spring 2000: Judith McClain, *In the Red Deep*
Very Short Fiction Award: Summer 2001: Daryl Siegel, *Gone Fishing*; Winter 2001: Brian Slattery, *The Things that Get You*; Summer 2000: Debra Innocenti, *Acacia*; Winter 2000: Al Sim, *Get the Can*.

Sponsoring Organization: Glimmer Train Press Inc.

Contact: Co-Editor Linda Davies.

Address: Glimmer Train Press Inc, 710 SW Madison St, Suite 504, Portland, OR 97205, USA. **Telephone:** (503) 221-0836. **Fax:** (503) 221-0837. **Internet:** www.glimmertrain.com.

Godage Literary Awards

An annual award for the best novel of the year, established in 1998 and sponsored by Godage Publishers, one of the leading book publishers in Sri Lanka. The winner is chosen from a shortlist of 12 novels. The awards do not carry cash prizes, but the winners are presented with trophies and certificates. During the first three years of the contest all entries were books published by Godage, but it is planned to extend this to other books for future editions. The award was primarily launched to assist new authors, although veteran authors are not barred from competing.

Recent Winners: 2000: Sepali Mayadunne, *Hath Adiyata Vina Kala Yaku*.

Sponsoring Organization: S. Godage & Brothers.

Address: S. Godage & Brothers, 675, Maradana Road, Colombo, 10, Sri Lanka. **E-mail:** godage@applesri.lk.

Gold Medallion Book Awards

Since 1978, the Evangelical Christian Publishers Association has awarded selected books the Gold Medallion based on content, literary quality, design, and significance. The winners are judged by Christian booksellers, reviewers, and other industry leaders.

Recent Winners: 2001: Kenneth L. Barker (Editor), *NASB Zondervan Study Bible*.

Sponsoring Organization: Evangelical Christian Publishers Association.

Address: 1969 E. Broadway Rd, Suite 2, Tempe, AZ 85282, USA. **Telephone:** (480) 966-3998. **Fax:** (480) 966-1944. **Internet:** www.ecpa.org/.

Gold/Platinum Book Awards

Established in 1990, the Gold/Platinum Book Awards recognize outstanding sales achievement in the publication of quality Christian literature.

Eligibility and Restrictions: Eligibility for these awards is attained whenever a book or a book series achieves the designated sales level in all of its print formats. These sales levels are as follows: Gold Book Award – presented when a book sells 500,000 copies; Platinum Book Award – presented when a book sells 1,000,000 copies.

Sponsoring Organization: Evangelical Christian Publishers Association.

Address: 1969 E. Broadway Rd, Suite 2, Tempe, AZ 85282, USA. **Telephone:** (480) 966-3998. **Fax:** (480) 966-1944.

Golden Kite Award

An annual award for children's fiction, non-fiction, picture book text and picture illustration, presented by the Society of Children's Book Writers and Illustrators. The Golden Kite Award is the only award presented to children's book authors and artists by their fellow authors and artists. Four Golden Kite Statuettes (for fiction, non-fiction, picture book text, and picture-illustration) are awarded each year. A certificate of acknowledgment is presented to the author of the picture-illustrated award books.

Eligibility and Restrictions: Only open to members of the Society; all books by members published during the previous year are eligible.

How to Apply: Three copies of each book (six copies if the book is to be entered for a writing award and the picture illustration award) are to be submitted between 1 February and 15 December of the year of original publication.

Recent Winners: Fiction: 2001: Virginia Euwer Wolfe, *True Believer*; 2000: Kathleen Karr, *The Boxer*; 1999: Laurie Halse Anderson, *Speak*

Non-fiction: 2001: Susan Campbell Bartoletti, *Black Potatoes: The Story of the Great Irish Famine*; 2000: Ellen Levine, *Darkness over Denmark*; 1999: Marianne J. Dyson, *Space Station Science: Life in Free Fall*
Picture book text: 2001: J. Patrick Lewis (author), Chris Sheban (illustrator), *The Shoe Tree of Chagrin*; 2000: Jane Kurtz (author), Neil Brennan (illustrator), *River Friendly, River Wild*; 1999: Deborah Hopkinson, *A Band of Angels*
Illustration: 2001: Beth Krommes (illustrator), Jacqueline Briggs Martin (author), *The Lamp, The Ice, and the Boat Called Fish*; 2000: David Shannon, *The Rain Came Down*; 1999: Amy Walrod, *The Little Red Hen (Makes a Pizza)*.

Sponsoring Organization: Society of Children's Book Writers and Illustrators.

Address: Society of Children's Book Writers and Illustrators, 8271 Beverly Blvd, Los Angeles, CA 90048, USA. **Telephone:** (323) 782-1010. **Fax:** (323) 782-1892. **Internet:** www.scbwi.org/goldkite.htm. **E-mail:** scbwi@scbwi.org.

Herman Gorterprijs

Established in 1945 by the City of Amsterdam, and awarded annually for a work of poetry. The winner is chosen by a three-member jury, and receives €7,000.

Eligibility and Restrictions: Open to Dutch language works only, published during the previous year. All books published by a Dutch or Flemish author are eligible.

How to Apply: There is no public application process; selection is made by the jury.

Recent Winners: 2001: Rob Schouten, *Infauste dienstprognose*; 2000: Hester Knibbe, *Antidood*; 1999: Ben Cami, *Ten Westen van Eden*; 1998: Kees Ouwens, *Van de verliezer & de lichtbron*; 1997: Nachoem M. Wijnberg, *Geschenken*.

Sponsoring Organization: Amsterdam Fund for the Arts.

Contact: Desmond Spruist.

Address: Stichting Amsterdams Fonds voor de Kunst, Herengracht 609, 1017 CE Amsterdam, Netherlands. **Telephone:** (20) 5200 556. **Fax:** (20) 623 8309. **Internet:** www.afk.nl. **E-mail:** afk@afk.nl.

Gouden Griffel/Gouden Zoen (Gold Pencil/Gold Kiss)

An annual award for the best original children's book, presented by the Collective Promotion of the Netherlands Book (CPBN). The prize is considered the most important Dutch prize for children's literature, and has an enormous effect on sales. Since 1997 a separate prize, the Gouden Zoen (Golden Kiss) has been awarded for works aimed at young readers aged 13 and over.

Recent Winners: Gouden Griffel: 2002: Peter van Gestel, *Winterijs*; 2001: André Sollie, *Wachten op Matroos*; 2000: Guus Kuijer, *Voor altijd samen, amen*; 1999: Annie Makkink, *Helden op sokken*; 1998: Wim Hofman, *Zwart als inkt*
Gouden Zoen: 2002: Anne Provoost, *De arkvaarders*; 2001: Marita de Sterck, *Wild vlees*; 2000: Edward van de Vendel, *De dagen van de bluegrassliefde*; 1999: Edward van de Vendel, *Gijsbrecht*; 1998: Anne Provoost, *De roos en het zwijn*.

Sponsoring Organization: Collective Promotion of the Netherlands Book/ Collectieve Propaganda van het Nederlandse Boek.

Address: Stichting CPNB, Postbus 10576, Keizersgracht 391, 1001 EN Amsterdam, Netherlands. **Telephone:** (20) 626 49 71. **Fax:** (20) 623 16 96. **Internet:** www.cpnb.nl/niv2/11bis/index.html. **E-mail:** info@cpnb.nl.

Gourmand World Cookbook Awards

The Gourmand World Cookbook Awards, formerly known as the World Cookbook Fair and Awards, were founded by Edouard Cointreau in 1995. Among their objectives was the desire to increase knowledge of, and respect for, food and wine culture, as well as to promote an international market for the publishers of food and wine books. For the first stage of selection, winning titles in each language are chosen, and these go on to compete for the Best in the World contest. In addition French entries are judged in a special category, the Prix La Mazille. The winners are chosen by an international jury. Entries are judged in 31 categories for cookbooks (including different types of food, different courses, and national or regional variations) and 15 for wine books.

Eligibility and Restrictions: Books must have been published between 1 November of the previous year and 15 October of the award year. Entries are only accepted in their original languages.

How to Apply: Books may be entered by anyone: authors, publishers or readers; there are no entry fees. Three copies of each entry should be submitted.

Recent Winners: There are 46 categories in total each year; see website for full listing. Main categories include:

Food Book of the Century: 2001: Alain Ducasse, *Le Grand Livre de Cuisine*
Prix La Mazille International 2001: Pierre Hermé, *Chocolate Desserts*
Best Book in French (Prix La Mazille): 2001: *La Cuisine Chez Regis Marcon*
Best Chef Book: 2001: Jean Claude Bourgueil, *Die Philosophie Der Grossen Küche*
Best Desserts Book: 2001: Richard Leach, *Sweet Seasons*
Best Fish and Seafood Book: 2001: Rick Stein, *Seafood*
Best Health and Nutrition: 2001: *Chinese Herb Cooking*
Best Children's Cookbook: 2001: J.Van Loon, Chantal Stewart and Gabriel Gaté, *The Chocolate Lovers*
Best Entertaining Book: 2001: Amy Weldon, *Taste, Koken voor Hollywood Sterren*
Best Vegetarian Book: 2001: Julia Ponsoby, *Gaia's Kitchen, Vegetarian Recipes for Family and Community from Schumacher College*
Best Wine Book in the World: 2001: C. Cocks, *Bordeaux et Ses Vins*
Best Book on Wine History: 2001: G. Lavignac, *Cepages du Sud Ouest, 2000 Ans d'Histoire*
Best Book on Spirits: 2001: *Historien Om Cognac, Calvados Og Armagnac*
Best Wine Atlas: 2001: Hugh Johnson and Jancis Robinson, *The World Atlas of Wine*.

Address: 2002 Pintor Rosales, 36–8° A, 28008 Madrid, Spain. **Telephone:** (91) 541 67 68. **Fax:** (91) 542 83 09. **Internet:** www.cookbookfair.com/press/gourmand. htm. **E-mail:** icr@virtualsw.es.

Governor General's Literary Awards

First awarded in 1937, the Governor General's Literary Awards have become Canada's premier literary awards. In 1959, The Canada Council assumed sponsorship of the awards, then known as the Canada Council Prizes for Literature. In 1988, The Canada Council Prizes for Children's Literature were renamed the Governor General's Literary Awards. There are separate prizes for entries in English and French; each winner receives C$10,000.

Recent Winners: Adult Fiction (English): 2001: Richard B. Wright, *Clara Callan*; 2000: Michael Ondaatje, *Anil's Ghost*; 1999: Matt Cohen, *Elizabeth and After*; 1998: Diane Schoemperlen, *Forms of Devotion*; 1997: Jane Urquhart, *The Underpainter*

Adult Fiction (French): 2001: Andrée A. Michaud, *Le ravissement*; 1999: Lise Tremblay, *La Danse juive*; 1998: Christiane Frenette, *La Terre Ferme*; 1997: Aude, *Cet imperceptible mouvement*
Poetry (English): 2001: George Elliott Clarke, *Execution Poems*; 2000: Don McKay, *Another Gravity*
Poetry (French): 2001: Paul Chanel Malenfant, *Des ombres portées*
Drama (English): 2001: Kent Stetson, *The Harps of God*
Drama (French): 2001: Normand Chaurette, *Le Petit Köchel*
Non-fiction (English): 2001: Thomas Homer-Dixon, *The Ingenuity Gap*
Non-fiction (French): 2001: Renée Dupuis, *Quel Canada pour les Autochtones?*
Children's Literature – Text (English): 2001: Arthur Slade, *Dust*; 2000: Deborah Ellis, *Looking for X*
Children's Literature – Illustration (English): 2001: Mireille Levert, *An Island in the Soup*
Children's Literature – Illustration (French): 2001: Bruce Roberts, *Fidèles éléphants*; 2000: Marie-Louise Gay (illustrator), Don Gillmor (author), *Yuck, A Love Story*
Children's Literature – Text (French): 2001: Christiane Duchesne, *Jomusch et le troll des cuisines*; 2000: Charlotte Gingras, *Un été de Jade*
Children's Literature – Illustration (French): 2000: Anne Villeneuve, *L'écharpe rouge*
Translation: 2001: Fred A. Reed and David Homel, *Fairy Ring* (English translation of *Le Cercle de Clara*, by Martine Desjardins) and Michel Saint-Germain, *No Logo: La Tyrannie des marques* (French translation of *No Logo: Taking Aim at the Brand Bullies*, by Naomi Klein).

Sponsoring Organization: Canada Council for the Arts/Bank of Montreal.

Address: Canada Council, 350 Albert St, POB 1047, Ottawa, ON K1P 5V8, Canada. **Telephone:** (613) 566-4305. **Internet:** www.canadacouncil.ca/prizes/ggla.

Gradam Litrochta Cló Iar-Chonnachta
(Cló Iar-Chonnachta Literary Award)

Established in 1995 by Micheal o Conghaile, writer and founder of Irish-language publisher Cló Iar-Chonnachta, to encourage Irish language writing. The prize, awarded each year, is €6,350 (IR£5,000), and publication of the winning manuscript. The winner is chosen by a panel of experts.

Eligibility and Restrictions: The award is made to a different type of work each year, either poetry, drama, novel or short story. The work must be written in Irish.

How to Apply: Entry form, entry fee and three copies of the manuscript should be submitted to Cló Iar-Chonnachta.

Recent Winners: 2001: Padraig ó Siadhail, *Na Seacht gCineál Meisce agus Finscéalta Eile*; 2000: Siobhán Ní Shúilleabháin, *Aistriu*; 1999: Liam ó Muirthile, *Walking Time agus Dánta Eile*; 1998: Joe Steve ó Neachtain, *Clochmhóin*; 1997: Pól Breathnach, *Do Lorg: Dánta agus Aortha*.

Sponsoring Organization: Údarás na Gaeltachta.

Contact: Gen. Man. Deirdre Ni Thuathail.

Address: Cló Iar-Chonnachta Teo, Indreabhán, Connemara, Ireland. **Telephone:** (91) 593307. **Fax:** (91) 593362. **Internet:** www.cic.ie. **E-mail:** cic@iol.ie.

Grand Prix de la Francophonie

The award was created in 1986 at the suggestion of the Canadian government, with support from the governments of France, Monaco and Morocco and several private sponsors. It is administered by the Académie Française, and aims to promote the influence of French-language literature. The winner receives €45,730 (300,000 francs).

Eligibility and Restrictions: Open to living authors of all ages; only published works may be submitted, and they must have appeared during the preceding year.

How to Apply: Two copies of the work should be sent by the author or publisher by 31 January.

Recent Winners: 2001: François Cheng.

Sponsoring Organization: Académie Française.

Address: Académie Française, Institut de France, 23 quai de Conti, 75006 Paris, France. **Telephone:** 1 44 41 43 00. **Fax:** 1 43 29 47 45. **Internet:** www.academie-francaise.fr. **E-mail:** contact@academie-francaise.fr.

Grand Prix Halperine-Kaminsky

An annual prize for translation, awarded in two categories, 'Consécration' given for a translator's whole body of work, and worth €7,000; and 'Découverte', to encourage a new translator, who receives €1,500.

Recent Winners: Consécration: 2001: Alain Pons
Découverte: 2001: Isabelle Kalinowski, *L'Ethique protestante et l'esprit du capitalisme* (translation of original work by Max Weber).

Sponsoring Organization: Société des Gens de Lettres de France.

Address: Société des Gens de Lettres de France, Hôtel de Massa, 38 rue du Faubourg St Jacques, 75014 Paris, France. **Telephone:** 1 53 10 12 00. **Fax:** 1 53 10 12 12. **Internet:** www.sgdl.org. **E-mail:** sgdlf@wanadoo.fr.

Grand Prix Littéraire de l'Afrique Noire

An annual prize given by Association des Ecrivains de Langue Française (ADELF) in recognition of outstanding achievements by an African writer. The prize was first presented in 1961.

Recent Winners: 2000: Ken Bugul, *Riwan ou le chemin de sable* and Alain Mabanckou, *Bleu-blanc-rouge*; previous winners include Alain Mabanckou; Ahmadou Kourouma (Côte d'Ivoire), Lamine Diakhate (Senegal), Aminata Sow Fall (Senegal), Jean-Marie Adiaffi (Côte d'Ivoire), Sony Labou Tansi (Congo), Modibo sounkalo Keita (Mali), Jean-Baptiste Tati Loutard (Congo).

Sponsoring Organization: Association des Ecrivains de Langue Française (ADELF).

Address: Association des Ecrivains de Langue Française (ADELF), 14 rue Broussais, 75014 Paris, France. **Telephone:** 1 43 21 95 99. **Fax:** 1 43 20 12 22.

Grand Prix Littéraire Poncetton

An annual prize of €3,000 awarded by the Société des Gens de Lettres for a complete body of work. The winner is selected by a jury of 24 writers.

How to Apply: Five copies of works should sent by 15 October.

Recent Winners: 2001: Gisèle Prassinos.

Sponsoring Organization: Société des Gens de Lettres de France.

Address: Société des Gens de Lettres, Hôtel de Massa, 38 rue du Faubourg St Jacques, 75014 Paris, France. **Telephone:** 1 53 10 12 00. **Fax:** 1 53 10 12 12. **Internet:** www.sgdl.org. **E-mail:** sgdlf@wanadoo.fr.

Grand Prix de Littérature Française hors de France/Prix Fondation Nessim Habif (Grand Prix for French Literature from Outside France)

Established following a 1960 bequest from Nessim Habif, amounting to 125,000 swiss francs for the creation of a prize to recognize a writer whose works in the French language are deemed 'worthy of French literature'.

Eligibility and Restrictions: Open to works in the French language, but writers of French nationality or whose parents are French may not enter.

Sponsoring Organization: Académie Royale de Langue et de Littérature Françaises.

Address: Académie Royale de Langue et de Littérature Françaises, Palais des Académies, 1 rue Ducale, 1000 Brussels, Belgium. **Telephone:** (2) 550 22 11. **Fax:** (2) 550 22 05.

Grand Prix de Littérature Henri Gal

An annual prize administered by the Académie française and sponsored by the Fondation Henri Gal. The winner, chosen for a lifetime's achievement, receives a prize of €30,400.

Recent Winners: 2002: Gilles Lapouge; 2001: Simon Leys.

Sponsoring Organization: Académie Française/Fondation Henri Gal.

Address: Académie Française, Institut de France, 23 quai de Conti, 75006 Paris, France. **Telephone:** 1 44 41 43 00. **Fax:** 1 43 29 47 45. **Internet:** www.academie-francaise.fr. **E-mail:** contact@academie-francaise.fr.

Grand Prix de Littérature Paul Morand

This prize, created in 1977, is biennial and alternates with the Grand Prix de Littérature de l'Académie Française. It is awarded to authors of one or more works characterized by their high quality of thought, style and spirit of independence and freedom. The winner receives a prize of €45,735 (300,000 francs).

Eligibility and Restrictions: Open to living authors of all ages; only published works may be submitted, and they must have appeared during the preceding two years.

How to Apply: Two copies of the work should be sent by the author or publisher by 31 January.

Recent Winners: 2002: Jean-Paul Kauffmann; 2000: Patrick Modiano.

Sponsoring Organization: Académie Française.

Address: Académie Française, Institut de France, 23 quai de Conti, 75006 Paris, France. **Telephone:** 1 44 41 43 00. **Fax:** 1 43 29 47 45. **Internet:** www.academie-francaise.fr. **E-mail:** contact@academie-francaise.fr.

Grand prix du livre de Montréal

Created by the city of Montreal, and relaunched in 1987, to recognize outstanding works of literature with a connection to the city and to promote literature from Quebec. The prize is given to a work of exceptional originality and workmanship. It is awarded annually in mid-November, and is judged by a five-member jury. The winning author receives $15,000, and the prize also attracts considerable publicity.

Eligibility and Restrictions: Open to works by authors or publishers from the Montreal area; entries may be in English or French, in the field of creative literature, analysis, literary reference, history, art, etc. Entries must have been published for the first time between October and September of the previous year.

How to Apply: Entries should be submitted by the publisher, accompanied by an entry form. Seven copies of submitted works must be sent by early May (for works published between October and March) or early October (for works published between April and September).

Recent Winners: 2001: Régine Robin, *Berlin chantiers*; 2000: Denis Vanier, *L'Urine des forêts*; 1999: Joël Des Rosiers, *Vétiver*; 1998: Gaétan Soucy, *L'Acquittement*; 1997: Willie Thomas, *Cristoforo – Récits insolites d'un singulier voyageur*.

Sponsoring Organization: City of Montreal.

Contact: Commr Normand Biron.

Address: Service de la Culture, Ville de Montréal, 5650 rue d'Iberville, 4e étage, Montreal, H2G 3E4, Canada. **Telephone:** (514) 872-1160. **Internet:** www.ville. montreal.qc.ca/culture/sectsout/gplmfs.htm.

Grand Prix Thyde Monnier

An annual prize of €3,000 awarded by the Société des Gens de Lettres (SGDL). The winner is selected by a jury of 24 writers. The SGDL also awards eight Thyde Monnier grants of €1,500 each year.

How to Apply: Five copies of works should sent by 15 October.

Recent Winners: 2001: Pierrette Fleutiaux, *Des phrases courtes, ma chérie*.

Sponsoring Organization: Société des Gens de Lettres de France.

Address: Société des Gens de Lettres de France, Hôtel de Massa, 38 rue du Faubourg St Jacques, 75014 Paris, France. **Telephone:** 1 53 10 12 00. **Fax:** 1 53 10 12 12. **Internet:** www.sgdl.org. **E-mail:** sgdlf@wanadoo.fr.

Grand Prix National des Arts et des Lettres (GPNAL)
(National Grand Prize for Arts and Letters)

An annual prize for literary, artistic and audiovisual achievements, awarded as part of the Semaine Nationale de la Culture (National Week of Culture). The National Week of Culture was set up to promote the cultural heritage of Burkina Faso, to encourage literary and artistic creation, and to provide a framework for exchange between artists and cultural figures from Burkina Faso and other countries.The prize, established in 1989, aims to promote young talent, and is judged by a jury of eminent professional figures, who select recipients for the first, second and third prizes. Awards are made in the fields of performance art, literature, visual arts, debate, cinema, culinary skill, and African struggle.

Recent Winners: Ernest Mingo Zougrana: 1st prize 1991, 2nd prize 1988, 1990, 1992, 1994, 3rd prize 1987.

Sponsoring Organization: Semaine Nationale de la Culture (SNC).

Address: SP / SNC, 01 BP 559, Bobo Dioulasso, Burkina Faso. **Telephone:** 98 02 35. **Fax:** 97 24 13. **Internet:** www.culture.gov.bf/site_ministere/evenements/evenement_snc.htm.

Grand Prix National des Lettres
(National Grand Prize for Literature)

One of a series of annual national prizes, which recognize outstanding artists in different fields. The National Grand Prize for Literature, first presented in 1951, was reorganized in 1988, to combine the previous separate awards for literature (letters), poetry, translation and history. Within the category of 'letters' a separate award is presented to a young author in recognition of new talent. The winner is selected by a jury of 10 eminent literary figures.

Recent Winners: 1999: Réjean Ducharme and Dominique Eddé; 1998: Michel Houellebecq; previous winners include Marguerite Yourcenar, Valéry Larbaud, Gaston Bachelard, Henri Michaux and Julien Green.

Sponsoring Organization: Ministère de la Culture et de la Communication (Ministry of Culture and Communication).

Address: Ministère de la Culture et de la Communication, Direction du Livre et de la Lecture, 3 rue de Valois, 75042 Paris, Cedex 01, France.

Grand Prix Ramuz

This prize was established in memory of the writer C. F. Ramuz, and is presented every five years to a writer for a whole body of work. A separate C. F. Ramuz poetry prize is also awarded every three years.

Recent Winners: 2000: Anne-Lise Grobéty; 1995: Nicolas Bouvier; 1990: Yves Meylan; 1985: Georges Haldas; 1980: Alice Rivaz.

Sponsoring Organization: Fondation C. F. Ramuz.

Address: Case Postale 181, 1009 Pully, Switzerland.

Grand Prix RTL-Lire

Originally known as the Prix RTL-Grand Public, this award was set up in 1975 and was given its current name in 1993. The award is sponsored by the radio station RTL and *Lire* magazine. The winning work is chosen by a jury drawn from 20 regional bookshops from a shortlist of five entries. The winner becomes the subject of a promotional campaign on RTL, and in the publications *L'Express* and *Lire*.

Eligibility and Restrictions: Entries must be novels written in French, which have appeared in the previous calendar year.

Recent Winners: 2002: Tonino Benacquista, *Quelqu'un d'autre*; 2001: Andreï Makine, *La musique d'une vie*; 2000: Anna Gavalda, *Je voudrais que quelqu'un m'attende quelque part*; 1999: La Galite, *Zacharie*; 1998: Jean-Christophe Grangé, *Les rivières pourpres*.

Sponsoring Organization: RTL/Lire.

Contact: Dominique Winter.

Address: SCP– RTL, 22 Rue Bayard, 75008 Paris, France. **Telephone:** 1 40 70 42 83. **Internet:** www.rtl.fr/players/livres_l/default.asp. **E-mail:** dominique.winter@rtl.fr.

Grand Prix de la Science-Fiction et du Fantastique Québécois

An annual prize established in 1984, awarded for an outstanding work of science fiction published during the previous year.

Recent Winners: 1997: Élisabeth Vonarburg, *Le Début du cercle* (short story), *Les Rêves de la mer* and *Le Jeu de la perfection* (novels); 1996: Daniel Sernine, *Sur la scène des siècles* (short story), *L'Arc-en-cercle* and *La Traversée de l'apprenti sorcier* (novels).

Address: Quebec, Canada.

Grande Prémio Calouste Gulbenkian de Literatura para Crianças e Jovens (Gulbenkian Grand Prix for Literature for Children and Young People)

Awarded to two distinguished works of literature for children or young people. The winners are chosen by a jury in the categories of illustrated book and literary text. The prize in the illustrated category is of 2,000 escudos, to be split between the author and the illustrator, and of 1,000 escudos for the literary category.

Eligibility and Restrictions: Works must be first editions appearing during the two previous years.

How to Apply: 10 copies of entries should be sent by 31 December.

Sponsoring Organization: Fundação Calouste Gulbenkian.

Address: Fundação Calouste Gulbenkian, Avenida de Berna n° 52 – 7°, 1067–001 Lisbon, Portugal. **Internet:** www.gulbenkian.pt/.

Kate Greenaway Medal

An annual award given in recognition of outstanding illustration in a children's book. The winner receives a gold medal and £1,000 of books to donate. In addition a bequest in 1999 led to the introduction of the Colin Mears Award of £5,000, which also goes to the Greenaway winner and was awarded for the first time in 2000. A shortlist for the medal is announced at the beginning of May and the winner is announced in July.

Eligibility and Restrictions: Entries must have been published in the UK in the preceding year.

Recent Winners: 2000: Lauren Child, *I Will Not Ever Never Eat a Tomato*; 1999: Helen Oxenbury, *Alice's Adventures in Wonderland*; 1998: Helen Cooper, *Pumpkin Soup*; 1997: P. J. Lynch, *When Jessie Came Across the Sea*; 1996: Helen Cooper, *The Baby Who Wouldn't Go To Bed*.

Sponsoring Organization: Youth Libraries Group.

Contact: Louisa Myatt.

Address: Chartered Institute of Library and Information Professionals, 7 Ridgmount St, London WC1E 7AE, UK. **Telephone:** (20) 7255 0650. **Fax:** (20) 7255 0501. **Internet:** www.cilip.org.uk. **E-mail:** marketing@cilip.org.uk.

Eric Gregory Trust Fund Award

Annual award for poets, established by the late Eric Gregory, and presented to poets aged under 30 who are likely to benefit from more time given to writing. Prize money of £25,000 is shared among several winners, on the strength of work submitted and taking into account the means of each winner.

How to Apply: Closing date for entries is 31 October.

Recent Winners: 2002: Caroline Bird, Christopher James, Jacob Polley, Luke Heeley, Judith Lal, David Briggs, Eleanor Rees, Kathryn Simmonds; 2001: Ross Cogan, Mathew Holis, Helen Ivory, Andrew Pideux, Owen Sheers, Dan Wyke; 2000: Eleanor Margolies, Antony Rowland, Antony Dunn, Karen Goodwin, Clare Pollard.

Sponsoring Organization: Society of Authors.

Address: Society of Authors, 84 Drayton Gdns, London SW10 9SB, UK. **Telephone:** (20) 7373 6642. **Fax:** (20) 7373 5768. **Internet:** www. societyofauthors.org. **E-mail:** info@societyofauthors.org.

J. Greshoff Prijs

This prize, named after Jan Greshoff, a Dutch poet, author and journalist, is given for an essay. The prize is of 10,000 DFL. It is presented biennially, in rotation with the Nienke van Hichtum Prize presented by the same foundation.

Recent Winners: 2000: Martin Reints, *Nacht- en dagwerk.*

Sponsoring Organization: Jan Campertstichting (Jan Campert Foundation).

Address: PO Box 12654, 2500 DP The Hague, Netherlands. **Telephone:** (353) 36 37. **Fax:** (353) 30 58.

Griffin Poetry Prize

The prize was launched in September 2000 to serve and encourage excellence in poetry written in English anywhere in the world. There are two annual prizes, each of C$40,000, one for a Canadian poet and one for an international poet. Winning entries are published in a special anthology.

Eligibility and Restrictions: Open to living poets from anywhere in the world who write in English. Translations are permitted; translators receive 60% of the prize and the poet 40%. To be eligible for the international prize, a book of poetry must be a first-edition poetry collection written in English, or translated into English, by a poet or translator from any part of the world. To be eligible for the Canadian prize a book of poetry must be a first-edition poetry collection written in English, or translated into English, by a Canadian citizen or permanent resident.

How to Apply: Eligible collections of poetry may be submitted by publishers in the calendar year of their publication; four copies should be sent by 31 December, accompanied by an entry form and author's details. See website for more details.

Recent Winners: Canadian prize: 2001: Anne Carson, *Men in the Off Hours* International prize: 2001: Nikolai Popov and Heather McHugh (translators), *Glottal Stop: 101 Poems by Paul Celan.*

Sponsoring Organization: Griffin Trust for Excellence in Poetry.

Contact: Manager Ruth Smith.

Address: The Griffin Trust For Excellence in Poetry, 6610 Edwards Blvd, Mississauga, ON L5T 2V6, Canada. **Telephone:** (905) 565-5993. **Fax:** (905) 564-3645. **Internet:** www.griffinpoetryprize.com. **E-mail:** info@griffinpoetryprize.com.

Apollon Grigoryev Prize

Named after the literary critic and poet Apollon Grigoryev, this award is similar to the American National Critics Circle award. The prize, which was first awarded in 1997, is sponsored jointly by the Literary Academy of Modern Russian Belles-Lettres and Rosbank, and carries a prize of $25,000.

Eligibility and Restrictions: Awarded for the best non-translated literary work.

Recent Winners: 2001: Olga Slavnikova, Andrei Dmitriev and Leonid Zorin; 2000: Nikolai Kononov, *Burial of the Grasshopper* and Vera Pavlova; 1999: Yuri Davydov, *Bestseller – A novel. Part 1.*

Sponsoring Organization: Literary Academy of Modern Russian Belles-Lettres/ Rosbank.

Address: Literary Academy of Modern Russian Belles-Lettres, Moscow, Russia.

Brüder-Grimm-Preis des Landes Berlin zur Förderung des Kinder- und Jugendtheaters

Established in 1961 by the Berlin State Senate, to promote theatre for children and young people, the prize is awarded every two years to a piece of drama, either in preparation or already performed. A special jury decides on the winner, who receives a prize of €10,000.

Eligibility and Restrictions: Open to German-language plays with a relevance to children and young people, and which promote harmonious co-existence.

How to Apply: Three copies should be sent by the beginning of June.

Recent Winners: 2001: Ingeborg von Zadow, for total body of work; 1999: Projekt Schulhofgeschichten (seven authors); 1995/96: GRIPS-Theater Berlin, *Eins auf die Fresse*; 1993: Gerd Knappe, *Struwwelpeter*; 1991/92: Kammertheater Neubrandenburg, *Zirkus der Kuscheltiere* and GRIPS-Theater Berlin, *Heimatlos* (joint winners).

Sponsoring Organization: Berlin State Senate.

Contact: Wofgang Meyer.

Address: Senatsverwaltung für Wissenschaft, Forschung und Kultur, IV E 12, Brunnenstr. 188–190, 10119 Berlin, Germany. **Telephone:** (30) 90228 536. **Fax:** (30) 90228 457.

Grosser Literaturpreis der Bayerischen Akademie der Schönen Künste

The prize has been awarded since 1950, but only adopted the name 'Grosser Literaturpreis' in 1986. It is given in honour of a body of work written in German and is sponsored by the region of Bavaria and the Friedrich-Baur-Stiftung. The winner receives a prize of €15,000.

Recent Winners: 2002: Urs Widmer; 2001: Uwe Timm; 2000: Anne Duden; 1999: Peter Kurzeck;1998: Wilhelm Genazino.

Sponsoring Organization: Friedrich-Baur-Stiftung/Land of Bavaria.

Contact: Christine Mrowiet.

Address: Bayerische Akademie der Schönen Künste, Max-Joseph-Platz 3, 80539 Munich, Germany. **Telephone:** (89) 290077-0. **Fax:** (89) 290077-23. **Internet:** www.badsk.de. **E-mail:** info@badsk.de.

Grosser Preis der Schweizerische Schillerstiftung

The Grosser Preis der Schweizerischen Schillerstiftung is one of a number of annual awards made by the Swiss Schiller Foundation in recognition either of an author's collected work or an individual work. The Grosser Preis der Schweizerischen Schillerstiftung was established in 1920 to honour exemplary literary work. It has been awarded every 4–6 years since then.

Recent Winners: 2000: Wanda Schmidt, *Friedhofsgeflüster*; 1999: Peter Bichsel, *Cherubin Hammer und Cherubin Hammer*, Jan Lurvink, *Windladen* and Ruth Schweikert, *Augen zu* (joint winners); 1998: Werner Bucher, *Unruhen*, Silvio Huonder, *Adalina* and Tim Krohn, *Dreigroschenkabinett* (joint winners); 1997: Christina Buchmüller, *Winterhaus*, Klaus Merz, *Jakob schläft* and Verena Wyss, *Verdecktes Spiel* (joint winners); 1996: Hansjörg Schertenleib, *Das Zimmer der Signora*, Mariella Mehr, *Das Kind* and Lukas Hartmann, *Die Mohrin* (joint winners).

Sponsoring Organization: Schweizerische Schillerstiftung/Fondation Schiller Suisse.

Address: Schweizerische Schillerstiftung/Fondation Schiller Suisse, Mattenway 4, 8126–3270 Aarberg, Switzerland.

Grosser Österreichischer Staatspreis für Literatur (Grand Austrian State Prize for Literature)

Established in 1949 , this prize alternates every three years with similar official prizes for music and visual art. The award carries a prize of 300,000 Sch (around €22,000); winners also become members of the national Art Senate.

Sponsoring Organization: Austrian Federal Culture Department.

Address: Bundeskanzleramt – Kunstsektion, Abt II/5, Schottengasse 1, 1014 Vienna, Austria.

Guardian Children's Fiction Award

An annual award of £1,500 for an outstanding work of fiction for children.

Eligibility and Restrictions: Entries must be written by a Commonwealth or British author and first published in the UK in the previous year. Picture books and previous winners are excluded.

Recent Winners: 2001: Kevin Crossley-Holland, *The Seeing Stone*; 1999: Jacqueline Wilson, *The Illustrated Mum*; 1999: Susan Price, *The Sterkarm Handshake*.

Sponsoring Organization: *The Guardian*.

Address: *The Guardian*, 72 Dukes Ave, London W4 2AF, UK. **Internet:** www.guardian.co.uk/books.

Guardian First Book Award

The prize was established in 1965 by the *Guardian*, adopting the current name in 1999. Originally open to all fiction, in 1999 it changed to focus on first books, whether in fiction, non-fiction or poetry. The winner is chosen by a panel of critics, writers and regional readers' groups, chaired by the Literary Editor of the *Guardian*, and receives a prize of £10,000.

Eligibility and Restrictions: Since 1999 the criteria have been extended, and the prize is no longer restricted to fiction.

How to Apply: Submissions are not accepted.

Recent Winners: 2001: Chris Ware, *Jimmy Corrigan*; 2000: Zadie Smith, *White Teeth*; 1999: Philip Gourevitch, *We Wish to Inform You That Tomorrow We Will be Killed with Our Families*; 1998: Jackie Kay, *Trumpet*; 1997: Anne Michaels, *Fugitive Pieces*.

Sponsoring Organization: *The Guardian.*

Address: The Guardian, 72 Dukes Ave, London W4 2AF, UK. **Internet:** www.guardian.co.uk/books.

Guild of Food Writers Awards

The Guild of Food Writers Awards, established in 1990, are awarded in recognition of outstanding achievement in all areas of food writing. Categories include the Derek Cooper Award for Investigative or Campaigning Food Writing (launched in 2002, and named after the presenter of BBC Radio 4's Food Programme), the Michael Smith Award for Work on British Food, the Jeremy Round Award for Best First Book, the Food Book of the Year, Cookery Book of the Year, as well as awards for best food and cookery journalists of the year. Each award is judged by a panel of up to five Guild of Food Writers members; each winner receives a trophy in the form of a wooden platter.

Eligibility and Restrictions: Work must have been published in the UK or Ireland in the previous calendar year.

How to Apply: One copy of the work should be sent to each of the five judges by mid-January; see website for further details.

Recent Winners: Michael Smith Award: 2002: Hugh Fearnley-Whittingstall, *The River Cottage Cookbook*; 2001: Sue Lawrence, *Scots Cooking*
Jeremy Round Award: 2002: Fuchsia Dunlop, *Sichuan Cookery*; 2001: Rowley Leigh, *No Place Like Home*
Food Book of the Year: 2002: Anthony Bourdain, *A Cook's Tour*; 2001: Andrew Dalby, *Dangerous Tastes*
Cookery Book of the Year: 2002: Gordon Ramsay and Roz Denny, *Just Desserts*; 2001: Donna Hay, *Flavours*
Derek Cooper Award: Andy Jones, *Eating Oil: Food Supply in a Changing Climate*.

Sponsoring Organization: Guild of Food Writers.

Contact: Administrator Christine Thomas.

Address: 48 Crabtree Lane, London SW6 6LW, UK. **Telephone:** (20) 7710 1180. **Fax:** (20) 7610 0299. **Internet:** www.gfw.co.uk. **E-mail:** awards@gfw.co.uk.

Friedrich Gundolf Preis für die Vermittlung deutscher Kultur im Ausland (Friedrich Gundolf Prize for the Promotion of German Culture Abroad)

Established in 1964 by the German Academy as a means to promote German culture in other countries. It is presented for a lifetime's achievement in the service abroad of German language and literature. The prize was originally only presented to foreign universities, but since the 1990s it has been extended beyond universities to include foreign individuals. The prize is worth €12,500.

Recent Winners: 2002: Massimo Cacciari (Venice); 2001: Fuad Rifka (Beirut); 2000: Ryszard Krynicki (Kraków); 1999: Thomas von Vegesack (Stockholm); 1998: Shulamit Volkov (Tel Aviv).

Sponsoring Organization: Deutsche Akademie für Sprache und Dichtung.

Address: Deutsche Akademie für Sprache und Dichtung, Alexandraweg 23, 64287 Darmstadt, Germany. **Telephone:** (6151) 40920. **Fax:** (6151) 409299. **Internet:** www.deutscheakademie.de.

Soren Gyldendal Prize

Awarded each year by the publisher Gyldendal in memory of Søren Gyldendal (1742–1802). The winner receives a prize of DKK150,000.

Recent Winners: 2002: Bo Lidegaard; 2001: Bent Vinn Nielsen; 2000: Frans Lasson; 1999: Suzanne Brøgger; 1998: Niels Birger Wamberg.

Sponsoring Organization: Gyldendalske Boghandel-Nordisk Forlag AS.

Address: Gyldendalske Boghandel-Nordisk Forlag AS, Kareboderne 3, 1001 Copenhagen, K, Denmark.

Gyldendal-prisen (Gyldendal Prize)

A long established prize for fiction, sponsored by the publisher Gyldendal and awarded annually since 1934. The winner is chosen by a jury made up of two professors, two literary critics and a senior manager from Gyldendal.

Recent Winners: 2001: Cecilie Løveid; 2000: Jan Erik Vold; 1999: Jon Fosse; 1998: Kjartan Fløgstad; 1997: Bjørn Aamodt.

Sponsoring Organization: Gyldendal Norsk Forlag AS.

Address: Gyldendal Norsk Forlag AS, PB 6860, St Olavs Pl., 0130 Oslo, Norway. **Telephone:** (22) 03 41 00. **Fax:** (22) 03 41 05. **Internet:** www.gyldendal.no. **E-mail:** gnf@gyldendal.no.

H-shi Shô (Mr H Prize)

Established in 1951 by the Association of Contemporary Japanese Poets (Nihon Gendaishijin Kai) in order to honour an outstanding anthology of poetry published during the previous year by a new poet. Cash prizes are awarded from a fund established by Hirasawa Teijirô ('Mr H'), who until 1960 remained anonymous as the award's benefactor. The winner receives a cash prize of 500,000 yen.

Sponsoring Organization: Association of Contemporary Japanese Poets (Nihon Gendaishijin Kai).

Address: Association of Contemporary Japanese Poets (Nihon Gendaishijin Kai), Tokyo, Japan.

Haidan Shô (Haidan Prize)

Established in 1986 by the haiku magazine *Haidan* (The Haiku Podium) and sponsored by the Hon'ami Shoten publishing company. An open competition in which candidates submit 30 previously unpublished haiku for consideration by a selection committee. The winner receives a certificate and a cash prize of 100,000 yen.

Recent Winners: 2002 Minakami Kojô, *Tsukiyo (A Moonlit Night)* and Itsukishima Fumie, *Matsusa oni:* (joint winners).

Sponsoring Organization: *Haidan* (The Haiku Podium).

Address: *Haidan* (The Haiku Podium), Tokyo, Japan.

Halldis Moren Vesaas-Prisen

An annual prize for poetry sponsored by the bookshop Norli.

Recent Winners: 2001: Haakon Dahlen; 2000: Øyvind Berg; 1999: Georg Johannesen; 1998: Torild Wardenær; 1997: Bjørn Aamodt.

Sponsoring Organization: Norlis Bokhandel AS.

Address: Norlis Bokhandel AS, Nedre Storgate 46, Postboks 473, Brakerøya, 3003 Drammen, Norway. **Telephone:** (32) 27 72 20. **Fax:** (32) 27 72 22. **Internet:** www.norli.no. **E-mail:** internett@norli.no.

Halldor Laxness Literary Prize

The annual Halldor Laxness Literary Prize, established in 1995, is presented by the publisher Vaka-Helgafell for a novel or collection of short stories. The winner is chosen by a panel of three judges, and receives $5,000 plus a bronze plaque, and publication of the winning manuscript.

Eligibility and Restrictions: Must be written in Icelandic by an Icelandic author.

Recent Winners: 2001: Bjarni Bjarneson; 2000: Gyrdir Eliasson; 1998: Sindri Freysson; 1997: Gvindur P. Eiriksson; 1996: S. Bjorn Gunnarsson.

Sponsoring Organization: Vaka-Helgafell.

Contact: Pétur Már Ólafsson.

Address: Sudurlandsbraut 12, 108 Reykjavík, Iceland. **Telephone:** 5222000. **Fax:** 5222022. **Internet:** www.vaka.is. **E-mail:** petur.olafsson@edda.is.

Hammett Awards

Named in honour of Dashiell Hammett, this award is given annually by the North American Branch of the International Association of Crime Writers to reward excellence in the genre of crime literature.

Eligibility and Restrictions: Open to American or Canadian writers.

Recent Winners: 2000: Margaret Atwood, *The Blind Assassin*; 1999: Martin Cruz Smith, *Havanna Bay*; 1998: William Hoffman, *Tidewater Blood*; 1997: William Deverell, *Trial of Passion*; 1996: Martin Cruz Smith, *Rose*; 1995: Mary Willis Walker, *Under the Beetle's Cellar*.

Sponsoring Organization: International Association of Crime Writers, North American Branch, USA.

Clarence H. Haring Prize

Established in honour of Clarence Haring (1885–1960), a noted Latin Americanist and long-time member of the American Historical Association (AHA), this prize is awarded every five years for the best work by a Latin American scholar in the field of Latin American history.

Recent Winners: 2001: Hilda Sabato, *La política en las calles: Entre el voto y la movilización – Buenos Aires, 1862–1880.*

Sponsoring Organization: American Historical Association.

Contact: Lynn Hunt.

Address: American Historical Asscn, 400 A St, SE, Washington, DC 20003–3889, USA. **Telephone:** (202) 544-2422. **Fax:** (202) 544-8307. **Internet:** www.theaha.org/prizes. **E-mail:** press@theaha.org.

Haryana Sahitya Akademi Awards

The Haryana Sahitya Akademi presents a number of prestigious awards for literature. The annual Bhai Santokh Singh award, which aims to to promote the Punjabi language in the state of Haryana, is given to a person for a lifetime's literary achievement. The award, which is named after an eminent writer from Kaithal, was established in 1999. It is presented to a Punjabi author, and carries a cash prize of Rs 21,000. The prestigious Sur Award of Rs 100,000 is presented to an author in recognition of a lifetime's contribution to Hindi literature. The Akademi also confers two separate Babu Balmukand Gupt Awards (for Hindi Literature and Hindi Journalism), as well as the the Maharshi Vedvyasa Award of Rs 15,000, the Pandit Lakhmi Chand Prize, and one or more Women Empowerment Awards of Rs 11,000 each.

How to Apply: Deadline for submissions is 31 January.

Recent Winners: Sur Award: 2002: Dr Harish Chander Verma
Babu Balmukand Gupt Award for Hindi Literature: 2002: Dr Naresh
Maharshi Vedvyasa Award: 2002: Dr Sansar Chand
Women Empowerment Awards: 2002: Shakuntala Brijmohan, Dr Sudha Jain and Dr Meera Gautam
Pandit Lakhmi Chand Prize: 2002: Dr Puran Chand Sharma.

Sponsoring Organization: Haryana Sahitya Akademi (Haryana Academy of Literature).

Address: Haryana Sahitya Akademi, 106 Sector 8, Panchkula, Haryana, 160 018, India.

Havmannprisen

A prize of 10,000 NOK, which was first presented in 1998, for works of high literary quality but with popular appeal. The winner is chosen by a four-member jury.

Recent Winners: 2000: Hanne Ørstavik, *Tiden det tar*; 1999: Laila Stien, *Gjennom glass*; 1998: Odd Klippenvåg, *Body & Soul.* Oslo, Norway.

123

Hawthornden Prize

The prize was established in 1919 by Miss Alice Warrender, and is awarded annually to an English writer for 'the best work of imaginative literature'. A panel of judges decides the winner. Young authors are particularly encouraged. The current value of the prize is £10,000.

Eligibility and Restrictions: Open to works of biography, travel, art history, etc, as well as fiction and drama.

How to Apply: No direct applications are accepted.

Recent Winners: 2001: Helen Simpson, *Hey Yeah Right Get a Life*; 2000: Michael Longley, *The Weather in Japan*; 1999: Antony Beevor, *Stalingrad*; 1998: Charles Nicholl, *Somebody Else*; 1997: John Lanchester, *The Debt to Pleasure*.

Address: 42A Hays Mews, Berkeley Square, London W1X 7RU, UK.

Thomas Head Raddall Fiction Prize

Established in 1990 to honour the best fiction writing (novel or collection of short stories) by an Atlantic Canadian. The winner is chosen by a peer jury, and receives C$10,000 plus an engraved medal.

Eligibility and Restrictions: Entries must have been published in the previous calendar year, and written by a writer who was born and has spent a considerable proportion of their working life in Atlantic Canada (Nova Scotia, New Brunswick, PEI, Newfoundland), or a writer who has lived there for 24 months prior to the deadline.

How to Apply: Four copies of eligible titles should reach the Writers' Federation of Nova Scotia by the first Friday in December.

Recent Winners: 2001: Carol Bruneau, *Purple for Sky*; 2000: Alistair MacLeod, *No Great Mischief*; 1999: Wayne Johnston, *The Colony of Unrequited Dreams*; 1998: Shree Ghatage, *Awake When All the World is Asleep*; 1997: Alfred Silver, *Acadia*.

Sponsoring Organization: Writers' Federation of Nova Scotia.

Contact: Exec. Dir Jane Buss.

Address: Writers' Federation of Nova Scotia, 1113 Marginal Rd, Halifax, NS B3H 4P7, Canada. **Telephone:** (902) 423-8116. **Fax:** (902) 422-0881. **Internet:** www.writers.ns.ca. **E-mail:** talk@writers.ns.ca.

Heinrich-Heine-Preis der Landeshauptstadt Düsseldorf

Established by the City of Düsseldorf in memory of the poet Heinrich Heine in 1972, the 175th anniversary of his birth. The medal is awarded for special achievements in helping understanding between people and promoting basic rights. The ceremony takes place on 13 December, Heine's birthday, or on 17 February, the anniversary of his death. The prize is of DM25,000.

How to Apply: There is no application process; winners are nominated.

Recent Winners: 2000: W. G. Sebald.

Sponsoring Organization: City of Düsseldorf.

Contact: Elisabeth Scheeben.

Address: Stadtverwaltung, 40200 Düsseldorf, Germany. **E-mail:** elisabeth. scheeben@stadt.duesseldorf.de.

124

W. H. Heinemann Award

Founded in 1944 with a bequest from W. H. Heinemann; the award aims to encourage 'genuine contributions to literature' and is given to a work – usually non-fiction – judged to be of 'outstanding literary distinction'. The prize of £5,000 is awarded in June of each year by three judges, who are Fellows of the Royal Society of Literature.

Eligibility and Restrictions: Generally awarded to a work of non-fiction, but fiction is not actually excluded. The book must be written in English, and translations are not eligible.

How to Apply: Publishers should apply for details from the Secretary, before submitting three copies to the judges. Entries are accepted from 15 October to 15 December each year.

Recent Winners: 2001: Miranda Carter, *Anthony Blunt: His Lives*; 2000: Catherine Merridale, *Night of Stone: Death and Memory in Russia*; 1999: Geoffrey Hill, *The Triumph of Love* and Anthony Sampson, *Mandela* (joint winners); 1998: Richard Holmes, *Coleridge: Darker Reflections*; 1997: Graham Robb, *Victor Hugo*.

Sponsoring Organization: Royal Society of Literature.

Contact: Asst Sec. Julia Abel Smith.

Address: Royal Society of Literature, Somerset House, Strand, London WC2R 1LA, UK. **Telephone:** (20) 7845 4676. **Fax:** (20) 7845 4679. **Internet:** www.rslit.org. **E-mail:** info@rslit.org.

Gustav-Heinemann-Friedenspreis für Kinder- und Jugendbücher (Gustav Heinemann Peace Prize for Children's Books)

An annual prize of around DM15,000 presented for works (or translations) for children and young people, in the field of human rights. The award is presented by the North Rhine Westfalia Ministry of Education and Research.

Eligibility and Restrictions: Books must have been published during the preceding 12 months.

How to Apply: Direct applications are not accepted.

Sponsoring Organization: Ministerium für Schule und Weiterbildung, Wissenschaft und Forschung des Landes Nordrhein-Westfalen.

Address: Ministerium für Schule und Weiterbildung, Wissenschaft und Forschung des Landes Nordrhein-Westfalen, Landeszentrale für politische Bildung, 40190 Düsseldorf, Germany. **Telephone:** (211) 679 77 56. **Fax:** (211) 679 77 33.

Hellenic Foundation for Culture Translation Award

The prize was established in 2002, and is presented for an outstanding translation of a literary work from Greek into English. The winner receives £1,000.

Eligibility and Restrictions: Entries must be a translation from modern Greek into English of a full-length work of prose, poetry or drama, first published within the last five years.

How to Apply: Closing date for entries is 31 December.

Sponsoring Organization: Society of Authors.

Contact: Dorothy Sym.
Address: Society of Authors, 84 Drayton Gdns, London SW10 9SB, UK.
Telephone: (20) 7373 6642. **Fax:** (20) 7373 5768. **E-mail:** info@societyofauthors.org.

Helsingin Sanomat Literary Award

Annual award presented by the leading daily newspaper *Helsingin Sanomat* to the best first work written in Finnish, with a prize of 50,000 markka. The award was established in 1964.

Recent Winners: 1999: Jyrki Vainonen, *Tutkimusmatkailija ja muita tarinoita (The Explorer and Other Stories)*.

Sponsoring Organization: *Helsingin Sanomat.*

Address: *Helsingin Sanomat*, Töölönlahdenkatu 2, POB 77, 00089 Sanomat, Finland. **Internet:** www.helsinginsanomat.fi/.

Ernest Hemingway Foundation/PEN Award for First Fiction

An annual award for a distinguished first novel or first collection of short fiction by a young and developing American writer. The winner receives $7,500. The award was established in 1976 by Mary Hemingway in honour of her husband.

Eligibility and Restrictions: Open to a first book-length work of fiction by a US writer published in the preceding year.

How to Apply: Entries may be submitted by agents, publishers or authors; four copies of entries should be sent, accompanied by an application form, by mid-December.

Recent Winners: 2001: Justin Cronin, *Mary and O'Neil*; 2000: Akhil Sharma, *An Obedient Father*; 1999: Jhumpa Lahiri, *Interpreter of Maladies*; 1998: Rosina Lippi, *Homestead*; 1997: Charlotte Bacon, *A Private State*.

Sponsoring Organization: PEN New England.

Contact: Mary Walsh.

Address: PEN New England, PO Box 400725, North Cambridge, MA 0210, USA. **Telephone:** (617) 499-9550. **Fax:** (617) 353-7134. **Internet:** www.pen-ne.org. **E-mail:** hemingway@pen-ne.org.

Cecil Hemley Memorial Award

The Cecil Hemley Memorial Award of $500, which is administered by the Poetry Society of America (PSA), was established by Jack Stadler and his late wife, Ralynn Stadler, for a lyric poem that 'addresses a philosophical or epistemological concern'.

Eligibility and Restrictions: Open to PSA members only. Poems should not exceed 100 lines in length.

How to Apply: Two copies of submissions should be sent accompanied by a cover sheet between 1 October and 21 December.

Recent Winners: 2002: Andrew Zawacki.

Sponsoring Organization: Poetry Society of America.

Address: Poetry Society of America, 15 Gramercy Park, New York, NY 10003, USA. **Telephone:** (212) 254-9628. **Internet:** www.poetrysociety.org.

Herder Prize

The prize is named after the 18th-century German philosopher and literary scientist, Johann Gottfried Herder, and it has been awarded since 1964 to artists and scientists in recognition of a significant contribution to the deepening of cultural and scientific relations among the nations of Central, Eastern and South-eastern Europe. Several prizes are awarded each year.

Recent Winners: 2000: Milan Kundera, Jan Bakos, Imre Kertesz, Arvo Pärt, Nikola Georgiev, Ivan Colovic and Karolos Mitsakis; former winners include Václav Frolec, Kamil Lhotak and Emil Skala.

Sponsoring Organization: F.V.S. Foundation.

Address: F.V.S. Foundation, Hamburg, Germany.

Hertzogprys (Hertzog Prize)

The long-established Hertzog Prize was inaugurated in 1914 after a bequest from J. B. M. Hertzog. It is considered to be the Academy's most prestigious award, and is the country's foremost honour for Afrikaans literature. It is presented for an outstanding work of prose, poetry or drama, although the winner's entire body of literary work is also taken into consideration for the award. The winner receives a gold medal and a cash prize of R17,000.

Eligibility and Restrictions: Open to works published in Afrikaans in the three preceding years.

Recent Winners: 2002: André Brink, *Donkermaan*; 2000: André Brink, *Die Jogger*; Ernst van Heerden, *Die Klop*; Etienne Leroux, *Magersfontein, O Magersfontein!*.

Sponsoring Organization: Suid-Afrikaanse Akademie vir Wetenskap en Kuns (South African Academy for Science and Arts).

Address: Die Suid-Afrikaanse Akademie vir Wetenskap en Kuns (South African Academy for Science and Arts), PO Box 538, Pretoria, 0001, South Africa. **Telephone:** (12) 328 5082. **Fax:** (12) 328 5091. **Internet:** www.akademie.co.za. **E-mail:** akademie@mweb.co.za.

Ed A. Hewett Book Prize

The Hewett Prize was established in 1994 in honour of a distinguished scholar in the field of East European research. It is awarded annually for an outstanding publication on the political economy of the centrally planned economies of the former Soviet Union and East Central Europe and their successors. The winner is selected by a committee, and receives a cash award.

Eligibility and Restrictions: Open to works published in English during the previous year. Textbooks, translations, bibliographies and reference works are not eligible.

How to Apply: Publishers, editors and authors should send copies of eligible works to each committee member by mid-May.

Recent Winners: 2001: Timothy Frye, *Brokers and Bureaucrats: Market Institutions in Russia*; 2000: Katharina Müller, *The Political Economy of Pension Reform in Central-Eastern Europe*; 1999: Stephen K. Wegren, *Agriculture and the State in Soviet and Post-Soviet Russia*; 1998: David L. Bartlett, *The Political Economy of Dual Transformations: Market Reform and Democratization in Hungary*; 1997: Clifford G. Gaddy, *The Price of the Past: Russia's Struggle with the Legacy of a Militarized Economy*.

Sponsoring Organization: American Association for the Advancement of Slavic Studies.

Address: American Association for the Advancement of Slavic Studies, 8 Story St, Cambridge, MA 02138, USA. **Telephone:** (617) 495-0677. **Fax:** (617) 495-0680. **E-mail:** aaass@hcs.harvard.edu.

Heywood Hill Literary Prize

This prize, established in 1995 by the Duke of Devonshire, is awarded for a lifetime's contribution to the enjoyment of books. A panel of four judges selects a winner. The annual competition carries a cash prize of £12,000 and is awarded during a summer party at Chatsworth, residence of the Duke.

Eligibility and Restrictions: There are no set restrictions on entries.

How to Apply: No direct submissions or nominations are accepted.

Recent Winners: 2001: Michael Holroyd; 2000: Charles Causley; 1999: Jane Gardam; 1998 Norman Lewis and Richard Ollard; 1997: John Nicoll.

Contact: Man. Dir John S. Smith.

Address: 10 Curzon St, London W1J 5HH, UK. **Telephone:** (20) 7629 0647. **Fax:** (20) 7408 0286. **Internet:** www.gheywoodhill.com. **E-mail:** books@gheywoodhill.com.

Louis Hiemstraprys vir nie-fiksie (Louis Hiemstra Prize for New Fiction)

A prize of R20,000 which was awarded for the first time in 2002. The prize is awarded every three years for a work of new fiction written in Afrikaans.

Eligibility and Restrictions: Entries must have been published in the three previous calendar years.

Recent Winners: 2002: Karel Schoeman, *Armosyn van die Kaap* and *Armosyn van die Kaap 2*.

Sponsoring Organization: Hiemstra Trust.

Address: Die Suid-Afrikaanse Akademie vir Wetenskap en Kuns (South African Academy for Science and Arts), PO Box 538, Pretoria, 0001, South Africa. **Telephone:** (12) 328 5082. **Fax:** (12) 328 5091. **E-mail:** akademie@mweb.co.za.

Cena Josefa Hlavky (Josef Hlavka Prize)

The Josef Hlavka Prize was established in 1993 by the Czech Literary Fund with the aim of promoting science and specialist literature. It is awarded for an original piece of academic or specialist literature. The winner is selected by a panel of experts, and receives a prize of 30,000 koruna.

Eligibility and Restrictions: Open to works published in book form in the Czech Republic in the field of science, social sciences, nature, medicine, mathematics, etc.

How to Apply: Publishers are invited to apply.

Recent Winners: 2000: Petr Cornej, *Velké dejiny zemí Koruny ceské V. (1402–1437)*; 1999: J. Schwabik, *Integration*; 1998: M. Horyna, *Map of Potential Natural Vegetation*; 1994: *Primeval History of Moravia*.

Sponsoring Organization: Czech Literary Fund/Josef, Marie and Zdenka Hlávkových Foundation.

Contact: Administrator Helena Hajkova.

Address: Pod Nuselskými schody 3, 120 00 Prague, 2, Czech Republic. **Telephone:** 222 560081-2. **Fax:** 222 560083. **Internet:** www.nclf.cz. **E-mail:** nclf@vol.cz.

Calvin and Rose G. Hoffmann Prize for a Distinguished Publication on Christopher Marlowe

Established by a bequest from the late Calvin Hoffman, as a memorial to himself and his wife. It is administered by the King's School, Canterbury, and is awarded for a distinguished publication on the life and works of Christopher Marlowe, in particular with regard to his possible authorship of works generally attibuted to William Shakespeare. The value of the prize is at least £6,000.

Eligibility and Restrictions: Open to all scholars and informed people anywhere in the world, for an unpublished essay written in English of no less than 5,000 words.

How to Apply: Submissions should be posted in duplicate to the Headmaster by 1 September.

Recent Winners: 2001: Prof. Michael Hattaway, *Myths of Empire, State and Nation in Marlovian and Shakespearean Texts* and Michael Rubbo, *Much Ado About Something* (joint winners); 2000: (prize not awarded); 1999: Prof. Kent Cartwright, *Bearing Witness to Tamburlaine*; 1998: Prof. David Riggs, *The Killing of Christopher Marlowe*; 1997: Jill Farringdon, *Attributing Marlowe and Shakespeare*.

Sponsoring Organization: Trustees of the Calvin & Rose G. Hoffmann Prize.

Contact: Headmaster's Secretary Linda Breaden.

Address: The King's School, Canterbury CT1 2ES, UK. **Telephone:** (1227) 595527. **Fax:** (1227) 595595. **Internet:** www.kings-school.co.uk. **E-mail:** headmaster@kings-school.co.uk.

Nils Holgersson Plaque

The Nils Holgersson Plaque, established by the Swedish Library Association in 1950, is presented to the author of the best Swedish children's book published during the previous year. It may also be given in recognition of the collected works of an author. The winner is selected by a committee, appointed for three years by the representative assembly of the Swedish Library Association, and made up of delegates from various public and school libraries. The plaque is named after a well-known character from *The Wonderful Adventures of Nils* by Selma Lagerlöf, first published in 1907.

Recent Winners: 1999: Annika Thor, *Havets djup*; 1998: Moni Nilsson-Brännström, *Bara Tsatsiki*; 1997: Per Nilsson, *Anarkai*; 1996: Helena Dahlbäck, *Jag Julia och Min läsebok*; 1995: Inger Edelfeldt, *Gravitation*.

Sponsoring Organization: Svensk biblioteksförening (Swedish Library Association).

Address: Svensk biblioteksförening (Swedish Library Association), PO Box 3127, 103 13 Stockholm, Sweden. **Internet:** www.biblioteksforeningen.org/.

Clarence L. Holt Literary Prize

The prize is awarded every two years for a work of excellence in literature and the humanities relating to the cultural heritage of Africa and the African diaspora.

Eligibility and Restrictions: Open to works by a living writer which makes a significant contribution to the cultural heritage of persons of African descent.

Sponsoring Organization: Phelps-Stoke Fund.

Address: 74 Trinity Place, Suite 1303, New York, NY, USA.

Winifred Holtby Memorial Prize

Founded in 1966 by Vera Brittain to honour the memory of Winifred Holtby. A prize of £1,000 is awarded in June each year to the best regional novel of the year; the winner is chosen by three judges who are Fellows of the Royal Society of Literature.

Eligibility and Restrictions: Open to fiction with a strong sense of a particular place. Entries must have been written in the English language (translations are not eligible) by a living citizen of the UK, the Republic of Ireland or the Commonwealth, and published in the year preceding the year in which the award is presented.

How to Apply: Publishers should apply for details from the Secretary, before submitting three copies to the judges. Entries are accepted from 15 October to 15 December each year.

Recent Winners: 2001: Anna Burns, *No Bones*; 2000: Donna Morrissey, *Kit's Law*; 1999: Andrew O'Hagan, *Our Fathers*; 1998: Giles Foden, *The Last King of Scotland*; 1997: Eden Robinson, *Traplines*.

Sponsoring Organization: Royal Society of Literature.

Address: Royal Society of Literature, Somerset House, Strand, London WC2R 1LA, UK. **Telephone:** (20) 7845 4676. **Fax:** (20) 7845 4679. **Internet:** www.rslit.org. **E-mail:** info@rslit.org.

Oles Honchar Prizes

Separate prizes are awarded for works of prose (Oles Honchar Prize, for best Ukrainian novel of the year) and for novels, short stories and works of literary criticism by young authors (Oles Honchar Ukrainian-German Prize). The prizes are named after a Ukrainian writer who was also President of the National Writers Union of Ukraine (NSPU).

Eligibility and Restrictions: For the Oles Honchar Ukrainian-German Prize, only authors aged up to 30 years may enter.

Recent Winners: Oles Honchar Prize: 1999: Natalia Dziubenko, *Apostle Andrew*.

Sponsoring Organization: National Writers Union of Ukraine (NSPU).

Contact: V. Yavorivsky.

Address: Blvd Bankova 2, 01024 Kiev, Ukraine. **Fax:** (44) 293-45-86. **Internet:** www.nspu.kiev.ua. **E-mail:** nspu@I.kiev.ua.

P. C. Hooft-prijs voor Letterkunde (P. C. Hooft Prize for Literature)

An annual award presented to a writer for a lifetime's achievement. The prize was established in 1947, to mark the 300th anniversary of the writer of the same name. Works of prose, essay and poetry are all considered for the prize.

Recent Winners: 2001: Gerrit Krol; 2000: Eva Gerlach; 1999: Arthur Lehning.

Sponsoring Organization: Stichting P. C. Hooft-prijs voor Letterkunde.

Address: Postbus 90515, Prins Willem, Alexanderhof 5, 2595 LM The Hague, Netherlands.

C. P. Hoogenhout Award

The award was created in 1960 to recognize outstanding works for children written in Afrikaans. The author and illustrator of the award-winning book receive a gold medal, and the publisher receives a certificate. The prize is named after the first author of a children's book in Afrikaans, C. P. Hoogenhout. Since 1982 the award has been given biennially.

Eligibility and Restrictions: Entries must be written in Afrikaans and be aimed at children aged 7 to 12 years.

Recent Winners: 1996: M. Preller, *Anderkantland*; 1992: B. Hough, *Droomwa*; 1986: L. Rode, *Goue lint my storie begint*.

Sponsoring Organization: South African Institute for Librarianship and Information Science/Suid-Afrikaanse Instituut vir Biblioteek- en Inligtingkunde.

Address: PO Box 36575, Menlo Park, Pretoria, 0102, South Africa. **Internet:** sunsite.wits.ac.za/conferen/sailis/sailis.html. **E-mail:** sailis@cis.co.za.

Lee Bennett Hopkins Promising Poet Award

Awarded every three years to a promising writer of poetry for children and young adults.

Recent Winners: 2001: Craig Crist-Evans, *Moon Over Tennessee: A Boy's Civil War Journal*.

Sponsoring Organization: International Reading Association.

Address: PO Box 8139, Newark, DE, New York, NY, USA. **Telephone:** (302) 731 1600. **Fax:** (303) 731-1051. **Internet:** www.reading.org. **E-mail:** jbutler@ reading.org.

Amelia Frances Howard-Gibbon Illustrator's Award

The Amelia Frances Howard-Gibbon Illustrator's Medal is awarded to an outstanding illustrator of a children's book published in Canada during the previous year.

Eligibility and Restrictions: To be eligible for this award, an illustrator must be a Canadian citizen or a permanent resident of Canada, and the text of the book must be worthy of the illustrations.

How to Apply: Nominations should be sent by 1 January each year to: Arlene Kissau, St Albert Public Library, 5 St Anne Street, St Albert, Alberta T8N 3Z9.

Recent Winners: 2001: Laura Fernandez and Rick Jacobson, *The Magnificent Piano Recital*; 2000: Zhong-Yang Huang, *The Dragon New Year: A Chinese Legend*; 1999: Kady MacDonald Denton, *A Child's Treasury of Nursery Rhymes*; 1998: Barbara Reid, *The Party*; 1997: Harvey Chan, *Ghost Train*.

Sponsoring Organization: National Book Service.

Address: Canadian Library Association, 328 Frank St, Ottawa, ON K2P 0X8, Canada. **Telephone:** (613) 232-9625. **Fax:** (613) 563-9895. **Internet:** www.cla.ca.

Peter-Huchel-Preis

Awarded annually since 1984 on 3 April, the birthday of Peter Huchel, the prize is sponsored by the Land of Baden-Württemberg and the radio station Südwestfunk Baden-Baden. The award is made for a work which is deemed to have made a notable contribution to developments in poetry in German. The winner receives a cash award of DM20,000.

Eligibility and Restrictions: Entries must have been first published during the previous year.

How to Apply: There is no direct application.

Recent Winners: 2000: Adolf Endler, *Der Pudding der Apokalypse*; 1999: Raoul Schrott, *Tropen*; 1998: Brigitte Oleschinski, *Your Passport ist Not Guilty*; 1997: Thomas Kling, *Morsch*; 1996: Gregor Laschen, *Jammerbugt-Notate*.

Sponsoring Organization: Baden-Württemberg /Südwestfunk Baden-Baden.

Address: Südwestfunk, Baden Baden, Germany. **Telephone:** (7221) 929 2203. **Internet:** www.swr.de.

Busken Huetprijs

Established in 1947 by the City of Amsterdam, and awarded annually for a work of biography or essay. The winner is chosen by a three-member jury, and receives €7,000.

Eligibility and Restrictions: Open to Dutch-language works only, published during the previous year. All books published by a Dutch or Flemish author are eligible.

How to Apply: There is no public application process; selection is made by the jury.

Recent Winners: 2001: Cyrille Offermans, *De ontdekking van de wereld*; 2000: Charlotte Mutsaers, *Zeepijn*; 1999: H. L. Wesseling, *Lopende Zaken*; 1998: Oek de Jong, *Een man die in de toekomst springt*; 1997: Elsbeth Etty, *Liefde is heel het leven niet*.

Sponsoring Organization: Amsterdam Fund for the Arts.

Contact: Desmond Spruist.

Address: Stichting Amsterdams Fonds voor de Kunst, Herengracht 609, 1017 CE Amsterdam, Netherlands. **Telephone:** (20) 5200 556. **Fax:** (20) 623 8309. **Internet:** www.afk.nl. **E-mail:** afk@afk.nl.

Hugo Award

The Hugo Award is awarded in memory of Hugo Gernsback, a pioneer of magazine science fiction. Also known as the Science Fiction Achievement Award, the Hugo Award is given annually by the World Science Fiction Society (WSFS). The winner is chosen by nominations from and a popular vote of the membership of WSFS.

Eligibility and Restrictions: Entries should have appeared during the previous year.

Recent Winners: Novel: 2001: J. K. Rowling, *Harry Potter and the Goblet of Fire*; 2000: Vernor Vinge, *A Deepness in the Sky*;1999: Connie Willis, *To Say Nothing of the Dog*
Novella: 2001: Jack Williamson, *The Ultimate Earth*; 2000: Connie Wills, *The Winds of Marble Arch*;1999: Greg Egan, *Oceanic*
Novelette: 2001: Kristine Kathryn Rusch, *Millennium Babies*; 2000: James Patrick Kelly, *1016 to 1*; 1999: Bruce Sterling, *Taklamakan*
Short Story: 2001: David Langford, *Different Kinds of Darkness*; 2000: Michael Swanwick, *Scherzo With Dinosaur*; 1999: Michael Swanwick, *The Very Pulse of the Machine*.

Sponsoring Organization: World Science Fiction Convention (Worldcon).

Address: World Science Fiction Society, POB 426159, Dendall Square Station, Cambridge, MA 02142, USA. **Internet:** worldcon.org.

Constantijn Huygens Prize

This prize, awarded for a lifetime's achievement, is named after an important 17th-century Dutch poet. The winner receives a prize of 20,000 DFL.

Recent Winners: 2000: Charlotte Mutsaers; 1999: Willem Jan Otten.

Sponsoring Organization: Jan Campertstichting (Jan Campert Foundation).

Address: PO Box 12654, 2500 DP The Hague, Netherlands. **Telephone:** (353) 36 37. **Fax:** (353) 30 58.

IBBY-Asahi Reading Promotion Award

Established in 1986, and presented every year to a group or institution which by its outstanding activities is judged to be making a lasting contribution to reading promotion. Nominations are submitted by National Sections of the International Board on Books for Young People (IBBY), while the final choice is made by a jury comprising members of the IBBY Executive Committee. The prize, sponsored by leading Japanese newspaper *Asahi Shimbun*, is of 1 million yen.

How to Apply: Nominations are made by National Sections of IBBY by invitation only.

Recent Winners: 2002: Por el derecho a leer (Argentina); 2001: Children's Reading Development Programme, Pechenga District (Russia); 2000: Tambogrande – Sowing a Reading Field (Peru); 1999: Mobile Library for Non-Violence and Peace (Palestine/Israel); 1998: Fureai Bunko Braille Library (Japan).

Sponsoring Organization: International Board on Books for Young People (IBBY)/ *Asahi Shimbun*.

Contact: Exec. Dir Leena Maissen.

Address: Nonnenweg 12, Postfach, 4003 Basel, Switzerland. **Telephone:** (61) 272 29 17. **Fax:** (61) 272 27 57. **Internet:** www.ibby.org. **E-mail:** ibby@eye.ch.

IBC International Book Award

An annual award established to honour a person or institution for outstanding services rendered to the cause of books.

Sponsoring Organization: International Book Committee (IBC).
Address: Mayerhofgasse 6, 1041 Vienna, Austria. **Telephone:** (1) 505 03 59.
Fax: (1) 505 03 59 17.

Icelandic Children's Book Prize

Awarded annually in the spring for the best children's books published the year before, one for an Icelandic book and one for a translated book. This prize is awarded by the educational council of Reykjavík.

Recent Winners: 1998: Gudmundur Olafsson; 1986 Gudmundur Olafsson, *Emil and Skundi.*

Sponsoring Organization: Fraedslurád Reykjavíkur (Educational Council of Reykjavík).

Address: Fraedslurád Reykjavíkur, Fríkirkjuvegi 1, IS-101 Reykjavík, Iceland. **Telephone:** 5355000. **Fax:** 5355050. **E-mail:** ggo@reykjavik.is.

Icelandic Literary Prize

Established by the Icelandic Publishers Association on its centenary anniversary in 1989, with the aim of encouraging Icelandic literature, writers and the publishing trade. The prize is awarded annually for two books, fiction (novels, short stories, children's books or poetry) and non-fiction, each chosen from a shortlist of five books. The prizes are presented by the President of Iceland at his residence. The shortlist for each year's published books is announced at the beginning of November and the prizes presented January/February of the next year. The amount of each prize is 750,000 IKR, and the winners also receive trophies.

Eligibility and Restrictions: Only open to books published in Iceland, in Icelandic, during the relevant year.

How to Apply: Publishers and others may nominate books to be considered for the shortlist upon payment of an entry fee.

Recent Winners: Fiction: 2001: Hallgrímur Helgason, *Höfundur Íslands*; 2000: Gyrðir Elíasson, *Gula húsið*; 1999: Andri Snær Magnússon, *Sagan af bláa hnettinum*; 1998: Thor Vilhjálmsson, *Morgunþula í stráum (Morning Verse in the Grass)*; 1997: Guðbergur Bergsson, *Faðir og módir og dulmagn bernskunnar (Father and Mother and the Mystery of Childhood)*
Non-fiction: 2001: Sigríður Dúna Kristmundsdóttir, *Björg – oevisaga Bjargar C. Þorláksson*; 2000: Guðmundur Páll Ólafsson, *Hálendið Í náttúru Íslands*; 1999: Páll Valsson, *Jónas Hallgrímsson, oevisaga*; 1998: Hörður Ágústsson, *Íslensk byggingararfleifð*; 1997: Guðjón Friðriksson, *Einar Benediktsson.*

Sponsoring Organization: Icelandic Publishers Association.
Contact: Man. Dir Vilborg Harðardóttir.
Address: Barónsstíg 5, 101 Reykjavík, Iceland. **Telephone:** 5118020. **Fax:** 5115020. **Internet:** www.bokautgafa.is. **E-mail:** baekur@mmedia.is.

ILAB-LILA Bibliography Prize

The ILAB Bibliographical Prize was started in the late 1960s, and awarded triennially until the 1990s when it became a quadrennial prize. It awards US$10,000.00 to the author of the best work, published or unpublished, of learned bibliography or of research into the history of the book or of typography, and books of general interest on the subject. The term 'bibliographical' is used in its widest sense. It covers: Bibliography (in the strict sense of the word); Book history; and Book trade/collectors' memoirs. The winner is selected by an international jury of eminent librarians and International League of Antiquarian Booksellers (ILAB) booksellers.

Eligibility and Restrictions: Entries must be submitted in a language which is universally used.

A published work must have appeared within the four years preceding the closing date for submission, or if it has an imprint bearing a date within those four years. Entries in the form of a specialized catalogue of one or more books destined for sale are not eligible, nor periodicals or public library catalogues.

How to Apply: Two copies of each work, whether published or unpublished, are to be submitted.

Recent Winners: L. H. Wüthrich, *Das druckgraphische Werk von Matthaeus Merian*; Jacob Blanck, *Bibliography of American Literature. Volumes 8–9*, edited and completed by Michael Winship; Eugène Rouir and Félicien Rops, *Catalogue raisonné de l'œuvre gravé et lithographié*.

Sponsoring Organization: International League of Antiquarian Booksellers (ILAB)/LILA.

Contact: Kay Craddock.

Address: International League of Antiquarian Booksellers, 156 Collins Street, Melbourne, Vic. 3000, Australia. **Telephone:** 3 9654 8506. **Fax:** 3 9654 7351. **Internet:** www.ilab-lila.com. **E-mail:** info@ilab-lila.com.

Gyula Illyes Prize

A prize for the best translation of a work of literature from French into Hungarian. Named after a Hungarian poet, the prize is twinned with the Prix Tristan Tzara in France (qv) which is presented for a translation from Hungarian into French.

Address: Budapest, Hungary.

Richard Imison Memorial Award

The award was established in 1994 in memory of Richard Imison, to acknowledge the encouragement he gave to writers working in the field of radio. The award, of £1,500, is administered by the Society of Authors. Its aim is to encourage new talent and high standards in writing drama for radio.

Eligibility and Restrictions: Eligibility is restricted to drama by a writer new to radio. The work must be an original piece for radio (not an adaptation of a piece already written for stage, TV or film), and it must be the first dramatic work by the writer or writers that has been broadcast. The award is judged by the Broadcasting Committee of the Society of Authors.

How to Apply: Submissions are accepted from any party, but must be accompanied by an entry form setting out details of transmission, with two copies of the writer's original script, by the end of January.

Recent Winners: 2002: Rhiannon Tise, *The Waltzer*; 2001: Murray Gold, *Electricity*; 2000: Peter Morgan, *A Matter of Interpretation*; 1999: Ben Cooper, *Skin Deep*; 1998: Katie Hims, *The Earthquake Girl*.

Sponsoring Organization: Society of Authors.

Contact: Asst Gen. Sec. Jo Hodder.

Address: Society of Authors, 84 Drayton Gdns, London SW10 9SB, UK. **Telephone:** (20) 7373 6642. **Fax:** (20) 7373 5768. **Internet:** www. societyofauthors.org. **E-mail:** info@societyofauthors.org.

Independent Foreign Fiction Prize

The prize was founded in 1990 by Robert Winder of the *Independent*. It is Britain's most valuable honour for translated literature, and is the country's only general competition for fiction first written in languages other than English. The prize, which is supported by the Arts Council of England and Champagne Taittinger, is of £10,000, shared between author and translator. The prize is awarded in spring of each year. The prize lapsed for five years from 1996 but was revived in 2000, with the next award being made in 2001.

Eligibility and Restrictions: Open to works of fiction by a living author, which have been translated into English from any other language and published in the UK during the previous year. Prize is awarded by a panel of judges (five in 2002), which changes each year.

How to Apply: Submissions of any literary works of prose fiction in translation are welcomed from UK publishers. There is no limit on the number of books submitted; publishers should apply as and when an appropriate title is published throughout the year, by sending six copies accompanied by an application form.

Recent Winners: 2002: W. G. Sebald, *Austerlitz* (translated by Anthea Bell); 2001: Marta Morazzoni, *The Alphonse Courrier Affair* (translated by Emma Rose); 1995: Gert Hofmann, *The Film Explainer* (translated by Michael Hofmann); 1994: Bao Ninh, *The Sorrow of War* (translated by Frank Palmos and Phan Thanh Hao); 1993: Jose Saramago, *The Year of the Death of Ricardo Reis* (translated by Giovanni Pontiero).

Sponsoring Organization: Arts Council of England/*The Independent*.

Contact: Asst Literary Officer Hilary Davidson.

Address: Literature Department, 14 Great Peter St, London SW1P 3NQ, UK. **Telephone:** (20) 7333 0100. **Fax:** (20) 7973 6590. **Internet:** www. artscouncil.org.uk. **E-mail:** info.literature@artscouncil.org.uk.

Innis-Gérin Medal

Established in 1966 in memory of historian Harold Innis and sociologist Léon Gérin, the medal is awarded every two years for a significant contribution to the literature of social sciences, including human geography and social psychology. The winner is chosen by a six-member selection committee, and receives a bronze medal.

Eligibility and Restrictions: Open to works of social science written by a Canadian citizen (or resident for five years) in either English or French.

How to Apply: Entries must be nominated by three persons, one of whom must be a member of the Society. Nomination forms must be submitted by 1 December, accompanied by a citation stating why the nominee should receive the award, a detailed appraisal of the nominee's work, a CV and supporting statements from other experts or scholars.

Recent Winners: 2001: Byrn P. Rourke; 1999: Rodolphe de Kononck; 1997: Norman S. Endler; 1995: Albert Legault; 1992: Thérèse Gouin-Décarie.

Sponsoring Organization: Royal Society of Canada.

Contact: Co-ordinator Sophie Buoro.

Address: Royal Society of Canada, 283 Sparks St, Ottawa, ON K1R 7X9, Canada. **Telephone:** (613) 991-6990. **Fax:** (613) 991-6996. **Internet:** www.rsc.ca.

Institutció de les Lletres Catalanes Translation Prize

Awarded every three years for literary translation both into and out of Catalan. Two prizes of 1 million ptas (€6,000) are awarded, one for translation into Catalan and one for translation out of Catalan.

Eligibility and Restrictions: The work must have appeared within the previous three years.

How to Apply: It is not possible to apply directly for the prize.

Sponsoring Organization: Institutció de les Lletres Catalanes.

Address: Institutció de les Lletres Catalanes, Portal de Santa Madrona 6–8, 08001 Barcelona, Spain. **Telephone:** (93) 316 27 80. **Fax:** (93) 316 27 98. **E-mail:** ilc@correu.gencat.es.

Institute of Historical Research Prize

A new award aimed at encouraging professional historians to write for a more general readership. The judges will be looking for original and interesting topics, ambition, accessibility to non-specialist readers, elegance of expression and accuracy. The winner will receive a publishing contract with Grove Atlantic worth £7,000.

Eligibility and Restrictions: Entrants must be professional historians who have, to date, published no trade history books in hardcover or paperback. Monographs, books published with university presses or recognizable academic publishers or imprints are not, for the purposes of the competition, defined as 'trade books'.

How to Apply: Closing date for submissions is early May.

Sponsoring Organization: Institute of Historical Research/Grove Atlantic.

Address: Institute of Historical Resarch, Senate House, London WC1E 7HU, UK. **Telephone:** (20) 7862 8740. **Internet:** www.ihrinfo.ac.uk.

International Einhard Prize

The International Einhard prize, the only international prize for biographies, was established in 1999 by the Einhard-Stiftung (Einhard Foundation). The award is named after the medieval biographer of Charlemagne who lived circa 775–840. The prize is valued at DM15,000 (around €8,000) and is presented every two years for an outstanding biography with a European connection. The jury is made up of three members, from Berlin, Paris and Rome.

Recent Winners: 2001: Brian Boyd, *Vladimir Nabokov: The American Years* and *Vladimir Nabokov: The Russian Years*; 1999: Otto Pflanze, *Bismarck and the Development of Germany*.

Sponsoring Organization: Einhard-Stiftung (Einhard Foundation).

Contact: Franz Preuschoff.

Address: Einhard-Stiftung, Am Breitenbach 4, 63500 Seligenstadt, Germany. **Telephone:** (6182) 93590. **Fax:** (6182) 22128.

International Imitation Hemingway Competition

Offered annually for an unpublished one-page parody in the style of Ernest Hemingway. The winner receives a pair of return air tickets to Italy, and the winning entry is published.

Eligibility and Restrictions: Entries should be up to 500 words, typed and double-spaced.

How to Apply: Authors are invited to send entries to the address given by 1 April; entries can be sent by mail, e-mail or fax, and should be accompanied by author's contact details.

Recent Winners: 2001: Timothy Smight, *Men Without Rabbits*.

Sponsoring Organization: Hemispheres/PEN Center USA West.

Address: PEN Center West, 672 South La Fayette Park Place, Suite 41, Los Angeles, CA 90057, USA. **Telephone:** (213) 365-8500. **Fax:** (213) 365-9616. **Internet:** www.pen-usa-west.org. **E-mail:** hemingway@pen-usa-west.org.

International IMPAC Dublin Literary Award

The prize was established in 1995 by Dublin City Council in partnership with IMPAC, a productivity improvement company which operates worldwide. The prize aims to promote quality literature on an international basis, and is presented annually to the best work of fiction written in or translated into English. With its prize money of €100,000, this is one of the world's richest books prize. If the winning title was originally written in English, the writer receives the whole amount; for a translated work, 25% goes to the translator. The winner also receives a Waterford Glass trophy.

Eligibility and Restrictions: Open to works of fiction written in or translated into English, published between January and December of a particular year. Titles published anywhere in the world are eligible. Libraries in major cities throughout the world submit nominations, which are considered by a panel of international judges, composed of writers and critics.

How to Apply: Submissions are not accepted from publishers, agents or authors, only from invited libraries. The award committee requests copies of the nominated titles from the relevant publishers.

Recent Winners: 2002: Michel Houellebecq, *Atomised*; 2001: Alistair MacLeod, *No Great Mischief*; 2000: Nicola Barker, *Wide Open*; 1999: Andrew Miller, *Ingenious Pain*; 1998: Herta Muller, *The Land of Green Plums*.

Sponsoring Organization: Dublin City Council/IMPAC.

Contact: Senior Librarian Clare Hogan.

Address: Dublin City Public Libraries, Cumberland House, Fenian St, Dublin, 2, Ireland. **Telephone:** (1) 664 4802. **Fax:** (1) 676 1628.

International Langhe Ceretto Prize for Food and Wine Culture

Founded in 1991 by brothers Bruno and Marcello Ceretto, the Langhe Ceretto Prize is awarded for an outstanding work in the field of food and wine – specifically the historic, scientific, dietary, gastronomic or sociological aspects. The prize is worth 15 million lire.

Recent Winners: 2001: Mohammed Hocine Benkheira, *Islam et interdits alimentaires: Juguler l'animalité* and Ariel Toaff, *Mangiare alla Giudea: la cucina ebraica in Italia dal Rinascimento all'età moderna* (joint winners).

Address: Segreteria del Premio, Biblioteca Civica 'G. Ferrero', Via Paruzza 1, 12051 Alba, Italy. **Telephone:** (173) 290092. **Internet:** www.enotecaregionaledelpiemonte.com/en/cs/cs0709.html.

International Lotus Prize for Poetry

This award, presented by the Afro-Asian Book Council for a litetime's achievement in literature, is often considered to be the Third World Nobel Prize.

Recent Winners: 1975 Chinua Achebe and Chi ha Kim; 1973: Ghassan Kanafani.

Sponsoring Organization: Afro-Asian Book Council.

Address: Afro-Asian Book Council (AABC), 4835/24 Ansari Road, Daryaganj, New Delhi, 110 002, India. **Telephone:** (11) 326 14 87. **Fax:** (11) 326 74 37.

International Playwriting Festival

An annual competition for full-length unperformed plays, established in 1985 and judged by a panel of theatre professionals. Entries are judged by a panel of distinguished theatre practitioners, and selected plays are given rehearsed readings during the festival week in November.

Eligibility and Restrictions: Entries are accepted from all over the world.

How to Apply: Entry form available on website. Closing date for submissions is 30 June.

Recent Winners: 2000: Andrew Bridgmont (UK), *Red on Black*, San Cassimally (Mauritius), *Chakala*, James Nicholson (USA), *Proud Flesh*, Andrew Shakeshaft (Wales), *Just Sitting*
1999: Roumen Shomov (Bulgaria), *The Dove*, Maggie Nevill (UK), *The Shagaround*.

Sponsoring Organization: Warehouse Theatre.

Address: Festival Administrator, Warehouse Theatre, Dingwall Road, Croydon CRO 2NF, UK. **Telephone:** (20) 8681 1257. **Fax:** (20) 8688 6699. **Internet:** www.warehousetheatre.co.uk. **E-mail:** warehous@dircon.co.uk.

International Vaptsarov Prize

The International Vaptsarov Prize, awarded by the Bulgarian government, recognizes foreign artists for distinguished artistic and social work. The award, which is named after the Bulgarian poet Nikola Y. Vaptsarov (1909–1942), is presented once every five years.

Recent Winners: 1979: William Meredith (USA).

Sponsoring Organization: Union of Bulgarian Writers.

Address: Union of Bulgarian Writers, Angel Kanchev 5, 1040 Sofia, Bulgaria.

Internationella Eeva Joenpelto-Litteraturpriset
(International Eeva Joenpelto Literary Prize)

Established by the city of Lohja and named after the novelist Eeva Joenpelto. The prize, which was first presented in 1988, is awarded irregularly and amounts to 75,000 markka. It is the only international literary prize awarded in Finland, and is presented to a writer whose work has influenced Finnish literature or who in his or her own country has made Finnish literature known.

Recent Winners: 1998: Andreï Makine (France/Russia); 1995: Sándor Csoóri (Hungary); 1992: Olof Lagercrantz (Sweden); 1988: Jaan Kross (Estonia).

Sponsoring Organization: City of Lohja.

Contact: Sec. Kaisa Rinne.

Address: Karstuntie 4, PL 71, 08101 Lohja, Finland. **Internet:** www.kaupunki. lohja.fi/kpalkinto/eevajeng.htm.

IODE Violet Downey Book Award

An award established in 1984 by the Imperial Order of the Daughters of the Empire (IODE), and presented annually for the best new English-language children's book. The winner receives a prize of C$3,000.

Eligibility and Restrictions: Open to English-language books published in Canada during the previous year for children 13 years of age and under. The book must be over 500 words long.

Recent Winners: 2002: Brian Doyle, *Mary Ann Alice*; 2001: Sharon E. McKay, *Charlie Wilcox*; 2000: Katherine Holubitsky, *Alone at Ninety Foot*; 1998: Celia Barker Lottridge, *Wings to Fly*; 1997: Janet McNaughton, *To Dance at the Palais Royale*.

Sponsoring Organization: Imperial Order of the Daughters of the Empire (IODE).

Address: National Chapter of Canada IODE, 40 Orchard View Blvd, Suite 254, Toronto, ON M4R 1B9, Canada. **Telephone:** (416) 487-4416. **Fax:** (416) 487-4417. **Internet:** www.iodecanada.ca. **E-mail:** iodecanada@sympatico.ca.

Dr Allama Muhammad Iqbal Award

The Pakistan Academy of Letters administers a series of annual prizes established in 1980 under the Hijra National Literary Awards Scheme. The aim of the awards is to promote literary activities and recognize outstanding contributions. The Dr Allama Muhammad Iqbal Award is an annual prize of Rs 50,000 for works of poetry, named after Pakistan's foremost Islamic poet. This award, since its inception in 1981, has been given for poetry in Urdu, Punjabi, Sindhi, Pushto, Siraiki, Baluchi and English language. Three eminent writers of each language are selected as judges, on whose decision the awards, are announced.

Recent Winners: 2000: Amjad Islam Amajd, *Sahiloon Ki Hawa*; 1999: Ahmad Faraz, *Ghazal Bhana Karoon*; 1998: Abbass Rizvi, *Khwabon Se Tarashe Huay Din*.

Sponsoring Organization: Pakistan Academy of Letters.

Contact: Deputy Dir Naseem Mahmood.

Address: Pitras Bokhari Road, Sector H-8/1, Islamabad, Pakistan. **Telephone:** 9257164. **Fax:** 9257159. **E-mail:** academy@apollo.net.pk.

Iranian Book of the Year Awards

A series of awards for categories including fiction, poetry, non-fiction and children's literature. The latter, also known as the Golden Bike Awards, are presented to the authors of the year's best books as selected by *Docharkheh (Bike)*, a weekly supplement of *Hamshahri* daily newspaper. The jury is made up mainly of young Iranian readers.

Recent Winners: Fiction: 2001: Freshteh Eqyan, *Green Love*
Poetry: 2001: Reza Saffarian, *Wisdom of the Shadows*
Children's: 2001: Mohammad Reza Youssefi, *The Myth of Belinas, the Witch*
Non-fiction: 2001: Dr Christophe Balai, *Excerpts from Iran's Historical Past*; Gholam Ali Hadad-Adel (Editor), *The Encyclopedia of Islamic Terms and Usage*; Ali Akbar Seif, *Changing Patterns of Behaviour and Psychological Behaviour Therapy*; and William Flore, *The History of Iranian Finances*
Children's Literary Award: 2001: Mehdi Mir-Kiani, *Where do You Come from, My Rose?*.
Sponsoring Organization: *Docharkheh (Bike)*.
Address: Hamshahri, Tehran, Iran.

Ireland Fund of Monaco Literary Award

A €50,000 prize, created in 2002 to commemorate the 20th anniversary of the death of Princess Grace of Monaco. The winners are chosen by a selection committee in Dublin.
Recent Winners: 2002: Colum McCann.
Sponsoring Organization: Ireland Fund of Monaco.
Address: Ireland Fund of Monaco, 9 rue Princesse Marie-de-Lorraine, Monaco Ville, MC98000, Monaco. **Internet:** www.pgil-eirdata.org/html/pgil_about/personnel/IrelandFund.htm.

Irish American Cultural Institute (IACI) Literary Awards

The Irish American Cultural Institute (IACI) makes a number of awards in different areas of the arts, including graphic arts, music and literature. Awards in the field of literature, each with a prize of $5,000, include the O'Shaughnessy Poetry Award, the IACI/Butler Literary Award for Poetry and the IACI/Butler Literary Award for Prose.
How to Apply: There is no application process.
Recent Winners: IACI/Butler Literary Award for Poetry: 1999: Colm Breathnach IACI/Butler Literary Award for Prose: 1999: Donal O'Kelly (playwright).
Sponsoring Organization: Irish American Cultural Institute.
Address: One Lackawanna Pl. Morristown, New Jersey, USA.

Irish Times International Fiction Prize

A biennial award for fiction; books are nominated by critics and editors. The prize is worth IR£7,500 (around €9,525). The *Irish Times* also runs a parallel Irish Literature Prize (qv).
Eligibility and Restrictions: Open to works of fiction written in English and published in Ireland, the UK, or the USA.
How to Apply: No submissions are accepted.

Recent Winners: 1999: Lorrie Moore, *Birds of America*; 1997: Seamus Deane, *Reading in the Dark*; 1995: J. M. Coetzee, *The Master of Petersburg*; 1993: E. Annie Proulx, *The Shipping News*; 1992: Norman Rush, *Mating*.

Sponsoring Organization: Irish Times Ltd.

Address: Irish Times Ltd, 10–16 D'Olier St, Dublin, 2, Ireland.

Irish Times Irish Literature Prizes

Founded in 1988 with the aim of 'offering Irish writers, novelists as well as those in other categories, a new opportunity to work towards a prize which is comparable with that available to writers in other countries'. The Irish Literature Prizes are awarded in four categories: Irish fiction; Irish non-fiction; Irish poetry; and Irish language. The winners are chosen from a shortlist by a panel of literary editors and critics, and receive a prize of IR£5,000 (€6,350) each. The *Irish Times* also runs a parallel International Fiction Prize (qv).

Eligibility and Restrictions: Authors must be born in Ireland or be an Irish citizen.

How to Apply: Books are nominated by critics and editors; no submissions are required.

Recent Winners: Fiction: 1999: Antonia Logue, *Shadow-box*; 1997: Seamus Deane, *Reading in the Dark*; 1995: Kathleen Ferguson, *A Maid's Tale*; 1992: Patrick McCabe, *The Butcher Boy*; 1990: John McGahern, *Amongst Women*
Non-fiction: 1999: Neil Belton, *The Good Listener*; 1997: Declan Kiberd, *Inventing Ireland*; 1995: Paddy Devlin, *Straight Left*; 1993: Brian Keenan, *An Evil Cradling*; 1991: J. J. Lee, *Ireland 1912–1985*
Poetry: 1999: Seamus Heaney, *Opened Ground*; 1997: Paul Muldoon, *New Selected Poems*; 1995: Robert Greacen, *Collected Poems*; 1992: Derek Mahon, *Selected Poems*; 1990: Ciaran Carson, *Belfast Confetti*.

Sponsoring Organization: Irish Times Ltd.

Address: Irish Times Ltd, 10–16 D'Olier St, Dublin, 2, Ireland.

Itô Sei Bungaku Shô (Itô Sei Prize for Literature)

Established in 1990 on the 20th anniversary of Itô's death by a group of residents in Otaru, Hokkaido, a city closely associated with the novelist and critic after whom the prize is named. The award is jointly sponsored by the Itô Sei Prize for Literature Committee, the City of Otaru, and the *Hokkaidô Shimbun*. The prize is awarded to outstanding works by established novelists and critics. The winner receives a bronze sculpture and a cash prize of 1 million yen.

Sponsoring Organization: jointly sponsored by the Itô Sei Prize for Literature Committee, the City of Otaru, and the *Hokkaidô Shimbun*.

Address: Hokkaidô Shimbun, Otaru, Japan.

Miroslav Ivanov Award for Non-Fiction

An annual award for non-fiction, established in 2001 by the Non-Fiction Literature Authors' Club. Categories include a lifetime achievement award; an award for original non-fiction work; and an award for an author below 35 years of age. The winners are selected by a seven-member jury.

Eligibility and Restrictions: Authors must be living.

Recent Winners: 2002: Antonín Bencík, *Utajovaná pravda o Alexandru Dubcekovi (The Hidden Truth About Alexander Dubcek)*, Milos Hubácek, *Odsouzená lod (The Condemned Ship)*, Jiré Kovarík, *Napoleonovo ruské tazeni 1812 (Napoleon's Russian Campaign 1812)*; 2001: Jindra Jarosová, *The Holy Heretics*
Author below 35 years: 2001: Frantisek Stellner, *The Seven-Year War in Europe*
Special Award: 2002: Vojtech Zamarovský
Lifetime Achievement Award: 2002: Robert Kvacek; 2001: Miloslav Moulis.
Sponsoring Organization: Non-Fiction Literature Authors' Club.
Address: Non-Fiction Literature Authors' Club, Národní 11, 111 47 Prague 1, Czech Republic. **Telephone:** 223 20924.

Izumi Kyôka Bungaku Shô (Izumi Kyôka Prize for Literature)

Established in 1973 by the city of Kanazawa to commemorate the 100th anniversary of the birth of novelist Izumi Kyôka and draw attention to the traditions and natural setting of the Kanazawa area. Awarded annually to a single-volume work published between August and the following July that demonstrates a notably 'romantic' quality. Recommendations are solicited from around 200 writers, critics, publishers, and newspapers, but the final decision is made by a five-member selection committee. The winner receives a mirror and a cash award of 1 million yen.

Recent Winners: 2001 (29th Izumi Kyôka Prize): Shôno Yoriko, *Yûrei morimusume ibun (The Strange Story of the Ghostly Girl of the Forest)*, and Kuze Teruhiko, *Shôshô-kan mokuroku (Catalogue of the Shôshô Residence)* (joint winners).
Address: Izumi Kyôka Prize for Literature (Izumi Kyôka Bungaku Shô), Kanazawa, Japan.

Jacob's Creek World Food Media Awards

Established in 1997, these awards, known as 'ladles', are presented for the best publications in the field of food and drink; there are also awards for television and photography. Winners are selected by an international panel of some 30 food, wine and media professionals. Categories for publications include: food book (separate categories for hard and soft covers); recipe book (separate categories for hard and soft covers); wine book; and food and/or wine guide book. The three best entries in each category receive gold, silver and bronze ladles.

Eligibility and Restrictions: Within the publication categories, entries are open to all examples, in any language, of television food books, recipe books, drink books, food and/or drink guide books, food and/or drink articles, restaurant reviews, food magazines, drink magazines, and food and/or drink sections within newspapers and magazines. All entries must be published for the first time in the country of origin in the two years preceding the award.

How to Apply: Closing date for applications is early June.

Recent Winners: Best Hard Cover Recipe Book: 2001: Jeffrey Alford and Naomi Duguid, *Hot Sour Salty Sweet: A Culinary Journey Through Southeast Asia*
Best Soft Cover Recipe Book: 2001: Dean Brettschneider and Lauraine Jacobs, *The New Zealand Baker*
Best Hard Cover Food Book: 2001: Gail and Kevin Donovan and Simon Griffiths, *Salute! Food, Wine & Travel in Southern Italy*
Best Soft Cover Food Book: 2001: Alex Barker, *Get Cracking*

Best Wine Book: 2001: Stephen Brook, *A Century of Wine*
Best Food and/or Wine Guide Book: 2001: Kath Kenny (et al.), *Out to Eat – Sydney 2001*.

Sponsoring Organization: Government of South Australia/Jacob's Creek.

Contact: Nicole Brewster-Jones.

Address: 7 Ellen Street, Subiaco, SA6008, Australia. **Telephone:** (8) 9388 8877. **Fax:** (8) 9388 8866. **Internet:** www.worldfoodmediaawards.com. **E-mail:** wfma2001@saugov.sa.gov.au.

Jefferson Cup Awards

An annual award given by the Youth Services Forum of the Virginia Library Association. The award, which was established in 1983, is presented for a distinguished biography, historical fiction, or American history book for young people.

Recent Winners: 2002: Elisa Carbone, *Storm Warriors*; 2000: Katherine Paterson, *Preacher's Boy*; 1999: Gary Paulsen, *Soldier's Heart*; 1998: Leon Walter Tillage, *Leon's Story*; 1997: Jean Thesman, *The Ornament Tree*.

Sponsoring Organization: Youth Services Forum of the Virginia Library Association.

Address: Youth Services Forum, Virginia Library Association, POB 8277, Norfolk, VA 23503–0277, USA. **Telephone:** (540) 372-1144. **E-mail:** rpurdy@crrl.org.

Barbara Jelavich Book Prize

The Jelavich Prize was established in 1995 in honour of a distinguished scholar in the field of Central European research. It is awarded annually for a distinguished monograph published on any aspect of Southeast European or Habsburg studies since 1600, or 19th or 20th century Russian or Ottoman diplomatic history. The winner is selected by a committee, and receives a cash award.

Eligibility and Restrictions: Open to works published in English in the USA during the previous year. Authors must be citizens or permanent residents of North America. Textbooks, translations, bibliographies and reference works are not eligible.

How to Apply: Publishers, editors and authors should send copies of eligible works to each committee member by mid-May.

Recent Winners: 2001: Alice Freifeld, *Nationalism and the Crowd in Liberal Hungary 1848–1914*; 2000: Lois C. Dubin, *The Port Jews of Habsburg Trieste: Absolutist Politics and Enlightenment Culture*; 1999: Melissa K. Bokovoy, *Peasants and Communists: Politics and Ideology in the Yugoslav Countryside 1941–53*; 1998: Anastasia N. Karakasidou, *Fields of Wheat, Hills of Blood: Passages to Nationhood in Greek Macedonia 1870–1990*; 1997: S. C. M. Paine, *Imperial Rivals: China, Russia and their Disputed Frontier*.

Sponsoring Organization: American Association for the Advancement of Slavic Studies.

Address: American Association for the Advancement of Slavic Studies, 8 Story St, Cambridge, MA 02138, USA. **Telephone:** (617) 495-0677. **Fax:** (617) 495-0680. **E-mail:** aaass@hcs.harvard.edu.

Jewish Quarterly-Wingate Prizes

Annual award for books of literary merit and which stimulate an interest in and awareness of themes of Jewish concern, in fiction and non-fiction categories. The winner in each category receives £4,000 and expenses to attend the Jerusalem Book Fair.

Eligibility and Restrictions: Books must be published in English in the UK during the previous year and authors must be citizens or residents of the UK, Ireland or the Commonwealth.

Recent Winners: Fiction: 2001: W. G. Sebald, *Austerlitz*; 2000: Howard Jacobson, *The Mighty Walzer*; 1999: Dorit Rabinyan, *Persian Brides*; 1998: Anne Michael, *Fugitive Pieces*
Non-fiction: 2001: Oliver Sacks, *Uncle Tungsten*; 2000: Wladislaw Szpilman, *The Pianist*; 1999: Edoth Velman, *Edith's Book*; 1998: Claudia Rodin, *The Book of Jewish Food*.

Sponsoring Organization: Harold Hyam Wingate Foundation.

Address: PO Box 2078, 146 Edgwarebury Lane, London W1A 1JR, UK. **Telephone:** (20) 7629 5004. **Fax:** (20) 7629 5110. **Internet:** www. jewishquarterly.org. **E-mail:** ed@jewquart.freeserve.co.uk.

Jnanpith Award

The Jnanpith Award was established in 1961, and the first award was made in 1965. The award is given every year to an Indian author for his/her outstanding contribution to creative Indian literature. Since 1982, the award has been given for overall contribution to literature rather than a specific title. The winner receives a cash prize of Rs 2.5 lakh, a citation and a bronze replica of Vagdevi.

Eligibility and Restrictions: Entries must be written in one of the 18 languages mentioned in the Indian constitution.

Recent Winners: 2002: Indira Goswami (Assam); 1999: Girish Karnad (Kannada); 1997: Ali Sardar Jafri (Urdu); 1996: Mahesweta Devi (Bengali); 1995: M. T. Vasudevan Nair (Malayalam).

Sponsoring Organization: Bharatiya Jnanpith.

Contact: Dinesh Misra, Hon. Dir Aditya Sharma.

Address: Bharatiya Jnanpith, 18, Institutional Area, Lodi Road, New Delhi New Delhi, 110 003, India. **Telephone:** (11) 462 6467/11- 465 4196. **Fax:** (11) 465 4197. **E-mail:** jnanpith@satyam.net.in / jnanpith@satyam.com.

BBC4 Samuel Johnson Prize for Non-Fiction

The Samuel Johnson Prize for Non-fiction is open to books in the area of current affairs, history, politics, science, sport, travel, biography, autobiography and the arts. The prize, formerly sponsored by an anonymous philanthropist, has been sponsored by BBC4 since 2002. With a prize of £30,000, the award represents Britain's richest non-fiction literary award.

Recent Winners: 2002: Margaret MacMillan, *Peacemakers*; 2001: Michael Burleigh, *The Third Reich: A New History*; 2000: David Cairns, *Berlioz: Vol 2*; 1999: Antony Beevor, *Stalingrad*.

Sponsoring Organization: BBC4.

Address: 206 Marylebone Rd, London NW1 6LY, UK. **Internet:** www. samueljohnsonprize.com.

Journey Prize

An annual award of C$10,000 for the best short story. In addition the literary journal that originally published the story receives $2,000.

Recent Winners: 2000: Timothy Taylor; 1999: Alissa York; 1998: John Brooke; 1997: Anne Simpson and Gabriella Goliger; 1996: Elyse Gasco.

Sponsoring Organization: National Library of Canada.

Address: National Library of Canada, 395 rue Wellington, Ottawa, ON K1A 0N4, Canada. **Telephone:** (613) 995-9481. **Fax:** (613) 943-1112. **Internet:** www.nlc-bnc.ca. **E-mail:** reference@nlc-bnc.ca.

Josef Jungmann Prize

An annual prize awarded by the Czech Translators' Guild in co-operation with the Ministry of Culture and the Czech Literature Foundation. The award, which is named after a poet and writer, is one of a number of awards of merit for the best translations of the year.

Recent Winners: 1999: K. Vinsová, *Zivot návod k pouzití* by G. Perec; 1998: M. Hilský, *Sonety* by W. Shakespeare; 1997: J. Pelán, *O pohybu a nehybnosti jámy* by Y. Bonnefoy.

Sponsoring Organization: Translators' Guild (Obec prekladatelu)/Ministry of Culture/Czech Literature Foundation.

Address: Pod Nuselskými schody 3, 120 00 Prague, 2, Czech Republic. **Telephone:** 222 564082. **Internet:** hyperlink.cz/obec/uvod_ang.html. **E-mail:** obecprekladatelu@hotmail.com.

Kadan Shô (Kadan Prize)

Established in 1990 by the magazine *Kadan (The Tanka Podium)* to commemorate its second anniversary, and sponsored by the Hon'ami Shoten publishing company. An open competition in which candidates submit 30 previously unpublished tanka for consideration by a selection committee. The winner receives 100,000 yen.

Recent Winners: 2001 (13th Kadan Prize): Tamura Hajime, *Uwakuchibiru ni hanabiru o (Flower Petals for the Upper Lip)*.

Sponsoring Organization: *Kadan (The Tanka Podium)*.

Address: Kadan (The Tanka Podium), Tokyo, Japan.

Franz Kafka Prize

The prize was established in October 2000 by the Franz Kafka Society, and the first prize was awarded in 2001. It is given to a writer from anywhere in the world in recognition of a life's literary achievement in any literary genre. The winner is chosen by an international jury (with members from Germany, Austria, USA, UK, France and the Czech Republic). The winner receives US $10,000 plus a diploma and a statuette.

Eligibility and Restrictions: There are no restrictions.

How to Apply: There is no direct application; nominations are made by an independent jury.

Recent Winners: 2001: Philip Roth.

Sponsoring Organization: Společnost Franze Kafky (Franz Kafka Society)/ Prague City Council.
Address: Společnost Franze Kafky, Maiselova 15, 5th Floor, 110 00 Prague, 1, Czech Republic. **Telephone:** 224 227452. **Fax:** 224 211850. **Internet:** www.franzkafka-soc.cz. **E-mail:** f.kafka.soc@ena.cz.

Kaikô Takeshi Shô (Kaikô Takeshi Prize)

Established in 1991 and sponsored by TBS Britannica. Presented annually to a work of fiction or non-fiction regardless of genre that displays the same sort of 'creative human insight' demonstrated by the author Kaikô, after whom it is named. The winner receives a commemorative gift from the Kaikô family and a cash prize of 3 million yen.

How to Apply: Works are solicited at large and reviewed by a selection committee.
Sponsoring Organization: TBS Britannica.
Address: TBS Britannica, Tokyo, Japan.

Kikuchi Hiroshi Shô (Kikuchi Hiroshi Prize)

Originally established as a literary award in 1938, and revived in 1953 to commemorate the achievements of the novelist and playwright Kikuchi Hiroshi (Kikuchi Kan). The prize is awarded annually to individuals and organizations who in the previous year have demonstrated notable innovation and creativity in any sphere of cultural activity, including literature, film, drama, journalism, broadcasting, and publishing. Sponsored by the Association for the Promotion of Japanese Literature (Nihon Bungaku Shinkô Kai). Winners receive a table clock and a cash prize of 1 million yen.

Sponsoring Organization: Association for the Promotion of Japanese Literature (Nihon Bungaku Shinkô Kai).
Address: Association for the Promotion of Japanese Literature (Nihon Bungaku Shinkô Kai), Bungei-Shunju Bldg, 3 Kioi-cho, Chiyoda-ku, Tokyo, 102, Japan.

Kalinga Prize

An annual award presented to someone who has popularized science through a distinguished career as a writer, editor, lecturer, director or producer. The winner receives a prize of £1,000.
Sponsoring Organization: UNESCO.
Address: c/o UNESCO, 7 place de Fontenoy, 75352 Paris, France.

Katapultpriset (Catapult Prize)

An annual prize presented by the Sveriges Författarförbund (Swedish Writers Union) for the best debut work of fiction by a new writer which has been published during the previous year. The winner receives a prize of SEK 35,000.

Recent Winners: 2002: Caterina Pascual Söderbaum, *Sonetten om andningen*; 2001: Mons Kallentoft, *Pesetas*; 2000: Robert Ståhl, *Om*; 1999: Mirja Unge, *Det var ur munnarna orden kom*.

Sponsoring Organization: Sveriges Författarförbund (Swedish Writers Union). **Address:** Sveriges Författarförbund, Drottninggatan 88 B, Box 3157, 103 63 Stockholm, Sweden. **Telephone:** (8) 545 132 00. **Fax:** (8) 545 132 10.

Katrine Harries Award

The prize was established in 1974 by the South African Institute for Library and Information Sciences (now Library and Information Association of South Africa), to recognize the work of a South African illustrator for a book published in the preceding two years. The illustrator must be a permanent South African resident. Since 1983 the award has been given biennially.

Recent Winners: 1997: D.Steward (author) and Jude Daly (illustrator), *Gift of the Sun*; 1995: Jeremy Grimsdell, *Kalinzu and the Oxpeckers*; 1993: Catherine Stock, *Armien's Fishing Trip*.

Sponsoring Organization: South African Institute for Librarianship and Information Science.

Address: PO Box 36575, Menlo Park, Pretoria, 0102, South Africa. **Internet:** sunsite.wits.ac.za/conferen/sailis/sailis.html. **E-mail:** sailis@cis.co.za.

Kawabata Yasunari Bungaku Shô (Kawabata Yasunari Prize for Literature)

Established in 1973 by the Kawabata Yasunari Memorial Association (Kawabata Yasunari Kinen Kai) to honour Japan's first Nobel Prize-winning novelist. The Nobel Prize award money was used to finance the Kawabata Yasunari Prize, which is presented annually to the year's most accomplished work of short fiction. The numbering of the award was restarted in 2000 to commemorate the 100th anniversary of Kawabata's birth. The winner receives 1 million yen, plus a certificate and a commemorative gift.

Recent Winners: 2001 (27th Kawabata Yasunari Prize): Kurumatani Chôkitsu, *Musashimaru* (in the collection *Hakuchi-gun*).

Address: Tokyo, Japan.

Eamon Keane Full Length Play Award

An annual award offered for the best new full-length play. The winner receives a prize of €2,000. The prize forms part of the annual Listowel Writers Week literary festival.

Eligibility and Restrictions: Entries must not have been published before in any form; no indication of the author's identity should appear on the entry. One-act plays are not eligible and plays submitted should be for stage presentation only. Works may be in English or Irish.

How to Apply: Send entry fee of €25 with each entry submitted. Closing date is 1 March.

Sponsoring Organization: Bank of Ireland.

Address: Writers Week, 24 The Square, Listowel, Co. Kerry, Ireland. **Telephone:** (68) 21074. **Fax:** (68) 22893. **Internet:** www.writersweek.ie. **E-mail:** writersweek@eircom.net.

Ezra Jack Keats New Writer's and New Illustrator's Award for Children's Books

Two annual awards, presented jointly by the New York Public Library and the Ezra Jack Keats Foundation, and given to an outstanding new writer and illustrator (since 2001) of picture books for children. The winners are selected by a committee of education specialists, librarians, illustrators and experts in children's literature. The winners each receive a silver medal and an honorarium of $1,000.

Eligibility and Restrictions: Open to writers and illustrators of books for children aged 9 and under. To be eligible, writers must have published no more than five books; candidates for the writer's award need not have also done the illustrations.

How to Apply: Publishers are invited to submit eligible entries.

Recent Winners: Illustrator's Award: 2002: Jerome Lagarrigue, *Freedom Summer*; 2001: Bryan Collier, *Uptown*
Writer's Award: 2002: Deborah Wiles, *Freedom Summer*; 2001: D. B. Johnson, *Henry Hikes to Fitchburg*; 2000: Soyung Pak, *Dear Juno* (illustrated by Susan Kathleen Hartung); 1999: Stephanie Stuve-Bodeen, *Elizabeti's Doll* (illustrated by Christy Hale); 1997: Juan Felipe Herrera, *Calling the Doves* (illustrated by Elly Simmons).

Sponsoring Organization: New York Public Library/Ezra Jack Keats Foundation.

Address: New York Public Library, Early Childhood Resource and Information Center, Hudson Park Library, 66 Leroy St, New York, NY, USA. **Telephone:** (212) 929-0815.

Keats–Shelley Prize

This annual prize, established in 1998, offers £3,000 for an essay or poem on any aspect of Keats' or Shelley's work or life.

Eligibility and Restrictions: Essays and poems must be in English and must be original and unpublished work; they must not have been submitted to a previous competition. Entries should be of 2,000–3,000 words, including quotations.

How to Apply: Two copies of entries must be submitted by 31 March. There is a fee of £5 sterling for a single entry, £3 for a second entry in the other category.

Recent Winners: Poetry: 2001: Robert Saxton, *The Nightingale Broadcasts*
Essay: 2001: Toby Venables, *Caroline Bertonèche*.

Sponsoring Organization: Keats–Shelley Memorial Association/The Folio Society.

Address: c/o Mrs Harriet Culten, 117 Cheyne Walk, London SW10 0ES, UK. **Internet:** users.ox.ac.uk/%7Escat1492/KSWeb/KSpages/KSframeset.html.

Frans Kellendonk-prijs

Established in 1993 by the Maatschappij der Nederlandse Letterkunde (MNL) following a bequest from the Stichting Frans Kellendonk Fonds. The prize recognizes a literary work reflecting quality, independence and original vision, and may be awarded for any type of literary work. The prize is awarded every three years. The winner is selected by a panel of experts, and receives €5,000.

Eligibility and Restrictions: Open to writers in the Dutch language. The work must not have been published more than five years before the award is given. Preference is given to authors aged 40 or under at the time of writing.

How to Apply: Application is open to anybody.

Recent Winners: 1999: Dirk van Weelden; 1996: Benno Barnard; 1993: Kristien Hemmerechts.

Sponsoring Organization: Maatschappij der Nederlandse Letterkunde (MNL) (Dutch Literature Association).

Address: Maatschappij der Nederlandse Letterkunde, Postbus 9501, 2300 RA Leiden, Netherlands. **Telephone:** (71) 5144962. **Fax:** (71) 5272836. **Internet:** www.leidenuniv.nl/host/mnl. **E-mail:** mnl@library.leidenuniv.nl.

Gottfried Keller Prize

The Gottfried Keller Prize is one of the oldest and most prestigious Swiss literary awards, having been established in 1921 in memory of Swiss poet and novelist Gottfried Keller (1819–1890). The prize is worth SFr 25,000, and is awarded every two or three years.

Recent Winners: 2001: Agota Kristof; previous winners include Heinrich Federer, C. F. Ramuz, Hermann Hesse, Gertrud von LeFort, Meinrad Inglin, Golo Homme, Ignazio Silone, Elias Canetti, Philippe Jaccottet, Gerhard Meier, Giovanni Orelli and Peter Bichsel.

Sponsoring Organization: Martin Bodmer-Siftung für einen Gottfried Keller-Preis.

Address: c/o Thomas Bodner, PO Box 1425, 8032 Zurich, Switzerland. **Internet:** www.gottfried-keller-preis.ch.

Kellgrenpriset (Kellgren Prize)

Established in 1979, for outstanding achievement in a range of literary genres. The prize is of SEK 125,000.

Recent Winners: 2001: Göran Malmqvist; 2000: Sven Lindqvist; 1999: Torsten Ekbom; 1998: Kjell Espmark; 1997: Johan Asplund.

Sponsoring Organization: Swedish Academy.

Contact: Sec. Bo Svensen.

Address: Swedish Academy, PO Box 2118, 103 13 Stockholm, Sweden.

Joan Kelly Memorial Prize

This annual prize was established in 1983 by the Coordinating Council for Women in History and is administered by the American Historical Association (AHA). It is offered, in recognition of the life and work of Joan Kelly (1928–1982), for the best work in women's history and/or feminist theory.

Recent Winners: 2001: Laura Wexler, *Tender Violence: Domestic Visions in an Age of US Imperialism*.

Sponsoring Organization: American Historical Association.

Contact: Lynn Hunt.

Address: American Historical Asscn, 400 A St, SE, Washington, DC 20003–3889, USA. **Telephone:** (202) 544-2422. **Fax:** (202) 544-8307. **Internet:** www. theaha.org/prizes. **E-mail:** press@theaha.org.

Kerala Sahitya Akademi Awards

The Academy presents a series of annual awards in order to recognize and honour the writers of Malayalam language and literature. Prizes are awarded to eminent works in various genres including poetry, drama (Padmanabha Swami Award), short story, biography, novel, literary criticism (Kuttippuzha Award), essays (C. B. Kumar Award), Vedic Literature (K. R. Namboodiri Award), linguistics (I. C. Chacko Award), humour and translation. Each award carries a prize of Rs10,000.

Recent Winners: Novel: 1999: Narayan, *Kocherathi*; 1998: N. Mohanan, *Innalathe Mazha*; 1997: M. Sukumaran, *Janithakam*; 1996: T.V. Kochubava, *Vridha Sadanam*; 1995: K.P. Ramanunni, *Soophi Paranja Katha*
Biography: 1999: Joseph Edamaruku, *Kodungattuyarthiya Kalam*; 1998: T.N. Gopakumar, *Sucheendram Rekhakal*; 1997: T. Venugopal, *Rajadrohiyaya Rajyasnehi*; 1996: A.V. Anil Kumar, *Charithathinoppam Natanna Oral*; 1995: Puthupally Raghavan, *Viplava Smaranakal*
Short Stories: 1999: Chandramathi, *Raindeer*; 1998: Asokan Charuvil, *Oru Rathrikkoru Pakakal*; 1997: Mundur Krishnankutty, *Aaswasathinte Manthracharadu*; 1996: N. Prabhakaran, *Rathrimozhi*; 1995: N.S. Madhavan, *Higwitta*
Poetry: 1999: A. Ayyappan, *Veyil Thinnunna Pakshi*; 1998: K. G. Sankara Pillai, *K.G. Sankarapillayude Kavithakal*; 1997: K. V. Ramakrishnan, *Aksharavidya*; 1996: Attoor Ravivarma, *Attoor Ravivarmayude Kavithakal*; 1995: Prabhavarma, *Arkkapoornima*
Lifetime achievement: 1999: N. P. Muhammed, Puthusseri Ramachandran and V. V. K. Valath; 1998: Vettur Raman Nair and G. Vivekanandan.

Sponsoring Organization: Kerala Sahitya Akademi.

Address: Kerala Sahitya Akademi, Town Hall Rd, Thrissur, 680 020, India. **Internet:** www.keralasahityaakademi.org/html/main-awards.htm.

Kerry Ingredients Irish Fiction Award

Established in 1995 under the sponsorship of Kerry Ingredients, in recognition of the growing importance of the work of the Irish writer. It is now considered one of the most influential awards in the Irish literary world, and is awarded annually at the Listowel Writers Week to the best fiction novel by an Irish author. The winner is chosen by a panel of leading literary critics and writers, and receives a prize of €10,000.

Eligibility and Restrictions: Open to works of fiction by Irish writers published in Ireland during the preceding year. Entries must not have been published before in any form, and may be in English or Irish.

How to Apply: Entries should be sent by 1 March, accompanied by the entry fee, to Literary Competitions, Writers' Week Ltd, 24 The Square, Listowel, County Kerry, Ireland.

Recent Winners: 2001: Anne Barnett, *The Largest Baby in Ireland after the Famine*; 2000: Michael Collins, *The Keepers of Truth*; 1999: J. M. O'Neill, *Bennett & Company*; 1998: John Banville, *The Untouchable*; 1997: Deirdre Madden, *One by One in Darkness*.

Sponsoring Organization: Kerry Ingredients (a division of Kerry Group PLC).

Contact: Dir Frank Hayes.

Address: Kerry Group, Prince's St, Tralee, Ireland. **Telephone:** (66) 118 2304. **Fax:** (66) 718 2972. **Internet:** www.kerrygroup.com. **E-mail:** corpaffairs@kerry.ie.

Khushhall Khan Khattak Award

The Pakistan Academy of Letters administers a series of annual prizes established in 1980 under the Hijra National Literary Awards Scheme. The aim of the awards is to promote literary activities and recognize outstanding contributions. The Khushhall Khan Khattak Award is an annual prize of Rs 50,000 for works written in Pushto language.

Recent Winners: 2000: Tahir Afridi, *Kanrro Ke Ragoona*; 1999: Saleem Raz, *Tanqeedi Karkhey*; 1998: Qamar Rahi, *Sera*.

Sponsoring Organization: Pakistan Academy of Letters.

Contact: Deputy Dir Naseem Mahmood.

Address: Pitras Bokhari Road, Sector H-8/1, Islamabad, Pakistan. **Telephone:** 9257164. **Fax:** 9257159. **E-mail:** academy@apollo.net.pk.

Khatulistiwa Literary Award (Indonesia's Best Fiction Award)

The Khatulistiwa Literary Award, which honours the country's best fiction, was established by Richard Oh from QB World Books. The award was intended to raise the image of Indonesian literature and to encourage more Indonesians to read. It has already become a prestigious award, with a main prize of Rp 30 million. The winner is chosen after three stages of judging by a jury of 45 people in total.

Eligibility and Restrictions: Open to works published in the previous year (year ending August).

Recent Winners: 2001: Goenawan Mohamad, *Sajak-sajak Lengkap (Complete Poems)*.

Sponsoring Organization: QB World Books.

Contact: Richard Oh.

Address: QB World Books, Plaza Senayan, 3rd floor, #310B&312B, Jl. Asia Afrika No. 8, Jakarta, 10270, Indonesia. **Telephone:** (21) 572 5267. **Fax:** (21) 424 8047. **Internet:** www.qbworld.com. **E-mail:** info@qbworld.com.

Kick Start Poets Open Poetry Competition

Kick Start Poets runs a series of open poetry competitions, with the sixth series launched on National Poetry Day, October 2002. The winner receives a cash prize of £500, with second-placed poem winning £250 and a third prize of £100. There are also four runners-up prizes of £25. The winning entries are posted on the Kick Start Poets website.

How to Apply: Entry forms are available on the website.

Recent Winners: 2002 (Fifth Competition): 1st Prize: Mario Petrucci, *Sinistra*.

Sponsoring Organization: Salisbury Arts Centre.

Contact: Adjudicator Mimi Khalvati.

Address: c/o Salisbury Arts Centre, Bedwin St, Salisbury SP1 3UT, UK. **Internet:** www.kickstartpoets.freeuk.com. **E-mail:** kspoets@aol.com.

Coretta Scott King Award

The award was set up to honour African-American authors and illustrators of outstanding books for children and young adults. The Award commemorates the life and work of Dr Martin Luther King Jr, and honours his widow, Coretta Scott

King; books are chosen by a seven-member national award jury. Winners receive a framed citation, an honorarium, and a set of *Encyclopaedia Britannica* or *World Book Encyclopedias*.

Recent Winners: 2002: Mildred D. Taylor, *The Land,* and Jerry Pinkney, *Goin' Someplace Special*; 2001: Jacqueline Woodson, *Miracle's Boys*; 2000: Christopher Paul Curtis, *Bud, Not Buddy*; 1999: Angela Johnson, *Heaven*; 1998: Sharon M. Draper, *Forged by Fire*.

Sponsoring Organization: American Library Association.

Address: American Library Association, 50 East Huron, Chicago, IL 60611–2795, USA. **Fax:** (312) 944-7671. **Internet:** www.ala.org/alsc. **E-mail:** alsc@ala.org.

King Fahd bin Abdulaziz Award for Initiative

The King Fahd bin Abdulaziz Award for Initiative was established in 2001, to be awarded in three categories: arts and literature; social and human studies; and basic and applied sciences. The first category includes plastic arts as well as poetry, novels, and literary criticism.

How to Apply: Nominations are accepted through either individuals or cultural and scientific institutions.

Sponsoring Organization: Gulf Co-operation Council (GCC).

Address: Gulf Co-operation Council (GCC), PO Box 7153, Riyadh, 11462, Saudi Arabia. **Telephone:** (1) 482-7777. **Fax:** (1) 482-9089.

Kiriyama Pacific Rim Book Prize

Founded in 1996 by the Kiriyama Institute to encourage the publication and readership of books that will contribute to further understanding among Pacific Rim peoples. Since 1999 the prize has been awarded annually to one fiction and one non-fiction book. There are two panels of five judges for each category. The prize money of $30,000 is divided between the two winners.

Eligibility and Restrictions: Books entered for the prize must be concerned with the Pacific Rim in a significant way and must be in English, either as original language or in translation. Pacific Rim includes countries of four sub-regions bordering the Pacific Ocean, together with the Indian subcontinent. Entries must have been published in the previous year (year ending 31 October).

How to Apply: Publishers from anywhere in the world may submit eligible entries. Entry forms are available from the address given or the website.

Recent Winners: Fiction: 2001: Patricia Grace, *Dogside Story*; 2000: Michael Ondaatje, *Anil's Ghost*; 1999: Cheng Ch'ing-win, *Three-legged Horse*
Non-fiction: 2001: Peter Hessler, *River Town: Two Years on the Yangtze*; 2000: Michael David Kwan, *Things That Must Not Be Forgotten: A Childhood in Wartime China*; 1999: Andrew X. Pham, *Catfish and Mandala: A Two-Wheeled Journey through the Landscape and Memory of Vietnam*.

Sponsoring Organization: Kiriyama Pacific Rim Institute.

Contact: Man Jeannine Cuevas.

Address: 650 Delancey St, Suite 101, San Francisco, CA 94107, USA. **Telephone:** (415) 777-1628. **Fax:** (415) 777-1646. **Internet:** www.kiriyamaprize. org. **E-mail:** admin@kiriyamaprize.org.

KOALA—Kids Own Australian Literature Awards

The KOALA (Kids Own Australian Literature Awards) awards are the NSW part of a series of Australian Children's Choice awards at both national and state level. The awards are presented in October of each year.

Recent Winners: Picture Book: 2001: Bob Graham, *Max*; 2000: Gillian Rubinstein and David Macintosh (illustrator), *Sharon Keep Your Hair On*; 1999: Rod Clement, *Grandad's Teeth*
Younger Readers: 2001: Bill Condon, *Miss Wolf and the Porkers*; 2000: Duncan Ball, *Selby Snowbound*; 1999: Di Bates and Stephen Axelson (illustrator), *Desert Dan the Dunny Man*
Older Readers: 2001: Andy Griffiths, *Just Crazy!*; 2000: Andy Griffiths and Terry Denton (illustrator), *Just Stupid!*; 1999: Andy Griffiths and Terry Denton (illustrator), *Just Annoying!*.

Address: POB 268, Artarmon, NSW 1570, Australia. **Fax:** (2) 9273 1248. **Internet:** www.koalabooks.com.au/koalanswawards.html.

Rudolf Koivu Prize

Established in 1949 to honour the work of the artist Rudolf Koivu, and awarded every two years for achievements in illustration of children's literature. The winner receives €5,046.

Eligibility and Restrictions: Open to Finnish illustrations for works of children's literature.

Recent Winners: 1999: Julia Vuoir; 1997: Mika Launis; 1995: Leena Lumme; 1993: Markus Majaluoma; 1991: Chris af Enehielm.

Sponsoring Organization: Grafia Ry (Finnish Association of Graphic Design).

Address: Grafia Ry, Uudenmaankatu 11B9, 00120 Helsinki, Finland. **Telephone:** (9) 601 941. **Fax:** (9) 601140. **Internet:** www.grafia.fi. **E-mail:** grafia@grafia.fi.

Gregory Kolovakos Award

The Gregory Kolovakos Award, established in 1992, is awarded every two years to an American literary translator, editor, or critic whose work is distinguished by a strong commitment to Hispanic literature and to expanding its English-language audience. The winner receives a prize of $2,000.

How to Apply: Writers, critics, or translators may be nominated for the award. Candidates may not nominate themselves.

Recent Winners: 2001: Gregory Rabassa and Alastair Reid (joint winners); 1998: Johannes Wilbert; 1996: Jean Franco and Suzanne Jill Levine (joint winners); 1994: Helen Lane.

Sponsoring Organization: PEN American Center.

Address: PEN American Center, 568 Broadway, New York, NY 10012–3225, USA. **Telephone:** (212) 334-1660. **Internet:** www.pen.org. **E-mail:** jm@pen.org.

Aleko Konstantinov Literary Prize

An international literary prize awarded each year to the authors of the best short works in prose. The prize was established in honour of the Bulgarian writer of that name (1863–1897).

Recent Winners: 2001: Yury Prokopenko (Ukraine).
Address: Sofia, Bulgaria.

Korean Literature Translation Award

Prizes are awarded for literary translations from Korean into other languages. The winners are selected by a Committee, composed of experts in literature and translation. Prizes are awarded in the categories Grand Prize and Work of Merit.

Recent Winners: Grand Prize: 2000: Sung-Il Lee, for the translation into English of *The Moonlit Pond: Korean Classical Poems in Chinese*
Work of Merit: 2000: Joung Kwon Tae for the translation into Spanish of *Selected Poems of Oh Sae Young* and Kao Jong-wen for the translation into Chinese of *Three Generations* by Yom Sang-Sop (joint winners).

Sponsoring Organization: Korean Culture and Fine Arts Foundation.

Address: PO Box Kwang Hwa Moon 947, Seoul, 110–510, Korea. **Internet:** www.kcaf.or.kr.

Kossuth Prize

The Kossuth Prize is Hungary's most distinguished artistic and literary honour. As the greatest official recognition by the state, it recognizes a lifetime's achievement in literature, as well as being awarded for music, sculpture and scientific achievement. The prize was created by the Hungarian Government in 1948, and is named after Lajos Kossuth (1802–1894), the 'Father of Hungarian Democracy'. The prize is awarded at two levels, Kossuth Prize, for individuals, and Grand Prize, for joint achievement. The winners receive a certificate, a monetary prize and a statuette of Lajos Kossuth. The level of the monetary prize is calculated by the Central Statistical Office, based on a multiple of the national average net earnings of the previous year; in 2002 the award was 3,950,000 FT, with winners of the Grand Prize receiving double this amount.

Eligibility and Restrictions: Hungarians and foreign nationals are eligible for the award; however, it cannot be awarded posthumously.

How to Apply: Nominations may be made by members of the Government, national governing bodies, previous prizewinners and leaders of national academic or artistic institutions. Anybody can approach the above people or organizations to recommend someone for nomination.

Recent Winners: Previous winners in the field of literature include: György Petri (1996), Otto Orbán (1989), Sándor Márai, Sándor Csoóri and György Faludy.

Sponsoring Organization: Office of the Hungarian President.

Address: Kossuth Prize Committee, Mueveloedesi Miniszterium, Kossuth Lajos-Ter 1–3, 1055 Budapest, Hungary. **Internet:** www.nkom.hu.

Katherine Singer Kovacs Prize

First awarded in 1991, the prize was established in memory of Professor Katherine Singer Kovacs, a specialist in Spanish and Latin American literature and film. It is awarded annually for an outstanding book in the field of Latin American and Spanish literature and culture. The winner is selected by a committee made up of members of the Modern Language Association of America (MLA), and receives $1,000 and a certificate.

Eligibility and Restrictions: Entries must be in English and be published during the previous year.

How to Apply: Publishers or authors may apply. Six copies should be sent to the address given by 1 May.

Recent Winners: 2001: Catherine Julien, *Reading Inca History*; 1999: Idelber V. Avelar, *The Untimely Present: Postdictatorial Latin American Fiction and the Task of Mourning*; 1998: Frances Aparicio, *Listening to Salsa, Gender, Latin Popular Music and Puerto Rican Culture* and Reacca Haidt, *Embodying Enlightenment: Knowing the Body in Eighteenth Century Spanish Literature and Culture* (joint winners); 1997: Kathryn Joy McKnight, *The Mystic of Tunja*; 1996: Diana Sorensen, *Facundo and the Construction of Argentine Culture*.

Sponsoring Organization: Modern Language Association of America (MLA).

Contact: Co-ordinator of Book Prizes and Special Projects.

Address: Modern Language Asscn of America, 26 Broadway, 3rd Floor, New York, NY 10004–1789, USA. **Telephone:** (646) 576-5141. **Fax:** (646) 458-0033. **Internet:** www.mla.org. **E-mail:** awards@mla.org.

Kraszna-Krausz Book Awards

Established in 1985 by Andor Kraszna-Krausz, founder of the Focal Press, to encourage and recognize outstanding achievements in the publishing and writing of books on the art, history, practice and technology of photography and the moving image. Awards for books on the moving image (film, television and video) alternate annually with those for books on still photography. Selection is made by a panel of three judges, each from a different country. There are two main prizes each year of £5,000 each, plus £1,000 for commendations.

Eligibility and Restrictions: Entries in each year cover books published in the previous two years. Books published in any language are eligible.

How to Apply: Publishers should send copies of entries to each of the three judges and one to the Administrator.

Recent Winners: Moving Image: 2001: Pearl Bowser and Louise Spence, *Writing Himself into History: Oscar Micheaux, His Silent Movies and His Audiences* and Richard Rickitt, *Special Effects: The History and Technique*; 1999: James Naremore, *More than Night: Film Noir in its Contexts* and R. W. Burns, *Television: An International History of the Formative Years*; 1997: Richard Taylor, *The Encyclopaedia of Animation Techniques* and Ruth Vasey, *The World According to Hollywood, 1918–1939*

Photography: 2000: Boris Mikhailov, *Case History* and Sidney F Ray, *Scientific Photography and Applied Imaging*; 1998: Herbert Molderings, *Umbo: Otto Umbehr 1902–1980* and Ann Thomas (Editor), *Beauty of Another Order: Photography in Science*.

Sponsoring Organization: Kraszna-Krausz Foundation.

Contact: Administrator Andrea Livingstone.

Address: Kraszna-Krausz Foundation, 122 Fawnbrake Ave, London SE24 0BZ, UK. **Telephone:** (20) 7738 6701. **Fax:** (20) 7738 6701. **Internet:** www.k-k.org.uk.

KROC—Kids Reading Oz Choice—Award

The KROC (Kids Reading Oz Choice) awards are the Darwin part of a series of Australian Children's Choice awards at both national and state level. The award is announced in October during Children's Week. The winner is chosen in a first-past-the-post voting system.

Eligibility and Restrictions: Open to all Australian books for children.

Recent Winners: 2000: Paul Jennings and Morris Gleitzman, *Wicked!*.

Sponsoring Organization: Darwin Library and Information Service.

Contact: Viki Chmielewski.

Address: Darwin Library and Information Service, Darwin, NT, Australia. **Telephone:** (8) 8982 2563. **E-mail:** v.chmielewski@darcity.nt.gov.au.

Kruyskamp-prijs

Established in 1992 and awarded for the first time in 1994. The prize is sponsored by the Maatschappij der Nederlandse Letterkunde (MNL), following a gift from the widow of Dr Kruyskamp. The prize recognizes the author of a work in one of the following categories: lexicography; lexicology; and annotation of old texts. The prize is awarded every three years, and the winner receives €2,500.

Eligibility and Restrictions: The work must have been published in the Dutch language within the preceding six years.

How to Apply: Application is open to anybody.

Recent Winners: 2000: Hans Luijten; 1997: Dr W. P. Gerritsen, Willem Wilmink, Soetje Oppenhuis de Jong and a group of students from the University of Utrecht; 1994: Dr F. M. W. Claes.

Sponsoring Organization: Maatschappij der Nederlandse Letterkunde (MNL) (Dutch Literature Association).

Address: Maatschappij der Nederlandse Letterkunde, Postbus 9501, 2300 RA Leiden, Netherlands. **Telephone:** (71) 5144962. **Fax:** (71) 5272836. **Internet:** www.leidenuniv.nl/host/mnl. **E-mail:** mnl@library.leidenuniv.nl.

Kulturdepartementets Premiering av Barne- og Ungdomslitteratur (Culture Department Literature Awards for Children and Young People)

The Culture Department makes an annual award for the year's best book for children and young people. The winner is chosen by a jury drawn from general and school librarians. Categories include children's book, non-fiction, illustration, translation, and debut book by a new writer. The winners receive a cash prize.

Recent Winners: Best Children's Book: 2001: Svein Nyhus, *Lille Lu og trollmannen Bulibar*
Best Picture Book: 2001: Tone Lie Böttinger and Akin Düzakin (illustrator), *Min storebror Apen*
Best Non-fiction: 2001: Anne B. Ragde, *Biografien om Sigrid Undset. Ogsaa en ung Pige*
Best First Book: 2001: Asgeir Helgestad, *Dyr i skogen*
Best Illustration: 2001: Bjørn Ousland (illustrator), Halvor Roll (author), *Frøken Bisk Glefs og femten andre*
Translation Prize: 2001: Lars S. Vikør, *Bror* by Ted van Lieshout.

Sponsoring Organization: Norwegian Culture Department.

Address: Statens Bibliotektilsyn, Munkedamsveien 62A, POB 8145 DEP, 0033 Oslo, Norway.

Lakeland Book of the Year Awards

The awards were established in 1984 by the Cumbrian Tourist Board and the Cumbrian author Hunter Davies to recognize and reward Cumbrian literature. There are a maximum of seven prizes awarded each year: the Hunter Davies Prize for the Lakeland Book of the Year (the overall prize); the Tullie House Prize for Best Book on the Cumbrian Environment (awarded for a book which best helps develop a greater appreciation of the art and the environment of Cumbria); the Barclays Bank Prize for Books About People (on any aspect of Cumbrian life, people or culture); the Border Television Prize for Best Illustrated Book (for a book which best illustrates the beauty and character of Cumbria); the Jennings Brothers Prize for the Best Small Book or Guide Book on Cumbria or the Lake District; the Ron Sands Prize for Best Book on a Cultural Theme; and the Titus Wilson Prize for Best Researched Book. The prize amounts to £100 for each category, plus a further £100 for the overall winner of the Lakeland Book of the Year title.

Eligibility and Restrictions: The winners are chosen by a panel of judges from entries submitted by publishers and local authors. Entries can be about any aspect of Cumbria, but must have been published in the last calendar year.

How to Apply: Entry forms are available from the Tourist Board; four copies of the book should be submitted to the address given by mid-March, with the winner announced at a charity literary luncheon in mid-June.

Recent Winners: Hunter Davies Prize for Lakeland Book of the Year: 2001: John and Eileen Malden, *Rex Malden's Whitehaven*
Barclays Bank Prize: 2001: David A. Cross, *A Striking Likeness: The Life of George Romney*
Border TV Prize: 2001: John and Eileen Malden, *Rex Malden's Whitehaven*
Bill Rollinson Award: 2001: Helen Caldwell, John Caldwell, Jennifer Forsyth, Beryl Offley, *Life on the Fell*
Ron Sands Prize: 2001: John Batchelor, *John Ruskin: No Wealth but Life*
Titus Wilson Prize: 2001: David W. V. Weston, *Carlisle Cathedral History*.

Sponsoring Organization: Cumbria Tourist Board.

Contact: Annette Vidler.

Address: Cumbria Tourist Board, Ashleigh, Holly Rd, Windermere LA23 2AQ, UK. **Telephone:** (15394) 44444. **Fax:** (15394) 44041. **Internet:** www.gocumbria.co.uk.

Lambda Literary Awards—Lammys

A set of annual awards in 20 categories, established in 1988 and presented in recognition of gay and lesbian literature.

Recent Winners: Gay Men's Fiction: 2002: Allan Gurganus, *The Practical Heart*
Lesbian Fiction: 2002: Achy Obejas, *Days of Awe*
Lesbian Poetry: 2002: Adrienne Rich, *Fox*
Gay Men's Poetry: 2002: Mark Doty, *The Source*
Lesbian Mystery: 2002: Ellen Hart, *Merchant of Venus*
Gay Men's Mystery: 2002: Michael Nava, *Rag and Bone*
Biography: 2002: Barry Werth, *The Scarlet Professor*
Memoir/Autobiography: 2002: Andrew Solomon, *Noonday Demon*
Anthologies (Fiction): 2002: Helen Sandler (Editor), *Diva Book of Short Stories*
Anthologies (Non-fiction): 2002: Delroy Constantine-Simms (Editor), *The Greatest Taboo*
Humour: 2002: David Rakoff, *Fraud*

Science Fiction/Fantasy: 2002: Lisa A. Barnett and Melissa Scott, *Point of Dreams*
Religion/Spirituality: 2002: Ken Stone (Editor), *Queer Commentary and the Hebrew Bible* and Bernard Duncan Mayes, *Escaping God's Closet* (joint winners)
Photography/Visual Arts: 2002: David Deitcher, *Dear Friends*
Children/Young Adult: 2002: Julia Watts, *Finding H. F.*
Erotica: 2002: Ian Philips, *See Dick Deconstruct*
Romance: 2002: Sylvia Brownrigg, *Pages for You.*

Sponsoring Organization: Lambda Literary Foundation.

Address: Lambda Literary Foundation, POB 73910, Washington, DC 20056–13910, USA. **Telephone:** (202) 682-0952. **Internet:** www.lambdalit.org. **E-mail:** llf@lambdalit.org.

Gerald Lampert Award

Annual award recognizing the best first book of poetry published by a Canadian in the preceding year. The winner receives a prize of C$1,000.

Recent Winners: 2001: Anne Simpson, *Light Falls Through You*; 2000: Shawna Lemay, *All the God-Sized Fruit*; 1999: Stephanie Bolster, *White Stone: The Alice Poems.*

Sponsoring Organization: League of Canadian Poets.

Address: League of Canadian Poets, 54 Wolseley St, Toronto, ON M5T 1A5, Canada. **Telephone:** (416) 504-1657. **Fax:** (416) 504-0096. **E-mail:** league@poets.ca.

Harold Morton Landon Translation Award

The award was established in 1976 by Mrs Harold Morton Landon in memory of her husband. Initially a biennial prize, since 1984 the competition has been held annually. It is given to an American for a published translation of poetry from any language into English. The winner is selected by a panel of judges, and receives a cash prize of $1,000.

Recent Winners: 2001: Clayton Eshleman, *Trilce* by César Vallejo; 2000: Cola Franzen, *Horses in the Air* by Jorge Guillén; 1999: W. D. Snodgrass, *Selected Translations.*

Sponsoring Organization: Academy of American Poets.

Address: Academy of American Poets, 584 Broadway, Suite 1208, New York, NY 10012, USA. **Telephone:** (212) 274-0343. **Fax:** (212) 274-9427. **Internet:** www.poets.org/academy. **E-mail:** academy@poets.org.

Lannan Literary Awards

Established in 1989 to honour established and new writers whose work is of exceptional quality. Recipients are chosen by the Foundation's Literary Committee, on recommendation from anonymous nominators. Awards are made in the areas of fiction, non-fiction and poetry, and are of $75,000 each for body of work rather than for a single publication. A Lifetime Achievement Award of $200,000 is also made.

How to Apply: There is no direct application process.

Recent Winners: Lifetime Achievement Award: 2001: Robert Creeley and Edward Said; 2000: Evan S. Connell; 1999: Adrienne Rich; 1998: John Barth; 1997: William H. Gass

Poetry: 2000: Herbert Morris, Jay Wright; 1999: Louise Glück, Dennis O'Driscoll; 1998: Frank Bidart, Jon Davis; 1997: Ken Smith
Fiction: 2000: Robert Coover, David Malouf, Cynthia Ozick, Leslie Marmon Silko; 1999: Gish Jen, Jamaica Kincaid, Richard Powers, Joanna Scott; 1998: J. M. Coetzee, Lydia Davis, Stuart Dybeck, Lois-Ann Yamanaka; 1997: John Banville, Anne Michaels, Grace Paley
Non-fiction: 2000: Bill McKibben, Carl Safina; 1999: Jared Diamond, Gary Paul Nabhan, Jonathan Schell; 1998: Chet Raymo, Lawrence Weschler, Howard Zinn; 1997: David Quammen.

Sponsoring Organization: Lannan Foundation.

Contact: Jeanie J. Kim, Director of Literary Programs.

Address: Lannan Foundation, 313 Read Street, Santa Fe, New Mexico, 87501 2628, USA. **Telephone:** (505) 986-8160. **Fax:** (505) 986-8195. **Internet:** www.lannan.org. **E-mail:** e-mail:jo@calannan.org.

Lao She Literary Prize

This biennial literary prize, named after the renowned Chinese writer Lao She (1898–1966), was established by the Lao She Art and Culture Foundation to promote the creation of more literary works. The award is presented to eminent works of literature which have 'in-depth and meaningful text with a distinct local flavour'.

Eligibility and Restrictions: Open to novels and works of drama.

Sponsoring Organization: Lao She Art and Culture Foundation., Beijing, China.

James Laughlin Award

The James Laughlin Award is given to commend and support a poet's second book of poetry. The award was established by a gift to the Academy of American Poets from the Drue Heinz Trust in honour of the poet and publisher James Laughlin (1914–1997). The winner, selected by a panel of judges, receives a cash award of $5,000, and the Academy purchases at least 8,000 hardcover copies of the winning entry.

Recent Winners: 2001: Peter Johnson, *Miracles and Mortifications*; 2000: Liz Waldner, *A Point is That Which Has No Part*; 1999: Tory Dent, *HIV, Mon Amour*.

Sponsoring Organization: Academy of American Poets.

Address: Academy of American Poets, 584 Broadway, Suite 1203, New York, NY 10012, USA. **Telephone:** (212) 274-0343. **Fax:** (212) 274-9427. **Internet:** www.poets.org/academy. **E-mail:** academy@poets.org.

Lazarillo Prize

This is the oldest Spanish prize for children's literature, having been established in 1958 in order to stimulate literature for children and young people. It has been administered since 1986 by Organización Española para Libro Infantil y Juvenil (OEPLI). Prizes are awarded in two categories, literary creation and illustration. Each award consists of 1 million ptas (€6,000), and two smaller runner-up awards are also presented. The winners are announced in December, during the celebration of the Semana del Libro Infantil y Juvenil (Children's and Young People's Book Week).

Eligibility and Restrictions: Open to works by young adults on any theme, written in any of the languages of Spain and particularly aimed at readers above 12. Entries should be between 80 and 125 pages in length (for narrative and drama) or 250 verses (poetry). The same works may be entered for both categories.

How to Apply: Three copies should be submitted by 1 July.

Recent Winners: Literary Creation: 2000: Ana Maria Fernández, *Amar e outros verbos*; 1999: Marilar Aleixandre, *A banda sen futuro*; 1998: Emilio Pascual, *Día de Reyes Magos*; 1997: Eliacer Cansino, *El misterio Velázquez*

Illustration: 2000: Saúl Oscar Rojas, *Los siete domingos*; 1999: Pablo Amargo, *No todas las vacas son iguales*; 1998: Judit Morales Villanueva, *No eres más que una pequeña hormiguita*; 1997: Manuel Barbero Richart, *El niño que dejó de ser pez*

Sponsoring Organization: Organización Española para Libro Infantil y Juvenil (OEPLI).

Address: Santiago Rusinol 8, 28040 Madrid, Spain. **Telephone:** (91) 553 08 21. **Fax:** (91) 553 99 90. **Internet:** www.oepli.org/ingles/bases_lit.htm. **E-mail:** oepli@arrakis.es.

Stephen Leacock Memorial Medal for Humour

An annual award made to a Canadian writer for excellence in a book, fictional or non-fictional, in which humour is a major element. The award is named after a celebrated humorist of the early 20th century. The winner receives a medal plus C$5,000.

Address: c/o Ms Judith Rapson, Frith House, 4223 Line 12 N., R.R. 2, Coldwater, ON L0K 1E0, Canada.

Waldo G. Leland Prize

This prize, established by the American Historical Association (AHA) Council in 1975, is offered every five years for the most outstanding reference tool in the field of history. It is named after Waldo Gifford Leland, a distinguished contributor to bibliographical guides, who served as secretary to the Association from 1909 to 1920.

Eligibility and Restrictions: Eligible works include bibliographies, indexes, encyclopedias, and other scholarly works.

Recent Winners: 2001: *American National Biography, 24 vols.*

Sponsoring Organization: American Historical Association.

Contact: Lynn Hunt.

Address: American Historical Asscn, 400 A St, SE, Washington, DC 20003–3889, USA. **Telephone:** (202) 544-2422. **Fax:** (202) 544-8307. **Internet:** www.theaha.org/prizes. **E-mail:** press@theaha.org.

Grace Leven Prize for Poetry

An award of A$200 in recognition of the best volume of poetry published in the previous year.

Eligibility and Restrictions: Entrants must be Australian by birth, or naturalized Australians resident in the country for over 10 years.

Address: c/o Perpetual Trustee Co Ltd, 39 Hunter St, Sydney, NSW 2000, Australia.

Fenia and Yaakov Leviant Memorial Prize

A new prize established in 2002, to be awarded each even-numbered year. This prize will be awarded alternately to an outstanding translation into English of a Yiddish literary work, and an outstanding scholarly work in the field of Yiddish.

Eligibility and Restrictions: For 2004, the prize will be awarded to an outstanding scholarly work in the field of Yiddish published between 1999 and 2003; cultural studies, critical biographies, or edited works in the field of Yiddish folklore or linguistic studies are eligible to compete. Translators need not be members of the Modern Language Association of America.

How to Apply: Four copies should be submitted by 1 May in even-numbered years.

Sponsoring Organization: Modern Language Association of America.

Contact: Co-ordinator of Book Prizes and Special Projects.

Address: Modern Language Asscn of America, 26 Broadway, 3rd Floor, New York, NY 10004–1789, USA. **Telephone:** (646) 576-5141. **Fax:** (646) 458-0033. **Internet:** www.mla.org. **E-mail:** awards@mla.org.

Libris Awards

The CBA Libris Awards honour outstanding achievement in Canada's bookselling industry. Awards are presented each year in several categories including Author of the Year, Fiction Book of the Year and Non-Fiction Book of the Year, and besides the book awards there are also various bookselling and publishing categories. Entries are nominated and voted on by members of the Canadian bookselling community. The awards are presented each June during BookExpo Canada. There is no monetary prize, but the winners receive an engraved trophy.

Recent Winners: Author of the Year: 2001: David Adams Richards; 1999: Alice Munro; 1998: Mordecai Richler; 1997: Margaret Atwood
Fiction Book of the Year: 2001: David Adams Richards, *Mercy Among the Children*; 2000: Alistair MacLeod, *No Great Mischief*; 1999: Alice Munro, *The Love of a Good Woman*; 1998: Ann Marie MacDonald, *Fall On Your Knees*
Non-Fiction Book of the Year: 2001: Don Gilmor and Pierre Turgeon, *Canada: A People's History*; 2000: Charlotte Gray, *Sisters in the Wilderness*; 1999: Katherine Barber, *The Canadian Oxford Dictionary*.

Sponsoring Organization: Canadian Booksellers Association.

Contact: Gen. Man. Susan Dayus.

Address: Canadian Booksellers Asscn, 789 Don Mills Rd, No 700, Toronto, ON M3C 1T5, Canada. **Telephone:** (416) 467-7883. **Internet:** www.cbabook.org/awards. **E-mail:** sdayus@cbabook.org.

Ruth Lilly Poetry Prize

Annual award to a US poet whose accomplishments warrant extraordinary recognition. The winner receives a prize of $100,000 to honour their lifetime achievement.

Eligibility and Restrictions: Open to US poets with a distinguished body of work.

How to Apply: There is no application process.

Recent Winners: 2002: Lisel Mueller; 2001: Yusef Komunyakaa; 2000: Carl Dennis; 1999: Maxine Kumin.

Sponsoring Organization: Modern Poetry Association.

Address: c/o Poetry, Modern Poetry Association, 60 West Walton St, Chicago, IL 60610, USA. **Telephone:** (312) 255-3703.

Astrid Lindgren Translation Prize

An international translation prize administered by the Fédération Internationale des Traducteurs (FIT). The prize aims to promote the translation of children's literature and draw attention to the role of translators in bringing the peoples of the world closer together in terms of culture. The prize is sponsored by the Astrid Lindgren Fund. The winner, chosen by an international jury consisting of five members appointed by the FIT Executive Committee, receives a Certificate of Merit and a sum of money.

Eligibility and Restrictions: Awarded either for a single translation of outstanding quality or for the entire body of work of a translator of books written for children or young people.

How to Apply: Candidates must be nominated by a FIT member and must be members of a similar organization. Nominations should be accompanied by the following information: a general report on the nominee's work, including his or her titles, any awards received and articles written about his or her work, and a detailed analysis of the merits of the translation under consideration or of the quality of all the works of the candidate. Nominations should be submitted in six copies, no later than six months prior to the opening of the Congress at which the prize will be awarded.

Recent Winners: 1999: Gunnel Malmstroem; 1996: Senta Kapoun; 1993: Jo Tenfjord; 1990: Anthea Bell; 1990: Lyudmïla Braude.

Sponsoring Organization: Fédération Internationale des Traducteurs/ International Federation of Translators.

Address: Fédération Internationale des Traducteurs, Dr-Heinrich-Maierstr 9, 1180 Vienna, Austria. **Internet:** www.fit-ift.org. **E-mail:** secretariat@fit-ift.org.

Literárna sútaz Poviedka (Slovakian Prize for Short Stories)

This annual award, presented since 1997 for the best short stories, attracts around 1,000 entrants each year and is the most popular literary competition in Slovakia. The aim of the competition is to encourage young authors and give them a chance for publication of their work. Twenty prizes are awarded in total, from the Grand Prix sponsored by EuroTel, to four smaller financial prizes with separate sponsors (*SME* newspaper, *Domino-forum* magazine, *inZineinternet* magazine, and Twist radio station), and 15 other smaller prizes.

Recent Winners: Recent winners include: Balla, *Tichy kut (Quiet Corner), Gravidita (Pregnancy), Leptokaria*; Pavol Rankov, *S odstupom casu (With Distance of Time), My a oni – Oni a my (Us and Them – Them and Us)*; Michal Hvorecky, *Silny pocit cistoty (Strong Feeling of Cleanness), Lovci & zberaci (Hunters & Collectors)*; Tomas Horvath, *Akozmia, Niekolko nahlych konfiguracii (A Few Speedy Configurations), Vrazda Marionet (Marionette Murder), Zverstvo (Atrocity)*.

Sponsoring Organization: EuroTel.

Contact: Chief Exec. Koloman Kertész Bagala.

Address: Literature and Culture Agency (LCA), POB 99, 810 00 Bratislava, 1, Slovakia. **Telephone:** (2) 5441 5366. **Fax:** (2) 5464 7393. **Internet:** www. POVIEDKA.sk. **E-mail:** LCA@LCA.sk.

Literary Achievement Award

An award for poetry and essay writing presented by the Writers' Union of the Philippines.

Recent Winners: 1985: José Maria Sison.

Sponsoring Organization: Writers' Union of the Philippines.

Address: Writers' Union of the Philippines, Manila, Philippines.

Literaturpreis der Landeshauptstadt Stuttgart

Established in 1978 by the City of Stuttgart to promote and encourage authors from Baden-Württemberg. Awarded every two years, with a prize of €17,900, shared between an author and a translator. The winner is chosen by an expert jury.

Eligibility and Restrictions: Open to writers with a strong connection to Baden-Württemberg (e.g. place of birth or residence). Entries must be written in German.

How to Apply: There is no direct application; the jury selects entries.

Recent Winners: 2000: Peter O. Chotjewitz (writer), Nikolaus Stingl (translator); 1998: Hermann Kinder (writer), Hildegard Grosche (translator); 1996: Maria Beig (writer), Willi Zurbrüggen (translator); 1994: Albracht Goes and Reinhard Gröper (writers), Barbara Heninges (translator); 1992: Tina Stroheker and Rolf Vollmann (writers), Helga Pfetsch (translator).

Sponsoring Organization: City of Stuttgart.

Address: Landeshauptstadt Stuttgart, Kulturamt, Postfach 106034, Eichstr 9, 70173 Stuttgart, Germany. **Telephone:** (711) 216 63 32. **Fax:** (711) 216 76 28.

Literaturpreis der Stadt Solothurn

The Literaturpreis der Stadt Solothurn is awarded for outstanding literary achievements written in German, and is the only Swiss literary prize which can be won by non-Swiss German-speaking authors. The prize is sponsored by Solothurn City Council, and has been awarded annually since 1994. The winner receives a prize of SFr 20,000.

Recent Winners: 2001: Anna Mitgutsch; 2000: Christoph Hein; 1999: Birgit Vanderbeke; 1998: Thomas Hürlimann; 1997: Christoph Ransmayr.

Sponsoring Organization: Stadtrat von Solothurn.

Address: Literaturpreis der Stadt Solothurn, Stadtrat, 4509 Solothurn, Switzerland. **Internet:** www.kat.ch/bm/solo6.htm.

Little Booker Prize

The Little Booker Prize was founded in 1992, at the same time as the Booker Russian Novel Prize (now the Booker/Open Russia Prize, qv). The categories for entry change each year. The prize aims to spotlight and encourage the most interesting and culturally relevant phenomena in Russian literature. The Little Booker prize money has always been one-half of the main Booker Prize. In 2000 the two prizes, formerly jointly administered, were separated.

Eligibility and Restrictions: Categories for entry change each year; for 2001 the prize was awarded to the best translation from English of a work of literary fiction. Entries must have been published in the last three years, although unpublished manuscripts will also be considered.

Recent Winners: 2000: URIATIN Foundation for the Advancement of Culture, Perm; 1999: Vladimir Bibikhin, *The New Renaissance*; 1998: Emma Gerstein, *Memoirs* and Mikhail Bezrodny, *End of Quote* (joint winners); 1997: Mikhail Gasparov, *Collected Essays* and Alexander Goldstein, *Farewell to Narcissus* (joint winners); 1996: Sergei Gandlevsky, *Opening the Scull*.

Sponsoring Organization: British Council/EXPOPARK.

Contact: coordinator: Natasha Perova.

Address: Expopark, Krymsky Val, 10, Moscow, Russia. **Telephone:** (95) 441 9157. **Fax:** (95) 441 9157. **E-mail:** perova@glas.msk.su.

Littleton-Griswold Prize

Originally created by Mrs Alice Griswold in honour of her father, William E. Littleton, and her husband, Frank T. Griswold, for research in American history and law, to fund a monograph series publication, the prize was changed in 1985, becoming instead a prize for the best book in any subject on the history of American law and society.

Recent Winners: 2001: Karl Jacoby, *Crimes Against Nature: Squatters, Poachers, Thieves, and the Hidden History of American Conservation*.

Sponsoring Organization: American Historical Association.

Contact: Lynn Hunt.

Address: American Historical Asscn, 400 A St, SE, Washington, DC 20003–3889, USA. **Telephone:** (202) 544-2422. **Fax:** (202) 544-8307. **Internet:** www. theaha.org/prizes. **E-mail:** press@theaha.org.

Elsie Locke Award

Known until 2002 as the Young People's Non-fiction Award, this was established in 1986 to recognize each year's most distinguished contribution to non-fiction for young people. The awards consists of an inscribed medal and a sum of money which is decided each year by the Library and Information Association of New Zealand Aotearoa (LIANZA) Council. LIANZA suspended its awards from 1999–2000 but reinstituted them in 2001.

Eligibility and Restrictions: Open to works of non-fiction for children, which have been published in the preceding year and written by a citizen or resident of New Zealand. Books must be an original work and longer than 14 pages. They must be still in print and available for public purchase. Reprints or new editions are not eligible.

How to Apply: Publishers may send in nominations, and are requested to provide three copies of each entry.

Recent Winners: 2001: Brian Parkinson, *The tuatara*; 1998: Andrew Crowe, *The Life-Size Guide to Native Trees and Other Common Plants in New Zealand's Native Forest*; 1997: Diane Noonan and Nic Bishop, *I Spy Wildlife: the Field*; 1996: Laura Ranger, *Laura's Poems*; 1995: Barbara Cairns and Helen Martin, *Shadows on the Wall*; 1994: Robyn Kahukiwa, *Paikea*.

Sponsoring Organization: Library and Information Association of New Zealand Aotearoa (LIANZA).

Contact: Office Man Steve Williams.

Address: LIANZA, POB 12–212, Wellington, 6001, New Zealand. **Telephone:** (4) 4735834. **Fax:** (4) 4991480. **Internet:** www.lianza.org.uk. **E-mail:** office@ lianza.org.nz.

London Writers Competition

A competition established in 1977 for writers in London. Awards are made annually in four categories: poetry, short story, play and children's (introduced in 2002). Each section has a first prize of £600, second prize of £250 and third prize of £100, with two runners-up receiving £25. Winners are published in a winner's booklet, and the winning play is given a public performance. A separate Promise prize is also awarded in each category.

Eligibility and Restrictions: Open to writers who live, work or study in the Greater London area. All entries must be in English, and must be original unpublished works.

How to Apply: Entry form can be downloaded from website; closing date is late June. Entries must be accompanied by an entry fee (between £3 and £6 per item in 2002). Author's name must not appear on manuscript.

Recent Winners: Play: 2001: Jon Osbaldeston, *Hard as Nails*
Short Story: 2001: Tanuja Desai Hidier, *The Border*
Poetry: 2001: Helen Clare, *Tired*.

Sponsoring Organization: Wandsworth Council/Roehampton University of Surrey/Waterstone's.

Address: Arts Office, Room 224A, Wandsworth Town Hall, High Street, London SW18 2PU, UK. **Telephone:** (20) 8871 7380. **Internet:** www.wandsworth.gov.uk.

Naomi Long Madgett Poetry Award

Created in 1993 by Lotus Press to recognize African American poets of high literary merit. The award is judged by two or three established poets. The winner receives $500 in cash, along with publication of their manuscript.

Eligibility and Restrictions: Poets must be African American and must not have had a collection of work previously published by Lotus Press. Collections entered should be approximately 60 to 80 pages in length, and must not include the name of the author on any of the pages.

How to Apply: Send three complete copies of the manuscript, with separate author details, between 1 April and 1 June. Entries should be accompanied by a signed statement confirming that all the poems are original and that the author is African American.

Recent Winners: 2001: Peggy Ann Tartt, *Among Bones*; 2000: James R. Whitley, *Immersion*; 1999: Jerry Wemple, *You Can See It From Here*; 1998: Ruth Ellen Kocher, *Desdemona's Fire*; 1997: Claude Wilkinson, *Reading the Earth*.

Sponsoring Organization: Lotus Press Inc.

Contact: Asst Ed. Constance Withers.

Address: Lotus Press Inc, POB 21607, Detroit, MI 48221, USA. **Telephone:** (313) 861-1280. **Fax:** (313) 861-4740. **E-mail:** lotuspress@aol.com.

Longman–History Today Book of the Year Award

Administered by *History Today* and awarded to an author's first or second non-fiction book on an historical subject written in English.

Recent Winners: 2002: Peter Biller, *Measure of Multitude – Population in Medieval Thought* and Jonathan Rose, *Intellectual Life of the British Working Classes* (joint winners); 2001: David Armitage, *Ideological Origins of the British*

Empire; 2000: Alexandra Walsham, *Providence in Early Modern England*; 1999: Amanda Vickery, *Gentleman's Daughter – Women's Lives in Georgian England*; 1998: Andrew Gordon, *Rules of the Game – Jutland and British Naval Command*.

Sponsoring Organization: History Today.

Address: History Today, 20 Old Compton St, London W1V 5PE, UK.

Lontar Literary Award

A new award established by the Lontar Foundation, which aims to promote Indonesia through its literature and culture. It inaugurated its award in 2001 by selecting works in the genres of poetry and short stories; each of the winning authors received Rp 5 million.

Recent Winners: 2001: Joko Pinurbo, *Celana* and Gustaf Sakai, *Kemilau Cahaya dan Perempuan Buta (The Dazzle of Light and the Blind Woman)*.

Sponsoring Organization: Lontar Foundation.

Address: Lontar Foundation, Jl. Danau Laut Tawar No. 53, Pejompongan, Jakarta, 10210, Indonesia. **Telephone:** (21) 574 6880. **Fax:** (21) 572 0353. **Internet:** www.lontar.org.

Los Angeles Times Book Prizes

The *Los Angeles Times* has awarded a set of book prizes annually since 1980. There are nine single-title categories: biography, current interest, fiction, first fiction (the Art Seidenbaum Award, named after the founder of the Book Prize programme), history, mystery/thriller, poetry, science and technology, and young-adult fiction. In addition, the Robert Kirsch Award (named after a novelist and editor who was book critic for the *Los Angeles Times*) recognizes the body of work by a writer living in and/or writing on the American West. The authors of each winning book and the Kirsch Award recipient each receive a citation and $1,000.

Eligibility and Restrictions: Entries must have been first published in English in the USA between January and December of the previous year. Translations are eligible and authors may be of any nationality. They should be alive at the time of their book's qualifying publication in the USA, although eligibility is also extended to significant new translations of the work of deceased writers.

Recent Winners: Biography: 2001: Edmund Morris, *Theodore Rex*; 2000: William J. Cooper, Jr, *Jefferson Davis, American*
Current Interest: 2001: Barbara Ehrenreich, *Nickel and Dimed*; 2000: Frances FitzGerald, *Way Out There in the Blue: Reagan, Star Wars and the End of the Cold War*
Fiction: 2001: Mary Robison, *Why Did I Ever?*; 2000: David Means, *Assorted Fire Events*
History: 2001: Rick Perlstein, *Before the Storm*; 2000: Alice Kaplan, *The Collaborator: The Trial and Execution of Robert Brasillach*
Mystery/Thriller: 2001: T. Jefferson Parker, *Silent Joe*; 2000: Val McDermid, *A Place of Execution: A Novel*
Poetry: 2001: Anne Carson, *The Beauty of the Husband*; 2000: Gjertrud Schnackenberg, *The Throne of Labdacus*
Science and Technology: 2001: Richard Hamblyn, *The Invention of Clouds*; 2000: James Le Fanu, *The Rise and Fall of Modern Medicine*
Young Adult Fiction: 2001: Mildred D. Taylor, *The Land*; 2000: Jacqueline Woodson, *Miracle's Boys*

Art Seidenbaum Award for First Fiction: 2001: Rachel Seiffert, *The Dark Room*; 2000: Pankaj Mishra, *The Romantics*
Robert Kirsch Award: 2001: Tillie Olsen; 2000: Lawrence Ferlinghetti.
Sponsoring Organization: Los Angeles Times.
Address: Los Angeles Times, Times Mirror Square, Los Angeles, CA 90053, USA.

Lu Xun Literature Awards

The Lu Xun Literature Awards represent the leading multi-category honours of their kind in China. Named after a pioneer of modern Chinese literature, Lu Xun, a short-story writer, essayist, critic, and literary theorist (1881–1936), the awards are sponsored by the Chinese Writers' Association, and aim to promote the creation of contemporary literature. They were first awarded in 1995–96. The winners are selected by an appraisal committee made up of eminent writers, theorists, critics and editors.

Eligibility and Restrictions: The awards include seven single categories selected every two years, and a major prize every four years. The awards for 1995–96 were presented to more than 60 works, while in 2001 more than 35 works were honoured. Categories include short story, novelette and translated work.

Recent Winners: Short story: 1996: *Old House in My Memory* and five others
Novelette: 1996: *Father is a Soldier* and nine other titles
Rainbow Prize for Translated Works: 1996: five works, led by *Selected Lyrics of Wordsworth*. Other award-winning pieces in each category are: 15 reportage works, including *Fall in Love in Jinzhou*; eight poetry collections including *Life Is a Blade of Leaf*; *Selected Essays of He Wei* and 14 others; and five articles on theoretical criticism, including *To Know Lao She*.

Sponsoring Organization: Chinese Writers' Association.
Address: Chinese Writers' Association, Dongtuchenglu 25 Hao, Beijing, China.

Lukas Prize Project

The Lukas Prize Project, established in memory of the Pulitzer Prize winner of that name, was founded in 1998 to honour the best in American non-fiction writing. The award is jointly administered by the Graduate School of Journalism at Columbia University and the Nieman Foundation at Harvard University. The award is in two parts: the J. Anthony Lukas Prize is given annually to a book-length work of narrative non-fiction on an American topic in recognition of its literary grace, commitment to serious research, and social concern. The winner receives $10,000. A parallel J. Anthony Lukas Work-in-Progress Award, to the amount of $45,000, is also given annually to aid in the completion of a significant work of non-fiction.

Eligibility and Restrictions: For the J. Anthony Lukas Prize books must have been published during the preceding year. For the work-in-progress award, applicants must already have a contract with a publisher to write a nonfiction book.

How to Apply: Anyone, including the author, may submit a book. Entry forms are available from the e-mail address given; submissions should be accompanied by four copies of the book (or, for the work-in-progress award, a copy of their original book proposal, a sample chapter from the book and evidence of a contract with a publisher), plus an entry fee of $50.

Recent Winners: J. Anthony Lukas Prize: 2002: Diane McWhorter, *Carry Me Home: Birmingham, Alabama, The Climactic Battle of the Civil Rights Revolution*; 2000: Witold Rybczynski, *A Clearing in the Distance: Frederick Law Olmsted and America in the Nineteenth Century*
J. Anthony Lukas Work-in-Progress Award: 2002: Jacques Leslie, *On Dams.*

Sponsoring Organization: Columbia University Graduate School of Journalism/Nieman Foundation.

Contact: Caroline Ladhani.

Address: Columbia University Graduate School of Journalism, 2950 Broadway, MC 3800, New York, NY 10027, USA. **Telephone:** (212) 854-8653. **Internet:** www.jrn.columbia.edu/prizes/lukas/2002/index.asp. **E-mail:** CL2059@columbia.edu.

Mark Lynton History Prize

The Mark Lynton History Prize is awarded every year to the book-length work of history, on any subject, that best combines intellectual or scholarly distinction with an excellent written style. The winner receives $10,000.

How to Apply: Anyone, including the author, may submit a book. Entry forms are available from the e-mail address given; submissions should be accompanied by four copies of the book plus an entry fee of $50.

Recent Winners: 2002: Mark Roseman, *A Past in Hiding: Memory and Survival in Nazi Germany*; 2000: John W. Dower, *Embracing Defeat: Japan in the Wake of World War II.*

Sponsoring Organization: Columbia University Graduate School of Journalism.

Address: Columbia University Graduate School of Journalism, 2950 Broadway, MC 3800, New York, NY 10027, USA. **Telephone:** (212) 854-8653. **Internet:** www.jrn.columbia.edu/prizes/. **E-mail:** vh2009@columbia.edu.

Lyric Poetry Award

The Lyric Poetry Award of $500, which is administered by the Poetry Society of America (PSA), was established under the will of Mrs Consuelo Ford (Althea Urn), and also in memory of Mary Carolyn Davies, for a lyric poem on any subject.

Eligibility and Restrictions: Open to PSA members only; poems should not exceed 50 lines.

How to Apply: Two copies of submissions should be sent accompanied by a cover sheet between 1 October and 21 December.

Recent Winners: 2002: Shira Dentz.

Sponsoring Organization: Poetry Society of America.

Address: Poetry Society of America, 15 Gramercy Park, New York, NY 10003, USA. **Telephone:** (212) 254-9628. **Internet:** www.poetrysociety.org.

M-Net Book Prize

The annual M-Net Book Prize for adult fiction was established in 1991 by Electronic Media Network, a commercial television station. The aim of the award is to encourage the writing of quality novels which could also be adapted for the screen. Prizes of R50,000 are presented to a winning novel in each of four language categories: English, Afrikaans, Nguni and Sotho.

Recent Winners: 2001: Etienne van Heerden, *Die swye van Mario Salvati* and Zoë Wicomb, *David's Story*; 1995: D. Hofmeyr, *Boikie, You Better Believe It*; 1992: T. Spencer-Smith, *The Man who Snarled at Flowers: A Fantasy for Children*; 1991: L. Beake, *A Cageful of Butterflies.*

Sponsoring Organization: Electronic Media Network.

Address: Electronic Media Network, Pretoria, South Africa.

Macallan/Scotland on Sunday Story Competition

An annual prize for a short story which has become one of Scotland's best known awards. The winner, selected by a jury of literary figures, receives £6,000, with runners-up prizes of £2,000 and £500 each; the best 20 stories are published in a collection supported by the Scottish Arts Council.

Eligibility and Restrictions: Open to short stories of less than 3,000 words written by authors born in Scotland, now living in Scotland or by Scots living abroad.

Recent Winners: 2000: Janette Munneke, *Christmas at Waipanoni Falls* and David Strachan, *Distances*; 1999: Michael Mail.

Sponsoring Organization: Scotland on Sunday.

Address: The Administrator, The Macallan/Scotland on Sunday Short Story Competition, 108 Holyrood Rd, Edinburgh EH8 8AS, UK. **Internet:** www. themacallan.com.

Bryan MacMahon Short Story Award

An annual award founded in 1971 and offered for the best short story on any subject. The winner receives a prize of €2,000. The prize forms part of the annual Listowel Writers Week literary festival.

Eligibility and Restrictions: Entries must not have been published before in any form; no indication of the author's identity should appear on the entry. Works may be in English or Irish. Entries should be up to 3,000 words in length.

How to Apply: Send entry fee of €6.50 with each entry submitted. Closing date is 1 March.

Sponsoring Organization: Ireland Funds.

Address: Writers Week, 24 The Square, Listowel, Co. Kerry, Ireland. **Telephone:** (68) 21074. **Fax:** (68) 22893. **Internet:** www.writersweek.ie. **E-mail:** writersweek@eircom.net.

Macmillan PEN Awards

A set of annual awards including the Macmillan Silver PEN for an outstanding collection of short stories (prize of £500 and a Dupont pen), the Stern Silver PEN for non-fiction (£1,000 plus sterling silver pen), the Macmillan Prize for short stories and the S. T. Dupont Gold PEN for a lifetime's literary achievement. The winners are chosen from nominations made by the Vice-Presidents and members of the PEN Executive Committee only.

Eligibility and Restrictions: Books must have been written in the English language by a living author of British nationality or long-term residence.

How to Apply: Entry is by nomination only.

Recent Winners: Stern Silver PEN Prize: 2001: Michela Wrong, *In the Footsteps of Mr Kurtz*; 1999: John Bayley, *Iris*
Macmillan Prize for Short Stories: 2001: William Trevor, *The Hill Bachelors; 1999: Peter Ho Davies, The Ugliest House in the World*
S. T. Dupont Gold PEN for a Lifetime's Literary Achievement: 1999: Penelope Fitzgerald.

Address: English Centre of International PEN, 152–156 Kentish Town Rd, London NW1 9QB, UK. **Telephone:** (20) 7267 9444. **Fax:** (20) 7267 9304. **Internet:** www.pen.org.uk. **E-mail:** enquiries@pen.org.uk.

Macmillan Prize for Children's Picture Book Illustration

This annual prize was established in 1986 to stimulate new work from young illustrators in art schools and help them start on a professional career. The award is judged in April/May by a panel of editors, art directors and children's book illustrators. The first prize is £1,000, with runners-up prizes of £500 and £250, and Macmillan Children's Books has the option to publish any of the prizewinners.

Eligibility and Restrictions: Entries should be illustrations for a children's colour picture book; open to art students in higher education establishments in the UK during the current academic year.

How to Apply: Entrants must submit pencil roughs or sketches and at least four double-page spreads, or three spreads and a front cover, of finished artwork, with a completed application form.

Recent Winners: 2001: Matthew Gould; 2000: Georgina Ripper; 1999: Candice Whatmore; 1998: Katherine Redfern; 1997: Angela Simpkin.

Sponsoring Organization: Macmillan Children's Books.

Contact: Marketing Dept.

Address: Macmillan Children's Books, 20 New Wharf Rd, London N1 9RR, UK. **Telephone:** (20) 7014 6000. **Fax:** (20) 7014 6001. **Internet:** www.panmacmillan.com.

Macmillan Writer's Prize for Africa

Established in January 2001 by Macmillan Publishers to encourage and promote African writing, this is a prize for unpublished work, and is split into several categories: Children's Literature Award: Junior: for an unpublished story in English for children between 8 and 12; the prize is of US$5,000; Senior: for an unpublished story in English for children between 13 and 17; the prize is of US$5,000. Adult Fiction Award: for a partial manuscript of an unpublished, original work of fiction; prize value is US$5,000. Special Award for Most Promising New Children's Writer, in either Junior or Senior category, with a prize of US$3,000. The prize is offered every two years; winners are chosen by a panel of judges.

Eligibility and Restrictions: Open to nationals or naturalized citizens of countries throughout Africa and writers born in those countries. Entries must be in English and be original and unpublished. Manuscripts must have a strong African content. Works submitted under pseudonym are not accepted. Conditions for the various categories are: Children's Literature Award, Junior: for entries up to 8,000 words. Senior: for entries between 14,000 and 18,000 words. Adult Fiction Award: maximum 5,000 words for a partial manuscript of a work either completed or in progress; short stories are excluded.

How to Apply: Contact the administrator for an entry form. Entrants should submit one copy to any Macmillan office in Africa or to Macmillan in Oxford at the address given. Closing dates are 30 June (children's categories), 30 Nov (adult category).

Recent Winners: Junior: 2001–02: Rosina Umelo (Nigeria), *Who Are You?*
Senior: 2001–02: Osman Conteh (Sierra Leone), *Unanswered Cries*
Adult: 2001–02: Yvonne Vera (Zimbabwe), *The Stone Virgins*
Special Award: 2001–02: Susan Mugizi Kajura (Uganda), *Daudi's Dream.*

Sponsoring Organization: Macmillan Education and Picador.

Address: Macmillan Oxford, Between Towns Rd, Oxford OX4 3PP, UK. **Telephone:** (1865) 405700. **Fax:** (1865) 405701. **Internet:** www.write4africa. com. **E-mail:** writersprize@macmillan.co.uk.

Mary McCarthy Prize in Short Fiction

The Mary McCarthy Prize in Short Fiction includes a $2,000 cash award, publication of a collection of short stories, novellas, or a short novel, and a standard royalty contract.

Eligibility and Restrictions: Open to any writer of English who is a citizen of the USA. Entries may be in the form of a collection of short stories, one or more novellas, or a short novel. Manuscripts must be between 150 and 250 pages. Works that have previously appeared in magazines or in anthologies may be included. Translations and previously self-published collections are excluded.

How to Apply: One copy of the manuscript should be submitted accompanied by entry form and entry fee of $20. Author's name or address should not appear anywhere on the manuscript.

Sponsoring Organization: Sarabande Books.

Address: Sarabande Books, 2234 Dundee Rd, Suite 200, Louisville, KY 40205, USA. **Telephone:** (502) 458-4028. **Fax:** (502) 458-4065.

McKitterick Prize

Annual award for a full-length work written in English and first published in the UK or previously unpublished. The winner receives £4,000.

Eligibility and Restrictions: Open to writers over 40 years old, who have had no previous work published other than that submitted.

Recent Winners: 2002: Manil Suri, *The Death of Vishnu*; 2001: Giles Waterfield, *The Long Afternoon*; 2000: Chris Dolan, *Ascension Day.*

Sponsoring Organization: Society of Authors.

Address: Society of Authors, 84 Drayton Gdns, London SW10 9SB, UK. **Telephone:** (20) 7373 6642. **Fax:** (20) 7373 5768. **Internet:** www. societyofauthors.org. **E-mail:** info@societyofauthors.org.

Enid McLeod Literary Prize

This prize, established in 1982, is awarded to a book that, in the judges' opinion, contributes the most to Franco-British understanding. There is a cash prize of £250.

Eligibility and Restrictions: Entries must be full-length works by a UK citizen, written in the English language. They must also be first published in the UK during the calendar year preceding the year in which the award is presented.

How to Apply: The winner is chosen from entries submitted by publishers and authors.

Recent Winners: 2001: Antonia Fraser, *Marie Antoinette*; 2000: Grahm Robb, *Rimbaud*; 1999: Ian Dunlop, *Louis XIV*; 1998: Hugo Young, *This Blessed Plot*; 1997: Jan Ousby, *Occupation – The Ordeal of France*.

Sponsoring Organization: Franco-British Society.

Address: Franco-British Society, Linen Hall, Rm 623, 162–168 Regent St, London W1R 5TB, UK. **Telephone:** (20) 7734 0815. **Fax:** (20) 7734 0815.

Mads Wiel Nygaards Legat (Mads Wiel Nygaards Foundation)

An annual prize of 50,000 NOK for a Norwegian author in the field of adult fiction, sponsored by the publisher Aschehoug.

Recent Winners: 2001: Odd W. Surén; 2000: Håvard Syvertsen; 1999: Toril Brekke; 1998: Unni Lindell; 1997: Torild Wardenær.

Sponsoring Organization: H. Aschehoug & Co.

Address: H. Aschehoug & Co, PB 363, Sentrum, 0102 Oslo, Norway. **Telephone:** (22) 400 400. **Internet:** www.aschehoug.no.

Magnesia Litera Awards

A series of new book awards for the best works of literature, with several categories including Book of the Year award. The awards were established by a group of enthusiasts who thought Czech literature deserved a wider-ranging approach, and were presented for the first time in 2002. Winners were selected by a 25-member committee, drawn from members of the Czech Translators' Guild, the Czech PEN Club, the Union of Czech Authors and the Czech Academy of Sciences as well as booksellers and librarians. Awards are presented in eight categories (best work of fiction, poetry, best translation, best non-fiction, best debut, most important event in publishing, contribution to Czech literature, and a special category for the book of the year). For the first edition there were no cash prizes, but the organisers hope to attract sponsorship in order to establish a cash prize in future.

Recent Winners: Book of the Year: 2002: Jürgen Serke, *Böhmische Dörfer (Bohemian Villages)*
Most Important Event in Publishing: 2002: Jürgen Serke, *Böhmische Dörfer (Bohemian Villages)*
Best Work of Fiction: 2002: Milos Urban, *Hastrman (The Water Goblin)*
Best Debut: 2002: Hana Andronikova, *Zvuk slunečnich hodin (The Sound of the Sundial)*.

Sponsoring Organization: Czech Translators' Guild/Czech PEN Club/Union of Czech Authors/Czech Academy of Sciences.

Address: Prague, Czech Republic.

Ramon Magsaysay Award

The Ramon Magsaysay Award Foundation sponsors this set of awards, which are often regarded as the Nobel Prizes of Asia. The Magsaysay awards are named in honour of the late Philippines president, Ramon Magsaysay, who died in a plane crash in 1957. The awards are presented in five categories: government service, public service, community leadership, international understanding, and journalism, literature, and creative communication arts. Up to five awards of $50,000 each are given annually.

Recent Winners: Journalism, Literature and Creative Communication Arts: 2002: Bharat Dutta Koirala (Nepal); 2001: K. W. D. Amaradeva.

Sponsoring Organization: Ramon Magsaysay Award Foundation.

Address: Ramon Magsaysay Award Foundation, Ramon Magsaysay Center, PO Box 3350, 1680 Roxas Boulevard, Manila, Philippines. **Telephone:** (2) 521-3166. **Fax:** (2) 521-8105. **Internet:** www.rmaf.org.ph. **E-mail:** rmaf@carmaf.org.ph.

Mail on Sunday/John Llewellyn Rhys Prize

This prize, administered by the Book Trust, was founded in 1942 by Jane Oliver in memory of her late husband John Llewellyn Rhys, a young writer who was killed in World War II. The winner receives £5,000, while runners-up get £500.

Eligibility and Restrictions: The prize is awarded annually for a book whose author is under 30 and is a citizen of Great Britain or the Commonwealth. Previous winners are not eligible.

How to Apply: Publishers are invited to submit entries.

Recent Winners: 2000: Edward Platt, *Leadville*; 1999: David Mitchell, *Ghostwritten*; 1998: Peter Ho Davies, *The Ugliest House in the World*; 1997: Phil Whitaker, *Eclipse of the Sun*; 1996: Nicola Barker, *Heading Inland*.

Sponsoring Organization: Book Trust.

Address: Book House, 45 East Hill, London SW18 2QZ, UK.

Andrei Malyshko Prize

Awarded for poetry published in the magazine *Dnipro*. The prize is administered by the National Writers Union of Ukraine (NSPU) and the editorial board of *Dnipro*.

Sponsoring Organization: National Writers Union of Ukraine (NSPU).

Contact: V. Yavorivsky.

Address: Blvd Bankova 2, 01024 Kiev, Ukraine. **Fax:** (44) 293-45-86. **Internet:** www.nspu.kiev.ua. **E-mail:** nspu@I.kiev.ua.

Man Booker Prize

This award, which is the best known British literary award, was established by Booker Brothers (now Booker Prize Foundation) as the Booker Prize in 1968. It is judged by literary critics, editors, writers and academics: the judging panel changes every year, and is selected by a Management Committee. The award, which was increased to £50,000 in 2002, is made to the judges' choice of the best novel of the year. Shortlisted writers receive £2,500 and a leather-bound copy of their novel. In 2002 a new five-year sponsorship deal was signed with Man Group, an alternative investment fund manager and broker, who announced plans to develop the prize under a new format, with the aim of raising its global profile. It was renamed the Man Booker Prize for Fiction. Possible changes include expanding the criteria and broadening the scope of the prize by opening it up to international writers.

Eligibility and Restrictions: Writers must be citizens of the Commonwealth or the Republic of Ireland; from 2004, however, the prize will be opened up to American writers. Only full-length novels written in English are considered. The prize may be awarded posthumously. Publishers must agree to spend certain amounts on publicity, should one of their publications reach the shortlist.

How to Apply: UK publishers may enter up to two novels per year; also any title by a former Booker Prize winner or shortlisted author (within the past 10 years) may be entered. Publishers may also submit a list of up to five further titles for consideration.

Recent Winners: 2001: Peter Carey, *True History of the Kelly Gang*; 2000: Margaret Atwood, *The Blind Assassin*; 1999: J. M. Coetzee, *Disgrace*; 1998: Ian McEwan, *Amsterdam*; 1997: Arundhati Roy, *The God of Small Things*.

Sponsoring Organization: Man Group.

Address: Book Trust, Book House, 45 East Hill, London SW18 2QZ, UK.

Manila Critics Circle National Book Awards

A set of prestigious awards presented annually by the Manila Critics Circle. Categories include fiction, poetry, drama, linguistics, essay, screenplay, children's book, anthology and literary crticism, as well as awards for editing and publisher of the year. The winners are announced during the annual Philippines book fair in September.

Eligibility and Restrictions: Books must be written, designed, and published in the Philippines.

Sponsoring Organization: Manila Critics Circle.

Address: Manila Critics Circle, Manila, Philippines.

Manitoba Literary Awards

A series of annual awards jointly sponsored by the Manitoba Writers' Guild and the Association of Manitoba Book Publishers. There are 10 separate categories: the McNally Robinson Book of the Year Award (prize of $3,000); the Eileen McTavish Sykes Award for Best First Book ($1,500); the Mary Scorer Award for Best Book by a Manitoba Publisher ($1,000); Le Prix littéraire Rue-Deschambault ($3,500); Manitoba Historical Society Margaret McWilliams Awards (with four sub-categories); the McNally Robinson Book for Young People Award (two prizes, each of $1,500); the Carol Shields Winnipeg Book Award ($5,000); the John Hirsch Award for Most Promising Manitoba Writer ($2,500); the Alexander Kennedy Isbister Award for Non-Fiction ($3,500); and the Margaret Laurence Award for Fiction ($3,500).

Eligibility and Restrictions: Entries must have been published during the previous year (with the exception of the John Hirsch Award for Most Promising Writer and the Prix littéraire Rue-Deschambault).

How to Apply: Deadlines and submission fees vary for each award. See website for entry form and full details.

Recent Winners: McNally Robinson Book of the Year: 2001: Miriam Toews, *Swing Low: A Life*
Eileen McTavish Sykes Award: 2001: Heather Frayne, *Last Night's Dream*
Mary Scorer Award: 2001: Jake MacDonald (Editor), *The Lake: An Illustrated History of Manitobans' Cottage Country*

Prix littéraire Rue-Deschambault: 2001: Jean-Pierre Dubé, *Ma cousine Germaine*
McNally Robinson Book for Young People Award: 2001: Young Adult: Linda
Holeman, *Raspberry House Blues*; Children: (no winner in 2001)
Carol Shields Winnipeg Book Award: 2001: Caelum Vatnsdal, *Kino Delerium: the
films of Guy Maddin*
John Hirsch Award: 2001: Alissa York
Alexander Kennedy Isbister Award: 2001: Miriam Toews, *Swing Low: A Life*
Margaret Laurence Award: 2001: Wayne Tefs, *Moon Lake*.

Sponsoring Organization: Manitoba Writers' Guild/Association of Manitoba
Book Publishers.

Address: Manitoba Writers' Guild, 206–100 Arthur St, Winnipeg, MB R3B 1H3,
Canada. **Telephone:** (204) 942-6134. **Fax:** (204) 942-5754. **Internet:** www.
mbwriter.mb.ca/mwapa.html. **E-mail:** mbwriter@escape.ca.

Thomas-Mann-Preis

A prize established by the city of Lübeck in 1975 in memory of the great German
writer Thomas Mann. It is awarded every three years for a complete body of work.
The winner receives €10,000.

Recent Winners: 2002: Hanns-Josef Ortheil.

Sponsoring Organization: City of Lübeck.

Address: Hansestadt Lübeck, Bereich Kunst und Kultur, Schildstr 12, 23539
Lübeck, Germany.

Mao Dun Literary Prize

One of China's best-known literary awards, presented every four years by the
Chinese Writers' Association for outstanding new full-length novels.

Recent Winners: 2000: Zhang Ping, *Jueze (Choose)*, Ah Lai, *Chen'ai Luo Ding
(The End)*, Wang Anyi, *Chang Hen Ge (The Ode of Endless Hatred)*, Charen
Sanbuqu (A Trilogy on Charen)*; 1994: Chen Zhongshi, *Bailu yuan (The White Deer
Plain)*; 1990: Alai, *Red Poppies*.

Sponsoring Organization: Chinese Writers' Association.

Address: Chinese Writers' Association, Dongtuchenglu 25 Hao, Beijing, China.

Eugène Maraisprys (Eugene Marais Prize)

The prize was established in 1961 and is named after a well-known South African
writer. It recognizes a first (or second) work by a promising new writer. The
winner receives a prize of R10,000.

How to Apply: Only open to works published in the preceding calendar year.

Recent Winners: 2002: Dine van Zyl, *Slagoffers*; 2001: Tom Dreyer,
Stinkafrikaaner; A. H. M. Scholtz, *A Place Called Vatmaar*.

Sponsoring Organization: Suid-Afrikaanse Akademie vir Wetenskap en Kuns
(South African Academy for Science and Arts).

Address: Die Suid-Afrikaanse Akademie vir Wetenskap en Kuns (South African
Academy for Science and Arts), PO Box 538, Pretoria, 0001, South Africa.
Telephone: (12) 328 5082. **Fax:** (12) 328 5091. **Internet:** www.akademie.co.za.
E-mail: akademie@mweb.co.za.

Howard R. Marraro Prize

A biennial prize awarded for an outstanding scholarly work on any phase of Italian literature or comparative literature involving Italian. The prize is awarded each even-numbered year, and consists of $1,000 from the Howard R. Marraro Endowment Fund and a certificate. From 1996–2000, the Howard R. Marraro Prize was awarded jointly with the Aldo and Jeanne Scaglione Prize for Italian Literary Studies, which is now awarded separately in odd-numbered years.

Eligibility and Restrictions: Books or articles published during the preceding two calendar years are eligible; authors must be members of the Modern Language Association of America (MLA).

How to Apply: Authors or publishers should send four copies by 1 May in even-numbered years.

Recent Winners: 1998–99: Margaret Brose, *Leopardi Sublime* and Nancy L. Canepa, *From Court to Forest: Giambattista Basile's Lo cunto de li cunti and the Birth of the Literary Fairy Tale*; 1996–97: Barbara Spackman, *Fascist Virilities: Rhetoric, Ideology, and Social Fantasy in Italy*; 1994–95: Robert S. Dombroski, *Properties of Writing: Ideological Discourse in Modern Italian Fiction* and Karen Pinkus, *Bodily Regimes: Italian Advertising under Fascism* (joint winners); 1992–93: Margaret F. Rosenthal, *The Honest Courtesan: Veronica Franco, Citizen and Writer in Sixteenth-Century Venice*.

Sponsoring Organization: Modern Language Association of America (MLA).

Contact: Co-ordinator of Book Prizes and Special Projects.

Address: Modern Language Asscn of America, 26 Broadway, 3rd Floor, New York, NY 10004–1789, USA. **Telephone:** (646) 576-5141. **Fax:** (646) 458-0033. **Internet:** www.mla.org. **E-mail:** awards@mla.org.

Howard R. Marraro Prize in Italian History

Established in 1973, to honour two historians of Italian culture, the Marraro Prize is offered annually for the best work in any epoch of Italian history, Italian cultural history, or Italian-American relations.

Eligibility and Restrictions: All submissions must be the work of resident citizens of the USA or Canada.

Recent Winners: 2001: Ronald G. Witt, *In the Footsteps of the Ancients: The Origins of Italian Humanism from Lovato to Bruni*; 2000: Anthony Grafton, *Cardano's Cosmos: The Worlds and Works of a Renaissance Astrologer*; 1999: Samuel L. Baily, *Immigrants in the Lands of Promise: Italians in Buenos Aires and New York City 1870–1914*.

Sponsoring Organization: American Historical Association.

Contact: Lynn Hunt.

Address: American Historical Asscn, 400 A St, SE, Washington, DC 20003–3889, USA. **Telephone:** (202) 544-2422. **Fax:** (202) 544-8307. **Internet:** www. theaha.org/prizes. **E-mail:** press@theaha.org.

Marsh Award for Children's Literature in Translation

The Marsh Award was established in 1996 to promote the translation into English and publication in the UK of children's books in translation. The award was founded by the National Centre for Research into Children's Literature (NRCL) and the Marsh Christian Trust. It is presented biennially, and the prize of £750 goes to the translator.

Eligibility and Restrictions: Books should have appeared in the two-year period preceding the award, and should be produced for children between 4 and 16 years of age. The translation must be from the original language; translations previously published in the USA or Australia are not eligible.

How to Apply: Submissions are accepted from publishers, who should send four copies of the translated work and one copy of the original by the end of June in the award year.

Recent Winners: 2000: David Gressman, *The Duel* (translated by Betsy Rosenberg); 1998: Gudrun Pausenrang, *The Final Journey* (translated by Patricia Crampton); 1996: Christine Nöstlinger, *A Dog's Life* (translated by Anthea Bell).

Sponsoring Organization: National Centre for Research into Children's Literature/Marsh Christian Trust.

Contact: Deputy Dir Dr Gillian Lathey.

Address: National Centre for Research into Children's Literature, Digby Stuart College, University of Surrey Roehampton, Roehampton Lane, London SW15 5PU, UK. **Telephone:** (20) 8392 3008. **Fax:** (20) 8392 3819. **E-mail:** nrcl@ roehampton.ac.uk.

Marsh Biography Award

Formerly known as the Marsh Christian Trust Award, this biennial award is presented for a significant new work of biography. The winner receives £3,500 and a silver trophy.

Eligibility and Restrictions: Open to works in the field of biography by a British author, published in the UK in the two preceding years.

How to Apply: Nominations are submitted by publishers.

Address: Authors' Club, 40 Dover St, London W1X 3RB, UK.

Lenore Marshall Poetry Prize

An annual award of $10,000 for the most outstanding book of poetry published in the USA in the previous year. The prize was established following an endowment from the New Hope Foundation in 1975 and is now administered by The Academy of American Poets in conjunction with *The Nation* magazine. The prize is named in honour of Lenore Marshall (1897–1971), a poet, novelist, essayist, and political activist.

How to Apply: Publishers are invited to submit books.

Recent Winners: 2001; Fanny Howe, *Selected Poems*; 2000: David Ferry, *Of No Country I Know: New and Selected Poems and Translations*; 1999: Wanda Coleman, *Bathwater Wine*; 1998: Mark Jarman, *Questions for Ecclesiastes*.

Sponsoring Organization: Academy of American Poets/The Nation.

Address: Academy of American Poets, 584 Broadway, Suite 1208, New York, NY 10012, USA. **Telephone:** (212) 274-0343. **Fax:** (212) 274-9427. **Internet:** www. poets.org/academy. **E-mail:** academy@poets.org.

Marten Toonder Award

An annual award of €10,000 which alternates between literature, music and visual arts.

How to Apply: There is no direct application; nominations are drawn up by the Arts Council.

Recent Winners: 2001: John F. Dean (writer and poet).

Sponsoring Organization: Arts Council/ An Chomhairle Ealaion.

Address: The Arts Council, 70 Merrion Square, Dublin, 2, Ireland. **Telephone:** (1) 618 0200. **Fax:** (1) 676 1302. **Internet:** www.artscouncil.ie. **E-mail:** info@artscouncil.ie.

Somerset Maugham Awards

Awarded to a writer on the strength of a published work. The prize of £12,000 is shared between two winners, and is designated to be used for foreign travel.

Eligibility and Restrictions: Writers must be aged under 35.

Recent Winners: 2002: Charlotte Hobson, *Black Earth City* and Marcel Theroux, *The Paperchase*; 2001: Edward Platt, *Leadville* and Ben Rice, *Pobby and Dingan*; 2000: Bella Bathurst, *The Lighthouse Stevensons* and Sarah Waters, *Affinity*.

Sponsoring Organization: Somerset Maugham Trust Fund/Society of Authors.

Address: Society of Authors, 84 Drayton Gdns, London SW10 9SB, UK. **Telephone:** (20) 7373 6642. **Fax:** (20) 7373 5768. **Internet:** www. societyofauthors.org. **E-mail:** info@societyofauthors.org.

Babai-e-Urdu Maulvi Abdul Haq Award

The Pakistan Academy of Letters administers a series of annual prizes established in 1980 under the Hijra National Literary Awards Scheme. The aim of the awards is to promote literary activities and recognize outstanding contributions. The Maulvi Abdul Haq Award is an annual award of Rs 50,000 for works of prose written in Urdu.

Recent Winners: 2000: Daud Rahbar, *Paraganda Tab'a Loag*; 1999: Zameer Ali Badayooni, *Jadeediat Aur Mabad-e-Jadeediat*; 1998: Daud Rahbar, *Culture Ke Ruhani Anaasir*.

Sponsoring Organization: Pakistan Academy of Letters.

Contact: Deputy Dir Naseem Mahmood.

Address: Pitras Bokhari Road, Sector H-8/1, Islamabad, Pakistan. **Telephone:** 9257164. **Fax:** 9257159. **E-mail:** academy@apollo.net.pk.

Lucille Medwick Memorial Award

The Lucille Medwick Memorial Award of $500, which is administered by the Poetry Society of America (PSA), was established by Maury Medwick in memory of his wife, the poet and editor. It is presented for an original poem in any form on a humanitarian theme.

Eligibility and Restrictions: Open to PSA members only; poems should not exceed 100 lines.

How to Apply: Two copies of submissions should be sent accompanied by a cover sheet between 1 October and 21 December.

Recent Winners: 2002: Minnie Bruce Pratt.

Sponsoring Organization: Poetry Society of America.

Address: Poetry Society of America, 15 Gramercy Park, New York, NY 10003, USA. **Telephone:** (212) 254-9628. **Internet:** www.poetrysociety.org.

Melsom-prisen (Melsom Prize)

An annual prize administered by the newspaper *Norske Samlaget*, established after a bequest in 1922 by Ferdinant Melsom. The prize was first awarded in 1924. It is presented to an author or translator.

Recent Winners: 2002: Brit Bildøen; 2001: Jon Fosse; 2000: Ingar Sletten Kolloen and Jan Inge Sørbø (joint winners); 1999: Johannes Gjerdåker; 1998: Marie Takvam.

Sponsoring Organization: Det Norske Samlaget.

Address: Det Norske Samlaget, Postboks 4672, Sofienberg, 0506 Oslo, Norway. **Telephone:** (22) 70 78 00. **Fax:** (22) 68 75 02. **Internet:** www.samlaget.no.

MER Prize

The MER Prize for youth literature was instituted in 1984. It is named after Maria Elizabeth (Mieme) Rothmann, a journalist and author who used her initials as her pen-name. The Nasionale Boekhandel Publishing Group (Tafelberg) sponsors the award, which recognizes the best children's book published in Afrikaans or English by members of the publishing group. The winner receives R5,000 and a gold medal.

Recent Winners: 2001: Dianne Hofmeyr, *The Waterbearer* and Jan Vermeulen, *Geraamtes dra nie klere nie*; 1996: J. Robeson, *One magic moment*; 1995: P. de Vos, *Moenie 'n miele kiele nie*; 1994: E. van der Merwe, *Koljander van die Karoo*.

Sponsoring Organization: Nasionale Boekhandel Publishing Group (Tafelberg).

Address: PO Box 879, 28 Wale St, Cape Town, 8000, South Africa. **Telephone:** (21) 424 1320. **Fax:** (21) 424 2510. **Internet:** www.tafelberg.com. **E-mail:** tafelbrg@tafelberg.com.

Johann-Heinrich-Merck-Preis für literarische Kritik und Essay (Johann-Heinrich-Merck Prize for Literary Criticism and Essays)

The prize was established in 1964 to encourage work in the genres of literary criticism and essays. It is named in honour of Johann Heinrich Merck (1741–1791), a renowned essayist. The award carries a prize of €12,500.

Recent Winners: 2002: Volker Klotz; 2001: Friedrich Dieckmann; 2000: Silvia Bovenschen; 1999: Gerhard R. Koch; 1998: Iso Camartin.

Sponsoring Organization: Deutsche Akademie für Sprache und Dichtung.

Address: Deutsche Akademie für Sprache und Dichtung, Alexandraweg 23, 64287 Darmstadt, Germany. **Telephone:** (6151) 40920. **Fax:** (6151) 409299. **Internet:** www.deutscheakademie.de.

Meyer-Whitworth Award

The Meyer-Whitworth Award is named after Carl Meyer, a wealthy philanthropist who inaugurated the appeal fund, and Geoffrey Whitworth, founder and director of the Shakespeare Memorial National Theatre Committee. The award, inaugurated in 1991, is supported by the Royal National Theatre Foundation and administered by the Arts Council of England, and aims to help further the careers of UK playwrights who are not yet established. The value of the award is up to £8,000.

Eligibility and Restrictions: Plays must be written in English and have been professionally produced in the UK for the first time in the previous calendar year (August–July). Candidates should have had no more than two of their plays professionally produced. No writer who has previously won the award may reapply, and no play that has previously been submitted is eligible. Translations are excluded.

How to Apply: Nominations are accepted from directors of professional theatre companies. Three copies of the script, accompanied by an application form, should be sent to the address given no later than 31 August.

Recent Winners: 2001: Ray Grewal, *My Dad's Corner Shop*; 2000: Kate Dean, *Down Red Lane*; 1999: David Harrower, *Kill the Old Torture Their Young*; 1998: Moira Buffini, *Gabriel* and Daragh Carville, *Language Roulette* (joint winners); 1997: Conor McPherson, *This Lime Tree Bower*.

Sponsoring Organization: Royal National Theatre Foundation/Arts Council of England.

Contact: Asst Drama Officer Jemima Lee.

Address: Drama Dept, Arts Council of England, 14 Great Peter St, London SW1P 3NQ, UK. **Telephone:** (20) 7973 6431. **Fax:** (20) 7973 6983. **Internet:** www.artscouncil.org.uk. **E-mail:** info.drama@artscouncil.org.uk.

James A. Michener Memorial Prize

The Michener Memorial Prize was initiated in October 1997, to run for a period of five years only; spring 2003 will be the final award. The winner is chosen by a panel of juges, and receives a prize of $10,000.

Eligibility and Restrictions: Open to first-time authors over the age of 40.

How to Apply: Entry is by nomination only; no direct applications are accepted.

Sponsoring Organization: Random House/Michener Center for Writers.

Address: Random House Inc, 1540 Broadway, New York, NY 10036, USA.

Kenneth W. Mildenberger Prize

First awarded in 1980, the prize is presented annually for an outstanding publication in the field of teaching foreign languages and literatures. It is awarded alternately to books (in even-numbered years) and articles (odd-numbered years). The winner is selected by a committee made up of members of the Modern Language Association of America (MLA), and receives $1,000 (for books) or $500 (for articles), a certificate and one-year membership of the MLA.

Eligibility and Restrictions: Entries must be published in the two years prior to the competition. Textbooks based on authors' original research are also eligible under certain circumstances.

How to Apply: Publishers or authors may apply. Four copies of the book should be submitted by 1 May.

Recent Winners: 2001: Hossein Nassaji and Gordon Wells, *What's the Use of Triadic Dialogue? An Investigation of Teacher-Student Interaction*; 1999: Guy Cook, *Language Play, Language Learning*; 1998: Richard Clément, Zoltán Dörnyei, Peter Macintyre, and Kimberly Noels, *Conceptualizing Willingness to Communicate in a L2: A Situational Model of L2 Confidence and Affiliation*; 1997: Peter Skehan, *A Cognitive Approach to Language Learning*; 1996: Lyle F. Bachman and Adrian S. Palmer, *Language Testing in Practice*.

Sponsoring Organization: Modern Language Association of America (MLA).

Contact: Co-ordinator of Book Prizes and Special Projects.

Address: Modern Language Asscn of America, 26 Broadway, 3rd Floor, New York, NY 10004–1789, USA. **Telephone:** (646) 576-5141. **Fax:** (646) 458-0033. **Internet:** www.mla.org. **E-mail:** awards@mla.org.

Ministry of Culture National Translation Prize

Four annual prizes of 25 million lire each, awarded for literary translation into and from Italian in both fiction and non-fiction, plus one for a foreign publisher of Italian works and one for an Italian publisher of foreign works. There is also a special prize of 5 million lire for special achievements in the field of cultural exchanges.

How to Apply: Biographical details and samples of the text should be submitted by 31 March.

Sponsoring Organization: Ministerio per i Beni Culturali e Ambientali.

Address: Ministerio per i Beni Culturali e Ambientali, Ufficio Centrale per i Beni Librari, per le Istituzioni Culturali e per l'Editoria, Via del Collegio Romano, 27, 100186 Rome, Italy.

Mishima Yukio Shô (Mishima Yukio Award)

Established in 1987 on the 20th anniversary of the founding of the Shinchô Society for the Promotion of the Literary Arts (Shinchô Bungei Shinkô Kai). One of the Four Shinchô Prizes (Shinchô yonshô); the others are the Yamamoto Shûgorô Award, the Shinchô Prize for Distinguished Scholarship, and the (non-literary) Grand Prize for Japanese Art; awarded annually to an outstanding work of fiction, criticism, poetry, or drama that is considered to have had a major impact on the literary world. The prize is 1 million yen plus a commemorative memorial.

Eligibility and Restrictions: Must be written in Japanese.

How to Apply: There is no public application.

Recent Winners: 2001: Shinji Aoyama , *Eureka* and Masaya Nakahara, *Arayuru basho ni hanataba ga... (Bouquets of Flowers Everywhere)* (joint winners); 2000: Tomoyuki Hoshino; 1999: Seigoh Suzuki and Toshiyaki Horie (joint winners); 1998: Kyoji Kobayashi; 1997: Satoru Higuchi.

Sponsoring Organization: Shinchô Society for the Promotion of the Literary Arts (Shinchô Bungei Shinkôkai).

Contact: Dir Masaharu Yokoyama.

Address: Shinchô Society for the Promotion of the Literary Arts (Shinchô Bungei Shinkô Kai), 71 Yarai-cho, Shinjuku, Tokyo, 162–8711, Japan. **Telephone:** (3) 3266 5411. **Fax:** (3) 3266 5534.

Kathleen Mitchell Award

A biennial award which aims to advance and improve Australian literature. The prize is of A$5,000.

Eligibility and Restrictions: Open to novels first published in the two calendar years preceding the award, by an author under 30 years of age at the time of publication. The author must be resident in Australia and be either Australian or British naturalized Australian.

How to Apply: Details available from Permanent Trustee Company Ltd.

Recent Winners: 2000: Julia Leigh, *The Hunter*; 1998: James Barclay, *Wrack*; 1996: Sonya Hartnett, *Sleeping Dogs*.

Sponsoring Organization: Permanent Trustee Company Ltd.

Contact: Linda Ingoldo.

Address: Permanent Trustee Company Ltd, 35 Clarence St, Sydney, NSW 2000, Australia. **Telephone:** (2) 8295 8100. **Fax:** (2) 8295 8659. **Internet:** www. permanentgroupcom.au. **E-mail:** linda.ingaldo@permanentgroupcom.au.

W. O. Mitchell Prize

This prize was established in 1997 in memory of novelist and playwright W. O. Mitchell. It is given to a Canadian author who has produced an outstanding body of work, has acted as a 'caring mentor,' and has published a work of fiction or a stage play in the last three years. The winner receives $15,000.

Recent Winners: 1999: Austin Clarke; 1998: Barry Callaghan.

Sponsoring Organization: Writers' Development Trust.

Address: Writers' Development Trust, 24 Ryerson Ave, Suite 201, Toronto, ON M5T 2P3, Canada.

Mitchell Prize for Art History/Eric Mitchell Prize

Two parallel prizes in the field of art history. The Mitchell Prize is awarded for an outstanding and original contribution to the understanding of the visual arts, while the Eric Mitchell Prize is given for the best first book in this field. The Mitchell Prize for Art History carries a prize of US $15,000, while the Eric Mitchell Prize is worth $5,000.

Eligibility and Restrictions: Entries must be written in English and published in the previous year.

Recent Winners: Mitchell Prize for Art History: 1999: David Anfam, *Mark Rothko: The Works on Canvas*
Eric Mitchell Prize: 1999: Frits Scholten (Editor), with contributions by Rosemarie Mulcahy and others, *Adriaen de Vries: Imperial Sculptor*.

Address: c/o The Burlington Magazine, 14–16 Duke's Rd, London WC1H 9AD, UK.

MLA Award for Lifetime Scholarly Achievement

First presented in 1996 and scheduled to be presented every three years thereafter, this award honours the lifetime scholarly achievement of a distinguished member of the Modern Language Association of America (MLA). The Committee on Honors and Awards reviews suggestions from members for recipients of the award and recommends names for consideration by the Executive Council.

How to Apply: Nominations should be sent to the Committee by 31 January.

Recent Winners: 1999: Carolyn Heilbrun; 1996: Maynard Mack.

Sponsoring Organization: Modern Language Association of America.

Contact: Co-ordinator of Book Prizes and Special Projects.

Address: Modern Language Asscn of America, 26 Broadway, 3rd Floor, New York, NY 10004–1789, USA. **Telephone:** (646) 576-5141. **Fax:** (646) 458-0033. **Internet:** www.mla.org. **E-mail:** awards@mla.org.

Modern Language Association Prize for a Distinguished Bibliography

First awarded in 1998, the prize recognizes an outstanding enumerative and descriptive bibliography published in the previous two years. The prize is awarded each even-numbered year. The winner is selected by a committee made up of members of the Modern Language Association of America (MLA), and receives $1,000 and a certificate.

Eligibility and Restrictions: Entries should fall within the scope of the MLA (modern languages and literature, composition theory, folklore, linguistics). Entries may be published in serial, monographic, book or electronic format; editors or compilers need not be members of the MLA.

How to Apply: Publishers or editors may apply; four copies of entries should be sent to the address given by 1 May in even-numbered years.

Recent Winners: 1996–97: Kathleen L. Scott, *Later Gothic Manuscripts, 1390–1490*; 1998–99: David W. Forbes, *Hawaiian National Bibliography, 1780–1900, I: 1780–1830*.

Sponsoring Organization: Modern Language Association of America (MLA).

Contact: Co-ordinator of Book Prizes and Special Projects.

Address: Modern Language Asscn of America, 26 Broadway, 3rd Floor, New York, NY 10004–1789, USA. **Telephone:** (646) 576-5141. **Fax:** (646) 458-0033. **Internet:** www.mla.org. **E-mail:** awards@mla.org.

Modern Language Association Prize for a First Book

First awarded in 1994, the prize is presented annually for an outstanding scholarly work as the first book-length publication by a current member of the Modern Language Association of America (MLA). The winner is selected by a committee made up of members of the MLA, and receives $1,000 and a certificate.

Eligibility and Restrictions: Open to first books in the field of literary or linguistic studies, critical editions of an important work, or critical biographies. Entries must be published during the preceding calendar year. Authors must be members of the MLA. Books that are primarily translations will not be considered.

How to Apply: Publishers or authors may apply. Six copies of the book should be submitted, accompanied by a letter confirming membership of the MLA, by 1 April.

Recent Winners: 2001: Patricia Crain, *The Story of A: The Alphabetization of America from The New England Primer to The Scarlet Letter*; 1999: Srinivas Aravamudan, *Tropicopolitans: Colonialism and Agency, 1688–1804*; 1998: Deidre Shauna Lynch, *The Economy of Character: Novels, Market Culture, and the Business of Inner Meaning*; 1997: Katie Trumpener, *Bardic Nationalism: The Romantic Novel and the British Empire*; 1996: Marc Redfield, *Phantom Formations: Aesthetic Ideology and the Bildungsroman* and John Rogers, *The Matter of Revolution: Science, Poetry, and Politics in the Age of Milton* (joint winners).

Sponsoring Organization: Modern Language Association of America.

Contact: Co-ordinator of Book Prizes and Special Projects.

Address: Modern Language Asscn of America, 26 Broadway, 3rd Floor, New York, NY 10004–1789, USA. **Telephone:** (646) 576-5141. **Fax:** (646) 458-0033. **Internet:** www.mla.org. **E-mail:** awards@mla.org.

Modern Language Association Prize for Independent Scholars

The prize was established in 1983 to recognize and further encourage the achievements and contributions of independent scholars. The prize is awarded annually for a distinguished scholarly book in the field of English or another modern language or literature. The winner is selected by a committee made up of members of the Modern Language Association of America (MLA), and receives $1,000 and a certificate.

Eligibility and Restrictions: Open to authors who are not enrolled in a programme leading to an academic degree and did not hold a tenured position in a post-secondary educational institution at the time of publication of the book.

How to Apply: Publishers or authors may apply. Six copies of the book should be submitted, accompanied by a completed application form, by 1 May.

Recent Winners: 2001: Joe Snader, *Caught between Worlds: British Captivity Narratives in Fact and Fiction*; 1999: Steven J. Holmes, *The Young John Muir: An Environmental Biography*; 1998: Janet Galligani Casey, *Dos Passos and the Ideology of the Feminine*; 1997: Gary Schmidgall, *Walt Whitman: A Gay Life*; 1996: Graham Robb, *Unlocking Mallarmé*.

Sponsoring Organization: Modern Language Association of America (MLA).

Contact: Co-ordinator of Book Prizes and Special Projects.

Address: Modern Language Asscn of America, 26 Broadway, 3rd Floor, New York, NY 10003–6981, USA. **Telephone:** (646) 576-5141. **Fax:** (646) 458-0033. **Internet:** www.mla.org. **E-mail:** awards@mla.org.

Monsudar Book Awards

An annual book award sponsored by Monsudar Printing House. A winner and eight runners-up are selected.

Recent Winners: 2000: D. Batbayar, *Mementog Buteehui (Create Mementoes)*.

Sponsoring Organization: Monsudar Printing House.

Address: Monsudar Printing House, Ulan Bator, Mongolia.

Montana New Zealand Book Awards

This wide-ranging award programme was established in 1996 following the amalgamation of the New Zealand Book Awards and the Montana Book Awards, and subsequently became known as the Montana New Zealand Book Awards. The awards recognize excellence in the best books published each year in New Zealand. They are managed by Booksellers New Zealand, with the support of the Book Publishers Association of New Zealand and the New Zealand Society of Authors. Awards are made in eight categories: Fiction, Poetry, Environment, Lifestyle, History and Biography, Illustrative Arts and Reference and Anthology. New Zealand readers can vote for their favourite book in the Readers' Choice Award. The winner in each category receives a prize of $NZ5,000. The A. W. Reed Lifetime Achievement Award is also presented in conjunction with the awards, while a separate set of Best First Book Awards is made for new authors in three different genres (see separate entries).

Eligibility and Restrictions: Entries are open to books published in a calendar year (April–March). Authors and/or illustrators must be New Zealand citizens by birth, naturalization, or immigration, or have been permanently resident in New Zealand for a period of at least five years. The work of authors deceased more than two years prior to the period of eligibility cannot be entered. Reprints of previously published works are not eligible unless they are new editions which contain substantial revision. Books by individual or multiple authors, including anthologies, are eligible, as are books published with the assistance of grants or subsidies.

How to Apply: Publisher submissions are invited in October and must be advised by 12 December. Deadline for receipt of entries is mid-March. An entry fee is charged for each submission.

Recent Winners: Poetry: 2001: Allen Curnow, *The Bells of St Babel's*; 2000: Elizabeth Smither, *The Lark Quartet*; 1999: Vincent O'Sullivan, *Seeing You Asked*
History and Biography: 2001: Te Miringa Hohaia, Gregory O'Brien and Lara Strongman (Editors), *Parihaka: The Art of Passive Resistance*; 2000: Chris Maclean, *Kapiti*; 1999: Kevin Ireland, *Under the Bridge and Over the Moon*
Environment: 2001: Philip Simpson, *Dancing Leaves*; 2000: Shaun Barnett and Rob Brown, *Classic Tramping in New Zealand*; 1999: Gerard Hutching, *The Natural World of New Zealand*
Lifestyle: 2001: Julie Biuso and Ian Batchelor, *Fresh*; 2000: Yvonne Cave and Valda Paddisson, *The Gardener's Encyclopedia of New Zealand Native Plants*; 1999: Heather Nicholson, *The Loving Stitch*
Illustrative Arts: 2001: Ian Wedde (Editor), *Ralph Hotere: Black Light*; 2000: Grahame Sydney, *The Art of Grahame Sydney*; 1999: Helen Schamroth, *100 New Zealand Craft Artists*
Readers' Choice Award: 2001: Michael King, *Wrestling with the Angel*; 2000: Grahame Sydney, *The Art of Grahame Sydney*; 1999: Elizabeth Knox, *The Vintner's Luck*
A. W. Reed Lifetime Achievement Award: 2001: Dame Fiona Kidman; 2000: Allen Curnow.

Sponsoring Organization: Booksellers NZ/Book Publishers Association of NZ/ NZ Society of Authors.

Contact: Promotions Team Leader Jayne Wasmuth.

Address: PO Box 11 377, Wellington, New Zealand. **Telephone:** (4) 4728678. **Fax:** (4) 4728628. **Internet:** www.booksellers.co.nz. **E-mail:** jaynewasmuth@ booksellers.co.nz.

Montana New Zealand Book Awards/Best First Book of Fiction Award

This prize for a best first book of fiction forms part of the broader Montana New Zealand Book Awards (see separate entry). This award, which is also known as the Hubert Church Fiction Award, carries a prize of $NZ1,000.

Eligibility and Restrictions: Entries are open to books published in the preceding calendar year (April–March). Authors and/or illustrators must be New Zealand citizens by birth, naturalization, or immigration, or have been permanently resident in New Zealand for a period of at least five years. The work of authors deceased more than two years prior to the period of eligibility cannot be entered. Reprints of previously published works are not eligible unless they are new editions which contain substantial revision. The Best First Book Awards recognize work of quality from an author for whom the entry is their first published book in any genre. Books by individual or multiple authors, including anthologies, are eligible, as are books published with the assistance of grants or subsidies.

How to Apply: Publisher submissions are invited in October and must be advised by 12 December. Deadline for receipt of entries is mid-March. An entry fee is charged for each submission.

Recent Winners: 2001: Karyn Hay, *Emerald Budgies*; 2000: Duncan Sarkies, *Stray Thoughts and Nosebleeds*; 1999: William Brandt, *Alpha Male*; 1998: Catherine Chidgey, *In a Fishbone Church*; 1997: Dominic Sheehan, *Finding Home*.

Sponsoring Organization: New Zealand Society of Authors.

Contact: Promotions Team Leader Jayne Wasmuth.

Address: PO Box 11 377, Wellington, New Zealand. **Telephone:** (4) 4728678. **Fax:** (4) 4728628. **Internet:** www.booksellers.co.nz. **E-mail:** jaynewasmuth@ booksellers.co.nz.

Montana New Zealand Book Awards/Best First Book of Non-Fiction Award

This prize for a best first book of non-fiction forms part of the broader Montana New Zealand Book Awards (see separate entry). This award, which is also known as the E. H. McCormick Non-Fiction Award, carries a prize of $NZ1,000.

Eligibility and Restrictions: Entries are open to books published in the preceding calendar year (April–March). Authors and/or illustrators must be New Zealand citizens by birth, naturalization, or immigration, or have been permanently resident in New Zealand for a period of at least five years. The work of authors deceased more than two years prior to the period of eligibility cannot be entered. Reprints of previously published works are not eligible unless they are new editions which contain substantial revision. The Best First Book Awards recognize work of quality from an author for whom the entry is their first published book in any genre. Books by individual or multiple authors, including anthologies, are eligible, as are books published with the assistance of grants or subsidies.

How to Apply: Publisher submissions are invited in October and must be advised by 12 December. Deadline for receipt of entries is mid-March. An entry fee is charged for each submission.

Recent Winners: 2001: Paul Tapsell, *Pukaki: A Comet Returns*; 2000: Peter Thomson, *Kava in the Blood*; 1999: Helen Schamroth,*100 New Zealand Craft Artists*; 1998: Genevieve Noser, *Olives: The New Passion*; 1997: Jessie Munro, *The Story of Suzanne Aubert*.

Sponsoring Organization: New Zealand Society of Authors.

Contact: Promotions Team Leader Jayne Wasmuth.

Address: PO Box 11 377, Wellington, New Zealand. **Telephone:** (4) 4728678. **Fax:** (4) 4728628. **Internet:** www.booksellers.co.nz. **E-mail:** jaynewasmuth@ booksellers.co.nz.

Montana New Zealand Book Awards/Best First Book of Poetry Award

This prize for a best first book of poetry forms part of the broader Montana New Zealand Book Awards (see separate entry). This award, which is also known as the Jessie Mackay Poetry Award, carries a prize of $NZ1,000.

Eligibility and Restrictions: Entries are open to books published in a calendar year (April–March). Authors and/or illustrators must be New Zealand citizens by birth, naturalization, or immigration, or have been permanently resident in New Zealand for a period of at least five years. The work of authors deceased more than two years prior to the period of eligibility cannot be entered. Reprints of previously published works are not eligible unless they are new editions which contain substantial revision. The Best First Book Awards recognize work of quality from an author for whom the entry is their first published book in any genre. Books by individual or multiple authors, including anthologies, are eligible, as are books published with the assistance of grants or subsidies.

How to Apply: Publisher submissions are invited in October and must be advised by 12 December. Deadline for receipt of entries is mid-March. An entry fee is charged for each submission.

Recent Winners: 2001: Stephanie de Montalk, *Animals Indoors*; 2000: Glenn Colquhoun, *The Art of Walking Upright*; 1999: Kate Camp, *Unfamiliar Legends of the Stars*; 1998: Kapka Kassabova, *All Roads Lead to the Sea*; 1997: Diane Brown, *Before the Divorce We Go to Disneyland*.

Sponsoring Organization: New Zealand Society of Authors.

Contact: Promotions Team Leader Jayne Wasmuth.

Address: PO Box 11 377, Wellington, New Zealand. **Telephone:** (4) 4728678. **Fax:** (4) 4728628. **Internet:** www.booksellers.co.nz. **E-mail:** jaynewasmuth@ booksellers.co.nz.

Montana New Zealand Book Awards/Deutz Medal

The Deutz Medal, introduced in 1998, recognizes a single outstanding work of fiction published in the 12-month period covered by the awards. All entries accepted for the fiction category of the Montana New Zealand Book Awards (qv) are also judged for the Deutz Medal. A shortlist of five titles is selected and from these the judges choose an overall winner and two runners-up.The winning author receives $15,000, with two runners-up each receiving $NZ2,500.

How to Apply: Publisher submissions are invited in October and must be advised by 12 December. Deadline for receipt of entries is mid-March. An entry fee is charged for each submission.

Recent Winners: 2001: Lloyd Jones,*The Book of Fame*; 2000: Owen Marshall, *Harlequin Rex*; 1999: Elizabeth Knox, *The Vintner's Luck*; 1998: Maurice Gee, *Live Bodies*.

Sponsoring Organization: New Zealand Society of Authors.

Contact: Promotions Team Leader Jayne Wasmuth.

Address: PO Box 11 377, Wellington, New Zealand. **Telephone:** (4) 4728678. **Fax:** (4) 4728628. **Internet:** www.booksellers.co.nz. **E-mail:** jaynewasmuth@ booksellers.co.nz.

Montana New Zealand Book Awards/Montana Medal

The Montana Medal, introduced in 1998, is awarded to one outstanding work of non-fiction, and carries a prize of $NZ10,000.

How to Apply: Publisher submissions are invited in October and must be advised by 12 December. Deadline for receipt of entries is mid-March. An entry fee is charged for each submission.

Recent Winners: 2001: Michael King, *Wrestling with the Angel*; 1999: Heather Nicholson, *The Loving Stitch*; 1998: Harry Orsman, *The Dictionary of New Zealand English*.

Sponsoring Organization: New Zealand Society of Authors.

Contact: Promotions Team Leader Jayne Wasmuth.
Address: PO Box 11 377, Wellington, New Zealand. **Telephone:** (4) 4728678.
Fax: (4) 4728628. **Internet:** www.booksellers.co.nz. **E-mail:** jaynewasmuth@
booksellers.co.nz.

Monteiro Lobato Award

A prize of 5,000 reais awarded for translation or illustration of a Brazilian book for
children or young people.

Eligibility and Restrictions: Only first editions are eligible. The original must
have appeared in Brazil in the year of the award; school textbooks and books with
a religious theme are excluded.

How to Apply: Publishers should submit three copies of the translation
accompanied by an application form.

Sponsoring Organization: Fundação Biblioteca Nacional/Dept Nacional do
Livro.

Address: Fundação Biblioteca Nacional, Dept Nacional do Livro, Elmer C. Corrêa
Barbosa, Av. Rio Branco 219, 20040–008 Rio de Janeiro, RJ, Brazil. **Telephone:**
(21) 2628 25 53 33. **Fax:** (21) 2628 25 53 36.

Oscar Moore Screenwriting Prize

An annual award established in 1997 with the aim of fostering new European
screenwriting talent. The award of £10,000 is intended to finance the second draft
of a promising screenplay, in a genre which changes each year (comedy in 2002).
The winner is chosen by a panel of film producers, and also receives a free place at
an editing workshop and a performed reading at The Script Factory.

Eligibility and Restrictions: The screenplay must be an original first draft in
English, and must be contemporary and European. The writer must be a
European national. The screenplay must be for a feature-length film, but no more
than 120 pages in length.

How to Apply: An official application form (available from the website) must
accompany each entry, along with an outline summary of the screenplay; closing
date is 1 August.

Recent Winners: 2001: Marcus Lloyd, *Cuckoo*; 2000: Tom Allen, *Grave Songs*;
1999: Matthew Cooper and James Wood, *Sober* and *Leaving George*; 1998: Lindsay
Shapero, *Bitten by a Zebra*.

Sponsoring Organization: Oscar Moore Foundation.

Contact: Administrator Ann Marie O'Connor.

Address: 33–39 Bowling Green Lane, London EC1R ODA, UK. **Telephone:** (20)
7505 8080. **Fax:** (20) 7505 8087. **Internet:** www.screendaily.com. **E-mail:**
annmarie.oconnor@media.emap.com.

Kathryn A. Morton Prize in Poetry

Named after an author and devotee of fine literature, this award is presented for a
full-length collection of poetry. The winner receives a prize of $2,000 cash, plus
publication of the winning entry and a standard royalty contract.

Eligibility and Restrictions: Open to any writer of English who is a citizen of the USA. Entries should comprise at least 48 pages of poetry. Individual poems from the manuscript may have been published previously in magazines or anthologies, but the collection as a whole must be unpublished. Translations and previously self-published books are not eligible.

How to Apply: One copy of the manuscript should be submitted accompanied by entry form and entry fee of $20. Author's name or address should not appear anywhere on the manuscript.

Sponsoring Organization: Sarabande Books.

Address: Sarabande Books, 2234 Dundee Rd, Suite 200, Louisville, KY 40205, USA. **Telephone:** (502) 458-4028. **Fax:** (502) 458-4065.

George L. Mosse Prize

The Mosse Prize is awarded annually for an outstanding major work of extraordinary scholarly distinction, creativity and originality in the intellectual and cultural history of Europe since the Renaissance. It was established in 2000 with funds donated by former students, colleagues and friends of Professor Mosse, an eminent scholar of European history.

Recent Winners: 2001: Lionel Gossman, *Basel in the Age of Burckhardt: A Study in Unseasonable Ideas.*

Sponsoring Organization: American Historical Association.

Contact: Lynn Hunt.

Address: American Historical Asscn, 400 A St, SE, Washington, DC 20003–3889, USA. **Telephone:** (202) 544-2422. **Fax:** (202) 544-8307. **Internet:** www. theaha.org/prizes. **E-mail:** press@theaha.org.

Mühlheimer Dramatikerpreis

The Mühlheimer Dramatikerpreis has been awarded to German-speaking dramatists annually since 1976 by the town of Mühlheim. The winner receives a prize of DM20,000.

Eligibility and Restrictions: Plays must have premiered in the previous theatrical season and been selected for performance at the Mühlheimer Theatertagen literary festival.

Recent Winners: 2000: Rainald Goetz, *Jeff Koons*; 1999: Oliver Bukowski, *Gäste*; 1998: Dea Loher, *Adam Geist*; 1997: Urs Widmer, *Top Dogs*; 1996: Werner Buhss, *Bevor wir Greise wurden.*

Sponsoring Organization: Mühlheim Town Council.

Address: Stadt Mühlheim am Main, Presse- und Öffentlichkeitsarbeit, Friedensstr. 20, 63165 Mühlheim am Main, Germany. **E-mail:** pressestelle@ rathaus.muehlheim.de.

Multatuli Prize

Established in 1945 by the City of Amsterdam, and awarded annually for a novel. The winner is chosen by a three-member jury, and receives €7,000.

Eligibility and Restrictions: Open to Dutch-language works only, published during the previous year. All books published by a Dutch or Flemish author are eligible.

How to Apply: No public application; selection is made by the jury.

Recent Winners: 2001: Jeroen Brouwers, *Geheime kamers*; 2000: Kees 't Hart, *De revue*; 1999: Marie Kessels, *Ongemakkelijke portretten*; 1998: Dirkje Kuik, *Broholm*; 1997: Maria Stahlie, *Honderd deuren*.

Sponsoring Organization: Amsterdam Fund for the Arts.

Contact: Desmond Spruist.

Address: Stichting Amsterdams Fonds voor de Kunst, Herengracht 609, 1017 CE Amsterdam, Netherlands. **Telephone:** (20) 5200 556. **Fax:** (20) 623 8309. **Internet:** www.afk.nl. **E-mail:** afk@afk.nl.

Myanmar Annual National Literary Awards

A series of annual awards for national literature, which are the country's highest literary honour. The awards cover 14 categories of both fiction and non-fiction, including novels, short stories, belles-lettres, poetry, children's literature, etc. The prizes were originally introduced in 1948, when the country won its independence, when they were known as the Sarpay Beikman Literary Awards; they were later renamed the National Literary Awards.

How to Apply: Entries are nominated by a 20-member panel of literary experts.

Recent Winners: 1995: U Htin Gyi, *History of Myanmar Newspapers and Journals*.

Sponsoring Organization: Myanmar Writers and Journalists Association.

Address: Myanmar Writers and Journalists Association, Yangon, Myanmar.

Mythopoeic Awards

In 1971 the Mythopoeic Society established its Mythopoeic Fantasy Award to honour the best of fantasy writing. In 1992 a separate children's literature prize was established alongside the adult category. The awards are given to the fantasy work that best exemplifies 'the spirit of the Inklings'. The children's category honours books for children or young adults which are in the tradition of *The Hobbit* or *The Chronicles of Narnia*. Winners are chosen by a volunteer committee of Mythopoeic Society members, and receive a statuette with a plaque.

Eligibility and Restrictions: Open to novels, multi-volume, or single-author story collections published during the previous year. Reissues (such as paperback editions) are eligible if no earlier edition was a finalist. Books from a series are eligible if they stand on their own; otherwise, the series is eligible the year its final volume appears.

How to Apply: Nominations are made by members of the Mythopoeic Society.

Recent Winners: Adult Literature: 2001: Midori Snyder, *The Innamorati*; 2000: Peter S. Beagle, *Tamsin*; 1999: Neil Gaiman and Charles Vess, *Stardust*; 1998: A. S. Byatt, *The Djinn in the Nightingale's Eye*; 1997: Terri Windling, *The Wood Wife* Children's Literature: 2001: Dia Calhoun, *Aria of the Sea*; 2000: Franny Billingsley, *The Folk Keeper*; 1999: Diane Wynne Jones, *Dark Lord of Derkholm*; 1998: Jane Yolen, *The Young Merlin Trilogy*; 1997: Diana Wynne Jones, *The Crown of Dalemark*.

Sponsoring Organization: Mythopoeic Society.

Contact: Administrator Eleanor M. Farrell.

Address: Mythopoeic Society, POB 320486, San Francisco, CA 94132–0486, USA. **Internet:** www.mythsoc.org/awards.html. **E-mail:** emfarrell@earthlink.net.

Mythopoeic Scholarship Awards

The Mythopoeic Society sponsors two scholarship prizes: the Mythopoeic Scholarship Award in Inklings Studies, established in 1971, is given to books on Tolkien, Lewis, and/or Williams that make significant contributions to Inklings scholarship, while the Mythopoeic Scholarship Award in General Myth and Fantasy Studies, established in 1992, is given to scholarly books on other specific authors in the Inklings tradition, or to more general works on the genres of myth and fantasy.

For both awards winners are chosen by a volunteer committee of Mythopoeic Society members, and receive a statuette with a plaque.

Eligibility and Restrictions: Books first published during the past three years are eligible, including finalists for previous years.

How to Apply: Nominations are made by members of the Mythopoeic Society.

Recent Winners: Inklings Studies: 2001: Tom Shippey, *J. R. R. Tolkien: Author of the Century*; 2000: J. R. R. Tolkien, *Roverandom* (edited by Wayne G. Hammond and Christina Scull); 1999: Walter Hooper, *C. S. Lewis: A Companion and Guide*; 1998: Verlyn Flieger, *A Question of Time: J. R. R. Tolkien's Road to Faerie*; 1997: Charles A. Huttar and Peter J. Schakel (Editors), *The Rhetoric of Vision*
General Myth and Fantasy Studies: 2001: Alan Lupack and Barbara Tepa Lupack, *King Arthur in America*; 2000: Carole G. Silver, *Strange and Secret Peoples: Fairies and Victorian Consciousness*; 1999: Donna R. White, *A Century of Welsh Myth in Children's Literature*; 1998: John Clute and John Grant (Editors), *The Encyclopedia of Fantasy*; 1997: Lois Rostow Kuznets, *When Toys Come Alive*.

Sponsoring Organization: Mythopoeic Society.

Contact: Administrator Eleanor M. Farrell.

Address: Mythopoeic Society, POB 320486, San Francisco, CA 94132–0486, USA. **Internet:** www.mythsoc.org/awards.html. **E-mail:** emfarrell@earthlink.net.

Shiva Naipaul Memorial Prize

An annual prize established by *The Spectator* magazine in 1985 in memory of the writer, Shiva Naipaul. The prize is awarded for travel writing which best demonstrates 'acute and profound observation of a culture alien to the writer'. The winner receives a cash prize of £3,000 and the winning entry is published in *The Spectator*.

Eligibility and Restrictions: The prize is open to English-language writers of any nationality under the age of 35 on the closing date for entries. Submissions should not previously have been published and should be not more than 4,000 words.

How to Apply: Closing date for submissions is 30 April.

Recent Winners: 2001: Matt Bannerman.

Sponsoring Organization: The Spectator.

Address: 56 Doughty St, London WC1L 2LL, UK. **Internet:** www.spectator.co.uk.

Nakahara Chûya Prize

Established in 1996 by the city of Yamaguchi, with the support of publishers Seidosha and Kadokawa Shoten, in honour of the city's native poet Nakahara Chûya (1907–37). The award is presented annually to an outstanding collection of contemporary poetry characterized by a 'fresh sensibility'. The winner receives a cash prize of 1 million yen, and the winning collection is published in an English translation.

Recent Winners: 2001: Arthur Binard, *Tsuriagete wa (Catch and Throw Back)*.

Sponsoring Organization: Seidosha and Kadokawa Shoten.

Address: Nakahara Chûya Prize, Yamaguchi, Japan.

Naoki Sanjûgo Shô (Naoki Prize)

Established at the same time as the Akutagawa Prize (1935) by Kikuchi Kan, editor of *Bungei Shunjû* magazine, in memory of novelist Naoki Sanjûgo. The prize is awarded twice a year to the best work of popular literature in any format by a new, rising, or (reasonably young) established author. Sponsored by the Society for the Promotion of Japanese Literature (Nihon Bungaku Shinkô Kai). The winner receives 1 million yen plus a watch.

Recent Winners: 126th Naoki Prize: shared by Yamamoto Ichiriki, *Akanezora (A Deep-Red Sky)*, and Yuikawa Kei, *Katagoshi no koibito (Over-the-Shoulder Lover)*; 125th Naoki Prize: Fujita Yoshinaga, *Ai no ryôbun (Love's Domain)*; 124th Naoki Prizes: Shigematsu Kiyoshi, *Bitamin F (Vitamin F)*, and Yamamoto Fumio, *Puranaria (Planaria)*.

Sponsoring Organization: Society for the Promotion of Japanese Literature (Nihon Bungaku Shinkô Kai).

Address: Society for the Promotion of Japanese Literature (Nihon Bungaku Shinkô Kai), Tokyo, Japan.

National Art Library Illustration Awards

The National Art Library Illustration Awards, sponsored by the Enid Linder Foundation, are intended to encourage the art of illustration in books and magazines. They were first awarded under their current name in 1995 (although their predecessor, the Francis Williams Awards, had been awarded at five-yearly intervals between 1972 and 1982; these were subsequently renamed the W. H. Smith Illustration Awards in recognition of their sponsor at that time). A first prize of £2,500 is awarded to the best overall magazine or book illustration (book-cover designs are ineligible). Two second prizes of £1,000 each are awarded: one for book illustration and the other for editorial illustration. There is also a selection of commended winners.

How to Apply: Nominations are sought from publishers and individuals.

Recent Winners: 2001: Wayne Anderson (illustrator), Nigel Suckling, *Gnomes and gardens: a field guide to the little people*; 1999: Satoshi Kitamura, *The ring of words: an anthology of poetry for children*; 1998: Posy Simmonds (illustrator), Hilaire Belloc, *Cautionary Tales and Other Verses*.

Sponsoring Organization: Enid Linder Foundation.

Address: Secretariat, National Art Library, Victoria and Albert Museum, South Kensington, London SW7 2LR, UK. **Internet:** www.nal.vam.ac.uk/exhibits/nalia2001.

National Artists Award

Every year 24 February is declared National Artist Day (birthday of the former King Rama II, 1767–1824), under the National Artists Programme launched in 1985 by the Office of the National Culture Commission, Ministry of Education. Its aim is to promote artists who have created works which add to the valuable national heritage. Among the awards is one in the field of literature, given for a lifetime's achievement.

Recent Winners: 2001: Literature: Khamphun Buntawi.

Sponsoring Organization: Office of the National Culture Commission, Ministry of Education.

Address: Office of the National Culture Commission, Ministry of Education, Ratchadapisek Rd, Huikwang, Bangkok, 10320, Thailand. **Telephone:** 645-2957. **Fax:** 645-2959. **Internet:** www.culture.go.th. **E-mail:** admin@culture.moe.go.th.

National Book Awards

Sponsored by the National Book Foundation, the National Book Awards were originally presented for fiction, non-fiction and poetry. Further categories were added from 1964 (such as children's and translation). Between 1980 and 1983 the awards were known as the American Book Awards; from 1984, however, they reassumed their original title, with a simplified structure based on the categories of fiction, non-fiction and poetry.

Recent Winners: Fiction: 2002: Jonathan Franzen, *The Corrections*; 2001: Susan Sontag, *In America*; 2000: Ha Jin, *Waiting*; 1999: Alice McDermott, *Charming Billy*; 1998: Charles Frazier, *Cold Mountain*
Non-fiction: 2002: Andrew Solomon, *The Noonday Demon: An Atlas of Depression*; 2001: Nathaniel Philbrick, *In the Heart of the Sea: The Tragedy of the Whaleship Essex*; 2000: John Dower, *Embracing Defeat*; 1999: Edward Ball, *Slaves in the Family*; 1998: Joseph Ellis, *American Sphinx*
Poetry: 2002: Alan Dugan, *Poems Seven*; 2001: Lucille Clifton, *Blessing the Boats: New and Selected Poems 1988–2000*; 2000: Ai, *Vice*; 1999: Gerald Stern, *This Time: New and Selected Poems*; 1998: William Meredith, *Effort at Speech: New & Selected Poems*
Distinguished Contribution to American Letters: 2002: Arthur Miller.

Sponsoring Organization: National Book Foundation.

Address: National Book Foundation, 260 Fifth Ave, 4th Floor, New York, NY 10001, USA.

National Book Contest

An annual contest administered by the National Book Development Committee of Thailand to promote the production and development of quality books, and presented during National Book Week. Entries are judged in 9 categories: non-fiction; poetry; novel; short story; book for children between 3 and 5 years old; book for children between 6 and 11 years old; book for children between 12 and 14 years old; cartoon; and most attractive book. The award winner in each category receives a cash prize of 30,000 baht (approx. US$750) and a trophy.

Eligibility and Restrictions: Books must have been printed in the previous year. All entries must be by Thai authors, published in Thailand and 'must not be harmful to the country's morality, ethics or security'.

Sponsoring Organization: National Book Development Committee of Thailand.

Address: National Book Development Committee of Thailand, Bangkok, Thailand.

The National Book Critics Circle Awards

The National Book Critics Circle consists of more than 700 book reviewers. Since its founding in 1974, the NBCC has awarded annual prizes for the best book in five categories: fiction, general non-fiction, biography/autobiography, poetry, and criticism. In addition, each year the NBCC awards the Ivan Sandrof Award for Contribution to American Arts and Letters and honours one member of the Circle with the Nona Balakian Citation for Excellence in Reviewing. There are no cash prizes.

Recent Winners: Fiction: 2001: W. G. Sebald, *Austerlitz*; 2000: Jim Crace, *Being Dead*; 1999: Jonathan Lethem, *Motherless Brooklyn*; 1998: Alice Munro, *The Love of a Good Woman*; 1997: Penelope Fitzgerald, *The Blue Flower*; 1996: Gina Berriault, *Women in Their Beds*
General Non-fiction: 2001: Nicholson Baker, *Double Fold: Libraries and the Assault on Paper*; 2000: Ted Conover, *Newjack: Guarding Sing Sing*; 1999: Jonathan Weiner, *Time, Love, Memory: A Great Biologist and His Quest for the Origins of Behavior*; 1998: Philip Gourevitch, *We Wish to Inform You That Tomorrow We Will be Killed With Our Families*; 1997: Anne Fadiman, *The Spirit Catches You and You Fall Down*
Biography and Autobiography: 2001: Adam Sisman, *Boswell's Presumptuous Task: The Making of the Life of Dr. Johnson*; 2000: Herbert P. Bix, *Hirohito and the Making of Modern Japan*; 1999: Henry Wiencek, *The Hairstons: An American Family in Black and White*; 1998: Sylvia Nasar, *A Beautiful Mind*; 1997: James Tobin, *Ernie Pyle's War: America's Eyewitness to World War II*
Poetry: 2001: Albert Goldbarth, *Saving Lives*; 2000: Judy Jordan, *Carolina Ghost Woods*; 1999: Ruth Stone, *Ordinary Words*; 1998: Marie Ponsot, *The Bird Catcher*; 1997: Charles Wright, *Black Zodiac*
Criticism: 2001: Martin Amis, *The War Against Cliché: Essays and Reviews, 1971–2000*; 2000: Cynthia Ozick, *Quarrel & Quandary*; 1999: Jorge Luis Borges, *Selected non-fiction*; 1998: Gary Giddins, *Visions of Jazz*; 1997: Mario Vargas Llosa, *Making Waves*
Ivan Sandrof Award for Contribution to American Arts and Letters: 2001: Jason Epstein; 1997: Leslie Fiedler; 1996: Albert Murray
Nona Balakian Excellence in Reviewing Award: 2001: Michael Gorra; 1997: Thomas Mallon; 1995: Laurie Stone.

Sponsoring Organization: National Book Critics Circle.

Address: The National Book Critics Circle, 245 West 17th, New York, NY 10016, USA. **Internet:** www.bookcritics.org/.

National Jewish Book Awards

The National Jewish Book Awards are administered by the Jewish Book Council. They are presented in a variety of categories to North American and Israeli authors to honour excellence, either for one book or for a lifetime of achievement. It is the oldest American awards programme in the field of Jewish literature and is recognized as the most prestigious. Categories include fiction, non-fiction, autobiography/memoir, children's literature, children's picture book and education. There are also a number of other categories for more specialized achievements. Each winner receives a cash award and a citation. The publisher of the award-winning book also receives a citation.

Recent Winners: Fiction: 2000: Philip Roth, *The Human Stain*; 1999: Steven Stern, *The Wedding Jester*; 1998: Aharon Applefeld, *The Iron Tracks*; 1997: Saul Bellow, *The Actual*
Non-fiction: 2000: Samuel Freedman, *Jew vs. Jew: The Struggle for the Soul of American Jewry*; 1999: Zvi Kolitz, *Yosl Rakover Talks to God*; 1998: Leon Wieseltier, *Kaddish*; 1997: Ruth Gay, *Unfinished People: Eastern European Jews Encounter America*
Children's Literature: 2000: Howard Schwartz, *The Day The Rabbi Disappeared*; 1999: Sandy Asher (editor), *With all my Heart, With all my Mind*; 1998: Norman Finkelstein, *Heeding the Call*; 1997: Barbara Rogasky (author), Trina Schart Hyman (illustrator), *The Golem*
Children's picture book (Louis Posner Memorial Award): 2000: Laura Krauss (author), David Slonim (illustrator), *Moishe's Miracle*; 1999: Simms Taback, *Joseph Had a Little Overcoat*; 1998: Francine Prose (author), Mark Podwal (illustrator), *You Never Know*; 1997: Kathryn Lasky (author), Kevin Hawkes (illustrator), *Marven of the Great North Woods*
Autobiography and memoir (Sandra Brand/Arik Weinstein Award): 2000: Cyrus H. Gordon, *A Scholar's Odyssey*; 1999: Stephen A. Sadow (editor), *King David's Harp*; 1998: Marcel Benabou, *Jacob, Menahem & Mimoun*; 1997: Elizabeth Ehrlich, *Miriam's Kitchen*
Education (Leon Jolson Award): 1999: Carol K. Ingall, *Transmission and Transformation: A Jewish Perspective on Moral Education*; 1998: Adrianne Bank and Ron Wolfson, (editors), *First Fruit: A Whizin Anthology of Jewish Family Education*.

Sponsoring Organization: Jewish Book Council.

Contact: Chair. Henry Everett.

Address: Jewish Book Council, 15 East 26th St, New York, NY 10010, USA. **E-mail:** jbc@jewishbooks.org.

National Kamal-E-Fun Award

The Pakistan Academy of Letters administers a series of annual prizes established in 1980 under the Hijra National Literary Awards Scheme. The aim of the awards is to promote literary activities and recognize outstanding contributions. The National Kamal-E-Fun Award is an annual award of Rs 50,000 given in recognition of lifetime services in the field of literature. The Award is considered to be the most prestigious award given to the most eminent literary personalities in recognition of their lifetime services to literature.

Recent Winners: 2000: Ahmad Faraz; 1999: Mushtaq Ahmad Yousufi; 1998: Intizar Hussain; 1997: Ahmad Nadeem Qasimi.

Sponsoring Organization: Pakistan Academy of Letters.

Contact: Deputy Dir Naseem Mahmood.

Address: Pitras Bokhari Road, Sector H-8/1, Islamabad, Pakistan. **Telephone:** 9257164. **Fax:** 9257159. **E-mail:** academy@apollo.net.pk.

National Outdoor Book Awards

Set up in 1996 to honour outstanding writing and publishing in the broad field of the outdoors. Prizes are awarded in seven categories: literature, history/biography, nature and environment, outdoor adventure guidebooks, nature guidebooks, instructional books and outdoor classics. The awards are presented annually in

November, and reward design and artistic merit. There are no monetary awards, but the winners receive certificates, and the winning books receive extensive publicity.

Eligibility and Restrictions: Must be newly published (except for the category classics), and written in English.

How to Apply: Publishers and authors are invited to nominate books; nine copies of each nomination should be sent to the address given.

Recent Winners: Literature: 2001: Erika Warmbrunn, *Where the Pavement Ends: One Woman's Bicycle Trip Through Mongolia, China and Vietnam*; 2000: Chris Duff, *On Celtic Tides: One Man's Journey Around Ireland by Sea Kayak*; 1999: Richard Bangs, *The Lost River: A Memoir of Life, Death, and Transformation on Wild Water*
History/biography: 2001: Donald Worster, *A River Running West: The Life of John Wesley Powell*; 2000: Peter and Leni Gillman, *The Wildest Dream: The Biography of George Mallory*; 1999: Sam Keith, *One Man's Wilderness: An Alaskan Odyssey*
Nature and Environment: 2001: Andrew Beattie and Paul Ehrlich, Christine Turnbull (illustrator), *Wild Solutions: How Biodiversity is Money in the Bank*; 2000: Terry Grosz, *Wildlife Wars: The Life and Times of a Fish and Game Warden* and Kevin Schafer, *Penguin Planet: Their World, Our World* (joint winners); 1999: Tim McNulty and Pat O'Hara (photographer), *Washington's Mount Rainier National Park: A Centennial Celebration* and Phillip Manning, *Islands of Hope: Lessons from North America's Great Wildlife Sanctuaries* (joint winners)
Outdoor Adventure Guidebooks: 2001: Mark Kroese, *Fifty Favorite Climbs: The Ultimate North American Tick List*; 2000: Roger Schumann and Jan Shriner, *Guide to Sea Kayaking Central and Northern California*; 1999: John Ross, *Trout Unlimited's Guide to America's 100 Best Trout Streams*
Nature Guidebooks: 2001: Jeffrey Glassberg, *Butterflies Through Binoculars: A Field Guide to the Butterflies of Western North America*; 2000: Kate Wynne and Malia Schwartz, Garth Mix (illustrator), *Guide to Marine Mammals and Turtles of the US Atlantic and Gulf of Mexico*; 1999: James Halfpenny and Todd Telander (illustrator), *Scats and Tracks of the Rocky Mountains: A Field Guide to the Signs of 70 Wildlife Species*
Instructional Books: 2001: Tom Rosenbauer and Rod Walinchus (illustrator), *The Orvis Fly-Tying Guide*; 2000: Mark Harvey, *The National Outdoor Leadership School's Wilderness Guide*; 1999: Mark F. Twight and James Martin, *Extreme Alpinism: Climbing Light, Fast and High*
Outdoor Classic: 2001: Roderick Nash, *Wilderness and the American Mind*; 2000: Aldo Leopold, *A Sand County Almanac: Sketches Here and There*; 1999: John J. Rowlands and Henry B. Kane (illustrator), *Cache Lake Country: Life in the North Woods*
Design and Artistic Merit: 2001: Art Wolfe (photographer), *The Living Wild*; 2000: Bradford Washburn (photographer) and Antony Decaneas (Editor), *Mountain Photography*; 1999: Leonard Adkins and Joe and Monica Cook (photographers), *Wildflowers of the Appalachian Trail*
Children's: 2001: Nancy White Carlstrom and Tim Ladwig (illustrator), *What Does the Sky Say?*; 2000: Ann Dixon and Evon Zerbetz (illustrator), *Blueberry Shoe* and Twig C. George, *The Life of Jellyfish* (joint winners); 1999: Mary Wallace, *The Inuksuk Book*.

Sponsoring Organization: Association of Outdoor Recreation and Education/ Idaho State University.

Contact: Chair. Ron Watters.

Address: Box 8128, Idaho State University, Pocatello, ID 83209, USA. **Telephone:** (208) 282-3912. **Fax:** (208) 282-4600. **Internet:** www.isu.edu/out-door/books. **E-mail:** wattron@isu.edu.

National Poetry Competition

Annual award for an unpublished poem of up to 40 lines by anyone over the age of 18. The winner receives a prize of £5,000; there are also runners-up prizes of £1,000 and £500. Winners are automatically entered for the Forward Prize.

How to Apply: Deadline is 31 October; entry forms available from the address given or the website.

Recent Winners: 2001: Beatrice Garland, *Undressing*; 2000: Ian Duhig, *The Lammas Hireling*.

Sponsoring Organization: Poetry Society.

Address: Poetry Society, 22 Betterton St, London WC2H 9BX, UK. **Telephone:** (20) 7420 9880. **Internet:** www.poetrysociety.org.uk.

National Writers Union of Ukraine Awards

The National Writers Union of Ukraine makes a series of literary awards, including the Oleksander Biletsky Prize (for works of literary and art criticism); the Leonid Hlibov Prize (founded by O. Deko and awarded for collections of fairy stories); the Volodymyr Korolenko Prize (for books of prose aimed at children and young people and written by Russian-language authors); the Ivan Kotlyarevsky Prize (named after dramatist and poet Ivan Kotlyarevsky, 1769–1838, and awarded for works of drama); the Mykola Ushakov Prize (for poetry books by Russian-language authors); the Ostap Vyshnya Prize (for humorous or satirical works of prose); the Vasyl Mysyk Literary Award (for collections of poetry and translations of poetic works from other languages); and the Maksym Rylsky Prize (for translations of works by foreign writers into Ukrainian).

Sponsoring Organization: National Writers Union of Ukraine (NSPU).

Contact: V. Yavorivsky.

Address: Blvd Bankova 2, 01024 Kiev, Ukraine. **Fax:** (44) 293-45-86. **Internet:** www.nspu.kiev.ua. **E-mail:** nspu@I.kiev.ua.

Native Writers Circle of the Americas Lifetime Achievement Award for Literature

A lifetime achievement award of $1,000, given to a Native American writer selected by fellow Native American writers.

How to Apply: There is no application process.

Recent Winners: 2002: Maurice Kenny (Mohawk); 2000: Louise Erdrich (Chippewa); 1998: Linda Hogan.

Sponsoring Organization: Native Writers Circle of the Americas.

Contact: Project Dir Geary Hobson.

Address: Native Writers Circle of the Americas, Department of English, 60 Van Vleet Oval, Room 113, University of Oklahoma, Norman, OK 73019–0240, USA. **Telephone:** (405) 325-6231.

NCTE Award for Excellence in Poetry for Children

Established in 1977 by the National Council of Teachers of English (NCTE) to recognize and foster excellence in children's poetry. The award was given annually until 1982; since then it has been presented every three years. The prize is judged on imagination, authenticity of voice, evidence of a strong persona, and universality. The winner receives a plaque.

Eligibility and Restrictions: Open to living American poets with a substantial body of work.

How to Apply: Nominations should be submitted to the NCTE Poetry Committee.

Recent Winners: 2000: X. J. Kennedy; 1997: Eloise Greenfield; 1994: Barbara Juster Esbensen; 1991: Valerie Worth; 1988: Arnold Adoff.

Sponsoring Organization: National Council of Teachers of English (NCTE).

Contact: Assoc. Exec. Dir Kathryn Egawa.

Address: National Council of Teachers of English, 1111 West Kenyon Rd, Urbana, IL 61081–1096, USA. **Telephone:** (800) 369-6283. **Fax:** (217) 328-0977. **Internet:** www.ncte.org. **E-mail:** kegawa@ncte.org.

Nebula Awards

The annual Nebula Awards were established in 1965 by the Science Fiction and Fantasy Writers of America, Inc (SFWA). Awards are presented to the best science fiction novel, novella, novelette, and short story. The prize is awarded at the Nebula Awards Banquet, which takes place each spring. Winners are selected by a jury, and receive the Nebula Trophy, and winning entries appear in a special anthology.

Eligibility and Restrictions: Entries are eligible for a Nebula Award nomination for a year after publication.

Recent Winners: Novel: 2001: Greg Bear, *Darwin's Radio*; 2000: Octavia Butler, *Parable of the Talents*; 1998: Vonda McIntyre, *The Moon and the Sun*
Novella: 2001: Linda Nagata, *Goddesses*; 2000: Ted Chaing, *Story of Your Life*; 1998: Jerry Oltion, *Abandon in Place*
Novelette: 2001: Walter Jon Williams, *Daddy's World*; 2000: Mary Turzillo, *Mars Is No Place for Children*; 1998: Nancy Kress, *The Flowers of Aulit Prison*
Short Story: 2001: Terry Bisson, *Macs*; 2000: Leslie What, *The Cost of Doing Business*; 1998: Jane Yolen, *Sister Emily's Lightship*.

Sponsoring Organization: Science Fiction and Fantasy Writers of America, Inc (SFWA).

Address: Science Fiction and Fantasy Writers of America, Inc, POB 877, Chestertown, MD 21620, USA.

Nestlé Smarties Book Prize

An annual award for children's fiction or poetry, sponsored by Nestlé. The award was established in 1985 by Book Trust and has become one of the UK's best known children's book prizes. Gold, Silver and Bronze awards are presented in three age categories. An initial shortlist is drawn up by a panel of adults; the eventual winners are picked by schoolchildren who have won a competition to become Young Judges.

Eligibility and Restrictions: The prize is awarded annually to a work of fiction or poetry for children written in English by a UK citizen, or an author resident in the UK in the year ending 31 October. Entries are judged in three age categories: under 5, 6–8 and 9–11.

How to Apply: Publishers may submit entries.

Recent Winners: Gold Award winners:
9–11 Years: 2001: Eva Ibbotson, *Journey to the River Sea*; 2000: William Nicholson, *The Wind Singer*; 1999: J. K. Rowling, *Harry Potter and the Prisoner of Azkaban*; 1998: J. K. Rowling, *Harry Potter and the Chamber of Secrets*; 1997: J. K. Rowling, *Harry Potter and the Philosopher's Stone*
6–8 Years: 2001: Emily Smith, *The Shrimp*; 2000: Jacqueline Wilson, *Lizzie Zipmouth*; 1999: Laurence Anholt, *Snow White and the Seven Aliens*; 1998: Harry Horse, *Last of the Gold Diggers*; 1997: Jenny Nimmo, *The Owl Tree*
0–5 Years: 2001: Catherine and Laurence Anholt, *Chimp and Zee*; 2000: Bob Graham, *Max*; 1999: Julia Donaldson, *The Gruffalo*; 1998: Sue Heap, *Cowboy Baby*; 1997: Charlotte Voake, *Ginger*.

Sponsoring Organization: Nestlé.

Contact: Tarryn McKay.

Address: Book Trust, Book House, 45 East Hill, London SW18 2QZ, UK. **Telephone:** (20) 8516 2972. **Fax:** (20) 8516 2978. **E-mail:** booktrust.org.uk.

Neuer deutscher Literaturpreis

Sponsored by the publisher Aufbau-Verlag and the magazine *neue deutsche Literatur*, the prize has been awarded every two years since 1998 to literary works which demonstrate mastery of narrative language. The competition is judged by a jury made up of employees of Aufbau-Verlag and *neue deutsche Literatur*. The winner, announced during the Frankfurt Book Fair, receives a prize of €10,000 and special hardback publication of the winning work.

Eligibility and Restrictions: Open to works written in the form of a traditional novel or novella. Science fiction, crime and fantasy are excluded. Manuscripts must be at least 100 pages long and be written in German.

How to Apply: Applications should be sent accompanied by biographical details to the Editorial Dept at Aufbau-Verlag by the end of March.

Recent Winners: 2000: Richard Wagner, *Miss Bukarest*; 1998: (no prize awarded).

Sponsoring Organization: Aufbau-Verlag.

Contact: Dr Jürgen Engler.

Address: Aufbau-Verlag, Neue Promenade 6, 10178 Berlin, Germany. **Telephone:** (30) 28 39 42 38. **Fax:** 930) 28 39 41 00. **Internet:** www.aufbau-verlag.de. **E-mail:** ndl@aufbau-verlag.de.

Neustadt International Prize for Literature

Established in 1969 by Dr Ivar Ivask (then Editor of *Books Abroad/World Literature Today*) and the University of Oklahoma, to honour a lifetime's outstanding achievement in fiction, poetry or drama. The prize is awarded every two years by a jury of 10–12 writers and translators which changes for each award. Each juror nominates one candidate, and the winner is selected by the jury six months later. The winner receives $50,000 plus a solid silver replica of an eagle feather, a hand-lettered certificate and a special issue of *World Literature Today*.

Eligibility and Restrictions: There are no linguistic or geographical restrictions, but a representative sample of each nominee's work must be available to the jury in English, Spanish or French.

How to Apply: Not open to general application; nominations are made only by the jurors.

Recent Winners: 2002: Álvaro Mutis (Colombia); 2000: David Malouf (Australia); 1998: Nuruddin Farah (Somalia); 1996: Assia Djebar (Algeria/France); 1994: Kamau Brathwaite (Barbados).

Sponsoring Organization: World Literature Today/University of Oklahoma.

Contact: Exec. Dir Prof. R C Davis-Undiano.

Address: World Literature Today, University of Oklahoma, 110 Monnet Hall, Norman, OK 73019–4033, USA. **Telephone:** (405) 325-4531. **Fax:** (405) 325-7495. **Internet:** www.ou.edu/worldlit. **E-mail:** rcdavis@ou.edu.

New Brunswick Excellence in the Arts Awards

These awards, established in 1984, recognize outstanding contributions to the arts in New Brunswick by a native or resident New Brunswicker; two awards (C$5,000) are awarded for the literary arts, one for work in English (Alden Nowlan Award) and one for work in French (Pascal Poirier Award).

How to Apply: The deadline for nominations is 1 October of each year.

Recent Winners: Pascal Poirier Award: 2002: Antonine Maillet; 2000: Claude LeBouthillier; 1998: Raymond Guy LeBlanc
Alden Nowlan Award: 2000: Elizabeth Harvor; 1999: Nancy Bauer; 1998: Robert Gibbs.

Sponsoring Organization: New Brunswick Arts Board.

Address: New Brunswick Arts Board, 634 Queen St, Suite 300, Fredericton, NB, E3B 1C2, Canada. **Telephone:** (506) 460-5888. **Fax:** (506) 460-5880. **E-mail:** nbabcanb@artsnb.ca.

New Letters Literary Awards

Established in 1985 to discover and reward new writers, to give them a chance to compete with more established writers, and to encourage the more established writers to try new genres or new work in competition. The awards are offered annually in the categories fiction (Alexander Patterson Cappon Fiction Prize), poetry (New Letters Poetry Prize) and creative non-fiction (Dorothy Churchill Cappon Prize). One winner and one runner-up are selected in each category, chosen by a distinguished panel of judges. The winners receive $1,000 and publication of their entry in *New Letters* magazine.

Eligibility and Restrictions: Only unpublished work is considered. Entries are not to exceed 5,000 words. Entrant's name and address should not appear on the manuscript.

How to Apply: Entries should be sent with contact details on a separate cover sheet, accompanied by an entry fee of $10; deadline is mid-May.

Recent Winners: Fiction: 2001: Gina Ochsner; 2000: Lou Fisher; 1999: Anne Panning
Poetry: 2001: Michael Campagnoli; 2000: Elizabeth Antalek; 1999: Joan I. Siegel
Non-fiction: 2001: Melita Schaum; 2000: M. Garrett Bauman; 1999: Debra Marquart.

Sponsoring Organization: New Letters magazine.

Address: UMKC, University House, 5101 Rockhill Rd, Kansas City, MO 64110–2499, USA. **Telephone:** (816) 235-1168. **Fax:** (816) 235-2611. **Internet:** www.umkc.edu/newletters. **E-mail:** newletters@umkc.edu.

New Millennium Writing Awards

Established in 1995 to promote writers and the written word in the new millennium. Awards are made in the categories fiction, poetry and non-fiction. Winners in each category receive $1,000, plus publication in a special anthology and on the *New Millennium Writings* website.

Eligibility and Restrictions: Entries must be previously unpublished in anything with a circulation greater than 5,000. There are no restrictions as to style or content. Each work of fiction or non-fiction is a separate entry and should total no more than 6,000 words. Each poetry entry may include up to three poems, not to exceed five pages in total.

How to Apply: Entry form available on internet at www.newmillennium writings.com/awards.html. Deadline is mid-June. Submission fee of $16 for each entry.

Recent Winners: Fiction: 2001: Toby Heaton, *Southern Revival* and Sari Rose, *The Daughter of Retail* (joint winners); 2000: Ann Bronston, *Reruns*
Poetry: 2001: Eduardo C. Corral, *For A Boy in a Bus Depot*; 2000: Donna Doyle, *My Mother, Climbing her Family Tree* and Elizabeth Haukaas, *The Hummingbird Heart* (joint winners)
Non-fiction: 2001: Trent Moorman, *Tilos*; 2000: Melita Schaum, *The Weight of Spring Wind*.

Sponsoring Organization: New Millennium Writings Anthology.

Contact: Editor Don Williams.

Address: NMW Room M2, POB 2463, Knoxville, TN 37901, USA. **Telephone:** (865) 428-0389. **Fax:** (865) 428-0389. **Internet:** www.writingawards.com. **E-mail:** donwilliams7@att.net.

New Writer Prose and Poetry Prizes

Sponsored by *The New Writer* magazine, the prize aims to encourage bold, incisive material in any genre. Up to 25 prizes (total prize money £2,500) are presented each year as well as publication for the prize-winning entries in *The New Writer Special Collection*. Preliminary judging is carried out by the magazine's editorial board with guest judges making the final selection.

Eligibility and Restrictions: Prizes are awarded in three categories: poetry (single poems up to 40 lines and collections of between 6 and 10 poems); fiction (short stories up to 4,000 words and serials/novellas up to 20,000 words, on any subject or theme and any genre except children's); and non-fiction (essays, articles and interviews covering any writing-related or literary theme, up to 2,000 words).

How to Apply: Entries should be sent to the address given accompanied by the entry form and fee (£4 per single poem, short story or non-fiction entry; £10 per collection of poetry or serial/novella), by the end of November.

Sponsoring Organization: New Writer.

Address: The New Writer Poetry Prizes, PO Box 60, Cranbrook, Kent TN17 2ZR, UK. **Telephone:** (1580) 212626. **Fax:** (1580) 212041. **Internet:** www.thenewwriter.com. **E-mail:** info@thenewwriter.com.

New Zealand Post Children's Book Awards

The awards are presented annually to provide recognition and reward for authors and illustrators of high-quality New Zealand books for children. Twenty outstanding entries are shortlisted in late January; the winners are presented with their prizes during the New Zealand Post Children's Book Festival in March. The awards are as follows: Senior Fiction Award (prize of $NZ5,000); Junior Fiction Award ($NZ5,000); Non-fiction Award ($NZ5,000); and Picture Book Award ($NZ5,000, split between author and illustrator). Additional prizes are given for the Children's Choice Award (presentation trophy), the Best First Book Award (chosen from among the other winners, and receives an additional $NZ1,000), and the Book of the Year (framed scroll and $NZ5,000).

Eligibility and Restrictions: Entries are judged in four categories: Senior Fiction (suitable for secondary school students); Junior Fiction (primary or intermediate school pupils); Non-fiction (excluding textbooks); and Picture Book (illustrations must comprise at least 50%). Anthologies are not eligible. All entries must be the work of New Zealand citizens, and must have been published during the previous year.

How to Apply: Submissions are accepted from publishers and booksellers; four copies are required.

Recent Winners: Senior Fiction Award: 2002: Joanna Orwin, *Owl*; 2001: Ken Catran, *Voyage with Jason*; 2000: Tessa Duder, *The Tiggie Thompson Show*
Junior Fiction: 2002: Sandy McKay, *Recycled*; 2001: Joy Cowley, *Shadrach Girl*; 2000: Vince Ford, *2MUCH4U*
Non-fiction: 2002: Lloyd Spencer Davis, *The Plight of the Penguin*; 2001: *The Zoo: Meet the Locals*; 2000: Hirini Melbourne and Te Maari Gardiner, *Te Wao Nui a Tane*
Picture Book: 2002: Joy Cowley and Chris Mousdale (illustrator), *Brodie*; 2001: Margaret Beames and Sue Hitchcock, *Oliver in the Garden*; 2000: Gavin Bishop, *The House that Jack Built*
Children's Choice: 2002: Joy Watson and Wendy Hodder, *Grandpa's Shorts*; 2001: Margaret Beames and Sue Hitchcock, *Oliver in the Garden*; 2000: Lunley Dodd, *Hairy Maclary and Zachary Quack*
Best First Book: 2002: Joy Cowley and Chris Mousdale (illustrator), *Brodie*; 2000: Vince Ford, *2MUCH4U*
Book of the Year: 2002: Lloyd Spencer Davis, *The Plight of the Penguin*; 2001: Ken Catran, *Voyage with Jason*; 2000: Gavin Bishop, *The House that Jack Built*.

Sponsoring Organization: Booksellers New Zealand/New Zealand Post/ Creative New Zealand.

Contact: Promotions Team Leader Jayne Wasmuth.

Address: PO Box 11–377, Wellington, New Zealand. **Telephone:** (4) 4728678. **Fax:** (4) 4728628. **Internet:** www.booksellers.co.nz. **E-mail:** jaynewasmuth@ booksellers.co.nz.

John Newbery Medal

Established in 1922 and named after John Newbery, an 18th century British bookseller; this medal, along with the Randolph Caldecott Medals, represents the most prestigious US award in children's literature. The medal is awarded annually to the writer of 'the most distinguished contribution to American literature for children' published in the USA in the previous year.

Eligibility and Restrictions: Writing of any form can be considered: fiction, non-fiction and poetry. The award may be made posthumously. Only original works are considered; reprints and compilations are not eligible. Authors must be citizens or residents of the USA and the work must not have been published originally outside the USA.

How to Apply: One copy of the book should be sent to the Association for Library Service to Children (ALSC) office, and one copy to the Chair of the Award Committee, by 31 December of the year of publication.

Recent Winners: 2002: Linda Sue Park, *A Single Shard*; 2001: Richard Peck, *A Year Down Yonder*; 2000: Christopher Paul Curtis, *Bud, Not Buddy*; 1999: Louis Sachar, *Holes*; 1998: Karen Hesse, *Out of the Dust*.

Sponsoring Organization: Association for Library Service to Children, a division of the American Library Association.

Address: Association for Library Service to Children, American Library Association, 50 East Huron, Chicago, IL 60611–2795, USA. **Fax:** (312) 944-7671. **Internet:** www.ala.org/alsc. **E-mail:** alsc@ala.org.

Newcastle Poetry Prize

The Newcastle Poetry Prize is one of the most prestigious poetry awards in Australia. There are three sections: the Open Section (prize of A$8,000), the New Media award for innovation in poetry production and presentation (A$2,000), and a special prize for a Newcastle poet.

Eligibility and Restrictions: For the Open category entries should be a poem or group of poems up to 200 lines, while the New Media section is for entries presented using new media.

How to Apply: Entries should be sent by 31 January accompanied by an entry fee of A$15.

Recent Winners: Open Section: 2001: Jo Gardiner, *Song to the Moon*, Emma Jones, *Fugue, or a Possible Poem* and John Watson, *A Jetty Completely Surrounded* (joint winners)
New Media: 2001: Mez Breeze, *Rictus Usage* and Jayne Keane, *Central Australia* (joint winners).

Sponsoring Organization: Coal River Press.

Address: Coal River Press, 246 Parry St, Newcastle West, NSW 2302, Australia. **Telephone:** (49) 611696. **Fax:** (49) 623959. **Internet:** www.artshunter.com.au. **E-mail:** npp@artshunter.com.au.

Nihon Horâ Shôsetsu Taishô (Japan Horror Story Grand Prize)

Established in 1994 by Kadokawa publishing company and Fuji Television with the aim of recognizing authors who have demonstrated exceptional talent in the genre of horror stories. Awarded annually to a previously unpublished novel in the genre of horror fiction. The winner receives 5 million yen; separate prizes are also given for the categories of long fiction (3 million yen) and short fiction (2 million yen), with total prize money amounting to 10 million yen. Winning stories are published by Kadokawa Shoten and dramatized and broadcast by Fuji Television.

Sponsoring Organization: Kadokawa Shoten Publishing Co., Ltd.

Address: Kadokawa Shoten Publishing Co, Ltd, 13–3 Fujimi, Chiyoda-ku, Tokyo, 102–0071, Japan. **Telephone:** (3) 3238 8501. **Fax:** 3-3262-7601.

Nihon SF Taishô (Japan Science Fiction Grand Prize)

Established in 1980 and jointly sponsored by the Science Fiction and Fantasy Writers of Japan and the Tokuma Shoten publishing company. The award is given annually to the best single-volume work of science fiction published between September and the following August. The winner receives 1 million yen plus a trophy.

Sponsoring Organization: Tokuma Shoten publishing company.

Address: Tokuma Shoten publishing company, Tokyo, Japan.

Martinus Nijhoff Prijs voor Vertalingen

An annual prize presented by the Prince Bernhard Cultural Foundation, first presented in 1955. The winner receives a prize of 100,000 DFL, of which 25,000 is a cash prize and the remaining 75,000 is for use on future work projects.

Recent Winners: 2000: Bertie van der Meij; 1999: Therese Cornips.

Sponsoring Organization: Prins Bernhard Fonds (Prince Bernhard Cultural Foundation).

Address: Postbus 19750, Herengracht 476, 1017 CB Amsterdam, Netherlands. **Telephone:** (20) 520 61 30. **Fax:** (20) 623 84 99. **Internet:** www. prinsbernhardcultuurfonds.nl/.

NIKE Literary Award

The NIKE Literary Prize was founded in 1997 by the publication *Gazeta Wyborcza* and Nicom Consulting to promote Polish literature, with particular focus on the novel. It has become the most prestigious award in Poland. Every year a nine-member jury selects the Polish book of the year from a shortlist of 20 nominee titles in a three-stage competition. The author of the winning book receives the NIKE statuette and a cash award of 80,000 zloty.

Eligibility and Restrictions: Open to literary works in all genres (including autobiographies, memoirs, etc. and works on the humanities). Works of criticism and by more than one author are excluded. The award is only made to living authors.

Recent Winners: 2001: Jerzy Pilch, *Pod Mocnym Aniolem*; 2000: Tadeusz Rózewicz, *Matka Odchodzi*; 1999: Stanislaw Baranczak, *Chirurgiczna Precyzja*; 1998: Czeslaw Milosz, *Piesek Przydrozny*; 1997: Wieslaw Mysliwski, *Widnokrag*.

Sponsoring Organization: Fundacja Nagrody Literackiej NIKE.

Address: Fundacja Nagrody Literackiej NIKE, ul. Wiertnicza 104, 02–952 Warsaw, Poland. **Telephone:** (22) 851 44 99. **Fax:** (22) 851 37 77. **Internet:** www.nike.org.pl.

Nobel Prize in Literature (Nobelpriset i litteratur)

Established by the will of Alfred Nobel, to be awarded to those who, in the preceding year 'shall have produced in the field of literature the most outstanding work in an ideal direction'. The first Nobel Prize was awarded in 1901. Besides the Nobel Prize in Literature, other Nobel prizes are awarded in Physics, Chemistry, Physiology or Medicine, Economic Sciences and Peace. The Literature laureate is chosen by the Swedish Academy, from writers nominated by members of academies, academics, presidents of societies of authors, professors of literature and languages, and previous prizewinners, via the Nobel Committee. Literature is defined by the statutes of the prize as including any writings which 'by virtue of their form and style, possess literary value'. The prize is awarded annually, along with the other Nobel Prizes, on 10 December (the anniversary of Alfred Nobel's death), and the prize is presented by the King of Sweden. In 2002 the prize was SEK 10,000,000.

Eligibility and Restrictions: The prize may be shared between two candidates, but no more than two.

How to Apply: Proposals must reach the Academy by 1 February; the prize-winner is chosen in October. It is not possible to propose oneself as a candidate.

Recent Winners: 2002: Imre Kertesz; 2001: V. S. Naipaul; 2000: Gao Xingjian; 1999: Günter Grass; 1998: José Saramago; 1997: Dario Fo; 1996: Wisława Szymborska; 1995: Seamus Heaney; 1994: Kenzaburo Oe; 1993: Toni Morrison; 1992: Derek Walcott; 1991: Nadine Gordimer; 1990: Octavio Paz.

Sponsoring Organization: Nobel Foundation.

Address: Swedish Academy, POB 2118, 103 13 Stockholm, Sweden. **Telephone:** (8) 10 65 24. **Fax:** (8) 24 42 25. **Internet:** www.nobel.se. **E-mail:** sekretariat@svenskaakademien.se.

NOMA Award for Publishing in Africa

The Noma Award was established in 1979 by the late Shoichi Noma, former President of the Japanese publisher Kodansha Ltd, to encourage work by African writers. It is awarded to an outstanding new book by an African writer. The Managing Committee of the Noma Award also acts as its jury. Its members are African scholars and book experts, as well as representatives of the international publishing community. The prize is of $10,000 plus a commemorative plaque.

Eligibility and Restrictions: The book must have been first published in Africa (and the African publisher must hold original rights to the book). Eligible categories are: scholarly or academic; children's books; and literature and creative writing. Entries may be submitted in any African language, either indigenous or European, and should have been published in the calendar year preceding the year in which the award is presented.

How to Apply: Only publishers may submit entries; six entries of each work entered should be sent by 28 February. The maximum number of entries is three per publisher.

Recent Winners: 2001: Abosede Emanuel, *Odun Ifa/Ifa Festival*; 2000: shared by Kimani Njogu and Rocha Chimerah, *Ufundishaji wa Fasihi. Nadharia na Mbinu*; 1999: Djibril Samb, *L'interprétation des rêves dans la région Sénégambienne*; 1998: Peter Adwok Nyaba, *The Politics of Liberation in South Sudan: An Insider's View*; 1996: Kitia Touré, *Destins Parallèles*.

Contact: Mary Jay.

Address: Secretary to the Managing Committee, POB 128, Witney OX8 5XU, UK. **Telephone:** (1993) 775235. **Fax:** (1993) 709265. **E-mail:** maryljay@aol.com.

Noma Bungei Shô (Noma Prize for Literature)

Established in 1941 by the Noma Service Association (Noma Hôkô Kai), an organization formed in accordance with the last wishes of Noma Seiji (1878–1938), founder and first president of the Kôdansha publishing company. Awarded annually to an outstanding new work in one of a variety of literary genres (including non-fiction) published between October and the following September. The winner receives 3 million yen, plus a commemorative plaque.

Sponsoring Organization: Noma Service Association.

Address: Otawa Daini Bldg, 2–12–21 Otawa 2-chrome, Bunkyo-ku, Tokyo, 112, Japan.

Noma Concours for Picture Book Illustrations

The Noma Concours for Picture Book Illustrations has been organized biennially since 1978 to encourage young illustrators, graphic designers and artists in Asia, the Pacific, Africa, Arab States, and Latin America. An international jury meets to select one Grand Prize winner, two Second Prize winners, 10 Runner-up winners and 20 Encouragement Prize winners. All winners receive a medal designed by Yutaka Sugita. In addition, the Grand Prize winner receives a prize of US $3,000, two Second Prize winners each receive $1,000, and the 10 Runners-up receive $300.

Eligibility and Restrictions: Open to original illustrations for picture books by artists in the countries of Asia and the Pacific, Africa, the Arab States, Latin America, and the Caribbean.

Recent Winners: 2000: Grand Prize: Nasrin Khosravi, *The Girl of the Wish Garden*.

Sponsoring Organization: Asia/Pacific Cultural Centre for UNESCO—ACCU.

Address: Asia/Pacific Cultural Centre for UNESCO—ACCU, 6 Fukuromachi, Shinjuku-ku, Tokyo, 162, Japan. **Internet:** www.accu.or.jp. **E-mail:** general@caaccu.or.jp.

Noma Literacy Prize

The Noma Literacy Prize is one of a series of five international literacy prizes presented in collaboration with UNESCO. It was created in 1980 by the late Shoichi Noma, President of Kodansha Ltd, a major Japanese publishing group. The prize is awarded annually in recognition of the services of institutions, organizations or individuals displaying outstanding merit and achieving special success in contributing to the fight against illiteracy. The winner receives a prize consisting of a cheque for US $15,000, a silver medal and a diploma.

Recent Winners: 2000: Philippines Non-formal Education Programme; 1999: National Literacy Mission (India); 1998: El Abrojo Institute for People's Education (Uruguay).

Sponsoring Organization: Kodansha/UNESCO.

Address: Otawa Daini Bldg, 2–12–21 Otawa 2-chome, Bunkyo-ku, Tokyo, 112, Japan.

Noma Literature Prize for New Writers

The Noma Literature Prize for New Writers is one of a series of awards sponsored by the major publishing company Kodansha. This prize, which recognizes an outstanding debut work by a young novelist, is among the most coveted of the Noma prizes.

Recent Winners: Recent winners include Haruki Murakami, *A Wild Sheep Chase*; Hideo Levy, *A Room Where the Star-Spangled Banner Cannot Be Heard*; and Fujino Chiya, *Oshaberi kaidan (A Chatty Ghost Story)*.

Sponsoring Organization: Kodansha.

Address: Otawa Daini Bldg, 2–12–21 Otawa 2-chome, Bunkyo-ku, Tokyo, 112, Japan.

Nordic Council Literature Prize

The Nordic Council's Literature Prize was founded in 1961, and is now regarded as one of the most distinguished Nordic prizes. Its aim is to promote the Nordic identity via the concept of Nordic literature, including sagas, folk tales and great authors.

Eligibility and Restrictions: The prize is awarded by a 10-member jury, with members drawn from each of the countries represented in the Nordic Council. The jury selects two works from each country, and decides on the winner by majority vote. Judgement is made on the basis of quality and originality. First editions published in the last two years are eligible.

How to Apply: Nominations should be made by 1 December.

Recent Winners: 2002: Lars Saabye Christensen, *The Half-Brother*; 2001: Jan Kjærstad, *The Discoverer*; 2000: Henrik Nordbrandt, *Drømmebroer (Dream Bridges)*; 1999: Pia Tafdrup, *Dronningeporten (The Queen's Gate)*; 1998: Tua Forsstrom, *Efter att ha tillbringat en natt bland hästar (After Having Spent a Night Among Horses)*; 1997: Dorrit Willumsen, *Bang. En roman om Herman Bang*; 1996: Øystein Lonn, *Hva skal vi gjøre i dag (What Shall We Do Today?)*; 1995: Einar Már Guðmundsson, *Englar alheimsins (Angels of the Universe)*.

Sponsoring Organization: Nordic Council, Swedish Delegation.

Address: Riksdagen, 100 12 Stockholm, Sweden. **Internet:** www.norden.org.

Nordisk Skolebibliotekarforenings Barnebokpris
(Norwegian School Library Association Children's Book Prize)

The prize was established by the Norwegian School Library Association in 1982, and is presented for a Norwegian book for children or young people. The winner receives a painting.

Recent Winners: 2001: Finn Øglænd, *Dei penaste jentene på TV*; 2000: Svein Nyhus, *Verden har ingen hjørner*; 1999: Bjørn Sortland, *Raudt, blått og litt gult*; 1998: Egil Hyldmo, *Ulveboka*; 1997: Tormod Haugen, *Georg og Gloria (og Edvard)*.

Sponsoring Organization: Nordisk skolebibliotekarforening.

Address: c/o Skolebibliotekar-foreningen I Norge, Torsvev 1, 7540 Kaebu, Norway.

Nordiska Priset (Nordic Prize)

Established in 1987, and awarded by the Swedish Academy to a writer in one of the Scandinavian countries who has made an important achievement in an area within the Academy's mandate. The award is of SEK 250,000.

How to Apply: No applications are accepted.

Sponsoring Organization: Swedish Academy.

Contact: Sec. Bo Svensen.

Address: Swedish Academy, PO Box 2118, 103 13 Stockholm, Sweden.

Norsk Kritikerlags Barnebokpris (Norwegian Critics' Children's Book Prize)

The prize was established in 1978 by the Norwegian Critics' Association, and has become one of the most important literary awards for children's literature in the country. It is awarded annually for the best work of children's fiction. The winner receives a piece of art.

Recent Winners: 2001: Rune Belsvik, *Verdas mest forelska par*; 2000: Anne Grete Hollup, *Engel*; 1999: Erna Ousland, *Salamanderryttaren*; 1998: Erlend Loe, *Kurt Quo Vadis*; 1997: Rønnaug Kleiva, *Ikkje gløym å klappe katten*.

Sponsoring Organization: Norsk Kritikerlags.

Address: Norsk Kritikerlags, Boks 352, Sentrum, 0101 Oslo, Norway. **E-mail:** norsk.kri@online.no.

Norsk Kritikerlags Pris (Norwegian Critics' Book Prize)

This is one of the major Norwegian awards, and has been presented every year since 1950 for the best work of adult fiction; a separate prize is awarded by the same organization for children's books.

Recent Winners: 2001: Ragnar Hovland, *Ei vinterreise*; 2000: Jonny Halberg, *Flommen*; 1999: Dag Solstad, *T. Singer*; 1998: Karl Ove Knausgård, *Ute av verden*; 1997: Hans Herbjørnrud, *Blinddøra*.

Sponsoring Organization: Norsk Kritikerlags.

Address: Norsk Kritikerlags, Boks 352, Sentrum, 0101 Oslo, Norway. **E-mail:** norsk.kri@online.no.

Norsk Sprakpris (Norwegian Language Prize)

An annual prize established in 1992 by the Norwegian Language Council. The winner is chosen by a four-member selection committee, and receives a cash prize and a diploma.

Recent Winners: 2002: (no award made); 2001: Arild Stubhaug; 2000: (no award made); 1999: Ottar Grepstad; 1998: Guri Hjeltnes.

Sponsoring Organization: Norsk Språkråd (Norwegian Language Council).

Address: Norsk Sprakrad, Postboks 8107 Dep, 0032 Oslo, Norway. **Telephone:** (24) 14 03 50. **Fax:** (24) 14 03 51. **Internet:** www.sprakrad.no/pris.htm.

Norske Akademis Pris til Minne om Thorleif Dahl (Norwegian Academy Thorleif Dahl Memorial Prize)

Each November the Norwegian Academy presents this prize to an outstanding work of fiction or non-fiction, either an original work or in translation. The prize is worth NOK 100,000.

Eligibility and Restrictions: Open to works of fiction or non-fiction written in Norwegian.

Recent Winners: 2001: Sven Kærup Bjørneboe; 2000: Georg Johannesen; 1999: Tor Åge Bringsværd; 1998: Hans Aaraas; 1997: Tove Lie.

Sponsoring Organization: Norske Akademi for Sprog og Litteratur (Norwegian Academy for Language and Literature).

Address: Norske Akademi for Sprog og Litteratur, Inkognitogt 24, 0256 Oslo, Norway. **Internet:** www.riksmalsforbundet.no/priser.html. **E-mail:** ordet@ riksmalsforbundet.no.

Norske Lyrikklubbens Pris (Norwegian Poetry Club Prize)

This prize, known until 1996 as the Hartvig Kirans Minnepris (Hartvig Kirans Memorial Prize), is presented annually for poetry.

Recent Winners: 2001: Øyvind Rimbereid; 2000: Inger Elisabeth Hansen; 1999: Arne Ruste; 1998: Torgeir Rebolledo Pedersen; 1997: Tone Hødnebø.

Sponsoring Organization: De Norske Bokklubbene.

Address: De Norske Bokklubbene, 0040 Oslo, Norway. **E-mail:** johann.grip@ bokklubbene.no.

North American Native Authors First Book Awards

The award is given for a book-length prose manuscript by a Native American of American Indian, Aleut, Inuit, or Metis ancestry who has not yet published a book. The winner receives $500 and a plaque, and the winning manuscript is submitted for publication to select presses specializing in Native American arts and letters.

Recent Winners: 2002: Edythe Hobson (Arkansas Quapaw), *An Inquest Every Sunday.*

Sponsoring Organization: Native Writers Circle of the Americas.

Address: Native Writers Circle of the Americas, Department of English, 60 Van Vleet Oval, Room 113, University of Oklahoma, Norman, OK 73019–0240, USA. **Telephone:** (405) 325-6231.

The Northern Palmira Prize

Awarded annually in June for works of prose, literary criticism and poetry.

Recent Winners: Sixth annual Northern Palmira literary prize: V. Popov (prose), E. Shvarz (poetry), E. Nevzglyadova (literary criticism).

Sponsoring Organization: Russian Academy of Arts.

Address: Russian Academy of Arts, ul. Prechistenka 21, 119034 Moscow, Russia. **Telephone:** (95) 290-20-88. **Fax:** (95) 954-33-20.

Northern Rock Foundation Writer Award

This new award represents Britain's most lucrative prize for an individual author, with its prize of £60,000; the winner receives three yearly instalments of £20,000. The award was established by the Northern Rock Foundation with the aim of helping developing writers flourish in the northern region as well as setting a trend for an increase in funding for literary awards. The first prize was awarded in 2002.

Eligibility and Restrictions: Open to writers in all genres, but authors have to be predominantly living and working in the North East of England (Teesside, County Durham, Tyneside or Northumberland).

Recent Winners: 2002: Anne Stevenson.

Sponsoring Organization: Northern Rock Foundation.

Address: The Northern Rock Foundation, 21 Lansdowne Terrace, Gosforth, Newcastle upon Tyne NE3 1HP, UK. **Internet:** www.nr-foundation.org.uk/index. cfm.

Northern Writers' Awards

The Northern Writers' Awards are co-ordinated by New Writing North (NWN) with funding from Northern Arts. Each year approximately £20,000 is granted to writers of new fiction and poetry to develop collections and to complete books. NWN has been running the awards schemes since 1999. A panel of professional writers shortlists and makes awards once a year.

Eligibility and Restrictions: Applicants must be resident in the Northern Arts region.

Recent Winners: Time to Write Awards: 2002: Richard Caddell (Durham), Chrissie Glazebrook (Newcastle) and Carol Clewlow (North Tyneside)
Northern Promise Awards: 2002: Barrie Darke (North Tyneside), Deborah Bruce (Newcastle), Christine Powell (County Durham), Joanna Boulter (County Durham), Victoria Bennett (Windermere), Marlynn Rosario (North Tyneside), Eileen Jennison (County Durham) and Kathleen Kenny (Newcastle).

Sponsoring Organization: New Writing North.

Contact: John McGagh.

Address: New Writing North, 7–8 Trinity Chare, Quayside, Newcastle upon Tyne NE1 3DF, UK. **Internet:** www.newwritingnorth.com. **E-mail:** subtext.nwn@ virgin.net.

NSW Premier's Literary Awards

A set of literary awards established from 1979 onwards to honour distinguished achievements by Australian writers. Entries are judged by an independent committee of peers, appointed by the New South Wales (NSW) Ministry for the Arts. The awards include the Gleebooks Prize for Literary or Cultural Criticism, the Community Relations Commission Award, the Script Award (for film, radio or TV scripts), the Play Award, the Ethel Turner Prize for Young People's Literature, the Patricia Wrightson Prize for Children's Literature, the Kenneth Slessor Prize for Poetry, the Douglas Stewart Prize for Non-fiction and the Christina Stead Prize for Fiction. Most of the awards carry a prize of A$15,000 plus a medallion, although for the Gleebooks award the amount is A$5,000, while for the Douglas Stewart and Christina Stead awards the prize money is A$20,000.

Eligibility and Restrictions: For all the awards the author must be living Australian citizens or hold permanent resident status. All works must be in English.

How to Apply: Nomination forms may be completed by authors or their representatives. Four copies of each work should be sent by the end of November.

Recent Winners: Gleebooks Prize for Literary or Cultural Criticism: 2001: Anna Haebich; 2000: Inga Clendinnen; 1999: Diane Bell; 1997: Alison MacKinnen; 1996: David McCooey
Community Relations Commission Award: 2001: Christine Olsen; 2000: Meme McDonald and Boori Monty Prior; 1999: George Alexander; 1997: Mark Raphael Baker; 1996: Hanifa Deen
Script Award: 2001: Christine Olsen; 2000: Melina Marchetta; 1999: Heather Rose, Frederick Stahl and Rolf de Heer; 1997: Trevor Graham; 1996: Ian David

Play Award: 2001: Margery and Michael Forde; 2000: Daniel Keene; 1999: Scott Rankin and Leah Purcell; 1997: Michael Gurr; 1996: John Misto
Ethel Turner Prize for Young People's Literature: 2001: Jaclyn Moriarty; 2000: Meme McDonald and Boori Monty Prior; 1999: Garry Disher; 1997: Junko Morimoto; 1996: David Metzenthen
Patricia Wrightson Prize for Children's Literature: 2001: Margaret Wild and Ron Brooks; 2000: Steven Herrick; 1999: Odo Hirsch
Kenneth Slessor Prize for Poetry: 2001: Ken Taylor; 2000: Jennifer Maiden; 1999: Lee Cataldi; 1997: Anthony Lawrence; 1996: Eric Beach and J. S. Harry

Douglas Stewart Prize for Non-fiction: 2001: Kim Mahood; 2000: Drusilla Modjeska; 1999: Ray Parkin; 1997: Alan Atkinson; 1996: Tom Griffiths
Christina Stead Prize for Fiction: 2001: Alex Miller; 2000: Michael Meehan; 1999: Roger McDonald; 1997: Robert Drewe; 1996: Sue Woolfe.

Sponsoring Organization: NSW Ministry for the Arts.

Address: POB A226, Sydney South, NSW 1235, Australia. **Telephone:** (2) 9228 5533. **Fax:** (2) 9228 4722. **Internet:** www.arts.nsw.gov.au. **E-mail:** www. ministry@arts.nsw.gov.au.

NSW Writer's Fellowship

Established in 1982 to assist the writing of new literary work by writers living in New South Wales (NSW). The prize is offered annually for works in any genre, and is awarded in conjunction with the NSW Premier's Literary Awards. The winner, chosen by an independent committee of peers, appointed by the NSW Ministry for the Arts, receives a cash award of A$20,000.

Eligibility and Restrictions: Author must live in NSW. The award is not given for the completion of university theses or to fund self-publication.

How to Apply: Writers should apply by 21 June sending a completed application form and 10 pages of supporting material.

Recent Winners: 2001: Ben Le Hunte; 2000: Merlinda Bobis; 1999: Coleen Burke; 1998: George Alexander.

Sponsoring Organization: NSW Ministry for the Arts.

Address: POB A226, Sydney South, NSW 1235, Australia. **Telephone:** (2) 9228 5533. **Fax:** (2) 9228 4722. **Internet:** www.arts.nsw.gov.au. **E-mail:** www. ministry@arts.nsw.gov.au.

Flannery O'Connor Award for Short Fiction

The award recognizes two winners each year for outstanding contributions to short fiction. Winners receive a cash prize of $1,000, and their collections are subsequently published by the University of Georgia Press.

Eligibility and Restrictions: Open to English-language works of short fiction, either published or unpublished. Novels or single novellas are not eligible; novellas are defined as being between 50 and 150 pages. Stories that have previously appeared in magazines or anthologies may be included; however, stories previously published in a book-length collection of the author's own work may not be included.

How to Apply: Authors may submit one or more manuscripts, each accompanied by a submission fee of $20 and a list of author's published work, during April and May.

Recent Winners: 2003: Eric Shade, *Eyesores*; 2002: Kellie Wells, *Compression Scars* and Gina Ochsner, *The Necessary Grace to Fall*; 2001: Dana Johnson, *Break Any Woman Down* and Bill Roorbach, *Big Bend*; 2000: Robert Anderson, *Ice Age* and Darrell Spencer, *Caution: Men in Trees*; 1999: Hester Kaplan, *The Edge of Marriage* and Mary Clyde, *Survival Rates*.

Sponsoring Organization: University of Georgia Press.

Contact: Co-ordinator Emily Montjoy.

Address: University of Georgia Press, 330 Research Dr., Athens, GA 30602–4901, USA. **Telephone:** (706) 369 6135. **Fax:** (706) 369-6131. **Internet:** www.uga.edu/ugapress. **E-mail:** books@ugapress.uga.edu.

Scott O'Dell Historical Fiction Award

An annual award of $5,000, established in 1981, and presented for a work of historical fiction for children or young adults. The winner is selected by the O'Dell Award Committee, headed by Zena Sutherland, Professor Emeritus of Children's Literature, at the University of Chicago.

Eligibility and Restrictions: To be eligible for the award, a book must have been published as a book intended for children or young people. It must be set in the New World (Canada, Central or South America, or the USA), and published by a publisher in the USA. All entries must be written in English by a citizen of the USA.

Recent Winners: 2001: Janet Taylor Lisle, *The Art of Keeping Cool*; 2000: Miriam Bat-Ami, *Two Suns in the Sky*; 1999: Harriette Gillem Robinet, *Forty Acres and Maybe a Mule*; 1998: Karen Hesse, *Out of the Dust*; 1997: Katherine Paterson, *Jip: His Story*.

Sponsoring Organization: University of Chicago.

Address: Dept of Literature, University of Chicago, 5801 S Ellis Ave, Chicago, IL 60637, USA. **Internet:** www.scottodell.com/sosoaward.html.

Oda Sakunosuke Shô (Oda Sakunosuke Prize)

Established in 1983 under the sponsorship of the Osaka Association for the Promotion of Literature (Osaka Bungaku Shinkô-kai) to commemorate the 70th anniversary of Oda's birth with the aim of carrying on the long tradition of Kamigata (Kansai) literature. Awarded annually to an outstanding work of fiction by a new author. The winner receives 500,000 yen plus a certificate and a commemorative gift; in addition, the winning story is published in Bungakukai magazine.

Sponsoring Organization: Osaka Association for the Promotion of Literature (Osaka Bungaku Shinkô-kai).

Address: Osaka Association for the Promotion of Literature (Osaka Bungaku Shinkô-kai), Osaka, Japan.

Oktober-Prisen

An annual prize for fiction sponsored by the publisher Oktober Forlag in collaboration with Kulturfondet Ikaros. The prize, with a value of 75,000 NOK, was first presented in 1992.

Recent Winners: 2001: Morten Øen; 2000: Hanne Ørstavik; 1999: Kjell Askildsen; 1998: Torgeir Rebolledo Pedersen; 1997: Lars Amund Vaage; 1996: Per Petterson.

Sponsoring Organization: Oktober Forlag AS/Kulturfondet Ikaros a/s.

Address: Oktober Forlag AS, PB 6848, St Olavs Plass, 0130 Oslo, Norway. **Telephone:** (23) 35 46 20. **Fax:** (23) 35 46 21. **Internet:** www.oktober.no/. **E-mail:** oktober@oktober.no.

Onassis Cultural Competition Prize

The Alexander S. Onassis Public Benefit Foundation established an international Cultural Competition in 1994, with the first prize awarded in 1997, to promote and enhance the dramatic arts. The prize is awarded every four years for the composition of an original theatrical play, and carries a monetary award of €150,000 for the winner, with two runners-up prizes. The winner is selected by three juries plus a panel of literary experts from the theatrical world.

Eligibility and Restrictions: Drama of any kind is accepted, although works of opera, pantomime or poetry are excluded. The script should be written in English, French, German, Greek, Italian or Spanish.

How to Apply: Entries for the 3rd Competition (2005) should be submitted by 30 June 2003 to the address given. Three copies of the script should be sent accompanied by biographical details and a letter of support from a professional playwrights' association from the entrant's country.

Recent Winners: 2001: Daniel du Plantis (USA), *Past Tenses Ever Present*; 1997: Manjula Padmanabhan (India), *Harvest*.

Sponsoring Organization: Alexander S. Onassis Public Benefit Foundation.

Contact: Admin. Sec. Barbara Charamis.

Address: Alexander S. Onassis Public Benefit Foundation, 7 Eschinou St, 105 58 Athens, Greece. **Telephone:** (1) 3713000. **Fax:** (1) 3713013. **Internet:** www.onassis.gr. **E-mail:** pubrel@caonassis.gr.

Orange Prize for Fiction

Established in 1996 to reward excellence and originality in novels and to promote the writing of women. The winner, chosen by a panel of five women judges from a shortlist of six titles, receives an award of £30,000 and a bronze figurine created by Grizel Niven ('Bessie'). The prize has developed a reputation for recognizing lesser-known talents, and has grown in stature to rank alongside the Man Booker and the Whitbread as one of Britain's foremost literary awards. In 2002 six new categories were introduced, and it was also announced that a new award, the Orange Prize for Translation, for women's fiction translated into the English language, was to be launched.

Eligibility and Restrictions: Novel must have been written in English by a woman of any nationality and published in the UK in the year preceding the award; translations are not eligible for the main Orange Prize, but a separate Orange Prize for Translation is planned.

How to Apply: All novels must either be submitted by publishers or called in by the judges; closing date for entries is 10 December.

Recent Winners: 2002: Ann Patchett, *Bel Canto*; 2001: Kate Grenville, *The Idea of Perfection*; 2000: Linda Grant, *When I Lived in Modern Times*; 1999: Suzanne Berne, *A Crime in the Neighbourhood*; 1998: Carol Shields, *Larry's Party*.

Sponsoring Organization: Orange, administered by Book Trust.

Contact: Tarryn McKay.

Address: Book Trust, Book House, 45 East Hill, London SW18 2QZ, UK. **Telephone:** (20) 8516 2972. **Fax:** (20) 8516 2978. **Internet:** www.orange.co.uk/about/sponsorship/culture/orange_prize.

Orbis Pictus Award for Outstanding Non-fiction for Children

An annual award aimed at promoting and recognizing excellence in the writing of non-fiction for children. It is named after a work by Johannes Amos Comenius, *Orbus Pictus – The World in Pictures* (1657), considered to be the first book actually planned for children. The winning entry is chosen for its accuracy, organization, design and style, as well as its broad appeal and choice of interesting and timely subject matter. The award consists of a plaque.

Eligibility and Restrictions: Any work of non-fiction informational literature may be nominated, including biography, although textbooks, historical fiction, folklore and poetry are excluded. Entries must have been published in the USA during the previous calendar year.

How to Apply: Nominations are accepted from members of the National Council of Teachers of English (NCTE) and the broader educational community. Closing date for nominations is 30 November.

Recent Winners: 2002: Susan Campbell Bartoletti, *Black Potatoes: The Story of the Great Irish Famine 1845–1850*; 2001: Jerry Stanley, *Hurry Freedom: African Americans in Gold Rush California*; 2000: Ruby Bridges, *Through My Eyes*; 1999: Jennifer Armstrong, *Shipwreck at the Bottom of the World: The Extraordinary True Story of Shackleton and the Endurance*; 1998: Laurence Pringle, *An Extraordinary Life: The Story of a Monarch Butterfly*.

Sponsoring Organization: National Council of Teachers of English (NCTE).

Contact: Assoc. Exec. Dir Kathy Egawa.

Address: National Council of Teachers of English, 1111 West Kenyon Rd, Urbana, IL 61081–1096, USA. **Telephone:** (800) 369-6283. **Fax:** (217) 328-0977. **Internet:** www.ncte.org. **E-mail:** kegawa@ncte.org.

Organization of American Historians Foreign Language Book Prize

A biennial prize sponsored by the Organization of American Historians (OAH) for the best book on American history published in a foreign language. The purpose of the prize is to expose American scholars to works originally published in a language other than English, to overcome the language barrier that keeps scholars apart. The winner receives $1,000 and a certificate.

Eligibility and Restrictions: Each entry must be published during the preceding two-year period (January–December). Entries should be concerned with the past (recent or distant) or with issues of continuity and change, and with events or processes with a link to the USA. Unpublished manuscripts will be considered. Books originally submitted for publication in English or by authors for whom English is their first language are not eligible.

How to Apply: Authors of eligible books are invited to nominate their work. Other nominations are also welcome. Four copies should be mailed to the address given by 1 May, accompanied by a one- to two-page essay (in English) explaining why the book is a significant and original contribution to an understanding of American history.

Recent Winners: 2001: Claudia Schnurmann, *Atlantic Worlds: English and Dutch People in the American–Atlantic Area, 1648–1713*; 1999: Jong Won Lee, *US-Korean Relations and Japan in East Asia's Cold War*; 1997: Jean Heffer, *The United States and the Pacific: The Story of a Frontier*; 1996: Marie-Jeanne Rossignol, *The Nationalist Ferment: At the Origins of American Foreign Policy, 1789–1812*; 1995: Ferdinando Fasce, *A Family in Stars and Stripes: The Great War and Corporate Culture in America*; 1994: Jacques Portes, *Une Fascination Réticente: Les États-Unis dans l'Opinion Française*.

Sponsoring Organization: Organization of American Historians (OAH).

Address: Organization of American Historians, 112 North Bryan Ave, Bloomington, IN 47408–4199, USA. **Telephone:** (812) 855-9852. **Fax:** (812) 855-0696. **Internet:** www.oah.org. **E-mail:** awards@oah.org.

Premio letterario Laura Orvieto (Laura Orvieto Literary Prize)

A biennial prize, awarded to an outstanding unpublished work for young readers on a theme which has relevance to the problems of growing up. It is named after a woman with a strong philanthropic attitude, who dedicated a large part of her life to children and their problems. The first prize is of 10 million lire, with a runner-up's prize of 5 million lire.

Eligibility and Restrictions: Open to unpublished manuscripts of up to 100 pages in length, written by an Italian author and aimed at young readers aged 11 to 14. Entries should deal with themes such as the psychological development of children, the relationship between different generations, racial integration and tolerance, the relationship with nature and the environment, school life and friends, or sport.

How to Apply: Deadline for submissions is 30 November.

Sponsoring Organization: Fondazione Premio Laura Oriveto.

Address: Archivio Contemporaneo del Gabinetto G. P. Vieusseuz Via Maggio 42, 00186 Florence, Italy. **Telephone:** (55) 697877.

Orwell Prize

The prize was established in 1993 by the George Orwell Memorial Fund and the editors of *The Political Quarterly*, and is awarded to encourage accessible writing about politics, political thinking or public policy. One prize is awarded for books and pamphlets; the other for newspaper or periodical articles.

Eligibility and Restrictions: Open to books aimed at the reading public, rather than academic books.

How to Apply: Deadline for submissions is mid-January.

Recent Winners: Books: 2001: Michael Ignatieff, *Virtual War*; 2000: Brian Cathcart, *The Case of Stephen Lawrence*; 1999: D. M. Thomas, *Alexander Solzhenitsyn: A Century in his Life*.

Sponsoring Organization: George Orwell Memorial Fund/The Political Quarterly.

Address: George Orwell Memorial Fund, UK.

Osaragi Jirô Shô (Osaragi Jirô Prize)

Established in 1974 by the Asahi Shimbun Company to commemorate the life and work of novelist Osaragi Jirô (1897–1973). Awarded annually to an outstanding prose work. Selection is made by a six-member committee based on recommendations submitted by *Asahi Shimbun* readers and various literary experts. The winner receives 2 million yen plus a commemorative plaque.

Recent Winners: 2001: 28th Osaragi Jirô Prize: Tsushima Yûko, *Warai-ôkami (The Laughing Wolf)* and Hagihara Nobutoshi, *Tôi gake Ânesuto Satô nikki shô (Distant Cliffs: Selections from the Journals of Ernest Satow).*

Sponsoring Organization: Asahi Shimbun Publishing Co.

Address: Osaragi Jiro Prize Office, 5–3–2 Tsukifi, Chou-ku, Tokyo, 104–11, Japan. **Internet:** www.mmip.or.jp.

Österreichischer Staatspreis für Europäische Literatur
(Austrian National Prize for European Literature)

An annual prize of 300,000 Sch (around €22,000), established in 1965. It is presented to a European writer, whose work is successful outside the writer's homeland, thanks to its translation. The winner is selected by an independent jury.

Eligibility and Restrictions: One or more editions of the work must be available in German.

Sponsoring Organization: Bundeskanzleramt–Kunstsektion (Austrian Federal Culture Department).

Address: Bundeskanzleramt–Kunstsektion, Abt II/5, Schottengasse 1, 1014 Vienna, Austria.

Österreichischer Staatspreis für Literarische Übersetzer
(Austrian National Prize for Literary Translators)

An official prize for translation of Austrian works into foreign languages, awarded for the first time in 1986. The award is presented in two categories: one to a translator for their complete body of work, and the other for work in a particular language.

Recent Winners: 2001: Erwin Köstler and Juan José del Solar Bardelli; previous winners include Josef Hirsal, Edda Werfel and Solomon Apt.

Sponsoring Organization: Austrian Federal Culture Dept.

Address: Bundeskanzleramt – Kunstsektion, Abt II/5, Schottengasse 1, 1014 Vienna, Austria.

Östersundsposten prize

An annual literary prize presented by the newspaper *Östersundsposten*. The prize is considered to be prestigious at a national level. The winner is selected by an award jury.

Recent Winners: 1998: Lennart Lundmark, *Så länge vi har marker.*

Sponsoring Organization: *Östersundsposten.*

Address: *Östersundsposten*, Box 720, 831 28 Östersund, Sweden. **Telephone:** (63) 61600. **Internet:** www.op.se/.

Ottakar's Faber National Poetry Competition

First awarded in 1997, the annual prize is run by Ottakar's Bookshops in association with the publisher Faber & Faber. Regional winners are selected from every county of the UK and then put forward into the national final, judged by the Poet Laureate Andrew Motion. Regional winners receive copies of Faber poetry books; national winners receive cash prizes of up to £500, and in addition the overall winning poem is published in a major national newspaper.

Eligibility and Restrictions: All work must be previously unpublished. Entrants are judged in four age categories (5–8, 9–11, 12–16, adult).

How to Apply: Entry forms are available via Ottakar's bookshops from August each year.

Recent Winners: Overall winner: 2001: Tessa Biddington, *Lantern Show, Scott Base*; 2000: Tiffany Atkinson; 1997: Tessa Biddington.

Sponsoring Organization: Ottakar's Bookshops/Faber & Faber.

Contact: Group Events Man. Jo James.

Address: Ottakar's plc, Rougemont House, Rougemont Close, Manor Road, Salisbury SP1 1LY, UK. **Telephone:** (1722) 428516. **Fax:** (1722) 428502. **Internet:** www.ottakars.co.uk. **E-mail:** jo.james@ottakars.co.uk.

Ôya Sôichi Nonfikushon Shô (Ôya Sôichi Prize for Non-fiction)

Established in 1969 by the Society for the Promotion of Japanese Literature (Nihonbungaku Shinkô Kai) in recognition of author Ôya's influential role in the Japanese media. The prize is intended to encourage outstanding new writers in the field of non-fiction. The winner receives a cash prize of 1 million yen.

Recent Winners: 2001: 32nd Ôya Sôichi Prize: Hiramatsu Tsuyoshi, *Hikari no Kyôkai: Andô Tadao no genba (The Church of Light: On-Site with Andô Tadao)*, and Hoshino Hiromi, *Korogaru Honkon no koke wa haenai (A Rolling Hong Kong Gathers No Moss)* (joint winners).

Sponsoring Organization: Society for the Promotion of Japanese Literature (Nihonbungaku Shinkô Kai).

Address: Bungei Shunju Publishing Co, 3–23 Kioi-cho, Chiyoda-ku, Tokyo, Japan.

P2-Lyttaranes Romanpris (P2 Listeners Novel Prize)

An annual prize established in 1997 for the year's best new fiction, sponsored by the NRK radio programme P2. A shortlist of six novels published in the last year is drawn up by a jury of professional critics and scholars, and this is then put to a second jury made up of listeners to the radio programme. The jury varies each year in its composition in terms of age and geographical spread. The winner receives a prize of 25,000 NOK.

Eligibility and Restrictions: Open to novels written in Norwegian and published during the preceding year.

Recent Winners: 2001: Carl Frode Tiller, *Skråninga*; 2000: Jonny Halberg, *Flommen*; 1999: Hanne Ørstavik, *Like sant som jeg er virkelig*; 1998: Erik Fosnes Hansen, *Beretninger om beskyttelse*; 1997 Jan Jacob Tønset, *Et vennskap*.

Sponsoring Organization: NRK (Norsk Rikskringkasting).

Contact: Marta Norheim.

Address: NRK (Norsk Rikskringkasting), Marienlyst, Oslo, Norway. **Telephone:** (815) 65 900. **Internet:** www.nrk.no/litteratur. **E-mail:** marta.norheim@nrk.no.

Margit Pahlson Prize

Established in 1981, and awarded by the Swedish Academy for achievements of particular significance to the Swedish language.

Sponsoring Organization: Swedish Academy.

Contact: Sec. Bo Svensen.

Address: Swedish Academy, PO Box 2118, 103 13 Stockholm, Sweden.

Pakokku U Ohn Pe Literary and Education Awards

In 1992 the Pakokku U Ohn Pe Literary Award Trust Fund was established, bearing the name of the benefactor who made a donation of Kyat 7,601,279 to set up a scheme with the aim of propagating Myanma literature and encouraging literary talents of all age groups from all walks of life. The Fund is administered by a management committee under the auspices of the Ministry of Information, while the selection committee is headed by the President of the Writers and Journalists Association. Prizes are awarded in five categories: novel, short stories, poetry, research work and treatise. Each award carries a cash prize of Kyat 40,000. There is also a special award conferred on one or more living writers who have devoted their whole life towards promotion and propagation of Myanmar literature, with a cash prize of Kyat 50,000.

Recent Winners: Lifetime achievement:1997: U Htin Gyi; 1996: Sayagyi U Htin Gyi (pen-name Tekkatho Htin Gyi); 1995: Sayagyi U Ko Lay (Zeyar Maung); 1994: Sayagyi U Yan Aung (Yan Aung) and Sayagyi U Thein Maung (Thu Kha); 1993: Sayagyi U Htin Fatt (Maung Htin), and Sayagyi U Tin Myint (Thinkhar).

Sponsoring Organization: Pakokku U Ohn Pe Literary Award Trust Fund.

Address: Pakokku U Ohn Pe Literary Award Trust Fund, Pakokku, Myanmar.

Don Carlos Palanca Memorial Awards

The Palanca Awards, presented by the Carlos Palanca Foundation Inc, are seen as the Philippines' highest literary prize. Prizes are awarded in 21 categories, in English, Filipino, and regional languages, and within each of these, categories for essay, novel, short story, children's literature, drama and poetry. The prize money varies according to category, from P3,000 for third prize in a smaller category up to P30,000.00 for the Novel Grand Prize. Writers who have won five first prizes in the contest also receive the Hall of Fame Award.

Eligibility and Restrictions: The awards are open to all Filipino citizens, or former Filipino citizens, except officers and employees of the Carlos Palanca Foundation, Inc. Authors may submit only one entry for each category, and works which have already been awarded a prize in any other contest are ineligible.

How to Apply: Four copies of entries should be submitted by 30 April.

Recent Winners: Former winners include Francis C. Macansantos, Priscilla S. Macansantos, Ruth Mabanglo and Edilberto K. Tiempo.

Sponsoring Organization: Carlos Palanca Foundation Inc.

Address: Carlos Palanca Foundation Inc, Ground Floor, CPJ Building 105 C. Palanca Jr St, Legaspi Village, Makati City, 1229, Philippines. **Telephone:** 818-36-81. **Fax:** 817-40-45. **E-mail:** cpawards@info.com.ph.

Pandora Award

Established in 1981, the Pandora Award is presented to a woman or women's organization for promoting positive images of women in publishing, bookselling or related trades.

Recent Winners: 2002: Honno (The Welsh Women's Press); 2000: Shahla Lahiji, Roshangaran Publishing and Urvashi Butalia, Kali for Women Publishers; 1999: Brenda Gardner, head of Piccadilly Press; 1998: Philippa Harrison, Publishers Association and Little, Brown.

Sponsoring Organization: Women in Publishing.

Address: Women in Publishing, 12 Dyott St, London WC1A 1DF, UK.

Jan Parandowski Prize

The Jan Parandowski Prize is the most prestigious award for literary achievement presented by the Polish PEN Club. The prize, first presented in 1988, is named in memory of the Polish writer (died 1978) who translated *The Odyssey* and wrote a biography of Petrarch.

Recent Winners: 1997: Tadeusz Rózewicz; 1996: Ryszard Kapuściński; 1995: Stanisław Baranczak.

Sponsoring Organization: Polish PEN Club.

Address: Krakówskie Przedmiescie 87/89, 00–079 Warsaw, Poland. **Telephone:** (22) 826 57 84. **Fax:** (22) 826 28 23. **Internet:** www.penclub.atomnet.pl. **E-mail:** penclub@ikp.atm.com.pl.

William Riley Parker Prize

An annual prize for works of literary criticism, first presented in 1964. The winner receives an award of $1,000.

How to Apply: Deadline for submissions is 1 May.

Recent Winners: 2001: Ian Baucom, *Globalit, Inc. or The Cultural Logic of Global Literary Studies*; 2000: Rita Felski, *Nothing to Declare: Identity, Shame, and the Lower Middle Class*; 1999: Phillip Novak, *Circles and Circles of Sorrow: In the Wake of Morrison's Sula*; 1998: Henry Staten, *Ethnic Authenticity, Class, and Autobiography: The Case of Hunger of Memory*; 1997: Jahan Ramazani, *The Wound of History: Walcott's Omeros and the Postcolonial Poetics of Affliction*.

Sponsoring Organization: Modern Language Association of America (MLA).

Contact: Co-ordinator of Book Prizes and Special Projects.

Address: Modern Language Asscn of America, 26 Broadway, 3rd Floor, New York, NY 10004–1789, USA. **Telephone:** (646) 576-5141. **Fax:** (646) 458-0033. **Internet:** www.mla.org. **E-mail:** awards@mla.org.

Parker Romantic Novel of the Year

This annual award was set up in 1981 to encourage and promote romantic fiction. It is administered by the Romantic Novelists' Association (RNA), with sponsorship from Parker Pen, and is awarded to the best modern or historical (i.e. set before 1950) romantic novel of the year. A shortlist is drawn up by a panel of readers, with the final winner chosen by a panel of three independent judges. The winner receives £10,000 and a silver Parker pen.

Eligibility and Restrictions: Authors must be resident in the UK, or, if overseas, must be members of the RNA. Entries must be written in English, and published in the UK in the year preceding the year in which the award is presented (usually December to November). Self-published and vanity-published novels are not eligible.

How to Apply: Entries may be submitted by authors, publishers or agents. Three copies should be sent to the address given.

Recent Winners: 2002: Philippa Gregory, *The Other Boleyn Girl*; 2001, Cathy Kelly, *Someone Like You*; 2000: Maureen Lee, *Dancing in the Dark*; 1999: Clare Chambers, *Learning to Swim*; 1998: Angela Lambert, *Kiss and Kin*; 1997: Sue Gee, *The Hours of the Night*.

Sponsoring Organization: Romantic Novelists' Association/Parker Pen.

Contact: Organizer Joan Emery.

Address: Romantic Novelists' Assocation, 2 Broad Oak Lane, Wigginton, York YO32 2SB, UK. **Telephone:** (1904) 765035.

Francis Parkman Prize

Awarded by the Society of American Historians to the book which 'best represents the union of the historian and the artist'.

Recent Winners: 2000: David M. Kennedy, *Freedom from fear: the American people in depression and war, 1929–1945*; 1999: Elliott West, *The contested plains: Indians, goldseekers, and the rush to Colorado*; 1998: John M. Barry, *Rising tide: the great Mississippi flood of 1927 and how it changed America*; 1997: Drew Gilpin Faust, *Mothers of invention: women of the slaveholding South in the American Civil War*; 1996: Robert D. Richardson, Jr, *Emerson: the mind on fire – a biography*.

Sponsoring Organization: Society of American Historians.

Address: Society of American Historians, Columbia University, 603 Fayerweather Hall, New York, NY 10027, USA.

Peer Poetry International Competition

Founded in 1992 to enable poets acclaimed by their peers to have a collection of their poetry published free of charge. Until 1998 a cash prize was given, but the award now comprises publication of the winning works in the succeeding edition of *Peer Poetry Magazine*. The winner is decided by vote from subscribers to the magazine.

Eligibility and Restrictions: The prize is judged on variety of style, imagination and technical brilliance, together with a sense of beauty in thought and language, including genres such as haiku, tanka, etc.

How to Apply: Dates for submission are end of April and October; entrants should submit at least three poems, up to 1,000 words in length, with an entry fee of £6.50/$10.

Recent Winners: 2002: Margaret Eddershaw and Idris Caffrey; April 1999: Audrey Morley and Marina Yedigaroff; October 1998: Joan Sheridan Smith and Isabella Strachan; April 1997: Richard Bonfield and Joan Sheridan Smith; October 1996: Chris Haslam and A. Grater; January 1996: Jim Norton and Noel Spence.

Sponsoring Organization: Peer Poetry Magazine.

Contact: Editor Paul Amphlett.

Address: 26 Arlington House, Bath St, Bath BA1 1QN, UK. **Telephone:** (1225) 445298. **Internet:** www.peerpoetryintnl.org. **E-mail:** paulamphlett@ peerpoetrymagazinefsworld.co.uk.

Pegasus Prize for Literature

The Pegasus Prize for Literature, created in 1977 and sponsored by Mobil Corporation, aims to foster literary excellence, especially for distinguished works of fiction from countries whose literature merits wider exposure to the outside world. In each country awarding the prize, the selection of the winner is made by a jury of the country's leading literary figures. Each jury, independent of Mobil, selects the winning work after reviewing the best works of a designated genre and period. The winning author receives a monetary award and the Pegasus Prize medallion. The winning work is also translated and published in a widely promoted English-language edition, bringing the chance for increased international readership.

Recent Winners: 1999: Ana Teresa Torres (Venezuela), *Doña Inés vs. Oblivion*; 1997: Mario de Carvalho (Portugal), *A God Strolling in the Cool of the Evening*; 1995: Francisco Rebolledo (Latin America), *Rasero*; 1994: Jia Pingwa (China), *Turbulence*; 1993: Kjartan Flogstad (Norway), *Dollar Road*.

Sponsoring Organization: Mobil Corporation/LSU Press.

Address: Exxon Mobil Corporation, 5959 Las Colinas Boulevard, Irving, TX 75039–2298, USA. **Internet:** www.exxonmobil.com/pegasus_prize/.

Pemenang Anugerah MAPIM-Fuji Xerox (MAPIM-Fuji Xerox Scholarly Book Award)

A new award set up by the Malaysian Scholarly Book Publishers Council (MAPIM) with sponsorship from Fuji Xerox, in order to promote the development of scholarly book publishing, especially in the Malay language. Awards are presented in the categories social sciences and science, technology and medicine.

Recent Winners: Social Sciences: 2002: Nik Azis Nik Pa, *Pendekatan Konstruktivisme Dalam Pendidikan Matematik (Constructive Approach in Mathematics Education)*
Science, Technology and Medicine: 2002: *Spektrometri Jisim*.

Sponsoring Organization: Malaysian Scholarly Book Publishers Council (MAPIM)/ Fuji Xerox.

Address: Anugerah Penerbitan Ilmiah MAPIM-Fuji Xerox, Penerbit Universiti Kebangsaan Malaysia, u.p. SETIAUSAHA, 43600 UKM, Bangi, Selangor D.E., Malaysia. **Internet:** www.mapim.com.

PEN Award for Poetry in Translation

An annual prize of $3,000 presented for a distinguished book-length translation of poetry, from any language into English, published in the current calendar year.

How to Apply: There is no application form. Two copies of entries should be submitted by publishers, agents, or the translators themselves; deadline is mid-December.

Recent Winners: 2001: Chana Bloch and Chana Kronfeld, *Open Closed Open* by Yehuda Amichai; 2000: James Brasfield and Oleh Lysheha, *Selected Poems* by Oleh Lysheha; 1999: Richard Zenith, *Fernando Pessoa & Co*; 1998: Eamon Grennan, *Selected Poems* by Giacomo Leopardi; 1997: Edward Snow, *Uncollected Poems* by Rainer Maria Rilke.

Sponsoring Organization: PEN American Center.

Address: PEN American Center, 568 Broadway, New York, NY 10012–3225, USA. **Telephone:** (212) 334-1660. **Internet:** www.pen.org. **E-mail:** jm@pen.org.

PEN/Architectural Digest Award for Literary Writing on the Visual Arts

This annual award is presented to an American writer for an outstanding book of criticism or commentary on one or more of the visual arts (including architecture, interior design, landscape studies, painting and sculpture). The winner receives $10,000 plus a medallion.

Eligibility and Restrictions: Entries must have been published in the calendar year under consideration.

Recent Winners: 2001: Leonard Barkan and Debora Silverman; 2000: Anne Hollander, *Feeding the Eye.*

Sponsoring Organization: American PEN.

Address: PEN American Center, 568 Broadway, New York, NY 10012–3225, USA. **Telephone:** (212) 334-1660. **Internet:** www.pen.org. **E-mail:** jm@pen.org.

PEN/Barbara Goldsmith Freedom to Write Awards

First presented in 1987, these awards are named after distinguished writer, historian, and PEN member Barbara Goldsmith who underwrites the prizes. They honour international literary figures who have been persecuted or imprisoned for exercising or defending the right to freedom of expression. Each award carries a stipend of $20,000.

How to Apply: Candidates are nominated by International PEN.

Recent Winners: 2002: Aung Myint (Myanmar) and Tohti Tunyaz (Xinjiang Uighur Autonomous Region); 2001 Shahla Lahiji (Iran), Mamadali Mahmudov (Uzbekistan); 2000: Xue Deyun (China).

Sponsoring Organization: American PEN.

Address: PEN American Center, 568 Broadway, New York, NY 10012–3225, USA. **Telephone:** (212) 334-1660. **Internet:** www.pen.org/freedom/pressrel/bga.htm. **E-mail:** jm@pen.org.

PEN/Book-of-the-Month Club Translation Prize

For a distinguished book-length translation, from any language into English, published in the current calendar year; a prize of $3,000 is awarded annually.

Eligibility and Restrictions: Although all eligible books must have been published in the USA, translators may be of any nationality. There are no restrictions on the subject matter of translated works, although eligible titles should be of a literary character; technical, scientific or bibliographical translations will not be considered.

How to Apply: There is no application form. Three copies of entries should be submitted by publishers, agents or translators.

Recent Winners: 2001: Tina Nunnally, Kristin Lavransdatter, *The Cross* by Sigrid Undset; 1999: Michael Hofmann, *The Tale of the 1002nd Night* by Joseph Roth; 1998: Peter Constantine, *Six Early Stories by Thomas Mann*; 1997: Arnold Pomerans, *The Letters of Vincent van Gogh*.

Sponsoring Organization: American PEN.

Address: PEN American Center, 568 Broadway, New York, NY 10012–3225, USA. **Telephone:** (212) 334-1660. **Internet:** www.pen.org. **E-mail:** jm@pen.org.

PEN Center USA West Annual Literary Awards

Since 1982 PEN Center USA West has sponsored a regional literary awards competition to recognize outstanding works published or produced by writers who live in the western USA. Winners are selected in 10 categories (fiction, creative non-fiction, research non-fiction, poetry, children's literature, translation, journalism, drama, screenplay, and teleplay). Winners are chosen by panels of judges comprising writers, editors, critics and booksellers. Each winner receives a $1,000 cash prize and is honoured at a ceremony in Los Angeles.

Eligibility and Restrictions: Open to writers and translators who live west of the Mississippi River. All entries must have been published or produced in the previous year. The book awards are given to works of outstanding literary merit in fiction, non-fiction, poetry, children's literature, and translation. Anthologies are not eligible. For literary journalism category entries must be long feature articles or a series of feature articles published in newspapers or magazines. For drama entries must be plays that have had their original full production in the preceding year. (They need not have been produced in the western USA.) Plays may be full-length, one-acts, or monologues. Teleplay category is open to feature-length produced scripts for television, either original works or adaptations. Screenplay refers to feature-length, produced scripts for films, either original works or adaptations.

How to Apply: Works maybe submitted by writers, their publishers or producers, agents, or publicists. Four copies of the entry should be submitted accompanied by a completed entry form (available on website) and a $25 entry fee for each submission. Exact deadline dates change every year: book deadlines are at the end of December, non-book categories, at the end of January.

Recent Winners: Previous winners include: Thom Gunn, Barbara Kingsolver, James Salter, Maxine Hong Kingston, Richard Reeves, Pete Dexter, Sandra Cisneros, William T. Vollmann, John E.Woods, Cherrié Moraga, and William Kittredge.

Sponsoring Organization: PEN Center USA West.

Contact: awards@pen-usa-west.org.

Address: PEN Center USA West, 672 South Lafayette Park Place, Suite 41, Los Angeles, CA 90057, USA. **Telephone:** (213) 365-8500. **Fax:** (213) 365-9616. **Internet:** www.penusa.org.

PEN/Faulkner Award for Fiction

An annual award established in 1981 to recognize the best work of fiction by an American citizen published in the preceding year. The winner receives a prize of $15,000; four finalists receive $5,000 each. As such this represents the largest annual juried prize for fiction in the USA.

Recent Winners: 2002: Ann Patchett, *Bel Canto*; 2001: Philip Roth, *The Human Stain*; 2000: Ha Jin, *Waiting*; 1999: Michael Cunningham, *The Hours*; 1998: Rafi Zabor, *The Bear Comes Home*.

Sponsoring Organization: Folger Shakespeare Library.

Contact: Pres., Susan Richards Shreve.

Address: Folger Shakespeare Library, 201 East Capitol St, SE, Washington, DC 20003, USA.

PEN/Jerard Fund Award

This prize of $4,000 is named after Elise Jerard, an amateur writer from New York. It is awarded every two years to a woman writer early in her career, for her work in progress on a book of general non-fiction demonstrating high literary quality.

Eligibility and Restrictions: Open to English-language book-length works in progress. Applicants should have had at least one magazine article published in a national publication or in a major literary magazine. Applicants must not have published more than one book of any kind. Applicants must be residents of the USA.

Recent Winners: 2001: Collette Brooks; 1999: Kim Todd; 1997: Judy Blunt; 1995: Kim Barnes.

Sponsoring Organization: American PEN.

Address: PEN American Center, 568 Broadway, New York, NY 10012–3225, USA. **Telephone:** (212) 334-1660. **Internet:** www.pen.org. **E-mail:** jm@pen.org.

PEN/Joyce Osterweil Award for Poetry

This award of $5,000 is given in odd-numbered years and alternates with the PEN/Voelcker Award for Poetry. The Osterweil Award recognizes the high literary character of the published work to date of a new and emerging American poet of any age and 'the promise of further literary achievement'.

Eligibility and Restrictions: Poets nominated for the award may not have published more than one book of poetry.

How to Apply: Applications are not accepted; nominations from PEN members are accepted, by the beginning of January.

Recent Winners: 2001: Richard Matthews, *The Mill Is Burning*; 1999: Nick Flynn, *Some Ether*.

Sponsoring Organization: American PEN.

Address: PEN American Center, 568 Broadway, New York, NY 10012–3225, USA. **Telephone:** (212) 334-1660. **Internet:** www.pen.org. **E-mail:** jm@pen.org.

PEN/Laura Pels Awards for Drama

The Laura Pels Awards for Drama are awarded each year in two categories: a medal is presented to an established American dramatist, in recognition of his or her body of work; and a stipend of $5,000 is awarded to an American playwright in mid-career for works demonstrating 'rich and striking language'.

How to Apply: Nominations are accepted for the mid-career category, but the award for the established dramatist is chosen by internal nomination.

Recent Winners: 2001: Richard Foreman and Charles L. Mee; 2000: Horton Foote and Suzan-Lori Parks; 1999: Edward Albee and Paula Vogel; 1998: Arthur Miller and Richard Greenberg.

Sponsoring Organization: PEN American Center.

Address: PEN American Center, 568 Broadway, New York, NY 10012–3225, USA. **Telephone:** (212) 334-1660. **Internet:** www.pen.org. **E-mail:** jm@pen.org.

PEN/Martha Albrand Award for First Non-fiction

An annual award presented for a first-published book of general non-fiction, characterized by literary excellence. The winner receives a cash prize of $1,000, plus residence at the Vermont Studio Center.

Eligibility and Restrictions: Entries must be written by an American writer and published in the current calendar year.

How to Apply: There is no application form. Three copies of each eligible book should be submitted by mid-December.

Recent Winners: 2001: Charles Seife, *Zero: The Biography of a Dangerous Idea*; 2000: Eileen Welsome, *The Plutonium Files*; 1999: Philip Gourevitch, *We Wish to Inform You That Tomorrow We Will Be Killed with Our Families*; 1998: Serge Schmemann, *Echoes of a Native Land*; 1997: Mark Doty, *Heaven's Coast*.

Sponsoring Organization: American PEN.

Address: PEN American Center, 568 Broadway, New York, NY 10012–3225, USA. **Telephone:** (212) 334-1660. **Internet:** www.pen.org. **E-mail:** jm@pen.org.

PEN/Martha Albrand Award for the Art of the Memoir

Presented to an American author for his or her first published memoir, distinguished by qualities of literary and stylistic excellence. The $1,000 prize was established following a bequest from the late PEN member and mystery writer Martha Albrand.

Eligibility and Restrictions: Entries must have been published in the current calendar year. Authors must be American citizens or permanent residents; they can have published books in any other literary genre, but the work submitted for this prize must be their first memoir to be published.

How to Apply: There is no application form. Three copies of entries should be submitted by mid-December.

Recent Winners: 2001: C. K. Williams, *Misgivings*; 2000: Ted Solotaroff, *Truth Comes in Blows*; 1999: Peter Balakian, *Black Dog of Fate*; 1998: Jeffrey Smith, *Where the Roots Reach for Water*.

Sponsoring Organization: American PEN.

Address: PEN American Center, 568 Broadway, New York, NY 10012–3225, USA. **Telephone:** (212) 334-1660. **Internet:** www.pen.org. **E-mail:** jm@pen.org.

PEN/Nabokov Award

A biennial prize of $20,000 for a living author whose works have been translated into English, and which demonstrate variety and originality. The award was established in memory of Vladimir Nabokov, and honours writers of 'enduring originality and consummate craftsmanship'.

Eligibility and Restrictions: Open to living authors (principally novelists) who have published a book in the USA within the past two years. Translations are eligible.

How to Apply: Selection is by internal nomination only.

Recent Winners: 2002: Margo Vargas Llosa (Peru); 2000: William Gass.

Sponsoring Organization: PEN American Center/Vladimir Nabokov Foundation.

Address: PEN American Center, 568 Broadway, New York, NY 10012–3225, USA. **Telephone:** (212) 334-1660. **Internet:** www.pen.org. **E-mail:** jm@pen.org.

PEN/Norma Klein Award

Named after a writer of children's books, this prize of $3,000 is awarded every two years to acknowledge a distinguished new entrant of literary merit among American writers of children's fiction.

Eligibility and Restrictions: Open to books for children from elementary school to young adult.

How to Apply: Nominations are welcomed from authors and editors of children's books, although authors may not nominate themselves.

Recent Winners: 1999: Valerie Hobbs; 1997: Rita Williams-Garcia; 1995: Angela Johnson.

Sponsoring Organization: American PEN.

Address: PEN American Center, 568 Broadway, New York, NY 10012–3225, USA. **Telephone:** (212) 334-1660. **Internet:** www.pen.org. **E-mail:** jm@pen.org.

PEN/Phyllis Naylor Working Writer Fellowship

An annual award of $5,000, which is presented to an emerging author of children's or young-adult fiction. The Fellowship aims to provide financial support to allow the recipient time to complete a book-length work in progress. The award, which is supported by a contribution from author and PEN member Phyllis Reynolds Naylor, is judged by a panel of three members of PEN who are authors of children's or young adult fiction.

Eligibility and Restrictions: Open to writers of children or young-adult fiction in financial need, who have published at least two books, and no more than three, during the past 10 years.

How to Apply: Writers must be nominated by an editor or a fellow writer. Three copies of no more than 100 pages of current work, (part of a new book) must be submitted by the beginning of January.

Recent Winners: 2001: Graham McNamee.

Sponsoring Organization: PEN American Center.

Address: PEN American Center, 568 Broadway, New York, NY 10012–3225, USA. **Telephone:** (212) 334-1660. **Internet:** www.pen.org. **E-mail:** jm@pen.org.

PEN/Ralph Manheim Medal for Translation

Given every three years to a translator whose career has demonstrated a commitment to excellence through the body of his or her work.

How to Apply: Entry is by internal nomination only.

Recent Winners: 2000: Edmund Keeley; 1997: Robert Fagles; 1994: Richard Wilbur; 1991: William Weaver.

Sponsoring Organization: American PEN.

Address: PEN American Center, 568 Broadway, New York, NY 10012–3225, USA. **Telephone:** (212) 334-1660. **Internet:** www.pen.org. **E-mail:** jm@pen.org.

PEN/Robert Bingham Fellowships for Writers

Three two-year fellowships (of $35,000 per year) are awarded to exceptionally talented fiction writers whose debut work – a first novel or collection of short stories published in during the two preceding years – represents distinguished literary achievement and suggests great promise. The fellowships were established by the family of writer Robert Bingham to commemorate his contribution to literary fiction.

Eligibility and Restrictions: Candidate's first (and only the first) novel or first collection of short fiction must have been published by a US publisher during the two previous years. Candidates must be US residents, but American citizenship not required. There are no restrictions on the candidate's age or on the style of his or her work.

How to Apply: Nominations are accepted from writers, editors and agents by mid-January; three copies of the candidate's book should be sent with nomination.

Sponsoring Organization: PEN American Center.

Address: PEN American Center, 568 Broadway, New York, NY 10012–3225, USA. **Telephone:** (212) 334-1660. **Internet:** www.pen.org. **E-mail:** jm@pen.org.

PEN/Spielvogel-Diamonstein Award for the Art of the Essay

An annual award presented to the author of the best book of previously uncollected essays on any subject; the winner receives a prize of $5,000.

Eligibility and Restrictions: Entries must be by an American writer and published in the current calendar year. Individual essays included in books may have been previously published in magazines, journals or anthologies. There are no restrictions on the subject matter of the essays.

How to Apply: Four copies of each eligible title should be submitted by publishers, agents or authors by mid-December.

Recent Winners: 2001: David Quammen, *The Boilerplate Rhino*; 2000: Annie Dillard, *For the Time Being*; 1999: Marilynne Robinson, *The Death of Adam*; 1998: Adam Hochschild, *Finding the Trapdoor*; 1997: Cynthia Ozick, *Fame & Folly*.

Sponsoring Organization: American PEN.

Address: PEN American Center, 568 Broadway, New York, NY 10012–3225, USA. **Telephone:** (212) 334-1660. **Internet:** www.pen.org. **E-mail:** jm@pen.org.

PEN/Voelcker Award for Poetry

A prize of $5,000 awarded every two years to an American poet whose distinguished and growing body of work to date represents a notable and accomplished presence in American literature, for whom the promise seen in earlier work has been fulfilled, and who has matured with each successive volume.

How to Apply: Nominations are only accepted from members of PEN.

Recent Winners: 2000: Heather McHugh; 1998: C.K. Williams; 1996: Franz Wright; 1994: Jane Kenyon.

Sponsoring Organization: American PEN.

Address: PEN American Center, 568 Broadway, New York, NY 10012–3225, USA. **Telephone:** (212) 334-1660. **Internet:** www.pen.org. **E-mail:** jm@pen.org.

Peterloo Poets Open Poetry Competition

The competition is in two parts, the Open Section, which was established in 1986 and carries a first prize of £2,000 (plus several runners-up prizes), and the Age Group Section, founded in 2000 for entrants aged 15 to 19, with five prizes of £100 each. Winners are selected from a shortlist of 100 poems by a panel of four experts (usually poets or editors).

Eligibility and Restrictions: Poems may be on any subject or theme and in any style or form but must be previously unpublished, 40 lines maximum and written in English.

How to Apply: There is an entry fee of £5 per poem (Open Section) or £2 per poem (Age Group Section). Up to 10 poems may be entered, but they must be accompanied by an entry form (available from address above or website). The deadline for receipt of entries is beginning of March.

Recent Winners: 2001: Jem Poster; 2000: Judy Gahagan; 1999: Alison Pryde; 1998: Philip Gross; 1997: M. R. Peacocke.

Contact: Dir Harry Chambers.

Address: The Old Chapel, Sand Lane, Calstock PL18 9QX, UK. **Telephone:** (1822) 833473. **Fax:** (1822) 833989. **Internet:** www.peterloopoets.co.uk. **E-mail:** poets@peterloo.fsnet.co.uk.

Petrarca-Prize for Translation

An annual prize presented for the best translation into German of a literary work. The winner receives a prize of 10,000 DM.

How to Apply: No direct applications are accepted.

Recent Winners: 1992: Michael Hamburger; 1991: Ilma Rakusa.

Sponsoring Organization: Carl Hanser Verlag.

Address: Carl Hanser Verlag, Michael Krüger, Postfach 86 04 20, 81631 Munich, Germany. **Telephone:** (89) 99 83 400. **Fax:** (89) 98 27119.

A. A. Phillips Prize

Awarded from time to time for a work of outstanding achievement in the field of Australian literary scholarship.

Recent Winners: 1999: Anna Rutherford; 1998: Clem Christesen, for services to Australian literature; 1996: Katharine Brisbane, for outstanding achievements as both writer and publisher on Australian theatre and drama; 1995: Judith Wright, for her long career as poet, critic and activist; 1992: Laurie Hergenhan, for services to Australian literature as editor of *Australian Literary Studies*.

Sponsoring Organization: Association for the Study of Australian Literature.

Address: Association for the Study of Australian Literature Ltd, Dept of English, University College, ADFA, Campbell, ACT 2600, Australia. **Internet:** idun.itsc.adfa.edu.au:16080/asal/Index.html.

Phoenix Award

Established 1985 by the Children's Literature Association (ChLA), the prize is awarded annually to a book of high literary merit orginally published in English 20 years previously which did not receive a major award at the time of its publication. The Phoenix Award is named after the fabled bird which rose from its ashes with renewed life and beauty, as a symbol of the renewed life which the winning books may achieve after years of obscurity. The winner is chosen each year by an elected committee of ChLA members, and receives a brass statuette of a Phoenix, individually cast and inscribed with the winner's name.

How to Apply: Nominations are made by ChLA members and others interested in promoting high critical standards in literature for children.

Recent Winners: 2002: Zibby O'Neal, *A Formal Feeling*; 2001: Peter Dickinson, *The Seventh Raven*; 2000: Monica Hughes, *The Keeper of the Isis Light*; 1999: E. L. Konigsburg, *Throwing Shadows*; 1998: Jill Paton Walsh, *A Chance Child*.

Sponsoring Organization: Children's Literature Association (ChLA).

Address: Children's Literature Association, POB 138, Battle Creek, MI 49016–0138, USA. **Internet:** ebbs.english.vt.edu/chla/.

Lorne Pierce Medal

Established in 1926 by Lorne Pierce, editor of Ryerson Press for 40 years and a major contributor to the development and appreciation of Canadian literature. The Medal is awarded biennially by the Royal Society of Canada for a lifetime's achievement of outstanding significance and merit in imaginative or critical literature. The award consists of a gold-plated silver medal.

Eligibility and Restrictions: Open to works of imaginative or critical literature written by a Canadian citizen (or resident for five years) in either English or French.

How to Apply: Entries must be nominated by three persons, one of whom must be a member of the Society. Nomination forms must be submitted by 1 December, accompanied by a citation stating why the nominee should receive the award, a detailed appraisal of the nominee's work, a CV and supporting statements from other experts or scholars.

Recent Winners: 2000: Jean-Louis Major; 1998: David Staines; 1996: Clément Moisan; 1993: Alice Munro; 1991: Gilles Marcotte.

Sponsoring Organization: Royal Society of Canada.

Contact: Co-ordinator Sophie Buoro.

Address: Royal Society of Canada, 283 Sparks St, Ottawa, ON K1R 7X9, Canada. **Telephone:** (613) 991-6990. **Fax:** (613) 991-6996. **Internet:** www.rsc.ca.

Pilgrim Award

The Pilgrim Award, established in 1970, honours a lifetime's contribution to science fiction and fantasy scholarship. The award is named after J. O. Bailey's pioneering book, *Pilgrims through Space and Time*.

Recent Winners: 2002: Mike Ashley; 2001: Dave Samuelson; 2000: Hal Hall; 1999: Brian Stableford; 1998: L. Sprague de Camp.

Sponsoring Organization: Science Fiction Research Association.

Address: Science Fiction Research Association, College of Arts and Humanities, Texas A&M University–Corpus Christi, Corpus Christi, TX 78412, USA. **Internet:** www.sfra.org/.

Edgar Allan Poe Awards

These awards, sponsored by The Mystery Writers of America, honour the best in mystery fiction and non-fiction produced the previous year. The awards, known as the 'Edgars', were established in 1954 and are named in memory of Edgar Allan Poe.

Eligibility and Restrictions: The 'Edgars' are awarded to authors of distinguished work in various categories. Categories include short stories, novels, critical studies, juvenile and young adult fiction, television and motion picture screenplays, first novels, paperback originals, fact crime, and critical/biographical work. A Grand Master Award is also presented for lifetime achievement.

Recent Winners: Best Novel: 2001: Joe R. Lansdale, *The Bottoms*; 2000: Jan Burke, *Bones*
Best First Novel: 2001: David Liss, *A Conspiracy of Paper*; 2000: Eliot Pattison, *The Skull Mantra*
Best Paperback Original: 2001: Mark Graham, *The Black Maria*; 2000: Ruth Birmingham, *Fulton County Blues*
Best Critical/Biographical Work: 2001: Robert Kuhn McGregor and Ethan Lewis, *Conundrums for the Long Week-End*; 2000: Daniel Stashower, *Teller of Tales: The Life of Arthur Conan Doyle*
Best Fact Crime: 2001: Dick Lehr and Gerard O'Neill, *Black Mass*; 2000: James B. Stewart, *Blind Eye*
Best Young Adult Fiction: 2001: Elaine Marie Alphin, *Counterfeit Son*; 2000: Vivian Vande Velde, *Never Trust a Dead Man*
Best Children's: 2001: Frances O'Roark Dowell, *Dovey Coe*; 2000: Elizabeth McDavid Jones, *The Night Flyers*
Grand Master Award: 2001: Edward D. Hoch; 2000: Mary Higgins Clark.

Sponsoring Organization: Mystery Writers of America.

Address: Mystery Writers of America, 174 East 47th St, New York, NY 10017, USA. **E-mail:** mwa_org@earthlink.net.

Poetry Life Open Poetry Competition

Sponsored by the magazine *Poetry Life*, the award of £250 aims to bring new and talented poets to a wider audience. Winning entries are published in a special edition, *Poetry Life Recommendations*.

Sponsoring Organization: Poetry Life.

Contact: Editor Adrian Bishop.

Address: 1 Blue Ball Corner, Water Lane, Winchester SO23 OER, UK. **Telephone:** (1962) 842621.

Poetry London Competition

An annual prize run by the magazine *Poetry London*, and judged by the poet Ciaran Carson. The first prize is of £1,000, with runners-up prizes of £500, £200 and £75, and the winning poems are published in the summer issue of the magazine.

Recent Winners: 2002: Alan Mumford, *Fragment*; 2001: Chris Beckett, *The dog who thinks he's a fish.*

Sponsoring Organization: Poetry London.

Address: Poetry London, PO Box 30104, London
London E17 4XR, UK. **Telephone:** (20) 8521 0776. **Fax:** (20) 8521 0776. **Internet:** www.poetrylondon.co.uk. **E-mail:** editors@plondon.demon.co.uk.

Renato Poggioli Translation Award

An annual award presented to a promising translator for work on a book-length translation from Italian into English. The winner receives a prize of $3,000.

Recent Winners: 2000: Wendell Ricketts, *La segretaria and other one-act plays of Natalia Ginzburg*; 1998: Minna Proctor, *Love in Vain: Selected Stories by Federigo Tozzi*; 1997: Ann McGarrell, *The Face of Isis* by Victoria Ronchley; 1996: Louise Rozier, *The Little Jesus of Sicily*, by Fortunato Pasqualino.

Sponsoring Organization: American PEN.

Address: PEN American Center, 568 Broadway, New York, NY 10012–3225, USA. **Telephone:** (212) 334-1660. **Internet:** www.pen.org. **E-mail:** jm@pen.org.

George Polk Awards

An annual award for journalism established by Long Island University in 1949 in memory of George Polk, a CBS correspondent who was killed covering the civil war in Greece. The award has become one of America's most coveted journalism honours. In addition to 12 categories for journalism, an occasional prize is awarded for outstanding books in the same field.

Eligibility and Restrictions: Entrants do not have to be US citizens and the media outlet does not have to be American, but all entries must be in English (translations are excluded).

How to Apply: There are no entry fees or application forms. Entries must be submitted by early January.

Recent Winners: Book Awards: 2000: Laurie Garrett, *Betrayal of Trust*; 1998: Philip Gourevitch, *The New Yorker*; 1997: Horst Faas and Tim Page, *Requiem*.

Sponsoring Organization: Long Island University.

Contact: Robert D. Spector.

Address: Long Island University, The Brooklyn Campus, 1 University Plaza, Brooklyn, New York, NY 11201–5372, USA. **Telephone:** (718) 488-1115.

Portico Prize for Literature

The prize was established in 1985 by the Portico Library to promote and reward the literature of the North West of England. The prize is awarded every two years to a book of general interest and literary merit set wholly or partly in the region. The award carries a prize of £3,000, along with a specially bound volume of the winning work. A panel of between three and five judges, consisting of authors, booksellers, librarians, readers or regional celebrities, draws up a shortlist and selects a final winner.

Eligibility and Restrictions: Entries must have been published in the two years prior to 31 August of the year in which the award is presented.

How to Apply: Publishers are invited on behalf of authors to submit four copies of entries to the librarian, accompanied by the official entry form.

Recent Winners: 2000: John Parkinson Bailey, *Manchester – an Architectural History*; 1997: Paul Wilson, *Do White Whales Sing at the Edge of the World?*; 1995: Richard Francis, *Taking Apart the Poco Poco*; 1993: Jenny Uglow, *Elizabeth Gaskell: A Habit of Stories*; 1991: Alan Hankinson, *Coleridge Walks the Fells*.

Sponsoring Organization: Portico Library Trust.

Contact: Librarian, Emma Marigliano.

Address: Portico Library, 57 Mosley St, Manchester M2 3HY, UK. **Telephone:** (161) 236 6785. **Fax:** (161) 236 6803. **Internet:** www.theportico.org.uk. **E-mail:** librarian@theportico.org.uk.

Gustav Prellerprys vir literatuurwetenskap en letterkundige kritiek (Gustav Preller Prize for Literary Criticism)

An annual prize for literary criticism, named after Gustav Preller, a major champion of the Afrikaans langauge. The prize was established in 1968 at the suggestion of the publisher Human & Rousseau. The winner receives a prize of R5,000 and a gold medal.

Recent Winners: 2001: H. P. van Coller.

Sponsoring Organization: Suid-Afrikaanse Akademie vir Wetenskap en Kuns (South African Academy for Science and Arts).

Address: Die Suid-Afrikaanse Akademie vir Wetenskap en Kuns (South African Academy for Science and Arts), PO Box 538, Pretoria, 0001, South Africa. **Telephone:** (12) 328 5082. **Fax:** (12) 328 5091. **Internet:** www.akademie.co.za. **E-mail:** akademie@mweb.co.za.

Premi d'Honor de les Lletres Catalanes (Prize of Honour of Catalan Letters)

An annual award which has been presented since 1969 by the Catalan organization Omnium Cultural (which also administers a number of other awards). The prize of €2,000 is given to an individual in recognition of their contribution to the cultural life of the Catalan-speaking area.

Recent Winners: 2002: Josep María Espinás; 2001; Teresa Pamies; 2000: Josep Vallverdú; 1999: Josep Palau i Fabre; 1998: Joaquim Molas.

Sponsoring Organization: Omnium Cultural., C/d'en Vilar, 5, (darrere de l'Ajuntament), 43201 Reus, Spain. **Telephone:** (977) 34 16 17. **Internet:** www.paisoscatalans.org/omniumbaixcamp/.

Premi de les Lletres Catalanes Ramon Llull

Created by José Manuel Lara Hernández to promote writing in the Catalan language. The winner receives a prize of €60,100.

Eligibility and Restrictions: Novelists of any nationality may enter unpublished works written in Catalan; authors must guarantee the originality of their works.

Recent Winners: 2002: Màrius Carol, *Les seduccions de Júlia*; 2001: Baltasar Porcel, *L'emperador o L'ull del vent*; 2000: Maria Mercè Roca, *Delictes d'amor*; 1999: Maria de la Pau Janer, *Lola*; 1998: Joan Barril, *Parada obligatòria*.

Sponsoring Organization: Editorial Planeta SA.

Address: Editorial Planeta, Còrsega 273–279, 08008 Barcelona, Spain. **Internet:** www.editorial.planeta.es.

Premi Nacional de Literatura de la Generalitat de Catalunya

An annual prize in recognition of an outstanding contribution to Catalan literature, presented every year since 1995.

Recent Winners: 2001: Carme Riera; 2000; Quim Monzó; 1999: Jordi-Pere Cerda; 1998; Miquel Marti i Pol; 1997: Pere Gimferrer;.

Sponsoring Organization: Generalitat de Catalunya.

Address: Generalitat de Catalunya, Secretaria General de Cultura, Rbla. de Sta. Mònica, 8 (Palau Marc), 08002 Barcelona, Spain. **Telephone:** (93) 316 27 00. **Fax:** (93) 316 27 01. **Internet:** cultura.gencat.es.

Premi Josep Pla (Josep Pla Prize)

Established in 1968 by the publisher Ediciones Destino SA to recognize outstanding works in Catalan. The award is made to works written in Catalan in the form of prose text demonstrating strong literary character. Works may be submitted in any genre (novel, short story, travel, memoire, biography, etc.). The winner receives a prize of €6,000.

Eligibility and Restrictions: Open to unpublished works of prose written in Catalan. Authors must guarantee the originality of their work.

Recent Winners: 2002: Eva Piquer, *Eva, Una Victoria Diferent*; 2001: Jordi Llavina, *Nitrato de Chile*; 2000: Empar Moliner, *Feli Estheticienne*; 1999: Francesc Puigpelat, *Apocalipsi Blanc*; 1998: Valenti Puig, *L'Home de l'Abric*.

Sponsoring Organization: Ediciones Destino SA.

Address: Provenza 260 40, 08008 Barcelona, Spain. **Internet:** www.edestino.es.

Premi Sèrie Negra

The award was established in 2000 by the publisher Planeta. It is awarded for a novel written in Catalan, on a police or crime theme. The winner is chosen by a five-member jury, and receives 1 million ptas (€6,000); the winning work is published by Editorial Planeta.

Eligibility and Restrictions: Open to all writers of original unpublished novels written in Catalan, of at least 150 pages, written on a police or crime theme.

How to Apply: Two copies of works should be sent to the address given by 15 July.

Recent Winners: 2002: Olga Xirinacs, *No jugueu al cementiri*; 2000: Albert Salvadó, *El rapte, el mort i el marsellès*.

Sponsoring Organization: Editorial Planeta SA.

Address: Editorial Planeta, Còrsega 273–279, 08008 Barcelona, Spain.

Premia Bohemica

An annual prize presented by the Czech Traditional Writers' Guild to a foreign translator for their contribution to the promotion of Czech literature. The prize is presented during the annual Prague Book Fair.

Recent Winners: 2002: Eero Balk; 1999: Ch. Rothmeier; 1998: O. Malevic and V. Kamenska; 1997: V. Rakovski.

Sponsoring Organization: Traditional Writers' Guild.

Address: Premia Bohemica, Prague, Czech Republic.

Prêmio Academia Brasileira de Letras de Poesia (ABL Poetry Prize)

The prize, established in 1995, is awarded every July to a Brazilian poet. Three nominations are made by a commission of three Academia Brasileira de Letras (ABL) members, and the final winner is chosen by a vote among all ABL members. The winner receives 12,000 reais and a diploma.

Eligibility and Restrictions: Only open to Brazilian poets.

How to Apply: No applications are accepted.

Recent Winners: 2001: Luiz de Miranda, *Trilogia do azul do mar, da madrugada e da ventania*; 2000: Dora Ferreira, *Poesia premiada* and Moacyr Félix, *Singular plural* (joint winners); 1999: Nauro Machado, *Antologia poética*; 1998: (no prize awarded); 1997: Bruno Tolentino, *A palavra do cárcere*.

Sponsoring Organization: Academia Brasileira de Letras.

Contact: Cultural Ass Leila Longo.

Address: Academia Brasileira de Letras, Av. Presidente Wilson 203, 20030–0221 Rio de Janeiro, RJ, Brazil. **Telephone:** (21) 2533-8800. **Fax:** (21) 2220-6095. **Internet:** www.academia.org.br. **E-mail:** llongo@academia.org.br.

Premio Academia Nacional de la Historia (National Academy of History Prize)

Biennial prize for the best work on the theme of Argentine history. The prize alternates between published and unpublished works.

Eligibility and Restrictions: Open either to original unpublished works or to works which have been published during the preceding four years (depending on the alternating award cycle). Works must be written in Spanish; works written by more than one author are permitted.

Sponsoring Organization: Academia Nacional de la Historia.

Address: Academia Nacional de la Historia, Balcarce 139, 1064AAC Buenos Aires, Argentina. **Telephone:** 4343-4416. **Internet:** www.an-historia.org.ar/actividades/Premios/index.htm. **E-mail:** admite@an-historia.org.

Premio Adonais de Poesía

An annual poetry prize established in 1943 and sponsored by publisher Ediciones Rialp since 1946, with the aim of encouraging new voices in Spanish poetry. There is no cash prize, but the author receives a sculpture and the winning entry is published by Rialp.

Eligibility and Restrictions: Open to poets aged 35 or under who have not previously won the prize.

How to Apply: Entries should be submitted by 15 October.

Recent Winners: 2001: José Antonio Gómez-Coronado, *El triunfo de los días*; 2000: Joaquín Pérez Azaústre, *Una interpretación*; 1999: Irene Sánchez Carrón, *Escenas principales de un actor secundario*; 1998: Luis Enrique Belmonte, *Inutil registro*; 1997: Luis Martínez-Falero, *Plenitud de la materia*.

Sponsoring Organization: Ediciones Rialp.

Address: Ediciones Rialp SA, 1998 Alcalá, 290 Madrid, Spain. **Telephone:** (91) 326 05 04. **Fax:** (91) 326 13 21. **Internet:** www.rialp.com. **E-mail:** ediciones@rialp.com.

Premio Alfaguara de Novela

First presented in 1998, the prize is offered by the publisher Alfaguara in recognition of the uniting power of the Spanish language. The winner receives a prize of €196,000.

Recent Winners: 2002: Tomás Eloy Martínez (Argentina), *El vuelo de la reina*; 2001: Elena Poniatowska (Mexico), *La piel del cielo*; 2000: Clara Sánchez (Spain), *Últimas noticias del paraíso*; 1999: Manuel Vicent (Spain), *Son de Mar*; 1998: Eliseo Alberto, *Caracol Beach* and Sergio Ramírez, *Margarita, está linda la mar* (joint winners).

Sponsoring Organization: Ediciones Alfaguara.

Address: Ediciones Alfaguara, Torrelaguna, 60, 28043 Madrid, Spain. **Telephone:** (91) 744 90 60. **Fax:** (91) 744 92 24. **Internet:** www.alfaguara.com/.

Premio Andalucía de Novela

An annual award for a novel, first presented in 1986.

Recent Winners: 2001: Juan Antonio Bueno Álvarez, *El último viaje de Eliseo Guzmán*; 2000: Antonio Orejudo Utrilla, *Ventajas de vivir en Tren*; 1999: Benjamín Prado, *No sólo el fuego*; 1998: Montserrat Fernández, *Gramática Griega*; 1997: Pepa Roma, *Mandala*.

Sponsoring Organization: BBVA/Alfaguara, Torrelaguna, 60, 28043 Madrid, Spain. **Telephone:** (91) 744 90 60. **Fax:** (91) 744 92 24. **Internet:** www.alfaguara.santillana.es.

Premio Anual de Ensayo Literario Hispanoamericano Lya Kostakowsky (Lya Kostakowsky Prize for a Latin American Literary Essay)

An annual prize of $25,000 for an unpublished literary essay; the topic changes each year.

Eligibility and Restrictions: Works must have been written in Spanish during the previous year (year ending August), and must be at least 50 pages in length.

Sponsoring Organization: Fundación Cultural Lya y Luis Cardoza y Aragón, A.C.

Address: Fundación Cultural Lya y Luis Cardoza y Aragón, A.C, Callejón de las Flores 1, esq. Puente San Francisco, Col. Barrio del Niño Jesús, CP 04000, Coyoacán, Mexico City, DF, Mexico. **Telephone:** (55) 55 54 40 10. **Fax:** (55) 54 40 10. **E-mail:** elrio@mail.internet.com.mx.

Premio Rolando Anzilotti

An international prize awarded for monographs in the field of literature for children and young people. Entries can take the form of essays, anthologies, critical dictionaries, theoretical discussions, and so on. The winner is selected by an international jury headed by Anna Maria Bernardinis, professor at the University of Padua.

Sponsoring Organization: Fondazione Nazionale Carlo Collodi.

Address: Fondazione Nazionale Carlo Collodi, Villa Arcangeli, Via Pasquinelli 6, 51014 Collodi (PT), Italy. **Telephone:** (572) 42 96 13. **Internet:** www.ricochet-jeunes.org/carnet/base15/fondcollodi.htm.

Premio Apel les Mestres

A prize for illustrated works for children, sponsored by the publisher Ediciones Destino SA and first given in 1981. The winner receives a prize of €4,500.

Eligibility and Restrictions: Open to illustrated works on any theme. Authors must guarantee the originality of their work. Works written in any of the Spanish languages are eligible, as well as English, French or Italian.

Recent Winners: 2002: Maria Teresa Cáceres and Anna Vila Badia, *A Mi no em Veu Ningu / A Mi no me Ve Nadie*; 1998: Sophie Fatus,*Tim a la Lluna*; 1997: Gisela Mehrem, *El Viatge d'Alexandre*; 1996: Davi, *Historias de Soles*; 1995: Moia and Biagio Bagini, *Berta la Modista*.

Sponsoring Organization: Ediciones Destino SA.

Address: Ediciones Destino SA, Provenza 260 40, 08008 Barcelona, Spain. **Internet:** www.edestino.es.

Premio Azorín

A prize established in 1994 as a collaboration between the Provincial Administration of Alicante and the publisher Editorial Planeta. The prize, which is awarded for a novel, is of 10 million ptas (€60,000).

Recent Winners: 2002: Eugenia Rico, *La muerte blanca*; 2001: Luisa Castro, *El secreto de la lejía*; 1999: José Luis Ferris, *Bajarás al reino de la tierra*; 1998: Daína Chaviano, *El hombre, la hembra y el hambre*.

Sponsoring Organization: Diputación Provincial de Alicante/Editorial Planeta SA.

Address: Diputación Provincial de Alicante, 08008 Alicante, Spain.

Premio Letterario Giuseppe Berto

The Giuseppe Berto literary prize was established in 1988 by the Commune of Mogliano in Veneto (birthplace of the writer Giuseppe Berto) to honour a first work of fiction. The prize aims to honour the name and the works of a writer who is recognized for his/her nonconformism. The winning title is chosen for its originality of form and its inspiration. It must be a first work, in the spirit of the writer Berto who fought to remove the obstacles facing talented young writers. The winner receives a prize of 10 million lire.

Eligibility and Restrictions: Awarded to a first work of narrative, published in Italian.

How to Apply: The jury chooses the winner from selected works of narrative which have appeared in the previous 12 months. Authors or publishers are invited to submit titles before the deadline of 30 April.

Recent Winners: 2001: Giuseppe Lupo, *L'Americano di Celenne*; 2000: Evelina Santangelo, *L'occhio cieco del mondo*; 1999: Elena Stancanelli, *Benzina*; 1998: Helena Janeczek, *Lezione di tenebra*; 1997: Francesco Piccolo, *Storie di primogeniti e figli unici*; 1996: Maria Luisa Magagnoli, *Un caffè molto dolce*.

Sponsoring Organization: Comune di Mogliano Veneto.

Address: Assessorato alle Attività Culturali, Segreteria Settore Politiche Culturali, Piazza Caduti, 3, 831021 Mogliano-Veneto (TV), Italy. **Telephone:** (41) 59 30 800. **Fax:** (41) 59 30 899. **E-mail:** cultura@comune.mogliano-veneto. tv.it.

Premio Biblioteca Breve

An annual prize for a novel established in 1958 by the publisher Editorial Seix Barral. The prize has been awarded annually since then, although it was suspended from 1972 until 1999. The prize now stands at €30,050. Its aim is to encourage young writers to participate in the movement for European renewal of literature, and to recognize innovation in theme, style or content in an outstanding work in a novel which best represents 'the spirit of our times'.

Eligibility and Restrictions: Open to novels written in Spanish.

Recent Winners: 2002: Mario Mendoza, *Satanás*; 2001: Juana Salabert, *Velódromo de Invierno*; 2000: Gonzalo Garcés, *Los impacientes*; 1999: Jorge Volpi, *En busca de Klingsor*.

Sponsoring Organization: Editorial Seix Barral.

Address: Editorial Seix Barral, 08008 Barcelona, Spain. **Internet:** www. seix-barral.es/portada.asp.

Premio Camões

This is one of the most important Portuguese literary awards, and is similar to the Spanish Cervantes prize. It was established in 1988 by the governments of Portugal and Brazil. The winner is selected by a six-member jury appointed by the Brazilian Minister of Culture and the Portuguese Secretary of Culture, and receives a prize of $100,000.

Eligibility and Restrictions: Open to Portuguese-speaking writers.

Recent Winners: 2002: Maria Velho de Costa (Portugal); 2001: Eugenio de Andrade (Portugal); 2000: Autran Dourado (Brazil); 1999: Sophia de Mello Breyner Andresen (Portugal); 1998: Antonio Candido de Melo e Sousa (Brazil).

Sponsoring Organization: Instituto Camões/Fundaçao Biblioteca Nacional/ Departamento Nacional do Livro.

Address: Rua Rodrigues Sampaio 113, 1150–279 Lisbon, Portugal. **Telephone:** (21) 3109100. **Internet:** www.instituto-camoes.pt. **E-mail:** geral@instituto-camoes.pt.

Premio Campiello (Campiello Prize)

The prize, one of the leading Italian literary awards, was established in 1962. The selection is made by a jury of 300 readers, from all social, cultural and professional areas throughout Italy. Readers are only permitted to take part in the jury for one year.

Recent Winners: 2001: Giuseppe Pontiggia, *Nati due volte*; 2000: Sandro Veronesi, *La forza del passato*; 1999: Ermanno Rea, *Fuochi fiammanti a un'hora di notte*; 1998: Cesare De Marchi, *Il talento*; 1997: Marta Morazzoni, *Il caso Courrier*.

Sponsoring Organization: Campieillo Foundation.

Address: Via Torino, 151/c, 30172 Mestre–Venezia, Italy. **Telephone:** (41) 2517520. **Fax:** (41) 2517576. **Internet:** www.premiocampiello.org/.

Premio Casa de las Americas

An annual award established in 1959 to stimulate literary works in the Americas. Prizes are presented for outstanding works in the categories novel, poetry, essay, children's literature, Caribbean or Creole works. Winning works are published in a special edition in collaboration with the Ministry of Culture of Colombia. Three special prizes are also awarded, the José Lezama Lima Prize (poetry), the José Maria Arguedas Prize (narrative) and the Ezequiel Martinez Estrada Prize (essay).

Eligibility and Restrictions: Works must have been written in Spanish during the preceding year by an author from Latin America.

How to Apply: Entries are put forward by an international nomination committee.

Recent Winners: Novel: 2002: Rafael Pinedo, *Plop*; 2001: Leonardo Peña Calderón, *Siempre es posible verlos al pasar*; 1997: Luis María Pescetti, *Ciudadano de mis zapatos*
Poetry: 2002: Luis Manuel Pérez Boitel, *Aún nos pertenece el otoño*
Essay: 2002: Álvaro Salvador Jofre, *El impuro amor de las ciudades*; 2001: Luis Fernando Ayerbe, *Los Estados Unidos y la América Latina. La construcción de la hegemonía*
Short story: 2001: Dante Medina, *Te ve, mi amor TV*
Drama: 2001: Walter Acosta, *El escorpión y la comadreja*
Brazilian literature: 2001: Walter Galbani, *La nave capitana*
Children's: 2002: Carlos Marianidis, *Nada detiene a las golondrinas*
Caribbean or Creole: 2002: Oonya Kempadoo, *Tide Running*
José Lezama Lima Prize: 2002: José Watanabe, *El guardián del hielo*
Jose Maria Arguedas Prize: 2002: Miguel Bonasso, *Diario de un clandestino*
Ezequiel Martinez Estrada Prize: 2002: Julio García Espinosa, *Un largo camino hacia la luz*.

Address: Casa de las Americas, Calle Tercera y G, El Vedado, Havana, 10400, Cuba. **Telephone:** (53 7) 552715. **Fax:** (53 7) 33-4554. **Internet:** www.casa. cult.cu. **E-mail:** cil@casa.cult.cu.

Premio Cervantes

The Cervantes Prize is considered to be the Hispanic equivalent of the Nobel prize. It was established in 1974, and honours an entire body of work. Nominations are presented by the Spanish Real Academia as well as those from other Spanish-speaking countries. The jury is headed by the Spanish Minister of Culture and Education. The award ceremony takes place in April, and the prize amounts to €90,000 (15 million ptas).

Recent Winners: 2001: Alvaro Mutis (Colombia); 2000: Francisco Umbral (Spain); 1999: Jorge Edwards (Chile); 1998: José Hierro (Spain); 1997: Guillermo Cabrera Infante (Cuba).

Sponsoring Organization: Dirección General del Libro y Bibliotecas, Ministerio de Cultura.

Address: Dirección General del Libro y Bibliotecas, Ministerio de Cultura, Plaza del Rey, 28004 Madrid, Spain.

Premio Demac

Annual award for biography or autobiography by Mexican women, the Demac Prize 'for women who dare to tell their story' carries a prize of $40,000 per category. The award is sponsored by Documentación y Estudios de Mujeres AC (DEMAC), an organization dedicated to promoting works of literature by women.

Eligibility and Restrictions: Open to Mexican women for an unpublished text in Spanish, of any length, in the field of biography or autobiography.

How to Apply: Deadline for submissions is the end of October.

Sponsoring Organization: Documentación y Estudios de Mujeres AC (DEMAC).

Address: Documentación y Estudios de Mujeres, AC, José de Teresa 253, Col. Tlacopac San Ángel, CP 01040, Álvaro Obregón, Mexico City, DF, Mexico. **Telephone:** (55) 56 63 37 45. **Fax:** (56) 62 52 08. **Internet:** www.starnet.net.mx/ demac/. **E-mail:** demac@starnet.net.mx.

Premio Destino-Guion

This prize is awarded alongside Premio Nadal (qv); entries to the Premio Nadal are automatically entered for this prize. An eight-member jury (made up of the jury for the Premio Nadal plus two people from the world of cinema) chooses the winner, based on its potential for adaptation into a cinematic screenplay. The winner receives a prize of 1.5 million ptas (€9,000).

Eligibility and Restrictions: Open to unpublished novels written in Spanish.

Recent Winners: 2002: Carlos Bardem, *Buziana o el Peso del Alma*; 2001: Yolanda García Serrano and Verónica Fernández, *¿De que va eso del Amor?*

Sponsoring Organization: Ediciones Destino SA.

Address: Ediciones Destino SA, Calle Provenza 260, 08008 Barcelona, Spain. **Internet:** www.edestino.es/enterate.htm.

Prêmio D. Diniz

The prize was established in 1980 by the Fundação da Casa de Mateus, to promote creativity and reading. The prize is awarded every year, preferably for a work published the year before. The jury comprises three members chosen by the Foundation. There is a prize of €7,500. Also awards the Prémio Morgado de Mateus.

Eligibility and Restrictions: The prize is only open to Portuguese writers, for works of fiction, non-fiction or poetry.

How to Apply: It is not possible to apply directly; the jury makes its own selection.

Recent Winners: 2001: Gastão Cruz, *Crateras*; 2000: Antonio Lobo Antunes, *Exortacão aos Crocodilos*; 1999: Lidia Jorge, *O Vale da Paixão*
1998: Jose Cardoso Pires, *De Profundis Valsa Lenta*; 1997: Fiama Hasse Pais Brandão, *Epistolas e Memorandos*.

Sponsoring Organization: Fundação da Casa de Mateus.

Contact: Fernando Albuquerque, President.
Address: Fundação da Casa de Mateus, Mateus, 5000–291 Vila Real, Portugal.
Telephone: (259) 323 121. **Fax:** (259) 326 553. **Internet:** www.utad.geira.pt/casa_mateus/. **E-mail:** casa.mateus@mail.telepac.pt.

Premio Esteban Echeverría

Awarded each year by the Asociación Gente de Letras in Buenos Aires for a complete body of work.

Recent Winners: 1999: Eduardo Gudiño Kieffer; 1995: Graciela Maturo; 1993: Abelardo Castillo; 1991: Juan Filloy; 1990: Antonio Requeni; other winners include Isidoro Blaisten, Luis Ricardo Furlan, Roberto Juarroz.

Sponsoring Organization: Asociación Gente de Letras.

Address: Asociación Gente de Letras, Buenos Aires, Argentina.

Premio Fastenrath

An annual prize administered by the Real Academia Española, awarded in recognition of a work of literary merit. The award rotates between the genres novel, poetry and essay. The winner receives a prize of 2 million ptas (€12,000).

Eligibility and Restrictions: Entries must have been published during the preceding three years.

Recent Winners: 2001 (poetry): D. Guillermo Carnero, *Verano inglés.*

Sponsoring Organization: Real Academia Española.

Address: Real Academia Española, Felipe IV, 4, 28014 Madrid, Spain. **Telephone:** (91) 420 14 78. **Fax:** (91) 420 00 79. **Internet:** www.rae.es/.

Premio Antonio Feltrinelli

The Feltrinelli Prizes have been awarded annually since 1950 by the Accademia Nazionale dei Lincei, following a bequest from Antonio Feltrinelli. The prizes honour the work, research and intelligence of individuals or organizations judged to have made a major contribution to the development of moral sciences, physics and mathematics, literature, fine arts, or medicine (the eligible categories rotate annually). Within the field of letters (literature), there is a €250,000 prize for classical philology, and four prizes of €65,000 for literary criticism, oriental literature, poetry and narrative.

Recent Winners: 2001: Operation Smile; former recipients of the Feltrinelli Prize include Günter Grass (1982), the International Red Cross (1969), Coretta Scott King (1969), Thomas Mann (1952) and Igor Stravinsky (1953).

Sponsoring Organization: Accademia Nazionale dei Lincei.

Address: Accademia Nazionale dei Lincei, Palazzo Corsini, Via della Lungara 10, 1000165 Rome, Italy. **Telephone:** (6) 68 02 71. **Fax:** (6) 689 36 16. **Internet:** www.lincei.it. **E-mail:** segreteria@lincei.it.

Premio Grinzane Cavour (Grinzane Cavour Prize)

An annual prize established in 1982 by Giuliano Soria, with the aim of drawing young readers closer to books by promoting the pleasure of reading books not strictly related to the school curriculum. The competition takes place in two stages, with an initial shortlist drawn up by a panel of literary experts, which is then judged by national and international panels of schoolchildren. Entries are judged in seven sections: published contemporary Italian fiction, contemporary foreign fiction translated and published in Italy, translations, essays, debut work by a young writer, an International Award (given in recognition of a life devoted to literature), and the Premio Grinzane Editoria, the Italian Publishing Award, in memory of Giulio Bollati, and presented to a national or international personality for their outstanding ethics and civil commitment.

Recent Winners: Italian narrative: 2002: Arnaldo Colasanti, *Gatti e scimmie*, Margaret Mazzantini, *Non ti muovere* and Romana Petri, *La donna delle Azzorre* Foreign narrative: 2002: Alfredo Bryce Echenique (Peru), *La tonsillite di Tarzan*, Christoph Hein (Germany), *Willenbrock* and Orhan Pamuk (Turkey), *Il mio nome è rosso*

International Prize: 2002: Daniel Pennac (France); former winners include Julien Green, Günter Grass, Czesław Miłosz, Carlos Fuentes, Bohumil Hrabal, Oe Kenzaburo, Yves Bonnefoy, Jean Starobinski, V. S. Naipaul, Manuel Vázquez Montalbán and Doris Lessing
Premio Grinzane Editoria: 2001: Hans Magnus Enzensberger (Germany)
Debut Writer: 2002: Davide Longo, *Un mattino a Irgalem*
Translation Prize: 2002: Ettore Capriolo.

Sponsoring Organization: Grinzane Cavour Prize Association.

Address: Grinzane Cavour Prize Association, Via Montebello 2, 10124 Turin, Italy. **Telephone:** (11) 81 00 111. **Fax:** (11) 812 54 56. **Internet:** www.grinzane.it. **E-mail:** info@grinzane.it.

Premio Hispanoamericano de Poesía Sor Juana Inés de la Cruz (Sister Juana Inés de la Cruz Latin American Poetry Prize)

An award created in 1997 for a work of poetry by a Hispanic writer. The award is named after a 17th century Catholic nun, and is sponsored by the Consejo Nacional para la Cultura y las Artes de México. The winner receives US $3,000, a diploma and publication of the work.

Eligibility and Restrictions: Open to all writers in Spanish living in Latin America; entries must be unpublished collections of poems of no more than 60 pages, which have not won any previous prizes.

Recent Winners: 2000: Germa'n Carrasco (Chile).

Sponsoring Organization: Consejo Nacional para la Cultura y las Artes de México.

Address: Centro Cultural de México, Los Yoses 4a., Entrada 250 S, PO Box 10107–1000, San José, Costa Rica.

Premio Internacional de Ensayo Mariano Picón Salas (Mariano Picón Salas International Essay Prize)

A new essay prize established in 2001 by the Centro de Estudios Latino-americanos Rómulo Gallegos (CELARG), with the aim of encouraging creativity in the form of a Spanish-language essay. The winner receives a prize of $20,000, plus a medal and a diploma. The winning entry will be also be published.

Eligibility and Restrictions: Open to unpublished works written in Spanish on any theme; authors may be resident in any country.

How to Apply: Entries should be sent under a pseudonym, with author's identity on a separate sheet. Four copies should be submitted by the end of June.

Sponsoring Organization: Centro de Estudios Latinoamericanos Rómulo Gallegos (CELARG).

Address: CELARG, Casa de Rómulo Gallegos, Av. Luis Roche con tercera transversal, Altamira, Caracas, 1062, Venezuela. **Telephone:** (285) 27 21. **Fax:** (285) 46 80. **Internet:** www.celarg.org.ve. **E-mail:** celarg2@reacciun.ve.

Premio Internacional de Novela Yolanda Vargas Dulché
(Yolanda Vargas Dulché International Novel Prize)

An annual award of $30,00 for a novel, sponsored by the publisher Grupo Editorial Vid. The latter also agrees to publish the winning entry and pay a 10% royalty to the author.

Eligibility and Restrictions: Open to all writers, either in Mexico or abroad, for an unpublished novel on any theme, written in Spanish. Works which have already won any other prize are excluded. Works must be between 100 and 200 pages in length.

How to Apply: Entries should be sent (under a pseudonym) by the end of January.

Sponsoring Organization: Grupo Editorial Vid.

Address: Departamento de Libros del Grupo Editorial Vid, S.A. de C.V, Calle Pino 1 Col. Florida, CP 01030, Álvaro Obregón, Mexico City, DF, Mexico. **Telephone:** (55) 53 22 13 00. **Internet:** www.mundovid.com/premioslit.htm. **E-mail:** cristinad@mundovid.com.

Premio Internacional de Novela Rómulo Gallegos

The award was created in 1964 by an official decree, and first presented in 1967 in honour of the Venezuelan novelist and former president Rómulo Gallegos. Since then it has become one of the most prestigious South American literary awards, and is presented once every five years. The winner, chosen by a jury drawn from countries across the whole of South America as well as Spain, receives a gold medal and a prize of $60,000.

Eligibility and Restrictions: Open to novels written in Spanish.

Recent Winners: 2001: Enrique Vila-Matas (Spain), *El Viaje Vertical*; 1991: Uslar Pietri, *Una visita en el tiempo (A Visit in Time)*; earlier winners include Mexican Carlos Fuentes in 1977, Colombian Gabriel García Márquez in 1972, and Peruvian Mario Vargas Llosa in 1967.

Sponsoring Organization: Centro de Estudios Latinoamericanos Rómulo Gallegos (CELARG).

Address: CELARG, Casa de Rómulo Gallegos, Av. Luis Roche con tercera transversal, Altamira, Caracas, 1062, Venezuela. **Telephone:** (285) 27 21. **Fax:** (285) 46 80. **Internet:** www.celarg.org.ve. **E-mail:** celarg2@reacciun.ve.

Premio Internacional Alfonso Reyes
(Alfonso Reyes International Prize)

An annual prize of $150,000 for works in the literary tradition of Mexican literary critic, scholar, poet, and diplomat Alfonso Reyes (1889–1959). The prize is awarded in recognition of a lifetime's achievement and contribution to promoting Mexican culture abroad.

How to Apply: Nominations are accepted from learned associations and writers' academies.

Recent Winners: 2001: Rafael Gutiérrez Girardot; 2000: Miguel Leon Portilla; 1998: Arturo Uslar Pietri; 1995: Juan Jose Arreola; 1994: German Arciniegas; previous winners include Francisco Zendejas, Jorge Luis Borges, Marcel Bataillon, Adolfo Bioy Casares and Octavio Paz.

Sponsoring Organization: Consejo Nacional para la Cultura y las Artes/ Instituto Nacional de Bellas Artes (INBA)/Sociedad Alfonsina Internacional, AC.

Address: Conaculta / Centro Nacional de Información y Promoción de la Literatura del INBA, Brasil 37, Col. Centro Histórico, CP 06020, Cuauhtémoc, 06029 Mexico City, DF, Mexico. **Telephone:** (55) 55 26 31 86. **E-mail:** cnipl@ data.net.mx.

Premio Internazionale Fregene

The Premio Fregene is awarded annually to artists and personalities who make an impact at an international level. The winner receives a statuette specially created by the Italian sculptor Angelo Canevari, and a cheque for 3 million lire. Besides the international prize, other awards are presented for narrative, children's fiction and new media.

How to Apply: Authors and publishers should send 15 copies of entries by 30 May.

Recent Winners: International Prize: 2001: Paulo Coelho, *The Devil and Miss Pym*; earlier winners include Melina Mercouri, the author Tennessee Williams, and the Russian poet Yevgeniy Yevtushenko
Narrative: 2001: Carlo Sgorlon, *La tredicesima notte*
Children's: 2001: Sandro Veronesi, *Ring City*.

Address: Via della Camilluccia, 201–00135 Rome, Italy. **Telephone:** (6) 35497720. **Fax:** (6) 35497720. **Internet:** www.premiofregene.it. **E-mail:** premiofregene@virgilio.it.

Premio Internazionale di Letteratura La Cultura del Mare

Established in 1988, this prize is awarded each July to a selection of outstanding works with an oceanic theme. The aim of the prize is to engender a greater respect and understanding of the sea and its heritage among the younger generation. The prize is awarded in a collaboration between the Parco Nazionale del Circeo, the Associations 'Amici del Mare' and 'Verso Sud' and the local communities of Sabaudia and San Felice Circeo.

Recent Winners: 2002: Giacomo Oreglia, *Dante*, Renato Laganà, *La Città del Mare*, Angelo Airol, *Le Isole mirabili*, Giovanna Bemporad, *Odissea*, Raffaele La Capria, *Capri e non più Capri* and Alessandro Baricco, *Oceano Mare*; 2000: Alvaro Mutis; special poetry prize awarded to Claudio Angelini, Antonio Benedetti and Martha Canfield, Enzo Siciliano, *Mia madre amava il mare*, Piero Angela, *Dentro il Mediterraneo*, Dava Sobel, *Longitude*, Raffaele Nigro, *Adriatico*, Fabrizia Romondino, *L'isola riflessa* and Maria Luisa Spaziani, *I misteri del Mare*; 1997: Folco Quilici, for collected works about the Italian seas.

Sponsoring Organization: Parco Nazionale del Circeo.

Address: Parco Nazionale del Circeo, Via Carlo Alberto, 107–04016 Sabaudia (LT), Italy. **Telephone:** (77) 3511385. **Fax:** (77) 3510503. **Internet:** www.parks.it/ parco.nazionale.circeo/man.html. **E-mail:** pn.Circeo@parks.it.

Prêmio Jabuti (Jabuti Prize)

Brazil's most prestigious literary award, administered by the Câmara Brasileira do Livro (Brazilian Book Chamber). Although the award brings a relatively small cash prize (1,000 reais, or $427), the winners enjoy considerable prestige. Prizes are awarded in numerous categories, including: romance, short stories, poetry, children/teens, literary and linguistic theory, economy, administration and law, natural and health sciences, science technology and computer, human sciences, pedagogy and psychology , media reporting and biography, school textbooks, and translation; there are also prizes for publishing. Two of the winners are also selected as Book of the Year in fiction and non-fiction, with a further prize of 15,000 reais ($6400).

Sponsoring Organization: Câmara Brasileira do Livro (Brazilian Book Chamber).

Address: Instituto Brasil–Estados Unidos, Ave NS de Copacabana 690, 11 andar, 22050–000 Rio de Janeiro, RJ, Brazil.

Premio Latinoamericano de Literatura Infantil y Juvenil Norma-Fundalectura (Norma-Fundalectura Latin American Prize for Children's Literature)

An international competition for the best works of literature (novels or short stories) for children, sponsored by the National Council for Culture and Art and the publisher Norma Ediciones. The winner receives a prize of $10,000.

Eligibility and Restrictions: Open to adult writers from any Latin American country, for unpublished works for children (aged 6 to 10), written in Spanish and up to 80 pages in length.

How to Apply: Entries may be submitted between December and April.

Sponsoring Organization: Norma Ediciones/Consejo Nacional para la Cultura y las Artes.

Address: Norma Ediciones, S.A. de C.V., Av. Cuauhtémoc 1093, Col. Del Valle, CP 36050, Benito Juárez, Mexico City, DF, Mexico. **Telephone:** (55) 56 05 44 94. **E-mail:** beario@carvajal.com.mx.

Prêmio Ler

This award, established in 1980 and named after *Ler* magazine, aims to discover new works which have never been published. The award is offered every two years. The winner is selected by a panel of five eminent figures from the literary world. The winner receives €15,000, plus publication of the book and payment of subsequent royalties.

Eligibility and Restrictions: Open to unpublished works of fiction of at least 200 pages. The manuscript must be submitted under a pseudonym to conceal the writer's identity.

How to Apply: Writers may apply by sending five copies of the work to the Fundação Círculo de Leitores at the address given.

Recent Winners: 2000: Miguel Real, *A visão de Túndalo por Eça de Queiroz*; 1998: Manuel Córrego, *Campo de Feno com Papoilas*; 1996: Rui Miguel Saramogo, *A fraude*; 1994: João Maria Mendes, *A mulher do terrrorista*; 1992: Helena Marques, *O último cais*.

Sponsoring Organization: Fundação Círculo de Leitores.

Contact: Dir Mafalda Lopes da Costa.
Address: Rua Prof. Jorge da Silva Horta, No 1, 1500–499 Lisbon, Portugal.
Telephone: (21) 7626000. **Fax:** (21) 7609592. **Internet:** www.circuloleitores.pt.
E-mail: fundacao@circuloleitores.pt.

Premio Letterario Isola d'Elba – Rafaello Brignetti
(Isle of Elba – Rafaello Brignetti Literary Award)

An annual prize, first awarded in 1962, for a work of fiction or poetry. The winner receives a prize of €5,165.

Eligibility and Restrictions: Entries must be written in Italian and published in the previous year (year ending February).

How to Apply: Deadline for submissions is 28 February.

Recent Winners: 2002: Desiato Luca, *Dal giardino murato*; 2001: Alessandro Barbero, *L'ultima rosa di Lautrec*; 2000: Fosco Maraini; 1999: Maurizo Bettini; 1998: Alvar Gonzales.

Sponsoring Organization: Premio Letterario Isola d'Elba – Rafaello Brignetti.

Address: c/o Consorzio Elba Promotion, Calata Italia 26, 57037 Portoferraio LI, Italy. **Telephone:** (56) 5960157. **Fax:** 956) 5917632. **E-mail:** elbapro@elba2000.it.

Premio Letterario Mondello Città di Palermo

An annual prize sponsored by the city of Palermo since 1974. Winners are chosen by a jury in several categories, including fiction, theatre, foreign novel, translation and first work.

Recent Winners: Drama: 2001: Claudio Magris, *La mostra*
Italian narrative: 2001: Roberto Alajmo, *Notizia del disastro*; 2000: Elio Bartolini, *Le quattro sorelle Bau*
Foreign narrative: 2000: Alexandar Tisma, *Il libro di Blam*
Translation: 2000: Sossio Giametta, *La stella danzante* by Friedrich Nietzsche
First work: 2000: Evelina Santangelo, *L'occhio cieco del mondo*.

Sponsoring Organization: Cultura del Comune di Palermo/Fondazione Premio Mondello.

Address: Fondazione Premio Mondello, Palermo, Italy. **Internet:** www.comune. palermo.it.

Premio del Libro

Established in 2001 by the Association of Madrid Booksellers, the prize recognizes a book which has had a major impact on booksellers and their customers during the previous year. The award is presented during the Madrid Book Fair in June. There is no cash prize.

Recent Winners: 2001: Eduardo Mendoza, *L'artiste des dames*.

Sponsoring Organization: Association of Madrid Booksellers.

Address: Association of Madrid Booksellers, Madrid, Spain.

Premio Literario Editorial Costa Rica

One of three awards sponsored by the publisher Editorial Costa Rica, the Premio Literario Carmen Lyra recognizes an outstanding short story on any theme. The winner receives a prize of 650,000 colones, and the winning work is published.

Eligibility and Restrictions: Open to authors of Costa Rican nationality or foreigners who are legally resident in the country. Entrants must be at least 18 years of age. Works submitted must be original, unpublished and not have won any previous prizes. Entries must be written in Spanish, and should be between 80 and 120 pages.

How to Apply: Three copies should be submitted under a pseudonym, with author's biographical details on a separate sheet, by mid-June.

Sponsoring Organization: Editorial Costa Rica.

Address: Editorial Costa Rica, Centro Cultural del Este, Guadalupe de Goicoechea, San José, 1000, Costa Rica. **Internet:** www.editorialcostarica.com/ certamenesliterar.htm. **E-mail:** difusion@editorialcostarica.com.

Premio Literario Joven Creación (Young Creation Literary Prize)

One of three awards sponsored by the publisher Editorial Costa Rica, the Premio Literario Joven Creación recognizes an outstanding novel on any theme by a young writer. The winner receives a prize of 250,000 colones, and the winning work is published.

Eligibility and Restrictions: Open to authors of Costa Rican nationality or foreigners who are legally resident in the country. Entrants must be at least 15 years of age, but less than 30. Works submitted must be original, unpublished and not have won any previous prizes. Entries must be written in Spanish, and should be between 50 and 100 pages.

How to Apply: Three copies should be submitted under a pseudonym, with author's biographical details on a separate sheet, by mid-June.

Sponsoring Organization: Editorial Costa Rica.

Address: Editorial Costa Rica, Centro Cultural del Este, Guadalupe de Goicoechea, San José, 1000, Costa Rica. **Internet:** www.editorialcostarica.com/ certamenesliterar.htm. **E-mail:** difusion@editorialcostarica.com.

Prêmio Literário José Saramago

The award was founded in 1998 in honour of the Portuguese novelist José Saramago, winner in that year of the Nobel Prize for Literature. The prize aims to promote young writers of any Portuguese-speaking country, and is offered every two years. The winner is selected by a panel of 5 to 10 eminent individuals from Portuguese-speaking countries, and receives €25,000.

Eligibility and Restrictions: Open to works by a young author (up to 35 years at date of publication) from any Portuguese-speaking country, who has had a work of fiction published in the last two years. Self-published works are excluded, as are works by authors no longer living.

How to Apply: Publishers or writers may apply by sending 10 copies of their work to the Fundação Círculo de Leitores at the address given.

Recent Winners: 2001: José Peixoto, *Nenhum Olhar*; 1999: Paulo José Miranda, *Natureza Morta*.

Sponsoring Organization: Fundação Círculo de Leitores.

Contact: Pres. Guilhermina Gomes.

Address: Rua Prof. Jorge da Silva Horta, No 1, 1500–499 Lisbon, Portugal. **Telephone:** (21) 7626000. **Fax:** (21) 7609592. **Internet:** www.circuloleitores.pt. **E-mail:** fundacao@circuloleitores.pt.

Premio de Literatura Ricardo Mimenza Castillo

An annual prize of $10,000 for a published work of any kind by a writer from Yucatán, sponsored jointly by the Instituto de Cultura de Yucatán, the Universidad Autónoma de Yucatán, the National Coucil for Culture and Art and the Association of Mexican Writers.

Eligibility and Restrictions: Open to published works in any genre by a writer from the Yucatán area; entries must have been published during the previous year.

Sponsoring Organization: Instituto de Cultura de Yucatán/Universidad Autónoma de Yucatán/Consejo Nacional para la Cultura y las Artes/Sociedad General de Escritores de México.

Address: ICY Av. Itzaes 501-C entre 59 y 65, Col. Centro, CP 97000, Mérida, Yucatán, Mexico. **Telephone:** (999) 928 00 90. **Internet:** www.icy.gob.mx/nuevo.htm. **E-mail:** literatura01@hotmail.com.

Premio de Literatura Infantil El Barco de Vapor
('Steamboat' Prize for Children's Literature)

An annual contest for children's literature, jointly sponsored by the National Council for Culture and Arts and the publisher Ediciones S. M. Cóndor. Prizes are awarded in several categories, depending on the age of the target readership: White, Blue, Orange, and Red. The prize is of US $150,000.

Eligibility and Restrictions: Open to writers resident in Mexico, for unpublished works of literature for children aged up to 14. Length limit for entries varies from 5 to 150 pages, depending on category.

How to Apply: Entries should be submitted between November and April of each year.

Sponsoring Organization: Consejo Nacional para la Cultura y las Artes/Ediciones S. M. Cóndor.

Address: Ediciones S. M. Cóndor, 240 Col. Las Águilas, CP 01710, Álvaro Obregón, Mexico City, Mexico. **Telephone:** (55) 56 60 20 90. **Fax:** (55) 56 60 19 61. **E-mail:** smedit@netra.net.

Premio de Literatura Juvenil Gran Angular

An annual prize of US $150,000, sponsored jointly by the publisher Ediciones S. M. Cóndor and theNational Council for Culture and Art, for an unpublished novel for children.

Eligibility and Restrictions: Entries must be written in Spanish, of at least 150 pages in length, and be aimed at readers up to 15. Applicants must be resident in Mexico.

How to Apply: Entries should be submitted between November and April.

Sponsoring Organization: Ediciones S. M. Cóndor/Consejo Nacional para la Cultura y las Artes.

Address: Ediciones S. M. Cóndor, 240 Col. Las Águilas, CP 01710, álvaro Obregón, Mexico City, DF, Mexico. **Telephone:** (55) 56 60 20 90. **Fax:** (55) 56 60 19 61. **E-mail:** smedit@netra.net.

Premio de Literatura Latinoamericana y del Caribe Juan Rulfo

Named after a great Mexican writer, the Premio Juan Rulfo is considered one of the most prestigious literary awards in Latin America. The awarding commission is made up of the following bodies: University of Guadalajara, Jalisco State Government, Fondo de Cultura Económica and the Consejo Nacional para la Cultura y las Artes. The jury comprises literary critics from throughout Latin America. The winner receives US $100,000.

Eligibility and Restrictions: Granted to a work of Latin American or Caribbean origin, published in one of the following languages: Spanish, Portuguese, French or English.

Recent Winners: 2002: Cintio Vitier (Cuba); 2001: Juan García Ponce (Mexico); 2000: Juan Gelman (Argentina); 1999: Sergio Pitol (Mexico); 1998: Olga Orozco (Argentina).

Address: Comisión de Premiación, Av. Francia 1747, Colonia Moderna, Jalisco, CP 44190, Guadalajara, Mexico. **Internet:** premiorulfo.udg.mx/.

Premio de Literatura José Fuentes Mares (José Fuentes Mares Literary Prize)

An annual prize for a published novel, sponsored by the Universidad Autónoma de Ciudad Juárez, through its Literary and Linguistics Studies Programme. The winner receives a prize of $50,000 and a special medal.

Eligibility and Restrictions: Open to works by Mexican authors published in the preceding 18 months (year ending August). Reprints and collections are excluded.

How to Apply: Entries should be submitted by the beginning of August.

Sponsoring Organization: Universidad Autónoma de Ciudad Juárez.

Address: Programa de Estudios Literarios y Lingüísticos de la UACJ, Henry Dunant 4016 y/o AP 1594-D, Col. Zona Pronaf, CP 32310, Juárez, Chihuahua, Mexico. **Telephone:** (656) 688 38 00. **Internet:** www.uacj.mx/Noticias/Mares/ContMares.htm. **E-mail:** lsalazar@uacj.mx.

Premio de Literatura para Niños Hunapuh e Ixbalamqué (Hunapuh e Ixbalamqué Prize for Children's Literature)

An annual competition organized by the Yucatán Institute of Culture, for an unpublished collection of short stories or a work of drama for children, in any style and on any theme. The winner receives $10,000, with a runner-up prize of $5,000.

Eligibility and Restrictions: Open to writers from the Yucatán area only.

Sponsoring Organization: Instituto de Cultura de Yucatán (ICY)/Sociedad General de Escritores de México.
Address: Instituto de Cultura de Yucatán (ICY), Av. Itzaes 501-C entre 59 y 65 Col. Centro, CP 97000, Mérida, Yucatán, Mexico. **Fax:** (999) 928 00 90. **Internet:** www.icy.gob.mx/nuevo.htm. **E-mail:** 01@hotmail.com.

Premio de Literatura Sor Juana Inés de la Cruz
(Sister Juana Inés de la Cruz Literary Prize)

An annual prize for women novelists, jointly organized by the Feria Internacional del Libro de Guadalajara (Guadalajara International Book Fair), the Escuela de Escritores SOGEM Guadalajara, the Asociación de Clubes del Libro and the Catholic University of Salta in Argentina. The winner receives a commemorative plaque, and publication of the winning work.

Eligibility and Restrictions: Open to novels written by women in Spanish or Portuguese during the previous year. Entries must be at least 120 pages long.

How to Apply: Entries are accepted from cultural or educational institutions, as well as from publishers and authors themselves. Six copies should be submitted accompanied by author's biographical details by the end of July.

Recent Winners: 2001: Cristina Rivera Garza; 1999: Sylvia Ipparaguirre; 1998: Sylvia Molina; 1997: Laura Restreppo; 1996: Elena Garro.

Sponsoring Organization: Feria Internacional del Libro de Guadalajara/ Escuela de Escritores SOGEM Guadalajara/Asociación de Clubes del Libro, AC/ Universidad Católica de Salta, Argentina.

Address: Feria Internacional del Libro, Av. Alemania 1370, Col. Moderna, CP 44190, Guadalajara, Mexico. **Telephone:** (33) 38 10 03 31. **Internet:** www.fil.com.mx. **E-mail:** cultura@fil.com.mx.

Premio Literario Carmen Lyra (Carmen Lyra Literary Prize)

One of three awards sponsored by the publisher Editorial Costa Rica, the Premio Literario Carmen Lyra recognizes an outstanding short story for children on any theme. The winner receives a prize of 450,000 colones, and the winning work is published.

Eligibility and Restrictions: Open to authors of Costa Rican nationality or foreigners who are legally resident in the country. Entrants must be at least 18 years of age. Works submitted must be original, unpublished and not have won any previous prizes. Entries must be written in Spanish, and should be between 50 and 80 pages.

How to Apply: Three copies should be submitted under a pseudonym, with author's biographical details on a separate sheet, by mid-June.

Sponsoring Organization: Editorial Costa Rica.

Address: Editorial Costa Rica, Centro Cultural del Este, Guadalupe de Goicoechea, San José, 1000, Costa Rica. **Internet:** www.editorialcostarica.com/ certamenesliterar.htm. **E-mail:** difusion@editorialcostarica.com.

Prêmio Machado de Assis

The Prize was created in 1941 in memory of the founder and first president of the Academia Brasileira de Letras (ABL). The prize is awarded every July for a lifetime's achievement, and consists of 30,000 reais and a diploma. Five writers are nominated by a special commission made up of three members of the ABL. Other members may add further nominations, and the final winner is decided upon by a vote among all ABL members.

Eligibility and Restrictions: Only open to Brazilian writers.

How to Apply: No applications are accepted.

Recent Winners: 2001: Ana Maria Machado; 2000: Antonio Torres; 1999: Fernando Sabino; 1998: Joel da Siveira; 1997: J. J. Veiga.

Sponsoring Organization: Academia Brasileira de Letras.

Contact: Cultural Asst Leila Longo.

Address: Academia Brasileira de Letras, Av. Presidente Wilson 203, 20030–0221 Rio de Janeiro, RJ, Brazil. **Telephone:** (21) 2533-8800. **Fax:** (21) 2220-6095. **Internet:** www.academia.org.br. **E-mail:** llongo@academia.org.br.

Prêmio Ricardo Malheiros (Ricardo Malheiros Prize)

A long-established prize for a best first book, presented by the Lisbon Academy of Science.

Recent Winners: Previous winners include: Lídia Jorge, *O Dia dos Prodígios*; Alvaro Manuel Machado, *Exílio*; Orlando Costa, *Signo de Ira*; José Maria Ferreira de Castro, *Terra Fria*; Augusto Abelaira, *As boas intenções*; other recipients include: Eça de Queirós, Aquilino Ribeiro, Ferreira de Castro, Joaquim Paço d'Arcos, Vitorino Nemésio, Alves Redol and Ruben A. Leitão.

Sponsoring Organization: Acedemia Das Ciencias de Lisboa (Lisbon Academy of Science).

Address: Rua Academia das Ciencias 19, 1200 Lisbon, Portugal. **Telephone:** (21) 321 97 30. **Fax:** (21) 342 03 95. **Internet:** www.acad-ciencias.pt/.

Premio Nacional de las Letras Españolas (National Prize of Spanish Literature)

Awarded in recognition of the complete body of literary work of a Spanish writer, for an outstanding contribution to current Spanish culture, in any genre (novel, essay, drama, poetry). The award, which was created in 1984, carries a prize of €30,000.

Recent Winners: 2001: Miguel Batllori i Munné; 2000: Martín de Riquer; 1999: Francisco Brines; 1998: Pere Gimferrer; 1997: Francisco Umbral.

Sponsoring Organization: Ministerio de Educación, Cultura y Deporte.

Address: Ministerio de Educación, Cultura y Deporte, Plaza del Rey 1, 28004 Madrid, Spain. **Internet:** www.mcu.es.

Premio Nacional de Literatura (National Prize for Literature)

A prestigious national prize awarded by the Secretary of Culture in the Ministry of Education. Categories include novel and children's literature.

Recent Winners: Recent winners include Hugo Wast, Desierto de Piedra and Ema Wolf.

Sponsoring Organization: Secretaría de Cultura de la Nación.

Address: Ministry of Education and Justice, Subsecretariat of Culture, Eizzurno 935, 1020 Buenos Aires, Argentina.

Premio Nacional de Literatura (National Prize for Literature)

Established in 1942, this prize represents the highest literary honour awarded by the Chilean state, via the Ministry of Education. It is one of a number of state prizes, including prizes for arts, science, journalism, etc. The prize is awarded every two years. The winner, chosen by a jury, receives a diploma, a one-off prize of $18,700, and a monthy pension for life.

Eligibility and Restrictions: Open to works of any literary genre by Chilean writers. May in exceptional circumstances be awarded to a foreign writer who has lived in Chile for a long time and whose work is deemed worthy of the prize. May be awarded to two or more writers who have worked together as a team.

Recent Winners: 2000: Raúl Zurita Canessa; 1998: Alfonso Calderón Squadritto; 1996: Miguel Arteche Salinas; 1994: Jorge Edwards Valdés; 1992: Gonzalo Rojas Pizarro.

Sponsoring Organization: Ministry of Education.

Contact: Co-ordinator Segio Aguilera Aguilera.

Address: Ministerio de Educación, Alameda No 1371, Oficina 710, Santiago, 1371, Chile. **Telephone:** 3904723. **Fax:** 3800364. **E-mail:** ministra@mineduc.cl.

Premio Nacional de Literatura (National Prize for Literature)

The Spanish National Literature Prize, sponsored by the Ministry of Culture, is awarded in the categories narrative, essay, poetry and drama. The prize for each genre is of €15,000. The narrative prize dates in its present form from 1977, while the category for essays (formerly a separate prize, the Premio Nacional de Ensayo) was added in 1987. The drama category dates from 1992. A separate prize is awarded for best illustration in a children's book.

Eligibility and Restrictions: All entries must be a Spanish writer, in any of the languages of Spain, and must have been published in Spain in the preceding year.

Recent Winners: Narrative: 2001: Juan Marsé, *Rabos de lagartija*; 2000, Luis Mateo Díez, *La ruina del cielo*; 1999: Miguel Delibes, *El hereje*; 1998: Alfredo Bryce, *Echenique, Reo de nocturnidad*; 1997: Álvaro Pombo, *Donde las mujeres*
Essay: 2001: Angel González García, *El resto – Una historia invisible del arte contemporáneo*; 2000: Javier Echeverría, *Los Señores del aire: Telépolis y el Tercer Entorno*; 1999: Claudio Guillén, *Múltiples moradas*; 1998: Jon Juaristi, *El bucle melancólico*; 1997: Alejandro Nieto, *Los primeros pasos del Estado Constitucional*
Poetry: 2001: José Angel Valente, *Fragmentos de un libro futuro*; 2000: Guillermo Carnero, *Verano Inglés*; 1999: José Hierro, *Cuaderno de Nueva York*; 1998: José Antonio Muñoz Rojas, *Objetos perdidos*; 1997: Diego Jesús Jiménez, *Itinerario para náufragos*
Drama: 2001: Jesús Campos García, *Naufragar en Internet*; 2000: Domingo Miras, *Una familia normal y Gente que prospera*; 1999: Agustín García Calvo, *Baraja del Rey Don Pedro*; 1998: Jerónimo López Mozo, *Ahlán*; 1997: Manuel Lourenzo Pérez, *Veladas indecentes*
Children's illustration: Judit Morales Villanueva, *No eres más que una pequeña hormiga*.

Sponsoring Organization: Ministerio de Cultura.

Address: Ministerio de Educación, Cultura y Deporte, Plaza del Rey 1, 28004 Madrid, Spain. **Internet:** www.mcu.es.

Premio Nacional de Literatura (National Literature Prize)

The most important official Cuban national prize for literature, this was established in 1983 and is awarded to Hispanic writers for the body of their work.

Recent Winners: 2000: Antón Arrufat; 1999: César López; 1998: Roberto Friol; 1997: Carilda Oliver Labra; 1996: Pablo Armando Fernández.

Sponsoring Organization: Instituto Cubano del Libro.

Address: Instituto Cubano del Libro, Havana, Cuba.

Premio Nacional de Literatura (National Literature Prize)

The most important literary prize in the Dominican Republic, which has been presented since 1990 by the Fundación Corripio and the Department of Education and Culture. A prize of 300 million pesos is awarded for an outstanding contribution to national culture and letters.

Recent Winners: 2002: Hilma Contreras Castillo; 2000: Victor Villegas; 1993: Pedro Mir.

Sponsoring Organization: Fundación Corripio.

Address: Fundación Corripio, Santo Domingo, Dominican Republic.

Premio Nacional de Literatura El Búho

An annual prize of $5,000 for short stories or poetry on any theme, sponsored by the magazine *Universo de El Búho*.

Eligibility and Restrictions: Open to Mexican writers for unpublished works up to four pages in length.

Sponsoring Organization: Universo de El Búho.

Address: Yácatas 242, Col. Narvarte, CP 03020, Benito Juárez, Mexico City, Mexico. **E-mail:** buhocult@hotmail.com.

Premio Nacional de Literatura Infantil y Juvenil (National Prize for Children's Literature)

The prize was created in 1978, but was reorganized in 1993. It aims to recognize and promote writing for children and young people, and carries a prize of 2.5 million ptas (€15,000).

Recent Winners: 2001: Miguel Angel Fernández, *Verdadera historia del perro Salomón*; 2000: Emilio Pascual, *Días de reyes magos*; 1999: Vicente Muñoz Puelles, *Oscar y el León de Correos*; 1998: Elvira Lindo, *Los trapos sucios*; 1997: Emili Teixidor, *L'amiga mès amiga de la formiga Piga*.

Sponsoring Organization: Ministerio de Educación, Cultura y Deporte.

Address: Ministerio de Educación, Cultura y Deporte, Plaza del Rey 1, 28004 Madrid, Spain. **Internet:** www.mcu.es.

Premio Nacional de Literatura Infantil y Juvenil Castillo de la Lectura (National Prize for Literature for Children and Young People)

Established in 2000 by the publishing house Ediciones Castillo to promote new writing for children. A shortlist is drawn up by an editorial committee, with final selection made by a panel of judges. Total prize fund stands at 500,000 pesos plus publication of the winning works.

Eligibility and Restrictions: Prizes are awarded in four categories: White Series (Age 5–7); Green Series (Age 7–9); Orange Series (Age 9–12); and Red Series (12 to adolescent).

Recent Winners: White Series: 2001: Roberta Andrey and Maria Eugenia, *El Kan Kanay*
Green Series: 2001: Gojira Gabriela and Aguileta Estrada, *La conspiración de las tías*
Orange Series: 2001: Yuca María Baranda, *Tulia y la tecla mágica*
Red Series: 2001: Bruno Díaz, Jaime Alfonso and M. Sandoval, *Confidencias de un superhéroe.*

Sponsoring Organization: Ediciones Castillo S.A. de C.V.

Address: Ediciones Castillo S.A. de C.V., Privada Francisco L. Rocha No. 7, Colonia San Jerónimo, Apdo Postal núm 1759, Monterrey, Mexico. **Telephone:** (83) 33-2498. **Fax:** (83) 47 62 15. **Internet:** www.castillodelalectura.com.mx. **E-mail:** castillo@edicionescastillo.com.

Premio Nacional a la mejor traducción (National Prize for the Best Translation)

Established in 1984, this prize was preceded by the Premio Fray Luis de León (established in 1956) and the Premio de traducción entre lenguas (1980–1984). It is awarded for the best translation from any foreign language by a Spanish translator into any of the Spanish languages. The winner receives 2.5 million ptas (€15,000).

Eligibility and Restrictions: Works must have appeared during the preceding year.

Recent Winners: 2001: Joan Francesc Mira, *La divina comedia* by Dante; 2000: José Luis Reina Palazón, *Obras completas* by Paul Celan; 1999: Lucía Rodríguez-Noriega Guillén, *Banquete de los eruditos* by Ateneo; 1998: Luis Angel Pujante, *La Tempestad* by William Shakespeare; 1997: Antonio Melero Bellido, *Sofistas: testimonios y fragmentos.*

Sponsoring Organization: Ministerio de Educación, Cultura y Deporte.

Address: Ministerio de Educación, Cultura y Deporte, Plaza del Rey 1, 28004 Madrid, Spain.

Premio Nacional de Narrativa Ignacio Manuel Altamirano

An annual prize of $40,000 for the best unpublished work of narrative (novel or short stories), sponsored by the Universidad Autónoma del Estado de México. In addition, the winning work is published.

Eligibility and Restrictions: Open to writers of Mexican nationality, or residence of at least one year, for a work of narrative of at least 120 pages.

Sponsoring Organization: Universidad Autónoma del Estado de México.
Address: Coordinación General de Difusión Cultural de la UAEM, Instituto Literario 100 Ote. Col. Centro, CP 50000, Toluca, Mexico. **Telephone:** (722) 214 01 77. **Fax:** (722) 213 71 16. **E-mail:** atellez@coatepec.uaemex.mx.

Premio Nacional de Novela José Rubén Romero

A national prize for the best novel, presented by the state via the Instituto Nacional de Bellas Artes (INBA) and the Instituto Michoacano de Cultura. The winner receives a prize of 80,000 pesos, and the winning work is published in a special co-edition by INBA and Tusquets.

Recent Winners: 2001: María Luisa 'la china' Mendoza, *De amor y lujo.*

Sponsoring Organization: Instituto Nacional de Bellas Artes (INBA)/Instituto Michoacano de Cultura.

Address: Auditorio Nacional, Bosque de Chapultepec, Miguel Hidalgo, 11580 Mexico City, DF, Mexico.

Premio Nacional a la obra de un traductor (National Prize for the Work of a Translator)

Created in 1989 to recognize the important role of literary translation, this award is given for the body of a work of a translator, and carries a prize of 2.5 million ptas (€15,000).

Recent Winners: 2001: Francisco Torres Oliver; 2000: José Luis López Muñoz; 1999: Luis Gil Fernández; 1998: Valentín García Yebra; 1997: Clara Janés.

Sponsoring Organization: Ministerio de Educación, Cultura y Deporte.

Address: Ministerio de Educación, Cultura y Deporte, Plaza del Rey 1, 28004 Madrid, Spain.

Premio Nacional de Poesía Tintanueva (Tintanueva National Poetry Prize)

An annual poetry award sponsored by the publisher Tintanueva. The winner receives a diploma, a commemorative plaque and a statuette, and the winning entry is published.

Eligibility and Restrictions: Open to Mexican poets aged over 21, for a collection of unpublished poems written in Spanish, on any theme and in any style, but between 12 and 24 pages in length.

How to Apply: Entries should be submitted by mid-July.

Sponsoring Organization: Tintanueva Editores.

Address: Tintanueva Editores, Av. Universidad 637–1, Col. Del Valle, CP 03100, Benito Juárez, Mexico City, DF, Mexico. **Telephone:** (55) 53 41 83 19. **Fax:** (53) 41 83 19. **E-mail:** tintanueva@starmedia.com.

Premio Nadal

The oldest literary prize in Spain, established in 1945 and sponsored by the publisher Ediciones Destino SA. It is awarded annually for unpublished novels in Spanish. The winner, chosen by a six-member jury, receives a prize of €18,000.

Eligibility and Restrictions: Open to unpublished works, written in Spanish, which have not won any prize previously. Authors must guarantee the originality of their works.

How to Apply: Entries must be submitted by the end of September.

Recent Winners: 2002: Angela Vallvey, *Los estados carenciales*; 2001: Fernando Marías, *El niño de los coroneles*; 2000: Lorenzo Silva, *El alquimista impaciente*.

Sponsoring Organization: Ediciones Destino SA.

Address: Ediciones Destino SA, Calle Provenza 260, 08008 Barcelona, Spain. **Internet:** www.edestino.es/nadal.htm.

Premio Napoli di Narrativa (Naples Prize for Fiction)

An annual award, first presented in 1970, for outstanding works of fiction. The total prize fund is €10,000; the winner also receives a statuette. Three winning works of fiction each receive 5 million lire; the Premio Napoli di Narrativa, worth an additional €2,500, is awarded to the overall winner chosen from the three finalists by majority vote from a jury of 300 readers randomly selected from the Naples area.

Eligibility and Restrictions: Open to works of fiction which have appeared as first editions during the previous year (year ending 28 February).

How to Apply: 20 copies of entries should be submitted by 10 April.

Recent Winners: 2000: Melania G. Mazzucco, *Lei così amata*; 1999: Giuseppe Montesano, *Nel Corpo di Napoli*; 1998: Gianni Riotta, *Il principe delle nuvole*; 1997: Elisabetta Rasy, *Posillipo*; 1996: Ermanno Rea, *Mistero napoletano*.

Sponsoring Organization: Fondazione Premio Napoli.

Address: Palazzo Reale Piazza Plebiscito, 80132 Naples, Italy. **Telephone:** (81) 403187. **Fax:** (81) 402023. **Internet:** www.fondazionepremionapoli.it/. **E-mail:** fpn@fondazionepremionapoli.it.

Premio de Narrativa Colima (Colima Prize for Fiction)

An annual prize of $40,000, jointly sponsored by the National Council for Culture and Art and the University of Colima, for the best new published works of fiction.

Eligibility and Restrictions: Works must have been first published in Mexico during the previous year (year ending July). Works which have already won any literary prizes are ineligible.

How to Apply: Authors, publishers or cultural institutes may submit entries; six copies should be sent by late August.

Recent Winners: 2001: Mónica Lavín, *Café cortado*; Salvador Elizondo, *El cantar del pecador*.

Sponsoring Organization: Consejo Nacional para la Cultura y las Artes/ Instituto Nacional de Bellas Artes/Universidad Autónoma de Colima.

Address: Universidad Autónoma de Colima, Dirección de Difusión Cultural Av. Universidad 333, Col. Las Víboras, CP 28040, Colima, Mexico. **Telephone:** (312) 312 69 96. **Internet:** www.conaculta.gob.mx/convoca/literatura/narrati.htm.

Premio Nazionale di Poesia Giosuè Carducci
(Giosuè Carducci National Poetry Prize)

An annual award for poetry, monographs and essays on poetry and poets, established in 1950. The prize is named after the great Italian poet Giosuè Carducci (1835–1907), winner of the Nobel Prize for Literature in 1906. The winner receives a prize of 1.5 million lire.

Recent Winners: 2001: Mario Luzi, *Opus Florentinum*.

Sponsoring Organization: Bologna University.

Address: Bologna University, Via Zamboni 33, 40100 Bologna, Italy.

Premio Nezahualcóyotl de Literatura en Lenguas Indígenas
(Nezahualcóyotl Prize for Literature in Native Languages)

An annual prize of $50,000 organized by the National Council for Culture and Art to promote contemporary literary works written in native Mexican languages.

Eligibility and Restrictions: Open to all writers of native Mexican origin, for an unpublished literary work written in their native language, with a translation into Spanish. Works of fiction, poetry or drama are eligible, but entries must be at least 50 pages long.

How to Apply: Entries should be submitted by 30 August.

Sponsoring Organization: Consejo Nacional para la Cultura y las Artes.

Address: Conaculta/Dirección General de Culturas Populares e Indígenas, Av. Revolución 1877, sexto piso, Col. San Ángel, CP 01000, Álvaro Obregón, Mexico City, DF, Mexico. **Telephone:** (54) 90 97 68. **Fax:** (54) 90 97 62. **Internet:** www.conaculta.gob.mx/convoca/neza.html. **E-mail:** cplitera@conaculta.gob.mx.

Premio de Novela Fernando Lara

The prize was established in 1996 as a collaboration between the Fundación José Manuel Lara and the publisher Editorial Planeta. The prize is in memory of José Manuel Lara Hernández, an executive of Grupo Planeta who died in 1995. The prize consists of 20 million ptas (€120,000).

Eligibility and Restrictions: The prize is open to unpublished novels written in Spanish.

Recent Winners: 2001: José Carlos Somoza, *Clara y la penumbra*; 2000: Ángeles Caso, *Un largo silencio*; 1999: Luis Racionero, *La sonrisa de la Gioconda*; 1998: Juan Eslava Galán, *Señorita*; 1997: Francisco Umbral, *La forja de un ladrón*.

Sponsoring Organization: Fundación José Manuel Lara/Editorial Planeta.

Address: Editorial Planeta, Còrsega 273–279, 08008 Barcelona, Spain. **Internet:** www.editorial.planeta.es.

Premio Fernándo Paz Castillo

The biennial award (annual until 1988) was created in 1982 by the Consejo Nacional de la Cultura (CONAC), and is now co-ordinated by Centro de Estudios Latinoamericanos Rómulo Gallegos (CELARG). The winner receives a prize of Bs1.5 million, and the winning work is published.

Eligibility and Restrictions: Open to unpublished works on any Latin American or Caribbean theme by Venezuelan authors aged up to 35 years.

How to Apply: Four copies of entries should be submitted by 31 July. Author's identity should not appear on the manuscript, but should be sent on a separate cover sheet.

Recent Winners: 2000: Hernán Zamora, *Desde el espejo del baño*; 1998: Alfredo Antonio Herrera Salas, *Cinco Árboles*; 1996: Luis Enrique Belmonte, *Cuerpo bajo lámpara*.

Sponsoring Organization: Centro de Estudios Latinoamericanos Rómulo Gallegos (CELARG).

Address: CELARG, Casa de Rómulo Gallegos, Av. Luis Roche con tercera transversal, Altamira, Caracas, 1062, Venezuela. **Telephone:** (285) 27 21. **Fax:** (285) 46 80. **Internet:** www.celarg.org.ve. **E-mail:** celarg2@reacciun.ve.

Premio Octavio Paz de Poesía y Ensayo

An annual award for a poet or essayist with high artistic, intellectual and critical qualities, following in the modern tradition that Octavio Paz represented. The winner receives a prize of US $100,000 and a diploma.

How to Apply: Nominations are invited from official bodies and learned institutions between August and December of each year.

Recent Winners: 2002: Juan Goytisolo; 2001: Blanca Varela; 2000: Tomás Segovia; 1999: Haroldo de Campos; 1998: Gonzalo Rojas.

Sponsoring Organization: Fundación Octavio Paz.

Address: Fundación Octavio Paz, Francisco Sosa 383, Col. Barrio de Santa Catarina, 04000 Mexico City, DF, Mexico. **Telephone:** (5) 659-5797. **Fax:** (5) 554-9705. **Internet:** www.fundacionpaz.org.mx..

Premio Pessoa

An annual prize promoted by the *Jornal Expresso* and Unisys; it is awarded to individuals for outstanding achievements in the field of literature, music, photography and other fields of art.

Recent Winners: 2001: João Bénard da Costa; 1988: Antonio Ramos Rosa, *Facilidad del aire*.

Sponsoring Organization: Jornal Expresso and Unisys.

Address: Rua Duque de Palmela, 7 – 3° Dto, 3rd Floor, 1269–200 Lisbon, Portugal. **Telephone:** (21) 3114000. **E-mail:** info@mail.expresso.pt.

Premio Planeta de Novela

The prize was established in 1952 by José Manuel Lara with the aim of encouraging Spanish writers, and is presented each year to an outstanding novel. The original prize money of 40,000 ptas has increased regularly, and now stands at €300,000.

Eligibility and Restrictions: Open to writers of any nationality for an original, unpublished novel written in Spanish.

Recent Winners: 2001: Rosa Regàs, *La canción de Dorotea*; 2000: Maruja Torres, *Mientras vivimos*; 1999: Espido Freire, *Melocotones helados*; 1998: Carmen Posadas, *Pequeñas infamias*.

Sponsoring Organization: Editorial Planeta SA.

Address: Editorial Planeta, Còrsega 273–279, 08008 Barcelona, Spain. **Internet:** www.editorial.planeta.es.

Premio de Poesía Ciudad de Medellín (City of Medellín Poetry Prizes)

During the annual poetry festival in Medellín poetry prizes are awarded in two categories, national and international. The winners are selected by a panel of international poets.

Eligibility and Restrictions: National category is open to Colombian poets born after 1970.

Recent Winners: International Prize: 2002: Roberto Mascaró (Uruguay); 2001: Marosa Di Giorgio (Uruguay), *Papeles salvajes*
National Prize: 2002: Yorlady Ruíz López.

Sponsoring Organization: City of Medellín.

Address: Calle 59 No 45–80, Medellín, Colombia. **Telephone:** 4) 2542033. **Fax:** (4) 2542033. **Internet:** www.epm.net.co/VIIfestivalpoesia/.

Premio de Poesía Mensajero (Mensajero Poetry Prize)

An annual poetry prize sponsored by the magazine *Equipo Mensajero*, with a prize of $500. The winning entry is published in the magazine.

Eligibility and Restrictions: Open to works of poetry up to 20 pages in length, written in Spanish, either published or unpublished.

How to Apply: Deadline for entries is 1 December.

Recent Winners: Poetry prize: 2001 and 2000: No award presented; 1999: Daniel Gutiérrez Pedreiro; 1998: No award presented; 1997: Gerardo Rodríguez Lara; 1996: Edgar René Pacheco Martínez; Category Horror: 2001, 2000 and 1999: No award presented; 1998: Roberto Fernando Pérez Morales; 1997: No award presented; 1996: Juan José Rojo Solís; 1995: Merari Fierro Villavicencio; Category Erotica: 2001, 2000 and 1999: No award presented; 1998: Svetlana Larrocha; 1997: Berenice Romano Hurtado.

Sponsoring Organization: Equipo Mensajero.

Contact: Sr Dir Janitzio Villamar.

Address: Equipo Mensajero, Elsa 35, Col. Guadalupe Tepeyac, CP 07840, Gustavo A. Madero, Mexico City, DF, Mexico. **Telephone:** (55) 55 17 87 24. **E-mail:** magurosa@prodigy.net.mx.

Premio Primavera de Novela

Jointly sponsored by the publisher Espasa Calpe and the retailer El Corte Inglés, this annual prize rewards an unpublished novel written in Spanish by a writer of any nationality. It is recognized as one of the most prestigious literary awards in Spain and Latin America. The winner receives €200,000.

Eligibility and Restrictions: Entries must be at least 150 pages long.

How to Apply: Entries are accepted between August and December each year.

Recent Winners: 2002: Juan José Millas, *Dos Mujeres en Praga*; 2001: Lucía Etxebarría, *De todo lo visible y lo invisible*; 2000: Ignacio Padilla, *Amphitryon*.

Sponsoring Organization: El Corte Inglés/Espasa Calpe.

Address: Editorial Espasa Calpe SA, Carr. de Irun, Km. 12,200, 28049 Madrid, Spain. **Internet:** www.espasa.com/index.html.

Premio Príncipe de Asturias (Prince of Asturias Award for Letters)

The prize is one of eight awarded by the Foundation, which were granted for the first time in 1981. (The others include Social Communication and Humanities, Arts, Sciences, Scientific Research and Technical Co-operation.) The prize is presented to a person, institution or group whose work represents an important contribution to the fields of linguistics and literature. The prize amounts to €50,000 plus a statuette by Joan Miró. The award is presented annually by Prince of Asturias in a solemn academic ceremony in Oviedo.

How to Apply: Nominations are invited from academies, cultural and research organisations, universities and other institutes of learning. A jury of between 8 and 15 people makes its decision based on synopses and documentation regarding the nominations. The award is presented to the individual, group, or institution that obtains the greatest number of votes cast by the members of the Jury.

Recent Winners: Prince of Asturias Award for Letters: 2002: Arthur Miller (USA); 2001: Doris Lessing (UK); 2000: Augusto Monterroso (Guatamala); 1999: Günter Grass (Germany); 1998: Francisco Ayala (Spain).

Sponsoring Organization: Fundación Príncipe de Asturias.

Address: Fundación Príncipe de Asturias, General Yague 2, 33004 Oviedo, Spain. **Internet:** www.fpa.es/esp/index.html.

Premio Alvarez Quintero (Alvarez Quintero Prize)

The award is presented every four years by the Real Academia Española, for an outstanding work of drama. The winner receives a prize of 2 million ptas (€12,000).

Eligibility and Restrictions: Open to works published during the last four years; however unpublished works are also eligible.

Sponsoring Organization: Real Academia Española.

Address: Real Academia Española, Felipe IV, 4, 28014 Madrid, Spain. **Telephone:** (91) 420 14 78. **Fax:** (91) 420 00 79. **Internet:** www.rae.es.

Premio Reina Sofía de Poesía Iberoamericana (Queen Sofia Poetry Prize for Spain and Latin America)

A poetry prize administered by the University of Salamanca, and awarded annually since 1992. The winner receives €42,000, in recognition of their complete body of poetic work.

Eligibility and Restrictions: Open to living poets writing in Spanish.

How to Apply: Candidates are nominated by the language academies of Latin American countries, the Real Academia Española and selected university departments.

Recent Winners: 2002: José Antonio Muñoz Rojas (Spain); 2001: Nicanor Parra (Chile); 2000: Pere Gimferrer (Catalonia); 1999: Mario Benedetti (Uruguay); 1998: José Angel Valente (Spain);.

Sponsoring Organization: Patrimonio Nacional y la Universidad de Salamanca.

Address: Patrimonio Nacional y la Universidad de Salamanca, Salamanca, Spain. **Internet:** w3.usal.es.

Premio del Rey Ocho Venado

An international competition for the best poem of the year, open to writers of any nationality. The prize consists of an expenses paid trip to Mexico (for a foreign winner) or to Paris (for a Mexican winner); in addition the winning work is published in a special anthology.

Eligibility and Restrictions: Open to poets anywhere in the world for works of poetry written in Spanish; entries may be on any subject and of any length. Poems written in other languages may be submitted accompanied by a Spanish translation.

How to Apply: Three poems should be sent by post or e-mail, but should be submittted under a pseudonym.

Sponsoring Organization: Centro de Estudios de la Cultura Mixteca.

Address: Centro de Estudios de la Cultura Mixteca, Trujano 39, CP 69000, Huajuapan de León, Mexico. **E-mail:** paisdelasnubes@mexico.com.

Premio Del Rey Prize

The award was established in 1990 following a gift from Rev. Robert I. Burns. It is awarded biennially for the best book written on the medieval periods in Spain's history and culture 500–1516 AD.

Recent Winners: 2000: Bernard F. Reilly, *The Kingdom of León-Castilla under King Alfonso VII, 1126–1157*; 1998: Simon Barton, *The Aristocracy in Twelfth-Century León and Castile*; 1996: David Nirenberg, *Communities of Violence: Persecution of Minorities in the Middle Ages*; 1994: Teofilo F. Ruiz, *Crisis and Continuity: Land and Town in Late Medieval Castile*; 1992: Paul H. Freedman, *The Origins of Peasant Servitude in Medieval Catalonia*.

Sponsoring Organization: American Historical Association.

Contact: Lynn Hunt.

Address: American Historical Asscn, 400 A St, SE, Washington, DC 20003–3889, USA. **Telephone:** (202) 544-2422. **Fax:** (202) 544-8307. **Internet:** www.theaha.org/prizes. **E-mail:** press@theaha.org.

Premio Rivadeneira (Rivadeneira Prize)

An annual prize presented by the Real Academia Española, for a new unpublished critical edition of a Spanish literary text dating from before 1900. The winner receives a prize of 1 million ptas (€6,000).

Eligibility and Restrictions: Only unpublished works in Spanish, which have not won any other prize, are eligible. Works may be written by more than one author.

How to Apply: Three copies of entries should be submitted by 30 September.

Recent Winners: 1999: D. Luigi Giuliani, *Tragedias de Lupercio Leonardo de Argensola*.

Sponsoring Organization: Real Academia Española.

Contact: José G. Muñoz.

Address: Real Academia Española, Felipe IV, 4, 28014 Madrid, Spain. **Telephone:** (91) 420 14 78. **Fax:** (91) 420 00 79. **Internet:** www.rae.es/. **E-mail:** guada@pa.

Prêmio Paulo Rónai

A prize awarded for the best translation of Brazilian literature of any genre. A prize of 5,000 reais is given.

Eligibility and Restrictions: The original work must have appeared in the year preceding the award; school textbooks and books with a religious theme are excluded.

How to Apply: Publishers and individuals may nominate entries. Three copies of the translation shoud be sent accompanied by an application form.

Sponsoring Organization: Fundação Biblioteca Nacional/Dept Nacional do Livro.

Address: Fundação Biblioteca Nacional, Dept Nacional do Livro, Elmer C. Corrêa Barbosa, Av. Rio Branco 219, 20040–008 Rio de Janeiro, RJ, Brazil. **Telephone:** (21) 2628 25 53 33. **Fax:** (21) 2628 25 53 36.

Premio La Sonrisa Vertical

An annnual prize for erotic fiction, sponsored by the publisher Tusquets Editores. The winner receives a bronze statuette by Joaquim Camps and an advance of €25,000 (with the winning entry being subsequently published by Tusquets).

Eligibility and Restrictions: Open to unpublished works in Spanish of between 100 and 200 pages.

How to Apply: Entries should be submitted under a pseudonym, with author's details on a separate sheet, between 1 April and 30 June.

Recent Winners: 2002: (no prize awarded); 2001: Andreu Martín, *Espera, ponte así*; 2000: Mayra Montero, *Púrpura profundo*; 1999: Luis Antonio de Villena, *El mal mundo*; 1998: Pedro de Silva, *Kurt*.

Sponsoring Organization: La Sonrisa Vertical, Tusquets Editores.

Address: Carretera del Prat 39, Parcela 45, Nave 5, Poligono Industrial Almeda, Cornella, 08940 Barcelona, Spain. **Telephone:** (93) 253 04 00. **Fax:** (93) 417 67 03. **Internet:** www.tusquets-editores.es.

Premio Strega

The Strega Prize originated in post-World War II Rome among a group of Italian writers, intellectuals, artists and musicians known as the Sunday Friends (Amici della domenica). In 1947 Maria and Goffredo Bellonci, along with Guido Alberti, decided to establish a new literary prize, which was to be decided by the votes of the members of the Sunday Friends. Alberti, the owner of the firm that produced the Strega brand of liqueur, provided the money for the prize and its name.

Recent Winners: 2001: Domenico Starnone, *Via Gemito*; 2000: Ernesto Ferrero, *N*; 1999: Dacia Maraini, *Buio*; 1998: Enzo Siciliano, *I bei momenti*; 1997: Claudio Magris, *Microcosmi*; 1996: Alessandro Barbero, *Bella vita e guerre altrui di Mr Pyle, gentiluomo*.

Sponsoring Organization: Fondazione Maria e Goffredo Bellonci.

Address: Strega Alberti Benevento, Corso Rinascimento 41, 1000186 Rome, Italy. **Internet:** www.strega.it/premio.html.

Premio UPC de ciencia ficción

An annual award of 1 million ptas (€6,000) for a short story in the field of science fiction. The winning work, chosen by a five-member jury, is published by the Universidad Politécnica de Cataluña (UPC) through the imprint Ediciones, in a special series of new science fiction works.

Eligibility and Restrictions: Open to unpublished works in the field of science fiction; entries must be written in Spanish, Catalan, English or French and be between 70 and 115 pages in length.

How to Apply: Two copies of entries should be sent by mid-December; works should be submitted under a pseudonym with author's details on a separate sheet.

Sponsoring Organization: Universidad Politécnica de Cataluña (UPC).

Address: Universidad Politécnica de Cataluña, Consell Social de la UPC, Edificio NEXUS, Gran Capità 2–4, 08034 Barcelona, Spain. **Telephone:** (93) 401 63 43. **Fax:** (93) 401 77 66. **E-mail:** consell.social@upc.es.

Premio Valle Inclán

Award for the best translation into English of a full-length Spanish work from any period, published in the UK in the preceding five years. The winner receives a prize of £1,000.

Sponsoring Organization: Translators Assocation.

Address: Translators Assocation, 84 Drayton Gardens, London SW10 9SB, UK. **Telephone:** (20) 7373 6642. **Fax:** (20) 7373 5768. **E-mail:** info@societyofauthors. org.

Premio Viareggio

An annual prize established in 1929 by Leonida Repaci, Carlo Salsa and Alberto Colantuoni, which has become one of the most important Italian literary awards.

Eligibility and Restrictions: Open to works in the genres of fiction, poetry and essay.

Recent Winners: 2001: Niccolò Ammaniti, *Io non ho paura*; 2000 Giorgio Van Straten, *Il mio nome a memoria* and Sandro Veronesi, *La forza del passato* (joint winners); 1999 Ernesto Franco, *Vite senza fine*; 1998 Giorgio Pressburger, *La neve e la colpa*; 1997: Claudio Piersanti, *Luisa e il silenzio*.

Address: Premio Viareggio, Via Francesco Borgatti 25, 100191 Rome, Italy.

Premios Literarios Fundación ARCIEN

The Arcien Foundation awards a number of prizes including the Literary Prize for novels, poetry and essays.

Sponsoring Organization: Fundación ARCIEN.

Address: Fundación ARCIEN, Avellaneda 3657, S3002GJC Santa Fe, Argentina. **Telephone:** 0342 453-4451. **Fax:** 0342 455-3439.

Premju Letterarju (Literary Award)

An annual literary award of 10,000 Lm, sponsored by the Ministry of Education and National Culture to promote and support literary production in Malta.

Sponsoring Organization: Ministry of Education and National Culture.
Address: Literary Award and Subsidy Selection Committee, Education Division, Floriana, CMR 02, Malta. **Telephone:** 21 221 401-4. **Fax:** 21 246 782.

President's Award for Pride of Performance

Pakistan's highest official honour, which is awarded to individuals for their pursuit of excellence in fields ranging from literature to arts and sciences.

Recent Winners: Literature winners: 2002: Himayat Ali Shair, Prof. Gilani Kamran, Ali Haider Joshi and Ghaos Bukhsh Sabir.

Sponsoring Organization: Pakistan Ministry of Education.

Address: Block D Pakistan Secretariat, Islamabad, Pakistan.

Mathew Prichard Award for Short Story Writing

The prize was established by Mathew Prichard, the grandson of Agatha Christie who inherited the royalties from her long-running play *The Mousetrap*. There is a prize of £2,000 awarded annually in an open competition for original short stories.

Eligibility and Restrictions: There are no restrictions except that the work should be an unpublished story in English, up to 2,500 words in length. The competition is open to everyone worldwide and entries may be on any topic.

How to Apply: There is an entry fee of £5. Entry forms from the address given. Closing date for applications is 28 February.

Sponsoring Organization: South and Mid Wales Association of Writers.

Contact: Sponsor Mathew Prichard.

Address: The Competition Secretary, 2 Rhododendron Close, Cardiff CF23 7HS, UK.

Prijs voor Meesterschap

Founded in 1920 by the Maatschappij der Nederlandse Letterkunde (MNL), to recognize authors for a lifetime's achievement in the fields of creative writing, philology and literature, and history. The prize is awarded every five years and alternates between categories. The winner receives a gold medal.

How to Apply: Direct applications are not accepted; entries are nominated by one of the three permanent committees of the MNL.

Recent Winners: 1999: Dr W. P. Gerritsen; 1994: Hugo Claus; 1989: Dr E. H. Kossmann; 1984: Dr C. C. de Bruin; 1979: Ida G. M. Gerhardt.

Sponsoring Organization: Maatschappij der Nederlandse Letterkunde (Dutch Literature Association).

Address: Maatschappij der Nederlandse Letterkunde, Postbus 9501, 2300 RA Leiden, Netherlands. **Telephone:** (71) 5144962. **Fax:** (71) 5272836. **Internet:** www.leidenuniv.nl/host/mnl. **E-mail:** mnl@library.leidenuniv.nl.

Prijs der Nederlandse Letteren (Dutch National Literature Prize)

The prize, awarded every three years, celebrates writers in the Dutch language, with categories for prose, poetry, essays and drama. It is awarded for a lifetime's achievement, or for a single work. The winner receives a prize of €16,000.

Recent Winners: 2001: Gerard Reve; 1998: Paul de Wispelaere.

Sponsoring Organization: Nederlandse Taalunie.

Address: Nederlandse Taalunie, Stadhoudersplantsoe 2, 2517 JL The Hague, Netherlands.

Prime Minister's Hebrew Literature Prize

The Fund's aim is to grant prizes to 14 Hebrew authors to enable them to undertake creative work. The award is equivalent to a year's salary for an experienced teacher, free of income tax.

Eligibility and Restrictions: Eligible to applicants resident in Israel.

How to Apply: Applications are accepted at the beginning of each Jewish year (around September). Applications should be accompanied by an outline of the request and relevant background material.

Sponsoring Organization: Prime Minister's Fund for Hebrew Literature Prizes.

Contact: Aharon Yadlin.

Address: Y. Levinbuk, 15 Lesin St, Tel Aviv, 6954586, Israel.

Thomas Pringle Award

Established in 1962 to honour achievements in five different categories: reviews, educational articles, literary articles, short stories or one-act plays, and poetry. Three categories are honoured each year, with a R2,000 prize for each. Winners are chosen by a panel of expert adjudicators from each field.

Eligibility and Restrictions: Entries must be written in English, by a Southern African writer, and published in Southern Africa.

Recent Winners: Review: 2001: Shaun de Waal, various film reviews
Educational Article: 2001: Rodrik Wade and Nicole Geslin, *Teaching Discourse Grammar in a Multimedia Program*
Literary Article: 2001: Peter Merrington
Poetry: 2001: Shabbir Banoobhai, *Sarajevo*.

Sponsoring Organization: FNB Vita/English Academy of Southern Africa.

Contact: Admin. Officer C. James.

Address: POB 124, Witwatersrand, 2050, South Africa. **Telephone:** (11) 717 9339. **Fax:** (11) 717 9339. **Internet:** www.englishacademy.co.za. **E-mail:** engac@ cosmos.wits.ac.za.

Michael L. Printz Award for Excellence in Young Adult Literature

The award, first given in 2000, honours the late Michael L. Printz, a school librarian from Kansas, who during his life continually strove to discover and promote quality books for young adults. The prize is selected annually by an award committee that can also name as many as four 'honor books'.

Eligibility and Restrictions: Entries can be fiction, non-fiction, poetry or an anthology, and can be a work of joint authorship or editorship. The book must be published between 1 January and 31 December of the preceding year and be designated by its publisher as being either a young-adult book or one published for the age range that Young Adult Library Services Association (YALSA) defines as young adult, i.e. ages 12 to 18. Publishers may not nominate their own titles.

How to Apply: Committee members may nominate an unlimited number of titles, but each nomination must be made in writing on an official nomination form. Each nomination should include the following information: author, title, publisher, price, ISBN, and an annotation specifying those qualities that justify a title for consideration. Field nominations (i.e. not from the committee) are also encouraged. To be eligible, they must be submitted on the official nomination form and must be seconded by a committee member. If, within 30 days, no second is forthcoming, the title will be dropped from consideration.
The deadline for nominations is 1 December.

Recent Winners: 2002: An Na, *A Step from Heaven*; 2001: David Almond, *Kit's Wilderness*; 2000: Walter Dean Myers, *Monster*.

Sponsoring Organization: American Library Association/Young Adult Library Services Association (YALSA).

Address: YALSA, American Library Association, 50 East Huron, Chicago, IL 60611–2795, USA. **Fax:** (312) 944-7671. **Internet:** www.ala.org/alsc. **E-mail:** alsc@ala.org.

V. S. Pritchett Memorial Prize

Founded in 1999 by the Royal Society of Literature in memory of the writer V. S. Pritchett. The award is for a previously unpublished short story, and comprises £1,000. The winner is chosen by three judges, all of whom are writers or publishers.

Eligibility and Restrictions: Open to previously unpublished short stories of 2,000–5,000 words. Nominees must be resident in or a citizen of the UK or Ireland.

How to Apply: Entrants should write to the Secretary enclosing a stamped addressed envelope. Multiple entries are allowed; there is a fee of £5 per entry.

Recent Winners: 2001: Somon Korner; 2000: Emma Barklamb; 1999: John Arden.

Sponsoring Organization: Royal Society of Literature.

Address: Royal Society of Literature, Somerset House, Strand, London WC2R 1LA, UK. **Telephone:** (20) 7845 4676. **Fax:** (20) 7845 4679. **Internet:** www.rslit.org. **E-mail:** info@rslit.org.

Private Eye Writers of America/SMP Contest

An award for the best private eye novel. The winning entry is published by St Martin's Press, and the author receives an advance against the future royalties of $10,000.

Eligibility and Restrictions: The contest is open to any professional or non-professional writer, regardless of race or nationality, who has never been the author of a published private eye novel. All manuscripts submitted must be original works of book length written in the English language.

How to Apply: All entries must be submitted by 1 August, accompanied by a double-spaced copy of the manuscript and a completed application form. Entries should be sent directly to the judge whose name appears on the application form.

Sponsoring Organization: Private Eye Writers of America (PWA)/St Martin's Press.

Address: Minotaur Books, Publicity Department, 175 5th Avenue, New York, NY 10010, USA. **Fax:** (212) 674-6132.

Prix de l'Académie des Sciences, Arts et Belles Lettres de Dijon

An annual award for an unpublished work, written in French, on a specific theme in the field of literature, art or science. The theme for the award is announced each year.

How to Apply: Entries should be submitted by the end of September.

Sponsoring Organization: Académie des Sciences, Arts et Belles Lettres de Dijon.

Address: Académie des Sciences, Arts et Belles Lettres de Dijon, Bibliothèque Municipale, 5 rue de l'Ecole de Droit, 21000 Dijon, France. **Telephone:** 3 80 44 94 14. **Fax:** 3 80 44 94 34. **Internet:** www.ac-dijon.fr/academ/rectorat/d-rect003.htm. **E-mail:** bmdijon@ville-dijon.fr.

Prix d'Ambronay

A prize for a novel presented by the town of Ambronay during its annual arts festival.

Recent Winners: 2000: Isabelle Callis-Sabot, *Le miracle de Mazières.*

Sponsoring Organization: Festival d'Ambronay.

Address: Festival d'Ambronay, BP 03, 01500 Ambronay, France. **Telephone:** 4 74 38 74 04. **Fax:** 4 74 38 10 93. **E-mail:** fest.ambronay@wanadoo.fr.

Prix des Amis du Monde diplomatique
(Friends of le Monde diplomatique prize)

A new annual prize created in February 2002 by supporters of the newspaper *le Monde diplomatique.* The prize aims to recognize outstanding works in the field of critical analysis of the contemporary international situation, presenting arguments about liberal society or alternative suggestions. Entries should take the form of essays or testimony. The winner will be chosen by an 11-member jury, from a shortlist of five entries.

Eligibility and Restrictions: Open to works which have appeared during the last two years.

How to Apply: Nominations are invited by phone, fax or e-mail.

Sponsoring Organization: Les Amis du Monde diplomatique.

Contact: Hélène Auclair.

Address: Les Amis du Monde diplomatique, BP 461–07, 75327 Paris, cedex 07, France. **Telephone:** 1 43 66 88 80. **Fax:** 1 43 66 88 80. **Internet:** www.amis. monde-diplomatique.fr/. **E-mail:** amis@monde-diplomatique.fr.

Prix des Amis du Scribe

A prize set up in 1996 by the bookshop Le Scribe to give readers a chance to vote for their favourite title, similar to the Prix du Livre Inter. Anyone who visits the shop or its website during March and April each year can vote for a book; the five most popular titles are then put before a seven-member jury. The eventual winner is displayed in the shop window and listed on the website. There is no cash prize. The bookshop itself remains independent of the whole selection process.

Eligibility and Restrictions: Entries must have been published in French during the last two years.

Recent Winners: 2002: Christian Gailly, *Un soir au club*; 2001: Tracy Chevalier, *La jeune fille à la perle*; 2000: Wallace Stegner, *La vie obstinée*; 1999: Tristan Egloff, *Le seigneur des porcheries*; 1998: Bernhard Schlink, *Le liseur*.

Sponsoring Organization: Librairie Le Scribe.

Address: Librairie Le Scribe, 115, Faubourg Lacapelle, 82000 Montauban, France. **Telephone:** 5 63 63 01 83. **Fax:** 5 63 91 20 08. **Internet:** www.lescribe. com. **E-mail:** info@lescribe.com.

Prix Apollinaire

A long-established poetry prize named after the noted French poet Apollinaire Guillaume.

Recent Winners: 2001: Alain Lance, *Temps criblé*; 2000: Alain Jouffroy, *C'est aujourd'hui toujours*; 1998: Anise Koltz, *Le mur du son*.

Address: 22 rue des Felibres, 91600 Savigny-sur-Orge, France.

Prix Antonin Artaud

An annual award established in 1951 by Jean Digot, awarded to a book of poems. The winner is selected by a panel of poets, and receives a prize of €1,600.

Eligibility and Restrictions: Must be written in French and published in the previous calendar year.

How to Apply: Publishers or individual poets should submit four copies of entries to the address given by 1 March each year.

Recent Winners: 2001: Joel Bastand, *Beule*; 2000: Chantal Dupuy, *Initiales*; 1999: Pierre Descamps, *Cantons*; 1998: Alain Lambert, *L'entretien d'Hiver*; 1997: Jean Marc Tixier, *L'oiseau de glaise*.

Sponsoring Organization: Association des Ecrivains du Rouerque.

Contact: Danielle Fenion.

Address: Association des Ecrivains du Rouerque, BP 307, 12003 Rodez, Cedex, France. **Telephone:** 5 65 42 47 80. **Internet:** www.perso.wanadoo.fr/d.f/journee-poesie.html. **E-mail:** danielle.fenion@wanadoo.fr.

Prix de l'Assemblée Nationale (National Assembly Prize)

Annual award created in 1990, with a prize of 60,000 francs (€9,000). The winner is selected by a jury made up of six members of parliament and five others. Since 1999 the focus of the awards has been on books for young people (10–14 years). Open to works by French authors or others writing in French, which help to make young people aware of contemporary political, economic, social and cultural problems, and to encourage them as good citizens to work towards a more just and tolerant society.

Recent Winners: 2001: Pascal Croci, *Auschwitz* and Magdeleine Lerasle and Hafida Favret, *À l'ombre de l'olivier* (joint winners); 2000: Xavier-Laurent Petit, *Fils de guerre*; 1999: Bernard Epin and Serge Bloch, *Le grand livre du jeune citoyen*.

Sponsoring Organization: National Assembly.

Address: 128 rue de l'Université, 75007 Paris, France. **Internet:** www.assemblee-nat.fr/evenements/prix.asp.

Prix Astrolabe–Étonnants Voyageurs

An annual prize awarded during the 'Étonnants voyageurs' festival in Saint Malo. The prize was established in 1989 by the Paris bookshop L'Astrolabe, and recognizes a book in the field of travel.

Recent Winners: 2002: Björn Larsson, *La sagesse de la mer, du cap de la Colère au Bout du monde*; 2001: Julia Leigh, *Le chasseur*; 2000: Nuruddin Farah, *Secrets*.

Sponsoring Organization: Festival Étonnants Voyageurs.

Address: Festival Étonnants Voyageurs, 48 bd Villebois Mareuil, 35000 Rennes, France. **Telephone:** 2 23 21 06 21. **Fax:** 2 23 21 06 29. **Internet:** www.etonnants-voyageurs.net. **E-mail:** info@etonnants-voyageurs.net.

Prix François-Joseph Audiffred

An annual prize presented to works which encourage virtue and morality and reject selfishness and envy, or which promote patriotism.

Recent Winners: 2000: Élisabeth Berrlioz, *La situation des départements et l'installation des premiers préfets en l'an VIII*.

Sponsoring Organization: Académie des Sciences Morales et Politiques.

Address: Académie des Sciences Morales et Politiques, Institut de France, 23 quai de Conti, 75270 Paris, Cedex 06, France.

Prix Marguerite Audoux

Named after a French writer (1863–1937) who grew up in Bourges and who won the prix Fémina in 1910, the prize is awarded to a living, French-speaking author.

Recent Winners: 2001: Maïssa Bey, *Cette fille-là*; 2000: Anne-Marie Garat, *Les Mal Famées*; 1999: Mathieu Belezi.

Address: Hôtel du département, place Marcel Plaisant, 18023 Bourges, Cedex, France.

Prix Augustin-Thierry

Established in 1998 and presented in October each year during the Rendez-vous de l'histoire festival. The prize, inaugurated following a donation by Mme Baptistine Augustin-Thierry in memory of her great-uncle, recognizes the author of a work of history for its contribution to historical research. The winner is chosen by a 15-member jury representing all areas of history, and receives a prize of €3,000.

Eligibility and Restrictions: Open to works of history written in French which have been published during the preceding year.

How to Apply: No direct application; entries are selected by the jury.

Recent Winners: 2001: Jérôme Baschet, *Le sein du père*; 2000: Jean-Pierre Chrétien, *L'Afrique des Grands Lacs*; 1999: Françoise Wacquet, *Le latin ou l'empire d'un signe, XVIe–XXe siècle*; 1998: Marc Olivier Baruch, *Servir l'Etat français: L'administration en France de 1940 à 1944*.

Sponsoring Organization: Les Rendez-vous de l'histoire.

Contact: Co-ordinator Rachel Menseau.

Address: Les Rendez-vous de l'histoire, 3 quai Abbé-Grégoire, 4100 Blois, France. **Telephone:** 2 54 56 09 50. **Fax:** 2 54 90 09 50. **Internet:** www.rdv-histoire.com. **E-mail:** rdv.histoire.blois@wanadoo.fr.

Prix Baobab de l'album

Inaugurated in 2000 to recognize works for children which help develop a taste for reading. The prize is awarded to an illustrated book in recognition of the inventiveness and quality of its illustration and text. The winner is chosen by a nine-member jury made up of artists, writers and editors, and receives a prize of €7,500 (50,000 francs).

Eligibility and Restrictions: Open to illustrated books published during the previous year. Translations are not eligible.

How to Apply: Publishers may submit up to three eligible works; 12 copies should be submitted for distribution among the jury and the press.

Recent Winners: 2001: Fred Bernard and François Roca, *Jésus Betz*; 2000: Ian Falconer, *Olivia*.

Sponsoring Organization: Le Monde/Salon du livre de jeunesse.

Contact: Nathalie Donikian.

Address: Salon du Livre de Jeunesse en Seine-Saint-Denis, 3 rue François Debergue, 93100 Montreuil, France. **Telephone:** 1 55 86 86 55. **Fax:** 1 48 57 04 62. **Internet:** www.ldj.tm.fr. **E-mail:** cplj@ldj.tm.fr.

Prix Laure Bataillon

The prize was created in 1986 by the cities of Nantes and Saint-Nazaire, and was given the name Laure Bataillon in honour of the Frenchwoman who translated works by Julio Cortazar. Since 1993 it has been administered by the Maison des Ecrivains Etrangers et des Traducteurs de Saint-Nazaire. The prize is of 100,000 francs (€15,000), shared between the author and the translator.

Eligibility and Restrictions: Recognizes the best work of fiction translated into French in the previous year.

Recent Winners: 2000: Mo Yan, *Le pays de l'alcool*; 1999: W. G. Sebald, *Les Emigrants* (translated by Patrick Charbonneau); 1998: Sergio Ramirez, *Le Bal des masques* (translated by Claude Fell); 1997: Bernhard Schlink, *Le liseur* (translated from German by Bernard Lortholary); 1996: Giuseppe O. Longo, *L'acrobate* (translated from Italian by Jean and Marie-Noëlle Pastureau); 1995: Hans Magnus Enzensberger, *Requiem pour une femme romantique* (translated from German by Georges Arès).

Sponsoring Organization: la Maison des Ecrivains Etrangers et des Traducteurs de Saint-Nazaire.

Address: La Maison des Ecrivains Etrangers et des Traducteurs de Saint-Nazaire, St Nazaire, France.

Prix Baudelaire

An annual prize awarded by the Société des Gens de Lettres de France for a translation of a literary work from English into French. The winner, chosen by a jury of 24 writers, receives a prize of €2,250.

Eligibility and Restrictions: Open to translations of work into French from English; original authors may be British or from any part of the Commonwealth.

Sponsoring Organization: Société des Gens de Lettres de France.

Address: Société des Gens de Lettres de France, Hôtel de Massa, 38 rue du Faubourg St Jacques, 75014 Paris, France. **Telephone:** 1 53 10 12 00. **Fax:** 1 53 10 12 12. **Internet:** www.sgdl.org. **E-mail:** sgdlf@wanadoo.fr.

Prix Daniel Bayon

This prize was created in 1998 in memory of a local writer who died in an accident in 1997. It is awarded to a piece of writing which reflects on life in the Bourbonnais region and demonstrates outstanding originality.

Recent Winners: 2001: Isabelle Lardot, *Diou sur Loire*; 2000: Jean-Marc Dete, *L'enclume et le gouyat*; 1999: Löys Mercurol, *Contes des lisières de la forêt de Tronçais*; 1998: J. L. Arnaud, *A Vichy, la marquise boit à 5 heures*.

Sponsoring Organization: Association Agir en Pays Jalignois.

Address: Mairie de Jaligny, 03220 Jaligny-sur-Besbre, France. **Telephone:** 4 70 34 69 91. **E-mail:** agirenpaysjalignois@wanadoo.fr.

Prix Anton Bergmann (Anton Bergmann Prize)

One of a number of awards presented by the Belgian Royal Academy, the Prix Anton Bergmann was established in 1875 and is worth €1,250. It is awarded for a recent work on the history of a town in the Flemish part of Belgium. The winner holds the title for a five-year period.

Eligibility and Restrictions: Entries must be written in Dutch; works must be written about a town or community, of any size, in the Flemish part of Belgium. Published works must have been printed in the previous five-year period, but manuscripts of work-in-progress are also eligible. Foreign writers may enter, but their entry must be written in Dutch and published in Belgium or the Netherlands.

Recent Winners: 1995–1999: A.-L. Van Bruaene.

Sponsoring Organization: Académie Royale de Belgique.

Contact: Jean-Luc De Paepe.

Address: Académie Royale de Belgique, Palais des Académies, 1 rue Ducale, 1000 Brussels, Belgium. **Telephone:** (2) 550 22 11. **Fax:** (2) 550 22 05. **Internet:** www.cfwb.be/arb/Fondations.

Prix François Billetdoux

The Prix François Billetdoux, created in 1998, is awarded each year to a young writer in the field of non-fiction. The winner receives a prize of 20,000 francs (€3,000).

Eligibility and Restrictions: Eligible categories are essays, memoirs, biography, travel and documentary-style novels; entries must have appeared in the previous year.

How to Apply: Publishers are invited to submit eligible titles by a deadline of 31 March.

Recent Winners: 2001: Evelyne Bloch-Dano, *Flora Tristan, la femme messie* and Michel Gall, *Le Maître des saveurs* (joint winners); 2000: Bernadette Chovelon, *Dans Venise la rouge* and Jean-Claude Lamy, *La belle inconnue* (joint winners); 1999: Daniel Timsit, *Algérie*; 1998: Michel Boujut, *Le jeune homme en colère*.

Sponsoring Organization: Société civile des auteurs multimedia (SCAM).

Address: Société civile des auteurs multimedia (SCAM), 5 avenue Vélasquez, 75008 Paris, France. **Telephone:** 1 56 69 58. **Fax:** 1 56 69 58 59. **Internet:** www.scam.fr/fr/evenement/prix/Litteraire/palmares%20litt/BodPalmareslitt.HTM.

Prix Bloc-Notes

A prize awarded by the listeners to RTBF radio, who choose a novel published during the last year from a shortlist of eight titles (drawn up earlier by a 16-member jury). The prize is presented during the annual Brussels book fair.

Recent Winners: 2002: Guy Goffette, *Un été autour du cou*.

Sponsoring Organization: RTBF Radio.

Address: RTBF Radio, Emission Bloc Notes, blvd Reyers 52, 1044 Brussels, Belgium.

Prix Bordin

A biennial prize awarded for an outstanding publication in the field of philosophy and morality. The prize is given in recognition of the public interest, humanity, scientific progress and national honour exhibited in the winning work.

Sponsoring Organization: Institut de France.

Address: Institut de France, Académie des Beaux Arts, 23 quai de Conti, 75006 Paris, France. **Telephone:** 1 44 41 43 26. **Fax:** 1 44 41 43 27. **Internet:** www.institut-de-france.fr/prixmecenat/asmp.htm.

Prix Bourbonnais

Established in 1989, this prize aims to reward authors for works about the Bourbonnais region. One or more prizes (of €381) may be awarded each year, during a literary festival in June, the Journées Littéraires du Bourbonnais.

How to Apply: Copies of entries must be sent to each member of the jury, plus two copies to the Association at the address given.

Recent Winners: 2001: Jean Desbordes, *L'Allier dans la guerre*; 2000: Pascal Chambriard, *Aux Sources de Vichy*; 1998: Christiane Keller and Léonard Leroux, *Bourbonnais de pierre et de lumière*; 1996: Jacky Boutonnet, *Tronçais, la forêt aux abois*; 1995: Robert Liris and Joseph Grivel, *Glozel, les graveurs du silence*.

Sponsoring Organization: Association Agir en Pays Jalignois.

Address: Mairie de Jaligny, 03220 Aligny-sur-Besbre, France. **Telephone:** 4 70 34 69 91. **E-mail:** agirenpaysjalignois@wanadoo.fr.

Prix BPT

The prize was established to honour and promote work in the field of Swiss Romande (French-language) literature, and is awarded to a work which has appeared in the previous year. The award is made by a jury of 11 to 15 members, drawn from cantons across French-speaking areas of Switzerland. Half of the available amount is earmarked for the purchase of a substantial number of books to be given to public libraries, in order for the work to become better known among the public. The other half goes to the author.

Recent Winners: 2001: Jean-Louis Kuffer, *L'ambassade du Papillon*; 2000: Jean-François Sonnay, *Un prince perdu*; 1999: Asa Lanova, *Le Blues d'Alexandrie*; 1998: Janine Massard, *Ce qui reste de Katharina*; 1997: Nicolas Couchepin, *Grefferic*.

Sponsoring Organization: Bibliothèque pour Tous.

Address: Bibliocentre de la Suisse romande, César-Roux 34, case postale 56, 1000 Lausanne, 4, Switzerland. **Internet:** www.svbbpt.ch/Literatur/francais/prix.htm.

Prix de Poésie et Prix d'Etudes Littéraires Maurice Carême

Named after a Belgian poet (1899–1978), himself the winner of several literary awards, the Prix Maurice Carême is awarded in two parts: a prize of 50,000 Belgian francs (around €1,239) for a poet, based on a recent collection, and a separate prize of 30,000 Belgian francs (around €750) for the author of a work about Maurice Carême.

Sponsoring Organization: Fondation Maurice Carême.

Address: Fondation Maurice Carême, ave Nellie Melba 14, 1070 Brussels, Belgium. **Telephone:** (2) 521 67 75. **Fax:** (2) 520 20 86.

Prix Louis Castex

An annual prize of €750, awarded by the Académie Française for works in the field of history.

Eligibility and Restrictions: Open to living authors of all ages; only published works may be submitted, and they must have appeared during the preceding year.

How to Apply: Two copies of the work should be sent by the author or publisher by 31 January.

Recent Winners: 2002: Joëlle Rostkowski, *Le renouveau indien aux États-Unis: Un siècle de reconquêtes*; 2001: Alfred Adler, *Le pouvoir et l'interdit: Royauté et religion en Afrique noire*.

Sponsoring Organization: Académie Française.

Address: Académie Française, Institut de France, 23 quai de Conti, 75006 Paris, France. **Telephone:** 1 44 41 43 00. **Fax:** 1 43 29 47 45. **Internet:** www.academie-francaise.fr. **E-mail:** contact@academie-francaise.fr.

Prix Cazes Brasserie Lipp

An annual award established in 1935. The winner receives a prize of €4,000 as well as €800 to spend in the restaurant of the Brasserie Lipp. The winner is chosen by a jury.

Recent Winners: 2002: Gérard de Cortanze, *Une chambre à Turin*; 2001: Marcel Jullian, *Mémoire buissonière*; 2000: Shan Pa, *Les quatre vies du Saule*.

Sponsoring Organization: Brasserie Lipp.

Address: Brasserie Lipp, 151, Bld Saint-Germain, 75006 Paris, France.

Prix du Champagne Lanson

An annual award in a series of categories (article, guide, book, CD ROM, radio/TV programme) about wine. The overall winner receives a prize of €2002 (increased by €1 each year) and a case of Lanson champagne. The other winners receive a magnum of Lanson Black Label.

Recent Winners: Black Label Award: 2001: John Stimpfig, series of articles in the *Financial Times*; 2000: Anthony Rose, series of articles in the *Independent* and *Wine Magazine*
Gold Label Award: 2001: Michael Schustere, *Essential Winetasting*; 2000: Stephen Brook, *The Wines of California*
Ivory Label Award: 2001: Jim Budd, *Investdrinks.org*; 2000: Andrew Jefford and Paul Kobrak
Rose Label Award: 2001: John Platter, *2001 Guide to South African Wines*; 2000: Monty Waldin, *Guide des Vins biologiques*

Noble Cuvée Award: 2001: Giles Fallowfield, series of articles in *Decanter*, *Harpers Wine & Spirit Gazette* and *Wine & Spirit International*; 2000: Margaret Rand, *100 ans de plus*.

Sponsoring Organization: Champagne Lanson Père et Fils.

Address: Champagne Lanson Père et Fils, BP 163, 12 boulevard Lundy, 51056 Reims, Cedex, France. **Telephone:** 3 26 78 50 50. **Fax:** 3 26 78 50 99. **Internet:** www.lansonpf.com/a_culture.htm. **E-mail:** info@lansonpf.com.

Prix Champlain

Created in 1957 with the aim of encouraging literary production by Francophones living outside Quebec, and to recognize the achievements of Francophones in other parts of North America as a minority group. The prize is awarded annually, and alternates between two categories: creative works (novels, short stories, novellas, drama, poetry, etc) and educational works (essays, collections of articles, social science or human studies, etc). The winner receives a prize of $1,500 and an official certificate.

Eligibility and Restrictions: Works must conform to the objectives of the Conseil de la vie française en Amérique (CVFA). Entries must be written in French and have been published, or at least be the subject of a publishing contract, before being entered for the prize. If an entry has been published it must be submitted to the jury within three years of publication. The same work may only be entered twice for the prize, and each candidate may only enter one work at a time.

How to Apply: Authors should send four copies of their work by 31 December to the CVFA, along with an application form plus CV and contact details.

Recent Winners: 2001: Françoise Lepage, *Histoire de la littérature pour la jeunesse. Québec et francophonies du Canada*; 2000: Jean-Marc Dalpé, *Un vent se lève qui éparpille*; 1999: Léonard Forest, *La jointure du temps*; 1998: Zachary Richard, *Faire Récolte*; 1997: Bernard Bocquel, *Au pays de CKSB: 50 ans de radio française au Manitoba*.

Sponsoring Organization: Le Conseil de la vie française en Amérique (CVFA).

Address: Le Conseil de la vie française en Amérique, 39 rue Dalhousie, Quebec, PQ G1K 8R8, Canada. **Internet:** www.cvfa.ca.

Prix Chrétien-de-Troyes

Established in 1987 by the Association Lecture et Loisirs (Reading and Leisure Association) to reward a children's picture book. The prize money of €1,500 is underwritten by the Maison du Boulanger Cultural Centre.

Eligibility and Restrictions: Book must be published during the previous year (year ending 30 April). Author and illustrator must be French-speaking.

How to Apply: Publishers or authors may apply by sending one copy to the address given.

Recent Winners: 2001: Dominique Derners and Stéphane Poulin, *Vieux Thomas et la petite fée*; 2000: Lionel le Neovanic, *Lucie Fer, un amour de sorcière*; 1999: Anaïs Vaugelade, *La guerre*; 1998: M. Voutch, *Le roi de la grande savane*; 1997: Mardana Sadat, *De l'autre côté de l'arbre*.

Sponsoring Organization: Salon Régional du Livre de Jeunesse de Troyes/ Maison du Boulanger.

Address: Salon Régional du Livre de Jeunesse de Troyes, 42 rue Paillot-de-Montabert, 10000 Troyes, France. **Telephone:** 3 25 73 14 43. **Fax:** 3 25 73 91 26. **Internet:** perso.wanadoo.fr/salondelivre.troyes. **E-mail:** slj.troyes@ wanadoo.fr.

Prix Chronos de Littérature pour la Jeunesse

An award created in 1996 by the Fondation Nationale de Gérontologie with the aim of making young people aware of the ageing process, emphasizing the value of different life stages, and the relationship between generations. Prizes are awarded for books in six age categories, from birth to 20 years, with winners chosen from a shortlist by a jury made up exclusively of young people.

Recent Winners: Pre-School: 2002: Martine Becke and Annie Bonhomme (illustrator), *Tu te souviens?*; 2001: Nigel Gray and Vanessa Cabban (illustrator), *Le Grand-père de Petit Ours*
Grades CE1-CE2: 2002: Christian and Edith Jolibois, *Batterie et lunettes noires*; 2001: Anne-Marie Desplat-Duc and Morgan (illustrator), *Plumette une poule super chouette*
Grades CM1-CM2: 2002: Gilles Fresse, *Supermamie*; 2001: Alan Temperley, Laurence Kiefe (translator) and Christophe Besse (illustrator), *Harry et les vieilles pommes*
Years 3–4: 2002: Maïa Brami and Claude K. Dubois (illustrator), *Vis ta vie*; 2001: Jacques Mazeau, *Jusqu'à la mer*
Years 5–6: 2002: Yaël Hassan and Serge Bloch (illustrator), *Le Professeur de musique*; 2001: Marie-Claude Berot and Nicolas Wintz (illustrator), *Ninon-Silence*.

Sponsoring Organization: Fondation Nationale de Gérontologie.

Address: Fondation Nationale de Gérontologie, 49 rue Mirabeau, 75016 Paris, France. **Telephone:** 1 55 74 67 08. **Fax:** 1 55 74 67 01. **Internet:** www.prix-chronos.org/. **E-mail:** prix-chronos.fng@wanadoo.fr.

Prix Ciné Roman Carte Noire

The prize was created in 2001 by Arlette Gordon and Patrick de Bourgues, with the aim of promoting French literature among professionals in the field of cinema, and of selecting a novel with potential to be made into a film. The winner receives €15,245, which is presented in April during the Paris Film Festival.

Recent Winners: 2002: Michel Houellebecq, *Plateforme*; 2001: Michel Quint, *Effroyables jardins*.

Sponsoring Organization: Paris Film Festival.

Address: Paris Film Festival, Paris, France.

Prix des Cinq Continents de la francophonie (Five Continents French-language Prize)

This prize was created in 2001 by the inter-governmental Francophone Agency, and is awarded every two years for a novel or a collection of short stories by a writer using the French language, but who is not of French origin. The winner receives a prize of 120,000 francs (€18,000) plus one year's marketing of the prize-winning title.

Eligibility and Restrictions: Open to French-language authors of origin other than French, who have not published more than five works.

How to Apply: Closing date for submissions is 31 May.

Recent Winners: 2001: Yasmine Khlat, *Le désespoir est un péché*.

Sponsoring Organization: Agence intergouvernementale de la Francophonie.

Address: 13 quai André Citroën, 75015 Paris, France. **Internet:** www.agence. francophonie.org/dernieres/home.cfm?quo_id=701.

Prix Maurice-Edgar Coindreau

An annual prize for translation of an American work, awarded by the Société des Gens de Lettres de France. It is named after the translator who brought the works of several great American writers (Faulkner, Steinbeck, Hemingway, Styron) to a French readership. The winner, chosen by a jury of 24 writers, receives a prize of €2,250.

Recent Winners: 2002: Sabine Porte, *Au présent* by Annie Dillard.

Sponsoring Organization: Société des Gens de Lettres de France.

Address: Société des Gens de Lettres de France, Hôtel de Massa, 38 rue du Faubourg St Jacques, 75014 Paris, France. **Telephone:** 1 53 10 12 00. **Fax:** 1 53 10 12 12. **Internet:** www.sgdl.org. **E-mail:** sgdlf@wanadoo.fr.

Prix Marcel-Couture

First presented in 2000, this award is for a single work, and is presented during the Montreal Book Festival.

Recent Winners: 2000: Bernard Andrès, *L'énigme de Sales Laterrière*.

Sponsoring Organization: Salon du livre de Montréal.

Address: Salon du livre de Montréal, 480 rue Saint-Laurent, bureau 403, Montreal, PQ H2Y 3Y7, Canada. **Internet:** www.slm.qc.ca.

Prix Franz Cumont

One of a number of awards presented by the Belgian Royal Academie, the Prix Franz Cumont was established in 1937 and is worth €2,500. It is awarded for a recent work on the history of religion or science during pre-Mohammedan times in the Mediterranean basin. The winner holds the title for a three-year period.

Eligibility and Restrictions: Open to writers of any nationality.

Recent Winners: 1997–1999: M. B. Vitrac.

Sponsoring Organization: Académie Royale de Belgique.

Contact: Jean-Luc De Paepe.

Address: Académie Royale de Belgique, Palais des Académies, 1 rue Ducale, 1000 Brussels, Belgium. **Telephone:** (2) 550 22 11. **Fax:** (2) 550 22 05. **Internet:** www.cfwb.be/arb/Fondations.

Prix Athanase-David

An annual prize set up in memory of Athanase David (1881–1953), the Secretary of Quebec who in 1922 founded the organization responsible for Les Prix du Québec. The prize recognizes an outstanding contribution to Québécois literature by a Canadian francophone author living in Quebec. The winner receives a prize of $30,000 and a medal.

Recent Winners: 1998: André Langevin; 1997: Gilles Marcotte; 1996: Monique Bosco; 1995: Jacques Poulin.

Sponsoring Organization: Québec Ministère de la Culture et des Communications..

Address: Québec Ministère de la Culture et des Communications, 225 Grande Allée Est, Bloc B, 2e étage, Quebec, PQ G1R 5G5, Canada.

Prix Décembre

Established in 1989, the Prix Décembre is presented to a novel and is worth 200,000 francs (€30,000). The prize, which was originally called the Prix Novembre, was set up as an anti-conformist alternative to the Prix Goncourt. The winner is selected by a special jury.

Recent Winners: 2001: Chloé Delaume, *Le Cri du sablier*; 2000: Anthony Palou, *Camille*; 1999: Claude Askolovitch, *Voyage au bout de la France: le Front national tel qu'il est*; 1998: Michel Houellebecq, *Les particules élémentaires*.

Address: Paris, France.

Prix Michel Dentan

The Prix Michel Dentan, first awarded in 1985, has become one of the most important literary awards in the field of Suisse Romande (French-language) literature. It is awarded each year by a nine-person jury, who make their selection from six or so works which have appeared in the preceding literary season. The prize is awarded to a work which is considered to be outstanding for the strength of writing, originality and powers of fascination and well-being in its content. The prize is supported by the weekly paper *Construire* and the daily title *Le Temps*, as well as the Cercle littéraire de Lausanne. The award comprises a cheque for SFr 8,000.

Recent Winners: 2001: Jean-Jacques Langendort, *La nuit tombe, Dieu écoute*; 2000: Frédéric Pajak, *L'Immense Solitude*; 1998: Claude Darbellay, *Les Prétendants*; 1997: Daniel Maggetti, *Chambre 112*; 1996: Claudine Roulet, *Rien qu'une écaille*.

Sponsoring Organization: University of Lausanne, Faculty of Literature.

Address: Uni Lausanne, Faculté des Lettres, 1015 Lausanne, Switzerland. **Internet:** www.unil.ch/fra/Dentan.htm.

Prix des Deux-Magots

A prize created in 1933 on the day when the novel *La Condition humaine* by André Malraux won the Prix Goncourt. It is presented every year at the famous Café des Deux Magots in Paris. The winner receives a prize of €7,622.45.

Recent Winners: 2002: Jean-Luc Coatalem, *Je suis dans les mers du sud*; 2001: François Bizot, *Le portail*; 2000: Philippe Hermann, *La vraie joie*; 1999: Marc Dugain, *La chambre des officiers*.

Sponsoring Organization: Café des Deux Magots.

Address: Café des Deux Magots, 6 place Saint Germain des Près, 75006 Paris, France. **Internet:** www.lesdeuxmagots.fr. **E-mail:** cmathivat@free.fr.

Prix Ernest Discailles

One of a number of awards presented by the Belgian Royal Academy, the Prix Ernest Discailles was established in 1907 and is worth €1,500. It is awarded every five years, and alternates between works on the history of French literature and on recent history. The period 2002–2006 is for recent history. The winner holds the title for a five-year period.

Eligibility and Restrictions: Entries must have been written during the previous ten years. Authors must be of Belgian nationality, or foreign students from the University of Ghent.

Recent Winners: History of French Literature (1997–2001 award): not yet awarded.

Sponsoring Organization: Académie Royale de Belgique.

Contact: Jean-Luc De Paepe.

Address: Académie Royale de Belgique, Palais des Académies, 1 rue Ducale, 1000 Brussels, Belgium. **Telephone:** (2) 550 22 11. **Fax:** (2) 550 22 05. **Internet:** www.cfwb.be/arb/Fondations.

Prix Jules Duculot

One of a number of awards presented by the Belgian Royal Academy, the Prix Jules Duculot was established in 1965 and is worth 120,000 Belgian francs (around €2,975). It is awarded for the best recent work on the subject of the history of philosophy. The winner holds the title for a five-year period.

Eligibility and Restrictions: Open to published works or unpublished manuscripts written in French; authors must be of Belgian nationality or be a resident academic at a Belgian university. Published works must have appeared in the previous five years.

Recent Winners: 1991–1995: M. L. Couloubaritsis.

Sponsoring Organization: Académie Royale de Belgique.

Contact: Jean-Luc De Paepe.

Address: Académie Royale de Belgique, Palais des Académies, 1 rue Ducale, 1000 Brussels, Belgium. **Telephone:** (2) 550 22 11. **Fax:** (2) 550 22 05. **Internet:** www.cfwb.be/arb/Fondations.

Prix Charles Duvivie

One of a number of awards presented by the Belgian Royal Academy, the Prix Charles Duvivie was established in 1905 and is worth €1,250. It is awarded every three years for a recent work on the history of Belgian or foreign law or the history of Belgian administrative, legal or political institutions. The winner holds the title for a three-year period.

Eligibility and Restrictions: Open to Belgian authors only.

Recent Winners: 1997–1999: M. J. Logie.

Sponsoring Organization: Académie Royale de Belgique.

Contact: Jean-Luc De Paepe.

Address: Académie Royale de Belgique, Palais des Académies, 1 rue Ducale, 1000 Brussels, Belgium. **Telephone:** (2) 550 22 11. **Fax:** (2) 550 22 05. **Internet:** www.cfwb.be/arb/Fondations.

Prix des Enfants (Children's Prize)

Established in 1992 by the Association Lecture et Loisirs (Reading and Leisure Association) to reward the author of a children's picture book. The prize money of €800 is underwritten by the Direction Départementale de la Jeunesse et des Sports (DDSS).

Eligibility and Restrictions: Book must have been published during the previous year (year ending 30 April). Author and illustrator must be French-speaking.

How to Apply: Publishers or authors may apply by sending one copy to the address given.

Recent Winners: 2001: Andrée Prigent, *Tibili et le chien du coiffeur*; 2000: Lionel le Neovanic, *Lucie Fer, un amour de sorcière*; 1999: J. Claude Mourlevat and J. Luc Bénazet, *Le jeune loup qui n'avait pas de nom*; 1998: Geoffroy de Pennart, *Le loup sentimental*; 1997: Jacques Taravant and Peter Sis, *Le marchand l'Ailes*.

Sponsoring Organization: Salon Régional du Livre de Jeunesse de Troyes/ Direction Départementale de la Jeunesse et des Sports (DDSS), 10000 Troyes, France.**Telephone:** 3 25 73 14 43. **Fax:** 3 25 73 91 26. **Internet:** perso.wanadoo.fr/ salondelivre.troyes. **E-mail:** slj.troyes@wanadoo.fr.

Prix Erckmann-Chatrian

The Erckmann-Chatrian Prize is an important regional prize created in 1924 for the Lorraine region. It is presented each year for a work of prose, preferably with a subject linked to the region. The prize is awarded in three categories: novel, history, and monograph (the latter two categories having been added in 1998, initially in the form of a grant).

Eligibility and Restrictions: Open to writers born or resident in Lorraine (Moselle, Meurthe et Moselle, Meuse, Vosges), or for works written about the area.

Recent Winners: Prix Erckmann-Chatrian: 2001: Jocelyne François, *Portrait d'un homme au crépuscule*; 2000: Joël Egloff, *Les Ensoleillés*; 1999: Philippe Claudel, *Meuse l'oubli*; 1998: Gaston-Paul Effa, *Mâ*; 1997: Georges Poull, *Les Fondateurs de l'industrie vosgienne de 1800 à 1870*
History: 2001: François Roth; 2000: Stéphanie Le Clerre-Chapotot, *Jardins du roi Stanislas en Lorraine*; 1999: Pierre Denis, *La Garnison de Metz 1914–1945*; 1998: Jean-Marie Moine, *René Boudot, le feu sacré*
Monograph: 2001: Jean Lanher; 2000: Bernard Lorraine, *Panorama de la littérature lorraine*; 1999: Gabriel Ladaique, *Origines lorraines de Frédéric Chopin*; 1998: Alain Dusart and François Moulin, *Art nouveau, épopée lorraine*.

Address: Nancy, France.

Prix Européen du Roman pour Enfant de la Ville de Poitiers

This award, founded in 1988, is jointly sponsored by the town of Poitiers, the Inspection Académique de la Vienne, CEMEA, Mediathèque and APPLAC. The prize is awarded in June of each year and the winner is selected by a panel of children from a shortlist of seven novels. The winner receives a cheque for €2,287.

Eligibility and Restrictions: Open to novels for children aged from 10 to 13 years. Must be written by an author resident in the European Community, and published in French between September and August of the preceding calendar year.

Contact: Christian Seigneurin.
Address: 5 avenue Rhin et Danube, 86000 Poitiers, France. **Telephone:** 5 49 01 02 55. **Fax:** 5 49 44 18 30.

Prix René Fallet

This prize was created in 1989 in memory of René Fallet, a writer from the Jalignois region, with the aim of recognizing an outstanding first novel by a young writer. The first award was made in 1990. A jury draws up a shortlist, which is then judged by a panel of readers spread across the region. The prize of €1,500 is awarded at a literary festival in June, the Journées Littéraires du Bourbonnais.

Eligibility and Restrictions: Entries must be written in French by an author aged not more than 40.

How to Apply: Copies of the novel must be sent to each member of the jury.

Recent Winners: 2001: A. Job, *La femme manquée*; 2000: Gérard Oberlé, *Nil rouge*; 1999: Marc Dugain, *La chambre des officiers*; 1998: Jean Baptiste Evette, *Jordan Fantosme*; 1997: Stéphanie Janicot, *Les Matriochkas*.

Sponsoring Organization: Association Agir en Pays Jalignois.

Address: Mairie de Jaligny, 03220 Jaligny-sur-Besbre, France. **Telephone:** 4 70 34 69 91; 04 70 34 69 91. **E-mail:** agirenpaysjalignois@wanadoo.fr Bureau.

Prix Fémina

Established in 1904 by 22 members of the periodical *La Vie heureuse*, in protest against the exclusion of women from the jury of the Prix Goncourt, the prize aims to encourage writing by women. It is awarded each year for a novel written in French by a woman. The winner is decided by an all-female jury. In 1986 the Prix Fémina Etranger, for foreign novels, was established to run alongside the Prix Fémina.

Recent Winners: 2001: Marie Ndiaye, *Rosie Carpe*; 2000: Camille Laurens, *Dans ces bras-là*; 1999: Maryline Desbiolles, *Anchise*; 1998: François Cheng, *Le Dit de Tianyi*; 1997: Dominique Noguez, *Amour noir*.

Address: Paris, France.

Prix Fémina Etranger

Established in 1986 to run alongside the long-established Prix Fémina, to provide an opportunity to recognize an outstanding work in the field of foreign novels; the winner is chosen by an all-female jury.

Recent Winners: 2001: Keith Ridgway, *Mauvaise pente*; 2000 Jamaica Kincaid, *Mon frère*; 1999: Hitonari Tsuji, *Le bouddha blanc*; 1998: Antonio Muñoz Molina, *Pleine lune*; 1997: Jia Pingwa, *La Capitale déchue*; 1996: Javier Marias, *Demain dans la bataille pense à moi*.

Address: Paris, France.

Prix du Festival de la Bande Dessinée de Sierre

Several awards are presented at the Cartoon Festival held each year in the Swiss town of Sierre. Categories include the Grand Prix de la Ville de Sierre, Prix Découverte, Prix Bande Dessinée Jeunesse, Prix Humour and the Prix Coup de

Cœur. Each award comprises a trophy and a cash prize, with total prize money standing at SFr 10,000. Selection is made throughout the year by specialists, although the awards are actually decided by a non-specialist jury.

Eligibility and Restrictions: Open to comic books only.

How to Apply: No direct application is possible.

Recent Winners: 2001: Ruben Pellejer (Spain), Sergio García (Spain), Yuan Yo Guarnido (France), Mann Larcenet (France), Matthias Gnehm (Switzerland).

Contact: Man Philippe Neyroud.

Address: Festival International de la Bande Dessinée de Sierre, CP 200, 3960 Sierre, Switzerland. **Telephone:** (27) 455 90 43. **Fax:** (27) 455 91 01. **Internet:** www.bdsierre.ch. **E-mail:** festival@bdsierre.ch.

Grand Prix Paul Féval de Littérature Populaire

An annual prize of €3,000 awarded by the Société des Gens de Lettres for a complete body of work. The winner is selected by a jury of 24 writers.

How to Apply: Five copies of works should sent by 31 March.

Recent Winners: 2000: Pierre Bordage, *Fables de l'Humpur.*

Sponsoring Organization: Société des Gens de Lettres de France.

Address: Société des Gens de Lettres de France, Hôtel de Massa, 38 rue du Faubourg St Jacques, 75014 Paris, France. **Telephone:** 1 53 10 12 00. **Fax:** 1 53 10 12 12. **Internet:** www.sgdl.org. **E-mail:** sgdlf@wanadoo.fr.

Prix FIT Aurore Boréale de la traduction
(Aurora Borealis Translation Prize)

Every three years the International Federation of Translators (FIT) awards two prizes for translation, one for fiction and one for non-fiction. The prize is sponsored by a generous donation from the Norwegian Association of Literary Translators (NO), and is financed by copyright revenues. The prize is awarded for either a single translation of outstanding quality or for the entire body of a translator's fiction work. The prize consists of a Certificate of Merit and a sum of money.

Eligibility and Restrictions: Open to works of translation in and out of any language of members of the FIT. Entrants must be members of a professional translators' organization which belongs to the FIT.

How to Apply: It is not possible to apply directly for the prize; member organizations nominate candidates. Six copies of the work, in either English or French, should be submitted at least six months before the FIT congress in September, with biographical details of the nominee.

Sponsoring Organization: International Federation of Translators/Fédération Internationale des Traducteurs (FIT).

Address: Fédération Internationale des Traducteurs, Dr-Heinrich-Maierstr. 9, 1180 Vienna, Austria. **Internet:** www.fit-ift.org.

Prix de Flore

Established in 1994 to recognize a promising new author of a work demonstrating modernity, youth and originality. The winner is selected by a jury made up of 13 journalists, and receives a cheque for 40,000 francs (€6,000) and an engraved Pouilly glass. The winner each year also writes a short story on the subject of the prize ceremony evening at the Café de Flore.

Recent Winners: 2001: Christophe Donner, *L'empire de la morale*; 2000: Nicolas Rey, *La mémoire courte*; 1998: Virginie Despentes, *Les jolies choses*.

Sponsoring Organization: Café de Flore.

Contact: cchretiennot@café-de-flore.com.

Address: Café de Flore, Saint-Germain-des-Prés, Paris, France.

Prix Fnac–Andersen du livre d'entreprise (Fnac–Andersen Prize for the Best Business Book)

An annual prize established in 2000 and jointly administered by Andersen, the firm of management consultants, the bookshop chain Fnac and the newspaper *Les Echos*. The award recognizes books which best describe current economic trends and their practical consequences for business. Prizes are awarded in four categories: Essay; Human Resources/Management; Law/Finance; and Strategy/ Marketing. In 2002 there was some doubt as to whether the prize was to be continued.

Eligibility and Restrictions: Entries must have been published during the previous year.

Recent Winners: Human Resources/Management: 2002: Philippe Détrie and Catherine Broyez, *La Communication interne au service du management*; 2001: Alain Meignant, *Ressources Humaines: déployer la stratégie*
Law/Finance: 2002: Alexandre K. Samii, *Stratégies logistiques*; 2001: Christiane Féral-Schuhl, *Cyber Droit*
Strategy/Marketing: 2002: Jérôme Barthélemy, *Stratégies d'externalisation*; 2001: Hermann Simon, Florent Jacquet and Franck Brault, *La stratégie Prix*
Essay: 2002: Peter Drucker, *Témoins du 20e siècle*; 2001: Jeremy Rifkin, *L'âge de l'accès*.

Sponsoring Organization: Andersen/Fnac/les Echos.

Address: Arthur Andersen, Paris, France. **Internet:** www.arthurandersen. com/website.nsf/content/ EuropeFranceEventsPrixFnac. **E-mail:** france@ arthurandersen.com.

Prix France Culture Français

The prize was created by radio presenter Alain Veinstein, and is decided by a jury made up of booksellers and producers of literary programmes.

Recent Winners: 2002: Dominique Rolin, *Le Futur immédiat* and Antonio Tabucchi, *Il se fait tard, de plus en plus tard* (joint winners); 2000: Christophe Gailly, *Nuage rouge*; 1999 Jean-Louis Schefer, *Paolo Uccelo, le déluge*; 1998: Pascal Quignard, *Vie secrète*.

Sponsoring Organization: France Culture.

Address: France Culture, Paris, France.

Prix France Télévision

Established in 1995 to recognize an outstanding novel, essay and book for children which have appeared during the previous year. The winning works are selected by a jury of television viewers from a shortlist of six titles drawn up by a panel of specialist readers. The three prizes are awarded at different times of the year:

May (essay), October (children's book) and November (novel). The prize takes the form of promotion of the winning titles on the channels France 2, France 3 and France 5.

Eligibility and Restrictions: Entries must be written in French and have appeared in the previous year.

Recent Winners: Essay: 2002: Patrick Declerck, *Les Naufragés*; 2001: Roger-Pol Droit, *101 expériences de philosophie quotidienne*; 2000: Dominique Jamet, *Un Petit Parisien*
Children's: 2001: Marie-Sabine Roger, *Attention fragiles*, Gilles Bonotaux and Hélène Lasserre, *Quand Mamie avait mon âge* and Jean-Louis Fonteneau and Olivier Schwartz, *Coups de feu à New York* (joint winners); 2000: Marie-Aude Murail, *Oh, boy* and Philippe Arrou-Vignod, *L'Omelette au sucre* (joint winners)
Novel: 2001: François Vallejo, *Madame Angeloso*; 2000: Philippe Claudel, *J'abandonne*.

Sponsoring Organization: France Télévision.

Address: France Télévision, 7, esplanade Henri-de-France, 75907 Paris, Cedex 15, France. **E-mail:** a.blaise@france2.fr.

Prix François 1er: prix Cognac de la critique littéraire
(François I Prize for Literary Criticism)

An award for literary criticism, established in 1990 by the Cognac-based Salon de la Littérature Européenne (European Literature Forum). The award is sponsored by Hennessy and carries a prize of 20,000 francs (€3,000).

Recent Winners: 1999: François Busnel, articles in *La 5e, les Dernières Nouvelles d'Alsace)*; 1998: Jean-Noël Pancrazi, articles in *Le Monde*; 1997: Jean Vedrines.

Sponsoring Organization: Hennessy.

Address: Salon de la Littérature Européenne, 59 rue Aristide Briand, 16100 Cognac, France. **Telephone:** 5 45 82 88 01. **Fax:** 5 45 36 00 48. **Internet:** www.ville-cognac.fr/subus/300.htm.

Prix Jean Freustié

A prize of €20,000 created in memory of writer Jean Freustié (whose real name was Jean-Pierre Teurlay, and who died in 1983). The prize is awarded for a French-language work of prose, either novel, short story, biography or essay.

Recent Winners: 2002: Jean Rolin, *La Clôture*; 2001: Charles Dantzig , *Nos vies hâtives*; 2000: Myriam Anissimov, *Sa majesté la mort*.

Address: Paris, France.

Prix Joseph Gantrelle

One of a number of awards presented by the Belgian Royal Academy, the Prix Joseph Gantrelle was established in 1890 and is worth €1,500. It is awarded every two years for a recent work on the subject of the philology.

Eligibility and Restrictions: Only Belgian authors may enter.

Recent Winners: 2000–2001: (not yet awarded); 1998–1999: A. Martin and O. Primavesi.

Sponsoring Organization: Académie Royale de Belgique.

Contact: Jean-Luc De Paepe.

Address: Académie Royale de Belgique, Palais des Académies, 1 rue Ducale, 1000 Brussels, Belgium. **Telephone:** (2) 550 22 11. **Fax:** (2) 550 22 05. **Internet:** www.cfwb.be/arb/Fondations.

Prix Théophile Gautier

An annual poetry prize, awarded by the Académie Française. The winner receives a silver medal.

Eligibility and Restrictions: Open to living authors of all ages; only published works may be submitted, and they must have appeared during the preceding year.

How to Apply: Two copies of the work should be sent by the author or publisher by 31 January.

Recent Winners: 2002: Michel Bénard, *Fragilité des signes*.

Sponsoring Organization: Académie Française.

Address: Académie Française, Institut de France, 23 quai de Conti, 75006 Paris, France. **Telephone:** 1 44 41 43 00. **Fax:** 1 43 29 47 45. **Internet:** www.academie-francaise.fr. **E-mail:** contact@academie-francaise.fr.

Prix Maurice-Genevoix

Established in 1985 by Yves Bodin, Mayor of Garches, in memory of Maurice Genevoix, a writer and member of the Académie Française, who was a frequent visitor to the town. The prize is awarded each May/June for a literary work such as a novel or biography, which honours the work and memory of Genevoix in its choice of theme and quality of style (nature, ecology, friendship, humanism, war, animals, etc). The winner, selected by an 11-member jury, receives €5,000.

Eligibility and Restrictions: Entries must have been published in French during the preceding calendar year (year ending May).

How to Apply: A copy of published entries should be sent to each member of the jury.

Recent Winners: 2002: Nicolas Vanier, *Le Chant du grand nord*; 2001: Jérôme Garcin, *C'était tous les jours tempête*; 2000: Pascale Roze, *Lettre d'été*; 1999: Geneviève Dormann, *Adieu, phénomène*; 1998: Jean-Marc Roberts, *Une petite femme*.

Sponsoring Organization: Mairie de Garches.

Contact: Sec Catherine Sart.

Address: Mairie de Garches, 92380 Garches, France. **Telephone:** 1 47 95 67 69. **Fax:** 1 47 95 67 00.

Prix Goblet d'Alviella

One of a number of awards presented by the Belgian Royal Academy, the Prix Goblet d'Alviella was established in 1926 and is worth €1,500. It is awarded for the recent work on the subject of the history of religion. The winner holds the title for a five-year period.

Eligibility and Restrictions: Open to works by Belgian authors only. Entries must be strictly objective and scientific in their treatment of the subject.

Recent Winners: 1996–2000: C. Van Liefferinge.

Sponsoring Organization: Académie Royale de Belgique.

Contact: Jean-Luc De Paepe.
Address: Académie Royale de Belgique, Palais des Académies, 1 rue Ducale, 1000 Brussels, Belgium. **Telephone:** (2) 550 22 11. **Fax:** (2) 550 22 05. **Internet:** www.cfwb.be/arb/Fondations.

Prix Goncourt

The Académie (Société littéraire des Goncourt) was established in 1900, and comprises ten members, who hold a salon on the first Tuesday of every month above the restaurant Drouant in Paris. The first Prix Goncourt was awarded in 1903, and has become regarded as France's most prestigious literary award. The winners, announced annually in December, are awarded a symbolic cheque for 50 French francs (€7.5).

Eligibility and Restrictions: Prizes are awarded in the categories of novels, first novels, biography, children's book and poetry.

Recent Winners: 2001: Jean-Christophe Rufin, *Rouge Brésil*; 2000: Jean-Jacques Schuhl, *Ingrid Caven*; 1999: Jean Echenoz, *Je m'en vais*; 1998: Paule Constant, *Confidence pour confidence*; 1997: Patrick Rambaud, *La Bataille*.

Sponsoring Organization: Académie Goncourt.

Address: c/o Drouant, place Gaillon, 75002 Paris, France. **Telephone:** 1 45 20 27 21. **Internet:** www.academie-goncourt.fr.

Prix Goncourt des Lycéens

Established in 1988, the Prix Goncourt des Lycéens, which represents younger readers, has become one of the many well-known French literary prizes.

Recent Winners: 2001: Shan Sa, *La joueuse de go*; 2000: Ahmadou Kourouma, *Allah n'est pas obligé*; 1999: Jean-Marie Laclavetine, *Première ligne*; 1998: Luc Lang, *Mille six cents ventres*; 1997: Jean-Pierre Milanoff, *Le Maître des paons*; 1996: Nancy Huston, *Instruments des ténèbres*.

Address: c/o Drouant, place Gaillon, 75002 Paris, France. **Internet:** 212.37.198.117/goncourt99/index.htm.

Prix Gouverneur de la Rosée du Livre et de la Littérature

The prize was created in 2001 by the former minister of culture, to recognize the achievements of Haitian writers, and to allow the public to become familiar with their country's leading cultural figures. The winner receives a bronze statuette and a prize of US $1,000.

Sponsoring Organization: Ministry of Culture.

Address: Ministry of Culture, Port-au-Prince, Haiti.

Prix Alain-Grandbois

The award was established in 1988 in honour of the poet Alain Grandbois, who was a founder member of the former Académie canadienne-française (now the Académie des lettres du Québec). The winner receives a prize of C$1,000.

Recent Winners: 2000: Normand de Bellefeuille, *La marche de l'aveugle sans son chien*.

Sponsoring Organization: Académie des lettres du Québec.

Address: Académie des lettres du Québec, 5724, chemin de la Côte-Saint-Antoine, Montreal, PQ H4A 1R9, Canada.

Prix Heredia

An annual poetry prize, awarded by the Académie Française. The winner receives a silver medal.

Eligibility and Restrictions: Open to living authors of all ages; only published works may be submitted, and they must have appeared during the preceding year.

How to Apply: Two copies of the work should be sent by the author or publisher by 31 January.

Recent Winners: 2002: Michel Guimbal, *Mon beau navire, ô ma mémoire*; 2001: Tristan Buridant, *L'Or des songes*.

Sponsoring Organization: Académie Française.

Address: Académie Française, Institut de France, 23 quai de Conti, 75006 Paris, France. **Telephone:** 1 44 41 43 00. **Fax:** 1 43 29 47 45. **Internet:** www.academie-francaise.fr. **E-mail:** contact@academie-francaise.fr.

Prix Joseph Houziaux

One of a number of awards presented by the Belgian Royal Academy, the Prix Joseph Houziaux was established in 1994 and is worth €1,500. It is awarded every three years, and alternates between works of research on the French language, and literary works written in dialect (Picard, Walloon, Lorraine or Champenois) or a study of dialects of Wallonia. (The award for 2000 to 2002 will be for works of research on the French language.) The winner holds the title for a three-year period.

Eligibility and Restrictions: Authors must be aged below 60; entries may be published works or manuscripts of work in progress, written in French, Spanish, Italian, German, English or Dutch (for the research category), or in a dialect from the greater Walloon region (for the dialect category).

How to Apply: Authors should send their work to the address given, accompanied by a letter providing biographical details and a list of author's publications.

Recent Winners: 1997–1999: M. Willems.

Sponsoring Organization: Académie Royale de Belgique.

Contact: Jean-Luc De Paepe.

Address: Académie Royale de Belgique, Palais des Académies, 1 rue Ducale, 1000 Brussels, Belgium. **Telephone:** (2) 550 22 11. **Fax:** (2) 550 22 05. **Internet:** www.cfwb.be/arb/Fondations.

Prix Infini

An annual prize established in 1993 to recognize an outstanding work of science fiction. The prize is sponsored by Infini, a French science fiction association, and is awarded during the French Science Fiction Convention.

Recent Winners: 2001: Pierre Gévart, *Comment les choses se sont vraiment passées*; 2000: no award given; 1999: no award given; 1998: Emmanuel Levilain-Clément, *Quand les dieux mènent boire leurs chevaux*; 1997: Marcel Divianadin, *Sur une fréquence lointaine existe un monde*.

Sponsoring Organization: Association Infini.

Address: 138, rue Gabriel Péri (2A), 93200 Saint-Denis, France.

Prix Interallié

The prize was established in 1930 by a group of journalists known as the Cercle Interallié, in response to the creation of the Prix Fémina. It aims to recognize a novel written by a journalist during the preceding year.

Recent Winners: 2002: Stéphane Denis, *Sisters*; 2001: Patrick Poivre d'Arvor, *L'irrésolu*; 1999: Jean-Christophe Rufin, *Les causes perdues*; 1998: Gilles Martin-Chauffier, *Les corrompus*; 1997: Éric Neuhoff, *La petite Française*.

Sponsoring Organization: Cercle Interallié.

Address: Cercle Interallié, 33 rue du Faubourg St Honoré, 75008 Paris, France.

Prix International Kadima (International Kadima Prize)

This prize, established in 1990, is awarded every two years with the aim of promoting multilingual creative writing and cultural diversity from young authors. It is named in honour of a linguist from Congo. The prize is administered by the Agence intergouvernementale de la Francophonie in collaboration with the Belgian-based Centre international des langues, littératures et traditions d'Afrique au service du développement (CILTADE), at the University of Louvain-la-Neuve, and Centre de linguistique théorique et appliquée de Kinshasa (CELTA). Three categories of award are made: language, literature and translation, with each winner receiving a prize of 30,000 francs (€4,500).

Eligibility and Restrictions: Open to anyone from countries of the Agence intergouvernementale de la Francophonie. Entries must be unpublished, written in an African, Creole or Arabic language (or a French translation of such a work). The language category is open to works of linguistic description or an educational nature; the literature prize is open to all kinds of works, both oral and written; the translation prize is for translation either into French or into one of the eligible languages.

How to Apply: Entry is free; three copies of the work should be sent to the address given (or to alternative addresses in the Democratic Republic of the Congo) by 1 March, accompanied by a summary in French. The author's identity must not be revealed on the work itself.

Recent Winners: Language: 2001: Kawata Ashem Tem (DRC), *Lingala dictionary*
Translation: 2001: Organisation sénégalaise d'appui au développement for works in wolof, pulal et sereer languages
Literature: 2001: Dramane Traoré (Mali), for a series of novels and essays in Bamanankan language.

Sponsoring Organization: Agence intergouvernementale de la Francophonie.

Contact: M. Bréhima Doumbia.

Address: 13 quai André Citroën, 75015 Paris, France. **Telephone:** 1 44 37 33 02. **Fax:** 1 44 37 32 42. **Internet:** www.agence.francophonie.org. **E-mail:** agence@ francophonie.org.

Prix Internet du Livre

This award for the best new novel was first presented in 2000, having been established with the aim of attracting interest among younger readers. The winner is chosen by public vote among users of the award's website, who are able to vote in two stages spread over a period of four weeks. The award is jointly sponsored by the magazine *l'Express* and the publisher France Loisirs.

Recent Winners: 2001: Marc Levy, *Et si c'était vrai*; 2000: Amélie Nothomb, *Stupeur et tremblements*.

Sponsoring Organization: l'Express and France Loisirs.

Address: France Loisirs, Paris, France. **Internet:** www.leprixinternet.com/.

Prix du Jeune Ecrivain (Young Writer's Prize)

Founded in 1985 by Marc Sebbah to reward and encourage young writers of French-language short stories. The prize has two sections, Le Prix du Jeune Ecrivain, for French writers, and the Prix du Jeune Ecrivain Francophone, for Francophone writers from other countries, and there are five or six awards in each section. The prize takes the form of books, travel, participation in arts festivals, etc., and the winning entries are published in a special anthology.

Eligibility and Restrictions: Applicants must be aged between 15 and 25 (or 27 for non-French writers). Entries must be unpublished short stories written in French, and should be between 5 and 40 pages in length.

How to Apply: Applicants should send three copies of their work to the address given.

Recent Winners: Prix du Jeune Ecrivain: 2001: Ilf Eddine Bencheikh, *Carrefour des fuites*; 1993: Antoine Bello; 1991: Dominique Mainard; 1988: Marie Darrieussecq; 1987: Florence Seyvos
Prix du Jeune Ecrivain Francophone: 2001: Andonirima Rakotonarivo (Madagascar), *L'enfant de la lune noire*; 2000: Nadine El Khoury (Lebanon), *L'obus siffla*.

Sponsoring Organization: Fondation Paribas and a number of other companies and organizations.

Contact: Pres. Marc Sebbah.

Address: Prix du Jeune Ecrivain, 6 Avenue Tissandie, 31600 Muret Cedex, France. **Telephone:** 5 61 56 13 15. **Fax:** 5 61 56 13 15. **Internet:** www.pjef.net. **E-mail:** pje@pjef.net.

Prix Stanislas Julien

This prize, administered by the Académie des Inscriptions et Belles Lettres, is named after the French sinologist Stanislas Julien. The prize is presented for a book about China, and is one of the most coveted and prestigious in the field of Chinese studies.

Recent Winners: 2000: Robert E. Hegel, *Reading Illustrated Fiction in Late Imperial China*; 1999: Elfriede Regina Knauer, *The Camel's Load in Life and Death*.

Sponsoring Organization: Académie des Inscriptions et Belles Lettres.

Address: Académie des Inscriptions et Belles Lettres, Institut de France, 23 quai de Conti, 75270 Paris, France.

Prix Joseph Kessel

In 1991 SCAM (the Société civile des auteurs multimedia) created a new literary prize, the Prix Scam du livre, which carried a prize of 30,000 francs (€4,500). In 1997 the prize was renamed the Prix Joseph Kessel. It is awarded to the author of a high quality documentary-style work (e.g. in the field of travel, biography, research, or essay).

Recent Winners: 2002: Gilles Lapouge, *La Mission des Frontières*; 2001: Bernard Ollivier, *Longue marche*; 2000: Geneviève Moll, *Yvonne de Gaulle*; 1999: Christian Millau, *Au galop des hussards*; 1998: Olivier Weber, *Lucien Bodard, un aventurier dans le siècle*.

Sponsoring Organization: Société civile des auteurs multimedia (SCAM).

Address: Société civile des auteurs multimedia (SCAM), 5 avenue Vélasquez, 75008 Paris, France. **Telephone:** 1 56 69 58. **Fax:** 1 56 69 58 59. **Internet:** www.scam.fr/fr/evenement/prix/Litteraire.

Prix de la Langue de France

An annual prize established in 1986 by the town of Brive with the aim of rewarding a work which demonstrates the quality and beauty of the French language. The prize is awarded during the Brive book fair in November; the winner is chosen by a jury and receives a prize of 100,000 francs (€15,000).

Recent Winners: 1998: Marcel Schneider; 1997: François Weyergans; 1996: René de Obaldia.

Address: Brive, France.

Prix Valéry Larbaud

An annual award created in 1967 and presented by the town of Vichy and the Association Internationale des Amis de Valéry Larbaud in memory of the writer of that name. It is awarded to a writer who has published a work 'which Larbaud would have liked'.

Recent Winners: 2002: Jean-Claude Pirotte, *Ange Vincent*; 1999: Gilles Leroy, *Machines à sous*; 1998: Gérard Macé, *Colportage I et II*; 1997: Jean-Paul Enthoven, *Les enfants de Saturne*; 1996: François Bott, *Radiguet*.

Sponsoring Organization: Town of Vichy/Association Internationale des Amis de Valéry Larbaud.

Address: Association Internationale des Amis de Valéry Larbaud, Vichy, France.

Prix Claude Le Heurteur

This prize is named after the poet Claude Le Heurteur who died in 1625. The prize was established in 1998 by a group of 10 writers, and is awarded to an outstanding novel. The winner is chosen by a jury of anonymous members. There is no official sponsor or cash prize.

Eligibility and Restrictions: Open to French language novels published during the previous year. Writers may be of any nationality, but translations are excluded.

Recent Winners: 2002: Marc Durin-Valois, *L'empire des solitudes*; 2001: Jacques Gélat, *La couleur inconnue*; 2000: Philippe S. Hadengue, *L'exode*; 1999: Marc Petit, *La Compagnie des Indes*.

Address: Paris, France. **Internet:** www.prixleheurteur.com/princip.htm. **E-mail:** claude@prixleheurteur.com.

Prix Léon Leclère

One of a number of awards presented by the Belgian Royal Academy, the Prix Léon Leclère was established in 1928 and is worth €1,300. It is awarded every five years, for the best debut work by a young Belgian historian. The winner holds the title for a five-year period.

Eligibility and Restrictions: Open to published works or manuscripts of works in progress, on the subject of Belgian history or general history.

Recent Winners: 1993–1997: J.-M. Wautelet.

Sponsoring Organization: Académie Royale de Belgique.

Contact: Jean-Luc De Paepe.

Address: Académie Royale de Belgique, Palais des Académies, 1 rue Ducale, 1000 Brussels, Belgium. **Telephone:** (2) 550 22 11. **Fax:** (2) 550 22 05. **Internet:** www.cfwb.be/arb/Fondations.

Prix des Lectrices de Elle

This prize, founded in 1970, is judged by a panel of 120 readers of *Elle* magazine, and is awarded for a novel and, since 1977, a document and a crime story. The winning titles are selected from a shortlist made up of a series of Books of the Month. The winners receive national publicity for their work and appear on the cover of the magazine.

How to Apply: Up to six entries are nominated by the Editorial Board of *Elle* magazine.

Recent Winners: Novel: 2002: Isabelle Hausser, *La Table des enfants*; 2000: Catherine Cusset, *Le problème avec Jane*; 1999: Manq Huston, *L'Empreinte de l'argent*; 1998: Tonino Benacquista, *Saga*; 1997: Élisabeth Gille, *Un paysage de cendres*
Document: 2002: Wladyslaw Szpilman, *Le Pianiste*; 1999: Laurent Greilsamer, *Le Prince foudroyé*; 1998: Evelyne Bloch-Dano, *Madame Zola*; 1997: Antoine de Baecque and Serge Toubiana, *François Truffaut*; 1996: Shusha Guppy, *Un jardin à Téhéran*
Crime Story: 2002: Fred Vargas, *Pars vite et reviens tard*.

Sponsoring Organization: Elle Magazine.

Address: Elle Magazine, Paris, France. **Internet:** www.elle.fr/elle_gouky/index.php.

Prix des Libraires

An annual prize awarded in two categories, a novel from Quebec, and a foreign novel.

Recent Winners: Novel from Quebec: 2001: Gil Courtemanche, *Un dimanche à la piscine à Kigali*; 2000: Nadine Bismuth, *Les gens fidèles ne font pas les nouvelles*; 1999: Marie Laberge, *La cérémonie des anges*; 1998: Bruno Hébert, *C'est pas moi, je le jure*; 1997: Marie Laberge, *Annabelle*

Foreign novel: 2001: Dai Sijie, *Balzac et la petite tailleuse chinoise*; 2000: Amélie Nothomb, *Stupeur et tremblements*; 1999: Nancy Huston, *L'empreinte de l'ange*; 1998: Alessandro Baricco, *Soie*; 1997: Bernhard Schlink, *Le Liseur*.

Sponsoring Organization: Association des libraires du Québec.

Address: Association des libraires du Québec, 1001, boulevard de Maisonneuve Est, Bureau 580, Montreal, H2L 4P9, Canada. **Telephone:** (514) 526-3349. **Fax:** (514) 526-3340. **Internet:** www.alq.qc.ca. **E-mail:** info@alq.qc.ca.

Prix des Librairies de Création

A prize for an outstanding second novel, established in 2001 by the Fondation Banques CIC pour le livre and ADELC.

Recent Winners: 2002: Laurent Mauvignier, *Apprendre à finir*; 2001: Lidia Jorge, *La couverture du soldat*.

Sponsoring Organization: Fondation Banques CIC pour le livre.

Address: Fondation Banques CIC pour le livre, Paris, France. **Internet:** www.cic-banques.fr.

Prix Littéraire de l'Age d'Or de France

First awarded in 2000, this prize recognizes a biography or autobiography, with varying criteria for entry being set each year. There is no official sponsor or cash prize.

Recent Winners: 2002: Paul Mourousy, *Alexandra, la dernière tsarine*; 2001: Alain Rémond, *Chaque jour est un adieu*; 2000: Marc Dugain, *La chambre des officiers*.

Address: 35 rue de Trevise, 75009 Paris, France. **Telephone:** 1 53 24 67 40. **Internet:** agedorfr.free.fr/AO_conferences.htm. **E-mail:** agedorfr@free.fr.

Prix Littéraire Henri Deschamps

The prize was established in 1975 in memory of Henri Deschamps (died 1958), a noted Haitian writer and educator. The prize aims to promote the country's literature and to encourage literary creation among young Haitian writers. The winner receives a prize of $1,000, and 1,000 copies of the work are published.

Eligibility and Restrictions: Open to unpublished works by Haitian writers.

How to Apply: Manuscripts should be submitted by 28 February.

Sponsoring Organization: Maison Henri Deschamps.

Address: Maison Henri Deschamps, BP 164, Port-au-Prince, Haiti. **Telephone:** 223-2215. **Fax:** 223-4975.

Prix Littéraire de l'ENS Cachan

The prize was established in 2001 at the suggestion of the Chroniques bookshop in Cachan, and is administered by the Ecole Normale Supérieure de Cachan, The winner, chosen by a jury from a shortlist of up to 15 titles, receives a work of art (painting or sculpture) donated by the town of Cachan.

Eligibility and Restrictions: Entries must have been published during the previous year. Open to novels, written in French or translated.

Recent Winners: 2002: Véronique Olmi, *Bord de Mer*; 2001: Jacque Gélat, *La couleur inconnue*.

Sponsoring Organization: Ecole Normale Supérieure de Cachan.

Contact: Sylviane Audet.

Address: 61 Ave de Président Wilson, 94235 Cachan, France. **Telephone:** 1 47 40 22 64. **Fax:** 1 47 40 23 73. **Internet:** www.ens-cachan.fr.

Prix Littéraire de la Gironde

An award sponsored by the regional Conseil Général de la Gironde and the weekly newspaper *Le Courrier Français*, established in 1990 with the aim of promoting reading, and to encourage contact between writers and readers from the Gironde region. The prize of €7,500 is awarded for a first or second novel. The competition is judged by a jury.

How to Apply: Publishers are invited to nominate submissions.

Recent Winners: 2002: Véronique Olmi, *Bord de mer*; 2001: Edouard Bernadac, *Ixxaun*; 2000: Patrick Retali, *Tricheur*; 1999: Florence Delaporte, *Je n'ai pas de château*; 1998: Daniel Meynard, *La jeune fille et la neige*.

Sponsoring Organization: Conseil Général de la Gironde/Le Courrier Français.

Address: Service du Livre et du Document, Esplanade Charles de Gaulle, Immeuble Croix du Palais – 5° étage, 33074 Bordeaux, Cedex, France. **Telephone:** 5 56 99 35 49. **Fax:** 5 56 99 35 61. **Internet:** www.cg33.fr. **E-mail:** barbe.dutarde@domade.fr.

Prix Littéraire des Mouettes

An annual prize administered by the regional Conseil Général de la Charente-Maritime. Prizes are awarded in two categories, creative writing and history/non-fiction. The winner is selected by a jury.

Recent Winners: Creative writing: 2001: Bernard Giraudeau, *Le marin à l'ancre*; 2000: Alberte van Herwynen, *L'arpenteur des lumières*
History/non-fiction: 2001: Francine Ducluzeau, *Histoire des Protestants Charentais*.

Sponsoring Organization: Conseil Général de la Charente-Maritime.

Address: Conseil Général de la Charente-Maritime, Charente-Maritime, France. **Telephone:** 5 46 317 200.

Prix Littéraire Prince Pierre-de-Monaco

An annual prize established in 1951 by the Prince Pierre de Monaco Foundation, which aims to reward a French-language writer for their whole body of work for its outstanding style, and whose recent works have been particularly praised. The winner is chosen by a jury of well-known writers, and receives a prize of €15,000.

Recent Winners: 2002: Marie-Claire Blais; 2001: Diane de Margerie.

Sponsoring Organization: Fondation Prince Pierre de Monaco.

Address: Le Winter Palace 4, boulevard des Moulins, 98000 Monte Carlo, Monaco.

Prix Littéraire de la Vocation

An annual prize established in 1960 by the Marcel Bleustein-Blanchet Foundation and awarded annually for literary work in French. The award aims to help a young author who has already had work published, and carries a prize of €7,700.

Eligibility and Restrictions: Open to authors aged between 18 and 35, who have already had work published by a French publisher.

Recent Winners: 2002: Tanguy Viel, *L'Absolue Perfection du crime*.

Sponsoring Organization: Fondation Marcel Bleustein-Blanchet de la Vocation.

Contact: Elisabeth Badinter.

Address: Fondation Marcel Bleustein-Blanchet de la Vocation, 60 ave Victor Hugo, 75116 Paris, France. **Telephone:** 1 45 01 29 28. **Fax:** 1 45 00 92 61.

Prix Littéraires de l'Académie Française

The Académie Française presents over 50 different awards, including many of the best-known, longest established and most prestigious French awards. In addition to numerous awards named after individuals, with prizes ranging from bronze or silver medals up to considerable cash prizes (e.g. the Grand Prix de Littérature Paul Morand, with a prize of €45,000 – see separate entry), the Academy presents an overall prize for a lifetime's achievement, the biennial Grand Prix de Littérature de l'Académie Française, and a number of prizes for specific genres, including the Grand Prix du Roman (Grand Prize for a Novel, of €7,500, established in 1918), the Grand Prix de Poésie (Poetry Grand Prize, €7,500), Grand Prix de la Biographie (€1,500, for historical biography), Prix de la Critique (€1,500, for literary criticism), Prix de l'Essai (€1,500, for essay), Prix du Théâtre (€1,500, for drama), and the Prix de la Nouvelle (€1,500, for short stories).

How to Apply: Two copies of the work should be sent by the author or publisher by 31 January.

Recent Winners: Grand Prix de Littérature: 2002: Milan Kundera
Grand Prix du Roman: 2002: Eric Neuhoff, *Un bien fou*
Grand Prix de Poésie: 2002: Alain Duault
Grand Prix de la Biographie: 2002: Simone Bertière, *Marie-Antoinette l'Insoumise*
Prix de la Critique: 2002: Pierre Jourde, *La Littérature sans estomac*
Prix de la Nouvelle: 2002: Mathieu Térence, *Les Filles de l'ombre*
Prix de l'Essai: 2002: Pierre Schneider, *Petite histoire de l'infini en peinture*
Prix du Théâtre: 2002: Jean-Michel Ribes.

Sponsoring Organization: Académie Française.

Address: Académie Française, Institut de France, 23 quai de Conti, 75006 Paris, France. **Telephone:** 1 44 41 43 00. **Fax:** 1 43 29 47 45. **Internet:** www.academie-francaise.fr. **E-mail:** contact@academie-francaise.fr.

Prix Littéraires du Ministère de la Jeunesse et des Sports
(Ministry of Youth and Sports Literary Awards)

A series of awards presented annually by the Ministry of Youth and Sports to encourage high-quality writing in French for young people and to discover new talent. Prizes are awarded in three categories: Young Novel (aimed at readers aged 10 to 14); Poetry for Young People; and the Prix Arthur Rimbaud, named after the French poet, for a collection of poetry by a young author (aged 18 to 25). The total prize money is €20,000.

How to Apply: Deadline for the novel category is early April; for poetry, early May.

Sponsoring Organization: Ministry of Youth and Sports.

Contact: Fabienne Coblence.

Address: Ministère de la Jeunesse et des Sports, 78 rue Olivier de Serres, 75739 Paris, Cedex 15, France. **Telephone:** 1 40 45 93 61. **Fax:** 1 40 45 92 92. **Internet:** www.jeunesse-sports.gouv.fr/ministere.

Prix Littéraires de la Société des Gens de Lettres (SDGL Literary Awards)

The Société des Gens de Lettres (SDGL) presents a series of prestigious annual awards for books in various fields including poetry, novel, art, history, and children's as well as two lifetime achievement awards. The prize money (including a number of grants) totals €75,000 each year, divided as follows: two lifetime achievement awards for a whole body of work (Grand Prix de Littérature and Grand Prix de Poésie), €7,000 each; Prix Paul Féval for popular literature and Prix de Poésie Louis Montalte: €3,000 each (see separate entries); Grand Prix Poncetton and Grand Prix Thyde Monnier: €3,000 each (see separate entries); Prix de Poésie Charles Vildrac: €1,500 (see separate entry); and prizes for a single work in each genre (novel, novella, essay, history, art, children's): €3,000 each. There are also separate prizes for multimedia and for websites.

Eligibility and Restrictions: Only published works are eligible; entries must have been published during the preceding year.

How to Apply: Five copies of entries should be sent to the address given by 31 March (spring session) or 15 October (autumn session).

Recent Winners: Complete body of work: 2002: Pierre Bergounioux
Poetry: 2002: Richard Rognet
Novel: 2002: Michel Vittoz, *L'Institut Giuliani*
Novella: 2002: Eric Holder, *Masculins, singuliers*
Essay: 2002: Roger Duchêne, *Les Précieuses*
Art: 2002: Pierre Schneider, *Petite histoire de l'infini en peinture*
History: 2002: Jean Nicolas, *La Rébellion française: mouvements populaires et conscience sociale, 1661–1779*
Children's: 2002: Virginie Lou and Joseph Périgot, *Les Pacom*
Multimedia: 2002: Philippe de Jonckheere, *Désordre*.

Sponsoring Organization: Société des Gens de Lettres (SDGL).

Address: Société des Gens de Lettres, Hôtel de Massa, 38 rue du Faubourg St Jacques, 75014 Paris, France. **Telephone:** 1 53 10 12 00. **Fax:** 1 53 10 12 12. **Internet:** www.sgdl.org. **E-mail:** sgdlf@wanadoo.fr.

Prix de littérature Émile Bernheim

The prize was established in 1959 by Émile Bernheim to promote Belgian literacy, with special emphasis on the humanist approach of the work. The prize is awarded every two years, and alternates between authors writing in French and Dutch. May be awarded for any literary genre – novel, drama, essay, criticism or poetry. The prize of €10,000 is awarded by a seven-member jury on the basis of a candidate's whole body of work.

Eligibility and Restrictions: Open to Belgian authors.

How to Apply: The jury reaches its decision independently, and no separate applications are sought.

Recent Winners: 2001: Christine D'Haen; 1999: Simon Leys; 1997: Hubert van Herreweghen; 1995: Fernand Verhesen; 1993: Paul de Wispelaere.

Sponsoring Organization: Fondation Bernheim.

Contact: Gen. Delegate Micheline Mardolyn.

Address: Fondation Bernheim, Place de l'Albertine 2, 1000 Brussels, Belgium. **Telephone:** (2) 213 1499. **Fax:** (2) 213 1795. **E-mail:** fondationbernheim@ online.be.

Prix du Livre Europe 1 (Europe 1 Book Prize)

This award, sponsored by the radio station Europe 1, recognizes a work of fiction which has not previously won any literary prizes. The winner receives €5,000, and also benefits from a two-week promotion campaign on the radio station. The winning entry is chosen by a jury made up of writers, booksellers and literary critics.

Recent Winners: 2002: Paula Jacques, *Gilda Stambouli souffre et se plaint*; 2001: Jean-Paul Enthoven, *Aurore*; 2000: Eric Fottorino, *Un territoire fragile*.

Sponsoring Organization: Europe 1.

Address: Europe 1, 26 bis, rue François 1er, 75008 Paris, France. **Telephone:** 1 820 31 90 00.

Prix du Livre Inter

Established in 1975 by Paul-Louis Mignon, the prize is awarded each year to a novel, with the winner chosen by vote among thousands of listeners to Radio France.

Recent Winners: 2002: Christian Gailly, *Un soir au club*; 2001: Laurent Mauvignier, *Apprendre à finir*; 2000: Antoine Volodine, *Des anges Mineurs*; 1999: Ahmadou Kourouma, *En attendant le vote des bêtes sauvages*; 1998: Martin Winckler, *La maladie de Sachs*.

Sponsoring Organization: Radio France.

Address: Radio France, 116 avenue du président Kennedy, 75220 Paris, cedex, France. **Internet:** www.radio-france.fr.

Prix du Livre Numérique NewsFam.com

An annual prize established in 2000 by the online news magazine *Newsfam.com* to recognize an outstanding contribution in book form in the field of news reporting. The winner is selected by a seven-member jury.

Recent Winners: 2001: Muna Hamzeh, *Jours ordinaires à Dheisheh*; 2000: Rouja Lazarova, *Cœurs Croisés*.

Sponsoring Organization: NewsFam.

Address: NewsFam.com, 18, rue du Faubourg du Temple, 75011 Paris, France. **Telephone:** 1 56 98 23 00. **Fax:** 1 56 98 23 07.

Prix du Livre de Picardie

An annual prize sponsored by the Conseil régional de Picardie for the year's best literary achievements in the Picardy region.

Recent Winners: 2000: Roger Wallet, *Portraits d'Automne*; 1998: Alain Trogneux.

Sponsoring Organization: Conseil régional de Picardie. Amiens, France. **Internet:** w2.amiens.com/jda/jda99/F_L_01.html.

Prix du Livre en Poitou-Charentes

A regional literary prize established by the Office du Livre in that region in 1987 to promote writing in Poitou-Charentes. Awarded each year to a title of exceptional quality with strong links to the region. The winner is chosen by a jury from a shortlist of five titles, and receives a prize of 25,000 francs (€3,750).

Eligibility and Restrictions: Open to works of literature in the genre of novels, poetry, drama, essay or cartoons. Entries must demonstrate a strong link to Poitou-Charentes, either through their author or publisher or their subject matter.

Recent Winners: 2001: Catherine Ternaux, *Olla-Podrida*; 2000: Georges Bonnet, *Un si bel été*; 1999: Jean-François Mathé, *Le Temps par moments*; 1998: Michel Boujut, *Le Jeune Homme en colère*; 1997: Raymond Bozier, *Lieu-dit*; 1996: La Galerie du Grand Écuyer, *L'Histoire de Troie au château d'Oiron*.

Sponsoring Organization: Office du Livre on Poitou-Charentes.

Address: Office du Livre on Poitou-Charentes, 14, rue Boncenne, 86000 Poitiers, France. **Telephone:** 5 49 88 33 60. **Fax:** 5 49 88 80 04.

Prix des Maisons de la Presse

A prize established in 1970 to recognize works with a broad appeal in the categories of novel or document, which have appeared during the preceding year. The winning works receive an advertising campaign in the national press.

Recent Winners: Document: 2002: Simone Berthière, *Marie Antoinette, l'insoumise*; 2001: Le Monde, *Il était minuit cinq à Bhopal*; 2000: Georges Coulonges, *L'été du grand bonheur*; 1999: Malika Oufkir and Michèle Fitoussi, *La prisonnière* Novel: 2002: Paul Couturiau, *Le Paravent de soie rouge*.

Sponsoring Organization: Syndicat national des dépositaires de presse.

Address: Syndicat national des dépositaires de presse, Paris, France.

Prix Médicis

Established in 1958, the Prix Médicis, recognized as one of the main French literary awards, aims to reflect contemporary literary trends. The winner is chosen by a jury of literary figures.

Recent Winners: 2001: Benoît Duteurtre, *Le Voyage en France*; 2000: Yann Apperry, *Diabolus in Musica*; 1999: Christian Oster, *Mon grand appartement*; 1998: Homeric, *Le Loup mongol*; 1997: Philippe Le Guillou, *Les sept noms du peintre*.

Sponsoring Organization: Association pour la Promotion des Prix Médicis.

Contact: Pres Francine Mallet.

Address: 25 rue Dombasle, 75015 Paris, France. **Telephone:** 1 48 28 76 90.

Prix Médicis de l'Essai (Médicis Essay Prize)

Awarded each autumn to an essay in French. The winner is selected by a jury.

Eligibility and Restrictions: Essays written in French and published in the year of the award are eligible.

How to Apply: One copy of entries should be sent to each member of the jury.

Recent Winners: 2001: Edwy Plenel, *Secrets de jeunesse*; 1999: Christine Jordis, *Gens de la Tamise et d'autres rivages*; 1998: Alberto Manguel, *Une histoire de la lecture*; 1997: Michel Winock, *Le Siècle des intellectuels*; 1996: Viviane Forrester, *L'horreur économique.*

Sponsoring Organization: Association pour la Promotion des Prix Médicis.

Contact: Pres Francine Mallet.

Address: 25 rue Dombasle, 75015 Paris, France. **Telephone:** 1 48 28 76 90.

Prix Médicis Etranger (Médicis Prize for Foreign Fiction)

Awarded each autumn to a novel which has been translated into French. The winner is selected by a jury.

Eligibility and Restrictions: Open to foreign novels which have appeared in translation in France during the previous year.

How to Apply: One copy of entries should be sent to each member of the jury.

Recent Winners: 2001: Antonio Skármeta, *La noce du poète*; 2000: Michael Ondaatje, *Le Fantôme d'Anil*; 1999: Björn Larsson, *Le capitaine et les rêves*; 1998: Jonathan Coe, *La maison du sommeil*; 1997: T. C. Boyle, *América* 1996: Michael Kruger, *Himmelfalb* and Ludmila Oulitskaia, *Sonietchka* (joint winners); 1995: Alessandro Baricco, *Châteaux de la colère.*

Sponsoring Organization: Association pour la Promotion des Prix Médicis.

Contact: Pres Francine Mallet.

Address: 25 rue Dombasle, 75015 Paris, France. **Telephone:** 1 48 28 76 90.

Prix Méditerranée (Mediterranean Literature Prize)

Established in 1985. The prize is awarded by an eminent jury composed of eminent literary personalities. Since 1993, it has become a tradition for the French Minister of Culture to be present at the prize-giving. The prize carries an award of 50,000 francs (€7,500).

Recent Winners: 2001: Edmonde-Charles Roux, *L'homme de Marseille*; 2000: Albert Cossery, *Les couleurs de l'infamie*; 1997: Jean-Christophe Ruffin, *L'abyssin*; 1996: Hector Bianchetti, *Ce que la nuit raconte au jour*; 1994: Tahar Ben Jelloun, *L'homme rompu.*

Sponsoring Organization: Centre for Mediterranean Literature (CML).

Contact: President André Bonet.

Address: Centre for Mediterranean Literature (CML), bis, rue Grande des Fabriques, 66 000 Perpignan, France. **Telephone:** 4 68 51 10 10. **Fax:** 4 68 51 42 44. **Internet:** www.mairie-perpignan.fr/.

Prix Méditerranée étranger (Mediterranean Prize for Foreign Novels)

Awarded each year in May for the best foreign novel to appear in France during the previous year.

Recent Winners: 2002: Umberto Eco, *Baudolino*; 2001: Arturo Perez-Reverte, *Le cimetière des bateaux sans nom.*

Sponsoring Organization: Centre for Mediterranean Literature (CML).

Address: Centre for Mediterranean Literature (CML), bis, rue Grande des Fabriques, 66 000 Perpignan, France. **Telephone:** 4 68 51 10 10. **Fax:** 4 68 51 42 44. **Internet:** www.mairie-perpignan.fr/.

Prix du Meilleur Livre Etranger (Prize for the Best Foreign Book)

An annual prize created in 1948 to celebrate the best foreign works published in France during the year. The jury is made up of literary figures. There is no cash prize.

Recent Winners: 2002: Enrique Vila Matas (Catalonia), *Bartleby et Cie*, Orhan Pamuk (Turkey), *Mon nom est Rouge* and J. M. Coetzee (South Africa), *Disgrâce*; earlier winners include Robert Musil, John Updike, Gabriel García Márquez, Mario Vargas Llosa, Guillermo Cabrera Infante and Elias Canetti.

Address: 24 rue de Oudinot, 75007 Paris, France.

Prix Arthur Merghelynck

A biennial prize, created in 1995 and worth €2,500, for a work in the field of genealogy and family history.

Recent Winners: 2001: (not yet awarded); 1999: M. J. Legge.

Sponsoring Organization: Koninklijke Academie voor Nederlandse Taal- en Letterkunde.

Address: Koninklijke Academie voor Nederlandse Taal- en Letterkunde, Koningstraat 18, 9000 Ghent, Belgium. **Internet:** www.cfwb.be/arb/FondationsL.htm.

Prix Jean Monnet de littérature européenne (Jean Monnet European Literature Prize)

A prize created in 1995 by the Cognac-based Salon de la Littérature Européenne (European Literature Forum), to recognize an outstanding novel written in French (or translated into French) during the previous year. The prize is 50,000 francs (€7,622.45).

Recent Winners: 2001: Jorge Semprun, *Le Mort qu'il faut*; 2000: Lidia Jorge (Portugal), *La couverture du soldat*; 1999: Harry Mulisch (Netherlands), *La découverte du Ciel*; 1998: Herbjorg Wassmo (Norway), *Ciel cruel*; 1997: Arturo Perez-Reverte (Spain), *La peau du tambour*.

Sponsoring Organization: Conseil Général de la Charente.

Address: Salon de la Littérature Européenne, 59 rue Aristide Briand, 16100 Cognac, France. **Telephone:** 5 45 82 88 01. **Fax:** 5 45 36 00 48. **Internet:** www.ville-cognac.fr/subfr/litterature/prix.htm.

Prix National des Bibliothécaires (National Booksellers Prize)

An award established in 1980, which has acquired considerable prestige on the French literary scene. It is awarded for a novel published during the last year, with the winning title selected from a shortlist of six by a jury of 7,000 booksellers.

Recent Winners: 2002: Pierrette Fleutiaux, *Des phrases courtes, ma chérie*; 2001: Eric Fottorino, *Un territoire fragile*; 2000: Jean-Claude Izzo, *Le Soleil des mourants*.

Sponsoring Organization: Union Nationale Culture et Bibliothèques pour Tous.

Address: Union Nationale Culture et Bibliothèques pour Tous, 18 bis, rue Violet, 75015 Paris, France. **Telephone:** 1 58 01 10 20. **Fax:** 1 58 01 10 21. **E-mail:** uncbpt.services@wanadoo.fr.

Prix Nautile de Cristal

Established in 1994 by the Salon du Livre de Troyes and Agence Nationale pour la Gestion des Déchets Radioactifs (ANDRA) to reward a work of non-fiction for children aged between 8 and 12. The prize money of €800 is underwritten by ANDRA.

Eligibility and Restrictions: Book must be published during the previous year (year ending 30 April).

How to Apply: Publishers or authors may apply by sending one copy to the address given.

Recent Winners: 2001: Michèle Mira-Pons, *Les aliments à petits pas*; 2000: Richard Platt and Chris Riddell, *Le journal de Geoffroy, un page au Moyen-Age*; 1999: Béatrice Fontanel, *Monstres, l'encyclopèdie des animaux les plus moches*; 1998: Walter Wick, *Gouttes d'eau*; 1997: Albert Lorenz, *Métropoles, dix villes, dix siècles*.

Sponsoring Organization: Salon Régional du Livre de Jeunesse de Troyes/ Agence Nationale pour la Gestion des Déchets Radioactifs (ANDRA).

Address: Salon Régional du Livre de Jeunesse de Troyes, 42 rue Paillot-de-Montabert, 10000 Troyes, France. **Telephone:** 3 25 73 14 43. **Fax:** 3 25 73 91 26. **Internet:** perso.wanadoo.fr/salondelivre.troyes. **E-mail:** slj.troyes@ wanadoo.fr.

Prix Émile-Nelligan

Established in 1979 in memory of the poet Émile Nelligan, the prize is awarded every spring and consists of a grant of $C5,000 and a medal.

Eligibility and Restrictions: Open to works of poetry published during the previous year by an author aged less than 35 years.

Recent Winners: 2000: Jean-Éric Riopel, *Papillons réfractaires*; 1999: Tony Tremblay, *Rue Pétrole-Océan*; 1997: Patrick Lafontaine, *L'Ambition du vide*; 1996: Carle Coppens, *Poèmes contre la montre*.

Sponsoring Organization: Secrétariat du Prix Émile-Nelligan.

Address: Secrétariat du Prix Émile-Nelligan, c/o Union des écrivaines et écrivains québécois, 3492 ave Laval, Montreal, PQ H2X 3C8, Canada.

Prix Gérard de Nerval

An annual prize of €3,000 awarded for translation of a German work into French. The winner is selected by a jury of 24 writers. The prize is twinned with the Paul Celan Preis (qv) for translation into German, which is awarded by a German jury.

Sponsoring Organization: Société des Gens de Lettres de France.

Address: Société des Gens de Lettres de France, Hôtel de Massa, 38 rue du Faubourg St Jacques, 75014 Paris, France. **Telephone:** 1 53 10 12 00. **Fax:** 1 53 10 12 12. **Internet:** www.sgdl.org. **E-mail:** sgdlf@wanadoo.fr.

Prix Octogone du livre de jeunesse (Octogone Prize for a Children's Book)

An annual prize established to recognize the best in literature aimed at children from birth to 13 years, created by the Centre International d'Etudes en Littérature de Jeunesse (CIELJ). A shortlist is drawn up by a reading committee, which is then opened to popular vote for a month via the Ricochet website (www.ricochet-jeunes.org). Winning works are selected for their use of complementary text and image. Prizes are awarded in eight categories (picture books, pre-school, poetry, short stories, non-fiction, novel, illustration and international illustration).

Eligibility and Restrictions: Works must have appeared during the previous year.

Recent Winners: Novel/prose: 2000: Alice Vieira, *Les yeux d'Ana Marta* and Laura Jaffé, *Poussière d'ange* (joint winners)
Non-fiction:2000: François Michel and Marc Boutavant (illustrator), *L'écologie à petits pas*
Poetry: 2000: Jean-Marie Henry, *Le tireur de langue*
Short story: 2000: Marie Sellier and Marion Lesage (illustrator), *L'Afrique Petit Chaka*
Pre-School: 2000: Voutch, *Pourquôôôa*
Illustration: 2000: Annick Tandavarayen, *Mon Tout Petit*.

Sponsoring Organization: Centre International d'Etudes en Littérature de Jeunesse—Ricochet.

Address: Centre International d'Etudes en Littérature de Jeunesse—Ricochet, Charleville-Mézières, France. **Internet:** asp.ricochet-jeunes.org/octogones01/octogone.htm.

Prix Littéraire du Parlement de la Communauté Française de Belgique

Awarded every year since 1975 to the author of a book illustrating the feelings of the French community in Belgium or its cultural heritage. The prize rotates between four genres: novel, poetry, drama and essay. The winner receives a prize of €3,718.5 (150,000 Belgian francs).

Eligibility and Restrictions: Open to works both unpublished and published; authors must be of Belgian nationality or have lived in Belgium for five years. Entries must have appeared during the last two years and must not have received any other literary award.

How to Apply: Five copies should be submitted by 1 February.

Recent Winners: Previous winners include: Gaston Compère, Marcel Lobet, Pierre Mertens, Charles Bertin, André Schmitz, Guy Goffette, Raymond Trousson, Liliane Wouters, William Cliff, Anne Richter and André-Marcel Adamek.

Sponsoring Organization: Parlement de la Communauté Française de Belgique.

Contact: M. Schumacher.

Address: Parlement de la Communauté Française, Rue de la Loi 6, 1000 Brussels, Belgium. **Telephone:** (2) 506 38 19.

Prix Pelléas

An annual award created in 1997 to reward a work of high literary quality in the field of music. It is presented every year at the famous Café des Deux Magots in Paris. The winner is chosen by a nine-member jury.

Recent Winners: 2001: Brina Svit, *Mort d'une prima donna slovène*; 2000: Philippe Beaussant, *Stradella*; 1999: Bruno Monsaingeon; 1998: Benoit Duteurtre; 1997: Laurent de Wilde.

Address: Café des Deux Magots, 6 place Saint Germain des Près, 75006 Paris, France. **Internet:** www.lesdeuxmagots.fr. **E-mail:** cmathivat@free.fr.

Prix de Poésie Louis Montalte

An annual prize of €3,000 awarded by the Société des Gens de Lettres for a complete body of work in the field of poetry. The winner is selected by a jury of 24 writers.

How to Apply: Five copies of works should sent by 15 October.

Recent Winners: 2001: Jean-Pierre Milovanoff.

Sponsoring Organization: Société des Gens de Lettres de France.

Address: Société des Gens de Lettres de France, Hôtel de Massa, 38 rue du Faubourg St Jacques, 75014 Paris, France. **Telephone:** 1 53 10 12 00. **Fax:** 1 53 10 12 12. **Internet:** www.sgdl.org. **E-mail:** sgdlf@wanadoo.fr.

Prix Polar

Established in 1998 to recognize the best writing in the field of crime novels. The award also aims to foster meetings between writers and their readers. The prize is presented in two categories: crime novels for adults, and for children. The winners are selected by a panel of experts (writers, critics, journalists, teachers, librarians, etc.) and each receive a prize of €1,500.

Eligibility and Restrictions: Open to works of fiction in the field of crime novels, either for adults or for children. Entries must have been published in the preceding calendar year (year ending June), and must be written in French.

How to Apply: Two copies of the entry should be submitted to the address given.

Recent Winners: Best Crime Novel: 2001: Jean Paul Nozière, *Trois petites mortes*; 2000: Thierry Serfaty, *Le sang des sirènes*
Best Crime Novel for Children: 2001: Xavier-Laurent Petit, *L'homme du jardin*.

Contact: Jean-Michel Pieuchon.

Address: Salon du Polar de Montigny-les-Cormeilles, Centre Picasso, Rue Guy de Maupassant, 95379 Montigny-les-Cormeilles, France. **Telephone:** 1 30 26 30 50. **Fax:** 1 30 26 30 59. **E-mail:** culture.montigny@wanadoo.fr.

Prix Edouard Privat

An annual prize for a work of historical literature, jointly sponsored by the newspaper *Dépêche du Midi*, the radio station Sud Radio and a publishing company, les Editions Privat. The latter undertakes to publish the winning entry.

Eligibility and Restrictions: Open to young writers in the field of history (whether international, French or more specific to the South of France) for a scholarly work showing originality and rich historical content. Novels and poetry are excluded. Entries should be between 100 and 150 pages in length.

Sponsoring Organization: La Dépêche du Midi/Sud Radio/les Editions Privat.

Address: Editions Privat, BP 828, 31080 Toulouse, Cedex 6, France. **Telephone:** 5 61 11 03 22. **Fax:** 5 61 13 74 41.

Prix Théophraste Renaudot

An annual award for a novel presented at the same time as the Prix Goncourt. The prize was established in 1926 by a group of journalists attending the Goncourt ceremony, who wanted to create an alternative prize. It is named after Théophraste Renaudot, a friend of Richelieu credited with establishing the first French newspaper. The winner is chosen by a ten-member jury, all of whom are journalists. There is no cash prize.

Recent Winners: 2001: Martine Le Coz, *Céleste*; 2000: Ahmadou Kourouma, *Allah n'est pas obligé*; 1999: Daniel Picouly, *L'Enfant léopard*; 1998: Dominique Bona, *Le Manuscrit de Port-Ebène*; 1997: Pascal Bruckner, *Les Voleurs de beauté*.

Address: c/o Drouant, place Gaillon, 75002 Paris, France. **Internet:** www.renaudot.com.

Prix RFI–témoin du monde

The prize was established in 1997 by the broadcaster Radio France International to reward a work of documentation or fiction that sheds a special light on a major issue in current affairs or culture. The winner is chosen by a jury made up leading journalists and writers, and receives an award of 25,000 francs (€3,850), as well as publicity from a major press campaign in varous media.

Eligibility and Restrictions: The award is made to a book published during the previous year (priority is given to French-language countries).

How to Apply: No direct application; a shortlist is drawn up by RFI's literary journalists.

Recent Winners: 2002: Gillian Slovo, *Poussière rouge*; 2000: Youri Rytkhéou, *Unna*.

Sponsoring Organization: Radio France International.

Address: RFI, avenue du Président-Kennedy, 75016 Paris, France. **Internet:** www.rfi.fr/Radio_Mondiale/Autres_Services/CONCOURS/decouvlitteraire.html.

Prix Roberval

Annual prize to recognize excellence in technical writing. Two literary awards are offered, the Prix Grand Public and the Prix Enseignement Supérieur (Higher Education Prize), as well as two other categories, Television and Multimedia.

How to Apply: Candidates should apply by e-mail or fax to the address above, giving their details, title of the work and relevant category. After receiving the appropriate entry form they should return this with copies of the work.

Recent Winners: Prix Grand Public: 2000: Bertrand Jordan, *Les imposteurs de la génétique*; 1999: Jacques Villain, *À la conquête de la lune*;1998: Pierre Barboza, *Les nouvelles images*; 1997: Jean and Nicole Dhombres, *Lazare Carnot*; 1996: Michel Rival, *Les apprentis sorciers*

Prix Enseignement Supérieur: 2000: Michel-Claude Girard and Colette-Marie Girard, *Traitement des données de télédétection*; 1999: Claude Flanzy (Editor), *Oenologie: fondements scientifiques et technologiques*; 1998: Étienne Guyon and Jean-Pierre Hulin, *Granites et fumées: un peu d'ordre dans le mélange*; 1997: Henri Heslot, *L'ingénierie des protéines et ses application*; 1996: André Fortin, *Analyse numérique pour ingénieurs*.

Sponsoring Organization: Conseil général de l'Oise et l'Université de Technologie de Compiègne. Paris, France. **Fax:** 1 44 23 52 19. **Internet:** prixroberval.utc.fr. **E-mail:** prix.roberval@utc.fr.

Prix Roman Historique de Blois (Blois Historical Novel Prize)

Established in 1998 and presented to a historical novel in October each year during the Rendez-vous de l'histoire festival. The winner is chosen by a panel of readers, made up of journalists, history teachers, critics, etc., and receives a prize of €3,000.

Eligibility and Restrictions: Open to historical novels in French; must have been published during the previous year (to end June).

How to Apply: Publishers may submit one or two novels to the jury; each member of the jury nominates one entry.

Recent Winners: 2001: David Haziot, *Le vin de la liberté*; 2000: Eric Deschot and Jean-Claude Lattés, *Le seul amant*; 1999: Jacques Baudouin, *Le mandarin blanc*; 1998: Gérard de Cortanze, *Les vice-rois*.

Contact: Helene Renard.

Address: Les Rendez-vous de l'histoire, 3 quai Abbé-Grégoire, 4100 Blois, France. **Telephone:** 2 54 56 13 53. **Fax:** 2 54 90 09 50. **Internet:** www.rdv-histoire.com. **E-mail:** rdv.histoire.blois@wanadoo.fr.

Prix Rosny-Aîné

Awarded since 1980 during the French Science Fiction Convention. Separate prizes are awarded for novels and short stories.

Recent Winners: Novels: 1999: Jean-Marc Ligny, *Jihad*; 1998: Roland C. Wagner, *L'Odyssée de l'espèce*; 1997: Serge Lehman, *F.A.U.S.T.*; 1996: Maurice Dantec, *Les Racines du mal*; 1995 Richard Canal, *Aube noire*
Short stories: 1999: Jean-Jacques Nguyen, *L'amour au temps de silicium*; 1998: Jean-Claude Dunyach, *Dechiffrer la trame*; 1997: Roland C. Wagner, *H.P.L.*; 1996: Serge Delsemme, *Voyage organisé*; 1995: Serge Lehman, *Dans l'abîme*.

Address: Paris, France.

Prix Victor-Rossel

The prize was established in 1938 by the newspaper *Le Soir* in memory of the son of its founder. The prize recognises a Belgian novel or collection of short stories. The prize, one of the major Belgian literary awards, is adjudicated by a jury. The winner receives 200,000 Belgian francs (€4,957).

Recent Winners: 1999: Daniel de Bruycker, *Silex*.

Sponsoring Organization: Le Soir.

Address: Le Soir, rue Royale 112, 1000 Brussels, Belgium. **Internet:** www. francophonie.philo.ulg.ac.be/CWB.Rossel.

Prix Baron de Saint-Genois

One of a number of awards presented by the Belgian Royal Academy, the Prix Baron de Saint-Genois was established in 1867 and is worth €1,250. It is awarded every five years for a recent work in Dutch on the subject of history or literature. The winner holds the title for a five-year period.

Recent Winners: 1996–2000: M. S. Vanderputten..

Sponsoring Organization: Académie Royale de Belgique.

Contact: Jean-Luc De Paepe.

Address: Académie Royale de Belgique, Palais des Académies, 1 rue Ducale, 1000 Brussels, Belgium. **Telephone:** (2) 550 22 11. **Fax:** (2) 550 22 05. **Internet:** www.cfwb.be/arb/Fondations.

Prix Saint Valentin

Awarded for best work of the year on the theme of 'l'amour' (love). Entries may be essays, documents or novels. The winner is selected by a 14-member jury.

Recent Winners: 2002: Thierry Luterbacher, *Un cerisier dans l'escalier*; 2000: Yann Andréa, *Cet amour-là*.

Sponsoring Organization: Académie Saint Valentin.

Address: 22 rue Lehot, 92600 Asnière-sur-Seine, France. **Telephone:** 6 70 06 47 21. **Internet:** www.prixsaintvalentin.com.

Prix Claude Sernet

An award established in 1976 by Jean Digot to recognize foreign poets writing in French. The winner is chosen by a jury of poets and members of the Association des Ecrivains du Rouerque (Writers' Association of Rouerque), and receives a prize of €800.

Eligibility and Restrictions: Open to works of poetry written in French by non-French writers. Works must have been published at least two years before the year of application.

How to Apply: Four copies of the entry should be sent to the address given by 1 March each year, accompanied by biographical details.

Recent Winners: 2001: Brigitte Gyr, *Avant je vous voyais en noir et blanc*; 2000: Jamel Edine Bencheikh, *L'aveugle au visage grêle*; 1999: Jeng N. Woo, *Blanchement*; 1998: Martin Ziegler, *Vitres griffées éteintes*; 1997: Denitza Bantcheva, *L'instant sur les ogives*.

Sponsoring Organization: Association des Ecrivains du Rouerque.

Contact: Danielle Fenion.

Address: Association des Ecrivains du Rouerque, BP 307, 12003 Rodez, Cedex, France. **Telephone:** 5 65 42 47 80. **Internet:** perso.wanadoo.fr/d.f/journeepoesie.html. **E-mail:** danielle.fenion@wanadoo.fr.

Prix Sorcières

An annual prize established in 1986 in recognition of the children's books considered by booksellers and librarians to have had the most impact during the year. Prizes are awarded in six categories.

Recent Winners: Pre-school: 2002: Ruth Brown, *Dix petites graines*; 2001: Voutch, *Pourquôôâa*; 2000: Antonin Louchard and Katy Couprie, *Tout un monde*; 1999: Christian Bruel, *Alboum*
Picture book: 2002: David Wiesner, *Les Trois Cochons*; 2001: Peter Sis, *Madlenka*; 2000: Michael Morpurgo, *La sagesse de Wombat*; 1999: Anthony Browne, *Une histoire à quatre voix*
Early Readers (8–9 years): 2002: Hubert Benkemoun and François Roca (illustrator), *Terriblement vert*; 2001: Stéphane Girel (illustrator), *Côté cœur*; 2000: Susie Morgenstern and Mireille d'Allancé (illustrator), *Joker*; 1999: Thierry Lenain, *Mademoiselle Zazie a t-elle un zizi ?*
Junior (9–12 years): 2002: Sylvie Weil, *Le Mazal d'Elvina*; 2001: Michael Morpurgo and François Place (illustrator), *Le royaume de Kensuke*; 2000: Jean-Claude Mourlevat, *L'enfant Océan*; 1999: J. K. Rowling, *Harry Potter à l'école des sorciers*
Teenage novel: 2002: Anne-Lise Grobéry, *Le Temps des mots à voix basse*; 2001: Louis Sachar, *Le passage*; 2000: Malika Ferdjoukh, *Sombres citrouilles*; 1999: Janine Teisson, *Au cinéma Lux*
Non-fiction: 2002: *Mondes rebelles junior*; 2001: Marie Sellier and Marion Lesage (illustrator), *L'Afrique, petit Chaka*; 2000: Chrystel Proupuech, *Yapa le petit aborigène d'Australie*; 1999: Pef, *Zappe la guerre*.

Sponsoring Organization: Association des librairies spécialisées jeunesse/ Association des bibliothécaires français.

Address: Association des Bibliothécaires Français, 31 rue de Chabrol, 75010 Paris, France. **Telephone:** 1 55 33 10 30. **Internet:** www.abf.asso.fr/ prixsorcieres/. **E-mail:** abf@abf.asso.fr.

Prix Auguste Teirlinck

One of a number of awards presented by the Belgian Royal Academie, the Prix Auguste Teirlinck was established in 1907 and is worth €1,250. It is awarded every five years for a recent work of literature in Dutch. The winner holds the title for a five-year period.

Recent Winners: 1996–2000: M. D. Cumps.

Sponsoring Organization: Académie Royale de Belgique.

Contact: Jean-Luc De Paepe.

Address: Académie Royale de Belgique, Palais des Académies, 1 rue Ducale, 1000 Brussels, Belgium. **Telephone:** (2) 550 22 11. **Fax:** (2) 550 22 05. **Internet:** www.cfwb.be/arb/Fondations.

Prix Tibet

Established in 1987 by the Association Lecture et Loisirs (Reading and Leisure Association) to reward a children's comic strip book. The prize money of €1,500 is underwritten by the Conseil Général de l'Aube.

Eligibility and Restrictions: Book must be published during the previous year (year ending 30 April). Author and illustrator must be French-speaking.

How to Apply: Publishers or authors may apply by sending one copy to the address given.

Recent Winners: 2001: Tatiana Domas and Denis-Pierre Filippi, *Theo – le jardin de Grand-mère*; 2000: Yann Degruel, *Genz Gys Khan au pays du vent*.

Sponsoring Organization: Salon Régional du Livre de Jeunesse de Troyes/ Conseil Général de l'Aube.

Address: Salon Régional du Livre de Jeunesse de Troyes, 42 rue Paillot-de-Montabert, 10000 Troyes, France. **Telephone:** 3 25 73 14 43. **Fax:** 3 25 73 91 26. **Internet:** perso.wanadoo.fr/salondelivre.troyes. **E-mail:** slj.troyes@ wanadoo.fr.

Prix Tour-Eiffel de Science-Fiction (Eiffel Tower Science Fiction Prize)

An annual prize established in 1997 and presented for a novel in the field of science fiction. The winner is chosen by a 30-member jury (booksellers, publishers and librarians), and receives a prize of 100,000 francs (€15,000). The prize alternates between a French writer and a foreign writer whose work has been translated into French.

Eligibility and Restrictions: Entries must have been published in France during the previous two years.

Recent Winners: 2001: Jean-Marc Ligny and Mandy (illustrator), *Les oiseaux de lumières*.

Sponsoring Organization: Société Nouvelle d'Exploitation de la Tour Eiffel (SNTE).

Address: Société Nouvelle d'Exploitation de la Tour Eiffel, Champ de Mars, 75007 Paris, France. **Telephone:** 1 44 11 23 11. **Internet:** www.tour-eiffel.fr/ teiffel/fr/documentation/dossiers/page/science_fiction.html.

Prix Tropiques de l'Agence Française de Développement

The Prix Tropiques is awarded annually for a work in the French language focusing on any aspect of development in the countries where the Agence Française de Développement (AFD) operates: Africa, Asia, the Caribbean, the Mediterranean, the Pacific, and the French Overseas Departments and Territories. The winner receives a prize of €4,575. In exceptional cases the judges may award an additional special prize of €3,050.

Recent Winners: 2001: Ryszard Kapuściński, *Ebène*; 2000: Boualen Sansal, *Le serment des barbares*; 1998: Ahmadou Kourouma, *En attendant le vote des bêtes sauvages*.

Sponsoring Organization: Agence Française de Développement.

Address: Agence Française de Développement (AFD), 5, rue Roland Barthes, 75598 Paris, Cedex 12, France. **Telephone:** 1 53 44 31 31. **Fax:** 1 44 87 99 39. **Internet:** www.afd.fr.

Prix Tristan Tzara de Traduction

A biennial prize of €1,500 awarded for translation of a Hungarian work into French. The winner is selected by a jury of 24 writers. The prize is twinned with the Gyula Illyes prize (qv) for translation into Hungarian, which is awarded by a Hungarian jury.

Sponsoring Organization: Société des Gens de Lettres de France.

Address: Société des Gens de Lettres de France, Hôtel de Massa, 38 rue du Faubourg St Jacques, 75014 Paris, France. **Telephone:** 1 53 10 12 00. **Fax:** 1 53 10 12 12. **Internet:** www.sgdl.org. **E-mail:** sgdlf@wanadoo.fr.

Prix Paul Verlaine

An annual poetry prize, named after the well-known French poet, and awarded by the Académie Française. The winner receives a silver medal.

Eligibility and Restrictions: Open to living authors of all ages; only published works may be submitted, and they must have appeared during the preceding year.

How to Apply: Two copies of the work should be sent by the author or publisher by 31 January.

Recent Winners: 2001: Philippe Chaunac-Lanzac, *Gravé dans l'éphémère*.

Sponsoring Organization: Académie Française.

Address: Académie Française, Institut de France, 23 quai de Conti, 75006 Paris, France. **Telephone:** 1 44 41 43 00. **Fax:** 1 43 29 47 45. **Internet:** www.academie-francaise.fr. **E-mail:** contact@academie-francaise.fr.

Prix Bernard Versele

An annual prize for children's literature established in 1979 in memory of Bernard Versele, a psychologist who worked with children. It is awarded for the best children's books from the previous year; the winning entries are chosen by a jury of thousands of children aged from 3 to 14 years. Winners are selected in five categories, from 1 chouette (one owl, for the youngest children) up to 5 chouettes (five owls, for older children).

Recent Winners: 1 chouette winner: 2002: Jules Feiffer, *Aboie, Georges*
2 chouettes winner: 2002: Jim Ayleswort, Wendy A. Halperin (illustrator), *Le bol magique*
3 chouettes winner: 2002: Pascal Teulade, J-C. Sarrazin (illustrator), *Bonjour Madame la Mort*
4 chouettes winner: 2002: Geneviève Brisac, *Monelle et les footballeurs*
5 chouettes winner: 2002: Michael Morpurgo, *Le royaume de Kensuke*.

Sponsoring Organization: Ligue des Familles.

Address: Ligue des Familles, Rue du Trône 127, 1050 Brussels, Belgium. **Telephone:** (2) 507 72 64. **Fax:** (2) 507 72 24. **Internet:** www.liguedesfamilles.be/vl/index.asp. **E-mail:** prix.versele@liguedesfamilles.be.

Prix Amerigo Vespucci

A prize established in 1990 to recognize an outstanding work in the field of travel or adventure. The award takes place alongside the annual Festival International de Géographie at Saint-Dié-des-Vosges. The winner receives a prize of €2,300 (15,087 francs).

Eligibility and Restrictions: Entries must have been published in French during the preceding year (year ending 15 July).

How to Apply: Fifteen copies of each entry should be submitted by 15 July.

Recent Winners: 2001: Jean-Luc Coatelem, *Je suis dans les mers du Sud, sur les traces de Paul Gauguin*; 2000: Ahmadou Kourouma, *Allah n'est pas obligé*; 1999: Gilles Lapouge, *Besoin de mirages*; 1998: Gisèle Pineau, *L'Âme prêtée aux oiseaux*; 1997: Éric Fottorino, *Coeur d'Afrique*.

Sponsoring Organization: Festival International de Géographie de Saint-Dié-des-Vosges.

Address: Secrétariat des Prix littéraires, Festival International de Géographie de Saint-Dié-des-Vosges, Hôtel de Ville, B. P. 275, 88107 Saint-Dié-des-Vosges,

Cedex, France. **Telephone:** 3 29 52 66 78. **Fax:** 3 29 56 09 31. **Internet:** www.wsf.fr/ecrivosges/prix_amerigo-vespucci.htm.

Prix Charles Vildrac de la Poésie

An annual prize of €1,500 awarded by the Société des Gens de Lettres for a published collection of poetry. The winner is selected by a jury of 24 writers.

Eligibility and Restrictions: Entries must have been published during the previous year.

How to Apply: Five copies of works should sent by 31 March.

Sponsoring Organization: Société des Gens de Lettres de France.

Address: Société des Gens de Lettres de France, Hôtel de Massa, 38 rue du Faubourg St Jacques, 75014 Paris, France. **Telephone:** 1 53 10 12 00. **Fax:** 1 53 10 12 12. **Internet:** www.sgdl.org. **E-mail:** sgdlf@wanadoo.fr.

Prix Voronca

An annual prize established in 1954 and given to works of poetry. The winner is chosen by a panel of poets and members of the Association des Ecrivains du Rouerque (Writers' Association of Rouerque). The winning entry is published in a special volume by Editions Jacques Bremond.

Eligibility and Restrictions: Open to works of poetry written in French, of up to 48 pages.

How to Apply: Two copies of the manuscript should be sent to the address given by 1 March each year, accompanied by submission payment and biographical details.

Recent Winners: 2001: Marlena Braester, *Oublier Avant*; 2000: Stephen Bertrand, *Ici la belle et immense table de la Pampa*; 1999: Marie Christine Gayffier, *Dans l'atelier*; 1998: Marie Mailat, *Klotho*; 1997: Marie Christine Masset, *L'Embrassée*.

Sponsoring Organization: Association des Ecrivains du Rouerque.

Contact: Danielle Fenion.

Address: Association des Ecrivains du Rouerque, BP 307, 12003 Rodez, Cedex, France. **Telephone:** 5 65 42 47 80. **Internet:** perso.wanadoo.fr/d.f/journeepoesie.html. **E-mail:** danielle.fenion@wanadoo.fr.

Prix Wepler–Fondation La Poste

An annual prize which seeks to reward works demonstrating a lively contemporary feel regardless of marketing pressures and commercial influences. The winner is chosen by a jury of members who are not associated with the Parisian literary scene.

Recent Winners: 2001: Yves Pagès, *Le Théoriste*; 2000: Laurent Mauvignier, *Apprendre à finir*.

Sponsoring Organization: Fondation La Poste.

Address: Fondation La Poste, Fondation de France, 40 ave Hoche, 75008 Paris, France. **Internet:** www.fondationlaposte.org/observatoire.cfm?action=LISTE_ARTICLES&rubrique=42.

Pulitzer Prizes in Journalism, Letters, Drama and Music

The famous Pulitzer Prizes were established in 1917 following a bequest from Joseph Pulitzer, a Hungarian-born journalist and pioneering publisher of American newspapers. The first Pulitzer Prizes were awarded in 1917 as an 'incentive to excellence'. The original bequest specified four awards in journalism, four in letters and drama, one for education, and four travel scholarships, but the Pulitzer Prize Board has since increased the number to 21 and introduced awards for poetry, music, and photography. The winners are chosen by an advisory board comprising newspaper publishers, the President of Columbia University and scholars; each winner receives a prize of $7,500.

Eligibility and Restrictions: In the category of 'Letters' (literature) awards are made in the fields of fiction, non-fiction and poetry, as well as biography/ autobiography, drama and history. Entries must be published during the previous calendar year. Only US writers are considered except in the history category where author may be of any nationality as long as the book deals with American history. Fiction awards are made preferably to books dealing with American life.

How to Apply: Four copies of the book should be submitted accompanied by a completed entry form (available from website or postal address given) and a $50 entry fee, by 1 November.

Recent Winners: Fiction: 2002: Richard Russo, *Empire Falls*; 2001: Michael Chabon, *The Amazing Adventures of Kavalier and Clay*; 2000: Jhumpa Lahiri, *Interpreter of Maladies*; 1999: Michael Cunningham, *The Hours*; 1998: Philip Roth, *American Pastoral*
Non-fiction: 2002: Diane McWhorter, *Carry Me Home*; 2001: Herbert P. Bix, *Hirohito and the Making of Modern Japan*; 2000: John W. Dower, *Embracing Defeat: Japan in the Wake of World War II*; 1999: John McPhee, *Annals of the Former World*; 1998: Jared Diamond, *Guns, Germs and Steel: The Fates of Human Societies*
Poetry: 2002: Carl Dennis, *Practical Gods*; 2001: Stephen Dunn, *Different Hours*; 2000: C. K. Williams, *Repair*; 1999: Mark Strand, *Blizzard of One*; 1998: Charles Wright, *Black Zodiac*
Biography: 2002: David McCullough, *John Adams*; 2001: David Levering Lewis, *W. E. B. Du Bois: The Fight for Equality and the American Century, 1919–63*; 2000: Stacy Schiff, *Vera (Mrs Vladimir Nabokov)*; 1999: A. Scott Bergh, *Lindbergh*; 1998: Katharine Graham, *Personal History*
Drama: 2002: Suzan-Lori Parks, *Topdog/Underdog*; 2001: David Auburn, *Proof*; 2000: Donald Margulies, *Dinner with Friends*; 1999: Margaret Edson, *Wit*; 1998: Paula Vogel, *How I learned to Drive*
History: 2002: Louis Menand, *The Metaphysical Club*; 2001: Joseph J. Ellis, *Founding Brothers: The Revolutionary Generation*; 2000: David M. Kennedy, *Freedom from Fear*; 1999: Edwin G. Burrows and Mike Wallace, *Gotham: A History of New York City to 1989*; 1998: Edward J. Larson, *Summer for the Gods*.

Sponsoring Organization: Columbia School of Journalism.

Address: Columbia University, Office of Public Affairs, 304 Low Library, MC 4321, 535 West 116th St, New York, NY 10027, USA. **Telephone:** (212) 854-3841. **Fax:** (212) 678-4817. **Internet:** www.pulitzer.org.

Pushcart Prize: Best of the Small Presses

Annual award for work published by a small press or literary journal. Works are nominated by editors and then reviewed by judges. The winning works are published in a special anthology.

Eligibility and Restrictions: Works of poetry, short fiction, essays, or self-contained extracts from books are eligible.

How to Apply: Submissions are accepted from editors only, who may nominate up to six works; deadline for entries is 1 December.

Recent Winners: Past winners include John Updike, Charles Simic, Robert Pinsky, Joyce Carol Oates, Raymond Carver, André Dubus, Margaret Atwood and Richard Ford.

Sponsoring Organization: Pushcart Press.

Address: Pushcart Press, POB 380, Wainscott, NY 11975, USA. **Telephone:** (516) 324-9300.

Pushkin Poetry Prize

In 1881, the Pushkin Prize was established in Russia, awarded to Russian (later Soviet) authors who achieved the highest standard of literary excellence. The prize is the highest prize awarded by the Russian Academy.

Recent Winners: 2001: Alexander Kushner; 1993: Dmitri Alexandrovich Prigov.

Sponsoring Organization: Russian Academy of Science.

Address: Russian Academy of Science, Leninsky pr. 14, 117901 Moscow, Russia. **Telephone:** (95) 954-29-05. **Fax:** (95) 954-33-20.

Queen's Gold Medal for Poetry

The King's Gold Medal for Poetry was instituted by King George V in 1933 at the suggestion of the then Poet Laureate, John Masefield. It became the Queen's Gold Medal for Poetry on the accession to the throne of Queen Elizabeth II in 1952. A small committee, under the chairmanship of the Poet Laureate, selects the winner. This choice is approved by the Queen and the Medal is presented at Buckingham Palace. It is not awarded every year.

Eligibility and Restrictions: The Medal is given for a book of verse published in the English language, but translations of exceptional merit may be considered. Since 1985 entrants from all Commonwealth Monarchies have been eligible for consideration.

Recent Winners: 2001: Michael Longley; 2000: Edwin Morgan; 1998: Les Murray.

Address: Buckingham Palace, London, UK.

Queensland Premier's Literary Awards

Established in 1999, this has become Australia's richest literary awards programme, offering A$150,000 in prize money and A$5,000 towards publication of the work of an emerging Queensland author. Prizes are given for best fiction, literary or media work advancing public debate, best manuscript of an emerging Queensland writer, history book, non-fiction book, children's book, young adult book, stage drama, film or television script.

Recent Winners: Best Emerging Queensland Author: 2001: Deborah Carlyon, *Mama Kuma: One Woman, Two Cultures*
Best Fiction Book: 2001: Peter Carey, *True History of the Kelly Gang*
Best Children's Book: 2001: Margaret Wild and Ron Brooks, *Fox*
Best History Book: 2001: Tim Bonyhady, *The Colonial Earth*
Best Non-Fiction Book: 2001: Brian Matthews, *A Fine and Private Place*

Best Literary or Media Work Advancing Public Debate: 2001: Michael Gordon, *Reconciliation: A Journey*
Best Stage Drama: 2001: Duong Le Quy, *Meat Party*
Best Film or Television Script: 2001: Christine Olsen, *Rabbit-proof Fence.*

Sponsoring Organization: Government of Queensland.

Address: Literary Awards Co-ordinator, Dept of the Premier and Cabinet, POB 185, Albert St, Brisbane, Qld 4002, Australia. **Telephone:** 3224 6206. **Internet:** www.premiers.qld.gov.au/literaryawards/2001/winners01.html. **E-mail:** literaryawards@premiers.qld.gov.au.

Raiziss/de Palchi Translation Award

Established in 1995, the award alternates between book and fellowship awards, recognizing outstanding translations of modern Italian poetry into English. The winner of the book prize receives $5,000; the fellowship carries a prize of $20,000, plus a residency at the American Academy in Rome.

How to Apply: No applications are accepted for the book prize, but submissions for the fellowship are accepted.

Recent Winners: Book Prize: 2001: Stephen Sartarelli, *Songbook: The Selected Poems of Umberto Saba*; 1999: John P. Welle and Ruth Feldman, *Peasants Wake for Fellini's Casanova* by Andrea Zanzotto; 1997: Michael Palma, *The Man I Pretend to Be: The Colloquies and Selected Poems of Guido Gozzano*
Fellowship: 2000: Emanuel di Pasquale, *Sharing a Trip: Selected Poems by Silvio Ramat*; 1998: Geoffrey Brock, *Poesie del disamore* by Cesare Pavese; 1996: Anthony Molino, *Esercizi di tiptologia* by Valerio Magrelli.

Sponsoring Organization: Academy of American Poets.

Address: Academy of American Poets, 584 Broadway, Suite 1208, New York, NY 10012, USA. **Telephone:** (212) 274-0343. **Fax:** (212) 274-9427. **Internet:** www.poets.org/academy. **E-mail:** academy@poets.org.

Rajasthan Urdu Academy Awards

The Rajasthan Urdu Academy presents a series of annual literary awards: the Mehmood Shirani Prize (named after a noted Urdu writer), of Rs11,000; the Bismil Saidi Prize for poetry and the Ahteramuddin Shagil Prize for prose (each worth Rs 7,000). The Academy also makes a separate award for best Urdu books and for journalism, and an occasional special award of Rs3,000 for special achievements in Urdu literature.

Recent Winners: Mehmood Shirani Prize: Ibn-e-Ahsan Bazmi
Bismil Saidi Prize: Haseen Kausari
Ahteramuddin Shagil Prize: Mashkoor Javed
Best Urdu Book: Zafar Ahmed Siddiqui, *Mohammedan College Se Muslim University Tak* and Mahendra Singh Tyagi, *Urdu Ka Apna Urooj Aur Shairi* (joint winners)
Special award: Musawwar Sabzwari, *Dhama* (collection of poems).

Sponsoring Organization: Rajasthan Urdu Academy.

Address: Rajasthan Urdu Academy, J-3,Subhash Marg, C-Scheme, Jaipur, 302 001, India.

Rancage Literary Award

Annual award presented to writers in the different Indonesian langugages for an outstanding contribution to the development of language and literature of their various regions.

Recent Winners: 2000: Chiye Retty Isnendes, *Kidang Kawisaya (A Deer Ensnared by Magic)*; Widodo, *Layang Saka Paran (Letters from Abroad)*; I Ketut Rida, *Sunari*; other winners include Dr H. Yus Rusyana, *Suparto Brata* and *I Gede Dharma*.

Sponsoring Organization: Rancage Foundation.

Address: Rancage Foundation, Palmerah Selatan 21, Jakarta, 10270, Indonesia.

Rauriser Förderungspreis (Rauriser Encouragement Award)

An annual prize sponsored by the region of Salzburg and the community of Rauris. The prize totals €3,643, and is presented for an unpublished prose manuscript on a specific topic. The winner is selected by a panel of experts.

Eligibility and Restrictions: Open to writers born or resident in Salzburg, aged up to 40, who have not previously won the prize.

How to Apply: Three copies of the unpublished manuscript should be submitted accompanied by biographical details.

Recent Winners: 2002: Roland Grünbart, Dirk Ofner and Kurt Rebol (joint winners); 2001: Herbert Reiter; 2000: Daniela Egger and Wolfgang Herman (joint winners); 1999: no prize given; 1998: Olivia Keglevic.

Sponsoring Organization: Salzburg Regional Government.

Contact: Dr Herbert Mayrhofer.

Address: Salzburger Landesregierung, Kulturabteilung, Postfach 527, 5010 Salzburg, Austria. **Telephone:** (662) 8042 2729. **Fax:** (662) 8042 2919. **Internet:** www.salzburg.gv.at. **E-mail:** kultur@salzburg.gv.at.

Rauriser Literaturpreis (Rauriser Literature Prize)

Presented to an outstanding first prose work by a German-speaking author published during the previous year. Awarded annually since 1972, it is sponsored by the Salzburger Landesregierung. The winner is chosen by a panel of experts, and receives €7,270 (100,000 Sch) and a certificate of honour.

Eligibility and Restrictions: Open to first works of prose published in the preceding year in German.

How to Apply: No direct applications are permitted.

Recent Winners: 2002: Julie Zeh, *Adler und Engel*; 2001: Corinna Soriat, *Leben zwischen den Seiten*; 2000: Gerhard Kelling, *Beckersons Buch*; 1999: Peter Stamm, *Agnes*; 1998: Bettina Galvagni, *Melancholia*; 1997: Felicitas Hoppe, *Picknick der Friseure* and Katrin Seebacher, *Morgen oder Abend* (joint winners).

Sponsoring Organization: Salzburger Landesregierung.

Contact: Dr Herbert Mayrhofer.

Address: Salzburger Landesregierung, Kulturabteilung, Postfach 527, 5010 Salzburg, Austria. **Telephone:** (662) 8042 2729. **Fax:** (662) 8042 2919. **Internet:** www.salzburg.gv.at. **E-mail:** kultur@salzburg.gv.at.

Rea Award for the Short Story

The $30,000 Rea Award for the Short Story is given annually to a writer who has made a significant contribution to the short story genre. The award was established in 1986 by Michael M. Rea and is sponsored annually by the Dungannon Foundation. Recipients are nominated and selected by a jury.

Eligibility and Restrictions: US and Canadian writers are eligible.

How to Apply: No direct applications are accepted; recipients are nominated and selected by a jury.

Recent Winners: 2001: Alice Munro; 2000: Deborah Eisenberg; 1999: Joy Williams; 1998: John Edgar Wideman; 1997: Gina Berriault.

Sponsoring Organization: Dungannon Foundation.

Contact: Pres. Elizabeth R. Rea.

Address: Dungannon Foundation, 131 East 66th St, New York, NY 10021, USA. **Internet:** www.reaaward.org.

Real Writers/Book Pl@ce Short Story Awards

Founded in 1994 as the Real Writers Short Story Competition, and renamed in 2001. Sponsored by The Book Pl@ce, an e-bookselling facility from Hammicks Bookshop. The prize aims to discover, reward and encourage excellence in the field of short fiction. There is a first prize of £2,500, and ten regional or section prizes of £100. The regional winners are chosen by small panels of journalists, writers and editors, while the overall winner is chosen by a leading literary figure. Prizewinning entries are published in a special anthology, and all winners have the opportunity to present their work for consideration by a major publisher.

Eligibility and Restrictions: Entries must be in English, not previously published, and no more than 5,000 words long. They may be in any style or genre.

How to Apply: Entries from all over the world are welcomed. Entry forms are available from the address or website given from May of each year. Entry fee payable of £5 per story.

Recent Winners: 2001: Kathy Barbour, *Goodbye Kisses*; 2000: Kate Long, *The Worst Word*; 1999: Robert Loughery, *The Real Thing*; 1998: Maxine Alterio, *Big Blue and the Potato War*; 1997: J. H. Tomkins, *An Acorn*.

Sponsoring Organization: Real Writers/the Book Pl@ce.

Contact: Awards Co-ordinator, Lynne Patrick.

Address: Real Writers/Book Pl@ce Short Story Awards, PO Box 170 Chesterfield, Derbyshire S40 1FE, UK. **Telephone:** (1246) 238492. **Fax:** (1246) 238492. **Internet:** www.real-writers.com. **E-mail:** info@real-writers.com.

Trevor Reese Memorial Prize

This prize was established in 1979 in memory of Trevor Reese, a distinguished scholar of imperial history, from the proceeds of contributions to a memorial fund from scholars in Britain and a large number of overseas countries. The prize of £1,000 is awarded biennially for a scholarly work, usually by a single author, in the field of Imperial and Commonwealth history.

Eligibility and Restrictions: Entries must have been published during the two previous years.

How to Apply: Publishers or authors are invited to submit one copy of the title to the Events and Publicity Officer by the end of May.

Sponsoring Organization: Institute of Commonwealth Studies.

Contact: Events and Publicity Officer, Stephanie Kearins.

Address: Institute of Commonwealth Studies, 28 Russell Square, London WC1B 5DS, UK. **Telephone:** (20) 7862 8825. **Fax:** (20) 7862 8820. **Internet:** www.sas.ac.uk/commonwealthstudies/. **E-mail:** ics@sas.ac.uk.

Rennyo Shô (Rennyo Prize)

Established in 1994 to commemorate the 500th anniversary of the death of Rennyo (1415–99), a Jôdo Shinshû (New Pure Land) priest. Sponsored by the Honganji Preservation Foundation with the support of the Kawade Shobô Shinsha publishing company, and awarded annually to an outstanding work of non-fiction (broadly interpreted to include criticism, biography, and other genres, and not restricted to religious topics). The winner receives 2 million yen plus a commemorative gift.

Sponsoring Organization: Kawade Shobô Shinsha publishing company.

Address: Kawade Shobô Shinsha publishing company, Tokyo, Japan.

Rhys Davies Short Story Competition

An annual award sponsored by The Welsh Academy in collaboation with the Rhys Davies Trust, a charity which has as its aim the fostering of Welsh writing in English. There is an overall prize of £1000, and ten further prizes of £250. The award is named after a Welsh writer, 1901–78, who published 19 novels.

Eligibility and Restrictions: Entries are restricted to those from writers either born in Wales or currently living in Wales. Works must be unpublished and written in English.

How to Apply: Three copies of entries, accompanied by an entry fee of £5 for each story, should be submitted by 30 March.

Recent Winners: 2000/01: Tristan Hughes, *A Sort of Homecoming*; 1999: Lewis Davies, *Mr Roopratna's Chocolate*.

Sponsoring Organization: Rhys Davies Trust/Welsh Academy.

Address: Rhys Davies Short Story Competition, P O Box 438, Cardiff CF10 5YA, UK. **Telephone:** (1222) 623359. **Fax:** (1222) 529202.. **Internet:** www. academi.org/english/info/info_rhys.html.

Evelyn Richardson Non-fiction Award

Established in 1977 by the Writers' Federation of Nova Scotia, the Evelyn Richardson Award is presented annually for a book of non-fiction written by a Nova Scotian. The prize honours the memory of Evelyn Richardson, and is awarded at the end of May. The winner is chosen by a peer jury, and receives C$1,000.

Eligibility and Restrictions: The author must have been born in Nova Scotia or been resident in the province for 24 months prior to the deadline.

How to Apply: Four copies of eligible titles should reach the Writers' Federation of Nova Scotia by the first Friday in November.

Recent Winners: 2001: Joan Baxter, *A Serious Pair of Shoes*; 2000: Marq de Villiers, *Water*; 1999: Silver Donald Cameron, *The Living Beach*; 1998: Harry Bruce, *An Illustrated History of Nova Scotia*; 1997: Harry Thurston, *The Nature of Shorebird: Nomads of the Wetlands*.

Sponsoring Organization: Writers' Federation of Nova Scotia.

Contact: Exec. Dir Jane Buss.

Address: Writers' Federation of Nova Scotia, 1113 Marginal Rd, Halifax, NS B3H 4P7, Canada. **Telephone:** (902) 423-8116. **Fax:** (902) 422-0881. **Internet:** www.writers.ns.ca. **E-mail:** talk@writers.ns.ca.

Fernando Rielo World Mystical Poetry Prize

An annual prize created by Fernando Rielo in 1981 with the aim of promoting mystical poetry. The prize is endowed with 1 million ptas (€6,000), and winning work is published in a special edition.

Eligibility and Restrictions: Entries must be written in Spanish or English or translated to one of these two languages. The entries must be unpublished and be between 600 and 1,300 verses.

Recent Winners: 2001: Julio Heladio Martín de Ximeno (Spain), *Mientras espero (While I Await)*; previous winners include: Manuel Álvarez Ortega, José García Nieto, Montserrat Maristany, Luis López Anglada, and Miguel de Santiago (Spain), Marin Sorescu (Romania); Alain Bosquet (France); Charles Carrère (Senegal); Daniel Ben Rafael Stawski (Israel); Takis Varvitsiotis (Greece); Laureano Albán (Costa Rica); and Mateja Matevski (Macedonia).

Sponsoring Organization: Fundación Fernando Rielo (Fernando Rielo Foundation).

Address: Fundación Fernando Rielo, Jorge Juan 102, No 2b, 28009 Madrid, Spain. **Telephone:** (91) 575 40 91. **Fax:** (91) 435 23 51. **Internet:** www.rielo.com. **E-mail:** santiago@caidt.net.

Klaus Rifbjergs Debutantpris for Lyrik

The prize,which was first awarded in 1984, is presented every other year to a new writer for a collection of poems. The winner receives DKK 6,000.

Eligibility and Restrictions: Open to writers who within the preceding two years have published a first collection of poems in the Danish, Faroese or Greenlandic languages.

How to Apply: No direct applications are accepted.

Recent Winners: 2000: Øverste Kirurgiske; 1998: Mikkel Thykier; 1996: Katrine Marie Guldager; 1994: Kirsten Hammann.

Sponsoring Organization: Danish Academy.

Contact: Administrator Dr Allan Philip.

Address: Det Danske Akademi, Rungstedlund, Rungsted Strandvej 111, 2960 Rungsted Kyst, Denmark. **Telephone:** 33 13 11 12. **Fax:** 33 32 80 45. **Internet:** www.danskeakademi.dk. **E-mail:** lawoffice@philip.dk.

Riksmalsprisen – Oslo og Baerum riksmalsforenings litteraturpris

An annual prize first presented in 1957 for outstanding new works of fiction using the Riksmal language. A separate children's category was introduced in 1988. The prize is presented to a Norwegian author or a translator of foreign works.

Recent Winners: General Prize: 2001: Britt Karin Larsen; 2000: Toril Brekke; 1999: Ingvar Ambjørnsen; 1998: Ketil Bjørnstad; 1997: Lars Saabye Christensen Children's Book: 2001: Charlotte Glaser Munch; 2000: Elin Brodin and Henning Hagerup; 1999: Tor Åge Bringsværd; 1998: Else Færden; 1997; Elisabeth Bjørnson.

Sponsoring Organization: Riksmalsforbundet.

Address: Riksmalsforbundet, Oslo, Norway. **Telephone:** (22) 56 29 50. **Fax:** (22) 55 37 43. **Internet:** www.riksmalsforbundet.no/priser.html.

River Styx International Poetry Contest

An annual poetry prize established in 1995. The final winner is selected by an expert judge, and receives $1,000. All the shortlisted poems are published in the August issue of the magazine.

Eligibility and Restrictions: Poems must be written in English; up to three poems may be entered per candidate, but must not exceed 14 pages.

How to Apply: Entries should be submitted by the end of May, accompanied by a reading fee of $20 (which includes a year's subscription to the magazine). Name and address should be included on cover sheet only.

Recent Winners: 2001: Roger Mitchell; 2000: Corrinee Clegg Hales; 1999: Kerri Webster; 1998: Dwaine Rieves; 1997: Andy Cox.

Sponsoring Organization: River Styx Magazine.

Contact: Editor Richard Newman.

Address: River Styx, 634 North Grand Blvd, 12th Floor, St Louis, MO 63103–1002, USA. **Telephone:** (314) 533-4541. **Fax:** (314) 533-3345. **Internet:** www.riverstyx.org. **E-mail:** r_t_newman@hotmail.com.

Rivertonprisen 'Den gylden revolver' (Riverton Golden Revolver Prize)

An annual prize for the best new novel in the field of crime literature, first presented in 1972. The prize is jointly sponsored by the radio broadcaster NRK and the Riverton Club. Works considered may be novels, short stories, drama, or scripts for radio, film or television.

Recent Winners: 2001: Jon Michelet, *Den frosne kvinnen*; 2000: Kjell Ola Dahl, *En liten gyllen ring*; 1999: Unni Lindell, *Drømmefangeren*; 1998: Jan Mehlum, *Kalde hender*; 1997: Jo Nesbø, *Flaggermusmannen*.

Sponsoring Organization: NRK (Norsk Rikskringkasting)/Rivertonklubben.

Address: NRK (Norsk Rikskringkasting), Marienlyst, Oslo, Norway. **Telephone:** (815) 65 900. **Internet:** www3.nrk.no/. **E-mail:** sigerson@online.no.

Colin Roderick Prize for Australian Literature

Founded in 1965 by Professor Colin Roderick to promote Australian literature. The prize is presented annually for the best work of Australian literature published in the previous year. The winner is selected by a panel of experts, and receives A$5,000 and a medal.

Eligibility and Restrictions: Open to any genre of Australian literature, which has been published in the previous year.

How to Apply: Entries should be sent to the Foundation for Australian Literary Studies at the address given.

Recent Winners: 2000: Peter Carey, *The True History of the Kelly Gang*; 1998: Robert Dessaix, *(and so forth)*.

Sponsoring Organization: Foundation for Australian Literary Studies (FALS).

Contact: Prof. Peter Piercer.

Address: James Cook University, Post Office James Cook University, Queensland, 4811, Australia. **Telephone:** (7) 40421497. **Fax:** (7) 40421290. **Internet:** www.jcu.edu.au.

Henriette Roland Holst-prijs

Originally founded in 1957 by the publishing house De Arbeiderspers and the Henriette Roland Holst Stichting (HRH Foundation), the prize has been sponsored since 1980 by the Maatschappij der Nederlandse Letterkunde (MNL—Dutch Literature Association). The prize recognizes a work of prose, poetry or drama, which reflects social concerns. The prize is awarded every three years, and the winner is chosen by a committee of experts. The winner receives €2,500.

Eligibility and Restrictions: The work must have been published in Dutch in the previous three years.

How to Apply: Application is open to anybody.

Recent Winners: 1999: Geert Mak; 1996: Inez van Dullemen; 1993: Lieve Joris; 1990: Wim de Bie; 1987: J. H. Donner.

Sponsoring Organization: Maatschappij der Nederlandse Letterkunde (MNL) (Dutch Literature Association).

Address: Maatschappij der Nederlandse Letterkunde, Postbus 9501, 2300 RA Leiden, Netherlands. **Telephone:** (71) 5144962. **Fax:** (71) 5272836. **Internet:** www.leidenuniv.nl/host/mnl. **E-mail:** mnl@library.leidenuniv.nl.

Romantic Novelists Association New Writers Award

An annual award sponsored by the Romantic Novelists Association for unpublished writers in the field of the romantic novel.

Eligibility and Restrictions: Open to non-members, but authors must be based in the UK.

Recent Winners: 2001: Anita Anderson, *Somebody*; 2000: Valerie-Anne Baglietto, *The Wrong Sort of Girl*; 1999: Donna Hay, *Waiting in the Wings*.

Sponsoring Organization: Romantic Novelists Association.

Address: Romantic Novelists Association, 2 Broad Oak Lane, Wigginton, York YO32 2SB, UK. **Telephone:** (1904) 765035.

Rooney Prize for Irish Literature

A non-competitive prize to reward and encourage young Irish talent. The winner is chosen by a panel of judges. Special awards are given on rare occasions where outstanding authors are honoured. The winner receives IR£5,000 (€6,350).

Eligibility and Restrictions: Writers must be Irish, under 40 years of age, and their work must be written in Irish or English.

How to Apply: No applications are accepted.

Recent Winners: 2000: Claire Keegan; 1999: Mark O'Rowe; 1998: David Wheatley.

Address: Strathlin, Templecarrig, Delgany, Ireland.

Lois Roth Award for a Translation of a Literary Work

A biennial award established in 1999 for an outstanding translation into English of a book-length literary work. The prize, which consists of $1,000 and a certificate, is offered in odd-numbered years and alternates with Scaglione Prize for a Translation of a Literary Work, offered in even-numbered years.

Eligibility and Restrictions: Open to translations published in the year preceding the year in which the award is given. Translators need not be members of the Modern Language Association of America (MLA).

How to Apply: Entrants should send six copies along with brief biographical and professional details, a total of 12–15 pages of the text in its original language, and a letter identifying the work, the translator, and the date of publication by 1 April.

Recent Winners: 2001: John Felstiner, *Selected Poems and Prose of Paul Celan*; 1998: Mark Harman, *The Castle*, by Franz Kafka.

Sponsoring Organization: Modern Language Association of America.

Contact: Co-ordinator of Book Prizes and Special Projects.

Address: Modern Language Asscn of America, 26 Broadway, 3rd Floor, New York, NY 10004–1789, USA. **Telephone:** (646) 576-5141. **Fax:** (646) 458-0033. **Internet:** www.mla.org. **E-mail:** awards@mla.org.

Royal Nepal Academy Awards

The Royal Nepal Academy presents two prestigious literary awards: the Prithvi Pragya Puraskar, for contributions to the advancement of arts and literature, and the Mahendra Pragya Puraskar, for contributions to Nepali literature.

Recent Winners: Arts and literature: 2000: Lain Soingh Bangdel
Nepali literature: 2000: Dev Kumari Thapa.

Sponsoring Organization: Royal Nepal Academy.

Address: Royal Nepal Academy, GPO Box: 3323, Kathmandu, Nepal. **Telephone:** (1) 547714. **Fax:** (1) 547713. **Internet:** www.ronast.org.np. **E-mail:** ronast@mos.com.np.

Runciman Award

This annual award, named in honour of Sir Steven Runciman, was established in 1986 in recognition of a work wholly or mainly about some aspect of Greece or the Hellenic scene. The winner is selected by a panel of judges, and receives a prize of not less than £5,000, sponsored by the National Bank of Greece. There were previously several awards each year, but since 2001 only one prize has been offered.

Eligibility and Restrictions: The award may be given for a work of fiction, non-fiction or drama, including history, arts, archaeology, biography or travel, and may be either academic or non-academic. Entries, which may have been translated from Greek, must have been published in their first English edition in the UK during the previous year.

How to Apply: Publishers should apply on behalf of the writer, sending five copies (one to each of the four judges, plus one to the Administrator). Entries are accepted during January and February.

Recent Winners: 2001: Cyprian Broodbank, *An Island Archaeology of the Early Cyclades*; 2000: J. V. Luce, *Celebrating Homer's Landscapes* and Reviel Netz, *The Shaping of Deduction in Greek Mathematics*; 1999: Ian MacNiven, *Lawrence Durrell: A Biography*, Christopher Stray, *Classics Transformed: Schools,*

Universities and Society in England 1830–1960 and Jenny March, *Dictionary of Classical Mythology*; 1998: George Cawkwell, *Thucydides and the Peloponnesian War*, Martin West, *The East Face of Helicon*, Robin Cormack, *Painting the Soul: Icons, Death Masks and Shrouds* and Patricia Storace, *Dinner with Persephone*; 1997: Andrew Dalby, *Siren Feasts: A History of Food and Gastronomy in Greece*, Oliver Rackham and Jennifer Moody, *The Making of the Cretan Landscape*, Gelina Harlaftis, *A History of Greek-owned Shipping* and Nigel Spivey, *Understanding Greek Sculpture*.

Sponsoring Organization: Anglo–Hellenic League/National Bank of Greece.

Contact: Administrator Lady Maria Fairweather.

Address: The Anglo-Hellenic League, 16–18 Paddington St, London W1U 4AS, UK. **Telephone:** (20) 7486 9410.

Walter McRae Russell Award

The Walter McRae Russell Award recognizes the best book of literary scholarship on an Australian subject published in the preceding calendar year. Until 1994 the award was made for an outstanding work of literary scholarship by a young or unestablished author (usually a first book).

How to Apply: No direct applications are accepted. No nominations are required, though Association for the Study of Australian Literature (ASAL) members are invited to propose books for consideration by the judging panel.

Recent Winners: 2001: Gillian Whitlock, *The Intimate Empire: Reading Women's Autobiography*; 1999: Helen Gilbert, *Sightlines: Race, Gender and Nation in Contemporary Australian Theatre*; 1998: David Carter, *A Career in Writing: Judah Waten and the cultural politics of a literary career*; 1997: Paul Carter, *The Lie of the Land*; 1996: Richard Fotheringham, *In Search of Steele Rudd*; 1995: Patrick Buckridge, *The Scandalous Penton*.

Sponsoring Organization: Association for the Study of Australian Literature.

Address: Association for the Study of Australian Literature Ltd, Department of English, University College, ADFA, Campbell, ACT 2600, Australia. **Internet:** idun.itsc.adfa.edu.au:16080/asal/.

James Russell Lowell Prize

This award, first presented in 1969, is offered annually for a scholarly work published in the previous year by a member of the Modern Language Association of America. The winner is selected by a committee made up of members of the MLA, and receives $1,000 and a certificate.

Eligibility and Restrictions: Authors must be members of the MLA, and entries must have been published during the previous calendar year. To qualify for entry a book must be an outstanding literary or linguistic study, a critical edition of an important work, or a critical biography. Books that are primarily translations are not eligible.

How to Apply: Publishers or authors may apply. Six copies should be submitted, accompanied by a letter confirming membership of the MLA, to the address given, by 1 March.

Recent Winners: 2001: Ann Rosalind Jones and Peter Stallybrass, *Renaissance Clothing and the Materials of Memory*; 1999: Mary Baine Campbell, *Wonder and Science: Imagining Worlds in Early Modern Europe*; 1998: Gauri Viswanathan,

Outside the Fold: Conversion, Modernity and Belief; 1997: David Wallace, *Chaucerian Polity: Absolutist Lineages and Associational Forms in England and Italy*; 1996: Joseph Roach, *Cities of the Dead: Circum-Atlantic Performance*.

Sponsoring Organization: Modern Language Association of America (MLA).

Contact: Co-ordinator of Book Prizes and Special Projects.

Address: Modern Language Asscn of America, 26 Broadway, 3rd Floor, New York, NY 10004–1789, USA. **Telephone:** (646) 576-5141. **Fax:** (646) 458-0033. **Internet:** www.mla.org. **E-mail:** awards@mla.org.

J. Russell Major Prize

The Major Prize is awarded annually for the best work in English on any aspect of French history. It was established in 2000 by Mrs Blair Major, in memory of her husband, a distinguished scholar of French history who served on the history faculty at Emory University from 1949 to 1990.

Recent Winners: 2001: Debora Silverman, *Van Gogh and Gauguin: The Search for Sacred Art*.

Sponsoring Organization: American Historical Association.

Contact: Lynn Hunt.

Address: American Historical Asscn, 400 A St, SE, Washington, DC 20003–3889, USA. **Telephone:** (202) 544-2422. **Fax:** (202) 544-8307. **Internet:** www. theaha.org/prizes. **E-mail:** press@theaha.org.

RÚV (Icelandic State Radio) Literary Award

The RÚV (Icelandic State Radio) Literary Award was established in 1956. It is given annually on 31 December to honour an author for their complete body of work, rather than a particular title. The winner is chosen by a five-member committee (one nominated by the Ministry of Culture and Education, two from the Writers Union and two from RÚV), and receives a prize of 500,000 IKR.

Recent Winners: 2001: Álfrún Gunnlaugsdóttir and Sigfús Bjartmarsson; 2000: Ingibjörg Haraldsdóttir and Þorvaldur Þorsteinsson; 1999: Sigurður Pálsson and Ólafur Gunnarsson; 1998: Pétur Gunnarsson and Sigurjón Birgir Sigurðsson; 1997: Kristín Ómarsdóttir and Kristján Árnason.

Sponsoring Organization: RÚV (Icelandic State Radio).

Address: Ríkisútvarpið, Styrkur Rithöfundasjóds, Efstaleiti 3, IS-103 Reykjavík, Iceland. **Telephone:** 5153000. **Fax:** 5153010. **E-mail:** isradio@ruv.is.

G H s'Gravesande Prize

Prize of 10,000 DFL awarded every three years in recognition of outstanding literary achievement.

Sponsoring Organization: Jan Campertstichting (Jan Campert Foundation).

Address: PO Box 12654, 2500 DP The Hague, Netherlands. **Telephone:** (353) 36 37. **Fax:** (353) 30 58.

Nelly-Sachs-Preis/Kulturpreis der Stadt Dortmund

The prize, awarded by the city of Dortmund, is named after a German Jewish writer, who herself was holder of the first Nelly Sachs Prize in 1961. A prize of DM25,000 (€12,782) is awarded every two years by a jury headed by the town Oberbürgermeister (mayor).

Recent Winners: 2001: Georges-Arthur Goldschmidt (Germany); 1999: Christa Wolff (Germany); 1997: Javier Marias (Spain); 1995: Michael Ondaatje (Canada); 1993: Juan Goytisolo (Morocco).

Sponsoring Organization: Kulturbüro der Stadt Dortmund.

Address: Kulturbüro der Stadt Dortmund, Kleppingstr. 21–23, 44122 Dortmund, Germany. **Telephone:** (231) 5025162. **Fax:** (231) 5025734. **Internet:** www. dortmund.de/inhalt_externe/kulturbuero.

Sagittarius Prize

An annual award established in 1990 to recognize a first published novel by an author over the age of 60. The winner receives a prize of £2,000.

Recent Winners: 2002: Zvi Jagendor, *Wolfy and the Strudelbakers*; 2001: Michael Richardson, *The Pig Bin*; 2000: David Crackanthorpe, *Stolen Marches*; 1999: Ingrid Mann, *The Danube Testament*.

Sponsoring Organization: Society of Authors.

Address: Society of Authros, 84 Drayton Gardens, London SW10 9SB, UK. **Telephone:** (20) 7373 6642. **Fax:** (20) 7373 5768. **Internet:** www. societyofauthors.org. **E-mail:** info@societyofauthors.org.

Sahitya Akademi Award

This is one of India's most prestigious literary prizes, awarded annually by the Sahitya Akademi (Indian Academy of Literature). Established in 1954, the prize recognizes the most outstanding books of literary merit published in any of the major Indian languages recognized by the Academy. The award carries a monetary prize of Rs 25,000, and a plaque. In total there are 22 awards for literary works in the various languages and an equal number for literary translations from and into the languages. The winners are chosen after a year-long process of scrutiny, discussion and selection. The aim of the awards is to recognize and promote excellence in Indian writing and to 'expand the very definition of Indian literature by acknowledging new trends and movements'. The Akademy also gives special awards called Bhasha Samman to significant contributions to the languages not formally recognized by the Academy.

Recent Winners: 1999: (Kannada language) D. R. Nagaraj, *Sahitya Kathana* (Essays); 1990: Amitav Ghosh, *The Shadow Lines*; earlier winners include Sundri Uttamchandani.

Sponsoring Organization: Sahitya Akademi (Indian Academy of Literature).

Address: Sahitya Akademi, Rabindra Bhavan, 35 Ferozshah Rd, New Delhi, 110 001, India. **Telephone:** 3386626/27/28/29. **Fax:** (11) 3382428. **Internet:** www. sahitya-akademi.org/sahitya-akademi/awa1.htm.

Saltire Society Literary Awards

These annual awards are arranged in three categories: Scottish Book of the Year; Scottish First Book of the Year; and Scottish History Book of the Year. The Scottish Book of the Year, established in 1982, carries a prize of £5,000; the First Book prize, established in 1988, is £1,500. The History category, established in 1965, comprises £500 and a bound and inscribed copy of the winning publication. Winners for all categories are chosen by a panel of experts.

Eligibility and Restrictions: Open to any book by an author of Scottish descent or living in Scotland, or to any book which deals with the work or life of a Scot, or with a Scottish question, event or situation. Eligible genres include poetry, novels, drama, biography, literary criticism or non-fiction. Entries for the First Book category must be by an author who has not previously published a book. Books must be published in the previous calendar year.

How to Apply: Nominations are invited from literary editors of newspapers and editors of magazines and reviews concerned with literature, as well as producers of book programmes on TV and radio and other interested parties. For the History category, the prize is selected from a shortlist of nominations from professors of Scottish history and editors of historical review publications. Closing date for nominations is early September.

Recent Winners: Scottish Book of the Year: 2001: Liz Lochead, *Medea*; 2000: Ronald Frame, *The Lantern Bearers*; 1999: George Bruce, *Pursuits*; 1998: Alan Warner, *The Sopranos*; 1997: Bernard MacLaverty, *Grace Notes*
First Book of the Year: 2001: Meaghan Delahunt, *In the Bluehouse*; 2000: Douglas Galbraith, *The Rising Sun*; 1999: Michael Faber, *Some Rain Must Fall*; 1998: Dennis O'Donnell, *Two Clocks Ticking* and Christopher Wallace, *The Pied Piper's Poison* (joint winners)
Scottish History Book of the Year: 2000: Marcus Merriman, *The Rough Wooings: Mary Queen of Scots 1542–51*; 1999: Eric Richards, *Patrick Sellar and the Highland Clearances*; 1998: William Ferguson, *The Identity of the Scottish Nation*; 1997: Dr Stephen Beardman *The Early Stewart Kings*.

Sponsoring Organization: Saltire Society.

Contact: Administrator Kathleen Munro.

Address: The Saltire Society, 9 Fountain Close, 22 High St, Edinburgh EH1 1TF, UK. **Telephone:** (131) 556 1836. **Fax:** (131) 557 1675. **Internet:** www.saltire-society.demon.co.uk. **E-mail:** saltire@saltire.org.uk.

Saltire Society/Times Educational Supplement Scotland Prize for Educational Publications

The prize, established in 1992, aims to enhance the teaching and learning of an aspect or aspects of the Scottish curriculum. It is awarded in April each year by a panel of experts, and carries a prize of £500 plus a certificate.

Eligibility and Restrictions: Open to published works of non-fiction, which must be relevant to Scottish schoolchildren aged between five and 18, although not necessarily the product of a Scottish author or publisher. To be eligible a work has to be a book or a package, the bulk of which comprises written words. Non-written elements such as videotapes or computer software may be included but must make up no more than 25% of the package.

How to Apply: Applications are open to publishers, and the closing date is in early November.

Recent Winners: Previous winners include: Hodder & Stoughton, Orian & Dolphin, Nelson Blackie & Scottish, Longman Education.

Sponsoring Organization: Saltire Society/Times Educational Supplement Scotland.

Contact: Administrator Kathleen Munro.

Address: The Saltire Society, 9 Fountain Close, 22 High St, Edinburgh EH1 1TF, UK. **Telephone:** (131) 556 1836. **Fax:** (131) 557 1675. **Internet:** www.saltire-society.demon.co.uk. **E-mail:** saltire@saltire.org.uk.

Samlagsprisen

An annual prize for a work of high-quality fiction, for adults or children, sponsored by the newspaper *Det Norske Samlaget*.

Recent Winners: 2002: Ragnar Hovland; 2001: Marit Kaldhol; 2000: Einar Økland; 1999: Oddmund Hagen; 1998: Rønnaug Kleiva.

Sponsoring Organization: Det Norske Samlaget.

Address: Det Norske Samlaget, Postboks 4672, Sofienberg, 0506 Oslo, Norway. **Telephone:** (22) 70 78 00. **Fax:** (22) 68 75 02. **Internet:** www.samlaget.no.

Sanlam Literary Award

The prize was established in 1984 by the insurance company Sanlam (Suid-Afrikaanse Nasionale Lewensassuransiemaatskappij) in collaboration with Tafelberg Publishers. The award recognizes outstanding writing for children, and originally comprised gold, silver, and bronze awards for authors of English and Afrikaans children's books. Since 1994 eligibility has been extended to include African languages, and the prize now offers R8,000 each for English, Afrikaans, Nguni and Sotho categories.

Recent Winners: 2001: Dan Sleigh, *Eilande*; 1998: J. Robson, *The denials of Kow-Ten* and R. Saunders, *Sons of Anubis*; 1996: B. van Niekerk, *Gamkab*, M. Preller, *In die tyd van die Esob*, J. Robson, *One magic moment*, P. Slingby, *The joining* and G. Smith, *Wheels!*.

Sponsoring Organization: Tafelberg Publishers, LitNet and RSG.

Address: PO Box 879, 28 Wale St, Cape Town, 8000, South Africa. **Telephone:** (21) 424-1320. **Fax:** (21) 424-2510. **Internet:** www.tafelberg.com. **E-mail:** tafelbrg@tafelberg.com.

Sapphire Awards

First given in 1995, the awards honour the best in the science fiction romance subgenre. Categories are best novel and short fiction, but the editors may award an occasional special award, for a person considered to have advanced the field of science fiction romance in a way other than by writing. The award is not monetary, but winners receive permanent placement on the website, a certificate and a heart-shaped sapphire.

Eligibility and Restrictions: Nominees are chosen by readers of the newsletter, with winners selected by a team of judges. Works must be novel-length books or short fiction with a first publication date (electronic, hard- or soft-cover) between December (of the preceding year) and November (of the current year). They may have been published in any genre, but both the science fiction and the romance must be intrinsic to the story.

Best novel: novel is defined as a single work of fiction of 40,000 words or more. Individual stories appearing as a collection are eligible only as individual stories and are not eligible taken together under the title of the collection.

Best short fiction: defined as a single work of fiction that is less than 40,000 words.

How to Apply: It is not possible to apply directly for the award. The first round nominees are selected by subscribers to the *Science Fiction Romance* newsletter and the winners are selected by a panel of judges.

Recent Winners: Novel: 2001: Linnea Sinclair, *Finders Keepers*; 2000: Saira Ramasastry, *Heir to Govandhara*; 1999: Lois McMaster Bujold, *A Civil Campaign*; 1998: Patricia White, *A Wizard Scorned*; 1997: Catherine Asaro, *Catch the Lightning*

Short fiction: 2001: Susan Krinard, *Kinsman*; 2000: Mary Janice Davidson, *Love's Prisoner*; 1999: Catherine Asaro, *Aurora in Four Voices*

Special Award 1999: Denise Little, Editor of the anthology *A Dangerous Magic*.

Sponsoring Organization: Science Fiction Romance Newletter.

Contact: Editor Jody Wallace.

Address: Science Fiction Romance Newletter, USA. **Internet:** www.sfronline. com. **E-mail:** editor@sfronline.

Sasakawa Haiku Prize

A biennial prize administered by The British Haiku Society and funded by The Great Britain Sasakawa Foundation, which is presented for original contributions in the field of haiku poetry. The winner receives a prize of £2,500, which is partly in the form of a return air ticket to Japan.

How to Apply: Full details and entry form, send stamped addressed envelope marked Sasakawa Prize to the address given.

Sponsoring Organization: British Haiku Society/The Great Britain Sasakawa Foundation.

Address: The British Haiku Society, Lenacre Ford, Woolhope, Hereford HR1 4RF, UK. **Internet:** www.britishhaikusociety.org/events.html.

Sasakawa Prize for Translation

This prize, organized by the Society of Authors, is awarded every two years to the best translation from Japanese into English of a full-length work of literary merit and general interest from any period.

Recent Winners: 1998: William I. Elliott and Kazuo Kawamura for their translation of *Selected Poems by Shuntaro Tanikawa*.

Sponsoring Organization: Society of Authors.

Contact: Dorothy Sym.

Address: Society of Authors, 84 Drayton Gdns, London SW10 9SB, UK. **Telephone:** (20) 7373 6642. **Fax:** (20) 7373 5768. **Internet:** www.gbsf.org.uk. **E-mail:** gbsf@cagbsf.org.uk.

Saskatchewan Book Awards

The Saskatchewan Book Awards were established in 1993 (with separate categories being added in later years), by the joint efforts of the Saskatchewan Writers Guild, the Saskatchewan Publishers Group and the Saskatchewan Library Association. The aim of the awards is to recognize and celebrate the achievements of Saskatchewan authors and publishers and help promote their books. There are nine writing awards as well as three separate awards for publishing, and each prize is sponsored by local businesses or institutions. One of the winners is also selected as Book of the Year.

How to Apply: Four copies of the book should be submitted, accompanied by an official entry form and an administration fee of $15 per title; deadlines vary according to publication date; check website for details.

Recent Winners: Book of the Year: 2001: Sandra Birdsell, *The Russländer*
Non-fiction: 2001: Warren Goulding, *Just Another Indian*
Anne Szumigalski Award for Poetry: 2001: Ken Howe, *Household Hints for the End of Time*
Fiction: 2001: Sandra Birdsell, *The Russländer*
Children's Literature: 2001: Arthur Slade, *Dust*
Brenda Macdonald Riches First Book Award: 2001: Katherine Lawrence, *Ring Finger, Left Hand*
Saskatoon Book Award: 2001: Glen Sorestad, *Leaving Holds Me Here*
Regina Book Award: 2001: Sandra Birdsell, *The Russländer*
Scholarly Writing: 2001: Peter Phillips and George Khachatourians, *The Biotechnology Revolution in Global Agriculture*
Publishing in Education: 2001: Native Law Centre, *Emerging Justice*.

Sponsoring Organization: Saskatchewan Writers Guild/Saskatchewan Publishers Group/Saskatchewan Library Association.

Address: Saskatchewan Book Awards, Box 1921, Regina, SK, S4P 3E1, Canada. **Telephone:** (306) 569-1585. **Fax:** (306) 569-4187. **Internet:** www. bookawards.sk.ca/. **E-mail:** director@bookawards.sk.ca.

SATI Award For Outstanding Translation

A new award established in 2000 by the South African Translators' Institute (SATI). The award recognizes translation work in the official languages of South Africa, with the aim of encouraging the publication of translations of original works in the indigenous languages of the country. The award is made annually on International Translation Day (popularly known as St Jerome's Day, 30 September). It alternates between fiction and non-fiction, and may be made either for a single translation of outstanding quality or for the entire body of a translator's fiction or non-fiction work. The award consists of a certificate of merit and a cash prize of R25,000.

How to Apply: Nominations must be made on an official form, accompanied by biographical and contact details. Six print copies and one electronic copy must be sent to the SATI Registrar by 31 July.

Recent Winners: 2000: Leon de Kock, for his translation from Afrikaans into English of *Triomf* by Marlene van Niekerk.

Sponsoring Organization: Billiton Development Trust/Die Taalsekretariaat/ Potchefstroom University's Chancellor's Trust Fund.

Address: South African Translators' Institute, PO Box 27711, Sunnyside, 0132, South Africa. **Telephone:** (11) 803-2681. **Fax:** (11) 803-2681. **E-mail:** sati@ intekom.co.za.

Aldo and Jeanne Scaglione Prize for Comparative Literary Studies

The prize, first presented in 1993, is awarded annually for an outstanding scholarly work in the field of comparative literary studies, involving at least two literatures. The winner is selected by a committee made up of members of the Modern Language Association of America (MLA), and receives $2,000 and a certificate.

Eligibility and Restrictions: Books must be published during the preceding calendar year. Authors must be members of the MLA. Books that are primarily translations will not be considered.

How to Apply: Publishers or authors may apply. Four copies of the book should be submitted by 1 May.

Recent Winners: 2001: Marie-Laure Ryan, *Narrative as Virtual Reality: Immersion and Interactivity in Literature and Electronic Media*; 1999: Leonard Barkan, *Unearthing the Past: Archaeology and Aesthetics in the Making of Renaissance Culture*; 1998: Dorrit Cohn, *The Distinction of Fiction*; 1997: Linda Haverty Rugg, *Picturing Ourselves: Photography and Autobiography*; 1996: Chana Kronfeld, *On the Margins of Modernism: Decentering Literary Dynamics*.

Sponsoring Organization: Modern Language Association of America (MLA).

Contact: Co-ordinator of Book Prizes and Special Projects.

Address: Modern Language Asscn of America, 26 Broadway, 3rd Floor, New York, NY 10004–1789, USA. **Telephone:** (646) 576-5141. **Fax:** (646) 458-0033. **Internet:** www.mla.org. **E-mail:** awards@mla.org.

Aldo and Jeanne Scaglione Prize for French and Francophone Studies

First awarded in 1993, the prize is presented annually for an outstanding scholarly work in the field of French or Francophone linguistic or literary studies. The winner is selected by a committee made up of members of the Modern Language Association of America (MLA), and receives $2,000 and a certificate.

Eligibility and Restrictions: Entries must be published in the calendar year preceding the competition. Authors must be members of the MLA. Books that are primarily translations will not be considered.

How to Apply: Publishers or authors may apply. Four copies of the book should be submitted, accompanied by a letter confirming membership of the MLA, by 1 May.

Recent Winners: 2001: Timothy Hampton, *Literature and Nation in the Sixteenth Century: Inventing Renaissance France*; 1999: Margaret Cohen, *The Sentimental Education of the Novel* and Philip Watts, *Allegories of the Purge: How Literature Responded to the Postwar Trials of Writers and Intellectuals in France* (joint winners); 1998: George Hoffmann, *Montaigne's Career*; 1997: Suzanne Guerlac, *Literary Polemics: Bataille, Sartre, Valéry, Breton* and Kathryn A. Hoffmann, *Society of Pleasures: Interdisciplinary Readings in Pleasure and Power during the Reign of Louis XIV* (joint winners); 1996: Lynn A. Higgins, *New Novel, New Wave, New Politics: Fiction and the Representation of History in Postwar France*.

Sponsoring Organization: Modern Language Association of America (MLA).

Contact: Co-ordinator of Book Prizes and Special Projects.

Address: Modern Language Asscn of America, 26 Broadway, 3rd Floor, New York, NY 10004–1789, USA. **Telephone:** (646) 576-5141. **Fax:** (646) 458-0033. **Internet:** www.mla.org. **E-mail:** awards@mla.org.

Aldo and Jeanne Scaglione Prize for Germanic Languages and Literatures

First awarded in 1994, the prize is presented in even-numbered years for an outstanding scholarly work on the linguistics or literature of the Germanic languages. The winner is selected by a committee made up of members of the Modern Language Association of America (MLA), and receives $2,000 and a certificate.

Eligibility and Restrictions: Germanic languages includes German, Icelandic, Norwegian, Swedish and Yiddish. Books must have been published during the previous two years. Authors must be members of the MLA. Books that are primarily translations will not be considered.

How to Apply: Publishers or authors may apply. Four copies of the book should be submitted, by 1 May of even-numbered years.

Recent Winners: 1998–99: Lutz Koepnick, *Walter Benjamin and the Aesthetics of Power*; 1996–97: Julia Hell, *Post-Fascist Fantasies: Psychoanalysis, History, and the Literature of East Germany*; 1994–95: James A. Schultz, *The Knowledge of Childhood in the German Middle Ages, 1100–1350*; 1992–93: Leslie A. Adelson, *Making Bodies, Making History: Feminism and German Identity*.

Sponsoring Organization: Modern Language Association of America (MLA).

Contact: Co-ordinator of Book Prizes and Special Projects.

Address: Modern Language Asscn of America, 26 Broadway, 3rd Floor, New York, NY 10004–1789, USA. **Telephone:** (646) 576-5141. **Fax:** (646) 458-0033. **Internet:** www.mla.org. **E-mail:** awards@mla.org.

Aldo and Jeanne Scaglione Prize for Italian Studies

First awarded in 1996, the prize is presented in odd-numbered years for an outstanding scholarly work on any phase of Italian literature or culture, or comparative literature involving Italian. The winner is selected by a committee made up of members of the Modern Language Association of America (MLA), and receives $2,000 and a certificate. The prize alternates with the Howard Marraro Prize (qv), which is presented in even-numbered years (between 1996 and 2000 the two prizes were awarded jointly).

Eligibility and Restrictions: Authors must be members of the MLA.

How to Apply: Publishers or authors may apply. Four copies of the book should be submitted, by 1 May of odd-numbered years.

Recent Winners: 2001: Gaetana Marrone-Puglia, *The Gaze and the Labyrinth: The Cinema of Liliana Cavani*; 1998–99: Margaret Brose, *Leopardi Sublime* and Nancy L. Canepa, *From Court to Forest: Giambattista Basile's Lo cunto de li cunti and the Birth of the Literary Fairy Tale*; 1996–97: Barbara Spackman, *Fascist Virilities: Rhetoric, Ideology, and Social Fantasy in Italy*; 1994–95: Robert S. Dombroski, *Properties of Writing: Ideological Discourse in Modern Italian Fiction* and Karen Pinkus, *Bodily Regimes: Italian Advertising under Fascism* (joint winners); 1992–93: Margaret F. Rosenthal, *The Honest Courtesan: Veronica Franco, Citizen and Writer in Sixteenth-Century Venice*.

Sponsoring Organization: Modern Language Association of America (MLA).

Contact: Co-ordinator of Book Prizes and Special Projects.

Address: Modern Language Asscn of America, 26 Broadway, 3rd Floor, New York, NY 10004–1789, USA. **Telephone:** (646) 576-5141. **Fax:** (646) 458-0033. **Internet:** www.mla.org. **E-mail:** awards@mla.org.

Aldo and Jeanne Scaglione Prize for Studies in Slavic Languages and Literatures

First awarded in 1995, the prize is presented in odd-numbered years for an outstanding scholarly work in the field of Slavic linguistic or literary studies. The winner is selected by a committee made up of members of the Modern Language Association of America (MLA), and receives $2,000 and a certificate.

Eligibility and Restrictions: Works of literary history, literary criticism, philology and literary theory are eligible. Entries must be published during the two calendar years preceding the competition. Authors need not be members of the MLA. Books that are primarily translations will not be considered.

How to Apply: Publishers or authors may apply. Four copies of the book should be submitted, by 1 May of odd-numbered years.

Recent Winners: 2001: Gabriella Safran, *Rewriting the Jew: Assimilation Narratives in the Russian Empire*; 1997–98: Harriet Murav, *Russia's Legal Fictions*; 1995–96: Alexander M. Schenker, *The Dawn of Slavic: An Introduction to Slavic Philology*; 1993–94: Robert Maguire, *Exploring Gogol*.

Sponsoring Organization: Modern Language Association of America (MLA).

Contact: Co-ordinator of Book Prizes and Special Projects.

Address: Modern Language Asscn of America, 26 Broadway, 3rd Floor, New York, NY 10004–1789, USA. **Telephone:** (646) 576-5141. **Fax:** (646) 458-0033. **Internet:** www.mla.org. **E-mail:** awards@mla.org.

Aldo and Jeanne Scaglione Prize for a Translation of a Literary Work

A biennial award for an outstanding translation into English of a book-length literary work. The award consists of $2,000 and a certificate. It is offered in even-numbered years and alternates with the Lois Roth Award, offered in odd-numbered years.

Eligibility and Restrictions: Open to translations published in the year preceding the year in which the award is given. Translators need not be members of the Modern Language Association of America (MLA).

How to Apply: Entrants should send six copies of the work, plus pages of text in original language, by 1 April in even-numbered years.

Recent Winners: 1998–99: Norman R. Shapiro, *One Hundred and One Poems by Paul Verlaine*; 1996–97: Peter Cole, *Selected Poems of Shmuel HaNagid*; 1994–95: David Ball, *Darkness Moves: An Henri Michaux Anthology, 1927–1984* and Carol Maier, *Memoirs of Leticia Valle*, by Rosa Chacel (joint winners); 1992–93: Estelle Gilson, *The Stories and Recollections of Umberto Saba*.

Sponsoring Organization: Modern Language Association of America (MLA).

Contact: Co-ordinator of Book Prizes and Special Projects.

Address: Modern Language Asscn of America, 26 Broadway, 3rd Floor, New York, NY 10004–1789, USA. **Telephone:** (646) 576-5141. **Fax:** (646) 458-0033. **Internet:** www.mla.org. **E-mail:** awards@mla.org.

Aldo and Jeanne Scaglione Prize for a Translation of a Scholarly Study of Literature

First awarded in 1995, the prize is presented in odd-numbered years for an outstanding translation into English of a book-length work of literary history, literary criticism, philology or literary theory. The winner is selected by a committee made up of members of the Modern Language Association of America (MLA), and receives $1,000 and a certificate.

Eligibility and Restrictions: Open to translations into English only; entries must have been published during the previous two years.

How to Apply: Publishers or translators may apply. Four copies of the book should be submitted, by 1 May of odd-numbered years.

Recent Winners: 1999–2000: Richard John Beardsworth, *The Confession of Augustine*, by Jean-François Lyotard; 1997–98: Marie-Claude Hays, *A Child Is Being Killed: On Primary Narcissism and the Death Drive*, by Serge Leclaire; 1995–96: John Charles Chasteen, *The Lettered City*, by Angel Rama, and Richard Heinemann and Bruce Krajewski, *Gadamer on Celan: "Who Am I and Who Are You?" and Other Essays, by Hans-Georg Gadamer* (joint winners); 1993–94: Joseph B. Solodow, *Latin Literature: A History*, by Gian Biagio Conte.

Sponsoring Organization: Modern Language Association of America (MLA).

Contact: Co-ordinator of Book Prizes and Special Projects.

Address: Modern Language Asscn of America, 26 Broadway, 3rd Floor, New York, NY 10004–1789, USA. **Telephone:** (646) 576-5141. **Fax:** (646) 458-0033. **Internet:** www.mla.org. **E-mail:** awards@mla.org.

Aldo and Jeanne Scaglione Publication Award for a Manuscript in Italian Literary Studies

An annual prize presented to an outstanding manuscript dealing with any aspect of the languages and literatures of Italy, including medieval Latin and comparative studies or intellectual history. The award consists of a $10,000 subvention to the press for the publication of the manuscript and a certificate for the author.

Eligibility and Restrictions: Open to manuscripts approved for publication before award deadline; authors must be current members of the Modern Language Association of America (MLA). Translations of classical works of prose and poetry produced in Italy prior to 1900 in any language (e.g. neo-Latin, Greek) or in a dialect of Italian may be entered. A manuscript may be in English or Italian but is eligible only if a not-for-profit press that is a member of the Association of American University Presses has favourably evaluated it.

How to Apply: Two copies of the manuscript, plus contact and biographical information, should be submitted by 1 August.

Recent Winners: 2001: Nelson Moe, *The View from Vesuvius: Italian Culture and the Southern Question*; 1999: Victoria Eulalia Kirkham, *Fabulous Vernacular: Boccaccio's Filocolo and the Art of Medieval Fiction*; 1998: Rebecca J. West, *Gianni Celati: The Craft of Everyday Storytelling*; 1997: Herman W. Haller, *The Other Italy: The Literary Canon in Dialect*.

Sponsoring Organization: Modern Language Association of America (MLA).

Contact: Co-ordinator of Book Prizes and Special Projects.

Address: Modern Language Asscn of America, 26 Broadway, 3rd Floor, New York, NY 10004–1789, USA. **Telephone:** (646) 576-5141. **Fax:** (646) 458-0033. **Internet:** www.mla.org. **E-mail:** awards@mla.org.

William Sanders Scarborough Prize

A new annual prize established in 2001 for an outstanding scholarly study of black American literature or culture. The prize is named after a distinguished man of letters and former university president, who was the first African American member of the Modern Language Association of America (MLA). The prize consists of $1,000 and a certificate.

Eligibility and Restrictions: For the inaugural prize books published between 1997 and 2001 were eligible; for future prizes they should have appeared during the previous calendar year. Authors need not be members of the MLA. Books that are primarily translations will not be considered.

How to Apply: Publishers are invited to send four copies by 1 May.

Sponsoring Organization: Modern Language Association of America (MLA).

Contact: Co-ordinator of Book Prizes and Special Projects.

Address: Modern Language Asscn of America, 26 Broadway, 3rd Floor, New York, NY 10004–1789, USA. **Telephone:** (646) 576-5141. **Fax:** (646) 458-0033. **Internet:** www.mla.org. **E-mail:** awards@mla.org.

Scheepersprys vir jeugliteratuur (Scheepers Prize for Young People's Literature)

The Scheepers Prize for Young People's Literature was established in 1956 by the South African Academy of Science and Arts, following a gift from Fred L. Scheepers. The prize is awarded every three years to an outstanding work in any literary genre for children. The winner receives a monetary prize and charter to the Academy.

Eligibility and Restrictions: Open to works published in Afrikaans in the previous three years.

Recent Winners: 2001: Jan Vermeulen, *Geraamtes dra nie klere nie*; 1989: C. Barnard, *Voetpad na Vergelegen*; 1986: D. van Niekerk, *Die Haasvanger*; 1983: F. Linde, *'n Tuiste vir Bitis*.

Sponsoring Organization: Suid-Afrikaanse Akademie vir Wetenskap en Kuns (South African Academy for Science and Arts).

Address: Die Suid-Afrikaanse Akademie vir Wetenskap en Kuns (South African Academy for Science and Arts), PO Box 538, Pretoria, 0001, South Africa. **Telephone:** (12) 328 5082. **Fax:** (12) 328 5091. **Internet:** www.akademie.co.za. **E-mail:** akademie@mweb.co.za.

Schlegel-Tieck Prize

An annual award for the best translation into English of a full-length 20th-century German literary work, published in the UK during the previous year. The winner receives £2,200.

Recent Winners: 2001: Krishna Winston, *Too Far Afield* by Günter Grass.

Sponsoring Organization: Translators Assocation.

Address: Translators Assocation, 84 Drayton Gardens, London SW10 9SB, UK. **Telephone:** 920) 7373 6642. **Fax:** (20) 7373 5768. **E-mail:** info@societyofauthors. org.

Olive Schreiner Prize

An annual prize, also known as the FNB Vita/Olive Schreiner prize, established in 1964 to honour new talent for excellence in prose, poetry and drama. Winners are chosen by a panel of experts, and receive R5,000 plus an illuminated certificate.

Eligibility and Restrictions: Open to works written in English by Southern African writers, and published in Southern Africa.

Recent Winners: Poetry: 2001: Mzi Mohola, *When Rains Come*; 1998: Dan Wylie Prose: 2000: Antjie Krog; 1997: Zakes Mda
Drama: 1999: Moira Lovell.

Sponsoring Organization: FNB Vita/English Academy of Southern Africa.

Contact: Admin. Officer C. James.

Address: POB 124, Witwatersrand, 2050, South Africa. **Telephone:** (11) 717 9339. **Fax:** (11) 717 9339. **Internet:** www.englishacademy.co.za. **E-mail:** engac@ cosmos.wits.ac.za.

Ruth Schwartz Children's Book Award

An annual award, established in 1976, for a picture book and a young-adult book picked by children from a shortlist of books compiled by booksellers. The award is presented by the Ontario Arts Council and Canadian Booksellers' Association (CBA) in honour of Ruth Schwartz, a respected Toronto bookseller. In the young-adult/middle reader book category the winning author receives a $2,000 prize; the $3,000 children's picture book prize is shared between the author and illustrator.

Eligibility and Restrictions: Entries must be published in Canada during the previous year and the author must be a Canadian citizen.

How to Apply: There is no application process; the shortlists of five books in each category are compiled by the CBA from nominations made by children's booksellers across the country.

Recent Winners: Picture Book Category: 2001: Stephanie S. McLellan (author) and Sean Cassidy (illustrator), *Chicken Cat*; 2000: Marie-Louise Gay, *Stella, Star of the Sea*; 1999: Celia Barker Lottridge (author) and Harvey Chan (illustrator), *Music for the Tsar of the Sea*
Young Adult Category: 2001: Janet McNaughton, *The Secret Under My Skin*; 2000: Kenneth Oppel, *Sunwing*; 1999: Eric Walters, *War of the Eagles*.

Sponsoring Organization: Ontario Arts Council Foundation/Canadian Booksellers' Association.

Address: Ontario Arts Council Foundation, 151 Bloor St West, 5th Floor, Toronto, ON M5S 1T6, Canada. **Telephone:** (416) 969-7438. **Fax:** (416) 969-7441.

Schweizer Jugendbuchpreis (Swiss Children's Book Prize)

The Schweizer Jugendbuchpreis is awarded to authors of children's literature and teenage literature either for their collected works or for an outstanding individual work. The prize has been awarded annually since 1943 and is sponsored by the Dachverband Schweizer Lehrerinnen und Lehrer (Swiss Teachers' Association).

Recent Winners: 2000: Angelika Waldis, *Tita und Leo*; 1999: *Zapp Zappina* (multiple authors); 1998: Christian Urech, *Schräge Typen*; 1997: (no prize awarded); 1996: Jürg Schubiger, *Als die Welt noch jung war*.

Sponsoring Organization: Dachverband Schweizer Lehrerinnen und Lehrer.

Address: Postfach 189, Ringstrasse 54, 8057 Zurich, Switzerland. **Telephone:** (1) 315 54 54.

Scott Moncrieff Prize

An annual award for the best translation into English of a full-length French literary work originally published in the last 150 years, published in the UK in the preceding year. The winner receives £1,000.

How to Apply: Closing date for entries is 31 December.

Recent Winners: 2001: Barbara Bray, *On Identity* by Amin Maalouf.

Sponsoring Organization: Translators Association.

Address: Translators Assocation, 84 Drayton Gardens, London SW10 9SB, UK. **Telephone:** (20) 7373 6642. **Fax:** (20) 7373 5768. **E-mail:** info@societyofauthors. org.

Scottish Arts Council Book of the Year Award

The award was inaugurated in 2002 in place of the former Scottish Arts Council Book Awards and Children's Book Awards, under which up to 10 adult and 5 children's awards of £1,000 were made annually. One winner is now chosen in each category of Adult and Children's Book of the Year, with prizes of £10,000 and £5,000 respectively. The aim of the award is to 'raise the profile and prestige of Scotland's thriving literary culture'.

Eligibility and Restrictions: Authors should be Scottish, resident in Scotland or have written works of Scottish interest.

How to Apply: Applications are accepted from publishers only.

Recent Winners: Book of the Year: 2002: Ali Smith, *Hotel World*
Children's Book of the Year: 2002: Alison Prince, *Oranges and Murder*.

Sponsoring Organization: Scottish Arts Council.

Address: Scottish Arts Council, 12 Manor Place, Edinburgh EH3 7DD, UK. **Telephone:** (131) 226 6051. **Internet:** www.scottishbooktrust.com.

Jaroslav Seifert Award

An annual literary award established in 1986 by the Charta 77 Foundation. The award is named after Jaroslav Seifert who in 1984 became the first Czech writer to be awarded the Nobel Prize for literature.

Eligibility and Restrictions: May be awarded for fiction or poetry.

Recent Winners: 2001: Zdenek Rotrekl, *Nezdené mesto*; other previous winners include Dominik Tatarka, Ludvík Vaculík, Ivan Divis, Jirík Kolár, Ivan Wernisch, Bohumil Hrabal, Milan Kundera, Jirík Kratochvil and Pavel Srut.

Sponsoring Organization: Charta 77 Foundation, Melantrichova 5, 110 00 Prague, 1, Czech Republic.

Selskabets Pris

The prize was awarded for the first time in 1968, and is awarded every other year for an outstanding cultural contribution in the field of literary criticism. The prizewinner is selected by members of the Danish Academy by a simple majority, and receives DKK 20,000.

Eligibility and Restrictions: Open only to Danish-language authors.

How to Apply: No direct applications are accepted.

Recent Winners: 2001: Jørgen Fafner; 1999: Thomas Bredsdorff; 1997: Jørgen Bonde Jensen; 1995: Jørgen Knudsen.

Sponsoring Organization: Danish Academy.

Contact: Administrator Dr Allan Philip.

Address: Det Danske Akademi, Rungstedlund, Rungsted Strandvej 111, 2960 Rungsted Kyst, Denmark. **Telephone:** 33 13 11 12. **Fax:** 33 32 80 45. **Internet:** www.danskeakademi.dk. **E-mail:** lawoffice@philip.dk.

Syed Waris Shah Award

The Pakistan Academy of Letters administers a series of annual prizes established in 1980 under the Hijra National Literary Awards Scheme. The aim of the awards is to promote literary activities and recognize outstanding contributions. The Syed Waris Shah Award is an annual prize of Rs 50,000 for works written in Punjabi.

Recent Winners: 2000: Munnu Bhai, *Ajay Qayamat Naeen Aaee*; 1999: Ilyas Ghuman, *Pind Dee Luj*; 1998: G. Mustafa Bismal, *Sufne Unndian Akhan*.

Sponsoring Organization: Pakistan Academy of Letters.

Contact: Deputy Dir Naseem Mahmood.

Address: Pitras Bokhari Road, Sector H-8/1, Islamabad, Pakistan. **Telephone:** 9257164. **Fax:** 9257159. **E-mail:** academy@apollo.net.pk.

Shamus Awards

The Shamus Awards are given annually by Private Eye Writers of America. The categories include novel, first novel, original paperback and short story. The 2002 award ceremony was cancelled out of respect for victims of the terrorist attacks in New York in September 2001.

Recent Winners: Fiction: 2001: Carolina Garcia-Aguilera, *Havana Heat*; 2000: Don Winslow, *California Fire and Life*; 1999: Bill Pronzini, *Boobytrap*; 1998: Terrance Faherty, *Come Back Dead*
Paperback: 2001: Thomas Lipinski, *Death in the Steel City*; 2000: Laura Lippman, *In Big Trouble*; 1999: Steven Womack, *Murder Manual*; 1998: Laura Lippman, *Charm City*
First Novel: 2001: Bob Truluck, *Street Level*; 2000: John Connolly, *Every Dead Thing*; 1999: Steve Hamilton, *A Cold Day in Paradise*; 1998: Rick Riordan, *Big Red Tequilla*
Short Story: 2001: Brendan Dubois, *The Road's End*; 2000: I. J. Parker, *Akitada's First Case*; 1999: Warren Murphy, *Another Day, Another Dollar*; 1998: Carolyn Wheat, *Love Me for My Yellow Hair Alone*.

Sponsoring Organization: Private Eye Writers of America.

Address: Private Eye Writers of America, 4342 Forest DeVille Dr., St Louis, MO 63129, USA.

Mina P. Shaughnessy Prize

First awarded in 1980, the prize is presented annually for an outstanding publication in the field of teaching English language, literature, rhetoric and composition. The winner is selected by a committee made up of members of the Modern Language Association of America (MLA), and receives $1,000, a certificate and one-year membership of the MLA.

Eligibility and Restrictions: Entries must be published in the calendar year preceding the competition. Textbooks based on authors' original research are also eligible under certain circumstances.

How to Apply: Publishers or authors may apply. Four copies of the book should be submitted by 1 May.

Recent Winners: 2001: Jacqueline Jones Royster, *Traces of a Stream: Literacy and Social Change among African American Women*; 1999: A. Suresh Canagarajah, *Resisting Linguistic Imperialism in English Teaching*; 1998: Sharon Crowley, *Composition in the University: Historical and Polemical Essays*; 1997: Thomas P. Miller, *The Formation of College English: Rhetoric and Belles Lettres in the British Cultural Provinces* and Marilyn S. Sternglass, *Time to Know Them: A Longitudinal Study of Writing and Learning at the College Level* (joint winners); 1996: James Crosswhite, *The Rhetoric of Reason: Writing and the Attractions of Argument*.

Sponsoring Organization: Modern Language Association of America (MLA).

Contact: Co-ordinator of Book Prizes and Special Projects.

Address: Modern Language Asscn of America, 26 Broadway, 3rd Floor, New York, NY 10004–1789, USA. **Telephone:** (646) 576-5141. **Fax:** (646) 458-0033. **Internet:** www.mla.org. **E-mail:** awards@mla.org.

Bernard Shaw Prize

A triennial award, funded by the Anglo-Swedish Literary Foundation, for the best translation into English of a full-length Swedish work, published in the UK in the three years prior to the award. The winner receives a prize of £1,000.

How to Apply: Entries are accepted from publishers only.

Sponsoring Organization: Translators Assocation.

Address: Translators Assocation, 84 Drayton Gardens, London SW10 9SB, UK. **Telephone:** (20) 7373 6642. **Fax:** (20) 7373 5768. **E-mail:** info@societyofauthors. org.

Shelley Memorial Award

The Shelley Memorial Award, which is administered by the Poetry Society of America (PSA), was established by the will of the late Mary P. Sears. The award, which was first presented in 1929, varies between $6,000 and $9,000 and is given to a living American poet.

How to Apply: There is no public application process; entry is by nomination only.

Recent Winners: 2002: Angela Jackson and Marie Ponsot (joint winners); 2001: Alice Notley and Michael Palmer (joint winners); 2000: Jean Valentine; 1999: Tom Sleigh; 1998: Eleanor Ross Taylor.

Sponsoring Organization: Poetry Society of America.

Address: Poetry Society of America, 15 Gramercy Park, New York, NY 10003, USA. **Telephone:** (212) 254-9628. **Internet:** www.poetrysociety.org.

Taras Shevchenko Award

The award was established in 1996 alongside eight other state awards, and is named after the famous Ukrainian poet Taras Hryhorovych Shevchenko. It has since become one of the most important Ukrainian prizes, and is presented in recognition of the winner's significant contribution and influence in the development of Ukrainian art and culture. In addition to the literary winners, prizes are also presented for music, art, acting and other areas.

Recent Winners: 1996: Volodymyr Bazylevskyj (poet), *Vertep*; Victor Minailo (novelist), *Vichnyj Ivan (Eternal Ivan)*; Iryna Zhylenko (poet), *Verchirka u starij vynarnij (An Evening in the Old Winery)*; Raisa Ivanchenko (writer), *Zrada, abo yak staty volodarem (Betrayal, or How to Become a Leader), Hniv Peruna (Perun's Anger), Zoloti Stremena (Golden Stir-ups)* and *Otruta dlya Knyahyn (Poison for the Princess)*; Vyacheslav Chornovil (publicist), *Pravosudya chy retsedyvy teroru (Justice or Relapses of Terror), Lykho z Rozumu (Evil with Wisdom)* and *Khronika taborovykh budniv (A Chronicle of Prison Days)*.

Sponsoring Organization: National Academy of Sciences of Ukraine.

Address: National Academy of Sciences of Ukraine, 54, Volodimirska St, Kiev, 01601, Ukraine. **Telephone:** (44) 224 5167. **Fax:** (44) 224 3243.

Yamamoto Shûgorô Shô (Yamamoto Shûgorô Award)

Established in 1987 on the 20th anniversary of the founding of the Shinchô Society for the Promotion of the Literary Arts (Shinchô Bungei Shinkô Kai). Along with the Mishima Yukio Award, the Shinchô Prize for Distinguished Scholarship, and the (non-literary) Grand Prize for Japanese Art, one of the so-called Four Shinchô Prizes (Shinchô yonshô). Awarded annually to a new work of fiction with excellent narrative; the winner receives a commemorative gift and a cash prize of 1 million yen.

Eligibility and Restrictions: Work must be written in Japanese and published between the previous April and March.

How to Apply: There is no public application process.

Recent Winners: 2001: Yûsaburô Otogawa, *Gonen no ume (Five-Year Plums)*, and Kaho Nakayama, *Shiroi bara no fuchi made (Until the Edge of the White Rose)* (joint winners); 2000: Shimako Iwai; 1999: Kiyoshi Shigematsu; 1998: Yang Sogiru; 1997: Yuhichi Shingo.

Sponsoring Organization: Shinchô Society for the Promotion of the Literary Arts (Shinchô Bungei Shinkô Kai).

Contact: Dir Masaharu Yokoyama.

Address: Shinchô Society for the Promotion of the Literary Arts (Shinchô Bungei Shinkô Kai), 71 Yarai -cho, Shinjuku-ku, Tokyo, 162–8711, Japan. **Telephone:** (3) 3266 5411. **Fax:** (3) 3266 5534.

Marshall Shulman Book Prize

The prize has been awarded since 1987 to encourage high-quality studies of the international behaviour of the countries of the former Communist Bloc. It is awarded for an outstanding monograph dealing with the international relations or foreign policy of any of the states of the former Soviet Union or Eastern Europe. The winner is selected by a committee, and receives a cash award.

Eligibility and Restrictions: Open to works published in English in the USA during the previous year. Authors must be American scholars or residents of the USA. Textbooks, translations, bibliographies and reference works are not eligible.

How to Apply: Publishers, editors and authors should send copies of eligible works to each committee member by mid-May.

Recent Winners: 2001: David Stone, *Hammer and Rifle: The Militarization of the Soviet Union 1926–1933* and Robert English, *Russia and the Idea of the West: Gorbachev, Intellectuals and the End of the Cold War* (joint winners); 2000: Matthew Evangelista, *Unarmed Forces: The Transnational Movement to End the Cold War*; 1999: William E. Odom, *The Collapse of the Soviet Military* and Ilya Prizel, *National Identity and Foreign Policy: Nationalism and Leadership in Poland, Russia and Ukraine* (joint winners); 1998: Paul Josephson, *New Atlantis Revisited: Akademgorodok, the Siberian City of Science*; 1997: Jane I. Dawson, *Eco-Nationalism: Anti-Nuclear Activism and National Identity in Russia, Lithuania and Ukraine*.

Sponsoring Organization: American Association for the Advancement of Slavic Studies/Harriman Institute of Columbia University.

Address: American Association for the Advancement of Slavic Studies, 8 Story St, Cambridge, MA 02138, USA. **Telephone:** (617) 495-0677. **Fax:** (617) 495-0680. **E-mail:** aaass@hcs.harvard.edu.

Robert F. Sibert Informational Book Award

The Robert F. Sibert Informational Book Award, established in 2001, is awarded annually to the author of the most distinguished informational book published during the preceding year. The award is named in honour of Robert F. Sibert, the long-time President of Bound to Stay Bound Books, Inc. of Jacksonville, Illinois, and is sponsored by the company. The Association for Library Service to Children (ALSC) administers the award.

How to Apply: One copy of the book should be sent to the ALSC office and one copy to the Chair of the Award Committee, by 31 December of the year of publication.

Recent Winners: 2002: Susan Campbell Bartoletti, *Black Potatoes: The Story of the Great Irish Famine, 1845–1850*; 2001: Marc Aronson, *Sir Walter Ralegh and the Quest for El Dorado*.

Sponsoring Organization: Association for Library Service to Children (American Library Association)/Bound to Stay Bound Books, Inc.

Address: Association for Library Service to Children, American Library Association, 50 East Huron, Chicago, IL 60611–2795, USA. **Fax:** (312) 944-7671. **Internet:** www.ala.org/alsc. **E-mail:** alsc@ala.org.

Sidewise Awards for Alternate History

Established in 1995 to honour excellence in alternative history writing; the first awards were announced in summer 1996. The award takes its name from Murray Leinster's 1934 short story *Sidewise In Time*. Two awards are presented each year at the World Science Fiction Convention, for long form and short form, and in addition the judging panel may also present a lifetime achievement award for work published prior to 1995. The prize consists of a plaque.

Eligibility and Restrictions: To be considered, a work must have had either first English-language publication or first American publication in the preceding calendar year. The short-form award is presented for the best work of less than

60,000 words. This includes short stories, novelettes and novellas, and poems. The long-form award is presented for the best work longer than 60,000 words. This category includes individual novels and longer works.

How to Apply: Six copies of the book or story should be sent to the judges.

Recent Winners: Short-form: 2000: Ted Chiang, *Seventy-Two Letters*; 1999: Alain Bergeron,*The Eighth Register*; 1998: Ian R. MacLeod, *The Summer Isles*; 1997: William Sanders, *The Undiscovered*; 1996: Walter Jon Williams, *Foreign Devils*

Long-form: 2000: Mary Gentle, *Ash: A Secret History*; 1999: Brendan DuBois, *Resurrection Day*; 1998: Stephen Fry, *Making History*; 1997: Harry Turtledove, *How Few Remain*; 1996: Stephen Baxter, *Voyage*

Lifetime Achievement: 1999: Randall Garrett, *The Lord Darcy Series*; 1997: Robert Sobel, *For Want of a Nail*.

Contact: Judge, Steven H. Silver.

Address: 707 Sapling Lane, Deerfield, IL 60015–3969, USA. **Telephone:** (847) 607-0776. **Fax:** (847) 607-778. **Internet:** www.uchronia.net/sidewise. **E-mail:** shsilver@sfsite.com.

Silas Prisen

Founded by Cecil Bødker in 1999, this award is presented every second or third year to an author for several children's books. The winner is selected by members of the Danish Academy, and receives DKK100,000.

Eligibility and Restrictions: Open to Danish language writers in the field of children's literature.

How to Apply: No direct applications are accepted.

Recent Winners: 2001: Bjarne Reuter.

Sponsoring Organization: Danish Academy.

Contact: Administrator Dr Allan Philip.

Address: Det Danske Akademi, Rungstedlund, Rungsted Strandvej 111, 2960 Rungsted Kyst, Denmark. **Telephone:** 33 13 11 12. **Fax:** 33 32 80 45. **Internet:** www.danskeakademi.dk. **E-mail:** lawoffice@philip.dk.

Vasyl Simonenko Prize

This prize, named after an eminent Ukrainian poet (1935–1963), was established by the National Writers Union of Ukraine (NSPU) in 1987 to recognize the best first book of poetry by a young poet.

Sponsoring Organization: National Writers Union of Ukraine (NSPU).

Contact: V. Yavorivsky.

Address: Blvd Bankova 2, 01024 Kiev, Ukraine. **Fax:** (44) 293-45-86. **Internet:** www.nspu.kiev.ua. **E-mail:** nspu@I.kiev.ua.

Singapore National Book Awards

The NBDCS organizes the Singapore National Book Awards, which are presented every two years for works of fiction, non-fiction, poetry and children's books written by Singaporeans and permanent residents in each of the four official languages.

Recent Winners: 1998: Abdul Ghani Abdul Hamid; 1995: Masuri S.N.; 1990: Muhammad Ariff, Jangan Tak Ada.

Sponsoring Organization: National Book Development Council of Singapore (NBDCS).

Contact: Elaine Kok.

Address: National Book Development Council of Singapore, No. 1, Temasek Avenue, #17–01 Millenia Tower, Singapore, 039192, Singapore. **Telephone:** (65) 4343651. **Fax:** (65) 8832393. **E-mail:** sp@reedexpo.com.

Skolebibliotekarforeningens Litteraturpris (Association of School Libraries Literary Prize)

A prize established by the Association of School Libraries in 1982, to recognize the best in new literature for children. The winner receives a piece of art.

Recent Winners: 2002: Thore Hansen; 2001: Finn Øglænd; 2000: Svein Nyhus; 1999: Bjørn Sortland; 1998: Egil Hyldmo.

Sponsoring Organization: Norsk Skolebibliotekarforening.

Address: Norsk Skolebibliotekarforening, Torsvev 1, 7540 Klaebu, Norway.

Jenny Smelik IBBY Prijs

A biennial prize presented to an author or illustrator for a work of children's literature which deals with the culture of ethnic minorities and promotes a better understanding of people with different backgrounds. The prize, which is named after a children's author, was formerly known as the Jenny Smelik-Kiggen Prijs.

Eligibility and Restrictions: Entries must have been published in the two years preceding the award; the prize is open to works of both fiction and non-fiction.

Recent Winners: 1998: Jos van Hest and Saskia van der Valk, *FeestVerHalen*; 1996: Naima El Bezaz, *De weg naar het noorden*; 1991: Marion Bloem.

Sponsoring Organization: Dutch Section of the International Board on Books for Young People (IBBY).

Address: PO Box 17162, 1001 JD Amsterdam, Netherlands.

Lilian Ida Smith Awards

Established to assist people aged over 35 to embark upon or further a literary career. The prize is awarded every two years, following a bequest by Lilian Ida Smith to NZ PEN (now the New Zealand Society of Authors—NZSA), and takes the form of a single biennial grant of $3,000.

Eligibility and Restrictions: Work may be fiction, non-fiction or poetry, for children or adults. Authors must be aged 35 or over and a member of NZSA. Applicants should not be holding a writer's bursary or grant from a similar source. Previous winners may not reapply within four years of earlier entry.

How to Apply: Applications must be received by 20 February; applicants should submit a synopsis of the work, or, failing that, a sample of previous work, and a CV with details of writing history.

Recent Winners: 2000: Jackie Davis; 1998: James Norcliffe, *Holden's Red Hunting Cap*; 1994: Jane Zusters; 1989: Elizabeth Smither.

Sponsoring Organization: New Zealand Society of Authors.

Address: PO Box 67 013, Mount Eden, Auckland, 3, New Zealand. **Internet:** www.authors.org.nz/nzsa/awards.html.

Society of Authors Medical Book Awards

The Society of Authors administers a number of book awards in various categories, sponsored by the Royal Society of Medicine. Prizes are awarded to the best English-language medical and dental books in several categories, including: Basic Book (undergraduate level, reviews, atlases); Advanced Authored Book (monographs, postgraduate level, specialities); Advanced Edited Book; Medical History/General Interest Book; Asher Prize (£1,000 for a first medical textbook with a maximum of three authors); The RSM Library Prize (£1,200 for a first edition specialist textbook priced under £50) and Dental Prize.

Eligibility and Restrictions: All books entered must have been published in the UK during the previous year (year ending 31 May).

How to Apply: Three copies of the book should be submitted by 31 May.

Recent Winners: Asher Prize: 2001: S. S. Nussey and S. A. Whitehead, *Endocrinology: An Integrated Approach*
First Edition Textbook: 2001: Louise Scheuer and Sue Black, *Developmental Juvenile Osteology*
First Edition Multi-Author Textbook: 2001: John D. Corson and Robin C. N. Williamson (Editors), *Surgery*
RSM Library Prize: 2001: Christopher M. Ball and Robert S. Phillips (Editors), *Acute Medicine Evidence-Based on Call*
Medical History Book: 2001: Harold Ellis, *A History of Surgery*
First Edition Dental Book: 2001: Linda Greenwall (Editor), *Bleaching Techniques in Restorative Dentistry*.

Sponsoring Organization: Royal Society of Medicine.

Address: Medical Writers Group, Society of Authors, 84 Drayton Gdns, London SW10 9SB, UK. **Telephone:** (20) 7373 6642. **Fax:** (20) 7373 5768. **Internet:** www.societyofauthors.org/medical/mwgawa.htm. **E-mail:** DSym@ societyofauthors.org.

Society of School Librarians International Book Awards

The Society of School Librarians International (SSLI) presents a series of annual awards in various categories to outstanding trade books for young people, published during the preceding year. There are seven categories divided up according to content (language, picture books, novels, social studies and science) and age of readers (elementary or secondary).

Sponsoring Organization: Society of School Librarians International.

Address: Society of School Librarians International, 19 Savage St, Charleston, SC 29401, USA.

Zulu Sofola Prize

The Zulu Sofola Prize is named after a Nigerian woman writer and dramatist born in 1938. It was established to encourage writing by women, and is valued at N25,000. The first award was presented in 2001.

Eligibility and Restrictions: Entries must not have won any prize previously. The award is open to works in any genres.

How to Apply: Entrants should submit four copies of the work to the address given.

Recent Winners: 2001: Akachi Ezeigbo, *House of Symbols*.

Sponsoring Organization: Association of Nigerian Authors (ANA).

Address: ANA House, 26, Oladipo Labinjo Crescent, off Akinsemoyin Street, off Bode Thomas Street, Surulere, Lagos, Nigeria.

Solzhenitsyn Prize for Russian Writing

The Solzhenitsyn Prize for Russian writing was established in 1997 by the Nobel Prize-winning author and his wife. The annual prize is worth $25,000 and is funded entirely from royalties for his novel *Gulag Archipelago*. The aim of the prize is to recognize works which 'help Russian society to understand itself and make a significant contribution to the development of [Russian] literary traditions'.

Recent Winners: 2000: Valentin Rasputin; 1999: Inna Lisnyanskaya; 1998: Vladimir Toporov.

Address: Solzhenitsyn Prize, Moscow, Russia.

Soong Ching Ling Children's Literature Prize

The Soong Ching Ling Children's Literature Prize was established in June 1986 with the aim of recognizing writers who have made an outstanding contribution to children's literature, and of promoting the creation of children's literature in China. The first prizes were presented in 1988. The prize is awarded every two years, with a different genre specified each time (e.g. drama in 1988, science/ science fiction in 1990, novels in 1992).

Eligibility and Restrictions: Open to works for children, with a different genre specified every two years.

Recent Winners: 1990: a series of popular science and science fiction books; 1988: Chu Xue and Zhan Nan, *The World that has been Found Back*.

Sponsoring Organization: Soong Ching Ling Foundation.

Address: Soong Ching Ling Foundation, No. 46, Houhai Bei Yan, Beijing, 100009, China. **Telephone:** 401-6304. **Fax:** 401-1354. **Internet:** www.wuta.com/ Wuta/soong.html#A04.

Southeast Asia (SEA) Write Award

The SEA Write Award is presented to prominent writers and poets of Association of South East Asian Nations (ASEAN) member nations. It is South East Asia's most prestigious literary award and is conferred for lifelong contribution to the publishing industry in each country. Awards are presented by the Crown Prince of Thailand at a dinner in honour of the winners, who each receive a prize of 100,000 baht.

How to Apply: Nominations for each country are made by national literary institutions.

Recent Winners: Myanmar: 2001: U Htin Gyi (pen-name: Tekkatho Htin Gyi); 2000: Daw Yin Yin (Saw Mon Hnyin); 1999: U Kyaw Aung (Kyaw Aung); 1998: Hsin Byu Kyun Aung Thein (U Kyi Aye)

Philippines: 1986: José Maria Sison, essay writing and poetry, chiefly for *Prison and Beyond*

Thailand: 2001: Chokechai Banditsilasak, *Ban Kao (Old House)*; 1982: Chart Korpjitti, *The Judgment*; 1980: Naowarat Phongphaibun; 1979, Khamphun Buntawi, *Luk Isan*.

Address: Southeast Asia (SEA) Write Award, Bangkok, Thailand.

Manès Sperber-Preis für Literatur

The prize was established in 1985 in memory of the writer and philosopher Manès Sperber. It is awarded for an outstanding literary work written in German. The sponsor is the Bundesministerium für Unterricht und Kunst (Ministry for Education and Art) in Vienna. The prize is awarded every two years, and the winner receives a prize of 100,000 Sch (€7,270).

How to Apply: No direct application; nominations are made by an independent jury.

Recent Winners: Previous winners include Siegfried Lenz, Albert Drach, Ilse Rechlinger and Fritz Habeck.

Sponsoring Organization: Bundesministerium für Unterricht und Kunst.

Address: Bundesministerium für Unterricht und Kunst, 1000 Vienna, Austria.

Språklig Samlings Litteraturpris

Established in 1963 by the Landslaget for Språklig Samling, an organization concerned with the promotion of good use of language, with funding from the Tomas Refsdal literary fund. The prize is awarded annually for literature of high quality, with good use of language, in the genres of poetry, novels, drama, essay or non-fiction.

Recent Winners: 2001: Jonny Halberg; 2000: Harald Rosenløw Eeg; 1999: Erling Kittelsen; 1998: Rune Christiansen; 1997: Magnar Mikkelsen.

Sponsoring Organization: Landslaget for Språklig Samling.

Address: Språklig Samling, Postboks 636, Sentrum, 0106 Oslo, Norway. **Internet:** home.no.net/lss/.

St Martin's Press/Malice Domestic Contest

A contest for the best first traditional mystery novel. The winning entry is published by St Martin's Press, and the author receives an advance against the future royalties of $10,000.

Eligibility and Restrictions: The contest is open to any professional or non-professional writer, regardless of nationality, who has never published a traditional mystery. Only one manuscript entry is permitted per writer. All manuscripts submitted must be original works of book length.

How to Apply: All entries must be submitted by October 25, accompanied by a double-spaced copy of the manuscript and a completed application form.

Sponsoring Organization: St Martin's Press.

Address: St Martin's Press, 175 5th Avenue, New York, NY 10010, USA. **Fax:** (212) 674-6132.

Staatliche Förderungspreise für junge Schriftstellerinnen und Schriftsteller (Bavarian State Encouragement Prize for Young Writers)

An annual prize sponsored by the Bavarian Ministry of Education and Culture to encourage young writers from Bavaria. Open to works of fiction, poetry, drama, non-fiction, children's literature, or translation into German of any of the above. The number of prizes awarded each year may vary, each of DM10,000.

Eligibility and Restrictions: Open to works which have been previously published by a writer aged not more than 40 who is resident in Bavaria.
How to Apply: It is not possible to apply directly for the prize.
Sponsoring Organization: Bayerisches Staatsministerium für Unterricht, Kultur, Wissenschaft und Kunst.
Address: Bayerisches Staatsministerium für Unterricht, Kultur, Wissenschaft und Kunst, Salvatorstr. 2, 80333 Munich, Germany. **Telephone:** (89) 21 86-12 67. **Fax:** (89) 21 86 12 81.

State Prize of the Russian Federation in Arts and Letters

An official state award, which carries a prize of around $10,000; the winner is announced with the signing of a decree by the President.
Recent Winners: 2000: Vladimir Voinovich, *Monumental Propaganda* and Andrei Volos, *Khurramabad* (joint winners); 1999: Daniil Granin.
Sponsoring Organization: Russian Federation in Arts and Letters.
Contact: Dr Sergei Losev.
Address: State Literature Museum, Petrovka 281, 103051 Moscow, Russia. **Telephone:** (95) 290-20-88. **Fax:** (95) 290-20-88.

State Prizes for Literature

An official prize awarded by the Ministry of Culture to recognize achievements in the field of literature. The winners receive a cash prize of €10,000.
Recent Winners: 2002: Markku Paasonen (poet), *Voittokulku*, and Anna-Maija Viitanen (translator), *The Little Girl Who Was Too Fond of Matches* by Gaétan Soucy; 2000: Juha Seppälä (author) and Erkki Kirjalainen (translator).
Sponsoring Organization: Ministry of Education.
Address: Ministry of Education, Meritullinkatu 10, 00171 Helsinki, Finland.

John Steinbeck Award

The Steinbeck Award, named after the Nobel Prize-winning author who lived his final years on the East End of Long Island, is awarded by Southampton College to an East End writer for their contribution to literature and humanity.
Recent Winners: 1996: Wilfrid Sheed; 1995: David Ignatow; 1994: Betty Friedan; 1993: Terrence McNally; 1992: Kurt Vonnegut.
Sponsoring Organization: Southampton College, Long Island University.
Address: Southampton College, Long Island University, 239 Montauk Highway, Southampton, NY 1968–4196, USA. **Telephone:** (631) 283-4000. **Fax:** (631) 287-8125.

Wallace Stevens Award

The Wallace Stevens Award was established in August 1994 by an anonymous gift of $2 million to the Academy of American Poets. The award recognizes outstanding and proven mastery in the art of poetry. The winner is chosen by a panel of judges and receives a prize of $150,000.
How to Apply: No applications are accepted.
Recent Winners: 2001: John Ashbery; 2000: Frank Bidart; 1999: Jackson Mac Low; 1998: A. R. Ammons; 1997: Anthony Hecht.

Sponsoring Organization: Academy of American Poets.

Address: Academy of American Poets, 584 Broadway, Suite 1208, New York, NY 10012, USA. **Telephone:** (212) 274-0343. **Fax:** (212) 274-9427. **Internet:** www.poets.org/academy. **E-mail:** academy@poets.org.

Otto Stoessl-Preis

A biennial prize of €4,000, awarded to an unpublished short story in German of 20 to 30 pages.

How to Apply: Deadline for submissions is 31 December.

Sponsoring Organization: Otto Stoessl-Stiftung (Otto Stoessl Foundation).

Contact: Administrator Dr Christoph Binder.

Address: Otto Stoessl-Stiftung, Semmelweisgasse 9, 8010 Graz, Austria.

Stora Priset (The Swedish Academy Great Prize)

Established in April 1786 by King Gustaf III, the award comprises a gold medal and is given to mark a lifetime's achievement. The prize is awarded infrequently.

How to Apply: There is no direct application process.

Sponsoring Organization: Swedish Academy.

Contact: Sec. Bo Svensen.

Address: Swedish Academy, POB 2118, 103 13 Stockholm, Sweden. **Telephone:** (8) 10 65 24. **Fax:** (8) 24 42 25. **Internet:** www.svenskaakademien.se. **E-mail:** sekretariat@svenskaakademien.se.

Den Store Pris

Established in 1961 by the Ministry of Culture. The prize is awarded every other year for a complete body of work, with the recipient chosen by members of the Danish Academy. The prize is DKK300,000.

Eligibility and Restrictions: Open only to Danish authors.

How to Apply: No direct applications are accepted.

Recent Winners: 2000: Kirsten Thorup; 1998: Cecil Bødker; 1996: Vibeke Grønfeldt; 1994: Ib Michael.

Sponsoring Organization: Danish Academy.

Contact: Administrator Dr Allan Philip.

Address: Det Danske Akademi, Rungstedlund, Rungsted Strandvej 111, 2960 Rungsted Kyst, Denmark. **Telephone:** 33 13 11 12. **Fax:** 33 32 80 45. **Internet:** www.danskeakademi.dk. **E-mail:** lawoffice@philip.dk.

Jan Strzelecki Prize

An award for essays presented by the Polish PEN Club.

Sponsoring Organization: Polish PEN Club.

Address: Krakówskie Przedmiescie 87/89, 00–079 Warsaw, Poland. **Telephone:** (22) 826 57 84. **Fax:** (22) 826 28 23. **Internet:** www.penclub.atomnet.pl. **E-mail:** penclub@ikp.atm.com.pl.

Theodore Sturgeon Memorial Award

The Theodore Sturgeon Award for the best short science fiction of the year was established in 1987 by James Gunn, Director of the Center for the Study of Science Fiction at the University of Kansas, and the heirs of Theodore Sturgeon.

Recent Winners: 2001: Ian McDonald, *Tendeléo's Story*; 2000: David Marusek, *The Wedding Album*; 1999: Ted Chiang, *Story of Your Life*; 1998: Michael Flynn, *House of Dreams*; 1997: Nancy Kress, *The Flowers of Aulit Prison*.

Sponsoring Organization: Center for the Study of Science Fiction.

Address: Center for the Study of Science Fiction, University of Kansas, Lawrence, Kansas, MO 66045, USA. **Telephone:** (785) 864-3380. **Internet:** falcon.cc.ukans.edu/~sfcenter/sturgeon.htm.

Sunday Telegraph Catherine Pakenham Memorial Award

Founded in 1970 in memory of Catherine Pakenham, who died in a car crash while working for the *Telegraph Magazine*. The winner receives £1,000 and the chance to write for a Telegraph publication.

Eligibility and Restrictions: Open to young women journalists aged 18–25 who have at least one piece of published work. Entries should be a previously unpublished non-fiction article of between 750 and 2,000 words.

How to Apply: Articles should be submitted by early May, accompanied by an entry form.

Recent Winners: Previous winners include Tina Brown and Polly Toynbee.

Sponsoring Organization: Sunday Telegraph.

Contact: PR Exec. Charlotte Ibarra.

Address: Corporate Affairs Department, The Sunday Telegraph, 1 Canada Sq. Canary Wharf, London E14 5DT, UK. **Fax:** (20) 7513 2512. **Internet:** www.telegraph.co.uk. **E-mail:** charlotte.ibarra@telegraph.co.uk.

Sunday Times Award for Literary Excellence

An annual award established in 1987 to fiction and non-fiction writers. Winners are chosen by a panel of judges consisting of *Sunday Times* writers, publishers and other leading figures from the publishing industry, and awarded at the discretion of the Literary Editor. The winner receives an inscribed silver trophy.

Recent Winners: 1997: Harold Pinter.

Sponsoring Organization: The Sunday Times.

Address: The Sunday Times, 1 Pennington St, London E1 9XW, UK.

Sunday Times Young Writer of the Year Award

Awarded to a writer under the age of 35 for a work of fiction, non-fiction or poetry published in the previous year. The winner receives £5,000.

Eligibility and Restrictions: The author must be a British citizen and resident in the UK.

Recent Winners: 2001: Zadie Smith, *White Teeth*; 2000: Sarah Waters, *Affinity*; 1999: Paul Farley, *The Boy From The Chemist Is Here To See You*; 1998: Patrick French, *Liberty Or Death*; 1997: Francis Spufford, *I May Be Some Time*.

Sponsoring Organization: Society of Authors.

Address: Society of Authors, 84 Drayton Gdns, London SW10 9SB, UK. **Telephone:** (20) 7373 6642. **Fax:** (20) 7373 5768. **E-mail:** authorsoc@ writers.org.uk.

Suomalaisen kirjallisuuden tiedotuskeskus (National Prize for Foreign Translators of Finnish Literature)

An annual prize of 40,000 markka awarded for translation of works of Finnish literature into other languages.

How to Apply: It is not possible to apply directly for the prize; nominations are put forward by the Institute of Finnish Literature.

Sponsoring Organization: Ministry of Education.

Contact: Bettina Wulff.

Address: Mariankatu 7 A 2, 00170 Helsinki, Finland. **Telephone:** (9) 13 13 32 91. **Fax:** (9) 656 380.

Suomen Nuorisokirjailijat Ry Awards

Suomen Nuorisokirjailijat Ry (Finnish Union of authors writing for children, youngsters and young adults) administers a number of awards for literature for children. The Union's oldest award is the Topelius Prize, founded in 1946 and presented annually for the best novel for young people. The Arvid Lydecken Prize, named after its founder, is awarded yearly for the best children's book. Other awards are given for the translation or publication of a high-quality book for young people, as well as a separate Finnish Picture Book Prize (partly sponsored by Children's Own Bookclub) for a Finnish picture book. In addition, every other year the Union awards an honorary diploma called Pääskynen (Swallow – named after the Union's former children's magazine) for a person or an institute promoting children's culture.

Sponsoring Organization: Suomen Nuorisokirjailijat Ry (Finnish Union of authors writing for children, youngsters and young adults).

Contact: Tuija Lethinen.

Address: Suomen Nuorisokirjailijat Ry, Palomäentie 13B, 02730 Espoo, Finland. **Telephone:** (9) 852 2176. **E-mail:** tuija.lehtinen@nuorisokirjailijat.fi.

Svenska Dagbladets Litteraturpris (Svenska Dagbladet Literary Award)

An annual prize of SEK 25,000, awarded by the daily newspaper *Svenska Dagbladet* for the year's best work of fiction.

Recent Winners: 2001: Maja Lundgren, *Pompeji*; 2000: Anne-Marie Berglund, *Jag vill stå träd nu*; 1999: Per Odensten, *En lampa som gör mörker*; 1999: Per Odensten, *En lampa som gör mörker*; 1998: Ellen Mattsson, *Resenärerna*; 1997: Carola Hansson, *Steinhof*.

Sponsoring Organization: Svenska Dagbladet.

Address: Ralambsvagen 7, 105 17 Stockholm, Sweden. **Internet:** www.svd.se.

Sveriges Radios Lyrikpris/Sveriges Radio P1:s Romanpris
(Swedish Radio Poetry Prize/Swedish Radio Novel Prize)

The Swedish radio station Sveriges Radio P1 presents annual literary awards for outstanding works in the genres poetry and novel, each with a prize of SEK 30,000. Winners are chosen by a jury drawn from listeners to the radio station.

Recent Winners: Poetry: 2001: Lars Mikael Raattamaa; 2000: Gunnar D. Hansson; 1999: Bruno K. Öijer; 1998: Eva-Stina Byggmäster; 1997: Stig Larsson Novel: 2002: Kerstin Norborg, *Min faders hus*; 2001: Agneta Pleijel, *Lord Nevermore*; 2000: Beate Grimsrud, *Jag smyger förbi en yxa*; 1999: Magnus Florin, *Syskonen*; 1998: Elisabeth Rynell, *Hohaj*.

Sponsoring Organization: Sveriges Radio.

Address: Sveriges Radio P1, 105 10 Stockholm, Sweden. **Telephone:** (8) 784 50 00. **Fax:** (8) 660 35 02. **Internet:** www.sr.se/p1/.

SWPA Audiobooks of the Year

The annual awards were set up in September 2001 to reward excellence in all areas of audiobook publishing. Winners are selected by a panel of 40 independent judges from the audio industry. Gold winners are awarded a trophy, while silver and bronze winners receive certificates. There are 18 main awards and four trade awards.

Eligibility and Restrictions: Categories include: TV/Film adaptation; drama; non-fiction; biography; children's; comedy; unabridged modern fiction; unabridged classic fiction; abridged modern fiction; abridged classic fiction; poetry; production; and abridgement.

How to Apply: Publishers may submit a maximum of two entries per category.

Recent Winners: Gold winners 2001: Abridged classic fiction: P. G. Wodehouse, *Thank You, Jeeves* (read by Simon Callow); Abridged modern fiction: Sebastian Faulks, *Birdsong* (read by Samuel West); Abridgement: Margaret Atwood, *The Blind Assassin* (read by Lorelei King); Biography: Felicity Kendal, *White Cargo* (read by Felicity Kendal); Children over 7: J. K. Rowling, *Harry Potter and the Prisoner of Azkaban* (read by Stephen Fry); Children under 7: Eric Hill, *Spot's Bedtime Storybook* (read by Christopher Timothy); Comedy: *Dead Ringers* (various readers); Drama: William Shakespeare, *King Richard III* (various readers); Non-fiction: David Timson, *The History of Theatre* (read by Derek Jacobi); Poetry: June Crebbin (Editor), *The Puffin Book of Fantastic First Poetry* (various readers); Production: Sheridan Morley, *Noel Coward: An Audio Biography* (read by Sheridan Morley); TV/Film adaptation: Bill Naughton, *Alfie* (read by Jason Flemyng); Unabridged classic fiction: James Joyce, *Dubliners II* (read by Jim Norton); Unabridged modern fiction: Robert Wilson, *A Small Death in Lisbon* (read by Sean Barrett).

Sponsoring Organization: Spoken Word Publishing Association (SWPA).

Contact: Event Organiser Gill Branston.

Address: BBC Spoken Word, A1047, Woodlands, 80 Wood Lane, London W12 OTT, UK. **Telephone:** (20) 7014 6041. **Fax:** (20) 7014 6141. **E-mail:** z.howes@ macmillan.co.uk.

Tabla Poetry Competition

An annual poetry competition, founded in 1991 by Stephen James and Emma Aylett, to encourage and canvass for new poetry. The prize fund totals £1,000, of which the first prize accounts for £500, second prize £200 and three runners-up prizes of £100 each. In addition the winning entries are published in the annual *Tabla Book of New Verse*.

Eligibility and Restrictions: Anyone over 16 may enter; open to poems in English from anywhere in the world, of any length and on any subject.

How to Apply: Send stamped addressed envelope or e-mail for details, or see website.

Recent Winners: 2001: Siobhan Anna Toman; 2000: Henry Shubman; 1999: Philip Gross; 1998: Paul F. Cowlan; 1997: Chris Becket.

Sponsoring Organization: Bristol University.

Contact: Editor Stephen James.

Address: Tabla, Dept of English, University of Bristol, 3–5 Woodland Rd, Bristol BS8 1TB, UK. **Fax:** (117) 928 8860. **Internet:** www.bristol.ac.uk/tabla. **E-mail:** stephenjames@bristol.ac.uk.

Takami Jun Shô (Takami Jun Prize)

Established in 1967 by the Association for the Promotion of Literature after a bequest by Takami Jun (Takami Jun Bungaku Shinkô Kai) in accordance with Takami's last wishes (Takami died in 1965). A proportion of Takami's royalties was set aside to start a fund that is now used to present an annual award to an outstanding collection of poetry based on the recommendations of poets, critics, and journalists. The winner receives 500,000 yen plus a commemorative gift.

Recent Winners: 31st Takami Jun Prize: Taguchi Inuo, *Mô Shôgun (General Moo)*.

Sponsoring Organization: Association for the Promotion of Literature.

Address: Association for the Promotion of Literature, Tokyo, Japan.

Tanizaki Jun'ichirô Shô (Tanizaki Jun'ichirô Prize)

Established in 1965 by the Chûô Kôronsha publishing company to commemorate its 80th anniversary. Awarded annually to the year's most representative work of fiction or drama by any professional writer. The winner receives 1 million yen plus a commemorative plaque.

Recent Winners: 2001 (37th Tanizaki Jun'ichirô Prize): Kawakami Hiromi, *Sensei no kaban (The Teacher's Briefcase)*; 1999: Nobuko Takagi, *Toko no ki (Lights Tinning Tree)*; 1991: Haruki Murakami, *Hard Boiled Wonderland and the End of the World*.

Sponsoring Organization: Chûô Kôronsha publishing company.

Address: Chûô Kôronsha publishing company, 2–8–7 Kyobashi, Chuo-ku, Tokyo, 104, Japan.

Tanning Prize

An annual award recognizing outstanding and proven mastery in the art of poetry. The winner receives a prize of $100,000.

How to Apply: No applications are accepted.

347

Recent Winners: 1998: A. R. Ammons; 1997: Anthony Hecht; 1996: Adrienne Riche.

Sponsoring Organization: Academy of American Poets.

Address: Academy of American Poets, 584 Broadway, Suite 1208, New York, NY 10012, USA. **Telephone:** (212) 274-0343. **Fax:** (212) 274-9427. **Internet:** www.poets.org/academy. **E-mail:** academy@poets.org.

Tano Aschehoug-Prisen/Idunn-Prisen

An annual prize, sponsored by the publisher H. Aschehoug & Co and presented for educational works written for high school or university level students. Eligible subjects include psychology, economics, law and social sciences.

How to Apply: Authors are invited to submit entries by mid-March.

Recent Winners: 2001: Britt Kroepelien, *Det virtuelle campus: visjon og virkelighet*; 2000: Sylvi Tenne, *Litteraturformidling i skolen*; 1999: Ariane Schjelderup, Øyvind Olsholt and Beate Børresen, *Filosofi i skolen*; 1998: Bjarne Bogen and Ludvig Munthe, *Lærebok i immunologi* and Eva Liestøl, *Dataspill: Innføring og analyse* (joint winners); 1997: Olga Herbjørnsen, *Rom, form og tall* and Tore Bjørgo, *Rasistiske grupper. Veier inn veier ut* (joint winners).

Sponsoring Organization: H. Aschehoug & Co.

Address: H. Aschehoug & Co, PB 363, Sentrum, 0102 Oslo, Norway. **Telephone:** (22) 400 400. **Internet:** www.aschehoug.no.

Tarjei Vesaas Debutanpris (Tarjei Vesaas Debutant Prize)

An annual prize first presented in 1964 by the Norwegian Authors' Union, in recognition of a debut novel by a young writer.

Recent Winners: 2001: Carl Frode Tiller, *Skråninga*; 2000: Mirjam Kristensen, *Dagene er gjennomsiktige*; 1999: Gunnar Wærness, *Kongesplint*; 1998: Trude Marstein, *Sterk sult, plutselig kvalme*; 1997: Lars Ramslie, *Biopsi*.

Sponsoring Organization: Den Norske Forfatterforening (Norwegian Authors' Union).

Address: Den Norske Forfatterforening, Boks 327 Sentrum, 0103 Oslo, 1, Norway. **Telephone:** (23) 35 76 20. **Internet:** www.litteraturnettet.no/dnf/index.html. **E-mail:** post@forfatterforeningen.no.

Tarlan Independent Prize

A new award established in 2000 by the Kazakhstan Club of Patrons of the Arts. Winners are to be selected in the categories of literature, science, music, theatre, art, cinematography and education. The prize consists of a US$10,000 prize and a statue of Tarlan (a famous horse in traditional Kazakh horse races), plus two smaller monetary awards. The awards programme will be held on a regular basis at the end of each year.

Sponsoring Organization: Kazakhstan Club of Patrons of the Arts.

Address: Kazakhstan Club of Patrons of the Arts, Almaty, Kazakhstan.

Sydney Taylor Book Awards (STBA)

An annual award established in 1968, to honour the author Sydney Taylor, and presented to the authors of outstanding books of positive Jewish content for children. Awards are made in two categories: picture book up to Grade 5, and Grade 6 upwards. Winners are chosen by a panel of librarians, and receive a prize of $2,000, plus a certificate and a stipend for attendance at a convention. An occasional STBA Body of Work Award is also presented to outstanding authors.

Eligibility and Restrictions: Entries must be new publications, written in English, and must be of high literary merit with positive religious or cultural Jewish content.

How to Apply: Publishers should send six copies of entries to the address given.

Recent Winners: Grade 6 upwards: 2001: Catherine Reef, *Sigmund Freud: A Pioneer of the Mind*; 2000: Ida Vos, *The Key is Lost* (translated by Therese Edelstein); 1999: Sybil Rosen, *Speed of Light*
Picture Book: 2001: Elsa Okon Rael (author) and Maryann Kovalski (illustrator), *Rivka's First Thanksgiving*; 2000: Eric A. Kimmel (author) and Jon. J. Muth (illustrator), *Gershon's Monster*; 1999: Maxine Rose Schur (author) and Kimberly Bulcken Root (illustrator), *The Peddlar's Gift*.

Sponsoring Organization: Association of Jewish Libraries.

Contact: Chair. Libby K. White.

Address: Association of Jewish Libraries, Beth Israel Congregation, 3706 Crondall Lane, Owings Mill, MD 21117, USA. **Telephone:** (410) 654-0803. **Fax:** (410) 581-0113. **Internet:** aleph.lib.ohio-state.edu/www/asl.html. **E-mail:** llibbylib@aol.com.

TDK Australian Audio Book Awards

The TDK Australian Audio Book Awards, established in 1988 by the National Library of Australia, are the country's leading audiobook awards. They are the only independent awards for Australian audiobooks and are open to both commercial and non-commercial publishers. They aim to improve the quality of Australian audio book production, to increase public awareness of books in this format, and to promote consumer access to a wide range of Australian audiobooks. Winners are presented with a special certificate and the winning entries receive extensive media publicity.

How to Apply: Entries should be sent to the address given accompanied by an entry form.

Recent Winners: Audio Books for Young People: 1999: John Marsden, *Staying Alive in Year 5* (narrated by Tim Ferguson)
Unabridged Fiction: 1999: Charles Frazier, *Cold Mountain* (narrated by Noel Hodda)
Unabridged Non-fiction: 1999: Caddie, *Caddie* (narrated by Helen Morse)
Narrator's Award (Trish Trinick Prize) 1999: Charles Dickens, *Oliver Twist* (narrated by Edgar Metcalf)
Special Award: 1999: *Wonder Tales of Earth and Sea – Traditional stories* (narrated by Jenni Cargill).

Sponsoring Organization: TDK.

Address: National Library of Australia, Parkes Pl., Canberra, ACT 2600, Australia. **Telephone:** (2) 6262 1139. **Fax:** (2) 6273 4493. **Internet:** www.nla.gov.au/events/tdk/tdk.html#back.

TDK Literary Award

Established in 1990 by the Turkish Language Institute (TDK) to promote a high standard of writing in Turkish. Awards are given in three categories: for academic works in the field of Turkish language and literature; for fiction; and for drama. The jury is made up of members of the Institute. The amount of prize money changes each year; in 2001 it was 5,000 million Turkish lira for drama and 1,000 million lira for fiction.

Eligibility and Restrictions: Entries must be written in Turkish, and must be of an academic nature. Only works by living authors are eligible.

How to Apply: Six copies of the entry should be submitted accompanied by biographical details.

Recent Winners: Academic work 2001: (no award made)
Fiction: 2001: Hatice Balkanlar, *KAPI*
Drama: 2001: Mustafa Nogay Kesim, *Pisti*.

Sponsoring Organization: Turkish Language Institute (Turk Dil Kurumu).

Address: Atatürk Bulvari, 217, Kavaklidere, Ankara 06680, Turkey. **Telephone:** (312) 4286100. **Fax:** (312) 4285288. **Internet:** www.tdk.gov.tr. **E-mail:** bim@tdk.gov.tr.

Te Kura Pounamu Award

Established in 1995 to recognize an outstanding contribution to literature for children or young people written in Te Reo Maori. The award consists of a Greenstone pendant (Taonga) and a sum of money which is decided each year by the Library and Information Association of New Zealand Aotearoa (LIANZA) Council ($1,000 in 2002). The winner is chosen by a panel of at least three judges. LIANZA suspended its awards from 1999–2000 but reinstituted them in 2001.

Eligibility and Restrictions: Authors must be citizens or residents of Aotearoa New Zealand. Books must be an original work written in Te Reo Maori and must be longer than 14 pages. They must be still in print and available for public purchase. Reprints or new editions are not eligible.

How to Apply: Judges may nominate books for consideration, or books may be submitted to the judges or the Executive Director of LIANZA. Publishers may also send in nominations, and are requested to provide three copies of each entry.

Recent Winners: 2001: Merito Tawhara, *Te Puriri*; 1998: Mere Clarke, *Whirikoki me tana Kekeno*; 1997: Katarina Mataira, *He Tino Kuia Taka Huia*; 1996: Katarina Mataira and Terewai Kemp, *Marama Tangiweta*.

Sponsoring Organization: Library and Information Association of New Zealand Aotearoa (LIANZA).

Contact: Office Man Steve Williams.

Address: LIANZA, POB 12–212, Wellington, 6001, New Zealand. **Telephone:** (4) 4735834. **Fax:** (4) 4991480. **Internet:** www.lianza.org.nz. **E-mail:** office@ lianza.org.nz.

Teixeira-Gomes Prize

Triennial award for translations into English of works from any period by a Portuguese national. Short stories and poems are eligible. The prize is also open to unpublished translations of works by Portuguese nationals. The winner receives £1,000.

Sponsoring Organization: Translators Assocation.

Address: Translators Assocation, 84 Drayton Gardens, London SW10 9SB, UK. **Telephone:** (20) 7373 6642. **Fax:** (20) 7373 5768. **E-mail:** info@societyofauthors. org.

Texas Institute of Letters Awards

A series of annual awards presented by the Texas Institute of Letters. The prizes include the $6,000 Jesse H. Jones Award for a novel; the $5,000 Best Book of Poetry Award; the $1,000 Natalie Ornish Poetry Award; the $1,000 Steven Turner Award for a novel; the $1,000 John Bloom Humor Award; the $1,000 Soeurette Diehl Fraser Translation Award; the O. Henry Award; and the $750 Brazos Bookstore Short Story Award.

Eligibility and Restrictions: Open to authors who have lived in Texas for two consecutive years or non-residents whose work concerns Texas; entries must have been published in the previous year.

Recent Winners: Jesse H. Jones Award: 2002: Sarah Bird, *The Yokota Officers Club*
Best Book of Poetry Award: 2002: Susan Wood, *Asunder*
Natalie Ornish Poetry Award: 2002: Ted Genoways, *Bullroarer*
Steven Turner Award: 2002: Katherine Tanney, *Carousel of Progress*
John Bloom Humor Award: 2002: Marco Perela, *Adventures of a No Name Actor*
Soeurette Diehl Fraser Translation Award: 2002: Wendy Barker and Saranindranath Tagore, *Rabindranath Tagore's Final Poems*
Brazos Bookstore Short Story Award: 2002: Tom McNeely, *Tickle Torture*
O. Henry Award: 2001: Mary Swan, *The Deep*; 2000: John Edgar Wideman, *Weight*; 1999: Peter Baida, *The Nurse's Story*; 1998: Lorrie Moore, *People Like That Are the Only People Here*.

Sponsoring Organization: Texas Institute of Letters.

Contact: Sec Paula Marks.

Address: Texas Institute of Letters, Literary Awards, Box 935, St Edward's University, Houston House, 217 Wook St, Austin, TX 78704, USA. **Telephone:** (512) 448-8702. **Internet:** www.stedwards.edu/newc/marks/til.

Tezuka Osamu Bunka Shô (Tezuka Osamu Cultural Prizes)

Established in 1997 by Asahi Shimbun in honour of Japanese cartoonist Tezuka Osamu. All single-volume 'manga' published in the preceding calendar year are eligible for the Grand Prize or Honourable Mention, and in addition special prizes are awarded in recognition of other significant contributions to the field. The Grand Prize for Manga brings the winner a bronze statuette and a cash prize of 2 million yen. Winners of Honourable Mention awards and special prizes receive a bronze statuette and 1 million yen in cash.

How to Apply: After a preliminary round which includes participation by ordinary readers, members of the selection committee rank the finalists in descending order, with the recipient of most votes receiving the Grand Prize for Manga and the second-place finisher receiving Honourable Mention.

Sponsoring Organization: Asahi Shimbun.

Address: Asahi Shimbun, Tokyo, Japan.

Theatre Book Prize

The Theatre Book Prize was first awarded in 1998 to celebrate the 50th anniversary of the Society for Theatre Research, and has become the UK's best-known award for books on the theatre.

Recent Winners: 2001: Jim Davis and Victor Emeljanow, *Reflecting the Audience: London theatregoing 1840–1880.*

Sponsoring Organization: Society for Theatre Research.

Address: Society for Theatre Research, c/o The Theatre Museum, 1E Tavistock St, London WC2E 7PA, UK. **Internet:** www.herts.ac.uk/UHPress/jdve.html.

David Thelen Prize

An annual prize, formerly known as the Foreign-Language Article Prize, for the best article on American history published in a foreign language. The winning article is translated into English and published in the *Journal of American History*. The author receives a certificate and a $500 prize.

Eligibility and Restrictions: Entries must have been published in the preceding calendar year, and be concerned with the past (recent or distant) or with issues of continuity and change. They should also be concerned with events or processes with a link to the USA, and should make a significant and original contribution to the understanding of US history. Unpublished manuscripts will be considered. Articles originally submitted for publication in English or by authors for whom English is their first language are not eligible.

How to Apply: Authors of eligible articles are invited to nominate their work. Other nominations are also welcome. Five copies should be mailed to the address given by 1 May, accompanied by a one- to two-page essay (in English) explaining why the article is a significant and original contribution to an understanding of American history.

Recent Winners: 2001: Axel R. Schäfer, *W. E. B. Du Bois and the Transatlantic Dimension of Progressivism, 1892–1909*; 2000: Mario Del Pero, *The United States and 'Psychological Warfare' in Italy, 1948–1955*; 1999: Gervasio Luis García, *I Am the Other: Puerto Rico in the Eyes of North Americans, 1898*; 1998: Catherine Collomp, *Immigrants, Labor Markets, and the State, a Comparative Approach: France and the United States, 1880–1930*; 1997: François Weil, *Capitalism and Industrialization in New England, 1815–1845.*

Sponsoring Organization: Organization of American Historians (OAH).

Address: Journal of American History, 1215 East Atwater Ave, Bloomington, IN 47401, USA. **Telephone:** (812) 855-9852. **Fax:** (812) 855-0696. **Internet:** www.oah.org. **E-mail:** awards@oah.org.

Theo Thijssen Prize for Children's and Youth Literature

The prize is awarded every three years in recognition of the whole body of work of a Dutch writer in the field of children's literature. It replaces the former Dutch State Prize for Children's and Youth Literature. The winner receives a prize of 125,000 DFL.

Recent Winners: 2000: Joke van Leeuwen; 1997: Toon Tellegen; 1994: Els Pelgrom; 1991: Wim Hofman; 1988: Willem Wilmink.

Sponsoring Organization: Stichting P. C. Hooft-prijs.

Address: Postbus 90515, Prins Willem, Alexanderhof 5, 2595 LM The Hague, Netherlands.

David St John Thomas Charitable Trust Awards

The Trust administers a wide range of awards for writers which aim to inspire creativity and individuality.

Eligibility and Restrictions: Categories include: the Open Poetry Competition (rhymed and unrhymed categories, each with prizes of £250), the Annual Ghost Story Competition (for a story 1,600 to 1,800 words, prize of £1,000 and silver cup), Annual Love Story Competition (for a story 1,600 to 1,800 words, prize of £1,000 and silver cup), Self-Publishing Awards (four categories, each with a prize of £250 plus a further £750 for Self-Published Book of the Year), Sea Story Prize (1,600–1,800 words, prize of £250), Narrative Poem Prize (up to 320 lines, £250), Crime Story Prize (1,600–1,800 words, prize of £250), and several others. From among all entries a Winner of Winners is chosen to receive a further £1,000 and a prestigious cup.

How to Apply: Closing date for all of the awards is 31 January; entry forms should be returned with entry fee.

Recent Winners: Winners' names and winning entries appear in October/November issue of *Writing Magazine* each year.

Sponsoring Organization: David St John Thomas Charitable Trust.

Contact: Competition Man. Lorna Edwardson.

Address: The David St John Thomas Charitable Trust, PO Box 6055, Nairn IV12 4YB, UK.

Thomas Cook/Daily Telegraph Travel Book Award

Annual award for best travel book published in the previous year. The winner receives a prize of £10,000.

Recent Winners: 2001: Stanley Stewart, *In the Empire of Genghis Khan*; 2000: Jason Elliot, *An Unexpected Light*; 1999: Philip Marsden, *The Spirit Wrestlers*.

Sponsoring Organization: Thomas Cook Group.

Address: Thomas Cook Group, 45 Berkeley St, London W1A 1EB, UK.

Lewis Thomas Prize

The Lewis Thomas Prize, established in 1993 by the Rockefeller University, honours scientists for their artistic achievements, usually in the form of literary publications. It is named after an award-winning author and scientist who received the first award in 1993.

Recent Winners: 2001: Oliver Sacks; 1999: Steven Weinberg; 1996: Freeman Dyson; 1995: Abraham Pais; 1994: François Jacob; 1993: Lewis Thomas.

Sponsoring Organization: Rockefeller University.

Contact: Marion E. Glick.

Address: Rockefeller University, 1230 York Avenue, New York, NY 10021–6399, USA. **Telephone:** (212) 327-8967. **Fax:** (212) 327-7876. **E-mail:** glickm@rockvax.rockefeller.edu.

Tidens Skjonnlitteraere Pris (Tidens Fiction Prize)

An annual prize for Norwegian fiction, sponsored by the publisher Tiden Norsk Forlag.

Recent Winners: 2001: Pål Christiansen; 2000: Einar O. Risa; 1999: Lars Ramslie; 1998: Kristine Næss; 1997: Nils Fredrik Dahl.

Sponsoring Organization: Tiden Norsk Forlag AS.

Address: Tiden Norsk Forlag AS, PB 8813, Youngstorget, 0028 Oslo, Norway. **Telephone:** (23) 32 76 60. **Fax:** (23) 32 76 97. **Internet:** www.tiden.no/tiden.html. **E-mail:** tiden@tiden.no.

Tienie Hollowaymedalje vir kleuterliteratuur (Tienie Holloway Medal)

The Tienie Holloway Medal was established in 1969, and is named after a writer who was noted for her verse for young children in the early part of the 19th century. This award is presented to authors or illustrators of the best books for children younger than 8 years of age (i.e. pre-school and kindergarten). The winner receives a gold medal.

Eligibility and Restrictions: Only open to works published in the preceding three calendar years. Entries must be written in Afrikaans, but in exceptional cases translated works may be considered. Entries may be poetry or drama, but preference is given to works in verse form.

Recent Winners: 2001: Verna Vels, *Liewe Heksie en die rekenaar* and other new Liewe Heksie-stories.

Sponsoring Organization: Suid-Afrikaanse Akademie vir Wetenskap en Kuns (South African Academy for Science and Arts).

Address: Die Suid-Afrikaanse Akademie vir Wetenskap en Kuns (the South African Academy for Science and Arts), P.O. Box 538, Pretoria, 0001, South Africa. **Telephone:** (12) 328 5082. **Fax:** (12) 328 5091. **Internet:** www.akademie.co.za. **E-mail:** akademie@mweb.co.za.

Tir Na N-og Awards

The awards were established with the aim of raising the standard of children's and young people's books in Wales and encouraging the buying and reading of good books. Three prizes of £1,000 each (Welsh Fiction, Welsh Non-fiction and English Section) are awarded to acknowledge the work of authors and illustrators. The prizes are sponsored by the Welsh Arts Council, the Welsh Libraries Association and the Welsh Books Council. The winners are chosen by a selection panel of three members.

Eligibility and Restrictions: The Welsh Fiction category is open to original Welsh-language novels, stories and picture books; all other Welsh-language books are eligible for the non-fiction category. Best English Book of the Year is awarded to the best English-language book with an authentic Welsh background.

How to Apply: Publishers are invited to submit books for consideration.

Recent Winners: Welsh Fiction: 2001: Bethan Gwanas, *Llinyn Trons*; 2000: Gwenno Hughes, *Ta-Ta Tryweryn*; 1999: John Owen, *Pam Fi eto, Duw?*; 1998: Gwen Redvers Jones, *Dyddiau Cwn*; 1997: John Owen, *Ydy Fe!*
Welsh Non-fiction: 2001: Myrddin ap Dafydd, *Jam Coch Mewn Pwdin Reis*; 2000: Rhiannon Ifans and Margaret Jones, *Chwedlau o'r Gwledydd Celtaidd*; 1999: Lis Jones, *Byw a Bod yn y Bath*; 1998: Tegwyn Jones and Jac Jones, *Stori Branwen*; 1997: Gareth F. Williams, *Dirgelwch Loch Ness*

English Section: 2001: Kevin Crossley-Holland, *The Seeing Stone*; 2000: Jo Dahn and Justin Baldwin, *Artworks on. . . Interiors*; 1999: Gillian Drake, *Rhian's Song*; 1998: Mary Oldham, *Alwena's Garden*; 1997: Sian Lewis and Jackie Morris, *Cities in the Sea*.

Sponsoring Organization: Cyngor Llyfrau Cymru/Welsh Books Council.

Contact: Menna Lloyd Williams.

Address: Welsh Books Council, Castell Brychan, Aberystwyth SY23 2JB, UK. **Telephone:** (1970) 624151. **Fax:** (1970) 625385. **Internet:** www.cllc.org.uk. **E-mail:** menna.lloydwilliams@cllc.org.uk.

Toronto Book Awards

Honours authors of books of literary merit – fiction and non-fiction books for adults and/or children – that are evocative of Toronto and are of literary and artistic merit. The total annual prize is C$15,000, with C$1,000 granted to each shortlisted author, and the remainder granted to the winner. Administered, annually, by the City of Toronto Book Award Committee.

Eligibility and Restrictions: Open to works of fiction and non-fiction published in English for adults and/or children. All entries must be evocative of Toronto. There are no separate categories: novels, short story collections, books of poetry, biographies, histories, social studies, books about sports, children's books, photographic collections, etc. are judged together. Reprints, textbooks and manuscripts are not eligible. Entries must have been published during the previous year.

How to Apply: Deadline for submissions is 28 February.

Recent Winners: 2001: Camilla Gibb, *The Spinster and The Prophet*; 2000: Camilla Gibb, *Mouthing the Words*; 1999: Richard Outram, *Benedict Abroad*; 1998: Helen Humphreys, *Leaving Earth*; 1997: Anne Michaels, *Fugitive Pieces*.

Address: c/o Toronto Protocol, City Clerk's West Tower, 10th Floor, City Hall, Toronto, ON M5H 2N2, Canada. **Internet:** www.city.toronto.on.ca/book_awards/.

Toyota/Children's Literature Foundation Award

This award, first presented in 1997, was established by the Ghana's Children's Literature Foundation, with sponsorship from the local car agency for Toyota, to encourage the production of books for children aged 3–12. The award recognizes an outstanding picture story book, and is planned to run every two years.

Eligibility and Restrictions: For the first award, entries were invited for picture story books published between 1990 and 1996. The award criteria included the art work, the balance between text and illustration and the overall design of the book.

Recent Winners: 1997: J. Campbell, *Anno's Kite*.

Sponsoring Organization: Toyota/Children's Literature Foundation.

Address: Toyota/Children's Literature Foundation Award, Accra, Ghana.

Georg Trakl Preis für Lyrik (Georg Trakl Poetry Prize)

Prize established by the region of Salzburg in memory of the Austrian poet Georg Trakl. First presented in 1952, the prize of €7,270 (100,000 Sch) accompanied by a certificate of honour is awarded for collected poetic work, at irregular periods around the anniversary of Trakl's years of birth and death. A parallel prize, the Georg Trakl Förderungspreis für Lyrik (Georg Trakl Encouragement Prize for Poetry), worth €2,907 (40,000 Sch), is also awarded.

Eligibility and Restrictions: Open to poetry by German-speaking writers. The Trakl Encouragement Prize is open to writers from Salzburg aged under 40, excluding former winners of the Trakl Prize.

How to Apply: No direct application is permitted; the winner is chosen by a jury. For the Encouragement prize, 15–20 unpublished poems should be submitted accompanied by biographical details.

Recent Winners: 2002: Andreas Okopenko; 1999: Elfriede Gerstl; 1997: Günter Kunert; 1994: Hans Raimund; 1992: Walter Helmut Fritz.

Sponsoring Organization: Salzburg Regional Government.

Contact: Dr Herbert Mayrhofer.

Address: Salzburger Landesregierung, Kulturabteilung, Postfach 527, 5010 Salzburg, Austria. **Telephone:** (662) 8042 2729. **Fax:** (662) 8042 2919. **Internet:** www.salzburg.gv.at. **E-mail:** kultur@salzburg.gv.at.

Translated Book Contest

An annual competition organized by the National Book Development Committee of Thailand under the jurisdiction of the Ministry of Education in order to promote the production and development of quality books translated into the Thai language. Entries are judged in seven categories: non-fiction, novel, poetry, short story, cartoon and/or illustrated book, book for children between 3 and 11 years old, and book for children between 12 and 18 years old. The winner of the first prize in each category receives a cash prize of 30,000 baht (approx. US$750) and a trophy.

Eligibility and Restrictions: Entries have been printed during the last four years. All books must be published in Thailand and 'must not be harmful to the country's morality, ethics or security'.

Sponsoring Organization: National Book Development Committee of Thailand/ Ministry of Education.

Address: Ministry of Education, Wang Chan Kasem, Thanon Ratchadamnoen Nok, Bangkok, 10300, Thailand. **Telephone:** 628-5620. **Fax:** 281-1753. **Internet:** www.moe.go.th.

Betty Trask Prize

A prestigious annual award of £8,000 for authors under 35 years old, for a first novel of a traditional or romantic nature. A series of Betty Trask Awards, of £5,000, £4,000 and £2,000 each, are also presented.

Eligibility and Restrictions: Open to first novels of a traditional or romantic nature, written by an author under 35; authors must be Commonwealth citizens.

Recent Winners: Betty Trask Prize: 2002: Hari Kunzru, *The Impressionist*; 2001: Zadie Smith, *White Teeth*
Betty Trask Awards: 2002: Rachel Seiffert, *The Dark Room*, Chloe Hooper, *A Child's Book of True Crime*, Shamim Sarif, *The World Unseen*, Helen Cross and Susanna Jones; 2001: Justin Hill, *The Drink and Dream Teahouse*, Maggie O'Farrell, *After You'd Gone*, Vivien Kelly, *Take One Young Man*, Mohsin Hamid, *Moth Smoke*, Patrick Neate, *Musungu Jim and the Great Chief Tuloko*, Jonathan Tulloch, *The Season Ticket*.

Sponsoring Organization: Society of Authors.
Address: Society of Authors, 84 Drayton Gdns, London SW10 9SB, UK. **Telephone:** (20) 7373 6642. **Fax:** (20) 7373 5768. **Internet:** www. societyofauthors.org. **E-mail:** info@societyofauthors.org.

Travelling Scholarship Fund

A non-competitive award shared between several winners, with the aim of enabling British writers to travel abroad. The prize money totals £6,000.

Recent Winners: 2002: Frank Kuppner, David Park, George Szirtes; 2001: Alan Judd, Christina Koning, Tessa Ransford, Maurice Riordan; 2000: Robert Edric, Georgina Hammick, Grace Ingoldby, Walter Perrie.

Sponsoring Organization: Society of Authors.
Address: Society of Authors, 84 Drayton Gdns, London SW10 9SB, UK. **Telephone:** (20) 7373 6642. **Fax:** (20) 7373 5768. **Internet:** www. societyofauthors.org. **E-mail:** info@societyofauthors.org.

Trillium Book Award/Prix Trillium

Established to recognize excellence, support marketing and to foster increased public awareness of the quality and diversity of Ontario writers and writing. The prize is co-ordinated by the Association of Canadian Publishers, in conjunction with the Ontario Ministry of Culture, Tourism and Recreation's Library and Community Information Branch. It is presented annually, to two authors (French and English language) resident in or native to Ontario; the award carries a prize of $12,000 for the author and $2,500 for the publisher.

Recent Winners: 1999: Alistair MacLeod, *No Great Mischief*; 1998: Andre Alexis, *Childhood*; 1998: Alice Munro, *Love of a Good Woman*.

Sponsoring Organization: Association of Canadian Publishers/Ontario Ministry of Culture, Tourism and Recreation Library and Community Information Branch.

Address: Association of Canadian Publishers, 110 Eglinton Ave West, Suite 401, Toronto, ON M4R 1A3, Canada.

Triumph Prize

A series of annual awards established by the Logovaz-Triumph Foundation, an independent charity, in 1992 to recognize outstanding literary achievement (as well as other areas of the arts, including music), and held alongside the Triumph Festival of Arts. This award is unofficially known as the Russian Nobel Prize; it carries a total prize fund of $250,000, of which $50,000 is awarded for literary achievement. Winners are selected by an independent jury of 13 eminent people drawn from all areas of the arts.

Recent Winners: 2002: Tatyana Tolstaya; 1999: Vasil Bykov, Alexander Volodin, Valery Gergiyev, Marina Neyolova, Vyacheslav Polunin; 1998: Aleksei German, Fasil Iskander, Gia Kancheli, Vera Krasovskaya, Yuri Lyubimov; 1997: Svetlana Aleksievich, Boris Grebenschikov, Victor Kosakovsky, Igor Moiseev, Arvo Pyart; 1996: Vladimir Voinovich, Rezo Gabriadze, Evgeni Kissin, Leonid Filatov, Rustam Khamdamov.

Sponsoring Organization: Logovaz-Triumph Foundation.

Contact: Jury Co-ordinator Zoya Boguslavskaya.

Address: Ul. Povarskaya 8, Moscow, Russia. **Telephone:** (95) 290-0361. **Fax:** (95) 291-4701. **Internet:** fondtriumph.ru. **E-mail:** triumph1@cityline.ru.

Tsubouchi Shôyô Taishô (Tsubouchi Shôyô Prize)

Established in 1994 by the city of Minokamo in Gifu Prefecture on the 40th anniversary of its incorporation to honour the memory of native son Tsubouchi Shôyô. The award is presented annually in recognition of activities related to the stage that contribute to a greater awareness of Shôyô's work. The winner receives a certificate, a plaque bearing a relief likeness of Shôyô, and a cash prize of 2 million yen.

Address: Tsubouchi Shôyô Prize, Minokamo, Japan.

Kingsley Tufts Poetry Prize

An annual award established in 1982 and given to a work by an emerging poet. The prize is among the poetry world's most prestigious awards. The Kate Tufts Discovery Award, an annual award for a first or very early work by a promising poet, is presented alongside the Kingsley Tufts Prize. The winner of the latter receives a prize of $100,000; the Kate Tufts Discovery Award carries a prize of $10,000.

Eligibility and Restrictions: The award is presented for a single work to writers who are considered to be in the middle of their careers.

Recent Winners: 2002: Carl Phillips, *The Tether*; 2001: Alan Shapiro, *The Dead Alive and Busy*; 2000: Robert Wrigley, *Reign of Snakes*.

Sponsoring Organization: Claremont Graduate University.

Address: Poetic Gallery for the Kingsley and Kate Tufts Poetry Awards, Claremont Graduate University, 60 E 10th St, Harper East B7, 1, Claremont, CA 91711–6165, USA. **Telephone:** (909) 621-8974. **Internet:** www.cgu.edu/tufts/.

Tun Seri Lanang Award

The award was one of three new literary awards introduced by the Malay Language Council of Singapore in 1993. It is the highest literary award for Malay Literature.

Recent Winners: 1998: Abdul Ghani Hamid; 1995: Masuri S.N.; 1993: Muhammad Ariff Ahmad.

Sponsoring Organization: Malay Language Council of Singapore.

Address: Malay Language Council of Singapore, Ministry of Information, Culture and the Arts, MITA Building, 140 Hill Street 02–02, Singapore, 179369, Singapore. **Telephone:** (62) 707988. **Fax:** (68) 379480. **E-mail:** mita_pa@mita.gov.sg.

Mark Twain Award for Short Fiction

An annual prize of $1,000 given to promote and reward the finest example of short fiction. The winning entry is also published in *Red Rock Review*.

Recent Winners: 2002: Cynthia Gregory, *Baby Blood*.

Sponsoring Organization: Red Rock Review.

Contact: Editor Richard Logsdon.

Address: Red Rock Review, Community College of Southern Nevada, English Department, J2A, 3200 East Cheyenne Avenue, Las Vegas, NV 89030, USA. **Telephone:** (702) 651-4005. **Internet:** www.ccsn.nevada.edu/ english/ redrockreview/index.html.

UBC Medal for Canadian Biography/UBC President's Medal in Biography

An annual award for the best biography with either a Canadian author or subject. The prize, also known as the President's Medal (as it was created by the University of British Columbia (UBC) president Norman MacKenzie), has been awarded annually since 1952.

Recent Winners: 1999: François Ricard, *Gabrielle Roy: A Life.*

Sponsoring Organization: University of British Columbia (UBC).

Address: University of British Columbia, 2329 West Mall, Vancouver, BC V6T 1Z4, Canada. **Internet:** www.ubc.ca.

Lesya Ukrainka Prize

Presented for works for children and young people, this award is named after a Ukrainian poet born in 1871.

Sponsoring Organization: National Writers Union of Ukraine (NSPU).

Contact: V. Yavorivsky.

Address: Blvd Bankova 2, 01024 Kiev, Ukraine. **Fax:** (44) 293-45-86. **Internet:** www.nspu.kiev.ua. **E-mail:** nspu@I.kiev.ua.

UNESCO Prize for Children's and Young People's Literature in the Service of Tolerance

UNESCO established this prize in order to carry the message of the United Nations Year for Tolerance beyond 1995. The Prize is awarded every two years in recognition of published works for the young that best embody the concepts and ideals of tolerance and peace, and promote mutual understanding based on respect for other peoples and cultures. The winner in each category receives US$8,000, donated by the Grupo Editorial SM of Spain.

Eligibility and Restrictions: Open to works in the following genres: novels; collections of short stories; and picture books. Entries should be suitable for either children up to 12 years old, or young people aged 13 to 18.

How to Apply: Only publishers may submit books (three copies) through the National Commission for UNESCO in their respective countries. Direct submissions to UNESCO will not be accepted, except from countries that do not have a National Commission for UNESCO.

Recent Winners: Books for Young Children: 2001: Anais Vaugelade (France), *La Guerre*; 1999: Meshack Asare (Ghana), *Sosu's Call*; 1997: Kathryn Cave and Chris Riddell (illustrator), *Something Else*
Books for Young People: 2001: Violet Razeghpanah (Iran), *Mir Space Station*; 1999: Ann R. Blakeslee (USA), *A Different Kind of Hero*; 1997: Chen Danyan, *Neun Leben.*

Sponsoring Organization: UNESCO.

Contact: Maha Bulos.

Address: Division of Arts and Cultural Enterprise, UNESCO, Division of Arts and Cultural Enterprise, 1 rue Miollis, 75732 Paris, Cedex 15, France. **Fax:** 1 45 68 55 95. **Internet:** www.unesco.org/culture/toleranceliterature/. **E-mail:** m.bulos@unesco.org.

Vaka-Helgafell Children's Book Award

The Vaka-Helgafell Children's Book Award is presented by the publisher Vaka-Helgafellin for an outstanding children's book.

Recent Winners: 1991: Idunn Steinsdóttir, *Gegnum Þyrnigerðið (Through the Thornhedge)*.

Sponsoring Organization: Vaka Helgafell/EDDA.

Contact: Pétur Már Ólafsson.

Address: Sudurlandsbraut 12, IS-108 Reykjavík, Iceland. **Telephone:** 5222000. **Fax:** 5222022. **E-mail:** petur.olafsson@edda.is.

Lucy B. & C. W. van der Hoogt Prize

Established in 1925 by the Maatschappij der Nederlandse Letterkunde (MNL) following a gift from C. W. van der Hoogt. The prize aims to encourage poets or writers of literary works written in Dutch or Afrikaans, and is awarded every year. The winner is selected by a committee of experts, and receives €6,000 and a commemorative plaque.

Eligibility and Restrictions: The work must be written in Dutch or Afrikaans, and must not have been published more than two years before the award is given.

Recent Winners: 2001: René Puthaar; 2000: Erwin Mortier; 1999: Erik Menkveld; 1998: Arthur Japin; 1997: Piet Gerbrandy.

Sponsoring Organization: Maatschappij der Nederlandse Letterkunde (MNL) (Dutch Literature Association).

Address: Universiteitsbibliotheek, Postbus 9501, 2300 RA Leiden, Netherlands. **Telephone:** (71) 5144962. **Fax:** (71) 5272836. **Internet:** www.leidenuniv.nl/host/mnl. **E-mail:** mnl@library.leidenuniv.nl.

Nienke van Hichtum Prize

A biennial prize for a children's book, presented in rotation with the J. Greshoffprijs, which is sponsored by the same foundation.

Recent Winners: 1999: Eva Gerlach, *Hee meneer Eland*; 1997: Rita Verschuur, *Vreemd land*; 1995: Veronica Hazelhoff, *Veren*; 1993: Annemie Heymans, *De prinses van de moestuin* and Mensje van Keulen, *Vrienden van de maan* (joint winners).

Sponsoring Organization: Jan Campertstichting (Jan Campert Foundation).

Address: PO Box 12654, 2500 DP The Hague, Netherlands. **Telephone:** (353) 36 37. **Fax:** (353) 30 58.

Mary Vaughan Jones Award

The award is in memory of author Mary Vaughan Jones for her outstanding contribution to children's books in the Welsh language. The prize is awarded every three years to a person who has, likewise, made an outstanding contribution to literature in the Welsh language over a considerable period of time. The prize is a silver trophy depicting characters from Mary Vaughan Jones's books. The winner is selected by the Children's Books Panel.

Recent Winners: 2000: J. Selwyn Lloyd; 1997: Roger Boore; 1994: W. J. Jones; 1991: T. Llew Jones; 1988: Emily Huws.

Sponsoring Organization: Cyngor Llyfrau Cymru/Welsh Books Council.

Contact: Menna Lloyd Williams.

Address: Welsh Books Council, Castell Brychan, Aberystwyth SY23 2JB, UK. **Telephone:** (1970) 624151. **Fax:** (1970) 625385. **Internet:** www.cllc.org.uk. **E-mail:** menna.lloydwilliams@cllc.org.uk.

Charles Veillon European Essay Prize

A prize of SFr 30,000 is awarded anually to a European writer or essayist for a piece offering a critical look at modern society's way of life and ideology. The prize was founded in 1975 as a tribute to Charles Veillon, a successful businessman and patron of the arts. The jury is made up of prominent figures drawn from different professional and linguistic backgrounds.

Eligibility and Restrictions: Open to European writers for a piece of work which contains a valuable personal testimony or puts forward a fruitful criticism of contemporary societies, lifestyles and ideologies.

How to Apply: Publishers or writers should send two copies of the work by the end of June each year.

Recent Winners: 2002: Jean-Claude Guillebaud, *La Principe d'humanité*; 2000: Peter Bichsel, *Alles von mir gelernt, Kolumnen 1995–1999*; 1999: Amin Maalouf, *Les Identités meurtrières*; 1998: Tzvetan Todorov, *Benjamin Constant – La passion démocratique*; 1997: Karl-Markus Gauss, *Das Europäische Alphabet*.

Sponsoring Organization: Charles Veillon Foundation.

Address: Charles Veillon Foundation, 1017 Lausanne, Switzerland. **Telephone:** (21) 706 9029. **Fax:** (21) 706 98 05. **Internet:** culturactif.ch/fondations/fondationcharlesveillon.htm. **E-mail:** fondation@veillon.ch.

Bill Venter/Altron Literary Award

The Bill Venter/Altron Literary Award was established by Dr Bill Venter in 1987 and is administered by the South African Universities Vice-Chancellors Association (SAUVCA). Its aim is to increase the awareness among the public of the importance of local research and of the excellence of South African universities. The Award is recognized as one of South Africa's premier awards in the field of research published in book form by academic writers. Each winner receives a cash prize of R25,000.

Eligibility and Restrictions: Open to works written by full-time members of staff at any one of the South African universities or technikons. The prize is awarded annually on an alternating basis for contributions from the humanities and the natural sciences. Published works in any of the country's eleven official languages qualify for submission and compete on an equal basis for the award.

Recent Winners: 2002: George Devenish, *A commentary of the South African Bill of Rights* and John Higgins, *Raymond Williams – Literature, Marxism and Cultural Materialism* (joint winners).

Sponsoring Organization: Allied Electronic Corporation (Altron).

Address: The Altron Group, Altron House, 4 Sherborne Road, Parktown, 2193 Gauteng, South Africa. **Telephone:** (11) 645-3600. **Fax:** (11) 726-5778. **Internet:** www.altron.co.za. **E-mail:** info@altron.co.za.

Ver Poets Open Competition

The competition was founded in 1970 by May Badman. Prizes are awarded in June each year, with £500 for the winner, £300 for the runner up and two further prizes of £100. The winning poems are published in a special anthology.

Eligibility and Restrictions: Poems of no more than 30 lines are invited on any subject and in any style. A different adjudicator, an established poet, reads all the submitted work each year. Entries must be unpublished work in English.

How to Apply: Entries should be submitted with an entry fee by 30 April.

Recent Winners: 2001: Margaret Morgan, John Godfrey, David Whitehead and Andrew Marstand-David; 2000: John Grove Stephensen, K. Close, Bill Headdon and Hubert Moore; 1999: Sean Body, Fiona Shackleton, Andre Mangeot and Daphne Gloag; 1998: Bill Headdon, Daphne Gloag, John Gallas and Suzanne Burrows; 1997: Kerry Hardy, Judith Everitt, Ruth Smith and Diana Stirling.

Sponsoring Organization: Ver Poets.

Contact: Organiser May Badman.

Address: Ver Poets, 61–63 Chiswell Green Lane, St Albans, Herts AL2 3AL, UK. **Telephone:** (1727) 867005.

The Verb Writing Competition BBC

A series of poetry and writing competitions running throughout the year, administered by The Verb, BBC Radio 3 language and literature series. The writing competition was established in April 2002, with the aim of encouraging listeners and online users to participate in the programme by submitting their own writing. Some submissions are read out on air.

Eligibility and Restrictions: Details of competitions are announced on air during the programme on Saturday evenings on Radio 3.

How to Apply: Original work can be submitted either via the website or in writing to the address given.

Sponsoring Organization: BBC Radio 3.

Contact: Liz Lindsay.

Address: Room 7090, BBC Broadcasting House, London W1A 1AA, UK. **Internet:** www.bbc.co.uk/radio3/speech/theverb. **E-mail:** theverb@bbc.co.uk.

Victorian Premier's Literary Awards

The Victorian Premier's Literary Awards are one of Australia's oldest and most prestigious annual literary awards. Financially supported by the Victorian Government, the Awards are national and reward Australian writers for the best Australian books and writing in the categories of fiction, non-fiction, young-adult fiction, poetry, drama, essay and literary translation. The Awards were established in 1985 to mark the centenary of the births of Vance and Nettie Palmer, distinguished writers and critics who made significant contributions to Victorian and Australian literary culture. The Awards aim to honour Australian literature, ideas, innovation and learning. The winners are chosen by professional panels of judges made up of actors, authors, playwrights, librarians, editors and book-sellers.

Eligibility and Restrictions: Awards are open to all living Australian citizens or legal permanent residents who have had a book published in the preceding year, or who have had a play performed in the preceding year (year ending 30 April). All works must be in English. Unpublished works and short stories are excluded. See website for further details of eligibility within each category.

How to Apply: Works may be submitted by writers, publishers, production companies or literary agents. Each entry must be accompanied by a completed and signed copy of the relevant nomination form plus entry fee where applicable. Deadline for submissions is 8 July.

Recent Winners: Vance Palmer Prize for Fiction: 2001: Peter Carey, *True History of the Kelly Gang*
Nettie Palmer Prize for Non-fiction: 2001: Anna Haebich, *Broken Circles: Fragmenting Indigenous Families 1800–2000*
Herald Sun Prize for Young Adult Fiction: 2001: James Moloney, *Touch Me*
C. J. Dennis Prize for Poetry: 2001: John Mateer, *Barefoot Speech*
Louis Esson Prize for Drama: 2001: Peta Murray, *Salt*
Alfred Deakin Prize for an Essay Advancing Public Debate: Malcolm Fraser, *My Country 2050*, Marcia Langton, *The Nations of Australia*, and Robert Manne, *A Personal Journey* (joint winners).

Sponsoring Organization: Government of Victoria state, administered by the State Library of Victoria.

Contact: Project Officer Barry Scott.

Address: State Library of Victoria, 328 Swanston St, Melbourne, Vic. 3000, Australia. **Telephone:** (3) 8664 7277. **Internet:** www.statelibrary.vic.gov.au/pla/. **E-mail:** pla@slv.vic.gov.au.

Vilenica International Literary Awards

The Vilenica International Literary Awards are an independent event organized by the Slovenian Writers' Association. The awards were established in 1986 to promote Slovenian literature abroad and foreign literature in Slovenia. The Vilenica International Award, of SIT 1,500,000, is presented every September at the Vilenica International Literary Festival in Lipica, in recognition of out-standing achievements in Central European literature. The winner is chosen by a special jury, headed by Iztok Osojnik, the Director of Vilenica. The award is financially supported by the Ministry of Culture of the Republic of Slovenia, the Central European Initiative, the Municipal Community of Sezana, and private sponsors. The association also presents the Kristal Vilenica Award, which is presented to one of the participants of the Vilenica International Literary Festival for the best text published in the Vilenica Almanac. The award is conferred by a special jury comprising at least five of the guests of the Vilenica Awards who are not themselves competing. The award winner receives a special crystal made from karst stone.

Eligibility and Restrictions: Open to works of fiction, drama or poetry by writers from Central European countries.

Recent Winners: Vilenica International Literary Award: 2001: Jaan Kaplinski (Estonia); 2000: Slavko Mihalic (Croatia); 1999: Erica Pedretti (Switzerland); 1998: Péter Nádas (Hungary); 1997: Pavel Vilikovský (Slovak Republic); 1996: Adam Zagajewski (Poland)

Kristal Vilenica Award: 2000: Vörös Istvan (Hungary); 1999: Angelo Cherchi (Italy); 1998: Peter Semolic (Slovenia); 1997: Nicole Mueller (Switzerland); 1996: Kaca Celan (Bosnia).
Sponsoring Organization: Slovenian Writers' Association.
Contact: Dir Iztok Osojnik.
Address: Tomsiceva 12, 1001 Ljubljana, Slovenia. **Telephone:** (1) 2514 144. **Fax:** (1) 4216430. **Internet:** www.vilenica.org. **E-mail:** iztok.osojnik@guest.arnes.si.

Herman Voaden National Playwriting Competition

A biennial award established in 1997 after a bequest by Herman Voaden, a pioneering Canadian playwright and theatre director. The award seeks to encourage the writing of Canadian drama and help develop a distinctively Canadian art of the theatre. All entries are judged by an initial group of judges, followed by a semi-final round and a final round judged by two prominent playwrights. The first prize is C$3,000, with a second prize of C$2,000 and third prize of C$1,000. First and second prize winners are also offered a one-week workshop and public reading by a professional director and cast.

Eligibility and Restrictions: Entrants must be Canadian citizens or landed immigrants. One play per entrant is permitted; only full-length plays in English are accepted. Plays must not have been professionally produced or published.

How to Apply: A bound and typed copy of the play should be submitted, along with a disk version, and a completed entry form, accompanied by an entry fee of $30. The deadline is 31 January.

Recent Winners: 2001: Michael Lewis MacLennan, *Last Romantics*; 1999: Brian Nelson, *North*.
Sponsoring Organization: Queen's University Drama Department.
Contact: Chair Tim Fort.
Address: Drama Dept, Queen's University, Kingston, ON K7L 3N6, Canada. **Telephone:** (613) 533-2104. **Fax:** (613) 533-6268. **Internet:** www.queensu.ca/drama. **E-mail:** hannaca@post.queensu.ca.

Vondel Translation Prize

Award for the best translation of a Dutch or Flemish literary work into English. Translations should have been published in the UK or the USA during the preceding two years.
Sponsoring Organization: Translators Assocation.
Address: Translators Assocation, 84 Drayton Gardens, London SW10 9SB, UK. **Telephone:** (20) 7373 6642. **Fax:** (20) 7373 5768. **E-mail:** info@societyofauthors. org.

Johann-Heinrich-Voss-Preis für Übersetzung (Johann Heinrich Voss Translation Prize)

An annual prize of €15,000 for translation into German of literary works in the genres poetry, drama or essay, as well as scientific works of high literary merit. The prize was established in 1958 but given this name only in 1977.

How to Apply: Applications are not accepted.

Recent Winners: 2002: Gisela Perlet; 2001: Burkhart Kroeber; 2000: Armin Eidherr; 1999: Harry Rowohlt; 1998: Gustav Just.

Sponsoring Organization: Deutsche Akademie für Sprache und Dichtung.

Address: Deutsche Akademie für Sprache und Dichtung, Alexandraweg 23, 64287 Darmstadt, Germany. **Telephone:** (6151) 40920. **Fax:** (6151) 409299. **Internet:** www.deutscheakademie.de.

Wayne S. Vucinich Book Prize

The prize has been awarded since 1983 for a distinguished monograph in Russian, Eurasian and East European Studies in any discipline of the humanities, including literature, the arts, film, etc. The winner is selected by a committee, and receives a cash award.

Eligibility and Restrictions: Open to works published in English in the USA during the previous year. Textbooks, translations, bibliographies and reference works are not eligible.

How to Apply: Publishers, editors and authors should send copies of eligible works to each committee member by mid-May.

Recent Winners: 2001: Alaina Lemon, *Between Two Fires: Gypsy Performance and Romani Memory from Pushkin to Post-Socialism*; 2000: Peter Gatrell, *A Whole Empire Walking: Refugees in Russia during World War I*; 1999: David D. Laitin, *Identity in Formation: The Russian Speaking Populations in the Near Abroad*; 1998: Stephen E. Hanson, *Time and Revolution: Marxism and the Design of Soviet Institutions*; 1997: Tomas Venclova, *Aleksandr Wat: Life and Art of an Iconoclast*.

Sponsoring Organization: American Association for the Advancement of Slavic Studies/Stanford University Center for Russian and East European Studies.

Address: American Association for the Advancement of Slavic Studies, 8 Story St, Cambridge, MA 02138, USA. **Telephone:** (617) 495-0677. **Fax:** (617) 495-0680. **E-mail:** aaass@hcs.harvard.edu.

Výrocní ceny Nadace

Awarded since 1997 by the Czech Literary Fund to promote literary quality. May be awarded to books in any genre, whether fiction, poetry, prose or essay. The winner is chosen by a panel of experts and receives a prize of 50,000 koruna.

Eligibility and Restrictions: Open to books in any genre published by Czech authors in the preceding year.

Recent Winners: 2001: Pavel Kosatík,*Ferdinand Peroutka – Pozdejsí zivot (1938–1978)*; 2000: Karel Siktanc, *Sarlat*; 1999: Jan Uikes, *True Plays*.

Sponsoring Organization: Czech Literary Fund.

Contact: Administrator Hana Kylianova.

Address: Pod Nuselskymi schody 3, 120 00 Prague, 2, Czech Republic. **Telephone:** 222 560081-2. **Fax:** 222 560083. **Internet:** www.nclf.cz. **E-mail:** nclf@vol.cz.

Vyšehrad Publishers Awards

The Prague publisher Vyšehrad presents a number of annual literary awards. In addition to prizes for best translation, best original work and best illustration, there is a lifetime achievement award and recognition of long-term co-operation with Vyšehrad Publishers.

Recent Winners: Translation: 2001: Zuzana Mayerová, *Ráj (Paradise)* by Toni Morrison; 2000: Radislav Hosek, *Aurelius Augustinus, A Roman – A Man – A Saint* Original work: 2001: Vera Frolcová, *Velikonoce v ceské lidové kulture (Easter in the Czech Folk Tradition)*; 2000: Jiri Kejr, *The John Huss Process* Illustration: 2001: Zdenek Ziegler; 2000: Adolf Born, illustrations of books by Jan Karon Lieftime Achievement: 2001: Václav Konzal; 2000: Bretislav Danek.

Sponsoring Organization: Vyšehrad Publishers.

Address: Vyšehrad, Bartolomíjská 9, Prague, 110 00, Czech Republic. **Telephone:** 232 6851. **Fax:** 224 221703. **E-mail:** vysehrad@login.cz.

W. H. Smith Literary Award

An annual literary award for an outstanding contribution to English literature in the year under review. The winner is chosen by a panel, and receives a prize of £10,000. The original W. H. Smith Award was established in 1959; in 2001 W. H. Smith reorganized the scheme, with the introduction of a separate set of popular awards selected by votes from the public – see separate entry for W. H. Smith Thumping Good Read Awards. The W. H. Smith Literary Award remains the only award not chosen by public vote.

Eligibility and Restrictions: Open to books written in English and published in the UK. Authors considered must be from the UK, the Commonwealth, or Ireland.

How to Apply: Writers cannot submit work themselves.

Recent Winners: 2002: Ian McEwan, *Atonement*; 2001: Philip Roth, *The Human Stain*; 2000: Melvyn Bragg, *The Soldier's Return*; 1999: Beryl Bainbridge, *Master Georgie*; 1998: Ted Hughes, *Tales From Ovid*.

Sponsoring Organization: W. H. Smith PLC.

Address: W. H. Smith PLC, Audrey House, Ely Place, London EC1N 6SN, UK. **Internet:** www.whsmith.co.uk/awards.

W. H. Smith Thumping Good Read Award

These awards, presented in eight categories, were set up in 2000 to run alongside the longstanding W. H. Smith Literary Award (see separate entry). They are the only British book awards chosen almost entirely by public vote. Each winner receives a prize of £5,000.

Recent Winners: Biography: 2002: Pamela Stephenson, *Billy*; 2001: David Starkey, *Elizabeth* Fiction: 2002: Nick Hornby, *How to be Good*; 2001: Maeve Binchy, *Scarlet Feather* Home and Leisure: 2002: Nigella Lawson, *Nigella Bites*; 2001: Jamie Oliver, *Return of the Naked Chef* Children's Fiction: 2002: Eoin Colfer, *Artemis Fowl*; 2001: J. K. Rowling, *Harry Potter and the Goblet of Fire* Business: 2002: Judi Bevan, *The Rise and Fall of Marks and Spencer*; 2001: Cynthia Crossen, *The Rich and How They Got That Way* General Knowledge: 2002: BBC, *The Blue Planet*; 2001: Simon Schama, *A History of Britain* New Talent: 2002: Emily Barr, *Backpack*; 2001: Zadie Smith, *White Teeth* Travel: 2002: Alex Garland and others, *The Weekenders*; 2001: Bill Bryson, *Down Under*.

Sponsoring Organization: W. H. Smith PLC.

Address: W. H. Smith PLC, Audrey House, Ely Place, London EC1N 6SN, UK. **Internet:** www.whsmith.co.uk/awards.

Wadsworth Prize for Business History

The annual Wadsworth Prize is presented by the Business Archives Council (BAC) for the best book on business history. The prize was established as an annual competition to honour John Wadsworth on his retirement in 1977 after over 40 years of association with the BAC.

How to Apply: Applications are accepted from publishers.

Recent Winners: 2001: Geoffrey Jones, *Merchants to Multinationals*; 2000: (no award given); 1999: David Kynaston, *City of London Vol. III*; 1998: Niall Ferguson, *The World's Banker: The History of the House of Rothschild*; 1997: Youssef Cassis, *Big Business: the European Experience in the Twentieth Century*.

Sponsoring Organization: Business Archives Council.

Address: Business Archives Council, 101 Whitechapel High St, London E1 7RE, UK. **Telephone:** (20) 7247 0024. **Fax:** (20) 7422 0026.

Walford Award for Contributions to Bibliography

Presented to an individual for a substantial contribution to the science and art of bibliography in the UK. The awards are sponsored by Whitaker and judged by panels of reference librarians and members of the Society of Indexers. The winner receives a certificate and a prize of £500.

How to Apply: Nominations are invited from Members, publishers and others.

Recent Winners: 2001: Prof. John McIlwaine.

Sponsoring Organization: Chartered Institute of Library and Information Professionals/Whitaker.

Contact: Reference Awards Administrator Mary Casteleyn.

Address: Chartered Institute of Library and Information Professionals, 7 Ridgmount St, London WC1E 7AE, UK. **Telephone:** (20) 7255 0500. **Fax:** (20) 7255 0501. **Internet:** www.cilip.org.uk. **E-mail:** info@cilip.org.uk.

David Watt Prize

An annual award for outstanding journalism, established in 1988 in memory of David Watt. The prize is given for an article which contributes to a better understanding of global, international or national issues, and is judged by a panel of eight people. The winner receives £7,500.

Eligibility and Restrictions: Open to articles published in English during the preceding year, of not more than 5,000 words.

How to Apply: Apply for rules and an entry form to the Administrator.

Recent Winners: 2000: Robert Fisk (the *Independent*); 1999: Edward Said (*London Review of Books*); 1998: Simon Jenkins (*The Times*); 1997: John Lloyd (*New Statesman*); 1996: Maire Nic Suibhne (the *Guardian*).

Sponsoring Organization: Rio Tinto Zinc plc.

Contact: Administrator Celia Beale.

Address: The Administrator, The David Watt Prize, Rio Tinto plc, 6 St James Square, London SW1Y 4LD, UK. **Telephone:** (20) 7753 2277. **Fax:** (20) 7753 2306. **E-mail:** davidwattprize@riotinto.com.

WAYRBA—West Australian Young Readers' Book Award

Established in 1980 by Mr and Mrs Hoffmann, the Award aims to promote reading, and to give recognition to those who read and write children's literature. The annual award comprises a glass and jarrah wood trophy, and is presented to a winner chosen by popular vote by students who have read the book. Prizes are presented in two categories, for older and younger readers (aged 8–10 and 4–7 respectively).

Eligibility and Restrictions: Open to works of fiction for children by a living author. Entries must have been published or reprinted during the preceding five years.

Recent Winners: Older Readers' List: 2001: Louis Sachar, *Holes*; 2000: John Marsden, *The Night is for Hunting*; 1999: John Marsden, *Burning for Revenge*; 1998: John Marsden, *The Third Day, the Frost*; 1997: Brian Jacques, *Salamandastron*
Younger Readers' List: 2001: J. K. Rowling, *Harry Potter and the Goblet of Fire*; 2000: J. K. Rowling, *Harry Potter and the Philosopher's Stone*; 1999: Alison Lester, *The Quicksand Pony*; 1998: Moses Aaron, *Lily and Me*; 1997: Duncan Ball, *Selby Supersnoop*.

Address: POB 256, Guildford, WA 6935, Australia. **Internet:** www.wayrba. iinet.net.au. **E-mail:** wayrba@hotmail.com.

Wellcome Trust Prize

An award set up with the aim of encouraging science writing that appeals to a non-scientific audience. A prize of £25,000 is presented to a previously unpublished professional life scientist, and the completed book is subsequently published by Weidenfeld & Nicolson.

Eligibility and Restrictions: Open to writers who are unpublished life scientists.

How to Apply: Entrants are asked to submit the opening chapter and a synopsis of their proposed book.

Recent Winners: 1999: Chris McManus, *Right Hand Left Hand*.

Sponsoring Organization: Wellcome Trust/Weidenfeld & Nicolson.

Address: Head of Consultation and Education, Medicine in Society Programme, Wellcome Trust, 210 Euston Rd, London NW1 2BE, UK. **Telephone:** (20) 7611 8846. **Fax:** (20) 7611 8416. **Internet:** www.wellcome.ac.uk. **E-mail:** press. office@wellcome.ac.uk.

Wesley-Logan Prize

Established in 1992, the Wesley-Logan Prize in African Diaspora History is sponsored jointly by the American Historical Association (AHA) and the Association for the Study of African-American Life and History (ASALH) to honour Charles H. Wesley and Rayford W. Logan, two pioneering historians in this field. It is awarded annually for an outstanding book on some aspect of the history of the dispersion, settlement, and adjustment and/or return of groups originally from Africa.

Recent Winners: 2001: Eric Arnesen, *Brotherhoods of Color: Black Railroad Workers and the Struggle for Equality.*

Sponsoring Organization: American Historical Association.

Contact: Lynn Hunt.

Address: American Historical Asscn, 400 A St, SE, Washington, DC 20003–3889, USA. **Telephone:** (202) 544-2422. **Fax:** (202) 544-8307. **Internet:** www.theaha.org/prizes. **E-mail:** press@theaha.org.

Western Australian Premier's Book Awards

These annual literary awards were inaugurated by the Western Australian Government in 1982 to honour and celebrate the literary achievements of Western Australian writers. Until 1990 they were known as the WA Week Literary Awards. The awards are presented in the categories of fiction, poetry, non-fiction (two prizes), children's books, books for young adults, and scripts. From these winners an overall winner is awarded the Premier's Prize. The judges are selected to provide a range of experience in literature, historical writing and writing for children. Each category winner receives A$5,000, while the winner of the Premier's Prize receives A$20,000 plus a trophy. In addition the winning book and a picture of the author are displayed in the State Library of Western Australia.

Eligibility and Restrictions: Entry is open to writers who fulfil at least one of the following conditions: born in Western Australia; resident in Western Australia; has been resident for at least 10 years; work has Western Australia as its primary focus. Entries must have been published during the previous calendar year; the award is presented in May of the following year.

How to Apply: Four copies of each book entered should be submitted to the address given accompanied by an official entry form.

Recent Winners: Premier's Prize: 2000: Michele Drouart, *Into the Wadi*; 1999: Kim Scott, *Benang: From the Heart*; 1998: Carolyn Polizzotto, *Pomegranate Season*; 1997: Robert Drewe, *The Drowner* and Gail Jones, *Fetish Lives* (joint winners); 1996: Banjo Woorunmurra and Howard Pederson, *Jandamarra and the Bunuba Resistance*

Fiction: 2000: Simone Lazaroo, *The Australian Fiancé*; 1999: Kim Scott, *Benang: From the Heart*; 1998: Pat Jacobs, *Going Inland*; 1997: Robert Drewe, *The Drowner* and Gail Jones, *Fetish Lives* (joint winners); 1996: Heather Grace, *The Lighthouse Spark* and Dave Warner, *City of Light* (joint winners)

Poetry: 2000: Mark Reid, *Parochial*; 1999: Tracy Ryan, *The Willing Eye*; 1998: John Kinsella, *The Hunt* and Fay Zwicky, *The Gatekeeper's Wife* (joint winners); 1997: Alec Choate, *The Wheels of Hama: Collected War Poems*; 1996: Dorothy Hewett, *Collected Poems*

Non-Fiction: 2000: Michele Drouart, *Into the Wadi* and Robert Drewe, *The Shark Net* (joint winners); 1999: Estelle Blackburn, *Broken Lives*; 1998: Quentin Beresford and Paul Omaji, *Our State of Mind: Racial Planning and the Stolen Generations*; 1997: Phillip Playford, *Carpet of Silver: the wreck of the Zuytdorp*; 1996: Banjo Woorunmurra and Howard Pederson, *Jandamarra and the Bunuba Resistance*

Children's Books: 2000: Kirsty Murray, *Zarconi's Magic Flying Fish*; 1999: Reg Bolton, *Showtime: Over 75 ways to put on a show*; 1998: Pat Lowe and Jimmy Pike, *Desert Dog*; 1997: Deborah Lisson, *A Place of Safety*; 1996: Helen Bell, *Idjhil*

Young Adults: 2000: Anthony Eaton, *The Darkness*; 1999: Glyn Parry, *Scooterboy*; 1998: Deborah Lisson, *Red Hugh*
Special Award: 1999: Victor France, Larry Mitchell and Alison Wright, *Abrolhos Islands Conversations*; 1998: Carolyn Polizzotto, *Pomegranate Season*; 1997: Women's Cancer Group, *Songs of Strength*; 1996: Mike Leonard, *The Kimberley – A Journey Through Northwest Australia*
Script: 1998: Ingle Knight, *Milk and Honey*; 1997: Dickon Oxenburgh and Andrew Ross, *Merry-Go-Round in the Sea*; 1996: Sarah Rossetti, *Culture Clash*.

Sponsoring Organization: Library and Information Service of Western Australia.

Contact: Consultant Julie Ham.

Address: Library and Information Service of Western Australia, Alexander Library Bldg, Perth Cultural Centre, Perth, WA 6000, Australia. **Telephone:** (8) 9427 3330. **Fax:** (8) 9427 3336. **Internet:** www.liswa.wa.gov.au/pba.html. **E-mail:** jham@liswa.wa.gov.au.

Westminster Prize

The Westminster Prize is Soho Theatre's annual playwriting competition for first-time playwrights who live or work in Westminster. Entrants submit a short play, which is approximately 10 minutes long for two characters, based on a photograph. All entries are read and assessed by a panel of readers made up of theatre professionals.

Eligibility and Restrictions: Prizes are awarded in two categories, for writers aged over 18 and under 18.

How to Apply: Details available on the website.

Recent Winners: Over 18: 2001: Gil Brailey, *Future Perfect* and Darren Murphy, *A Road in Winter* (joint winners)
Under 18: 2001: Lidonia Lawrence, *Butt Naked on a Broadway*.

Sponsoring Organization: Soho Theatre and Writers Centre/City of Westminster/Getty Images.

Address: 21 Dean Street, London W1D 3NE, UK. **Telephone:** (20) 7287 5060. **Internet:** www.sohotheatre.com.

Wheatley Medal for an Outstanding Index

Awarded jointly with the Society of Indexers, for an outstanding printed index published in the UK. The award is sponsored by Whitaker and judged by panels of reference librarians and members of the Society of Indexers. The winner receives a golden medal, a certificate and a prize of £500.

How to Apply: Nominations are invited from Members, publishers and others.

Recent Winners: 2001: David and Hilary Crystal, *Words on Words*.

Sponsoring Organization: Chartered Institute of Library and Information Professionals/Whitaker/Society of Indexers.

Contact: Reference Awards Administrator Mary Casteleyn.

Address: Chartered Institute of Library and Information Professionals, 7 Ridgmount St, London WC1E 7AE, UK. **Telephone:** (20) 7255 0500. **Fax:** (20) 7255 0501. **Internet:** www.cilip.org.uk. **E-mail:** info@cilip.org.uk.

Whitbread Book of the Year and Literary Awards

The Whitbread Awards, which were established by Whitbread company in 1971, have joined the ranks of the UK's most prestigious literary awards. Panels of three judges select prizewinners (with the assistance of three young judges for the Children's Book of the Year). The total prize money is £50,000: £5,000 for the winners of the First Novel, Novel, Poetry and Biography categories; £10,000 for the Children's Book of the Year; and £25,000 for the Book of the Year (2001).

Eligibility and Restrictions: Awards are made annually at a presentation dinner in January in the categories First Novel, Novel, Poetry, Biography and Children's Book of the Year; an overall winner is awarded the Book of the Year prize.

Recent Winners: Book of the Year: 2001: Philip Pullman, *The Amber Spyglass*; 2000: Matthew Kneale, *English Passengers*; 1999: Seamus Heaney, *Beowulf: A New Verse Translation*; 1998: Ted Hughes, *Birthday Letters*; 1997: Ted Hughes, *Tales from Ovid*
First Novel: 2001: Sid Smith, *Something Like A House*; 2000: Zadie Smith, *White Teeth*; 1999: Tim Lott, *White City Blue*; 1998: Giles Foden, *The Last King of Scotland*; 1997: Pauline Melville, *The Ventriloquist's Tale*
Novel: 2001: Patrick Neate, *Twelve Bar Blues*; 2000: Matthew Kneale, *English Passengers*; 1999: Rose Tremain, *Music and Silence*; 1998: Justin Cartwright, *Leading the Cheers*; 1997: Jim Crace, *Quarantine*
Poetry: 2001: Selima Hill, *Bunny*; 2000: John Burnside, *The Asylum Dance*; 1999: Seamus Heaney, *Beowulf: A New Verse Translation*; 1998: Ted Hughes, *Birthday Letters*; 1997: Ted Hughes, *Tales from Ovid*
Biography: 2001: Diana Souhami, *Selkirk's Island*; 2000: Lorna Sage, *Bad Blood–A Memoir*; 1999: David Cairns, *Berlioz Volume 2*; 1998: Amanda Foreman, *Georgiana, Duchess of Devonshire*; 1997: Graham Robb, *Victor Hugo*
Children's Book of the Year: 2001: Philip Pullman, *The Amber Spyglass*; 2000: Jamila Gavin, *Coram Boy*; 1999: J. K. Rowling, *Harry Potter and the Prisoner of Azkaban*; 1998: David Almond, *Skellig*; 1997: Andrew Norriss, *Aquila*.

Sponsoring Organization: Whitbread/Karen Earl Sponsorship.

Contact: Administrator Denise Bayat.

Address: Booksellers Association of the United Kingdom and Ireland, Minister House, 272 Vauxhall Bridge Road, London SW1V 1BA, UK. **Internet:** www.whitbread-bookawards.co.uk.

White Ravens

Every year since 1996 the Internationale Jugendbibliothek (International Youth Library) has drawn up a list of the best books for children from around the world which have appeared during the previous year. The list, known as the White Ravens catalogue, includes books of international interest which deserve a wider reception on account of their universal theme and/or their exceptional or innovative artistic and literary style and design. The list, which is compiled by experts in children's literature for all the major languages, appears each year just before the Children's Book Fair in Bologna.

How to Apply: Publishers are invited to send review copies to the address given.

Recent Winners: The list for 2001 contained 250 titles in 28 languages from 46 countries. Full details can be found on the website.

Sponsoring Organization: Internationale Jugendbibliothek (International Youth Library).
Address: Internationale Jugendbibliothek, Schloss Blutenburg, 81247 Munich, Germany. **Internet:** www.ijb.de.

Whitfield Prize

The Whitfield Prize is offered annually for a new book on British history. It carries a value of £1,000.

Eligibility and Restrictions: To be eligible a book must be on a subject within a field of British history, and have been published in the UK during the previous year. It should also be the author's first solely written history book.

Recent Winners: 2001: Adam Fox, *Oral and Literate Culture in England, 1500–1700*.

Sponsoring Organization: Royal Historical Society.

Contact: Exec. Sec. Joy McCarthy.

Address: Royal Historical Society, University College London, Gower St, London WC1E 6BT, UK. **Telephone:** (20) 7387 7532. **Fax:** (20) 7387 7532. **Internet:** www.rhs.ac.uk. **E-mail:** royalhistsoc@ucl.ac.uk.

John Whiting Award

This annual award was inaugurated in 1965 in memory of John Whiting, a member of the Drama Panel of the Arts Council of Great Britain. The award is intended to help further the careers and enhance the reputations of British playwrights. The award is made for a play in which the writing is of special quality, and which has relevance and importance to contemporary life. The winner is chosen by a panel of judges, and receives £6,000.

Eligibility and Restrictions: The play must have been written during the previous calendar year, but does not have to have received a production. No writer who has previously won the award may reapply, and plays that have previously been submitted are excluded, as are translations.

How to Apply: Writers who have had an offer of an award under the Arts Council Writing Schemes, or who have received a commission from certain theatre companies, may apply by sending three copies of the script accompanied by biographical details to the address given by the beginning of February.

Recent Winners: 2000: Zinnie Harris, *Further than the Furthest Thing*; 1999: Tanika Gupta, *The Waiting Room*; 1998: David Greig, *The Cosmonaut's Last Message to the Woman He Once Loved in the Former Soviet Union*; 1997: Roy Williams, *Starstruck*; 1996: Ayub Khan Din, *East is East*.

Sponsoring Organization: Arts Council of England.

Contact: Asst Drama Officer Jemima Lee.

Address: Drama Dept, Arts Council of England, 14 Great Peter St, London SW1P 3NQ, UK. **Telephone:** (20) 7973 6431. **Fax:** (20) 7973 6983. **Internet:** www.artscouncil.org.uk. **E-mail:** info.drama@artscouncil.org.uk.

Whiting Writers' Awards

A set of annual awards presented to emergent writers in recognition of their writing achievement and future promise in four categories: fiction, poetry, non-fiction and drama. Winners receive a prize of $35,000.

Recent Winners: Poetry: 2000: Albert Mobilio, James Thomas Stevens/ Aronhiota, Claude Wilkinson
Fiction: 2000: Robert Cohen, Samantha Gillison, Lily King, John McManus, Colson Whitehead
Non-fiction: 2000: Andrew X. Pham
Drama: 2000: Kelly Stuart.

Sponsoring Organization: Mrs Giles Whiting Foundation.

Address: Mrs Giles Whiting Foundation, 1133 Ave of the Americas, New York, NY 10036, USA.

Walt Whitman Award

The Walt Whitman Award was established in 1975 to make possible the publication of a poet's first full-length collection. The competition is judged by a distinguished poet, and the winning manuscript is published by a prominent literary publishing house. In addition the winner receives a cash prize of $5,000, and a one-month residency at the Vermont Studio Center.

Eligibility and Restrictions: Open to any citizen of the USA who has neither published nor committed to publish a book of poetry 40 pages or more in length and in an edition of 500 or more copies.

How to Apply: Book-length manuscripts (50 to 100 pages) may be submitted to the Academy between 15 September and 15 November of each year, accompanied by an entry form and fee.

Recent Winners: 2002: Sue Kwock Kim, *Notes from the Divided Country*; 2001: John Canaday, *The Invisible World*; 2000: Ben Doyle, *Radio, Radio*; 1999: Judy Jordan, *Carolina Ghost Woods*; 1997: Barbara Ras, *Bite Every Sorrow*.

Sponsoring Organization: Academy of American Poets.

Address: Academy of American Poets, 584 Broadway, Suite 1208, New York, NY 10012, USA. **Telephone:** (212) 274-0343. **Fax:** (212) 274-9427. **Internet:** www.poets.org/academy. **E-mail:** academy@poets.org.

Christoph-Martin-Wieland-Preis

Established in 1979, the Wieland-Preis recognizes translation of literary works into German. A prize of 20,000 DM is awarded every other year, alternating with the Helmut-M.-Braem-Preis (qv), with the winner chosen by a panel of experts.

Eligibility and Restrictions: Translation must be published by a German publisher, and be readily available.

How to Apply: Entries should be submitted accompanied by biographical details, a copy of the original work and two copies of the translation.

Recent Winners: 2001: Frank Günther.

Sponsoring Organization: Freundeskreis zur internationalen Förderung literarischer und wissenschaftlicher Übersetzungen.

Contact: Pres. Ragni Maria Gschwend.

Address: Freundeskreis zur internationalen Förderung literarischer und wissenschaftlicher Übersetzungen, Ragni Maria Gschwend, Runzstr. 56, 79102 Freiburg im Breisgau, Germany. **Telephone:** (76) 12 61 98. **Internet:** www. literaturuebersetzer.de.

Elie Wiesel Prize in Ethics Essay Contest

The Elie Wiesel Prize in Ethics Essay Contest was created in 1989 to challenge college students to contemplate the various significant ethical issues facing them in today's complex society and to analyze their own perception and thoughts on ethics. A distinguished panel of readers evaluates all contest entries and a jury, including Elie Wiesel, chooses the winners. The winner receives a prize of $5,000, while the runners-up receive $2,500 and $1,500.

Eligibility and Restrictions: Students should submit an original essay of 3,000–4,000 words on one of the suggested topics or a topic of their choice, so long as it pertains to ethics. Undergraduate full-time third- and fourth-year students at colleges and universities in the USA and Canada are welcome to apply. European and international students may enter only if they are studying at a US or Canadian college or university and fulfill certain other requirements.

How to Apply: Information and application forms can be found on the website given; faxed or emailed applications are not accepted.

Recent Winners: 2001: James D. Long IV, *Deaths in Paradise: Genocide and the Limits of Imagination in Rwanda*; 2000: Alexa R. Kolbi-Molinas, *The Secret of Redemption–Memory and Resistance: A Lesson for the 21st Century*; 1999: Sami F. Halabi, *The Bosnian Women*; 1998: Laura Overland, *Their Lives in Our Hands: Fulfilling Our Ethical Obligations to the Terminally Ill Enrolling in Research Studies*; 1997: Tamara Duker, *Ethics and One February Morning*.

Sponsoring Organization: Elie Wiesel Foundation for Humanity.

Contact: Programme Co-ordinator Annika Wadenius.

Address: Elie Wiesel Foundation for Humanity, 529 Fifth Ave, Suite 1802, New York, NY 10017, USA. **Telephone:** (212) 490-7777. **Fax:** (212) 490 6006 212-490-6006. **Internet:** www.eliewieselfoundation.org. **E-mail:** info@eliewieselfoundation.org.

D. R. Wijewardene Memorial Award

An annual award established in 1984 by the Lake House Bookshop in memory of a great nationalist, D. R. Wijewardene, who also established Lake House newspapers. The award, of Rs40,000, is presented to the best Sinhala novel in manuscript form.

Recent Winners: 1999: Arambawatege Yasawardena Rodrigo, *Viparyasaya*; 1998: Shanthi Dissanayake, *Vara Mal*; 1997: J. C. P. S. Siriwardene, Pambaya; 1996: Seetha Kumarihamy, *Aratu*; 1995: (no award presented).

Sponsoring Organization: Lake House Bookshop.

Address: Lake House Bookshop, 100, Sir Chittampalam Gardiner, Mawatha, Colombo, 2, Sri Lanka. **Telephone:** (1) 430581. **Fax:** (1) 432104.

Laura Ingalls Wilder Award

Established in 1954, when the first medal was presented to Laura Ingalls Wilder, this prize is awarded to a writer or illustrator whose books published in the USA have made 'a substantial and lasting contribution to literature for children' over a number of years. From 1960–80 the award was made every five years, and between 1980 and 2001 it was made every three years. Since 2001 the award has been made every two years. The winner receives a bronze medal.

Recent Winners: 2001: Milton Meltzer; 1998: Russell Freedman; 1995: Virginia Hamilton; 1992: Marcia Brown; 1989: Elizabeth George Speare.

Sponsoring Organization: Association for Library Service to Children, a division of the American Library Association.

Address: Association for Library Service to Children, American Library Association, 50 East Huron, Chicago, IL 60611–2795, USA. **Fax:** (312) 944-7671. **Internet:** www.ala.org/alsc. **E-mail:** alsc@ala.org.

William Hill Sports Book of the Year

Established in 1988, this is awarded to the year's best sports book. It is judged by a panel of sports broadcasters and journalists, and carries a prize of £15,000.

Eligibility and Restrictions: The book must be available in the UK, and must have appeared in the year preceding the year in which the prize is awarded.

How to Apply: Entry forms are available from the office.

Recent Winners: 2001: Laura Hillonbrand, *Sea Biscuit*; 2000: Lance Armstrong, *It's Not About the Bike*; 1999: Derek Briley, *A Social History of English Cricket*.

Sponsoring Organization: William Hill.

Contact: Romaine Snijder.

Address: William Hill Organization, 50 Station Rd, London N22 7TP, UK. **Telephone:** (20) 818 3731. **Fax:** (20) 8918 3728. **Internet:** www. williamhillmedia.com. **E-mail:** pressoffice@williamhill.co.uk.

William Carlos Williams Award

The William Carlos Williams Award, which is administered by the Poetry Society of America (PSA), is a prize of between $500 and $1,000 for a book of poetry published by a small press, non-profit, or university press. The award is endowed by the family and friends of Geraldine Clinton Little, a poet and author of short stories and former vice-president of the PSA.

Eligibility and Restrictions: Open to books of poetry published by a small press, non-profit or university press. Only original works by a single author who is a permanent resident of the USA will be considered. Translations are excluded.

How to Apply: Submissions can only be entered by publishers; two copies should be sent accompanied by a cover sheet and entry fee (non-members) between 1 October and 21 December.

Recent Winners: 2002: Li-Young Lee, *Book of My Nights*.

Sponsoring Organization: Poetry Society of America.

Address: Poetry Society of America, 15 Gramercy Park, New York, NY 10003, USA. **Telephone:** (212) 254-9628. **Internet:** www.poetrysociety.org.

Raymond Williams Community Publishing Prize

Established in 1989 to recognize published works which reflect the lives of people of particular communities. The prize is named after Raymond Williams who was a critic and academic, and member of the Arts Council. Awarded to a work (fiction or non-fiction) which offers outstanding imaginative and creative qualities and which exemplifies the values of ordinary people and their lives. The winner receives £3,000, of which £2,000 goes to the publisher and £1,000 to the author. The runner-up receives £2,000 (publisher £1,500, author £500).

Eligibility and Restrictions: Must be a work of community publishing which has been published in the calendar year preceding the year in which the award is presented.

How to Apply: The winner is chosen from entries submitted by non-profit-making publishers (one entry only per year). Applications may be made from anywhere in the UK; four copies of the book should be submitted accompanied by four application forms.

Recent Winners: 2001: Tim Smith, Michelle Winslow; 2000: Jackie Gay (Editor), Julia Bell; 1999: Origins Literature Development Project; 1998 Brian Lewis (Editor); 1997: Sharon Whetler, Liz Bartlett.

Sponsoring Organization: Arts Council of England.

Address: Arts Council of England, 14 Great Peter St, London SW1P 3NQ, UK. **Telephone:** (20) 7973 6442. **Fax:** (20) 7973 6520. **Internet:** www.artscouncil. org.uk. **E-mail:** pippa.shoubridge@artscouncil.org.uk.

Robert H. Winner Memorial Award

The Robert H. Winner Memorial Award of $2,500, which is administered by the Poetry Society of America (PSA), was established by the family and friends of Robert H. Winner, a poet whose first book of poems appeared when he was almost 50. The prize aims to reward significant work written by someone in mid-life who has not had substantial recognition.

Eligibility and Restrictions: Open to poets over 40 who have published no more than one book. Entries should comprise a manuscript of 10 poems (up to 20 pages); previously published work may be included.

How to Apply: Two copies of submissions should be sent accompanied by a cover sheet and entry fee (non-members) between 1 October and 21 December.

Recent Winners: 2002: Margo Berdeshevsky.

Sponsoring Organization: Poetry Society of America.

Address: Poetry Society of America, 15 Gramercy Park, New York, NY 10003, USA. **Telephone:** (212) 254-9628. **Internet:** www.poetrysociety.org.

Paul A. Witty Short Story Award

Offered to the author of an original short story in a periodical for children, which sets a high literary standard and encourages younger readers to read periodicals. The award carries a $1,000 prize.

Eligibility and Restrictions: Entries must have been published for the first time during the preceding year.

How to Apply: Entries must be received by 1 December.

Recent Winners: 2001: G. Clifton Wiler, *The Orange Armband*.

Sponsoring Organization: International Reading Association.

Address: PO Box 8139, Newark, DE, New York, NY, USA. **Telephone:** (302) 731 1600. **Fax:** (303) 731-1051. **Internet:** www.reading.org. **E-mail:** jbutler@ reading.org.

Wolfson History Prize

Established in 1972 to promote and encourage standards of excellence in the writing of history for the general public. The prize is awarded annually by a panel of experts for a history book that is accessible to the lay reader. The amount awarded varies, but totalled £35,000 for three prizes in 2000.

Eligibility and Restrictions: Books must be published in the UK in the same calendar year as the award. The author must be a British subject.

How to Apply: Publisher should contact the Wolfson Foundation.

Recent Winners: 2000 (three prizes): Ian Kershaw, *Hitler, 1936–1945: Nemesis*; Mark Mazower, *The Balkans*; Roy Porter, *Enlightenment: Britain and the Creation of the Modern World*; 1999 (three prizes): Lord Briggs, for his contribution to the writing of history; Andrew Roberts, *Salisbury: Victorian Titan*; Joanna Bourke, *An Intimate History of Killing*; 1998 (two prizes): Antony Beevor, *Stalingrad*; Amanda Vickery, *The Gentleman's Daughter*; 1997 (two prizes): John Brewer, *The Pleasures of the Imagination: English Culture in the Eighteenth Century*; Patricia Hollis, *Jennie Lee: A Life*; 1996 (two prizes): Orlando Figes, *A People's Tragedy: The Russian Revolution 1891–1924*; Prof. Eric J. Hobsbawn for his contribution to the writing of history.

Sponsoring Organization: Wolfson Foundation.

Contact: Administrator Yee-Lin Tan.

Address: Wolfson Foundation, 8 Queen Anne St, London W1G 9LD, UK. **Telephone:** (20) 7323 5730 ext 213. **Fax:** (20) 7323 3241.

David T.K. Wong Prize for Short Fiction

Established in 2000, this international prize is presented every other year to promote literary excellence in the form of the short story written in English. Unpublished stories are welcome from writers worldwide. The winner receives a prize of £7,500.

Eligibility and Restrictions: Open to unpublished stories of between 2,500 and 6,000 words; entries must incorporate one or more of International PEN's ideals as set out in its Charter (details on website).

How to Apply: Entries must be submitted via one of International PEN's centres; the closing date is the end of September.

Recent Winners: 2001: Rachel Seiffert, *The Crossing*.

Sponsoring Organization: International PEN.

Address: International PEN, 9/10 Charterhouse Buildings, Goswell Road, London EC1M 7AT, UK. **Telephone:** (20) 7253 4308. **Fax:** (20) 7253 5711. **Internet:** www.oneworld.org/internatpen. **E-mail:** intpen@dircon.co.uk.

World Book of the Year Prize

Initiated in 1994 by the Ministry of Culture and Islamic Guidance, the Book of the Year Festival selects outstanding books in the categories Islamic Studies and Iranian Studies. The awards aim to provide a forum for publishers to co-operate and contribute to the advancement of Iranian national culture. The winners are chosen in consultation with Islamic scholars and theoreticians.

Eligibility and Restrictions: Books must have been published during the previous year.

Sponsoring Organization: Ministry of Culture and Islamic Guidance.

Address: Ministry of Culture and Islamic Guidance, Tehran, Iran.

World Wide Writers Competition

World Wide Writers runs a series of competitions, including a £3,000 short story competition, and a £100 poetry prize. Winning entries are published in a special anthology.

Eligibility and Restrictions: Poetry competition is open to unpublished poems up to 40 lines in length. There are no restrictions on subject or theme.

How to Apply: Readers are invited to enter their poems for a competition to be held in each issue of *Writers' Forum*, accompanied by the appropriate entry fee. There are four deadlines per year.

Sponsoring Organization: Writers' International.

Address: Writers' International Ltd, PO Box 3229, Bournemouth BH1 1ZS, UK. **Internet:** www.worldwidewriters.com. **E-mail:** writintl@globalnet.co.uk.

Writer Magazine/Emily Dickinson Award

The Writer/Emily Dickinson Award of $250, which is administered by the Poetry Society of America (PSA), was established in honour of Charles Angoff. The award aims to honour the memory and poetry of Emily Dickinson.

Eligibility and Restrictions: Open to PSA members only. Entries should be poems of up to 30 lines inspired by Dickinson though not necessarily in her style.

How to Apply: Two copies of submissions should be sent accompanied by a cover sheet between 1 October and 21 December.

Recent Winners: 2002: Mary Ann Samyn.

Sponsoring Organization: Poetry Society of America.

Address: Poetry Society of America, 15 Gramercy Park, New York, NY 10003, USA. **Telephone:** (212) 254-9628. **Internet:** www.poetrysociety.org.

Writer's Digest Annual Writing Competition

Established in 1931 to help unpublished writers gain recognition and get their works published. Prizes are given to 1,001 winners each year, and the prize money totals more than $25,000; the First Place Winner in each of the ten categories receives $750, with other prizes for runners-up. The categories are: Inspirational Writing; Memoirs/Personal Essay; Feature Article; Short Story (Genre); Short Story (Mainstream/Literary); Poetry (Rhyming); Poetry (Non-rhyming); Stage Play; TV/Movie Script; Children's Fiction.

Eligibility and Restrictions: Entries must be original, unpublished and unproduced. Manuscripts must not exceed the word count for the relevant category (between 2,000 and 4,000 words – see website for details).

How to Apply: Application forms may be obtained from the website or by email. Entries may be submitted online or by post, but must be accompanied by entry fee ($5 or $10 per entry depending on category); deadline is mid-May.

Recent Winners: Full list of recent winners (1,001 each year) is available on website.

Sponsoring Organization: Writer's Digest.

Contact: Promotion Asst Terri Boes.

Address: Writer's Digest, 4700 E Galbraith Rd, Cincinnati, OH 45236, USA. **Telephone:** (513) 531-2690. **Fax:** (513) 531-0798. **Internet:** www.writersdigest. com. **E-mail:** competitions@fwpubs.com.

Writer's Journal Annual Short Story Contest

Established in 1980 to offer aspiring writers a forum to compete with other writers. The three best entries in each round win cash prizes of up to $300, and are published in the *Writer's Journal* magazine.

Eligibility and Restrictions: Entries must not exceed 2,000 words and must be previously unpublished. Categories for entries include short story, horror/ghost story, romance, travel writing and poetry.

How to Apply: Submit entries to the address given accompanied by a separate cover sheet giving contact details; author's name should not appear on the manuscript itself. A reading fee is payable for each entry submitted. Deadlines vary by category; check website for details.

Sponsoring Organization: Val-Tech Media.

Contact: Editor Leon Ogroske.

Address: Val-Tech Media Inc, POB 394, Perham, MN 56573–0394, USA. **Telephone:** (218) 346-7921. **Fax:** (218) 346-7924. **Internet:** www. writersjournal.com. **E-mail:** writersjournal@lakesplus.com.

Writers' Alliance of Newfoundland and Labrador Provincial Book Awards

The Writers' Alliance administers four provincial book awards, presented bi-annually on alternate years. The awards are financed mainly by corporate and private sponsors, each of whom contributes $3,000 towards the administration of the awards, which includes a cash prize of $1,000 for the winners. Non-fiction and poetry alternate with fiction and children's literature/young adult.

Eligibility and Restrictions: Only books written by residents of Newfoundland and Labrador are eligible.

How to Apply: Submissions are accepted from either authors or publishers; four copies of each title should be submitted.

Recent Winners: 2002: Janet McNaughton, *The Secret Under My Skin* and Ed Kavanagh, *The Confessions of Nipper Mooney*; 2001: Al Pittman, *Thirty-for-Sixty* and Mary Pratt, *A Personal Calligraphy*; 2000: Janet McNaughton, *Make or Break Spring* and Carmelita McGrath, *Stranger Things Have Happened*; 1999: Berni Stapleton, *They Let Down Baskets* and John Steffler, *That Night We Were Ravenous*.

Sponsoring Organization: Writers' Alliance of Newfoundland and Labrador.

Address: Writers' Alliance of Newfoundland and Labrador, Box 2681, St John's, NF A1C 5M5, Canada. **Telephone:** 709 739 5215. **Fax:** 709 739 5931. **Internet:** www.writersalliance.nf.ca/main.html.

Writers' Week Poetry Competition

The prize forms part of the annual Listowel Writers' Week literary festival. Prizes are awarded in two categories: €650 for the best single poem, and €650 for the best collection of poems. The winners also receive financial support towards the publication of a special winning anthology.

Eligibility and Restrictions: Only open to those who have not yet published a volume of poetry.

How to Apply: Send entry fee of €6.50 for each poem submitted and 20 euros for each collection.

Sponsoring Organization: Ireland Funds.

Address: Writers' Week, 24 The Square, Listowel, Co. Kerry, Ireland. **Telephone:** (68) 21074. **Fax:** (68) 22893. **Internet:** www.writersweek.ie. **E-mail:** writersweek@eircom.net.

Würdigungspreis für Literatur (Literature Appreciation Prize)

An annual prize established in 1979 and presented alongside similar prizes for art, music, and cinema. An independent jury selects the winner, who receives a prize of 150,000 Sch (€10,905).

Sponsoring Organization: Lower Austria Culture Dept.

Address: Amt der Niederösterreichischen Landesregierung – Kulturabteilung, Landhausplatz 1, 3109 St Polten, Austria.

YARA—Young Australian Readers' Awards

The YARA awards are part of a series of Australian Children's Choice awards at both national and state level. They were established in 2001. The winners are chosen by online voting during October by students around the country.

Recent Winners: Older Readers: 2001: Andy Griffiths, *The Day My Bum Went Psycho*
Younger Readers: 2001: Libby Gleeson, *Dear Writer*
Picture Books: 2001: Alan Brown and Kim Michelle Toft, *Turtle Song*.

Address: YARA committee, Palmerston District Primary School, Palmerston, ACT 2913, Australia. **Internet:** www.teachers.ash.org.au/ozreading/yara.

Yokomizo Seishi Shô (Yokomizo Seishi Prize)

Established in 1980 under the sponsorship of the Kadokawa Shoten publishing company and the Tokyo Broadcasting System (TBS) in honour of detective-fiction writer Yokomizo Seishi (1902–1981). Awarded annually to a previously unpublished full-length mystery novel. The winner receives 10 million yen plus a statuette in the shape of fictional detective Kindaichi Kôsuke. In addition, the winning story is published by Kadokawa Shoten and dramatized and broadcast nationally by TBS.

Recent Winners: 19th Yokomizo Seishi Prize (1999): Inoue Monta, *Ka-shite aranami (Storm Wave Metamorphosis)*.

Sponsoring Organization: Kadokawa Shoten publishing company.

Address: Kadokawa Shoten publishing company, 13–3 Fujimi, Chiyoda-ku, Tokyo, 102–0071, Japan.

Yomiuri Bungaku Shô (Yomiuri Prize for Literature)

First established in 1950 by the Yomiuri Shimbun Company with the aim of building a 'cultural nation'. Prizes are awarded in six major categories: novels, plays, essays and travel journals, criticism and biography, poetry, and academic studies and translation. The winners are selected by a screening panel of 12 Japanese novelists, poets and critics. The prize is 2 million yen plus a commemorative inkstone.

Eligibility and Restrictions: Works must be written in Japanese in one of the six categories.

How to Apply: No direct application from the public is sought; instead nominations are selected by a screening panel.

Recent Winners: 1999: Kunio Ogawa, *Hassissi gang (Hashish Gang)*; 1997: Haruki Murakami, *The Wind-Up Bird Chronicle*; 1995: Masajo Suzuki, *Miyakodori (Black-headed Gull)*; 1995: Keizo Hino, *Hikari (Light)*; 1992: Harue Tsutsumi, *Kanadehon Hamlet*; 1990: Yoshikichi Furui; 1988: Dr Kazuo Mizuta, *On the Pacific Age – Promoting a Pacific University*.

Sponsoring Organization: Yomiuri Shimbun Company.

Address: Yomiuri Shimbun Company, 1–7–1 Ohtemachi Chiyoda-ku, Tokyo, 100–55, Japan. **Telephone:** (3) 3217 8167. **Fax:** (3) 3217 8321. **E-mail:** c-awa@ yomiuri.com.

Yorkshire Post Awards

A series of annual awards in the following categories: Book of the Year Award, with a prize of £1,200; Author of the Year (£1,000); Art and Music Awards (£1,000 each), given to the authors whose work has contributed most to the understanding and appreciation of art and music.

Eligibility and Restrictions: Open to works of fiction or non-fiction by a British writer or one resident in the UK, published in the UK in the preceding year. Entrants for Author of the Year Award must be authors of fiction or non-fiction born in Yorkshire.

How to Apply: Up to four books may be submitted by any one publisher.

Sponsoring Organization: Yorkshire Post Newspapers Ltd.

Address: Yorkshire Post Newspapers Ltd, POB 168, Wellington St, Leeds LS1 1RF, UK.

Yoshikawa Eiji Bungaku Shinjin Shô (Yoshikawa Eiji Prize for New Writers)

Established in 1980 by the Yoshikawa Eiji Citizens' Cultural Promotion Association (Yoshikawa Eiji Kokumin Bunka Shinkô Kai) to recognize the most promising work of fiction by a new writer published during the preceding year. The winner receives 1 million yen plus a commemorative plaque.

Recent Winners: 22nd Yoshikawa Eiji Prize for New Writers: Nozawa Takashi, *Shinku (Crimson)*.

Sponsoring Organization: Yoshikawa Eiji Citizens' Cultural Promotion Association (Yoshikawa Eiji Kokumin Bunka Shinkô Kai).

Address: Yoshikawa Eiji Citizens' Cultural Promotion Association (Yoshikawa Eiji Kokumin Bunka Shinkô Kai), Otawa Daini Bldg, 2–12–21 Otawa, Bunkyo-ku, Tokyo, 112, Japan.

Yoshikawa Eiji Bungaku Shô (Yoshikawa Eiji Prize for Literature)

Established in 1967, along with the Yoshikawa Eiji Prize for Culture, by the Yoshikawa Eiji Citizens' Cultural Promotion Association (Yoshikawa Eiji Kokumin Bunka Shinkô Kai) to commemorate the work of novelist Yoshikawa Eiji. The prize is awarded annually to an outstanding work in a variety of literary genres based on recommendations submitted by several hundred professionals working in the arts, media, and other fields. The winner receives 3 million yen plus a commemorative plaque.

Recent Winners: 35th Yoshikawa Eiji Prize for Literature: Miyagidani Masamitsu, *Shisan (Birth)*.

Sponsoring Organization: Yoshikawa Eiji Citizens' Cultural Promotion Association (Yoshikawa Eiji Kokumin Bunka Shinkô Kai).

Address: Yoshikawa Eiji Citizens' Cultural Promotion Association (Yoshikawa Eiji Kokumin Bunka Shinkô Kai), Otawa Daini Bldg, 2–12–21 Otawa, Bunkyo-ku, Tokyo, 112, Japan.

Young Wine Writer Award

Inaugurated in 2001 to encourage young UK-based wine writers. The award is to enable a writer to travel to a wine region to gain first-hand experience to develop a book or article based on that experience; the prize is £1,000.

Eligibility and Restrictions: The award is open to any wine writer under 30 who has not yet had a book published and is not an established contributor or columnist.

How to Apply: Applicants should submit a synopsis of the proposed book to Websters by 31 January, plus examples of previous work and a full CV.

Recent Winners: 2001: Peter Richards, *The Wines of Catalonia: An Alternative France?*.

Sponsoring Organization: Websters International/Circle of Wine Writers.

Contact: Nick Skinner.

Address: Websters International Publishers, 2nd Floor, Axe and Bottle Court, 70 Newcomen St, London SE1 1YT, UK. **Telephone:** (20) 7940 4714. **Fax:** (20) 7940 4701. **Internet:** www.websters.co.uk. **E-mail:** nicksk@websters.co.uk.

Zimbabwean Publishers' Literary Awards

The Zimbabwean Publishers' Literary Awards include four categories: books written in English, in Ndebele, in Shona, and for children. The committees announce the awards at the annual Zimbabwe Book Fair in August.

Eligibility and Restrictions: Only books published by local publishers in Africa are considered.

Recent Winners: Previous winners include: Herbert Chimhundu, *Duramazwi Rechishona* (Non-fiction: 1997), Herbert Chimhundu, *Chakwesha* (Shona fiction: 1992), Chirikure Chirikure, *Rukuvhute* (1990), Chenjerai Hove (1989) and Irene Vera.

Sponsoring Organization: Zimbabwe International Book Fair.

Address: Zimbabwe International Book Fair, PO Box CY 1179, Causeway, Harare, Zimbabwe. **Telephone:** (4) 702104/8. **Fax:** (4) 702129. **Internet:** www.zibf.org. **E-mail:** execdir@zibf.org.zw.

Charlotte Zolotow Award

Established in 1998, the award is given annually to the author of the best picture book text published in the USA in the preceding year. The award, named after a distinguished author and editor of children's books, is administered by the Cooperative Children's Book Center (CCBC) at the University of Wisconsin–Madison. Each year a committee of children's literature experts selects the winner from the books published in the preceding year. The winner receives a cash prize of $1,000 and a bronze medallion.

Eligibility and Restrictions: Any picture book for young children (up to age seven), first published in the USA and written by a US citizen or resident, is eligible. Open to any genre of writing (fiction, nonfiction, or folklore) as long as it is presented in a picture-book format and aimed at an audience of young children.

How to Apply: The winner is selected from a shortlist of titles, selected by the CCBC professional staff. Committee members may suggest additional titles they think should be included on the shortlist; however, all titles are subject to the approval of the CCBC staff.

Recent Winners: 2002: Margaret Willey, *Clever Beatrice*; 2001: Kate Banks (author), Georg Hallensleben (illustrator), *The Night Worker*; 2000: Molly Bang, *When Sophie gets Angry – Really, Really Angry*; 1999: Uri Shulevitz, *Snow*; 1998: Vera B. Williams, *Lucky Song*.

Sponsoring Organization: Co-operative Children's Book Center.

Address: Co-operative Children's Book Center, 4290 Helen C. White Hall, 600 North Park St, Madison, WI 53706, USA. **Telephone:** (608) 263-3720. **Fax:** (608) 262-4933. **Internet:** www.soemadison.wisc.edu/ccbc/zolotow.htm. **E-mail:** ccbcinfo@education.wisc.edu.

INDEX OF AWARDS

A. A. Phillips Prize.. 229
AAAS/Orbis Books Prize for Polish Studies.. 1
Abell (Kjeld) Prisen   *see* Kjeld Abell Prisen
Academia Brasileira de Letras Children's Literature Prize 1
Academia Brasileira de Letras Essay Prize... 2
Academia Brasileira de Letras Fiction Prize.. 2
Academy of American Poets Fellowship... 2
Ackerley (J. R.) Prize for Autobiography   *see* J. R. Ackerley Prize for Autobiography
Adamji Prize 3
Addison Metcalf Award   *see* American Academy of Arts and Letters Annual Awards
Adelbert-von-Chamisso-Preis der Robert-Bosch-Stiftung 62
Adikarya Book Awards.. 4
Aesop Prize 4
Africa's 100 Best Books of the Twentieth Century 4
Aftonbladets litteraturpris... 5
Agatha Awards.. 5
AIP Science Writing Awards in Physics and Astronomy 6
Akademieprys vir Vertaalde Werk... 6
Akademiets Oversætterpris.. 6
Akron Poetry Prize... 7
Akutagawa Ryûnosuke Shô 7
Al-Uweis Literary Award 8
Alba Bouwerprys vir Kinderliteratuur 44
Albert J. Beveridge Award... 34
Alberta Book Awards.. 8
Albrand (Martha) Award for First Non-fiction
      see PEN/Martha Albrand Award for First Non-fiction
Albrand (Martha) Award for the Art of the Memoir
      see PEN/Martha Albrand Award for the Art of the Memoir
Aldeburgh Poetry Festival First Collection Prize... 8
Aldo and Jeanne Scaglione Prize for Comparative Literary Studies.. 326
Aldo and Jeanne Scaglione Prize for French and Francophone Studies 326
Aldo and Jeanne Scaglione Prize for Germanic Languages and Literatures... 327
Aldo and Jeanne Scaglione Prize for Italian Studies... 327
Aldo and Jeanne Scaglione Prize for Studies in Slavic Languages and Literatures 328
Aldo and Jeanne Scaglione Prize for a Translation of a Literary Work.. 328
Aldo and Jeanne Scaglione Prize for a Translation of a Scholarly Study of Literature...................... 329
Aldo and Jeanne Scaglione Publication Award for a Manuscript in Italian Literary Studies............ 329
Aleko Konstantinov Literary Prize 154
Alex Awards.. 9
Alexander Prize 9
Alfred Fagon Award.. 91
Alfred-Döblin-Preis 82
Ali (Mast Tauq) Award   *see* Mast Tauq Ali Award
Alice Fay di Castagnola Award 61
Altamirano (Ignacio Manuel), Premio Nacional
      see Premio Nacional de Narrativa Ignacio Manuel Altamirano
Altron Literary Award   *see* Bill Venter/Altron Literary Award
Amazon.com/Books in Canada First Novel Award.. 10
Ambassador Book Awards.. 10
Amelia Frances Howard-Gibbon Illustrator's Award.. 131
American Academy of Arts and Letters Annual Awards 11

American Academy of Arts and Letters Gold Medal 11

An duais don bhfiliocht as Gaeilge.. 83

ANA/Cadbury Prize for Poetry   *see* Association of Nigerian Authors Literature Prizes

Andersen (H. C.) Prize   *see* H. C. Andersen Prize

Andersen (Hans Christian) Awards   *see* Hans Christian Andersen Awards

Andrei Malyshko Prize... 174

André-Gide-Preis für deutsch-französische Literaturübersetzungen 104

Aniara Priset 12

Anisfield-Wolf Book Awards 12

Annett (R. Ross) Award for Children's Literature   *see* Alberta Book Awards

Anthony Awards.. 13

Anti-Booker Prize.. 13

Anugerah Persuratan (Bidang Esei Sastera)... 13

Anzilotti (Rolando) Premio   *see* Premio Rolando Anzilotti

Apollon Grigoryev Prize 118

Arar Literary Award... 13

Arguedas (José Maria) Prize   *see* Premio Casa de las Americas

Arreola (Juan José), Concurso Nacional   *see* Concurso Nacional de Cuento Juan José Arreola

Artaud (Antonin) Prix   *see* Prix Antonin Artaud

Arthur C. Clarke Award for Science Fiction.. 69

Arthur Ellis Awards... 88

Arts Council Bursaries and Commissions... 14

Arts Council of England Children's Award.. 14

Arts Council of England Writers' Awards... 15

Arts Council of Wales Book of the Year Awards.. 15

Arvon Poetry Competition... 15

Aschehougprisen... 16

Aschehougs debutantpris   *see* Aschehougprisen

ASF Translation Prize.. 16

Asham Award for Women 17

Asher Prize   *see* Society of Authors Medical Book Awards

Aspekte-Literatur-Preis.. 17

Associated Writing Programs (AWP) Award Series in Poetry, Fiction and Creative Non-fiction 17

Association of Nigerian Authors Literature Prizes 18

Astrid Lindgren Translation Prize.. 163

Asturias (Príncipe de), Premio   *see* Premio Príncipe de Asturias

Atlanta Review Poetry Competition 18

Atlantic History Prize.. 19

Atlantic Poetry Prize 19

Attila (Jozsef) Prize   *see* József Attila Prize

Audiffred (François-Joseph), Prix   *see* Prix François-Joseph Audiffred

Audoux (Marguerite), Prix   *see* Prix Marguerite Audoux

Augustin-Thierry, Prix   *see* Prix Augustin-Thierry

Augustpriset 20

Aurealis Awards... 20

Auschwitz Foundation Prize... 21

Australia Council Literature Board Emeritus Awards... 21

Australian Christian Book of the Year.. 21

Australian Christian Children's Book of the Year   *see* Australian Christian Book of the Year

Australian Literature Society Gold Medal.. 22

Australian Science Fiction Achievement Awards—Ditmars 22

Australian/Vogel Literary Award... 23

Austrian Award of Merit for Children's Literature.. 23

Austrian National Award for Poetry for Children 24

Austrian National Children's and Juvenile Book Awards 24
Authors' Club Best First Novel Award... 24
Aventis Prize 25
Awgie Awards... 25
BA/Book Data Author of the Year.. 25
Babai-e-Urdu Maulvi Abdul Haq Award... 179
Bachmann (Ingeborg) Preis   *see* Ingeborg Bachmann Preis
Bad Sex in Fiction Awards 26
Balakian (Nona) Citation   *see* The National Book Critics Circle Awards
Balzan Prize for Culture 26
Bancroft Prizes 26
Bank of New Zealand Essay Award... 27
Bank of New Zealand Katherine Mansfield Memorial Awards.. 27
Bank of New Zealand Novice Writer's Award... 28
Bank of New Zealand Young Writer's Award.. 28
Barbara Jelavich Book Prize 144
Bargate (Verity) Award   *see* Verity Bargate Award
Bastian Prize 29
Bataillon (Laure) Prix   *see* Prix Laure Bataillon
Batchelder (Mildred L.) Award   *see* Mildred L. Batchelder Award
Baxter Adams (Herbert) Prize   *see* Herbert Baxter Adams Prize
Bayon (Daniel), Prix   *see* Prix Daniel Bayon
BBC Wildlife Magazine Literary Awards... 30
BBC Wildlife Magazine Nature Writing Award   *see* BBC Wildlife Magazine Literary Awards
BBC Wildlife Magazine Poet of the Year Award   *see* BBC Wildlife Magazine Literary Awards
BBC4 Samuel Johnson Prize for Non-Fiction... 145
Beatriceprisen.. 30
Beaufort (Henriëtte de) prijs   *see* Henriëtte de Beaufort-prijs
Beer (George Louis) Prize   *see* George Louis Beer Prize
Bellmanpriset 31
Belpré (Pura) Award   *see* Pura Belpré Award
Benson Medal 32
Bergmann (Anton) Prix   *see* Prix Anton Bergmann
Berliner Preis für deutschsprachige Gegenwartsliteratur 32
Bernard Shaw Prize... 334
Bernheim (Emile) Prix de littérature   *see* Prix de littérature Émile Bernheim
Bernstein (Mordechai) Literary Prizes   *see* Mordechai Bernstein Literary Prizes
Berry (David) Prize   *see* David Berry Prize
Berto (Giuseppe), Premio Letterario   *see* Premio Letterario Giuseppe Berto
Best First Book of Fiction Award
     see Montana New Zealand Book Awards
Best First Book of Non-Fiction Award
     see Montana New Zealand Book Awards/Best First Book of Non-Fiction Award
Best First Book of Poetry Award
     see Montana New Zealand Book Awards
Besterman/McColvin Medals 33
Betty Trask Prize... 356
Beveridge (Albert J.) Award   *see* Albert J. Beveridge Award
Bhakta (Bhanu) Memorial Award   *see* Bhanu Bhakta Memorial Award
Bhanu Bhakta Memorial Award 34
Bhitaee (Shah Abdul Latif) Award   *see* Shah Abdul Latif Bhitaee Award
Bialik Prize for Literature 35
Bienek (Horst) Preis fur Lyrik   *see* Horst Bienek Preis für Lyrik
Biennial of Illustrations Bratislava (BIB)... 35

BILBY—Books I Love Best Yearly—Award 36

Biletsky (Oleksander) Prize   *see* National Writers Union of Ukraine Awards

Bill Venter/Altron Literary Award.. 361

Billetdoux (François) Prix   *see* Prix François Billetdoux

Bilson (Geoffrey) Award   *see* Geoffrey Bilson Award for Historical Fiction for Young People

Bingham (Robert) Fellowships for Writers   *see* PEN/Robert Bingham Fellowships for Writers

Binkley–Stephenson Award 36

Biographers' Club Prize.. 37

Birdsall (Paul) Prize   *see* Paul Birdsall Prize in European Military and Strategic History

Black (James Tait) Memorial Prizes   *see* James Tait Black Memorial Prizes

Blagovist Prize.. 38

Blixen (Karen) Medaljen   *see* Karen Blixen Medaljen

Bloom (John) Humor Award   *see* Texas Institute of Letters Awards

Blue Peter Children's Book Awards... 38

Blyth (R. H.) Award   *see* R. H. Blyth Award

BMA (British Medical Association) Medical Book Competition 39

Boardman Tasker Award 40

Bogin (George) Memorial Award   *see* George Bogin Memorial Award

Bokhandlerprisen... 41

Böll (Heinrich) Preis der Stadt Köln   *see* Heinrich-Böll-Preis der Stadt Köln

Bollingen Prize in Poetry 41

Bologna New Media Prize (BNMP).. 41

Bologna Ragazzi Award.. 42

Bolt (Carol) Drama Award   *see* Canadian Authors Association Literary Awards

Bonniers (Gerard) Pris   *see* Gerard Bonniers Pris

Book Sense Book of the Year Award 42

Booker Prize for Fiction   *see* Man Booker Prize

Booker/Open Russia Prize.. 43

Border Television Prize   *see* Lakeland Book of the Year Awards

Boston Globe–Horn Book Award... 44

Bourne (Louise Louis/Emily) Student Poetry Award
    see Louise Louis/Emily F. Bourne Student Poetry Award

Bouwer (Alba) prys vir Kinderliteratuur   *see* Alba Bouwerprys vir Kinderliteratuur

BP Natural World Book Prize 45

Bradt Travel Writing Award   *see* BBC Wildlife Magazine Literary Awards

Braem (Helmut M.) Preis   *see* Helmut M. Braem Preis

Brageprisen... 45

Brand (Sarah) and Weinstein (Arik) Award   *see* National Jewish Book Awards

Branford Boase Award 46

Breasted (James H.) Prize   *see* James H. Breasted Prize

Bremen Literatur Förderungspreis.. 47

Bridport Prize... 47

Briggs (Katharine) Folklore Award   *see* Katharine Briggs Folklore Award

Brignetti (Rafaello), Premio   *see* Premio Letterario Isola d'Elba – Rafaello Brignetti

British Academy Book Prize 48

British Book Awards.. 48

British Columbia Book Prizes 49

British Comparative Literature Association Translation Prize... 50

British Fantasy Awards 50

British Science Fiction Association Awards 51

Broumovska literarni cena... 51

Brüder-Grimm-Preis des Landes Berlin zur Förderung des Kinder- und Jugendtheaters 118

Bryan MacMahon Short Story Award 170

Bucharest Writers' Association Prizes 52

Büchner (Georg) Preis   *see* Georg-Büchner-Preis

Bukhari (Pitras) Award   *see* Pitras Bukhari Award

Bulwer-Lytton Fiction Contest 53

Bungakukai Shinjin Shô 54

Busken Huetprijs 132

Butler Literary Awards   *see* Irish American Cultural Institute (IACI) Literary Awards

Buxtehuder Bulle 54

C. H. Currey Memorial Fellowship 75

C. P. Hoogenhout Award 131

CAA Air Canada Award 54

Caine Prize for African Writing 55

Caldecott (Randolph) Medal   *see* Randolph Caldecott Medal

California Young Reader Medal 56

Calvin and Rose G. Hoffmann Prize for a Distinguished Publication on Christopher Marlowe 129

Calwer Hermann-Hesse-Preis 56

Campbell (John W.) Memorial Award
      see John W. Campbell Memorial Award for the Best New Writer

Canada-Switzerland Literary Prize 57

Canadian Authors Association Literary Awards 57

Canadian Library Association Book of the Year for Children Award 58

Canadian Library Association Young Adult Book Award 58

Canadian Literary Awards 59

Cao Yu Drama Literature Prize 59

Čapek (Karel) Award for Literary Achievement
      see Karel Čapek Award for Literary Achievement

Cappelen-prisen 60

Cappon (Alexander Patterson) Fiction Prize   *see* New Letters Literary Awards

Cappon (Dorothy Churchill) Prize   *see* New Letters Literary Awards

Carducci (Giosue), Premio Nazionale di Poesia
      see Premio Nazionale di Poesia Giosuè Carducci

Carnegie Medal 60

Cartier Diamond Dagger   *see* CWA Awards

Carême (Maurice), Prix de Poésie
      see Prix de Poésie et Prix d'Etudes Littéraires Maurice Carême

Cassidy (Lar) Award   *see* Lar Cassidy Award

Castagnola (Alice Fay di) Award   *see* Alice Fay di Castagnola Award

Castex (Louis) Prix   *see* Prix Louis Castex

Castillo (Ricardo Mimenza), Premio de Literatura
      see Premio de Literatura Ricardo Mimenza Castillo

Cavour (Grinzane) Premio   *see* Premio Grinzane Cavour

Cecil Hemley Memorial Award 126

Celan (Paul) Preis   *see* Paul-Celan-Preis

Cena Josefa Hlavky 128

Chalmers (Floyd S.) Canadian Play Awards
      see Chalmers Awards for Creativity and Excellence in the Arts

Chalmers (Jack) Poetry Award   *see* Canadian Authors Association Literary Awards

Chalmers Awards for Creativity and Excellence in the Arts 61

Chamisso (Adelbert von) Preis   *see* Adelbert-von-Chamisso-Preis der Robert-Bosch-Stiftung

Chapters/Books in Canada Award 62

Charles Veillon European Essay Prize 361

Charlotte Zolotow Award 382

Chicano/Latino Literary Prize 63

Children's Award (Arts Council of England)   *see* Arts Council of England Children's Award

Children's Book Award 63

389

Children's Book Awards 63
Children's Book Guild Award for Non-fiction 64
Children's Book of the Year Awards 64
Children's eBook Award   *see* Bologna New Media Prize (BNMP)
Children's Laureate 65
Children's Literature Association Book Awards 65
China Literature Foundation Awards 65
Chôkû Shô 66
Cholmondeley Awards 66
Chrichton Award for Book Illustration 66
Christie's (Mr) Book Awards   *see* Mr Christie's Book Awards
Christoph-Martin-Wieland-Preis 373
Christopher Awards 67
Christopher Ewart-Biggs Memorial Prize 90
Christy Awards 68
Chuang (C. W.) Literary Prize   *see* China Literature Foundation Awards
Church (Hubert) Fiction Award
      see Montana New Zealand Book Awards
City of Vancouver Book Award 68
Clarence H. Haring Prize 123
Clarence L. Holt Literary Prize 130
Clark (Russell) Award   *see* Russell Clark Award
Clarke (Arthur C.) Award for Science Fiction   *see* Arthur C. Clarke Award for Science Fiction
CNA Letterkunde Toekenning 70
Cohen (David) British Literature Prize   *see* David Cohen British Literature Prize
Cohen (Morton N.) Award   *see* Morton N. Cohen Award for a Distinguished Edition of Letters
Coindreau (Maurice-Edgar) Prix   *see* Prix Maurice-Edgar Coindreau
Colin Roderick Prize for Australian Literature 316
Colorado Prize 71
Commonwealth Writers Prize 71
Concurso Annual de Literatura 72
Concurso Literario Premio Emecé 73
Concurso Nacional de Cuento Juan José Arreola 73
Concurso Nacional de Dramaturgia Teatro Nuevo 74
Concurso de Prosa y Poesia Timón de Oro 73
Constantijn Huygens Prize 133
Cool Awards 74
Cooper (Derek) Award   *see* Guild of Food Writers Awards
Cooper (Duff) Prize   *see* Duff Cooper Prize
Coretta Scott King Award 152
County of Cardiff International Poetry Competition 75
Couture (Marcel) Prix   *see* Prix Marcel-Couture
Crawshay (Rose Mary) Prize   *see* Rose Mary Crawshay Prize
Creasey (John) Memorial Dagger   *see* CWA Awards
Cultural Center of the Philippines Literary Awards 75
Cumont (Franz), Prix   *see* Prix Franz Cumont
Currey (C. H.) Memorial Fellowship   *see* C. H. Currey Memorial Fellowship
Curtius (Ernst-Robert) Preise für Essayistik   *see* Ernst-Robert-Curtius-Preise für Essayistik
CWA Awards 76
CYBER—Children's Yearly Best-Ever Reads—Award 77
D. R. Wijewardene Memorial Award 374
Dahl (Thorlief), Norske Akademis Pris   *see* Norske Akademis Pris til Minne om Thorleif Dahl
Danish Ministry of Culture Children's Book Prize 77
Dartmouth Medal 77

Darton (Harvey) Award   *see* Harvey Darton Award

David (Athanase) Prix   *see* Prix Athanase-David

David Berry Prize 33

David Cohen British Literature Prize 71

David Gemmell Cup Short Story Competition 103

David St John Thomas Charitable Trust Awards 353

David T.K. Wong Prize for Short Fiction 377

David Thelen Prize 352

David Watt Prize 367

Davies (Hunter) Prize   *see* Lakeland Book of the Year Awards

Dazai Osamu Shô 78

De la Cruz (Sor Juana), Premio de Literatura
    see Premio de Literatura Sor Juana Inés de la Cruz

de Nerval (Gérard), Prix   *see* Prix Gérard de Nerval

De Troyes (Chrétien), Prix   *see* Prix Chrétien-de-Troyes

Den Store Pris 343

Denis Devlin Memorial Award for Poetry 81

Dennis (C. J.) Prize for Poetry   *see* Victorian Premier's Literary Awards

Dentan (Michel) Prix   *see* Prix Michel Dentan

Derleth (August) Award   *see* British Fantasy Awards

Deutscher (Isaac and Tamara) Memorial Prize
    see Isaac and Tamara Deutscher Memorial Prize

Deutscher Jugendliteraturpreis 79

Deutscher Jugendliteraturpreis Sonderpreis 80

Deutscher Kinder- und Jugendtheaterpreis 80

Deutscher-Krimi-Preis 80

Deutz Meda   *see* Montana New Zealand Book Awards/Deutz Medal

Devlin (Denis) Memorial Award for Poetry   *see* Denis Devlin Memorial Award for Poetry

Dewan Bahasa dan Pustaka Prize 82

Diagram Group Prize 82

Dickinson (Emily) Award   *see* Writer Magazine/Emily Dickinson Award

Diniz (D.) Prêmio   *see* Prêmio D. Diniz

Discailles (Ernest), Prix   *see* Prix Ernest Discailles

Discovery/The Nation Joan Leiman Jacobson Poetry Prizes 82

Ditmars   *see* Australian Science Fiction Achievement Awards—Ditmars

Dixon Ryan Fox Manuscript Prize 98

Döblin (Alfred) Preis   *see* Alfred-Döblin-Preis

Dobloug Priset 83

Don Carlos Palanca Memorial Awards 219

Donner Prize 83

Downey (Violet) Book Award   *see* IODE Violet Downey Book Award

Dr Allama Muhammad Iqbal Award 140

Dr Wijnaendts Francken-prijs 99

Duculot (Jules) Prix   *see* Prix Jules Duculot

Duff Cooper Prize 74

Dulché (Yolanda Vargas), Premio Internacional
    see Premio Internacional de Novela Yolanda Vargas Dulché

Dundee Book Prize 84

Dunne (Thomas) Books Award for the Novel   *see* Thomas Dunne Books Award for the Novel

Dunning (Jonh H.) Prize   *see* John H. Dunning Prize

Dupont (S. T.) Gold PEN   *see* Macmillan PEN Awards

Duvivie (Charles), Prix   *see* Prix Charles Duvivie

DV Cultural Award 85

Dymocks Children's Choice Awards 85

Dymocks Singapore Literature Prize 85
Eamon Keane Full Length Play Award 148
Echeverría (Esteban), Premio   *see* Premio Esteban Echeverría
Ed A. Hewett Book Prize 127
Edgar Allan Poe Awards 231
Edgars   *see* Edgar Allan Poe Awards
Edwards (Margaret) Award   *see* Margaret A. Edwards Award
Eesti Kirjanduse Aastapreemia 86
Eggleston (Wilfred) Award for Non-Fiction   *see* Alberta Book Awards
Egyptian Literary Award 87
Ehrenpreis des Österreichischen Buchhandels für Toleranz in Denken und Handeln 87
Elder (Ann) Poetry Award   *see* Fellowship of Australian Writers Literature Awards
Eleanor Farjeon Award 93
Elie Wiesel Prize in Ethics Essay Contest 374
Eliot (T. S.) Prize   *see* T. S. Eliot Prize
Ellis (Arthur) Awards   *see* Arthur Ellis Awards
Elsie Locke Award 165
Emerson-Thoreau Medal 88
Encore Award 89
Engel (Marian) Award   *see* Marian Engel Award
Enid McLeod Literary Prize 172
Eric Gregory Trust Fund Award 117
Erich-Fried-Preis 100
Ernest Hemingway Foundation/PEN Award for First Fiction 126
Ernst-Robert-Curtius-Preise für Essayistik 76
Esther Glen Award 106
Estrada (Ezequiel Martinez) Prize   *see* Premio Casa de las Americas
Eugène Maraisprys 176
European Jewish Publication Society Grant to Publishers 89
European Online Journalism (EOJ) Award 90
Evans (Hubert) Non-Fiction Prize   *see* British Columbia Book Prizes
Evelyn Richardson Non-fiction Award 314
Evens Foundation European Prize for Literature 90
Ewart-Biggs (Christopher) Memorial Prize   *see* Christopher Ewart-Biggs Memorial Prize
Ezra Jack Keats New Writer's and New Illustrator's Award for Children's Books 149
F. Bordewijkprijs 44
Faber (Geoffrey) Memorial Prize   *see* Geoffrey Faber Memorial Prize
Fagg (John E.) Prize   *see* John E. Fagg Prize
Fagon (Alfred) Prize   *see* Alfred Fagon Award
Fairbank (John K.) Prize   *see* John K. Fairbank Prize
Fairlight Talking Book Award of New South Wales 92
Faisal (King) International Prize   *see* King Faisal International Prize for Arabic Literature
Fallet (René), Prix   *see* Prix René Fallet
Farber (Norma) First Book Award   *see* Norma Farber First Book Award
Farid (Khwaja Ghulam) Award   *see* Khwaja Ghulam Farid Award
Feis (Herbert) Prize   *see* Herbert Feis Prize
Fellowship of Australian Writers Literature Awards 93
Feltrinelli (Antonio) Premio   *see* Premio Antonio Feltrinelli
Fenia and Yaakov Leviant Memorial Prize 162
Fernando Rielo World Mystical Poetry Prize 315
Féval (Paul), Grand Prix   *see* Grand Prix Paul Féval de Littérature Populaire
Finlandia Award 94
Firecracker Alternative Book Awards 94
Fitzpatrick (Percy) Medal   *see* Percy Fitzpatrick Medal

Flannery O'Connor Award for Short Fiction 212

Fleck (Norma) Award for Children's Non-Fiction
    see Norma Fleck Award for Children's Non-Fiction

Fleming (Ian) Steel Dagger   *see* CWA Awards

Fletcher (Sir Banister) Prize of the Authors' Club
    see Sir Banister Fletcher Prize of the Authors' Club

Florio (John) Prize   *see* John Florio Prize

FNB VITA Poetry Award 96

Förderungspreis für Literatur 97

Foreign-Language Article Prize   *see* David Thelen Prize

Forkosch (Morris D.) Prize   *see* Morris D. Forkosch Prize

Forward Prizes for Poetry 97

Fox (Dixon Ryan) Manuscript Prize   *see* Dixon Ryan Fox Manuscript Prize

Fraenkel Prize in Contemporary History 98

Francis Parkman Prize 221

Francken-prijs (Dr Wijnaendts)   *see* Dr Wijnaendts Francken-prijs

Franklin (Miles) Award   *see* Miles Franklin Award

Franko (Ivan) Prize   *see* Ivan Franko Prize

Frans Kellendonk-prijs 149

Franz Kafka Prize 146

Freud (Sigmund) Preis   *see* Sigmund-Freud-Preis für wissenschaftliche Prosa

Freustié (Jean), Prix   *see* Prix Jean Freustié

Fried (Erich) Preis   *see* Erich-Fried-Preis

Friedenspreis des Deutschen Buchhandels 101

Friedrich Gundolf Preis für die Vermittlung deutscher Kultur im Ausland 121

Friedrich-Glauser-Preis—Krimipreis der Autoren 105

Frogmore Poetry Prize 101

Frost Medal 101

Fujin Kôron Literary Prize 101

Füst Milan Literary Prize 102

G H s'Gravesande Prize 320

Gal (Henri), Grand Prix de Littérature   *see* Grand Prix de Littérature Henri Gal

Gallegos (Romulo) Premio Internacional de Novela
    see Premio Internacional de Novela Rómulo Gallegos

Gantrelle (Joseph), Prix   *see* Prix Joseph Gantrelle

Gautier (Théophile) Prix   *see* Prix Théophile Gautier

Gay, Lesbian, Bisexual and Transgendered Book Awards 102

Gelsted (Otto) prisen   *see* Otto Gelstedprisen

Gemmell (David) Short Story Competition   *see* David Gemmell Cup Short Story Competition

Genevoix (Maurice) Prix   *see* Prix Maurice-Genevoix

Geoffrey Bilson Award for Historical Fiction for Young People 36

Geoffrey Faber Memorial Prize 90

Georg-Büchner-Preis 52

Georg Trakl Preis für Lyrik 355

George Bogin Memorial Award 40

George L. Mosse Prize 190

George Louis Beer Prize 31

George Polk Awards 232

Gerald Lampert Award 159

Gerard Bonniers Pris 42

Gershoy (Leo) Prize   *see* Leo Gershoy Prize

Geschwister-Scholl-Preis 103

Gide (André) Preis   *see* André-Gide-Preis

Giller Award 104

Gironde, Prix Littéraire   *see* Prix Littéraire de la Gironde

Gladstone History Book Prize... 105

Glassco (John) Prize for Literary Translation
    see John Glassco Prize for Literary Translation

Glauser (Friedrich) Preis—Krimipreis der Autoren
    see Friedrich-Glauser-Preis—Krimipreis der Autoren

Gleebooks Prize for Literary or Cultural Criticism   *see* NSW Premier's Literary Awards

Glen (Esther) Award   *see* Esther Glen Award

Glenfiddich Food & Drink Awards... 106

Glimmer Train Literary Awards.. 107

Godage Literary Awards 107

Gold Medallion Book Awards 108

Gold/Platinum Book Awards... 108

Golden Bike Awards   *see* Iranian Book of the Year Awards

Golden Kite Award 108

Goldsmith (Barbara) Award   *see* PEN/Barbara Goldsmith Freedom to Write Awards

Gottfried Keller Prize 150

Gouden Griffel/Gouden Zoen... 109

Gouden Zoen   *see* Gouden Griffel/Gouden Zoen

Gourmand World Cookbook Awards... 110

Governor General's Literary Awards.. 110

Grace Leven Prize for Poetry.. 161

Gradam Litrochta Cló Iar-Chonnachta.. 111

Grand Prix de Biographie de l'Académie Française
    see Prix Littéraires de l'Académie Française

Grand Prix de la Francophonie 112

Grand Prix Halperine-Kaminsky... 112

Grand Prix Littéraire de l'Afrique Noire... 112

Grand Prix Littéraire Poncetton 112

Grand Prix de Littérature Française hors de France/Prix Fondation Nessim Habif......... 113

Grand Prix de Littérature Henri Gal 113

Grand Prix de Littérature Paul Morand 113

Grand prix du livre de Montréal 114

Grand Prix National des Arts et des Lettres (GPNAL)... 114

Grand Prix National des Lettres... 115

Grand Prix Paul Féval de Littérature Populaire 281

Grand Prix de Poésie de l'Académie Française   *see* Prix Littéraires de l'Académie Française

Grand Prix Ramuz 115

Grand Prix du Roman de l'Académie Française   *see* Prix Littéraires de l'Académie Française

Grand Prix RTL-Lire 115

Grand Prix de la Science-Fiction et du Fantastique Québécois 116

Grand Prix Thyde Monnier.. 114

Grand Prix de la Ville de Sierre   *see* Prix du Festival de la Bande Dessinée de Sierre

Grandbois (Alain) Prix   *see* Prix Alain-Grandbois

Grande Prémio Calouste Gulbenkian de Literatura para Crianças e Jovens.................... 116

Greenaway (Kate) Medal   *see* Kate Greenaway Medal

Gregory (Eric) Trust Fund Award   *see* Eric Gregory Trust Fund Award

Gregory Kolovakos Award... 154

Griffin Poetry Prize.. 117

Grigoryev (Apollon) Prize   *see* Apollon Grigoryev Prize

Grosser Literaturpreis der Bayerischen Akademie der Schönen Kunste.......................... 118

Grosser Österreichischer Staatspreis für Literatur 119

Grosser Preis der Schweizerische Schillerstiftung.. 119

Guardian Children's Fiction Award.. 119

Guardian First Book Award 120
Guild of Food Writers Awards 120
Gulbenkian (Calouste), Grande Prémio de Literatura
    see Grande Prémio Calouste Gulbenkian de Literatura para Crianças e Jovens
Gundolf (Fiedrich) Preis
    see Friedrich Gundolf Preis für die Vermittlung deutscher Kultur im Ausland
Gustav Prellerprys vir literatuurwetenskap en letterkundige kritiek 233
Gustav-Heinemann-Friedenspreis für Kinder- und Jugendbücher 125
Gyldendal (Soren) Prize   *see* Soren Gyldendal Prize
Gyldendal-prisen 121
Gyula Illyes Prize 135
H-shi Shô 121
H. C. Andersen Prize 12
Habif (Nessim), Prix Fondation
    see Grand Prix de Littérature Française hors de France/Prix Fondation Nessim Habif
Haidan Shô 122
Halldis Moren Vesaas-Prisen 122
Halldor Laxness Literary Prize 122
Hammett Awards 122
Hans Christian Andersen Awards 11
Harbourfront Reading Series' short stories award   *see* Journey Prize
Haring (Clarence H.) Prize   *see* Clarence H. Haring Prize
Harold Morton Landon Translation Award 159
Harries (Katrine) Award   *see* Katrine Harries Award
Harvey Darton Award 78
Haryana Sahitya Akademi Awards 123
Havmannprisen 123
Hawthornden Prize 124
Head Raddall (Thomas) Fiction Prize   *see* Thomas Head Raddall Fiction Prize
Heine (Heinrich) Medaille   *see* Heinrich-Heine-Preis der Landeshauptstadt Düsseldorf
Heinemann (W. H.) Award   *see* W. H. Heinemann Award
Heinrich-Böll-Preis der Stadt Köln 41
Heinrich-Heine-Preis der Landeshauptstadt Düsseldorf 124
Hellenic Foundation for Culture Translation Award 125
Helmut M. Braem Preis 45
Helsingin Sanomat Literary Award 126
Hemingway (Ernest) Foundation/PEN Award
    see Ernest Hemingway Foundation/PEN Award for First Fiction
Hemley (Cecil) Memorial Award   *see* Cecil Hemley Memorial Award
Henriëtte de Beaufort-prijs 31
Henriette Roland Holst-prijs 317
Henry (O.) Award   *see* Texas Institute of Letters Awards
Herb Barrett Award 29
Herbert Baxter Adams Prize 30
Herbert Feis Prize 93
Herder Prize 127
Herman Gorterprijs 109
Herman Voaden National Playwriting Competition 364
Hertzogprys 127
Hewett (Ed A.) Book Prize   *see* Ed A. Hewett Book Prize
Heywood Hill Literary Prize 128
Hiemstra (Louis) prys vir nie-fiksie   *see* Louis Hiemstraprys vir nie-fiksie
Hlavky (Josef) Prize   *see* Cena Josefa Hlavky
Hlibov (Leonid) Prize   *see* National Writers Union of Ukraine Awards

Hoffmann (Calvin and Rose G.) Prize   *see* Calvin and Rose G. Hoffmann Prize
  for a Distinguished Publication on Christopher Marlowe
Holgersson (Nils) Plaque   *see* Nils Holgersson Plaque
Holloway (Tienie) Medal   *see* Tienie Hollowaymedalje vir kleuterliteratuur
Holt (Clarence L.) Literary Prize   *see* Clarence L. Holt Literary Prize
Honchar (Oles) Ukrainian-German Prize   *see* Oles Honchar Prizes
Hooft (P. C.) prijs voor Letterkunde   *see* P. C. Hooft-prijs voor Letterkunde
Hopkins (Lee Bennett) Promising Poet Award
  see Lee Bennett Hopkins Promising Poet Award
Horst Bienek Preis für Lyrik 35
Houziaux (Joseph), Prix   *see* Prix Joseph Houziaux
Howard R. Marraro Prize 177
Howard R. Marraro Prize in Italian History 177
Howard-Gibbon (Amelia Frances) Illustrator's Award
  see Amelia Frances Howard-Gibbon Illustrator's Award
Huchel (Peter) Preis   *see* Peter-Huchel-Preis
Huetprijs (Busken)   *see* Busken Huetprijs
Hugo Award 132
Hunapuh e Ixbalamqué, Premio de Literatura
  see Premio de Literatura para Niños Hunapuh e Ixbalamqué
Huygens (Constantijn) Prize   *see* Constantijn Huygens Prize
IBBY-Asahi Reading Promotion Award 133
IBC International Book Award 133
Icelandic Children's Book Prize 134
Icelandic Literary Prize 134
Idunn-prisen   *see* Tano Aschehoug-Prisen/Idunn-Prisen
ILAB-LILA Bibliography Prize 134
Illyes (Gyula) Prize   *see* Gyula Illyes Prize
Imison (Richard) Memorial Award   *see* Richard Imison Memorial Award
Independent Foreign Fiction Prize 136
Ingeborg Bachmann Preis 26
Innis-Gérin Medal 136
Institutció de les Lletres Catalanes Translation Prize 137
Institute of Historical Research Prize 137
International Einhard Prize 137
International Imitation Hemingway Competition 138
International IMPAC Dublin Literary Award 138
International Langhe Ceretto Prize for Food and Wine Culture 138
International Lotus Prize for Poetry 139
International Playwriting Festival 139
International Vaptsarov Prize 139
Internationella Eeva Joenpelto-Litteraturpriset 140
IODE Violet Downey Book Award 140
Iqbal (Dr Allama Muhammad) Award   *see* Dr Allama Muhammad Iqbal Award
Iranian Book of the Year Awards 141
Ireland Fund of Monaco Literary Award 141
Irish American Cultural Institute (IACI) Literary Awards 141
Irish Times International Fiction Prize 141
Irish Times Irish Literature Prizes 142
Isaac and Tamara Deutscher Memorial Prize 81
Itô Sei Bungaku Shô 142
Ivan Franko Prize 100
Ivanov (Miroslav) Award for Non-Fiction   *see* Miroslav Ivanov Award for Non-Fiction
Izumi Kyôka Bungaku Shô 143

J. Greshoff Prijs.. 117
J. R. Ackerley Prize for Autobiography 3
J. Russell Major Prize 320
Jacinto Prado Coelho Award... 70
Jacob's Creek World Food Media Awards 143
Jacobson (Joan Leiman) Poetry Prizes
    see Discovery/The Nation Joan Leiman Jacobson Poetry Prizes
James A. Michener Memorial Prize.. 181
James H. Breasted Prize.. 46
James Laughlin Award 160
James Russell Lowell Prize 319
James Tait Black Memorial Prizes 37
Jan Campert Prize.. 57
Jan Parandowski Prize... 220
Jan Strzelecki Prize 343
Jane Addams Children's Book Award 3
Jaroslav Seifert Award 332
Jefferson Cup Awards... 144
Jelavich (Barbara) Book Prize   *see* Barbara Jelavich Book Prize
Jenny Smelik IBBY Prijs 338
Jewish Quarterly-Wingate Prizes.. 145
Jnanpith Award... 145
Joan Kelly Memorial Prize 150
Joenpelto (Eeva), Internationella Litteraturpriset
    see Internationella Eeva Joenpelto-Litteraturpriset
Johann-Heinrich-Merck-Preis für literarische Kritik und Essay 180
Johann-Heinrich-Voss-Preis für Übersetzung... 364
John E. Fagg Prize 91
John Florio Prize.. 96
John Glassco Prize for Literary Translation/Prix de Traduction John-Glassco................ 105
John H. Dunning Prize 85
John K. Fairbank Prize 91
John Newbery Medal.. 203
John Steinbeck Award 342
John W. Campbell Memorial Award for the Best New Writer.. 57
John Whiting Award.. 372
Johnson (Samuel) Prize   *see* BBC4 Samuel Johnson Prize for Non-Fiction
Jolson (Leon) Award   *see* National Jewish Book Awards
Jones (Jesse H.) Award   *see* Texas Institute of Letters Awards
Josef Jungmann Prize 146
Journey Prize... 146
Jozsef Attila Prize 19
Jubilee Award for Short Stories   *see* Canadian Authors Association Literary Awards
Julien (Stanislas), Prix   *see* Prix Stanislas Julien
Jungmann (Josef) Prize   *see* Josef Jungmann Prize
Kadan Shô... 146
Kafka (Franz) Prize   *see* Franz Kafka Prize
Kaikô Takeshi Shô.. 147
Kalinga Prize 147
Karel Čapek Award for Literary Achievement 59
Karen Blixen Medaljen 38
Katapultpriset 147
Kate Greenaway Medal.. 116
Katharine Briggs Folklore Award 47

Katherine Singer Kovacs Prize 155
Kathleen Fidler Award 94
Kathleen Mitchell Award 182
Kathryn A. Morton Prize in Poetry 189
Katrine Harries Award 148
Kaufman (Sue) Prize for First Fiction
    see American Academy of Arts and Letters Annual Awards
Kawabata Yasunari Bungaku Shô 148
Keane (Eamon) Full Length Play Award   *see* Eamon Keane Full Length Play Award
Keats (Ezra Jack) Awards
    see Ezra Jack Keats New Writer's and New Illustrator's Award for Children's Books
Keats–Shelley Prize 149
Kellendonk (Frans)-prijs   *see* Frans Kellendonk-prijs
Keller (Gottfried) Prize   *see* Gottfried Keller Prize
Kellgrenpriset 150
Kelly (Joan) Memorial Prize   *see* Joan Kelly Memorial Prize
Kenneth W. Mildenberger Prize 181
Kerala Sahitya Akademi Awards 151
Kerry Ingredients Irish Fiction Award 151
Kessel (Joseph) Prix   *see* Prix Joseph Kessel
Khattak (Khushhall Khan) Award   *see* Khushhall Khan Khattak Award
Khatulistiwa Literary Award 152
Khushhall Khan Khattak Award 152
Khwaja Ghulam Farid Award 93
Kick Start Poets Open Poetry Competition 152
Kikuchi Hiroshi Shô 147
King (Coretta Scott) Award   *see* Coretta Scott King Award
King Fahd bin Abdulaziz Award for Initiative 153
King Faisal International Prize for Arabic Literature 92
Kingsley Tufts Poetry Prize 358
Kiriyama Pacific Rim Book Prize 153
Kirsch (Robert) Award   *see* Los Angeles Times Book Prizes
Kjeld Abell Prisen 1
Klaus Rifbjergs Debutantpris for Lyrik 315
Klein (Norma) Award   *see* PEN/Norma Klein Award
KOALA—Kids Own Australian Literature Awards 154
Koivu (Rudolf) Prize   *see* Rudolf Koivu Prize
Kolovakos (Gregory) Award   *see* Gregory Kolovakos Award
Konstantinov (Aleko) Literary Prize   *see* Aleko Konstantinov Literary Prize
Korean Literature Translation Award 155
Korolenko (Volodymyr) Prize   *see* National Writers Union of Ukraine Awards
Kossuth Prize 155
Kostakowsky (Lya), Premio Annual
    see Premio Anual de Ensayo Literario Hispanoamericano Lya Kostakowsky
Kotlyarevsky (Ivan) Prize   *see* National Writers Union of Ukraine Awards
Kovacs (Katherine Singer) Prize   *see* Katherine Singer Kovacs Prize
Kraszna-Krausz Book Awards 156
Kreisel (Henry) Award for Best First Book   *see* Alberta Book Awards
Kristal Vilenica Award   *see* Vilenica International Literary Awards
KROC—Kids Reading Oz Choice—Award 156
Kruyskamp-prijs 157
Kulturdepartementets Premiering av Barne- og Ungdomslitteratur 157
Kumar (C. B.) Award   *see* Kerala Sahitya Akademi Awards
Kuttippuzha Award   *see* Kerala Sahitya Akademi Awards

Ladles   *see* Jacob's Creek World Food Media Awards

Lakeland Book of the Year Awards 158

Lambda Literary Awards—Lammys 158

Lampert (Gerald) Award   *see* Gerald Lampert Award

Landon (Harold Morton) Translation Award   *see* Harold Morton Landon Translation Award

Lannan Literary Awards 159

Lanson (Champagne) Prix   *see* Prix du Champagne Lanson

Lao She Literary Prize 160

Lar Cassidy Award 60

Lara (Fernando) Premio   *see* Premio de Novela Fernando Lara

Larbaud (Valéry), Prix   *see* Prix Valéry Larbaud

Laughlin (James) Award   *see* James Laughlin Award

Laura Ingalls Wilder Award 374

Lazarillo Prize 160

Le Heurteur (Claude) Prix   *see* Prix Claude Le Heurteur

Leacock (Stephen) Memorial Medal for Humour
        see Stephen Leacock Memorial Medal for Humour

Leclère (Léon), Prix   *see* Prix Léon Leclère

Lee Bennett Hopkins Promising Poet Award 131

Leland (Walso G.) Prize   *see* Waldo G. Leland Prize

Lenore Marshall Poetry Prize 178

Leo Gershoy Prize 103

Lesya Ukrainka Prize 359

Leven (Grace) Prize for Poetry   *see* Grace Leven Prize for Poetry

Leviant (Fenia and Yaakov) Memorial Prize   *see* Fenia and Yaakov Leviant Memorial Prize

Lewis Thomas Prize 353

LIANZA Young People's Non-fiction Award   *see* Elsie Locke Award

Libris Awards 162

Lilian Ida Smith Awards 338

Lilly (Ruth) Poetry Prize   *see* Ruth Lilly Poetry Prize

Lima (José Lezama) Prize   *see* Premio Casa de las Americas

Lindgren (Astrid) Translation Prize   *see* Astrid Lindgren Translation Prize

Literárna sútaz Poviedka 163

Literary Achievement Award 164

Literaturpreis der Landeshauptstadt Stuttgart 164

Literaturpreis der Stadt Solothurn 164

Little Booker Prize 164

Littleton-Griswold Prize 165

Llull (Ramon) Premi   *see* Premi de les Lletres Catalanes Ramon Llull

Locke (Elsie) Award   *see* Elsie Locke Award

Lois Roth Award for a Translation of a Literary Work 318

London Writers Competition 166

Long Madgett (Naomi) Poetry Award   *see* Naomi Long Madgett Poetry Award

Longman–History Today Book of the Year Award 166

Lontar Literary Award 167

Lorne Pierce Medal 230

Los Angeles Times Book Prizes 167

Louis Hiemstraprys vir nie-fiksie 128

Louise Louis/Emily F. Bourne Student Poetry Award 44

Lu Xun Literature Awards 168

Lucille Medwick Memorial Award 179

Lucy B. & C. W. van der Hoogt Prize 360

Lukas (J. Anthony) Prize   *see* Lukas Prize Project

Lukas Prize Project 168

Lydecken (Arvid) Prize   *see* Suomen Nuorisokirjailijat Ry Awards

Lynton (Mark) History Prize   *see* Mark Lynton History Prize

Lyra (Carmen), Premio   *see* Premio Literario Carmen Lyra

Lyric Poetry Award 169

M-Net Book Prize 169

Macallan Gold/Silver Dagger   *see* CWA Awards

Macallan/Scotland on Sunday Story Competition 170

Mackay (Jessie) Poetry Award
     see Montana New Zealand Book Awards

MacMahon (Bryan) Short Story Award   *see* Bryan MacMahon Short Story Award

Macmillan PEN Awards 170

Macmillan Prize   *see* Macmillan PEN Awards

Macmillan Prize for Children's Picture Book Illustration 171

Macmillan Silver PEN   *see* Macmillan PEN Awards

Macmillan Writer's Prize for Africa 171

McCarthy (Mary) Prize in Short Fiction   *see* Mary McCarthy Prize in Short Fiction

McColvin Medal   *see* Besterman/McColvin Medals

McCormick (E. H.) Non-Fiction Award
     see Montana New Zealand Book Awards/Best First Book of Non-Fiction Award

McKitterick Prize 172

McLeod (Enid) Literary Prize   *see* Enid McLeod Literary Prize

McNally Robinson Book of the Year Award   *see* Manitoba Literary Awards

McNamara (Peter) Convenors' Award for Excellence   *see* Aurealis Awards

McTavish Sykes (Eileen) Award for Best First Book   *see* Manitoba Literary Awards

Mads Wiel Nygaards Legat 173

Magnesia Litera Awards 173

Magsaysay (Ramon) Award   *see* Ramon Magsaysay Award

Mahendra Pragya Puraskar   *see* Royal Nepal Academy Awards

Mail on Sunday/John Llewellyn Rhys Prize 174

Malheiros (Ricardo), Prêmio   *see* Prêmio Ricardo Malheiros

Malyshko (Andrei) Prize   *see* Andrei Malyshko Prize

Man Booker Prize 174

Manheim (Ralph) Medal for Translation   *see* PEN/Ralph Manheim Medal for Translation

Manila Critics Circle National Book Awards 175

Manitoba Literary Awards 175

Mann (Thomas) Preis   *see* Thomas-Mann-Preis

Mansfield (Katherine) Award
     see Bank of New Zealand Katherine Mansfield Memorial Awards

Manès Sperber-Preis für Literatur 341

Mao Dun Literary Prize 176

Marais (Eugene) prys   *see* Eugène Maraisprys

Mares (José Fuentes), Premio de Literatura   *see* Premio de Literatura José Fuentes Mares

Margaret A. Edwards Award 86

Margit Pahlson Prize 219

Marian Engel Award 89

Mark Lynton History Prize 169

Mark Twain Award for Short Fiction 358

Marlowe Award for Best International Crime Novel
     see Raymond Chandler Society's 'Marlowe' Award for Best International Crime Novel

Marraro (Howard R.) Prize   *see* Howard R. Marraro Prize

Marraro (Howard R.) Prize   *see* Howard R. Marraro Prize in Italian History

Marsh Award for Children's Literature in Translation 177

Marsh Biography Award 178

Marshall (Lenore) Poetry Prize   *see* Lenore Marshall Poetry Prize

Marshall Shulman Book Prize 335
Marten Toonder Award 178
Martinus Nijhoff Prijs voor Vertalingen 205
Mary Gilmore Award 104
Mary McCarthy Prize in Short Fiction 172
Mary Vaughan Jones Award 360
Mast Tauq Ali Award 10
Mathew Prichard Award for Short Story Writing 264
Maulvi Abdul Haq (Babai-e-Urdu) Award   see Babai-e-Urdu Maulvi Abdul Haq Award
Mears (Colin) Award   see Kate Greenaway Medal
Medwick (Lucille) Memorial Award   see Lucille Medwick Memorial Award
Melbourne University Literature Award
          see Fellowship of Australian Writers Literature Awards
Melsom-prisen 180
MER Prize 180
Merck (Johann-Heinrich) Preis
          see Johann-Heinrich-Merck-Preis für literarische Kritik und Essay
Merghelynck (Arthur), Prix   see Prix Arthur Merghelynck
Meyer-Whitworth Award 180
Michael L. Printz Award for Excellence in Young Adult Literature 265
Michael Smith Award   see Guild of Food Writers Awards
Michener (James A.) Memorial Prize   see James A. Michener Memorial Prize
Milán Füst Literary Prize 102
Mildenberger (Kenneth W.) Prize   see Kenneth W. Mildenberger Prize
Mildred L. Batchelder Award 29
Miles Franklin Award 100
Mina P. Shaughnessy Prize 334
Ministry of Culture National Translation Prize 182
Miroslav Ivanov Award for Non-Fiction 142
Mishima Yukio Shô 182
Mitchell (Eric) Prize   see Mitchell Prize for Art History/Eric Mitchell Prize
Mitchell (Kathleen) Award   see Kathleen Mitchell Award
Mitchell (W. O.) Prize   see W. O. Mitchell Prize
Mitchell Prize for Art History/Eric Mitchell Prize 183
MLA Award for Lifetime Scholarly Achievement 183
Modern Language Association Prize for a Distinguished Bibliography 184
Modern Language Association Prize for a First Book 184
Modern Language Association Prize for Independent Scholars 185
Monnet (Jean), Prix   see Prix Jean Monnet de littérature européenne
Monnier (Thyde), Grand Prix   see Grand Prix Thyde Monnier
Monsudar Book Awards 185
Montalte (Louis) Prix de Poésie   see Prix de Poésie Louis Montalte
Montana Medal   see Montana New Zealand Book Awards/Montana Medal
Montana New Zealand Book Awards 185
Montana New Zealand Book Awards/Best First Book of Fiction Award 186
Montana New Zealand Book Awards/Best First Book of Non-Fiction Award 187
Montana New Zealand Book Awards/Best First Book of Poetry Award 187
Montana New Zealand Book Awards/Deutz Medal 188
Montana New Zealand Book Awards/Montana Medal 188
Monteiro Lobato Award 189
Moore (Oscar) Screenwriting Prize   see Oscar Moore Screenwriting Prize
Morand (Paul), Grand Prix   see Grand Prix de Littérature Paul Morand
Mordechai Bernstein Literary Prizes 33
Morris D. Forkosch Prize 97

Morton (Kathryn A.) Prize in Poetry   *see* Kathryn A. Morton Prize in Poetry
Morton Dauwen Zabel Award   *see* American Academy of Arts and Letters Annual Awards
Morton N. Cohen Award for a Distinguished Edition of Letters 70
Mosse (George L.) Prize   *see* George L. Mosse Prize
Mr Christie's Book Awards 67
Mr H Prize   *see* H-shi Shô
Mühlheimer Dramatikerpreis 190
Multatuli Prize 190
Myanmar Annual National Literary Awards 191
Mythopoeic Awards 191
Mythopoeic Fantasy Award for Adult Literature   *see* Mythopoeic Awards
Mythopoeic Fantasy Award for Children's Literature   *see* Mythopoeic Awards
Mythopoeic Scholarship Award in General Myth   *see* Mythopoeic Scholarship Awards
Mythopoeic Scholarship Award in Inklings Studies   *see* Mythopoeic Scholarship Awards
Mythopoeic Scholarship Awards 192
Nabokov Award   *see* PEN/Nabokov Award
Naipaul (Shiva) Memorial Prize   *see* Shiva Naipaul Memorial Prize
Nakahara Chûya Prize 192
Namboodiri (K. R.) Award   *see* Kerala Sahitya Akademi Awards
Naoki Sanjûgo Shô 193
Naomi Long Madgett Poetry Award 166
National Art Library Illustration Awards 193
National Artists Award 193
National Book Awards 194
National Book Contest 194
National Book Critics Circle Awards 195
National Jewish Book Awards 195
National Kamal-E-Fun Award 196
National Outdoor Book Awards 196
National Poetry Competition 198
National Writers Union of Ukraine Awards 198
Native Writers Circle of the Americas Lifetime Achievement Award for Literature 198
Naylor (Phyllis) Working Writer Fellowship
      see PEN/Phyllis Naylor Working Writer Fellowship
NCTE Award for Excellence in Poetry for Children 199
Nebula Awards 199
Nelligan (Émile) Prix   *see* Prix Émile-Nelligan
Nelly-Sachs-Preis/Kulturpreis der Stadt Dortmund 321
Nestlé Smarties Book Prize 199
Neuer deutscher Literaturpreis 200
Neustadt International Prize for Literature 200
New Brunswick Excellence in the Arts Awards 201
New Letters Literary Awards 201
New Millennium Writing Awards 202
New Writer Prose and Poetry Prizes 202
New Zealand Post Children's Book Awards 203
Newbery (John) Medal   *see* John Newbery Medal
Newcastle Poetry Prize 204
Nibbies   *see* British Book Awards
Nienke van Hichtum Prize 360
Nihon Horâ Shôsetsu Taishô 204
Nihon SF Taishô 205
Nijhoff (Martinus) Prijs voor Vertalingen   *see* Martinus Nijhoff Prijs voor Vertalingen
NIKE Literary Award 205

Nils Holgersson Plaque 129
Nobel Prize in Literature 205
NOMA Award for Publishing in Africa.. 206
Noma Bungei Shô 206
Noma Concours for Picture Book Illustrations... 207
Noma Literacy Prize 207
Noma Literature Prize for New Writers 207
Nordic Council Literature Prize 208
Nordisk Skolebibliotekarforenings Barnebokpris 208
Nordiska Priset 208
Norma Farber First Book Award 92
Norma Fleck Award for Children's Non-Fiction 95
Norsk Kritikerlags Barnebokpris 209
Norsk Kritikerlags Pris 209
Norsk Sprakpris 209
Norske Akademis Pris til Minne om Thorleif Dahl 209
Norske Lyrikklubbens Pris 210
North American Native Authors First Book Awards.. 210
Northern Palmira Prize... 210
Northern Rock Foundation Writer Award 210
Northern Writers' Awards... 211
Nowlan (Alden) Award   *see* New Brunswick Excellence in the Arts Awards
NSW Premier's Literary Awards... 211
NSW Writer's Fellowship.. 212
O'Connor (Flannery) Award for Short Fiction   *see* Flannery O'Connor Award for Short Fiction
O'Dell (Scott) Historical Fiction Award   *see* Scott O'Dell Historical Fiction Award
O'Shaughnessy Poetry Award   *see* Irish American Cultural Institute (IACI) Literary Awards
Ocho Venado (Rey), Premio   *see* Premio Demac
Oda Sakunosuke Shô.. 213
Okigbo (Christopher) Prize   *see* Association of Nigerian Authors Literature Prizes
Oktober-Prisen.. 213
Oles Honchar Prizes 130
Olive Schreiner Prize.. 331
Onassis Cultural Competition Prize 214
Orange Prize for Fiction.. 214
Orange Prize for Translation   *see* Orange Prize for Fiction
Orbis Pictus Award for Outstanding Non-fiction for Children 215
Organization of American Historians Foreign Language Book Prize 215
Ornish (Natalie) Poetry Award   *see* Texas Institute of Letters Awards
Oro (Timón de), Concurso   *see* Concurso de Prosa y Poesía Timón de Oro
Orvieto (Laura), Premio letterario   *see* Premio letterario Laura Orvieto
Orwell Prize... 216
Osaragi Jirô Shô... 217
Oscar Moore Screenwriting Prize... 189
Österreichischer Staatspreis für Europäische Literatur 217
Österreichischer Staatspreis für Literarische Übersetzer... 217
Östersundsposten prize 217
Osterweil (Joyce) Award for Poetry   *see* PEN/Joyce Osterweil Award for Poetry
Ottakar's Faber National Poetry Competition.. 218
Otto Gelstedprisen 102
Otto Stoessl-Preis.. 343
Ôya Sôichi Nonfikushon Shô 218
P. C. Hooft-prijs voor Letterkunde... 131
P2-Lyttaranes Romanpris 218

Pääskynen   see Suomen Nuorisokirjailijat Ry Awards

Pahlson (Margit) Prize   see Margit Pahlson Prize

Pakokku U Ohn Pe Literary and Education Awards 219

Palanca (Don Carlos) Memorial Awards   see Don Carlos Palanca Memorial Awards

Palmer (Nettie) Prize for Non-fiction   see Victorian Premier's Literary Awards

Palmer (Vance) Prize for Fiction   see Victorian Premier's Literary Awards

Pandora Award 220

Parandowski (Jan) Prize   see Jan Parandowski Prize

Parker (William Riley) Prize   see William Riley Parker Prize

Parker Romantic Novel of the Year 221

Parkman (Francis) Prize   see Francis Parkman Prize

Paul A. Witty Short Story Award 376

Paul Birdsall Prize in European Military and Strategic History 37

Paul-Celan-Preis 61

Paz (Octavio), Premio de Poesía y Ensayo   see Premio Octavio Paz de Poesía y Ensayo

Paz Castillo (Fernando), Premio   see Premio Fernándo Paz Castillo

Peer Poetry International Competition 221

Pegasus Prize for Literature 222

Pels (Laura) Awards for Drama   see PEN/Laura Pels Awards for Drama

Pemenang Anugerah MAPIM-Fuji Xerox 222

PEN Award for Poetry in Translation 223

PEN Center USA West Annual Literary Awards 224

PEN/Architectural Digest Award for Literary Writing on the Visual Arts 223

PEN/Barbara Goldsmith Freedom to Write Awards 223

PEN/Book-of-the-Month Club Translation Prize 223

PEN/Faulkner Award for Fiction 225

PEN/Jerard Fund Award 225

PEN/Joyce Osterweil Award for Poetry 225

PEN/Laura Pels Awards for Drama 226

PEN/Martha Albrand Award for the Art of the Memoir 226

PEN/Martha Albrand Award for First Non-fiction 226

PEN/Nabokov Award 227

PEN/Norma Klein Award 227

PEN/Phyllis Naylor Working Writer Fellowship 227

PEN/Ralph Manheim Medal for Translation 228

PEN/Robert Bingham Fellowships for Writers 228

PEN/Spielvogel-Diamonstein Award for the Art of the Essay 228

PEN/Voelcker Award for Poetry 229

Percy Fitzpatrick Medal 95

Peter-Huchel-Preis 132

Peterloo Poets Open Poetry Competition 229

Peters (Ellis) Historical Dagger   see CWA Awards

Petrarca-Prize for Translation 229

Phillips (A. A.) Prize   see A. A. Phillips Prize

Phoenix Award 230

Pierce (Lorne) Medal   see Lorne Pierce Medal

Pilgrim Award 231

Pitras Bukhari Award 53

Pla, (Josep) Premi   see Premi Josep Pla

Poe (Edgar Allen) Awards   see Edgar Allan Poe Awards

Poetry Life Open Poetry Competition 231

Poetry London Competition 232

Poggioli (Renato) Translation Award   see Renato Poggioli Translation Award

Poirier (Pascal) Award   see New Brunswick Excellence in the Arts Awards

Polk (George) Awards   *see* George Polk Awards
Portico Prize for Literature 232
Posner (Louis) Memorial Award   *see* National Jewish Book Awards
Pownall (Eve) Award for Information Books   *see* Children's Book of the Year Awards
Preller (Gustav) Prize
     see Gustav Prellerprys vir literatuurwetenskap en letterkundige kritiek
Premi d'Honor de les Lletres Catalanes 233
Premi Josep Pla 234
Premi de les Lletres Catalanes Ramon Llull 233
Premi Nacional de Literatura de la Generalitat de Catalunya 234
Premi Sèrie Negra 234
Premia Bohemica 235
Prêmio Academia Brasileira de Letras de Poesia 235
Premio Academia Nacional de la Historia 235
Premio Adonais de Poesía 235
Premio Alfaguara de Novela 236
Premio Alvarez Quintero 260
Premio Andalucía de Novela 236
Premio Antonio Feltrinelli 241
Premio Anual de Ensayo Literario Hispanoamericano Lya Kostakowsky 236
Premio Apel les Mestres 237
Premio Azorín 237
Premio Biblioteca Breve 238
Premio Camões 238
Premio Campiello 238
Premio Casa de las Americas 239
Premio Cervantes 239
Premio del Rey Ocho Venado 261
Premio Del Rey Prize 261
Premio Demac 240
Premio Destino-Guion 240
Prêmio D. Diniz 240
Premio Esteban Echeverría 241
Premio Fastenrath 241
Premio Fernándo Paz Castillo 257
Premio Grinzane Cavour 241
Premio Grinzane Editoria   *see* Premio Grinzane Cavour
Premio Hispanoamericano de Poesía Sor Juana Inés de la Cruz 242
Premio Internacional Alfonso Reyes 243
Premio Internacional de Ensayo Mariano Picón Salas 242
Premio Internacional de Novela Rómulo Gallegos 243
Premio Internacional de Novela Yolanda Vargas Dulché 243
Premio Internazionale Fregene 244
Premio Internazionale di Letteratura La Cultura del Mare 244
Prêmio Jabuti 245
Premio La Sonrisa Vertical 262
Premio Latinoamericano de Literatura Infantil y Juvenil Norma-Fundalectura 245
Prêmio Ler 245
Premio Letterario Giuseppe Berto 237
Premio Letterario Isola d'Elba – Rafaello Brignetti 246
Premio letterario Laura Orvieto 216
Premio Letterario Mondello Città di Palermo 246
Premio del Libro 246
Premio Literario Carmen Lyra 250

Premio Literario Editorial Costa Rica 247
Prêmio Literário José Saramago 247
Premio Literario Joven Creación 247
Premio de Literatura Infantil El Barco de Vapor 248
Premio de Literatura José Fuentes Mares 249
Premio de Literatura Juvenil Gran Angular 248
Premio de Literatura Latinoamericana y del Caribe Juan Rulfo 249
Premio de Literatura para Niños Hunapuh e Ixbalamqué 249
Premio de Literatura Ricardo Mimenza Castillo 248
Premio de Literatura Sor Juana Inés de la Cruz 250
Prêmio Machado de Assis 250
Premio Nacional de las Letras Españolas 251
Premio Nacional de Literatura 252
Premio Nacional de Literatura 253
Premio Nacional de Literatura 252
Premio Nacional de Literatura 253
Premio Nacional de Literatura 251
Premio Nacional de Literatura El Búho 253
Premio Nacional de Literatura Infantil y Juvenil 253
Premio Nacional de Literatura Infantil y Juvenil Castillo de la Lectura 254
Premio Nacional a la mejor traducción 254
Premio Nacional de Narrativa Ignacio Manuel Altamirano 254
Premio Nacional de Novela José Rubén Romero 255
Premio Nacional a la obra de un traductor 255
Premio Nacional de Poesía Tintanueva 255
Premio Nadal 255
Premio Napoli di Narrativa 256
Premio de Narrativa Colima 256
Premio Nazionale di Poesia Giosue Carducci 257
Premio Nezahualcóyotl de Literatura en Lenguas Indígenas 257
Premio de Novela Fernando Lara 257
Premio Octavio Paz de Poesía y Ensayo 258
Prêmio Paulo Rónai 262
Premio Pessoa 258
Premio de Poesía Ciudad de Medellín 259
Premio de Poesía Mensajero 259
Premio Planeta de Novela 258
Premio Primavera de Novela 259
Premio Príncipe de Asturias 260
Premio Reina Sofía de Poesía Iberoamericana 260
Prêmio Ricardo Malheiros 251
Premio Rivadeneira 261
Premio Rolando Anzilotti 237
Premio Strega 262
Premio UPC de ciencia ficción 263
Premio Valle Inclán 263
Premio Viareggio 263
Premios Literarios Fundación ARCIEN 263
Premju Letterarju 263
President's Award for Pride of Performance 264
Prichard (Mathew) Award for Short Story Writing
    see Mathew Prichard Award for Short Story Writing
Prijs voor Meesterschap 264
Prijs der Nederlandse Letteren 264

Prime Minister's Hebrew Literature Prize.. 265
Pringle (Thomas) Award   see Thomas Pringle Award
Printz (Michael L.) Award   see Michael L. Printz Award for Excellence
Pritchett (V. S.) Memorial Prize   see V. S. Pritchett Memorial Prize
Prithvi Pragya Puraskar   see Royal Nepal Academy Awards
Privat (Edouard), Prix   see Prix Edouard Privat
Private Eye Writers of America/SMP Contest.. 266
Prix de l'Académie des Sciences, Arts et Belles Lettres de Dijon 267
Prix Alain-Grandbois.. 285
Prix d'Ambronay.. 267
Prix Amerigo Vespucci... 307
Prix des Amis du Monde diplomatique... 267
Prix des Amis du Scribe 267
Prix Anton Bergmann... 271
Prix Antonin Artaud 268
Prix Apollinaire 268
Prix Arthur Merghelynck 298
Prix de l'Assemblée Nationale 268
Prix Astrolabe–Etonnants Voyageurs... 269
Prix Athanase-David.. 276
Prix Auguste Teirlinck 305
Prix Augustin-Thierry 269
Prix Baobab de l'album 270
Prix Baron de Saint-Genois 304
Prix Baudelaire 270
Prix Bernard Versele 307
Prix Bloc-Notes.. 272
Prix Bordin 272
Prix Bourbonnais... 272
Prix BPT.. 272
Prix Cazes Brasserie Lipp.. 273
Prix du Champagne Lanson 273
Prix Champlain 274
Prix Charles Duvivie 278
Prix Charles Vildrac de la Poésie.. 308
Prix Chrétien-de-Troyes 274
Prix Chronos de Littérature pour la Jeunesse 275
Prix Ciné Roman Carte Noire 275
Prix des Cinq Continents de la francophonie 275
Prix Claude Le Heurteur 289
Prix Claude Sernet... 304
Prix Daniel Bayon... 271
Prix Décembre 277
Prix des Deux-Magots... 277
Prix Edouard Privat.. 301
Prix Émile-Nelligan 299
Prix des Enfants.. 279
Prix Erckmann-Chatrian... 279
Prix Ernest Discailles... 278
Prix Européen du Roman pour Enfant de la Ville de Poitiers 279
Prix Fémina... 280
Prix Fémina Etranger 280
Prix du Festival de la Bande Dessinée de Sierre.. 280
Prix FIT Aurore Boréale de la traduction... 281

Prix de Flore 281
Prix Fnac–Andersen du livre d'entreprise 282
Prix France Culture Français 282
Prix France Télévision 282
Prix Franz Cumont 276
Prix François 1er: prix Cognac de la critique littéraire 283
Prix François Billetdoux 271
Prix François-Joseph Audiffred 269
Prix Gérard de Nerval 299
Prix Goblet d'Alviella 284
Prix Goncourt 285
Prix Goncourt des Lycéens 285
Prix Gouverneur de la Rosée du Livre et de la Littérature 285
Prix Heredia 286
Prix Infini 286
Prix Interallié 287
Prix International Kadima 287
Prix Internet du Livre 288
Prix Jean Freustié 283
Prix Jean Monnet de littérature européenne 298
Prix du Jeune Ecrivain 288
Prix Joseph Gantrelle 283
Prix Joseph Houziaux 286
Prix Joseph Kessel 289
Prix Jules Duculot 278
Prix La Mazille   *see* Gourmand World Cookbook Awards
Prix de la Langue de France 289
Prix Laure Bataillon 270
Prix des Lectrices de Elle 290
Prix Léon Leclère 290
Prix des Libraires 290
Prix des Librairies de Création 291
Prix Littéraire de l'Age d'Or de France 291
Prix Littéraire de l'ENS Cachan 291
Prix Littéraire de la Gironde 292
Prix Littéraire Henri Deschamps 291
Prix Littéraire des Mouettes 292
Prix Littéraire du Parlement de la Communauté Française de Belgique 300
Prix Littéraire Prince Pierre-de-Monaco 292
Prix Littéraire de la Vocation 292
Prix Littéraires de l'Académie Française 293
Prix Littéraires du Ministère de la Jeunesse et des Sports 293
Prix Littéraires de la Société des Gens de Lettres 294
Prix de littérature Émile Bernheim 294
Prix du Livre Europe 1 295
Prix du Livre Inter 295
Prix du Livre Numérique NewsFam.com 295
Prix du Livre de Picardie 295
Prix du Livre en Poitou-Charentes 296
Prix Louis Castex 273
Prix des Maisons de la Presse 296
Prix Marcel-Couture 276
Prix Marguerite Audoux 269
Prix Maurice-Edgar Coindreau 276

Prix Maurice-Genevoix 284
Prix Médicis 296
Prix Médicis de l'Essai 296
Prix Médicis Etranger 297
Prix Méditerranée 297
Prix Méditerranée étranger 297
Prix du Meilleur Livre Etranger 298
Prix Michel Dentan 277
Prix National des Bibliothécaires 298
Prix Nautile de Cristal 299
Prix Octogone du livre de jeunesse 300
Prix Paul Verlaine 307
Prix Pelléas 301
Prix de Poésie Louis Montalte 301
Prix de Poésie et Prix d'Etudes Littéraires Maurice Carême 273
Prix Polar 301
Prix René Fallet 280
Prix RFI–témoin du monde 302
Prix Roberval 302
Prix Roman Historique de Blois 303
Prix Rosny-Aîné 303
Prix Saint Valentin 304
Prix Sorcières 304
Prix Stanislas Julien 288
Prix Théophile Gautier 284
Prix Théophraste Renaudot 302
Prix Tibet 305
Prix Tour-Eiffel de Science-Fiction 306
Prix Tristan Tzara de Traduction 306
Prix Tropiques de l'Agence Française de Développement 306
Prix Valéry Larbaud 289
Prix Victor-Rossel 303
Prix Voronca 308
Prix Wepler–Fondation La Poste 308
Promise Prize   *see* London Writers Competition
Pulitzer Prizes in Journalism, Letters, Drama and Music 309
Pura Belpré Award 32
Pushcart Prize: Best of the Small Presses 309
Pushkin Poetry Prize 310
Queen's Gold Medal for Poetry 310
Queensland Premier's Literary Awards 310
Quintero (Alvarez) Premio   *see* Premio Alvarez Quintero
R. H. Blyth Award 39
Raiziss/de Palchi Translation Award 311
Rajasthan Urdu Academy Awards 311
Ramon Magsaysay Award 173
Ramuz (C. F.), Grand Prix   *see* Grand Prix Ramuz
Rancage Literary Award 312
Randolph Caldecott Medal 55
Rauriser Förderungspreis 312
Rauriser Literaturpreis 312
Raymond Chandler Society's 'Marlowe' Award for Best International Crime Novel 62
Raymond Williams Community Publishing Prize 375
Rea Award for the Short Story 313

Real Writers/Book Pl@ce Short Story Awards 313
Reed (A. W.) Lifetime Achievement Award   see Montana New Zealand Book Awards
Reese (Trevor) Memorial Prize   see Trevor Reese Memorial Prize
Renato Poggioli Translation Award 232
Renaudot (Théophraste) Prix   see Prix Théophraste Renaudot
Rennyo Shô 314
Reyes (Alfonso) Premio Internacional   see Premio Internacional Alfonso Reyes
Rhône-Poulenc Prize   see Aventis Prize
Rhys Davies Short Story Competition 314
Richard Imison Memorial Award 135
Richardson (Evelyn) Non-fiction Award   see Evelyn Richardson Non-fiction Award
Rielo (Fernando) World Mystical Poetry Prize   see Fernando Rielo World Mystical Poetry Prize
Rifbjergs (Klaus) Debutantpris for Lyrik   see Klaus Rifbjergs Debutantpris for Lyrik
Riksmalsprisen – Oslo og Baerum riksmalsforenings litteraturpris 315
Rimbaud (Arthur), Prix   see Prix Littéraires du Ministère de la Jeunesse et des Sports
River Styx International Poetry Contest 316
Rivertonprisen 'Den gylden revolver' 316
Robert F. Sibert Informational Book Award 336
Robert H. Winner Memorial Award 376
Roderick (Colin) Prize for Australian Literature
        see Colin Roderick Prize for Australian Literature
Roland Holst (Henriette) prijs   see Henriette Roland Holst-prijs
Romantic Novelists Association New Writers Award 317
Romero (José Rubén), Premio Nacional de Novela
        see Premio Nacional de Novela José Rubén Romero
Rónai (Paulo), Premio   see Prêmio Paulo Rónai
Rooney Prize for Irish Literature 317
Rose Mary Crawshay Prize 75
Rosenthal (Richard and Hinda) Foundation Award
        see American Academy of Arts and Letters Annual Awards
Rossel (Victor) Prix   see Prix Victor-Rossel
Roth (Lois) Award   see Lois Roth Award for a Translation of a Literary Work
Round (Jeremy) Award   see Guild of Food Writers Awards
Royal Nepal Academy Awards 318
RSM Library Prize   see Society of Authors Medical Book Awards
Rudolf Koivu Prize 154
Rulfo (Juan) Premio   see Premio de Literatura Latinoamericana y del Caribe Juan Rulfo
Runciman Award 318
Russell (Walter McRae) Award   see Walter McRae Russell Award
Russell Clark Award 69
Russell Lowell (James) Prize   see James Russell Lowell Prize
Russell Major (J.) Prize   see J. Russell Major Prize
Russian Booker Prize   see Booker/Open Russia Prize
Ruth Lilly Poetry Prize 162
Ruth Schwartz Children's Book Award 331
RÚV (Icelandic State Radio) Literary Award 320
s'Gravesande (G H) Prize   see G H s'Gravesande Prize
Sachs (Nelly) Preis   see Nelly-Sachs-Preis/Kulturpreis der Stadt Dortmund
Sagittarius Prize 321
Sahitya Akademi Award 321
Saidi (Bismil) Prize   see Rajasthan Urdu Academy Awards
Saint-Genois (Baron de) Prix   see Prix Baron de Saint-Genois
Salas (Mariano Picón), Premio   see Premio Internacional de Ensayo Mariano Picón Salas
Saltire Society Literary Awards 322

Saltire Society/Times Educational Supplement Scotland Prize for Educational Publications............ 322

Samlagsprisen 323

Sandrof (Ivan) Award   *see* The National Book Critics Circle Awards

Sands (Ron) Prize   *see* Lakeland Book of the Year Awards

Sanlam Literary Award... 323

Sapphire Awards.. 323

Saramago (José) Prémio Literário   *see* Prêmio Literário José Saramago

Sasakawa Haiku Prize 324

Sasakawa Prize for Translation 324

Saskatchewan Book Awards... 324

SATI Award For Outstanding Translation 325

Scaglione (Aldo and Jeanne) Prize
    see Aldo and Jeanne Scaglione Prize for Comparative Literary Studies

Scaglione (Aldo and Jeanne) Prize
    see Aldo and Jeanne Scaglione Prize for French and Francophone Studies

Scaglione (Aldo and Jeanne) Prize
    see Aldo and Jeanne Scaglione Prize for Germanic Languages and Literatures

Scaglione (Aldo and Jeanne) Prize
    see Aldo and Jeanne Scaglione Prize for Italian Studies

Scaglione (Aldo and Jeanne) Prize
    see Aldo and Jeanne Scaglione Prize for Studies in Slavic Languages and Literatures

Scaglione (Aldo and Jeanne) Prize
    see Aldo and Jeanne Scaglione Prize for a Translation of a Literary Work

Scaglione (Aldo and Jeanne) Prize
    see Aldo and Jeanne Scaglione Prize for a Translation of a Scholarly Study of Literature

Scaglione (Aldo and Jeanne) Prize
    see Aldo and Jeanne Scaglione Publication Award for a Manuscript in Italian Literary Studies

Scarborough (William Sanders) Prize   *see* William Sanders Scarborough Prize

Scheepersprys vir jeugliteratuur... 330

Schiller, Grosser Preis   *see* Grosser Preis der Schweizerische Schillerstiftung

Schlegel-Tieck Prize 330

Scholz (Hugo) Prize   *see* Broumovska literarni cena

Schreiner (Olive) Prize   *see* Olive Schreiner Prize

Schwartz (Ruth) Children's Book Award   *see* Ruth Schwartz Children's Book Award

Schweizer Jugendbuchpreis.. 331

Science Fiction Achievement Award   *see* Hugo Award

Scorer (Mary) Award   *see* Manitoba Literary Awards

Scott Moncrieff Prize 332

Scott O'Dell Historical Fiction Award.. 213

Scottish Arts Council Book of the Year Award... 332

Scottish Book of the Year   *see* Saltire Society Literary Awards

Scottish First Book of the Year   *see* Saltire Society Literary Awards

Scottish History Book of the Year   *see* Saltire Society Literary Awards

Seidenbaum (Art) Award   *see* Los Angeles Times Book Prizes

Seifert (Jaroslav) Award   *see* Jaroslav Seifert Award

Selskabets Pris... 333

Sernet (Claude) Prix   *see* Prix Claude Sernet

Shagil (Ahteramuddin) Prize   *see* Rajasthan Urdu Academy Awards

Shah (Syed Waris) Award   *see* Syed Waris Shah Award

Shah Abdul Latif Bhitaee Award.. 34

Shamus Awards... 333

Shaughnessy (Mina P.) Prize   *see* Mina P. Shaughnessy Prize

Shaw (Bernard) Prize   *see* Bernard Shaw Prize

Shelley Memorial Award... 334

INDEX OF AWARDS

Shevchenko (Taras) Award   *see* Taras Shevchenko Award

Shirani (Mehmood) Prize   *see* Rajasthan Urdu Academy Awards

Shiva Naipaul Memorial Prize 192

Shûgorô (Yamamoto) Shô   *see* Yamamoto Shûgorô Shô

Shulman (Marshall) Book Prize   *see* Marshall Shulman Book Prize

Sibert (Robert F.) Informational Book Award   *see* Robert F. Sibert Informational Book Award

Sidewise Awards for Alternate History 336

Sigmund-Freud-Preis für wissenschaftliche Prosa 100

Silas Prisen 337

Simonenko (Vasyl) Prize   *see* Vasyl Simonenko Prize

Singapore National Book Awards 337

Singh (Bhai Santokh) Award   *see* Haryana Sahitya Akademi Awards

Sino-American Literary Exchange Prize   *see* China Literature Foundation Awards

Sir Banister Fletcher Prize of the Authors' Club 96

Sjöberg (Leif and Inger) Prize   *see* ASF Translation Prize

Skolebibliotekarforeningens Litteraturpris 338

Slessor (Kenneth) Prize for Poetry   *see* NSW Premier's Literary Awards

Smirnoff-Booker Prize   *see* Booker/Open Russia Prize

Smith (Lilian Ida) Awards   *see* Lilian Ida Smith Awards

Society of Authors Medical Book Awards 339

Society of School Librarians International Book Awards 339

Sofola (Zulu) Prize   *see* Zulu Sofola Prize

Solzhenitsyn Prize for Russian Writing 340

Somerset Maugham Awards 179

Soong Ching Ling Children's Literature Prize 340

Soren Gyldendal Prize 121

Southeast Asia (SEA) Write Award 340

Spectrum Prize   *see* Association of Nigerian Authors Literature Prizes

Sperber (Manès) Preis für Literatur   *see* Manès Sperber-Preis für Literatur

Spielvogel-Diamonstein Award
     see PEN/Spielvogel-Diamonstein Award

Språklig Samlings Litteraturpris 341

St John Thomas (David) Charitable Trust Awards
     see David St John Thomas Charitable Trust Awards

St Martin's Press/Malice Domestic Contest 341

Staatliche Förderungspreise für junge Schriftstellerinnen und Schriftsteller 341

State Prize of the Russian Federation in Arts and Letters 342

State Prizes for Literature 342

Stead (Christina) Award   *see* Fellowship of Australian Writers Literature Awards

Stephen Leacock Memorial Medal for Humour 161

Stern Silver PEN Prize   *see* Macmillan PEN Awards

Stevens (Wallace) Award   *see* Wallace Stevens Award

Stewart (Douglas) Prize for Non-fiction   *see* NSW Premier's Literary Awards

Stoessl (Otto) Preis   *see* Otto Stoessl-Preis

Stora Priset 343

Stryjova (Marie) Prize   *see* Broumovska literarni cena

Strzelecki (Jan) Prize   *see* Jan Strzelecki Prize

Sturgeon (Theodore) Memorial Award   *see* Theodore Sturgeon Memorial Award

Sunday Telegraph Catherine Pakenham Memorial Award 344

Sunday Times Award for Literary Excellence 344

Sunday Times Young Writer of the Year Award 344

Suomalaisen kirjallisuuden tiedotuskeskus 345

Suomen Nuorisokirjailijat Ry Awards 345

Sur Award   *see* Haryana Sahitya Akademi Awards

Svenska Dagbladets Litteraturpris 345
Sveriges Radios Lyrikpris/Sveriges Radio P1:s Romanpris 346
SWPA Audiobooks of the Year 346
Sydney Taylor Book Awards (STBA) 349
Syed Waris Shah Award 333
T. S. Eliot Prize 87
T. S. Eliot Prize for Poetry 88
Tabla Poetry Competition 347
Takami Jun Shô 347
Tanizaki Jun'ichirô Shô 347
Tanning Prize 347
Tano Aschehoug-Prisen/Idunn-Prisen 348
Taras Shevchenko Award 335
Tarjei Vesaas Debutanpris 348
Tarlan Independent Prize 348
Taylor (Sydney) Book Awards   see Sydney Taylor Book Awards (STBA)
TDK Australian Audio Book Awards 349
TDK Literary Award 350
Te Kura Pounamu Award 350
Teirlinck (Auguste), Prix   see Prix Auguste Teirlinck
Teixeira-Gomes Prize 350
Texas Institute of Letters Awards 351
Tezuka Osamu Bunka Shô 351
Theatre Book Prize 352
Thelen (David) Prize   see David Thelen Prize
Theo Thijssen Prize for Children's and Youth Literature 352
Theodore Sturgeon Memorial Award 344
Thomas (Lewis) Prize   see Lewis Thomas Prize
Thomas Cook/Daily Telegraph Travel Book Award 353
Thomas Dunne Books Award for the Novel 84
Thomas Head Raddall Fiction Prize 124
Thomas Pringle Award 265
Thomas-Mann-Preis 176
Tibor-Déry-Preis 78
Tidens Skjonnlitteraere Pris 353
Tienie Hollowaymedalje vir kleuterliteratuur 354
Tir Na N-og Awards 354
Tolman Cunard Prize   see Forward Prizes for Poetry
Toonder (Martin) Award   see Marten Toonder Award
Topelius Prize   see Suomen Nuorisokirjailijat Ry Awards
Toronto Book Awards 355
Toyota/Children's Literature Foundation Award 355
Trakl (Georg) Preis für Lyrik   see Georg Trakl Preis für Lyrik
Translated Book Contest 356
Trask (Betty) Awards   see Betty Trask Prize
Trask (Betty) Prize   see Betty Trask Prize
Travelling Scholarship Fund 357
Trevor Reese Memorial Prize 313
Trillium Book Award/Prix Trillium 357
Trinick (Trish) Prize   see TDK Australian Audio Book Awards
Triumph Prize 357
Tsubouchi Shôyô Taishô 358
Tufts (Kate) Discovery Award   see Kingsley Tufts Poetry Prize
Tufts (Kingsley) Poetry Prize   see Kingsley Tufts Poetry Prize

Tullie House Prize   *see* Lakeland Book of the Year Awards
Tun Seri Lanang Award 358
Turner (Ethel) Prize for Young People's Literature
     see NSW Premier's Literary Awards
Turner (Steven) Award   *see* Texas Institute of Letters Awards
Twain (Mark) Award for Short Fiction   *see* Mark Twain Award for Short Fiction
Tzara (Tristan), Prix de Traduction   *see* Prix Tristan Tzara de Traduction
UBC Medal for Canadian Biography/UBC President's Medal in Biography 359
Ukrainka (Lesya) Prize   *see* Lesya Ukrainka Prize
UNESCO Prize for Children's and Young People's Literature in the Service of Tolerance 359
Ushakov (Mykola) Prize   *see* National Writers Union of Ukraine Awards
V. S. Pritchett Memorial Prize 266
Vaka-Helgafell Children's Book Award 360
Valentin (Saint), Prix   *see* Prix Saint Valentin
van Hichtum (Nienke) Prize   *see* Nienke van Hichtum Prize
Vaptsarov (International) Prize   *see* International Vaptsarov Prize
Vasyl Simonenko Prize 337
Vaughan Jones (Mary) Award   *see* Mary Vaughan Jones Award
Vedvyasa (Maharshi) Award   *see* Haryana Sahitya Akademi Awards
Veillon (Charles) European Essay Prize   *see* Charles Veillon European Essay Prize
Venter (Bill) Literary Award   *see* Bill Venter/Altron Literary Award
Ver Poets Open Competition 362
Verb Writing Competition BBC 362
Verity Bargate Award 28
Verlaine (Paul) Prix   *see* Prix Paul Verlaine
Versele, Prix Bernard   *see* Prix Bernard Versele
Vespucci (Amerigo), Prix   *see* Prix Amerigo Vespucci
Victorian Premier's Literary Awards 362
Vildrac (Charles), Prix de la Poésie   *see* Prix Charles Vildrac de la Poésie
Vilenica International Literary Awards 363
Virgin Books Newcomer of the Year Award   *see* British Book Awards
Voaden (Herman) National Playwriting Competition
     see Herman Voaden National Playwriting Competition
Vondel Translation Prize 364
Voss (Johann Heinrich)-Preis für Übersetzung
     see Johann-Heinrich-Voss-Preis für Übersetzung
Vucinich (Wayne S.) Book Prize   *see* Wayne S. Vucinich Book Prize
Vursell (Harold D.) Memorial Award
     see American Academy of Arts and Letters Annual Awards
Výrocní ceny Nadace 365
Vysehrad Publishers Awards 365
W. H. Heinemann Award 125
W. H. Smith Children's Book of the Year   *see* British Book Awards
W. H. Smith Literary Award 366
W. H. Smith Thumping Good Read Award 366
W. O. Mitchell Prize 183
Wadsworth Prize for Business History 367
Waldo G. Leland Prize 161
Walford Award for Contributions to Bibliography 367
Wallace Stevens Award 342
Walt Whitman Award 373
Walter McRae Russell Award 319
Waterstone's Prize   *see* Forward Prizes for Poetry
Watt (David) Prize   *see* David Watt Prize

Wayne S. Vucinich Book Prize 365
WAYRBA—West Australian Young Readers' Book Award 368
Wellcome Trust Prize 368
Wesley-Logan Prize 368
Western Australian Premier's Book Awards 369
Westminster Prize 370
Wheatley Medal for an Outstanding Index 370
Whitbread Book of the Year and Literary Awards 371
White Ravens 371
Whitfield Prize 372
Whiting (John) Award   *see* John Whiting Award
Whiting Writers' Awards 372
Whitman (Walt) Award   *see* Walt Whitman Award
Wieland (Christoph-Martin) Preis   *see* Christoph-Martin-Wieland-Preis
Wiesel (Elie) Prize in Ethics Essay Contest
     see Elie Wiesel Prize in Ethics Essay Contest
Wijewardene (D. R.) Memorial Award   *see* D. R. Wijewardene Memorial Award
Wilder (Laura Ingalls) Award   *see* Laura Ingalls Wilder Award
William Carlos Williams Award 375
William Hill Sports Book of the Year 375
William Riley Parker Prize 220
William Sanders Scarborough Prize 330
Williams (Raymond) Community Publishing Prize
     see Raymond Williams Community Publishing Prize
Williams (William Carlos) Award   *see* William Carlos Williams Award
Willner (Ernst) Prize   *see* Ingeborg Bachmann Preis
Wilson (Ethel) Fiction Priz   *see* British Columbia Book Prizes
Wilson (Titus) Prize   *see* Lakeland Book of the Year Awards
Wine Book of the Year Gold Label Award   *see* Prix du Champagne Lanson
Winifred Holtby Memorial Prize 130
Winner (Robert H.) Memorial Award   *see* Robert H. Winner Memorial Award
Wittig (Joseph) Prize   *see* Broumovska literarni cena
Witty (Paul A.) Short Story Award   *see* Paul A. Witty Short Story Award
Wolfson History Prize 376
Wong (David T.K) Prize for Short Fiction
     see David T.K. Wong Prize for Short Fiction
World Book of the Year Prize 377
World Wide Writers Competition 377
Wrightson (Patricia) Prize   *see* NSW Premier's Literary Awards
Writer Magazine/Emily Dickinson Award 378
Writer's Digest Annual Writing Competition 378
Writer's Journal Annual Short Story Contest 378
Writers' Alliance of Newfoundland and Labrador Provincial Book Awards 379
Writers' Week Poetry Competition 379
Würdigungspreis für Literatur 380
Yamamoto Shûgorô Shô 335
YARA—Young Australian Readers' Awards 380
Yokomizo Seishi Shô 380
Yomiuri Bungaku Shô 380
Yorkshire Post Awards 381
Yoshikawa Eiji Bungaku Shinjin Shô 381
Yoshikawa Eiji Bungaku Shô 381
Young Wine Writer Award 382
Yukio (Mishima) Shô   *see* Mishima Yukio Shô

INDEX OF AWARDS

Zimbabwean Publishers' Literary Awards 382
Zolotow (Charlotte) Award   *see* Charlotte Zolotow Award
Zulu Sofola Prize 339

INDEX OF AWARDING ORGANIZATIONS

92nd Street Y Unterberg Poetry Center/The Nation 82
Academi, Cardiff/ Welsh Academy 75
Academia Brasileira de Letras 1, 2, 235, 250
Academia Das Ciencias de Lisboa (Lisbon Academy of Science) 251
Académie Française 112, 113, 273, 284, 286, 293, 307
Académie Française/Fondation Henri Gal 113
Académie Goncourt 285
Academia Nacional de la Historia 235
Académie des Inscriptions et Belles Lettres 288
Académie des lettres du Québec 285
Académie Royale de Belgique 271, 276, 278, 278, 283, 284, 286, 290, 304, 305
Académie Royale de Langue et de Littérature Françaises 113
Academie Saint Valentin 304
Académie des Sciences, Arts et Belles Lettres de Dijon 267
Académie des Sciences Morales et Politiques 269
Academy of American Poets 2, 159, 160, 311, 342, 347, 373
Academy of American Poets/The Nation 178
Accademia Nazionale dei Lincei 241
Africa Centre 55
Afro-Asian Book Council 139
Aftonbladet 5
Agence Française de Développement 306
Agence intergouvernementale de la Francophonie 275, 287
Al Hussein Cultural Centre 13
Aldeburgh Poetry Trust 8
Alexander S. Onassis Public Benefit Foundation 214
Allen & Unwin Publishers 23
Allied Electronic Corporation (Altron) 361
American Academy of Arts and Letters 11
American Academy of Arts and Sciences 88
American Association for the Advancement of Slavic Studies 127, 144
American Association for the Advancement of Slavic Studies/Harriman Institute
   of Columbia University 335
American Association for the Advancement of Slavic Studies/Orbis
   Books Ltd 1
American Association for the Advancement of Slavic Studies/Stanford
   University Center for Russian and East European Studies 365
American Booksellers Association 42
American Historical Association 19, 30, 31
American Institute of Physics 6
American Historical Association 34, 37, 46, 85, 91, 93, 97, 103, 123, 150, 161, 165, 177,
   190, 261, 320, 368
American Library Association 102, 152
American Library Association/Dartmouth College 77
American Library Association/School Library Journal 86
American Library Association/Young Adult Library Services Association (YALSA) 265
American PEN 223, 223, 225, 226, 226, 228, 228, 232
American-Scandinavian Foundation 16
Amis du Monde diplomatique 267
Amsterdam Fund for the Arts 109, 132, 190
Andersen/Fnac/les Echos 282
Anglo–Hellenic League/National Bank of Greece 318

INDEX OF AWARDING ORGANIZATIONS

Arts Council of England 14, 15, 372, 375
Arts Council of England/The Independent 136
Arts Council of Wales 15
Arts Council/An Chomhairle Ealaion 60, 81, 83, 178
Asahi Shimbun 351
Asahi Shimbun Publishing Co 217
Asham Literary Endowment Trust/Waterstone's 17
Asia/Pacific Cultural Centre for UNESCO—ACCU 207
Asociación Gente de Letras 241
Asociación de la Heroica Escuela Naval Militar A.C/Instituto de
    Cultura de la Ciudad de México 73
Asociatiei Scriitorilor din Bucuresti 52
Associated Writing Program 17, 84
Association Agir en Pays Jalignois 271, 272, 280
Association of Canadian Publishers/Ontario Ministry of Culture, Tourism
    and Recreation Library and Community Information Branch 357
Association of Contemporary Japanese Poets (Nihon Gendaishijin Kai) 121
Association des Ecrivains de Langue Française (ADELF) 112
Association des Ecrivains du Rouerque 268, 304, 308
Association Infini 286
Association of Jewish Libraries 349
Association des libraires du Québec 290
Association des librairies spécialisées jeunesse/Association des bibliothécaires français 304
Association for Library Service to Children (American Library Association) 29, 32, 55, 203, 374
Association of Madrid Booksellers 246
Association of Nigerian Authors (ANA) 18, 339
Association of Outdoor Recreation and Education/Idaho State University 196
Association for the Promotion of Japanese Literature (Nihon Bungaku Shinkô Kai) 7, 147
Association for the Promotion of Literature 347
Association pour la Promotion des Prix Médicis 296, 297
Association for the Study of Australian Literature 229, 319, 22, 104
Atlanta Review 18
Aufbau-Verlag 200
Aurealis magazine 20
Auschwitz Foundation 21
Australia Council Literature Board 21
Australian Capital Territory (ACT) Public Library 74
Australian Christian Literature Society 21
Australian Writers' Guild 25
Austrian Federal Culture Dept 23, 24, 97, 119, 217
Authors' Club 96
Aventis – Institut de France 25
Baden-Württemberg /Südwestfunk Baden-Baden 132
Bank of Ireland 148
Bank of New Zealand 27, 28
Bayerische Akademie der Schönen Künste/Robert-Bosch-Stiftung 62
Bayerisches Staatsministerium für Unterricht, Kultur, Wissenschaft und Kunst 341
BBC Radio 3 362
BBC Wildlife Magazine/BBC Worldwide 30
BBC4 145
BBVA/Alfaguara 236
Berlin State Senate 118
Bharatiya Jnanpith 145
Bibliothèque pour Tous 272

Billiton Development Trust/Die Taalsekretariaat/Potchefstroom
    University's Chancellor's Trust Fund 325
Boardman Tasker Charitable Trust 40
Bochumer Krimi Archiv 80
Bologna Book Fair 42
Bologna University 257
Book Publishers Association of Alberta/Writers Guild of Alberta 8
Book Trust 174
Book Trust Scotland 94
BookExpo America Convention 94
Booksellers Association of the UK and Ireland Ltd 25
Booksellers New Zealand/New Zealand Post/Creative New Zealand 203
Booksellers NZ/Book Publishers Association of NZ/NZ Society of Authors 185
Börsenverein des deutschen Buchhandels eV 101
Boston Globe 44
Bouchercon—the World Mystery Convention 13
BP Amoco, in association with the Wildlife Trusts, administered by the Book Trust 45
Brasserie Lipp 273
Bridport Arts Centre 47
Bristol University 347
British Academy 48, 75
British Comparative Literature Association/British Centre for Literary Translation 50
British Council/EXPOPARK 164
British Fantasy Society 50
British Haiku Society/The Great Britain Sasakawa Foundation 324
British Medical Association/Board of Science 39
British Science Fiction Association 51
Bundeskanzleramt-Kunstsektion (Austrian Federal Culture Department) 217
Bundesministerium für Familie, Senioren, Frauen und Jugend/Arbeitskreis
    für Jugendliteratur eV 79, 80
Bundesministerium für Unterricht und Kunst 341
Bungakukai magazine 54
Business Archives Council 367
Café des Deux Magots 277
Café de Flore 281
California Library Association 56
Câmara Brasileira do Livro (Brazilian Book Chamber) 245
Campieillo Foundation 238
Canada Council 57
Canada Council for the Arts/Bank of Montreal 110
Canadian Authors Association (CAA)/Air Canada 54
Canadian Authors Association/Canada Council for the Arts 57
Canadian Booksellers Association 162
Canadian Broadcasting Corporation/Saturday Night Magazine/The Canada Council 59
Canadian Children's Book Centre 36, 95
Canadian Library Association 58
Carl Hanser Verlag 229
Carlos Palanca Foundation Inc 219
Center for the Study of Science Fiction 344
Central News Agency 70
Centre International d'Etudes en Littérature de Jeunesse—Ricochet 300
Centre for Mediterranean Literature (CML) 297
Centro de Estudios de la Cultura Mixteca 261
Centro de Estudios Latinoamericanos Rómulo Gallegos (CELARG) 242, 243, 257

Centro Português da Associação International de Críticos Literários 70
Centrum Broumov.. 51
Cercle Interallié.. 287
Champagne Lanson Père et Fils 273
Charles Veillon Foundation 361
Charta 77 Foundation 332
Chartered Institute of Library and Information Professionals/Whitaker.. 33, 367
Chartered Institute of Library and Information Professionals/Whitaker/Society of Indexers 370
Children's Book Circle 93
Children's Book Council of Australia... 64
Children's Book Council of Australia (Queensland Branch) 36
Children's Book Council of Australia (Victoria Branch).. 66
Children's Book Guild/Washington Post.. 64
Children's Books History Society (CBHS) 78
Children's Folklore Section of the American Folklore Society.. 4
Children's Literature Association (ChLA).. 65, 230
Children's Software Revue and The Bologna Children's Book Fair... 41
China Literature Foundation.. 65
Chinese Dramatists' Association 59
Chinese Writers' Association 168, 176
Christie Brown & Co (a division of Nabisco) 67
Christophers 67
Chûô Kôronsha publishing company 101, 347
City of Bremen 47
City of Buxtehude 54
City of Cologne 41
City of Discovery Campaign/Dundee University 84
City of Düsseldorf... 124
City of Klagenfurt 26
City of Lohja 140
City of Lübeck 176
City of Medellin.. 259
City of Mitaka 78
City of Montreal 114
City of Stuttgart 164
City of Vancouver Office of Cultural Affairs 68
Claremont Graduate University... 358
Cleveland Foundation... 12
Co-operative Children's Book Center.. 382
Coal River Press... 204
Collective Promotion of the Netherlands Book/Collectieve
    Propaganda van het Nederlandse Boek 109
Colorado Review... 71
Columbia School of Journalism 309
Columbia University Graduate School of Journalism 169
Columbia University Graduate School of Journalism/Nieman Foundation 168
Columbia University Trustees.. 26
Commonwealth Foundation.. 71
Comune di Mogliano Veneto.. 237
Conseil général de l'Oise et l'Université de Technologie de Compiègne.. 302
Conseil Général de la Charente.. 298
Conseil Général de la Charente-Maritime 292
Conseil Général de la Gironde/Le Courrier Français 292
Conseil régional de Picardie 295

Conseil de la vie française en Amérique (CVFA) 274
Consejo Nacional para la Cultura y las Artes 257
Consejo Nacional para la Cultura y las Artes de México 242
Consejo Nacional para la Cultura y las Artes/Ediciones S.M. Cóndor 248
Consejo Nacional para la Cultura y las Artes/Instituto Nacional de Bellas
    Artes (INBA)/Sociedad Alfonsina Internacional, AC 243
Consejo Nacional para la Cultura y las Artes/Instituto Nacional de Bellas
    Artes/Universidad Autónoma de Colima 256
Crime Writers Association/The Macallan 76
Crime Writers of Canada 88
Cultura del Comune di Palermo/Fondazione Premio Mondello 246
Cultural Center of the Phillippines (CCP) 75
Cultural Foundation 8
Cumbria Tourist Board 158
Cyngor Llyfrau Cymru/Welsh Books Council 354, 360
Czech Literary Fund 365
Czech Literary Fund/Josef, Marie and Zdenka Hlávkových Foundation 128
Czech PEN Centre 59
Czech Translators' Guild/Czech PEN Club/Union of Czech Authors/Czech Academy
    of Sciences 173
Dachverband Schweizer Lehrerinnen und Lehrer 331
Daily Mail/Biographers' Club 37
Daily Telegraph 15
Danish Academy 6, 30, 38, 315, 333, 337, 343
Darwin Library and Information Service 156
David Berry Trust/Royal Historical Society 33
David Cohen Family Charitable Trust/Arts Council of England 71
David St John Thomas Charitable Trust 353
Dépêche du Midi/Sud Radio/les Editions Privat 301
Deutsche Akademie für Sprache und Dichtung 52, 100, 121, 180, 364
Deutscher Literaturfonds eV 61
Dewan Bahasa dan Pustaka 82
Diputación Provincial de Alicante/Editorial Planeta SA 237
Dirección de Cultura/Departamento de Letras 72
Direccion General del Libro y Biblioteccas, Ministerio de Cultura 239
Docharkheh (Bike) 141
Documentación y Estudios de Mujeres AC (DEMAC) 240
Donner Canadian Foundation 83
Dublin City Council/IMPAC 138
Dungannon Foundation 313
Dutch Section of the International Board on Books for Young People 338
DV 85
Dymocks Pty Ltd 85
Ecole Normale Supérieure de Cachan 291
Ediciones Alfaguara 236
Ediciones Castillo S.A. de C.V. 254
Ediciones Destino SA 234, 237, 240, 255
Ediciones Rialp 235
Ediciones S.M. Cóndor/Consejo Nacional para la Cultura y las Artes 248
Editorial Costa Rica 247, 247, 250
Editorial Planeta SA 233, 234, 258
Editorial Seix Barral 238
Eesti Kultuurkapital 86
Einhard-Stiftung (Einhard Foundation) 137

INDEX OF AWARDING ORGANIZATIONS

El Corte Inglés/Espasa Calpe 259
Electronic Media Network 169
Elie Wiesel Foundation for Humanity 374
Elle Magazine 290
Emecé Editores SA 73
English Centre of International PEN 3
English-Speaking Union of the United States (ESU) 10
Enid Linder Foundation 193
Equipo Mensajero 259
Europe 1 295
European Jewish Publication Society 89
EuroTel 163
Evangelical Christian Publishers Association 108
Evens Foundation 90
F.V.S. Foundation 127
Faber and Faber Ltd 90
Fairlight Inc 92
Federation of Children's Book Groups 63
Fellowship of Australian Writers 93
Feria Internacional del Libro de Guadalajara/Escuela de Escritores SOGEM
    Guadalajara/Asociación de Clubes del Libro, AC/Universidad Católica de Salta, Argentina 250
Festival d'Ambronay 267
Festival Étonnants Voyageurs 269
Festival International de Géographie de Saint-Dié-des-Vosges 307
First National Bank 96
FIT (Fédération Internationale des Traducteurs)/International Federation of Translators 163
FNB Vita/English Academy of Southern Africa 265, 331
Folger Shakespeare Library 225
Folklore Society 47
Fondation Banques CIC pour le livre 291
Fondation Bernheim 294
Fondation La Poste 308
Fondation Marcel Bleustein-Blanchet de la Vocation 292
Fondation Maurice Carême 273
Fondation Nationale de Gérontologie 275
Fondation Paribas (and others) 288
Fondation Prince Pierre de Monaco 292
Fondazione Maria e Goffredo Bellonci 262
Fondazione Nazionale Carlo Collodi 237
Fondazione Premio Laura Oriveto 216
Fondazione Premio Napoli 256
Forward Arts Foundation 97
Foundation for Australian Literary Studies (FALS) 316
Foundation C. F. Ramuz 115
Fraedslurád Reykjavíkur (Educational Council of Reykjavik) 134
France Culture 282
France Télévision 282
Franco-British Society 172
Freundeskreis zur internationalen Förderung literarischer und wissenschaftlicher
    Übersetzungen 45, 373
Friedrich Baur-Stiftung/Land of Bavaria 118
Frogmore Foundation 101
Fundação Biblioteca Nacional/Dept Nacional do Livro 189, 262
Fundação Calouste Gulbenkian 116

Fundação Círculo de Leitores 245, 247
Fundação da Casa de Mateus 240
Fundación ARCIEN 263
Fundación Corripio 253
Fundación Cultural Lya y Luis Cardoza y Aragón, A.C. 236
Fundación Fernando Rielo (Fernando Rielo Foundation) 315
Fundación José Manuel Lara/Editorial Planeta. 257
Fundación Octavio Paz 258
Fundación Príncipe de Asturias 260
Fundacja Nagrody Literackiej NIKE 205
Generalitat de Catalunya 234
George Orwell Memorial Fund/The Political Quarterly 216
Glenfiddich 106
Glimmer Train Press Inc. 107
Government of Queensland 310
Government of South Australia/Jacob's Creek 143
Government of Victoria state, administered by the State Library of Victoria 362
Grafia Ry (Finnish Association of Graphic Design) 154
Griffin Trust for Excellence in Poetry 117
Grinzane Cavour Prize Association 241
Grupo Editorial Vid 243
Guardian 119, 120
Guild of Food Writers 120
Gulf Cooperation Council (GCC) 153
Gyldendal Norsk Forlag AS 121
Gyldendalske Boghandel-Nordisk Forlag AS 121
H. Aschehoug & Co 16, 173, 348
Haidan (The Haiku Podium) 122
Hamilton Haiku Press 29
Harold Hyam Wingate Foundation 145
Haryana Sahitya Akademi (Haryana Academy of Literature) 123
Hastings Writers Group 103
Hauptverband des Österreichischen Buchhandels 87
Helsingin Sanomat 126
Hemispheres/PEN Center USA West 138
Hennessy 283
Hermann-Hesse-Stiftung (Hermann Hesse Foundation) 56
Hiemstra Trust 128
History Today 166
Horst Bienek Stiftung 35
Hungarian Academy of Sciences 102
Icelandic Publishers Association 134
Ikatan Penerbit Indonesia (IKAPI) (Indonesian Book Publishers Association) 4
Imperial Order of the Daughters of the Empire (IODE) 140
Institut de France 272
Institutció de les Lletres Catalanes 137
Institute of Commonwealth Studies 313
Institute of Contemporary History/Wiener Library 98
Institute of Historical Research/Grove Atlantic 137
Instituto Camões/Fundaçao Biblioteca Nacional/Departamento Nacional do Livro 238
Instituto Cubano del Libro 253
Instituto de Cultura de Yucatán (ICY)/Sociedad General de Escritores de México 249
Instituto de Cultura de Yucatán/Universidad Autónoma de Yucatán/Consejo Nacional
    para la Cultura y las Artes/Sociedad General de Escritores de México 248

INDEX OF AWARDING ORGANIZATIONS

Instituto Nacional de Bellas Artes (INBA)/Instituto Michoacano de Cultura 255
International Association of Crime Writers, North American Branch 122
International Balzan Foundation 26
International Board on Books for Young People (IBBY) 11, 65
International Board on Books for Young People (IBBY)/Asahi Shimbun.. 133
International Book Committee (IBC)... 133
International Federation of Translators/Fédération Internationale des Traducteurs (FIT) 281
International League of Antiquarian Booksellers (ILAB)/LILA 134
International PEN 377
International Reading Association 63, 131, 376
Internationale Erich-Fried-Gesellschaft 100
Internationale Jugendbibliothek (International Youth Library) 371
Ireland Fund of Monaco 141
Ireland Funds 170, 379
Irish American Cultural Institute.. 141
Irish Times Ltd 141, 142
Isaac Deutscher Memorial Foundation... 81
J. W. Cappelens Forlag AS 60
Jan Campertstichting (Jan Campert Foundation) 44, 57, 117, 133, 320, 360
Jane Addams Peace Association/Women's International
    League for Peace and Freedom 3
Jewish Book Council.. 195
Jornal Expresso and Unisys 258
Kadan (The Tanka Podium.. 146
Kadokawa Foundation for the Promotion of Culture (Kadokawa Bunka Shinkô Zaidan) 66
Kadokawa Shoten Publishing Co., Ltd.. 204, 380
Kawade Shobô Shinsha publishing company.. 314
Kazakhstan Club of Patrons of the Arts 348
Keats–Shelley Memorial Association/The Folio Society 149
Kerala Sahitya Akademi 151
Kerry Ingredients (a division of Kerry Group PLC)... 151
Kinder- und Jugendtheaterzentrum in der Bundesrepublik Deutschland... 80
King Faisal Foundation 92
Kiriyama Pacific Rim Institute.. 153
Kjeld Abellfondet/Danish Academy 1
Kodansha 207
Kodansha/UNESCO 207
Koninklijke Academie voor Nederlandse Taal- en Letterkunde... 298
Korean Culture and Fine Arts Foundation 155
Kraszna-Krausz Foundation 156
Kulturbüro der Stadt Dortmund 321
L'Express and France Loisirs 288
Lake House Bookshop.. 374
Lambda Literary Foundation 158
Landeshauptstadt München/ Verband Bayerischer Verlage und Buchhandlungen............................. 103
Landslaget for Språklig Samling.. 341
Lannan Foundation 159
Lao She Art and Culture Foundation... 160
Le Monde/Salon du livre de jeunesse 270
Le Soir 303
League of Canadian Poets.. 159
Librairie Le Scribe 267
Library and Information Association of New Zealand Aotearoa (LIANZA) 69, 106, 165, 350
Library and Information Service of Western Australia.. 369

Ligue des Familles 307
Literary Academy of Modern Russian Belles Lettres/Rosbank 118
Literary Review 26
Literary Translators' Association of Canada 105
Logovaz-Triumph Foundation 357
Long Island University 232
Lontar Foundation 167
Los Angeles Times 167
Lotus Press Inc. 166
Lower Austria Culture Dept 380
Maatschappij der Nederlandse Letterkunde (MNL)
    (Dutch Literature Association) 31, 99, 149, 264, 317, 360
Macmillan Children's Books 171
Macmillan Education and Picador 171
Mairie de Garches 284
Maison des Ecrivains Etrangers et des Traducteurs de Saint-Nazaire 270
Maison Henri Deschamps 291
Malay Language Council of Singapore 358
Malaysian Scholarly Book Publishers Council (MAPIM/ Fuji-Xerox 222
Malice Domestic international mystery convention 5
Man Group 174
Manila Critics Circle 175
Manitoba Writers' Guild/Association of Manitoba Book Publishers 175
Marsh ChristianTrust 24
Martin Bodmer-Siftung für einen Gottfried Keller-Preis 150
Media Tenor South Africa/Institute for Media Analysis 95
Ministère de la Culture et de la Communication (Ministry of Culture and Communication) 115
Ministerio per i Beni Culturali e Ambientali 182
Ministerio de Cultura 252
Ministerio de Educación, Cultura y Deporte 251, 253, 254, 255
Ministerium für Schule und Weiterbildung,
    Wissenschaft und Forschung des Landes Nordrhein-Westfalen 125
Ministry of Culture 87, 285
Ministry of Culture and Education 19
Ministry of Culture and Islamic Guidance 377
Ministry of Culture/Media and Grants Secretariat 12, 77
Ministry of Culture/Slovak Commission for UNESCO/BIBIANA
    International House of Art for Children 35
Ministry of Education 252, 342, 345
Ministry of Education and National Culture 263
Ministry of Youth and Sports 293
Mobil Corporation/LSU Press 222
Modern Language Association of America (MLA) 70, 155, 162, 181, 184, 185, 220,
                                                                    326, 326, 327, 328, 330, 334
Modern Poetry Association 162
Monsudar Printing House 185
Mordechai Bernstein Literary Prizes Association 33
Mrs Giles Whiting Foundation 372
Mühlheim Town Council 190
Myanmar Writers and Journalists Association 191
Mystery Writers of America 231
Mythopoeic Society 192
Nasionale Boekhandel Publishing Group (Tafelberg) 180
National Academy of Sciences of Ukraine 335

INDEX OF AWARDING ORGANIZATIONS

National Assembly 268
National Book Critics Circle 195
National Book Development Committee of Thailand 194
National Book Development Committee of Thailand/Ministry of Education 356
National Book Development Council of Singapore (NBDCS) 85, 337
National Book Foundation 194
National Book Service 58, 131
National Centre for Research into Children's Literature/Marsh Christian Trust 177
National Council of Teachers of English (NCTE) 199, 215
National Library of Canada 62, 104, 146
National Writers Union of Ukraine (NSPU) 38, 100, 130, 174, 198, 337, 359
Native Writers Circle of the Americas 198, 210
Nederlandse Taalunie 264
Nepal Sikshya Parisad (Nepal Education Council) 34
Nestlé 199
New Brunswick Arts Board 201
New Letters magazine 201
New Millennium Writings Anthology 202
New Writer 202
New Writing North 211
New York Public Library/Ezra Jack Keats Foundation 149
New York State Historical Association 98
New Zealand Society of Authors 186, 187, 188, 338
NewsFam 295
Nobel Foundation 205
Noma Service Association 206
Non-Fiction Literature Authors' Club 142
Nordic Council, Swedish Delegation 208
Nordisk skolebibliotekarforening 208
Norlis Bokhandel AS 122
Norma Ediciones/Consejo Nacional para la Cultura y las Artes 245
Norsk Kritikerlags 209, 209
Norsk Skolebibliotekargorening 338
Norsk Språkråd (Norwegian Language Council) 209
Norske Akademi for Sprog og Litteratur (Norwegian Academy for Language and Literature) 209
Norske Bokhandlerforening (Association of Norwegian Bookdealers) 41
Norske Bokklubbene 210
Norske Forfatterforening (Norwegian Authors' Union) 348
Norske forleggerforeningen (Norwegian Publishers Association) 45
Norske Samlaget 180, 323
Northern Rock Foundation 210
Norwegian Association of Literary Translators 29
Norwegian Culture Department 157
NRK (Norsk Rikskringkasting) 218
NRK (Norsk Rikskringkasting)/Rivertonklubben 316
NSW Ministry for the Arts 211, 212
Office of the Hungarian President 155
Office du Livre on Poitou-Charentes 296
Office of the National Culture Commission, Ministry of Education 193
Oktober Forlag AS/Kulturfondet Ikaros a/s 213
Omnium Cultural 233
Ontario Arts Council Foundation 61
Ontario Arts Council Foundation/Canadian Booksellers' Association 331
Orange, administered by Book Trust 214

Organización Española para Libro Infantily Juvenil (OEPLI) 160
Organization of American Historians (OAH) 36, 215, 352
Osaka Association for the Promotion of Literature (Osaka Bungaku Shinkô-kai)............... 213
Oscar Moore Foundation 189
Östersundsposten 217
Ottakar's Bookshops/Faber & Faber... 218
Otto Gelsteds Mindefond/Danish Academy.. 102
Otto Stoessl-Stiftung (Otto Stoessl Foundation).. 343
Pakistan Academy of Letters...10, 34, 53, 93, 140, 152, 179, 196, 333
Pakistan Ministry of Education.. 264
Pakistan Writers Guild 3
Pakokku U Ohn Pe Literary Award Trust Fund 219
Parco Nazionale del Circeo 244
Paris Film Festival 275
Parlement de la Communauté Française de Belgique.. 300
Patrimonio Nacional y la Universidad de Salamanca 260
Peer Poetry Magazine... 221
PEN American Center... 154, 223, 226, 228
PEN American Center/Vladimir Nabokov Foundation... 227
PEN Center USA West.. 224
PEN New England 126
Permanent Trustee Company Ltd... 182
Phelps-Stoke Fund 130
Poetry Book Society 87
Poetry Life 231
Poetry London 232
Poetry Society... 198
Poetry Society of America 40, 44, 61, 92, 101, 126, 169, 179, 334, 375, 376, 378
Polish PEN Club 220, 343
Portico Library Trust.. 232
Premio Letterario Isola d'Elba – Rafaello Brignetti 246
Preussische Seehandlung... 32
Prime Minister's Fund for Hebrew Literature Prizes.. 265
Prins Bernhard Fonds (Prince Bernhard Cultural Foundation)... 205
Private Eye Writers of America 333
Private Eye Writers of America/St Martin's Press.. 266
Publishing News.. 48
Pushcart Press... 309
QB World Books 152
Québec Ministère de la Culture et des Communications. 276
Queen's University Drama Department... 364
Radio France.. 295
Radio France International... 302
Rajasthan Urdu Academy 311
Ramon Magsaysay Award Foundation 173
Rancage Foundation 312
Random House/Michener Center for Writers.. 181
Raymond Chandler Society.. 62
Real Academia Española 241, 260, 261
Real Writers/the Book Place 313
Red Rock Review.. 358
Rendez-vous de l'histoire.. 269
Rhys Davies Trust/Welsh Academy 314
Riksmalsforbundet 315

INDEX OF AWARDING ORGANIZATIONS

Rio Tinto Zinc plc 367
River Styx Magazine 316
Rockefeller University 353
Rocket Publishing 69
Romantic Novelists Association 317
Romantic Novelists' Association/Parker Pen 221
Royal Historical Society 9, 105, 372
Royal National Theatre Foundation/Arts Council of England 180
Royal Nepal Academy 318
Royal Society of Canada 136, 230
Royal Society of Literature 32, 125, 130, 266
Royal Society of Medicine 339
RTBF Radio 272
RTL/Lire 115
Russian Academy of Arts 210
Russian Academy of Science 310
Russian Booker Foundation/Open Russia 43
Russian Federation in Arts and Letters 342
RÚV (Icelandic State Radio) 320
S. Godage & Brothers 107
Sahitya Akademi (Indian Academy of Literature) 321
Salisbury Arts Centre 152
Salon du livre de Montréal 276
Salon Régional du Livre de Jeunesse de Troyes/Conseil Général de l'Aube 305
Salon Régional du Livre de Jeunesse de Troyes/Maison du Boulanger 274
Saltire Society 322
Saltire Society/Times Educational Supplement Scotland 322
Salzburg Regional Government 312, 355
Salzburger Landesregierung 312
San José State University English Department 53
Sarabande Books 172, 189
Saskatchewan Writers Guild/Saskatchewan Publishers Group/Saskatchewan
    Library Association 324
Schweizerische Schillerstiftung/Fondation Schiller Suisse 119
Science Fiction and Fantasy Writers of America, Inc (SFWA) 199
Science Fiction Research Association 231
Science Fiction Romance Newletter 323
Scotland on Sunday 170
Scottish Arts Council 332
Scottish Arts Council/University of Edinburgh 37
Scottish Book Trust 38
Secretaría de Cultura de la Nación 251
Secretaría de Cultura/Sociedad General de Escritores de México/Instituto Politécnico Nacional 74
Secrétariat du Prix Émile-Nelligan 299
Seidosha and Kadokawa Shoten 192
Semaine Nationale de la Culture(SNC) 114
Shinchô Society for the Promotion of the Literary Arts (Shinchô Bungei Shinkô Kai) 335, 182
Singapore Malay Language Council 13
Slovenian Writers' Association 363
Société civile des auteurs multimedia (SCAM) 271, 289
Société des Gens de Lettres (SDGL) 294
Société des Gens de Lettres de France 112, 114, 270, 276, 281, 299, 301, 306, 308
Société Nouvelle d'Exploitation de la Tour Eiffel (SNTE) 306
Society for the Promotion of Japanese Literature (Nihon Bungaku Shinkô Kai) 193, 218

Society for Theatre Research 352
Society of American Historians 221
Society of Authors 66, 89, 117, 125, 135, 172, 321, 324, 344, 356, 357
Society of Children's Book Writers and Illustrators 108
Society of School Librarians International... 339
Soho Theatre and Writers Centre 28
Soho Theatre and Writers Centre/City of Westminster/Getty Images 370
Somerset Maugham Trust Fund/Society of Authors 179
Sonrisa Vertical, Tusquets Editores 262
Soong Ching Ling Foundation 340
South African Institute for Librarianship & Information Science/Suid-Afrikaanse
    Instituut vir Biblioteek- en Inligtingkunde... 131, 148
South and Mid Wales Association of Writers 264
Southampton College, Long Island University.. 342
Spectator 192
Spoken Word Publishing Association (SWPA).. 346
Spolecnost Franze Kafky (Franz Kafka Society)/Prague City Council... 146
St Martin's Press... 341
Stadtrat von Solothurn... 164
State Library of NSW Press 75
Stichting P. C. Hooft-prijs 352
Stichting P. C. Hooft-prijs voor Letterkunde 131
Stiftung Alfred-Döblin-Preis/Günter Grass 82
Suid-Afrikaanse Akademie vir Wetenskap en Kuns
    (South African Academy for Science and Arts)..................................... 6, 44, 127, 176, 233, 330, 354
Sunday Telegraph 344
Sunday Times... 344
Suomen kirjasäätiö (Finland Book Foundation)... 94
Svensk biblioteksförening (Swedish Library Association) 12, 129
Svenska Dagbladet... 345
Svenska Förläggareföreningen (Swedish Publishers' Association)... 20
Sveriges Författarförbund (Swedish Writers Union) 147
Sveriges Radio 346
Swedish Academy... 31, 42, 83, 150, 208, 219, 343
Syndicat national des dépositaires de presse 296
Tafelberg Publishers, LitNet and RSG... 323
TBS Britannica... 147
TDK 349
Tel-Aviv—Yafo Municipality.. 35
Texas Institute of Letters.. 351
Thomas Cook Group 353
Tiden Norsk Forlag AS... 353
Tintanueva Editores 255
Tokuma Shoten publishing company 205
Town of Vichy/Association Internationale des Amis de Valery Larbaud.. 289
Toyota/Children's Literature Foundation.. 355
Traditional Writers' Guild 235
Translators Assocation 96, 263, 330, 332, 334, 350, 364
Translators' Guild (Obec prekladatelu)/Ministry of Culture/Czech Literature Foundation 146
Truman State University Press.. 88
Trustees of the Calvin and Rose G. Hoffmann Prize 129
Turkish Language Institute (Turk Dil Kurumu).. 350
Údarás na Gaeltachta.. 111
UNESCO 147, 359

INDEX OF AWARDING ORGANIZATIONS

Union of Bulgarian Writers 139
Union Nationale Culture et Bibliothèques pour Tous 298
Universidad Autónoma de Ciudad Juárez 249
Universidad Autónoma del Estado de México 254
Universidad Politécnica de Cataluña (UPC) 263
Universitätsbuchhandlung Bouvier 76
University of Akron Press 7
University of British Columbia (UBC) 359
University of California 63
University of Chicago 213
University of Georgia Press 212
University of Guadalajara 73
University of Lausanne, Faculty of Literature 277
Universo de El Búho 253
Vaka Helgafell 122
Vaka Helgafell/EDDA 360
Val-Tech Media 378
Ver Poets 362
Vysehrad Publishers 365
W. H. Smith PLC 366
Wandsworth Council/Roehampton University of Surrey/Waterstone's 166
Warehouse Theatre 139
Websters International/Circle of Wine Writers 382
Wellcome Trust/ Weidenfeld & Nicolson 368
West Coast Book Prize Society 49
Whitbread/Karen Earl Sponsorship 371
William Hill 375
Wolfson Foundation 376
Women in Publishing 220
World Haiku Club 39
World Literature Today/University of Oklahoma 200
World Science Fiction Convention (Worldcon) 132
World Science Fiction Society (WSFS)/Davis Publications/Dell Publications 57
Writer's Digest 378
Writers' Alliance of Newfoundland and Labrador 379
Writers' Development Trust 183
Writers' Federation of Nova Scotia 19, 124, 314
Writers' International 377
Writers' Union of the Philippines 164
Writers' Development Trust 89
Yomiuri Shimbun Company 380
Yorkshire Post Newspapers Ltd 381
Yoshikawa Eiji Citizens' Cultural Promotion Association
    (Yoshikawa Eiji Kokumin Bunka Shinkô Kai) 381
Young Adult Library Services Association (YALSA) 9
Youth Libraries Group 60, 116
Youth Services Forum of the Virginia Library Association 144
Zimbabwe International Book Fair 382
Zimbabwe International Book Fair/Kingdom Securities Holdings Ltd 4
Zweites Deutsches Fernsehen (ZDF) 17

INDEX OF AWARDS BY COUNTRY

Australia

A. A. Phillips Prize.. 229
Aurealis Awards 20
Australia Council Literature Board Emeritus Awards.. 21
Australian Christian Book of the Year... 21
Australian Christian Children's Book of the Year   *see* Australian Christian Book of the Year
Australian Literature Society Gold Medal... 22
Australian Science Fiction Achievement Awards—Ditmars 22
Australian/Vogel Literary Award.. 23
Awgie Awards.. 25
BILBY—Books I Love Best Yearly—Award 36
C. H. Currey Memorial Fellowship 75
Children's Book of the Year Awards.. 64
Chrichton Award for Book Illustration... 66
Colin Roderick Prize for Australian Literature 316
Cool Awards.. 74
Currey (C. H.) Memorial Fellowship   *see* C. H. Currey Memorial Fellowship
CYBER—Children's Yearly Best-Ever Reads—Award 77
Dennis (C .J.) Prize for Poetry   *see* Victorian Premier's Literary Awards
Ditmars   *see* Australian Science Fiction Achievement Awards—Ditmars
Dymocks Children's Choice Awards.. 85
Elder (Ann) Poetry Award   *see* Fellowship of Australian Writers Literature Awards
Fairlight Talking Book Award of New South Wales... 92
Fellowship of Australian Writers Literature Awards.. 93
Franklin (Miles) Award   *see* Miles Franklin Award
Gleebooks Prize for Literary or Cultural Criticism   *see* NSW Premier's Literary Awards
Grace Leven Prize for Poetry... 161
ILAB-LILA Bibliography Prize.. 134
Jacob's Creek World Food Media Awards 143
Kathleen Mitchell Award 182
KOALA—Kids Own Australian Literature Awards... 154
KROC—Kids Reading Oz Choice—Award 156
Ladles   *see* Jacob's Creek World Food Media Awards
Leven (Grace) Prize for Poetry   *see* Grace Leven Prize for Poetry
McNamara (Peter) Convenors' Award for Excellence   *see* Aurealis Awards
Mary Gilmore Award 104
Melbourne University Literature Award
     see Fellowship of Australian Writers Literature Awards
Miles Franklin Award 100
Mitchell (Kathleen) Award   *see* Kathleen Mitchell Award
Newcastle Poetry Prize... 204
NSW Premier's Literary Awards... 211
NSW Writer's Fellowship.. 212
Palmer (Nettie) Prize for Non-fiction   *see* Victorian Premier's Literary Awards
Palmer (Vance) Prize for Fiction   *see* Victorian Premier's Literary Awards
Phillips (A. A.) Prize   *see* A. A. Phillips Prize
Pownall (Eve) Award for Information Books   *see* Children's Book of the Year Awards
Queensland Premier's Literary Awards 310
Roderick (Colin) Prize for Australian Literature
          see Colin Roderick Prize for Australian Literature
Russell (Walter McRae) Award   *see* Walter McRae Russell Award

Slessor (Kenneth) Prize for Poetry   *see* NSW Premier's Literary Awards

Stead (Christina) Award   *see* Fellowship of Australian Writers Literature Awards

Stewart (Douglas) Prize for Non-fiction   *see* NSW Premier's Literary Awards

TDK Australian Audio Book Awards 349

Trinick (Trish) Prize   *see* TDK Australian Audio Book Awards

Turner (Ethel) Prize for Young People's Literature   *see* NSW Premier's Literary Awards

Victorian Premier's Literary Awards 362

Walter McRae Russell Award 319

WAYRBA—West Australian Young Readers' Book Award 368

Western Australian Premier's Book Awards 369

Wrightson (Patricia) Prize   *see* NSW Premier's Literary Awards

YARA—Young Australian Readers' Awards 380

Austria

Astrid Lindgren Translation Prize 163

Austrian Award of Merit for Children's Literature 23

Austrian National Award for Poetry for Children 24

Austrian National Children's and Juvenile Book Awards 24

Bachmann (Ingeborg) Preis   *see* Ingeborg Bachmann Preis

Ehrenpreis des Österreichischen Buchhandels für Toleranz in Denken und Handeln 87

Erich-Fried-Preis 100

Förderungspreis für Literatur 97

Fried (Erich) Preis   *see* Erich-Fried-Preis

Georg Trakl Preis für Lyrik 355

Grosser Österreichischer Staatspreis für Literatur 119

IBC International Book Award 133

Ingeborg Bachmann Preis 26

Lindgren (Astrid) Translation Prize   *see* Astrid Lindgren Translation Prize

Manès Sperber-Preis für Literatur 341

Österreichischer Staatspreis für Europäische Literatur 217

Österreichischer Staatspreis für Literarische Übersetzer 217

Otto Stoessl-Preis 343

Prix FIT Aurore Boréale de la traduction 281

Rauriser Förderungspreis 312

Rauriser Literaturpreis 312

Sperber (Manès) Preis für Literatur   *see* Manès Sperber-Preis für Literatur

Stoessl (Otto) Preis   *see* Otto Stoessl-Preis

Trakl (Georg) Preis für Lyrik   *see* Georg Trakl Preis für Lyrik

Willner (Ernst) Prize   *see* Ingeborg Bachmann Preis

Würdigungspreis für Literatur 380

Argentina

Concurso Literario Premio Emecé 73

Echeverría (Esteban), Premio   *see* Premio Esteban Echeverría

Premio Academia Nacional de la Historia 235

Premio Esteban Echeverría 241

Premio Nacional de Literatura 251

Premios Literarios Fundación ARCIEN 263

Belgium

Auschwitz Foundation Prize 21

Bergmann (Anton) Prix   *see* Prix Anton Bergmann

Bernheim (Emile) Prix de littérature   *see* Prix de littérature Émile Bernheim

Carême (Maurice), Prix de Poésie
       see Prix de Poésie et Prix d'Etudes Littéraires Maurice Carême

Cumont (Franz), Prix   *see* Prix Franz Cumont

Discailles (Ernest), Prix   *see* Prix Ernest Discailles

Duculot (Jules) Prix   *see* Prix Jules Duculot

Duvivie (Charles), Prix   *see* Prix Charles Duvivie

Evens Foundation European Prize for Literature 90

Gantrelle (Joseph), Prix   *see* Prix Joseph Gantrelle

Grand Prix de Littérature Française hors de France/Prix Fondation Nessim Habif 113

Habif (Nessim), Prix Fondation
       see Grand Prix de Littérature Française hors de France/Prix Fondation Nessim Habif

Houziaux (Joseph), Prix   *see* Prix Joseph Houziaux

Leclère (Léon), Prix   *see* Prix Léon Leclère

Merghelynck (Arthur), Prix   *see* Prix Arthur Merghelynck

Prix Anton Bergmann 271

Prix Arthur Merghelynck 298

Prix Auguste Teirlinck 305

Prix Baron de Saint-Genois 304

Prix Bernard Versele 307

Prix Bloc-Notes 272

Prix Charles Duvivie 278

Prix Ernest Discailles 278

Prix Franz Cumont 276

Prix Goblet d'Alviella 284

Prix Joseph Gantrelle 283

Prix Joseph Houziaux 286

Prix Jules Duculot 278

Prix Littéraire du Parlement de la Communauté Française de Belgique 300

Prix de littérature Émile Bernheim 294

Prix Léon Leclère 290

Prix de Poésie et Prix d'Etudes Littéraires Maurice Carême 273

Prix Victor-Rossel 303

Rossel (Victor) Prix   *see* Prix Victor-Rossel

Saint-Genois (Baron de) Prix   *see* Prix Baron de Saint-Genois

Teirlinck (Auguste), Prix   *see* Prix Auguste Teirlinck

Versele, Prix Bernard   *see* Prix Bernard Versele

Brazil

Academia Brasileira de Letras Children's Literature Prize 1

Academia Brasileira de Letras Essay Prize 2

Academia Brasileira de Letras Fiction Prize 2

Monteiro Lobato Award 189

Prêmio Academia Brasileira de Letras de Poesia 235

Prêmio Jabuti 245

Prêmio Machado de Assis 250

Prêmio Paulo Rónai 262

Rónai (Paulo), Premio   *see* Prêmio Paulo Rónai

Bulgaria

Aleko Konstantinov Literary Prize 154

International Vaptsarov Prize 139

Konstantinov (Aleko) Literary Prize   *see* Aleko Konstantinov Literary Prize

Vaptsarov (International) Prize   *see* International Vaptsarov Prize

Burkina Faso

Grand Prix National des Arts et des Lettres (GPNAL) 114

Canada

Alberta Book Awards 8

Amazon.com/Books in Canada First Novel Award 10

Amelia Frances Howard-Gibbon Illustrator's Award 131

Annett (R. Ross) Award for Children's Literature   *see* Alberta Book Awards

Arthur Ellis Awards 88

Atlantic Poetry Prize 19

Bilson (Geoffrey) Award   *see* Geoffrey Bilson Award for Historical Fiction for Young People

Bolt (Carol) Drama Award   *see* Canadian Authors Association Literary Awards

British Columbia Book Prizes 49

CAA Air Canada Award 54

Canada-Switzerland Literary Prize 57

Canadian Authors Association Literary Awards 57

Canadian Library Association Book of the Year for Children Award 58

Canadian Library Association Young Adult Book Award 58

Canadian Literary Awards 59

Chalmers (Floyd S.) Canadian Play Awards
     see Chalmers Awards for Creativity and Excellence in the Arts

Chalmers (Jack) Poetry Award   *see* Canadian Authors Association Literary Awards

Chalmers Awards for Creativity and Excellence in the Arts 61

Chapters/Books in Canada Award 62

Christie's (Mr) Book Awards   *see* Mr Christie's Book Awards

City of Vancouver Book Award 68

Couture (Marcel) Prix   *see* Prix Marcel-Couture

David (Athanase) Prix   *see* Prix Athanase-David

Donner Prize 83

Downey (Violet) Book Award   *see* IODE Violet Downey Book Award

Eggleston (Wilfred) Award for Non-Fiction   *see* Alberta Book Awards

Ellis (Arthur) Awards   *see* Arthur Ellis Awards

Engel (Marian) Award   *see* Marian Engel Award

Evans (Hubert) Non-Fiction Prize   *see* British Columbia Book Prizes

Evelyn Richardson Non-fiction Award 314

Fleck (Norma) Award for Children's Non-Fiction
     see Norma Fleck Award for Children's Non-Fiction

Geoffrey Bilson Award for Historical Fiction for Young People 36

Gerald Lampert Award 159

Giller Award 104

Glassco (John) Prize for Literary Translation
     see John Glassco Prize for Literary Translation

Governor General's Literary Awards 110

Grand prix du livre de Montréal 114

Grand Prix de la Science-Fiction et du Fantastique Québécois 116
Grandbois (Alain) Prix   *see* Prix Alain-Grandbois
Griffin Poetry Prize 117
Harbourfront Reading Series' short stories award   *see* Journey Prize
Head Raddall (Thomas) Fiction Prize   *see* Thomas Head Raddall Fiction Prize
Herb Barrett Award 29
Herman Voaden National Playwriting Competition 364
Howard-Gibbon (Amelia Frances) Illustrator's Award
     see Amelia Frances Howard-Gibbon Illustrator's Award
Innis-Gérin Medal 136
IODE Violet Downey Book Award 140
John Glassco Prize for Literary Translation/Prix de Traduction John-Glassco 105
Journey Prize 146
Jubilee Award for Short Stories   *see* Canadian Authors Association Literary Awards
Kreisel (Henry) Award for Best First Book   *see* Alberta Book Awards
Lampert (Gerald) Award   *see* Gerald Lampert Award
Leacock (Stephen) Memorial Medal for Humour
     see Stephen Leacock Memorial Medal for Humour
Libris Awards 162
Lorne Pierce Medal 230
McNally Robinson Book of the Year Award   *see* Manitoba Literary Awards
McTavish Sykes (Eileen) Award for Best First Book   *see* Manitoba Literary Awards
Manitoba Literary Awards 175
Marian Engel Award 89
Mitchell (W. O.) Prize   *see* W. O. Mitchell Prize
Mr Christie's Book Awards 67
Nelligan (Émile) Prix   *see* Prix Émile-Nelligan
New Brunswick Excellence in the Arts Awards 201
Norma Fleck Award for Children's Non-Fiction 95
Nowlan (Alden) Award   *see* New Brunswick Excellence in the Arts Awards
Pierce (Lorne) Medal   *see* Lorne Pierce Medal
Poirier (Pascal) Award   *see* New Brunswick Excellence in the Arts Awards
Prix Alain-Grandbois 285
Prix Athanase-David 276
Prix Champlain 274
Prix Émile-Nelligan 299
Prix des Libraires 290
Prix Marcel-Couture 276
Richardson (Evelyn) Non-fiction Award   *see* Evelyn Richardson Non-fiction Award
Ruth Schwartz Children's Book Award 331
Saskatchewan Book Awards 324
Schwartz (Ruth) Children's Book Award   *see* Ruth Schwartz Children's Book Award
Scorer (Mary) Award   *see* Manitoba Literary Awards
Stephen Leacock Memorial Medal for Humour 161
Thomas Head Raddall Fiction Prize 124
Toronto Book Awards 355
Trillium Book Award/Prix Trillium 357
UBC Medal for Canadian Biography/UBC President's Medal in Biography 359
Voaden (Herman) National Playwriting Competition
     see Herman Voaden National Playwriting Competition
W. O. Mitchell Prize 183
Wilson (Ethel) Fiction Priz   *see* British Columbia Book Prizes
Writers' Alliance of Newfoundland and Labrador Provincial Book Awards 379

Chile

Premio Nacional de Literatura 252

China (People's Republic)

China Literature Foundation Awards 65
Chuang (C. W.) Literary Prize   see China Literature Foundation Awards
Lao She Literary Prize 160
Lu Xun Literature Awards 168
Mao Dun Literary Prize 176
Sino-American Literary Exchange Prize   see China Literature Foundation Awards
Soong Ching Ling Children's Literature Prize 340

Colombia

Premio de Poesía Ciudad de Medellín 259

Costa Rica

Lyra (Carmen), Premio   see Premio Literario Carmen Lyra
Premio Hispanoamericano de Poesía Sor Juana Inés de la Cruz 242
Premio Literario Carmen Lyra 250
Premio Literario Editorial Costa Rica 247
Premio Literario Joven Creación 247

Cuba

Arguedas (José Maria) Prize   see Premio Casa de las Americas
Estrada (Ezequiel Martinez) Prize   see Premio Casa de las Americas
Lima (José Lezama) Prize   see Premio Casa de las Americas
Premio Casa de las Americas 239
Premio Nacional de Literatura 253

Czech Republic

Broumovska literarni cena 51
Čapek (Karel) Award for Literary Achievement
       see Karel Čapek Award for Literary Achievement
Cena Josefa Hlavky 128
Franz Kafka Prize 146
Hlavky (Josef) Prize   see Cena Josefa Hlavky
Ivanov (Miroslav) Award for Non-Fiction
       see Miroslav Ivanov Award for Non-Fiction
Josef Jungmann Prize 146
Kafka (Franz) Prize   see Franz Kafka Prize
Karel Čapek Award for Literary Achievement 59
Magnesia Litera Awards 173
Miroslav Ivanov Award for Non-Fiction 142
Premia Bohemica 235
Scholz (Hugo) Prize   see Broumovska literarni cena
Stryjova (Marie) Prize   see Broumovska literarni cena
Výrocní ceny Nadace 365

Vysehrad Publishers Awards 365
Wittig (Joseph) Prize   *see* Broumovska literarni cena

Denmark

Abell (Kjeld) Prisen   *see* Kjeld Abell Prisen
Akademiets Oversætterpris 6
Andersen (H. C.) Prize   *see* H. C. Andersen Prize
Beatriceprisen 30
Blixen (Karen) Medaljen   *see* Karen Blixen Medaljen
Danish Ministry of Culture Children's Book Prize 77
Gelsted (Otto) prisen   *see* Otto Gelstedprisen
Gyldendal (Soren) Prize   *see* Soren Gyldendal Prize
H. C. Andersen Prize 12
Karen Blixen Medaljen 38
Kjeld Abell Prisen 1
Klaus Rifbjergs Debutantpris for Lyrik 315
Otto Gelstedprisen 102
Rifbjergs (Klaus) Debutantpris for Lyrik   *see* Klaus Rifbjergs Debutantpris for Lyrik
Selskabets Pris 333
Silas Prisen 337
Soren Gyldendal Prize 121
Store Pris 343

Dominican Republic

Premio Nacional de Literatura 253

Egypt

Egyptian Literary Award 87

Estonia

Eesti Kirjanduse Aastapreemia 86

Finland

Finlandia Award 94
Helsingin Sanomat Literary Award 126
Internationella Eeva Joenpelto-Litteraturpriset 140
Joenpelto (Eeva), Internationella Litteraturpriset
    see Internationella Eeva Joenpelto-Litteraturpriset
Koivu (Rudolf) Prize   *see* Rudolf Koivu Prize
Lydecken (Arvid) Prize   *see* Suomen Nuorisokirjailijat Ry Awards
Pääskynen   *see* Suomen Nuorisokirjailijat Ry Awards
Rudolf Koivu Prize 154
State Prizes for Literature 342
Suomalaisen kirjallisuuden tiedotuskeskus 345
Suomen Nuorisokirjailijat Ry Awards 345
Topelius Prize   *see* Suomen Nuorisokirjailijat Ry Awards

France

Artaud (Antonin) Prix   *see* Prix Antonin Artaud
Audiffred (François-Joseph), Prix   *see* Prix François-Joseph Audiffred
Audoux (Marguerite), Prix   *see* Prix Marguerite Audoux
Augustin-Thierry, Prix   *see* Prix Augustin-Thierry
Bataillon (Laure) Prix   *see* Prix Laure Bataillon
Bayon (Daniel), Prix   *see* Prix Daniel Bayon
Billetdoux (François) Prix   *see* Prix François Billetdoux
Castex (Louis) Prix   *see* Prix Louis Castex
Coindreau (Maurice-Edgar) Prix   *see* Prix Maurice-Edgar Coindreau
de Nerval (Gérard), Prix   *see* Prix Gérard de Nerval
De Troyes (Chrétien), Prix   *see* Prix Chrétien-de-Troyes
Fallet (René), Prix   *see* Prix René Fallet
Féval (Paul), Grand Prix   *see* Grand Prix Paul Féval de Littérature Populaire
Freustié (Jean), Prix   *see* Prix Jean Freustié
Gal (Henri), Grand Prix de Littérature   *see* Grand Prix de Littérature Henri Gal
Gautier (Théophile) Prix   *see* Prix Théophile Gautier
Genevoix (Maurice) Prix   *see* Prix Maurice-Genevoix
Gironde, Prix Littéraire   *see* Prix Littéraire de la Gironde
Grand Prix de Biographie de l'Académie Française
     see Prix Littéraires de l'Académie Française
Grand Prix de la Francophonie 112
Grand Prix Halperine-Kaminsky 112
Grand Prix Littéraire de l'Afrique Noire... 112
Grand Prix Littéraire Poncetton 112
Grand Prix de Littérature Henri Gal 113
Grand Prix de Littérature Paul Morand 113
Grand Prix National des Lettres... 115
Grand Prix Paul Féval de Littérature Populaire 281
Grand Prix de Poésie de l'Académie Française   *see* Prix Littéraires de l'Académie Française
Grand Prix du Roman de l'Académie Française   *see* Prix Littéraires de l'Académie Française
Grand Prix RTL-Lire 115
Grand Prix Thyde Monnier.. 114
Julien (Stanislas), Prix   *see* Prix Stanislas Julien
Kalinga Prize 147
Kessel (Joseph) Prix   *see* Prix Joseph Kessel
Lanson (Champagne) Prix   *see* Prix du Champagne Lanson
Larbaud (Valéry), Prix   *see* Prix Valéry Larbaud
Le Heurteur (Claude) Prix   *see* Prix Claude Le Heurteur
Monnet (Jean), Prix   *see* Prix Jean Monnet de littérature européenne
Monnier (Thyde), Grand Prix   *see* Grand Prix Thyde Monnier
Montalte (Louis) Prix de Poésie   *see* Prix de Poésie Louis Montalte
Morand (Paul), Grand Prix   *see* Grand Prix de Littérature Paul Morand
Privat (Edouard), Prix   *see* Prix Edouard Privat
Prix de l'Académie des Sciences, Arts et Belles Lettres de Dijon 267
Prix d'Ambronay.. 267
Prix Amerigo Vespucci.. 307
Prix des Amis du Monde diplomatique.. 267
Prix des Amis du Scribe 267
Prix Antonin Artaud 268
Prix Apollinaire 268
Prix de l'Assemblée Nationale 268
Prix Astrolabe–Etonnants Voyageurs.. 269

Prix Augustin-Thierry 269
Prix Baobab de l'album 270
Prix Baudelaire 270
Prix Bordin 272
Prix Bourbonnais.. 272
Prix Cazes Brasserie Lipp.. 273
Prix du Champagne Lanson 273
Prix Charles Vildrac de la Poésie.. 308
Prix Chronos de Littérature pour la Jeunesse 275
Prix Chrétien-de-Troyes 274
Prix Ciné Roman Carte Noire 275
Prix des Cinq Continents de la francophonie 275
Prix Claude Le Heurteur 289
Prix Claude Sernet... 304
Prix Daniel Bayon.. 271
Prix Décembre 277
Prix des Deux-Magots.. 277
Prix Edouard Privat... 301
Prix Erckmann-Chatrian.. 279
Prix Européen du Roman pour Enfant de la Ville de Poitiers 279
Prix Fémina 280
Prix de Flore 281
Prix Fnac–Andersen du livre d'entreprise 282
Prix France Culture Français... 282
Prix France Télévision... 282
Prix François 1er: prix Cognac de la critique littéraire.. 283
Prix François Billetdoux... 271
Prix François-Joseph Audiffred 269
Prix Goncourt 285
Prix Goncourt des Lycéens.. 285
Prix Gérard de Nerval 299
Prix Heredia 286
Prix Infini... 286
Prix Interallié 287
Prix International Kadima... 287
Prix Internet du Livre 288
Prix Jean Freustié 283
Prix Jean Monnet de littérature européenne.. 298
Prix du Jeune Ecrivain.. 288
Prix Joseph Kessel.. 289
Prix de la Langue de France 289
Prix Laure Bataillon 270
Prix des Lectrices de Elle.. 290
Prix des Librairies de Création 291
Prix Littéraire de l'Age d'Or de France.. 291
Prix Littéraire de l'ENS Cachan 291
Prix Littéraire de la Gironde... 292
Prix Littéraire des Mouettes.. 292
Prix Littéraire de la Vocation.. 292
Prix Littéraires de l'Académie Française 293
Prix Littéraires du Ministère de la Jeunesse et des Sports.. 293
Prix Littéraires de la Société des Gens de Lettres 294
Prix du Livre Europe 1.. 295
Prix du Livre Inter... 295

Prix du Livre Numérique NewsFam.com 295
Prix du Livre de Picardie 295
Prix du Livre en Poitou-Charentes 296
Prix Louis Castex 273
Prix des Maisons de la Presse 296
Prix Marguerite Audoux 269
Prix Maurice-Edgar Coindreau 276
Prix Maurice-Genevoix 284
Prix Médicis 296
Prix Médicis de l'Essai 296
Prix Médicis Etranger 297
Prix Méditerranée 297
Prix Méditerranée étranger 297
Prix du Meilleur Livre Etranger 298
Prix National des Bibliothécaires 298
Prix Nautile de Cristal 299
Prix Octogone du livre de jeunesse 300
Prix Paul Verlaine 307
Prix Pelléas 301
Prix de Poésie Louis Montalte 301
Prix Polar 301
Prix René Fallet 280
Prix RFI–témoin du monde 302
Prix Roberval 302
Prix Roman Historique de Blois 303
Prix Rosny-Aîné 303
Prix Saint Valentin 304
Prix Sorcières 304
Prix Stanislas Julien 288
Prix Théophile Gautier 284
Prix Théophraste Renaudot 302
Prix Tibet 305
Prix Tour-Eiffel de Science-Fiction 306
Prix Tristan Tzara de Traduction 306
Prix Tropiques de l'Agence Française de Développement 306
Prix Valéry Larbaud 289
Prix Voronca 308
Prix Wepler–Fondation La Poste 308
Renaudot (Théophraste) Prix   see Prix Théophraste Renaudot
Rimbaud (Arthur), Prix   see Prix Littéraires du Ministère de la Jeunesse et des Sports
Sernet (Claude) Prix   see Prix Claude Sernet
Tzara (Tristan), Prix de Traduction   see Prix Tristan Tzara de Traduction
UNESCO Prize for Children's and Young People's Literature in the Service of Tolerance 359
Valentin (Saint), Prix   see Prix Saint Valentin
Verlaine (Paul) Prix   see Prix Paul Verlaine
Vespucci (Amerigo), Prix   see Prix Amerigo Vespucci
Vildrac (Charles), Prix de la Poésie   see Prix Charles Vildrac de la Poésie
Wine Book of the Year Gold Label Award   see Prix du Champagne Lanson

Germany

Adelbert-von-Chamisso-Preis der Robert-Bosch-Stiftung 62
Alfred-Döblin-Preis 82

André-Gide-Preis für deutsch-französische Literaturübersetzungen 104

Aspekte-Literatur-Preis 17

Berliner Preis für deutschsprachige Gegenwartsliteratur 32

Bienek (Horst) Preis fur Lyrik   *see* Horst Bienek Preis für Lyrik

Böll (Heinrich) Preis der Stadt Köln   *see* Heinrich-Böll-Preis der Stadt Köln

Braem (Helmut M.) Preis   *see* Helmut M. Braem Preis

Bremen Literatur Förderungspreis 47

Brüder-Grimm-Preis des Landes Berlin zur Förderung des Kinder- und Jugendtheaters 118

Büchner (Georg) Preis   *see* Georg-Büchner-Preis

Buxtehuder Bulle 54

Calwer Hermann-Hesse-Preis 56

Celan (Paul) Preis   *see* Paul-Celan-Preis

Chamisso (Adelbert von) Preis   *see* Adelbert-von-Chamisso-Preis der Robert-Bosch-Stiftung

Christoph-Martin-Wieland-Preis 373

Curtius (Ernst-Robert) Preise für Essayistik   *see* Ernst-Robert-Curtius-Preise für Essayistik

Deutscher Jugendliteraturpreis 79

Deutscher Jugendliteraturpreis Sonderpreis 80

Deutscher Kinder- und Jugendtheaterpreis 80

Deutscher-Krimi-Preis 80

Döblin (Alfred) Preis   *see* Alfred-Döblin-Preis

Ernst-Robert-Curtius-Preise für Essayistik 76

Freud (Sigmund) Preis   *see* Sigmund-Freud-Preis für wissenschaftliche Prosa

Friedenspreis des Deutschen Buchhandels 101

Friedrich Gundolf Preis für die Vermittlung deutscher Kultur im Ausland 121

Friedrich-Glauser-Preis—Krimipreis der Autoren 105

Georg-Büchner-Preis 52

Geschwister-Scholl-Preis 103

Gide (André) Preis   *see* André-Gide-Preis

Glauser (Friedrich) Preis—Krimipreis der Autoren
        see Friedrich-Glauser-Preis—Krimipreis der Autoren

Grosser Literaturpreis der Bayerischen Akademie der Schönen Kunste 118

Gundolf (Fiedrich) Preis
        see Friedrich Gundolf Preis für die Vermittlung deutscher Kultur im Ausland

Gustav-Heinemann-Friedenspreis für Kinder- und Jugendbücher 125

Heine (Heinrich) Medaille   *see* Heinrich-Heine-Preis der Landeshauptstadt Düsseldorf

Heinrich-Böll-Preis der Stadt Köln 41

Heinrich-Heine-Preis der Landeshauptstadt Düsseldorf 124

Helmut M. Braem Preis 45

Herder Prize 127

Horst Bienek Preis für Lyrik 35

Huchel (Peter) Preis   *see* Peter-Huchel-Preis

International Einhard Prize 137

Johann-Heinrich-Merck-Preis für literarische Kritik und Essay 180

Johann-Heinrich-Voss-Preis für Übersetzung 364

Literaturpreis der Landeshauptstadt Stuttgart 164

Mann (Thomas) Preis   *see* Thomas-Mann-Preis

Marlowe Award for Best International Crime Novel
        see Raymond Chandler Society's 'Marlowe' Award for Best International Crime Novel

Merck (Johann-Heinrich) Preis
        see Johann-Heinrich-Merck-Preis für literarische Kritik und Essay

Mühlheimer Dramatikerpreis 190

Nelly-Sachs-Preis/Kulturpreis der Stadt Dortmund 321

Neuer deutscher Literaturpreis 200

Paul-Celan-Preis 61

Peter-Huchel-Preis 132
Petrarca-Prize for Translation 229
Raymond Chandler Society's 'Marlowe' Award for Best International Crime Novel 62
Sachs (Nelly) Preis   *see* Nelly-Sachs-Preis/Kulturpreis der Stadt Dortmund
Sigmund-Freud-Preis für wissenschaftliche Prosa 100
Staatliche Förderungspreise für junge Schriftstellerinnen und Schriftsteller 341
Thomas-Mann-Preis 176
Voss (Johann Heinrich)-Preis für Übersetzung
        see Johann-Heinrich-Voss-Preis für Übersetzung
White Ravens 371
Wieland (Christoph-Martin) Preis   *see* Christoph-Martin-Wieland-Preis

Ghana

Toyota/Children's Literature Foundation Award 355

Greece

Onassis Cultural Competition Prize 214

Haiti

Prix Gouverneur de la Rosée du Livre et de la Littérature 285
Prix Littéraire Henri Deschamps 291

Hungary

Attila (Jozsef) Prize   *see* József Attila Prize
Gyula Illyes Prize 135
Jozsef Attila Prize 19
Kossuth Prize 155
Milán Füst Literary Prize 102
Tibor-Déry-Preis 78

Iceland

DV Cultural Award 85
Halldor Laxness Literary Prize 122
Icelandic Children's Book Prize 134
Icelandic Literary Prize 134
RÚV (Icelandic State Radio) Literary Award 320
Vaka-Helgafell Children's Book Award 360

India

Haryana Sahitya Akademi Awards 123
International Lotus Prize for Poetry 139
Jnanpith Award 145
Kerala Sahitya Akademi Awards 151
Kumar (C. B.) Award   *see* Kerala Sahitya Akademi Awards
Kuttippuzha Award   *see* Kerala Sahitya Akademi Awards
Namboodiri (K. R.) Award   *see* Kerala Sahitya Akademi Awards

Rajasthan Urdu Academy Awards 311
Sahitya Akademi Award 321
Saidi (Bismil) Prize   *see* Rajasthan Urdu Academy Awards
Shagil (Ahteramuddin) Prize   *see* Rajasthan Urdu Academy Awards
Shirani (Mehmood) Prize   *see* Rajasthan Urdu Academy Awards
Singh (Bhai Santokh) Award   *see* Haryana Sahitya Akademi Awards
Sur Award   *see* Haryana Sahitya Akademi Awards
Vedvyasa (Maharshi) Award   *see* Haryana Sahitya Akademi Awards

Indonesia

Adikarya Book Awards 4
Khatulistiwa Literary Award 152
Lontar Literary Award 167
Rancage Literary Award 312

Iran

Golden Bike Awards   *see* Iranian Book of the Year Awards
Iranian Book of the Year Awards 141
World Book of the Year Prize 377

Ireland

An duais don bhfiliocht as Gaeilge... 83
Bryan MacMahon Short Story Award 170
Cassidy (Lar) Award   *see* Lar Cassidy Award
Denis Devlin Memorial Award for Poetry 81
Eamon Keane Full Length Play Award 148
Gradam Litrochta Cló Iar-Chonnachta... 111
International IMPAC Dublin Literary Award 138
Irish Times International Fiction Prize... 141
Irish Times Irish Literature Prizes.. 142
Keane (Eamon) Full Length Play Award   *see* Eamon Keane Full Length Play Award
Kerry Ingredients Irish Fiction Award... 151
Lar Cassidy Award 60
MacMahon (Bryan) Short Story Award   *see* Bryan MacMahon Short Story Award
Marten Toonder Award 178
Rooney Prize for Irish Literature... 317
Toonder (Martin) Award   *see* Marten Toonder Award
Writers' Week Poetry Competition.. 379

Israel

Bernstein (Mordechai) Literary Prizes   *see* Mordechai Bernstein Literary Prizes
Bialik Prize for Literature 35
Mordechai Bernstein Literary Prizes... 33
Prime Minister's Hebrew Literature Prize.. 265

Italy

Anzilotti (Rolando) Premio   *see* Premio Rolando Anzilotti
Balzan Prize for Culture 26

Berto (Giuseppe), Premio Letterario   *see* Premio Letterario Giuseppe Berto

Bologna Ragazzi Award 42

Brignetti (Rafaello), Premio   *see* Premio Letterario Isola d'Elba – Rafaello Brignetti

Carducci (Giosue), Premio Nazionale di Poesia
       see Premio Nazionale di Poesia Giosuè Carducci

Cavour (Grinzane) Premio   *see* Premio Grinzane Cavour

Feltrinelli (Antonio) Premio   *see* Premio Antonio Feltrinelli

International Langhe Ceretto Prize for Food and Wine Culture 138

Ministry of Culture National Translation Prize 182

Orvieto (Laura), Premio letterario   *see* Premio letterario Laura Orvieto

Premio Antonio Feltrinelli 241

Premio Campiello 238

Premio Grinzane Cavour 241

Premio Grinzane Editoria   *see* Premio Grinzane Cavour

Premio Internazionale Fregene 244

Premio Internazionale di Letteratura La Cultura del Mare 244

Premio Letterario Giuseppe Berto 237

Premio Letterario Isola d'Elba – Rafaello Brignetti 246

Premio letterario Laura Orvieto 216

Premio Letterario Mondello Città di Palermo 246

Premio Napoli di Narrativa 256

Premio Nazionale di Poesia Giosue Carducci 257

Premio Rolando Anzilotti 237

Premio Strega 262

Premio Viareggio 263

Japan

Akutagawa Ryûnosuke Shô 7

Bungakukai Shinjin Shô 54

Chôkû Shô 66

Dazai Osamu Shô 78

Fujin Kôron Literary Prize 101

H-shi Shô 121

Haidan Shô 122

Itô Sei Bungaku Shô 142

Izumi Kyôka Bungaku Shô 143

Kadan Shô 146

Kaikô Takeshi Shô 147

Kawabata Yasunari Bungaku Shô 148

Kikuchi Hiroshi Shô 147

Mishima Yukio Shô 182

Mr H Prize   *see* H-shi Shô

Nakahara Chûya Prize 192

Naoki Sanjûgo Shô 193

Nihon Horâ Shôsetsu Taishô 204

Nihon SF Taishô 205

Noma Bungei Shô 206

Noma Concours for Picture Book Illustrations 207

Noma Literacy Prize 207

Noma Literature Prize for New Writers 207

Oda Sakunosuke Shô 213

Osaragi Jirô Shô 217

Ôya Sôichi Nonfikushon Shô 218
Rennyo Shô 314
Shûgorô (Yamamoto) Shô   *see* Yamamoto Shûgorô Shô
Takami Jun Shô 347
Tanizaki Jun'ichirô Shô 347
Tezuka Osamu Bunka Shô 351
Tsubouchi Shôyô Taishô 358
Yamamoto Shûgorô Shô 335
Yokomizo Seishi Shô 380
Yomiuri Bungaku Shô 380
Yoshikawa Eiji Bungaku Shinjin Shô 381
Yoshikawa Eiji Bungaku Shô 381
Yukio (Mishima) Shô   *see* Mishima Yukio Shô

Jordan

Arar Literary Award... 13

Kazakhstan

Tarlan Independent Prize 348

Korea (Republic)

Korean Literature Translation Award.. 155

Malaysia

Dewan Bahasa dan Pustaka Prize.. 82
Pemenang Anugerah MAPIM-Fuji Xerox... 222

Malta

Premju Letterarju 263

Mexico

Altamirano (Ignacio Manuel), Premio Nacional
    see Premio Nacional de Narrativa Ignacio Manuel Altamirano
Arreola (Juan José), Concurso Nacional   *see* Concurso Nacional de Cuento Juan José Arreola
Castillo (Ricardo Mimenza), Premio de Literatura
    see Premio de Literatura Ricardo Mimenza Castillo
Concurso de Prosa y Poesía Timón de Oro 73
Concurso Nacional de Cuento Juan José Arreola 73
Concurso Nacional de Dramaturgia Teatro Nuevo 74
De la Cruz (Sor Juana), Premio de Literatura
    see Premio de Literatura Sor Juana Inés de la Cruz
Dulché (Yolanda Vargas), Premio Internacional
    see Premio Internacional de Novela Yolanda Vargas Dulché
Hunapuh e Ixbalamqué, Premio de Literatura
    see Premio de Literatura para Niños Hunapuh e Ixbalamqué
Kostakowsky (Lya), Premio Annual
    see Premio Anual de Ensayo Literario Hispanoamericano Lya Kostakowsky

Mares (José Fuentes), Premio de Literatura   *see* Premio de Literatura José Fuentes Mares
Ocho Venado (Rey), Premio   *see* Premio Demac
Oro (Timón de), Concurso   *see* Concurso de Prosa y Poesía Timón de Oro
Paz (Octavio), Premio de Poesía y Ensayo   *see* Premio Octavio Paz de Poesía y Ensayo
Premio Anual de Ensayo Literario Hispanoamericano Lya Kostakowsky 236
Premio del Rey Ocho Venado.. 261
Premio Demac 240
Premio Internacional Alfonso Reyes 243
Premio Internacional de Novela Yolanda Vargas Dulché 243
Premio Latinoamericano de Literatura Infantil y Juvenil Norma-Fundalectura................................ 245
Premio de Literatura Infantil El Barco de Vapor 248
Premio de Literatura José Fuentes Mares... 249
Premio de Literatura Juvenil Gran Angular 248
Premio de Literatura Latinoamericana y del Caribe Juan Rulfo... 249
Premio de Literatura para Niños Hunapuh e Ixbalamqué 249
Premio de Literatura Ricardo Mimenza Castillo 248
Premio de Literatura Sor Juana Inés de la Cruz... 250
Premio Nacional de Literatura El Búho... 253
Premio Nacional de Literatura Infantil y Juvenil Castillo de la Lectura 254
Premio Nacional de Narrativa Ignacio Manuel Altamirano 254
Premio Nacional de Novela José Rubén Romero... 255
Premio Nacional de Poesía Tintanueva.. 255
Premio de Narrativa Colima... 256
Premio Nezahualcóyotl de Literatura en Lenguas Indígenas.. 257
Premio Octavio Paz de Poesía y Ensayo... 258
Reyes (Alfonso) Premio Internacional   *see* Premio Internacional Alfonso Reyes
Romero (José Rubén), Premio Nacional de Novela
        see Premio Nacional de Novela José Rubén Romero
Rulfo (Juan) Premio   *see* Premio de Literatura Latinoamericana y del Caribe Juan Rulfo

Monaco

Ireland Fund of Monaco Literary Award 141
Prix Littéraire Prince Pierre-de-Monaco 292

Mongolia

Monsudar Book Awards 185

Myanmar

Myanmar Annual National Literary Awards 191
Pakokku U Ohn Pe Literary and Education Awards 219

Nepal

Bhanu Bhakta Memorial Award 34
Mahendra Pragya Puraskar   *see* Royal Nepal Academy Awards
Prithvi Pragya Puraskar   *see* Royal Nepal Academy Awards
Royal Nepal Academy Awards... 318

Netherlands

Beaufort (Henriëtte de) prijs   *see* Henriëtte de Beaufort-prijs
Busken Huetprijs 132
Constantijn Huygens Prize 133
Dr Wijnaendts Francken-prijs 99
F. Bordewijkprijs 44
Francken-prijs (Dr Wijnaendts)   *see* Dr Wijnaendts Francken-prijs
Frans Kellendonk-prijs 149
G H s'Gravesande Prize 320
Gouden Griffel/Gouden Zoen 109
Gouden Zoen   *see* Gouden Griffel/Gouden Zoen
Henriette Roland Holst-prijs 317
Henriëtte de Beaufort-prijs 31
Herman Gorterprijs 109
Hooft (P. C.) prijs voor Letterkunde   *see* P. C. Hooft-prijs voor Letterkunde
Huetprijs (Busken)   *see* Busken Huetprijs
Huygens (Constantijn) Prize   *see* Constantijn Huygens Prize
J. Greshoff Prijs... 117
Jan Campert Prize 57
Jenny Smelik IBBY Prijs 338
Kellendonk (Frans)-prijs   *see* Frans Kellendonk-prijs
Kruyskamp-prijs 157
Lucy B. & C. W. van der Hoogt Prize... 360
Martinus Nijhoff Prijs voor Vertalingen.. 205
Multatuli Prize 190
Nienke van Hichtum Prize... 360
Nijhoff (Martinus) Prijs voor Vertalingen   *see* Martinus Nijhoff Prijs voor Vertalingen
P. C. Hooft-prijs voor Letterkunde... 131
Prijs der Nederlandse Letteren 264
Prijs voor Meesterschap 264
Roland Holst (Henriette) prijs   *see* Henriette Roland Holst-prijs
s'Gravesande (G H) Prize   *see* G H s'Gravesande Prize
Theo Thijssen Prize for Children's and Youth Literature.. 352
van Hichtum (Nienke) Prize   *see* Nienke van Hichtum Prize

New Zealand

Bank of New Zealand Essay Award.. 27
Bank of New Zealand Katherine Mansfield Memorial Awards 27
Bank of New Zealand Novice Writer's Award 28
Bank of New Zealand Young Writer's Award.. 28
Best First Book of Fiction Award
    see Montana New Zealand Book Awards
Best First Book of Non-Fiction Award
    see Montana New Zealand Book Awards/Best First Book of Non-Fiction Award
Best First Book of Poetry Award
    see Montana New Zealand Book Awards
Church (Hubert) Fiction Award
    see Montana New Zealand Book Awards
Clark (Russell) Award   *see* Russell Clark Award
Deutz Meda   *see* Montana New Zealand Book Awards/Deutz Medal
Elsie Locke Award 165
Esther Glen Award 106

Glen (Esther) Award   *see* Esther Glen Award

LIANZA Young People's Non-fiction Award   *see* Elsie Locke Award

Lilian Ida Smith Awards 338

Locke (Elsie) Award   *see* Elsie Locke Award

Mackay (Jessie) Poetry Award
    see Montana New Zealand Book Awards

McCormick (E. H.) Non-Fiction Award
    see Montana New Zealand Book Awards/Best First Book of Non-Fiction Award

Mansfield (Katherine) Award
    see Bank of New Zealand Katherine Mansfield Memorial Awards

Montana Medal   *see* Montana New Zealand Book Awards/Montana Medal

Montana New Zealand Book Awards 185

Montana New Zealand Book Awards/Best First Book of Fiction Award 186

Montana New Zealand Book Awards/Best First Book of Non-Fiction Award 187

Montana New Zealand Book Awards/Best First Book of Poetry Award 187

Montana New Zealand Book Awards/Deutz Medal 188

Montana New Zealand Book Awards/Montana Medal 188

New Zealand Post Children's Book Awards 203

Reed (A. W.) Lifetime Achievement Award   *see* Montana New Zealand Book Awards

Russell Clark Award 69

Smith (Lilian Ida) Awards   *see* Lilian Ida Smith Awards

Te Kura Pounamu Award 350

Nigeria

ANA/Cadbury Prize for Poetry   *see* Association of Nigerian Authors Literature Prizes

Association of Nigerian Authors Literature Prizes 18

Okigbo (Christopher) Prize   *see* Association of Nigerian Authors Literature Prizes

Sofola (Zulu) Prize   *see* Zulu Sofola Prize

Spectrum Prize   *see* Association of Nigerian Authors Literature Prizes

Zulu Sofola Prize 339

Norway

Aschehougprisen 16

Aschehougs debutantpris   *see* Aschehougprisen

Bastian Prize 29

Bokhandlerprisen 41

Brageprisen 45

Cappelen-prisen 60

Dahl (Thorlief), Norske Akademis Pris
    see Norske Akademis Pris til Minne om Thorleif Dahl

Gyldendal-prisen 121

Halldis Moren Vesaas-Prisen 122

Havmannprisen 123

Idunn-prisen   *see* Tano Aschehoug-Prisen/Idunn-Prisen

Kulturdepartementets Premiering av Barne- og Ungdomslitteratur 157

Mads Wiel Nygaards Legat 173

Melsom-prisen 180

Nordisk Skolebibliotekarforenings Barnebokpris 208

Norsk Kritikerlags Barnebokpris 209

Norsk Kritikerlags Pris 209

Norsk Sprakpris 209

Norske Akademis Pris til Minne om Thorleif Dahl 209

Norske Lyrikklubbens Pris 210
Oktober-Prisen.. 213
P2-Lyttaranes Romanpris 218
Riksmalsprisen – Oslo og Baerum riksmalsforenings litteraturpris.............................. 315
Rivertonprisen 'Den gylden revolver' 316
Samlagsprisen 323
Skolebibliotekarforeningens Litteraturpris... 338
Språklig Samlings Litteraturpris... 341
Tano Aschehoug-Prisen/Idunn-Prisen 348
Tarjei Vesaas Debutanpris.. 348
Tidens Skjonnlitteraere Pris.. 353

Pakistan

Adamji Prize 3
Ali (Mast Tauq) Award   see Mast Tauq Ali Award
Babai-e-Urdu Maulvi Abdul Haq Award.. 179
Bhitaee (Shah Abdul Latif) Award   see Shah Abdul Latif Bhitaee Award
Bukhari (Pitras) Award   see Pitras Bukhari Award
Dr Allama Muhammad Iqbal Award 140
Farid (Khwaja Ghulam) Award   see Khwaja Ghulam Farid Award
Iqbal (Dr Allama Muhammad) Award   see Dr Allama Muhammad Iqbal Award
Khattak (Khushhall Khan) Award   see Khushhall Khan Khattak Award
Khushhall Khan Khattak Award 152
Khwaja Ghulam Farid Award 93
Mast Tauq Ali Award 10
Maulvi Abdul Haq (Babai-e-Urdu) Award
      see Babai-e-Urdu Maulvi Abdul Haq Award
National Kamal-E-Fun Award.. 196
Pitras Bukhari Award 53
President's Award for Pride of Performance... 264
Shah (Syed Waris) Award   see Syed Waris Shah Award
Shah Abdul Latif Bhitaee Award.. 34
Syed Waris Shah Award 333

Philippines

Cultural Center of the Philippines Literary Awards 75
Don Carlos Palanca Memorial Awards.. 219
Literary Achievement Award.. 164
Magsaysay (Ramon) Award   see Ramon Magsaysay Award
Manila Critics Circle National Book Awards... 175
Palanca (Don Carlos) Memorial Awards   see Don Carlos Palanca Memorial Awards
Ramon Magsaysay Award 173

Poland

Jan Parandowski Prize.. 220
Jan Strzelecki Prize 343
NIKE Literary Award... 205
Parandowski (Jan) Prize   see Jan Parandowski Prize
Strzelecki (Jan) Prize   see Jan Strzelecki Prize

Portugal

Diniz (D.) Prêmio   *see* Prêmio D. Diniz
Grande Prémio Calouste Gulbenkian de Literatura para Crianças e Jovens 116
Gulbenkian (Calouste), Grande Prémio de Literatura
      see Grande Prémio Calouste Gulbenkian de Literatura para Crianças e Jovens
Jacinto Prado Coelho Award 70
Malheiros (Ricardo), Prêmio   *see* Prêmio Ricardo Malheiros
Premio Camões 238
Prêmio D. Diniz 240
Prêmio Ler 245
Prêmio Literário José Saramago 247
Prêmio Ricardo Malheiros 251
Saramago (José) Prémio Literário   *see* Prêmio Literário José Saramago

Romania

Bucharest Writers' Association Prizes 52

Russia

Anti-Booker Prize 13
Apollon Grigoryev Prize 118
Booker/Open Russia Prize 43
Grigoryev (Apollon) Prize   *see* Apollon Grigoryev Prize
Little Booker Prize 164
Northern Palmira Prize 210
Pushkin Poetry Prize 310
Russian Booker Prize   *see* Booker/Open Russia Prize
Smirnoff-Booker Prize   *see* Booker/Open Russia Prize
Solzhenitsyn Prize for Russian Writing 340
State Prize of the Russian Federation in Arts and Letters 342
Triumph Prize 357

Saudi Arabia

Faisal (King) International Prize   *see* King Faisal International Prize for Arabic Literature
King Fahd bin Abdulaziz Award for Initiative 153
King Faisal International Prize for Arabic Literature 92

Singapore

Anugerah Persuratan (Bidang Esei Sastera) 13
Dymocks Singapore Literature Prize 85
Singapore National Book Awards 337
Tun Seri Lanang Award 358

Slovakia

Biennial of Illustrations Bratislava (BIB) 35
Literárna sútaz Poviedka 163

Slovenia

Kristal Vilenica Award   *see* Vilenica International Literary Awards

Vilenica International Literary Award   *see* Vilenica International Literary Awards

Vilenica International Literary Awards 363

South Africa

Akademieprys vir Vertaalde Werk 6

Alba Bouwerprys vir Kinderliteratuur 44

Altron Literary Award   *see* Bill Venter/Altron Literary Award

Bill Venter/Altron Literary Award 361

Bouwer (Alba) prys vir Kinderliteratuur   *see* Alba Bouwerprys vir Kinderliteratuur

C. P. Hoogenhout Award 131

CNA Letterkkunde Toekenning 70

Eugène Maraisprys 176

Fitzpatrick (Percy) Medal   *see* Percy Fitzpatrick Medal

FNB VITA Poetry Award 96

Gustav Prellerprys vir literatuurwetenskap en letterkundige kritiek 233

Harries (Katrine) Award   *see* Katrine Harries Award

Hertzogprys 127

Hiemstra (Louis) prys vir nie-fiksie   *see* Louis Hiemstraprys vir nie-fiksie

Holloway (Tienie) Medal   *see* Tienie Hollowaymedalje vir kleuterliteratuur

Katrine Harries Award 148

Louis Hiemstraprys vir nie-fiksie 128

M-Net Book Prize 169

Marais (Eugene) prys   *see* Eugène Maraisprys

MER Prize 180

Olive Schreiner Prize 331

Percy Fitzpatrick Medal 95

Preller (Gustav) Prize
      see Gustav Prellerprys vir literatuurwetenskap en letterkundige kritiek

Pringle (Thomas) Award   *see* Thomas Pringle Award

Sanlam Literary Award 323

SATI Award For Outstanding Translation 325

Scheepersprys vir jeugliteratuur 330

Schreiner (Olive) Prize   *see* Olive Schreiner Prize

Thomas Pringle Award 265

Tienie Hollowaymedalje vir kleuterliteratuur 354

Venter (Bill) Literary Award   *see* Bill Venter/Altron Literary Award

Spain

Asturias (Príncipe de), Premio   *see* Premio Príncipe de Asturias

Fernando Rielo World Mystical Poetry Prize 315

Gourmand World Cookbook Awards 110

Institutció de les Lletres Catalanes Translation Prize 137

Lara (Fernando) Premio   *see* Premio de Novela Fernando Lara

Lazarillo Prize 160

Llull (Ramon) Premi   *see* Premi de les Lletres Catalanes Ramon Llull

Pla, (Josep) Premi   *see* Premi Josep Pla

Premi d'Honor de les Lletres Catalanes 233

Premi Josep Pla 234

Premi de les Lletres Catalanes Ramon Llull...233
Premi Nacional de Literatura de la Generalitat de Catalunya...234
Premi Sèrie Negra 234
Premio Adonais de Poesía..235
Premio Alfaguara de Novela..236
Premio Alvarez Quintero...260
Premio Andalucía de Novela...236
Premio Apel les Mestres...237
Premio Azorín..237
Premio Biblioteca Breve 238
Premio Cervantes..239
Premio Destino-Guion...240
Premio Fastenrath 241
Premio La Sonrisa Vertical..262
Premio del Libro..246
Premio Nacional de las Letras Españolas..251
Premio Nacional de Literatura..252
Premio Nacional de Literatura Infantil y Juvenil...253
Premio Nacional a la mejor traducción 254
Premio Nacional a la obra de un traductor..255
Premio Nadal..255
Premio de Novela Fernando Lara 257
Premio Planeta de Novela..258
Premio Primavera de Novela...259
Premio Príncipe de Asturias 260
Premio Reina Sofía de Poesía Iberoamericana 260
Premio Rivadeneira 261
Premio UPC de ciencia ficción..263
Prix La Mazille   *see* Gourmand World Cookbook Awards
Quintero (Alvarez) Premio   *see* Premio Alvarez Quintero
Rielo (Fernando) World Mystical Poetry Prize   *see* Fernando Rielo World Mystical Poetry Prize

Sri Lanka

D. R. Wijewardene Memorial Award 374
Godage Literary Awards 107
Wijewardene (D. R.) Memorial Award   *see* D. R. Wijewardene Memorial Award

Sweden

Aftonbladets litteraturpris 5
Aniara Priset 12
Augustpriset 20
Bellmanpriset 31
Bonniers (Gerard) Pris   *see* Gerard Bonniers Pris
Dobloug Priset 83
Gerard Bonniers Pris...42
Holgersson (Nils) Plaque   *see* Nils Holgersson Plaque
Katapultpriset 147
Kellgrenpriset 150
Margit Pahlson Prize 219
Nils Holgersson Plaque 129
Nobel Prize in Literature 205

Nordic Council Literature Prize 208
Nordiska Priset 208
Östersundsposten prize 217
Pahlson (Margit) Prize   *see* Margit Pahlson Prize
Stora Priset 343
Svenska Dagbladets Litteraturpris 345
Sveriges Radios Lyrikpris/Sveriges Radio P1:s Romanpris 346

Switzerland

Andersen (Hans Christian) Awards   *see* Hans Christian Andersen Awards
Charles Veillon European Essay Prize 361
Dentan (Michel) Prix   *see* Prix Michel Dentan
Gottfried Keller Prize 150
Grand Prix Ramuz 115
Grand Prix de la Ville de Sierre   *see* Prix du Festival de la Bande Dessinée de Sierre
Grosser Preis der Schweizerische Schillerstiftung 119
Hans Christian Andersen Awards 11
IBBY-Asahi Reading Promotion Award 133
Keller (Gottfried) Prize   *see* Gottfried Keller Prize
Literaturpreis der Stadt Solothurn 164
Prix BPT 272
Prix du Festival de la Bande Dessinée de Sierre 280
Prix Michel Dentan 277
Ramuz (C. F.), Grand Prix   *see* Grand Prix Ramuz
Schiller, Grosser Preis   *see* Grosser Preis der Schweizerische Schillerstiftung
Schweizer Jugendbuchpreis 331
Veillon (Charles) European Essay Prize   *see* Charles Veillon European Essay Prize

Thailand

National Artists Award 193
National Book Contest 194
Southeast Asia (SEA) Write Award 340
Translated Book Contest 356

Turkey

TDK Literary Award 350

United Arab Emirates

Al-Uweis Literary Award 8

Ukraine

Andrei Malyshko Prize 174
Biletsky (Oleksander) Prize   *see* National Writers Union of Ukraine Awards
Blagovist Prize 38
Franko (Ivan) Prize   *see* Ivan Franko Prize
Hlibov (Leonid) Prize   *see* National Writers Union of Ukraine Awards
Honchar (Oles) Ukrainian-German Prize   *see* Oles Honchar Prizes
Ivan Franko Prize 100

Korolenko (Volodymyr) Prize   *see* National Writers Union of Ukraine Awards
Kotlyarevsky (Ivan) Prize   *see* National Writers Union of Ukraine Awards
Lesya Ukrainka Prize 359
Malyshko (Andrei) Prize   *see* Andrei Malyshko Prize
National Writers Union of Ukraine Awards 198
Oles Honchar Prizes 130
Shevchenko (Taras) Award   *see* Taras Shevchenko Award
Simonenko (Vasyl) Prize   *see* Vasyl Simonenko Prize
Taras Shevchenko Award 335
Ukrainka (Lesya) Prize   *see* Lesya Ukrainka Prize
Ushakov (Mykola) Prize   *see* National Writers Union of Ukraine Awards
Vasyl Simonenko Prize 337

United Kingdom

Ackerley (J. R.) Prize for Autobiography   *see* J. R. Ackerley Prize for Autobiography
Aldeburgh Poetry Festival First Collection Prize 8
Alexander Prize 9
Alfred Fagon Award 91
Arthur C. Clarke Award for Science Fiction 69
Arts Council Bursaries and Commissions 14
Arts Council of England Children's Award 14
Arts Council of England Writers' Awards 15
Arts Council of Wales Book of the Year Awards 15
Arvon Poetry Competition 15
Asham Award for Women 17
Asher Prize   *see* Society of Authors Medical Book Awards
Authors' Club Best First Novel Award 24
Aventis Prize 25
BA/Book Data Author of the Year 25
Bad Sex in Fiction Awards 26
Bargate (Verity) Award   *see* Verity Bargate Award
BBC Wildlife Magazine Literary Awards 30
BBC Wildlife Magazine Nature Writing Award   *see* BBC Wildlife Magazine Literary Awards
BBC Wildlife Magazine Poet of the Year Award   *see* BBC Wildlife Magazine Literary Awards
BBC4 Samuel Johnson Prize for Non-Fiction 145
Benson Medal 32
Bernard Shaw Prize 334
Berry (David) Prize   *see* David Berry Prize
Besterman/McColvin Medals 33
Betty Trask Prize 356
Biographers' Club Prize 37
Black (James Tait) Memorial Prizes   *see* James Tait Black Memorial Prizes
Blue Peter Children's Book Awards 38
Blyth (R. H.) Award   *see* R. H. Blyth Award
BMA (British Medical Association) Medical Book Competition 39
Boardman Tasker Award 40
Booker Prize for Fiction   *see* Man Booker Prize
Border Television Prize   *see* Lakeland Book of the Year Awards
BP Natural World Book Prize 45
Bradt Travel Writing Award   *see* BBC Wildlife Magazine Literary Awards
Branford Boase Award 46
Bridport Prize 47

Briggs (Katharine) Folklore Award   *see* Katharine Briggs Folklore Award

British Academy Book Prize 48

British Book Awards 48

British Comparative Literature Association Translation Prize 50

British Fantasy Awards 50

British Science Fiction Association Awards 51

Caine Prize for African Writing 55

Calvin and Rose G. Hoffmann Prize for a Distinguished Publication on Christopher Marlowe 129

Carnegie Medal 60

Cartier Diamond Dagger   *see* CWA Awards

Children's Award (Arts Council of England)   *see* Arts Council of England Children's Award

Children's Book Award 63

Children's Laureate 65

Cholmondeley Awards 66

Christopher Ewart-Biggs Memorial Prize 90

Clarke (Arthur C.) Award for Science Fiction   *see* Arthur C. Clarke Award for Science Fiction

Cohen (David) British Literature Prize   *see* David Cohen British Literature Prize

Commonwealth Writers Prize 71

Cooper (Derek) Award   *see* Guild of Food Writers Awards

Cooper (Duff) Prize   *see* Duff Cooper Prize

County of Cardiff International Poetry Competition 75

Crawshay (Rose Mary) Prize   *see* Rose Mary Crawshay Prize

Creasey (John) Memorial Dagger   *see* CWA Awards

CWA Awards 76

Darton (Harvey) Award   *see* Harvey Darton Award

David Berry Prize 33

David Cohen British Literature Prize 71

David Gemmell Cup Short Story Competition 103

David St John Thomas Charitable Trust Awards 353

David T.K. Wong Prize for Short Fiction 377

David Watt Prize 367

Davies (Hunter) Prize   *see* Lakeland Book of the Year Awards

Derleth (August) Award   *see* British Fantasy Awards

Deutscher (Isaac and Tamara) Memorial Prize
       see Isaac and Tamara Deutscher Memorial Prize

Diagram Group Prize 82

Duff Cooper Prize 74

Dundee Book Prize 84

Dupont (S. T.) Gold PEN   *see* Macmillan PEN Awards

Eleanor Farjeon Award 93

Eliot (T. S.) Prize   *see* T. S. Eliot Prize

Encore Award 89

Enid McLeod Literary Prize 172

Eric Gregory Trust Fund Award 117

European Jewish Publication Society Grant to Publishers 89

European Online Journalism (EOJ) Award 90

Ewart-Biggs (Christopher) Memorial Prize   *see* Christopher Ewart-Biggs Memorial Prize

Faber (Geoffrey) Memorial Prize   *see* Geoffrey Faber Memorial Prize

Fagon (Alfred) Prize   *see* Alfred Fagon Award

Fleming (Ian) Steel Dagger   *see* CWA Awards

Fletcher (Sir Banister) Prize of the Authors' Club
       see Sir Banister Fletcher Prize of the Authors' Club

Florio (John) Prize   *see* John Florio Prize

Forward Prizes for Poetry 97

Fraenkel Prize in Contemporary History 98
Frogmore Poetry Prize 101
Gemmell (David) Short Story Competition   see David Gemmell Cup Short Story Competition
Geoffrey Faber Memorial Prize 90
Gladstone History Book Prize 105
Glenfiddich Food & Drink Awards 106
Greenaway (Kate) Medal   see Kate Greenaway Medal
Gregory (Eric) Trust Fund Award   see Eric Gregory Trust Fund Award
Guardian Children's Fiction Award 119
Guardian First Book Award 120
Guild of Food Writers Awards 120
Harvey Darton Award 78
Hawthornden Prize 124
Heinemann (W. H.) Award   see W. H. Heinemann Award
Hellenic Foundation for Culture Translation Award 125
Heywood Hill Literary Prize 128
Hoffmann (Calvin and Rose G.) Prize   see Calvin and Rose G. Hoffmann Prize
    for a Distinguished Publication on Christopher Marlowe
Imison (Richard) Memorial Award   see Richard Imison Memorial Award
Independent Foreign Fiction Prize 136
Institute of Historical Research Prize 137
International Playwriting Festival 139
Isaac and Tamara Deutscher Memorial Prize 81
J. R. Ackerley Prize for Autobiography 3
James Tait Black Memorial Prizes 37
Jewish Quarterly-Wingate Prizes 145
John Florio Prize 96
John Whiting Award 372
Johnson (Samuel) Prize   see BBC4 Samuel Johnson Prize for Non-Fiction
Kate Greenaway Medal 116
Katharine Briggs Folklore Award 47
Kathleen Fidler Award 94
Keats–Shelley Prize 149
Kick Start Poets Open Poetry Competition 152
Kraszna-Krausz Book Awards 156
Lakeland Book of the Year Awards 158
London Writers Competition 166
Longman–History Today Book of the Year Award 166
Macallan Gold/Silver Dagger   see CWA Awards
Macallan/Scotland on Sunday Story Competition 170
Macmillan PEN Awards 170
Macmillan Prize   see Macmillan PEN Awards
Macmillan Prize for Children's Picture Book Illustration 171
Macmillan Silver PEN   see Macmillan PEN Awards
Macmillan Writer's Prize for Africa 171
McColvin Medal   see Besterman/McColvin Medals
McKitterick Prize 172
McLeod (Enid) Literary Prize   see Enid McLeod Literary Prize
Mail on Sunday/John Llewellyn Rhys Prize 174
Man Booker Prize 174
Marsh Award for Children's Literature in Translation 177
Marsh Biography Award 178
Mary Vaughan Jones Award 360
Mathew Prichard Award for Short Story Writing 264

Mears (Colin) Award   *see* Kate Greenaway Medal

Meyer-Whitworth Award 180

Michael Smith Award   *see* Guild of Food Writers Awards

Mitchell (Eric) Prize   *see* Mitchell Prize for Art History/Eric Mitchell Prize

Mitchell Prize for Art History/Eric Mitchell Prize 183

Moore (Oscar) Screenwriting Prize   *see* Oscar Moore Screenwriting Prize

Naipaul (Shiva) Memorial Prize   *see* Shiva Naipaul Memorial Prize

National Art Library Illustration Awards 193

National Poetry Competition 198

Nestlé Smarties Book Prize 199

New Writer Prose and Poetry Prizes 202

Nibbies   *see* British Book Awards

NOMA Award for Publishing in Africa 206

Northern Rock Foundation Writer Award 210

Northern Writers' Awards 211

Orange Prize for Fiction 214

Orange Prize for Translation   *see* Orange Prize for Fiction

Orwell Prize 216

Oscar Moore Screenwriting Prize 189

Ottakar's Faber National Poetry Competition 218

Pandora Award 220

Parker Romantic Novel of the Year 221

Peer Poetry International Competition 221

Peterloo Poets Open Poetry Competition 229

Peters (Ellis) Historical Dagger   *see* CWA Awards

Poetry Life Open Poetry Competition 231

Poetry London Competition 232

Portico Prize for Literature 232

Premio Valle Inclán 263

Prichard (Mathew) Award for Short Story Writing
    see Mathew Prichard Award for Short Story Writing

Pritchett (V. S.) Memorial Prize   *see* V. S. Pritchett Memorial Prize

Promise Prize   *see* London Writers Competition

Queen's Gold Medal for Poetry 310

R. H. Blyth Award 39

Raymond Williams Community Publishing Prize 375

Real Writers/Book Pl@ce Short Story Awards 313

Reese (Trevor) Memorial Prize   *see* Trevor Reese Memorial Prize

Rhône-Poulenc Prize   *see* Aventis Prize

Rhys Davies Short Story Competition 314

Richard Imison Memorial Award 135

Romantic Novelists Association New Writers Award 317

Rose Mary Crawshay Prize 75

Round (Jeremy) Award   *see* Guild of Food Writers Awards

RSM Library Prize   *see* Society of Authors Medical Book Awards

Runciman Award 318

Sagittarius Prize 321

Saltire Society Literary Awards 322

Saltire Society/Times Educational Supplement Scotland Prize for Educational Publications 322

Sands (Ron) Prize   *see* Lakeland Book of the Year Awards

Sasakawa Haiku Prize 324

Sasakawa Prize for Translation 324

Schlegel-Tieck Prize 330

Scott Moncrieff Prize 332

Scottish Arts Council Book of the Year Award 332
Scottish Book of the Year   *see* Saltire Society Literary Awards
Scottish First Book of the Year   *see* Saltire Society Literary Awards
Scottish History Book of the Year   *see* Saltire Society Literary Awards
Shaw (Bernard) Prize   *see* Bernard Shaw Prize
Shiva Naipaul Memorial Prize 192
Sir Banister Fletcher Prize of the Authors' Club 96
Society of Authors Medical Book Awards 339
Somerset Maugham Awards 179
St John Thomas (David) Charitable Trust Awards
      see David St John Thomas Charitable Trust Awards
Stern Silver PEN Prize   *see* Macmillan PEN Awards
Sunday Telegraph Catherine Pakenham Memorial Award 344
Sunday Times Award for Literary Excellence 344
Sunday Times Young Writer of the Year Award 344
SWPA Audiobooks of the Year 346
T. S. Eliot Prize 87
Tabla Poetry Competition 347
Teixeira-Gomes Prize 350
Theatre Book Prize 352
Thomas Cook/Daily Telegraph Travel Book Award 353
Tir Na N-og Awards 354
Tolman Cunard Prize   *see* Forward Prizes for Poetry
Trask (Betty) Awards   *see* Betty Trask Prize
Trask (Betty) Prize   *see* Betty Trask Prize
Travelling Scholarship Fund 357
Trevor Reese Memorial Prize 313
Tullie House Prize   *see* Lakeland Book of the Year Awards
V. S. Pritchett Memorial Prize 266
Vaughan Jones (Mary) Award   *see* Mary Vaughan Jones Award
Ver Poets Open Competition 362
Verb Writing Competition BBC 362
Verity Bargate Award 28
Virgin Books Newcomer of the Year Award   *see* British Book Awards
Vondel Translation Prize 364
W. H. Heinemann Award 125
W. H. Smith Children's Book of the Year   *see* British Book Awards
W. H. Smith Literary Award 366
W. H. Smith Thumping Good Read Award 366
Wadsworth Prize for Business History 367
Walford Award for Contributions to Bibliography 367
Waterstone's Prize   *see* Forward Prizes for Poetry
Watt (David) Prize   *see* David Watt Prize
Wellcome Trust Prize 368
Westminster Prize 370
Wheatley Medal for an Outstanding Index 370
Whitbread Book of the Year and Literary Awards 371
Whitfield Prize 372
Whiting (John) Award   *see* John Whiting Award
William Hill Sports Book of the Year 375
Williams (Raymond) Community Publishing Prize
      see Raymond Williams Community Publishing Prize
Wilson (Titus) Prize   *see* Lakeland Book of the Year Awards
Winifred Holtby Memorial Prize 130

Wolfson History Prize 376
Wong (David T.K) Prize for Short Fiction   *see* David T.K. Wong Prize for Short Fiction
World Wide Writers Competition 377
Yorkshire Post Awards 381
Young Wine Writer Award 382

United States of America

AAAS/Orbis Books Prize for Polish Studies 1
Academy of American Poets Fellowship 2
Addison Metcalf Award   *see* American Academy of Arts and Letters Annual Awards
Aesop Prize 4
Agatha Awards 5
AIP Science Writing Awards in Physics and Astronomy 6
Akron Poetry Prize 7
Albert J. Beveridge Award 34
Albrand (Martha) Award for First Non-fiction
          see PEN/Martha Albrand Award for First Non-fiction
Albrand (Martha) Award for the Art of the Memoir
          see PEN/Martha Albrand Award for the Art of the Memoir
Aldo and Jeanne Scaglione Prize for Comparative Literary Studies 326
Aldo and Jeanne Scaglione Prize for French and Francophone Studies 326
Aldo and Jeanne Scaglione Prize for Germanic Languages and Literatures 327
Aldo and Jeanne Scaglione Prize for Italian Studies 327
Aldo and Jeanne Scaglione Prize for Studies in Slavic Languages and Literatures 328
Aldo and Jeanne Scaglione Prize for a Translation of a Literary Work 328
Aldo and Jeanne Scaglione Prize for a Translation of a Scholarly Study of Literature 329
Aldo and Jeanne Scaglione Publication Award for a Manuscript in Italian Literary Studies 329
Alex Awards 9
Alice Fay di Castagnola Award 61
Ambassador Book Awards 10
American Academy of Arts and Letters Annual Awards 11
American Academy of Arts and Letters Gold Medal 11
Anisfield-Wolf Book Awards 12
Anthony Awards 13
ASF Translation Prize 16
Associated Writing Programs (AWP) Award Series in Poetry, Fiction and Creative Non-fiction 17
Atlanta Review Poetry Competition 18
Atlantic History Prize 19
Balakian (Nona) Citation   *see* The National Book Critics Circle Awards
Bancroft Prizes 26
Barbara Jelavich Book Prize 144
Batchelder (Mildred L.) Award   *see* Mildred L. Batchelder Award
Baxter Adams (Herbert) Prize   *see* Herbert Baxter Adams Prize
Beer (George Louis) Prize   *see* George Louis Beer Prize
Belpré (Pura) Award   *see* Pura Belpré Award
Beveridge (Albert J.) Award   *see* Albert J. Beveridge Award
Bingham (Robert) Fellowships for Writers   *see* PEN/Robert Bingham Fellowships for Writers
Binkley–Stephenson Award 36
Birdsall (Paul) Prize   *see* Paul Birdsall Prize in European Military and Strategic History
Bloom (John) Humor Award   *see* Texas Institute of Letters Awards
Bogin (George) Memorial Award   *see* George Bogin Memorial Award
Bollingen Prize in Poetry 41
Bologna New Media Prize (BNMP) 41

Book Sense Book of the Year Award 42
Boston Globe–Horn Book Award 44
Bourne (Louise Louis/Emily) Student Poetry Award
    see Louise Louis/Emily F. Bourne Student Poetry Award
Brand (Sarah) and Weinstein (Arik) Award   *see* National Jewish Book Awards
Breasted (James H.) Prize   *see* James H. Breasted Prize
Bulwer-Lytton Fiction Contest 53
Butler Literary Awards   *see* Irish American Cultural Institute (IACI) Literary Awards
Caldecott (Randolph) Medal   *see* Randolph Caldecott Medal
California Young Reader Medal 56
Campbell (John W.) Memorial Award
    see John W. Campbell Memorial Award for the Best New Writer
Cappon (Alexander Patterson) Fiction Prize   *see* New Letters Literary Awards
Cappon (Dorothy Churchill) Prize   *see* New Letters Literary Awards
Castagnola (Alice Fay di) Award   *see* Alice Fay di Castagnola Award
Cecil Hemley Memorial Award 126
Charlotte Zolotow Award 382
Chicano/Latino Literary Prize 63
Children's Book Awards 63
Children's Book Guild Award for Non-fiction 64
Children's eBook Award   *see* Bologna New Media Prize (BNMP)
Children's Literature Association Book Awards 65
Christopher Awards 67
Christy Awards 68
Clarence H. Haring Prize 123
Clarence L. Holt Literary Prize 130
Cohen (Morton N.) Award   *see* Morton N. Cohen Award for a Distinguished Edition of Letters
Colorado Prize 71
Coretta Scott King Award 152
Dartmouth Medal 77
David Thelen Prize 352
Dickinson (Emily) Award   *see* Writer Magazine/Emily Dickinson Award
Discovery/The Nation Joan Leiman Jacobson Poetry Prizes 82
Dixon Ryan Fox Manuscript Prize 98
Dunne (Thomas) Books Award for the Novel   *see* Thomas Dunne Books Award for the Novel
Dunning (Jonh H.) Prize   *see* John H. Dunning Prize
Ed A. Hewett Book Prize 127
Edgar Allan Poe Awards 231
Edgars   *see* Edgar Allan Poe Awards
Edwards (Margaret) Award   *see* Margaret A. Edwards Award
Elie Wiesel Prize in Ethics Essay Contest 374
Emerson-Thoreau Medal 88
Ernest Hemingway Foundation/PEN Award for First Fiction 126
Ezra Jack Keats New Writer's and New Illustrator's Award for Children's Books 149
Fagg (John E.) Prize   *see* John E. Fagg Prize
Fairbank (John K.) Prize   *see* John K. Fairbank Prize
Farber (Norma) First Book Award   *see* Norma Farber First Book Award
Feis (Herbert) Prize   *see* Herbert Feis Prize
Fenia and Yaakov Leviant Memorial Prize 162
Firecracker Alternative Book Awards 94
Flannery O'Connor Award for Short Fiction 212
Foreign-Language Article Prize   *see* David Thelen Prize
Forkosch (Morris D.) Prize   *see* Morris D. Forkosch Prize
Fox (Dixon Ryan) Manuscript Prize   *see* Dixon Ryan Fox Manuscript Prize

Francis Parkman Prize... 221
Frost Medal.. 101
Gay, Lesbian, Bisexual and Transgendered Book Awards.. 102
George Bogin Memorial Award 40
George L. Mosse Prize... 190
George Louis Beer Prize... 31
George Polk Awards... 232
Gershoy (Leo) Prize   *see* Leo Gershoy Prize
Glimmer Train Literary Awards 107
Gold Medallion Book Awards 108
Gold/Platinum Book Awards.. 108
Golden Kite Award 108
Goldsmith (Barbara) Award   *see* PEN/Barbara Goldsmith Freedom to Write Awards
Gregory Kolovakos Award.. 154
Haring (Clarence H.) Prize   *see* Clarence H. Haring Prize
Harold Morton Landon Translation Award 159
Hemingway (Ernest) Foundation/PEN Award
        see Ernest Hemingway Foundation/PEN Award for First Fiction
Hemley (Cecil) Memorial Award   *see* Cecil Hemley Memorial Award
Henry (O.) Award   *see* Texas Institute of Letters Awards
Herbert Baxter Adams Prize 30
Herbert Feis Prize.. 93
Hewett (Ed A.) Book Prize   *see* Ed A. Hewett Book Prize
Holt (Clarence L.) Literary Prize   *see* Clarence L. Holt Literary Prize
Hopkins (Lee Bennett) Promising Poet Award
        see Lee Bennett Hopkins Promising Poet Award
Howard R. Marraro Prize... 177
Howard R. Marraro Prize in Italian History 177
Hugo Award 132
International Imitation Hemingway Competition.. 138
Irish American Cultural Institute (IACI) Literary Awards 141
J. Russell Major Prize 320
Jacobson (Joan Leiman) Poetry Prizes
        see Discovery/The Nation Joan Leiman Jacobson Poetry Prizes
James A. Michener Memorial Prize.. 181
James H. Breasted Prize 46
James Laughlin Award 160
James Russell Lowell Prize 319
Jane Addams Children's Book Award 3
Jefferson Cup Awards... 144
Jelavich (Barbara) Book Prize   *see* Barbara Jelavich Book Prize
Joan Kelly Memorial Prize 150
John E. Fagg Prize.. 91
John H. Dunning Prize.. 85
John K. Fairbank Prize 91
John Newbery Medal... 203
John Steinbeck Award.. 342
John W. Campbell Memorial Award for the Best New Writer... 57
Jolson (Leon) Award   *see* National Jewish Book Awards
Jones (Jesse H.) Award   *see* Texas Institute of Letters Awards
Katherine Singer Kovacs Prize.. 155
Kathryn A. Morton Prize in Poetry... 189
Kaufman (Sue) Prize for First Fiction
        see American Academy of Arts and Letters Annual Awards

Keats (Ezra Jack) Awards
    see Ezra Jack Keats New Writer's and New Illustrator's Award for Children's Books
Kelly (Joan) Memorial Prize   *see* Joan Kelly Memorial Prize
Kenneth W. Mildenberger Prize 181
King (Coretta Scott) Award   *see* Coretta Scott King Award
Kingsley Tufts Poetry Prize 358
Kiriyama Pacific Rim Book Prize 153
Kirsch (Robert) Award   *see* Los Angeles Times Book Prizes
Klein (Norma) Award   *see* PEN/Norma Klein Award
Kolovakos (Gregory) Award   *see* Gregory Kolovakos Award
Kovacs (Katherine Singer) Prize   *see* Katherine Singer Kovacs Prize
Lambda Literary Awards—Lammys 158
Landon (Harold Morton) Translation Award   *see* Harold Morton Landon Translation Award
Lannan Literary Awards 159
Laughlin (James) Award   *see* James Laughlin Award
Laura Ingalls Wilder Award 374
Lee Bennett Hopkins Promising Poet Award 131
Leland (Walso G.) Prize   *see* Waldo G. Leland Prize
Lenore Marshall Poetry Prize 178
Leo Gershoy Prize 103
Leviant (Fenia and Yaakov) Memorial Prize   *see* Fenia and Yaakov Leviant Memorial Prize
Lewis Thomas Prize 353
Lilly (Ruth) Poetry Prize   *see* Ruth Lilly Poetry Prize
Littleton-Griswold Prize 165
Lois Roth Award for a Translation of a Literary Work 318
Long Madgett (Naomi) Poetry Award   *see* Naomi Long Madgett Poetry Award
Los Angeles Times Book Prizes 167
Louise Louis/Emily F. Bourne Student Poetry Award 44
Lucille Medwick Memorial Award 179
Lukas (J. Anthony) Prize   *see* Lukas Prize Project
Lukas Prize Project 168
Lynton (Mark) History Prize   *see* Mark Lynton History Prize
Lyric Poetry Award 169
McCarthy (Mary) Prize in Short Fiction   *see* Mary McCarthy Prize in Short Fiction
Manheim (Ralph) Medal for Translation   *see* PEN/Ralph Manheim Medal for Translation
Margaret A. Edwards Award 86
Mark Lynton History Prize 169
Mark Twain Award for Short Fiction 358
Marraro (Howard R.) Prize   *see* Howard R. Marraro Prize
Marraro (Howard R.) Prize   *see* Howard R. Marraro Prize in Italian History
Marshall (Lenore) Poetry Prize   *see* Lenore Marshall Poetry Prize
Marshall Shulman Book Prize 335
Mary McCarthy Prize in Short Fiction 172
Medwick (Lucille) Memorial Award   *see* Lucille Medwick Memorial Award
Michael L. Printz Award for Excellence in Young Adult Literature 265
Michener (James A.) Memorial Prize   *see* James A. Michener Memorial Prize
Mildenberger (Kenneth W.) Prize   *see* Kenneth W. Mildenberger Prize
Mildred L. Batchelder Award 29
Mina P. Shaughnessy Prize 334
MLA Award for Lifetime Scholarly Achievement 183
Modern Language Association Prize for a Distinguished Bibliography 184
Modern Language Association Prize for a First Book 184
Modern Language Association Prize for Independent Scholars 185
Morris D. Forkosch Prize 97

Morton (Kathryn A.) Prize in Poetry   see Kathryn A. Morton Prize in Poetry
Morton Dauwen Zabel Award   see American Academy of Arts and Letters Annual Awards
Morton N. Cohen Award for a Distinguished Edition of Letters.. 70
Mosse (George L.) Prize   see George L. Mosse Prize
Mythopoeic Awards.. 191
Mythopoeic Fantasy Award for Adult Literature   see Mythopoeic Awards
Mythopoeic Fantasy Award for Children's Literature   see Mythopoeic Awards
Mythopoeic Scholarship Award in General Myth   see Mythopoeic Scholarship Awards
Mythopoeic Scholarship Award in Inklings Studies   see Mythopoeic Scholarship Awards
Mythopoeic Scholarship Awards.. 192
Nabokov Award   see PEN/Nabokov Award
Naomi Long Madgett Poetry Award 166
National Book Awards.. 194
National Book Critics Circle Awards.. 195
National Jewish Book Awards... 195
National Outdoor Book Awards.. 196
Native Writers Circle of the Americas Lifetime Achievement Award for Literature 198
Naylor (Phyllis) Working Writer Fellowship
     see PEN/Phyllis Naylor Working Writer Fellowship
NCTE Award for Excellence in Poetry for Children 199
Nebula Awards.. 199
Neustadt International Prize for Literature.. 200
New Letters Literary Awards... 201
New Millennium Writing Awards 202
Newbery (John) Medal   see John Newbery Medal
Norma Farber First Book Award 92
North American Native Authors First Book Awards... 210
O'Connor (Flannery) Award for Short Fiction   see Flannery O'Connor Award for Short Fiction
O'Dell (Scott) Historical Fiction Award   see Scott O'Dell Historical Fiction Award
O'Shaughnessy Poetry Award   see Irish American Cultural Institute (IACI) Literary Awards
Orbis Pictus Award for Outstanding Non-fiction for Children 215
Organization of American Historians Foreign Language Book Prize 215
Ornish (Natalie) Poetry Award   see Texas Institute of Letters Awards
Osterweil (Joyce) Award for Poetry   see PEN/Joyce Osterweil Award for Poetry
Parker (William Riley) Prize   see William Riley Parker Prize
Parkman (Francis) Prize   see Francis Parkman Prize
Paul A. Witty Short Story Award 376
Paul Birdsall Prize in European Military and Strategic History.. 37
Pegasus Prize for Literature.. 222
Pels (Laura) Awards for Drama   see PEN/Laura Pels Awards for Drama
PEN Award for Poetry in Translation.. 223
PEN Center USA West Annual Literary Awards 224
PEN/Architectural Digest Award for Literary Writing on the Visual Arts.. 223
PEN/Barbara Goldsmith Freedom to Write Awards... 223
PEN/Book-of-the-Month Club Translation Prize 223
PEN/Faulkner Award for Fiction 225
PEN/Jerard Fund Award 225
PEN/Joyce Osterweil Award for Poetry... 225
PEN/Laura Pels Awards for Drama.. 226
PEN/Martha Albrand Award for the Art of the Memoir 226
PEN/Martha Albrand Award for First Non-fiction 226
PEN/Nabokov Award.. 227
PEN/Norma Klein Award... 227
PEN/Phyllis Naylor Working Writer Fellowship.. 227

PEN/Ralph Manheim Medal for Translation 228
PEN/Robert Bingham Fellowships for Writers 228
PEN/Spielvogel-Diamonstein Award for the Art of the Essay 228
PEN/Voelcker Award for Poetry 229
Phoenix Award 230
Pilgrim Award 231
Poe (Edgar Allen) Awards   see Edgar Allan Poe Awards
Poggioli (Renato) Translation Award   see Renato Poggioli Translation Award
Polk (George) Awards   see George Polk Awards
Posner (Louis) Memorial Award   see National Jewish Book Awards
Premio Del Rey Prize 261
Printz (Michael L.) Award   see Michael L. Printz Award for Excellence
Private Eye Writers of America/SMP Contest 266
Pulitzer Prizes in Journalism, Letters, Drama and Music 309
Pura Belpré Award 32
Pushcart Prize: Best of the Small Presses 309
Raiziss/de Palchi Translation Award 311
Randolph Caldecott Medal 55
Rea Award for the Short Story 313
Renato Poggioli Translation Award 232
River Styx International Poetry Contest 316
Robert F. Sibert Informational Book Award 336
Robert H. Winner Memorial Award 376
Rosenthal (Richard and Hinda) Foundation Award
        see American Academy of Arts and Letters Annual Awards
Roth (Lois) Award   see Lois Roth Award for a Translation of a Literary Work
Russell Lowell (James) Prize   see James Russell Lowell Prize
Russell Major (J.) Prize   see J. Russell Major Prize
Ruth Lilly Poetry Prize 162
Sandrof (Ivan) Award   see The National Book Critics Circle Awards
Sapphire Awards 323
Scaglione (Aldo and Jeanne) Prize
        see Aldo and Jeanne Scaglione Prize for Comparative Literary Studies
Scaglione (Aldo and Jeanne) Prize
        see Aldo and Jeanne Scaglione Prize for French and Francophone Studies
Scaglione (Aldo and Jeanne) Prize
        see Aldo and Jeanne Scaglione Prize for Germanic Languages and Literatures
Scaglione (Aldo and Jeanne) Prize
        see Aldo and Jeanne Scaglione Prize for Italian Studies
Scaglione (Aldo and Jeanne) Prize
        see Aldo and Jeanne Scaglione Prize for Studies in Slavic Languages and Literatures
Scaglione (Aldo and Jeanne) Prize
        see Aldo and Jeanne Scaglione Prize for a Translation of a Literary Work
Scaglione (Aldo and Jeanne) Prize
        see Aldo and Jeanne Scaglione Prize for a Translation of a Scholarly Study of Literature
Scaglione (Aldo and Jeanne) Prize
        see Aldo and Jeanne Scaglione Publication Award for a Manuscript in Italian Literary Studies
Scarborough (William Sanders) Prize   see William Sanders Scarborough Prize
Science Fiction Achievement Award   see Hugo Award
Scott O'Dell Historical Fiction Award 213
Seidenbaum (Art) Award   see Los Angeles Times Book Prizes
Shamus Awards 333
Shaughnessy (Mina P.) Prize   see Mina P. Shaughnessy Prize
Shelley Memorial Award 334

Shulman (Marshall) Book Prize   *see* Marshall Shulman Book Prize

Sibert (Robert F.) Informational Book Award   *see* Robert F. Sibert Informational Book Award

Sidewise Awards for Alternate History 336

Sjöberg (Leif and Inger) Prize   *see* ASF Translation Prize

Society of School Librarians International Book Awards... 339

Spielvogel-Diamonstein Award
    see PEN/Spielvogel-Diamonstein Award

St Martin's Press/Malice Domestic Contest 341

Stevens (Wallace) Award   *see* Wallace Stevens Award

Sturgeon (Theodore) Memorial Award   *see* Theodore Sturgeon Memorial Award

Sydney Taylor Book Awards (STBA) 349

T. S. Eliot Prize for Poetry... 88

Tanning Prize 347

Taylor (Sydney) Book Awards   *see* Sydney Taylor Book Awards (STBA)

Texas Institute of Letters Awards 351

Thelen (David) Prize   *see* David Thelen Prize

Theodore Sturgeon Memorial Award... 344

Thomas (Lewis) Prize   *see* Lewis Thomas Prize

Thomas Dunne Books Award for the Novel... 84

Tufts (Kate) Discovery Award   *see* Kingsley Tufts Poetry Prize

Tufts (Kingsley) Poetry Prize   *see* Kingsley Tufts Poetry Prize

Turner (Steven) Award   *see* Texas Institute of Letters Awards

Twain (Mark) Award for Short Fiction   *see* Mark Twain Award for Short Fiction

Vucinich (Wayne S.) Book Prize   *see* Wayne S. Vucinich Book Prize

Vursell (Harold D.) Memorial Award
    see American Academy of Arts and Letters Annual Awards

Waldo G. Leland Prize.. 161

Wallace Stevens Award... 342

Walt Whitman Award.. 373

Wayne S. Vucinich Book Prize 365

Wesley-Logan Prize... 368

Whiting Writers' Awards... 372

Whitman (Walt) Award   *see* Walt Whitman Award

Wiesel (Elie) Prize in Ethics Essay Contest   *see* Elie Wiesel Prize in Ethics Essay Contest

Wilder (Laura Ingalls) Award   *see* Laura Ingalls Wilder Award

William Carlos Williams Award.. 375

William Riley Parker Prize.. 220

William Sanders Scarborough Prize 330

Williams (William Carlos) Award   *see* William Carlos Williams Award

Winner (Robert H.) Memorial Award   *see* Robert H. Winner Memorial Award

Witty (Paul A.) Short Story Award   *see* Paul A. Witty Short Story Award

Writer Magazine/Emily Dickinson Award.. 378

Writer's Digest Annual Writing Competition 378

Writer's Journal Annual Short Story Contest 378

Zolotow (Charlotte) Award   *see* Charlotte Zolotow Award

Uruguay

Concurso Annual de Literatura... 72

Venezuela

Gallegos (Romulo) Premio Internacional de Novela
    see Premio Internacional de Novela Rómulo Gallegos
Paz Castillo (Fernando), Premio   *see* Premio Fernándo Paz Castillo
Premio Fernándo Paz Castillo 257
Premio Internacional de Ensayo Mariano Picón Salas 242
Premio Internacional de Novela Rómulo Gallegos 243
Salas (Mariano Picón), Premio   *see* Premio Internacional de Ensayo Mariano Picón Salas

Zimbabwe

Africa's 100 Best Books of the Twentieth Century 4
Zimbabwean Publishers' Literary Awards 382

INDEX OF AWARDS BY SUBJECT

Adult Fiction

Academia Brasileira de Letras Fiction Prize 2

Adamji Prize 3

Addison Metcalf Award   *see* American Academy of Arts and Letters Annual Awards

Adelbert-von-Chamisso-Preis der Robert-Bosch-Stiftung 62

Africa's 100 Best Books of the Twentieth Century 4

Aftonbladets litteraturpris 5

Agatha Awards 5

Akutagawa Ryûnosuke Shô 7

Alberta Book Awards 8

Aleko Konstantinov Literary Prize 154

Alex Awards 9

Alfred-Döblin-Preis 82

Altamirano (Ignacio Manuel), Premio Nacional

      see Premio Nacional de Narrativa Ignacio Manuel Altamirano

Amazon.com/Books in Canada First Novel Award 10

American Academy of Arts and Letters Annual Awards 11

American Academy of Arts and Letters Gold Medal 11

ANA/Cadbury Prize for Poetry   *see* Association of Nigerian Authors Literature Prizes

Aniara Priset 12

Anisfield-Wolf Book Awards 12

Annett (R. Ross) Award for Children's Literature   *see* Alberta Book Awards

Anthony Awards 13

Anti-Booker Prize 13

Apollon Grigoryev Prize 118

Arguedas (José Maria) Prize   *see* Premio Casa de las Americas

Arreola (Juan José), Concurso Nacional   *see* Concurso Nacional de Cuento Juan José Arreola

Arthur C. Clarke Award for Science Fiction 69

Arthur Ellis Awards 88

Arts Council of England Writers' Awards 15

Arts Council of Wales Book of the Year Awards 15

Aschehougprisen 16

Aschehougs debutantpris   *see* Aschehougprisen

Asham Award for Women 17

Aspekte-Literatur-Preis 17

Associated Writing Programs (AWP) Award Series in Poetry, Fiction and Creative Non-fiction 17

Association of Nigerian Authors Literature Prizes 18

Audoux (Marguerite), Prix   *see* Prix Marguerite Audoux

Augustpriset 20

Aurealis Awards 20

Australian Literature Society Gold Medal 22

Australian Science Fiction Achievement Awards—Ditmars 22

Australian/Vogel Literary Award 23

Authors' Club Best First Novel Award 24

BA/Book Data Author of the Year 25

Babai-e-Urdu Maulvi Abdul Haq Award 179

Bachmann (Ingeborg) Preis   *see* Ingeborg Bachmann Preis

Bad Sex in Fiction Awards 26

Balakian (Nona) Citation   *see* The National Book Critics Circle Awards

Bank of New Zealand Katherine Mansfield Memorial Awards 27

Bank of New Zealand Novice Writer's Award 28
BBC Wildlife Magazine Literary Awards.. 30
BBC Wildlife Magazine Nature Writing Award   *see* BBC Wildlife Magazine Literary Awards
BBC Wildlife Magazine Poet of the Year Award   *see* BBC Wildlife Magazine Literary Awards
Beatriceprisen.. 30
Bernheim (Emile) Prix de littérature   *see* Prix de littérature Émile Bernheim
Bernstein (Mordechai) Literary Prizes   *see* Mordechai Bernstein Literary Prizes
Berto (Giuseppe), Premio Letterario   *see* Premio Letterario Giuseppe Berto
Best First Book of Fiction Award
        see Montana New Zealand Book Awards
Betty Trask Prize.. 356
Bhitaee (Shah Abdul Latif) Award   *see* Shah Abdul Latif Bhitaee Award
Bingham (Robert) Fellowships for Writers   *see* PEN/Robert Bingham Fellowships for Writers
Black (James Tait) Memorial Prizes   *see* James Tait Black Memorial Prizes
Blagovist Prize.. 38
Bloom (John) Humor Award   *see* Texas Institute of Letters Awards
Boardman Tasker Award 40
Bokhandlerprisen.. 41
Böll (Heinrich) Preis der Stadt Köln   *see* Heinrich-Böll-Preis der Stadt Köln
Bolt (Carol) Drama Award   *see* Canadian Authors Association Literary Awards
Bonniers (Gerard) Pris   *see* Gerard Bonniers Pris
Book Sense Book of the Year Award 42
Booker Prize for Fiction   *see* Man Booker Prize
Booker/Open Russia Prize.. 43
Border Television Prize   *see* Lakeland Book of the Year Awards
Bradt Travel Writing Award   *see* BBC Wildlife Magazine Literary Awards
Brageprisen... 45
Brand (Sarah) and Weinstein (Arik) Award   *see* National Jewish Book Awards
Bremen Literatur Förderungspreis.. 47
Bridport Prize... 47
Briggs (Katharine) Folklore Award   *see* Katharine Briggs Folklore Award
Brignetti (Rafaello), Premio   *see* Premio Letterario Isola d'Elba – Rafaello Brignetti
British Book Awards... 48
British Columbia Book Prizes 49
British Fantasy Awards 50
British Science Fiction Association Awards 51
Broumovska literarni cena... 51
Bryan MacMahon Short Story Award 170
Bucharest Writers' Association Prizes.. 52
Bukhari (Pitras) Award   *see* Pitras Bukhari Award
Bulwer-Lytton Fiction Contest 53
Bungakukai Shinjin Shô 54
Butler Literary Awards   *see* Irish American Cultural Institute (IACI) Literary Awards
CAA Air Canada Award... 54
Caine Prize for African Writing.. 55
Campbell (John W.) Memorial Award
        see John W. Campbell Memorial Award for the Best New Writer
Canada-Switzerland Literary Prize 57
Canadian Authors Association Literary Awards... 57
Canadian Library Association Book of the Year for Children Award.. 58
Canadian Library Association Young Adult Book Award 58
Canadian Literary Awards 59
Cappelen-prisen.. 60
Cappon (Alexander Patterson) Fiction Prize   *see* New Letters Literary Awards

Cappon (Dorothy Churchill) Prize   *see* New Letters Literary Awards
Cartier Diamond Dagger   *see* CWA Awards
Cassidy (Lar) Award   *see* Lar Cassidy Award
Castillo (Ricardo Mimenza), Premio de Literatura
      see Premio de Literatura Ricardo Mimenza Castillo
Cavour (Grinzane) Premio   *see* Premio Grinzane Cavour
Chalmers (Jack) Poetry Award   *see* Canadian Authors Association Literary Awards
Chamisso (Adelbert von) Preis   *see* Adelbert-von-Chamisso-Preis der Robert-Bosch-Stiftung
Chapters/Books in Canada Award 62
Chicano/Latino Literary Prize 63
Christopher Awards 67
Christy Awards 68
Church (Hubert) Fiction Award
      see Montana New Zealand Book Awards
City of Vancouver Book Award 68
Clarke (Arthur C.) Award for Science Fiction   *see* Arthur C. Clarke Award for Science Fiction
CNA Letterkkunde Toekenning 70
Colin Roderick Prize for Australian Literature 316
Commonwealth Writers Prize 71
Concurso Annual de Literatura 72
Concurso Literario Premio Emecé 73
Concurso Nacional de Cuento Juan José Arreola 73
Concurso de Prosa y Poesía Timón de Oro 73
Couture (Marcel) Prix   *see* Prix Marcel-Couture
Creasey (John) Memorial Dagger   *see* CWA Awards
CWA Awards 76
D. R. Wijewardene Memorial Award 374
Dahl (Thorlief), Norske Akademis Pris   *see* Norske Akademis Pris til Minne om Thorlief Dahl
David (Athanase) Prix   *see* Prix Athanase-David
David Gemmell Cup Short Story Competition 103
David St John Thomas Charitable Trust Awards 353
David T.K. Wong Prize for Short Fiction 377
Davies (Hunter) Prize   *see* Lakeland Book of the Year Awards
Dazai Osamu Shô 78
De la Cruz (Sor Juana), Premio de Literatura
      see Premio de Literatura Sor Juana Inés de la Cruz
Dennis (C. J.) Prize for Poetry   *see* Victorian Premier's Literary Awards
Dentan (Michel) Prix   *see* Prix Michel Dentan
Derleth (August) Award   *see* British Fantasy Awards
Deutscher-Krimi-Preis 80
Deutz Meda   *see* Montana New Zealand Book Awards/Deutz Medal
Dewan Bahasa dan Pustaka Prize 82
Diniz (D.) Prémio   *see* Prêmio D. Diniz
Ditmars   *see* Australian Science Fiction Achievement Awards—Ditmars
Döblin (Alfred) Preis   *see* Alfred-Döblin-Preis
Dobloug Priset 83
Don Carlos Palanca Memorial Awards 219
Dulché (Yolanda Vargas), Premio Internacional
      see Premio Internacional de Novela Yolanda Vargas Dulché
Dundee Book Prize 84
Dunne (Thomas) Books Award for the Novel   *see* Thomas Dunne Books Award for the Novel
Dupont (S. T.) Gold PEN   *see* Macmillan PEN Awards
Dymocks Singapore Literature Prize 85
Edgar Allan Poe Awards 231

Edgars   *see* Edgar Allan Poe Awards

Eggleston (Wilfred) Award for Non-Fiction   *see* Alberta Book Awards

Egyptian Literary Award 87

Elder (Ann) Poetry Award   *see* Fellowship of Australian Writers Literature Awards

Ellis (Arthur) Awards   *see* Arthur Ellis Awards

Encore Award 89

Engel (Marian) Award   *see* Marian Engel Award

Ernest Hemingway Foundation/PEN Award for First Fiction 126

Estrada (Ezequiel Martinez) Prize   *see* Premio Casa de las Americas

Eugène Maraisprys 176

European Jewish Publication Society Grant to Publishers.. 89

Evans (Hubert)Non-Fiction Prize   *see* British Columbia Book Prizes

F. Bordewijkprijs... 44

Fairlight Talking Book Award of New South Wales.. 92

Fallet (René), Prix   *see* Prix René Fallet

Farid (Khwaja Ghulam) Award   *see* Khwaja Ghulam Farid Award

Fellowship of Australian Writers Literature Awards 93

Feltrinelli (Antonio) Premio   *see* Premio Antonio Feltrinelli

Finlandia Award 94

Firecracker Alternative Book Awards 94

Flannery O'Connor Award for Short Fiction... 212

Fleming (Ian) Steel Dagger   *see* CWA Awards

Franklin (Miles) Award   *see* Miles Franklin Award

Frans Kellendonk-prijs.. 149

Franz Kafka Prize 146

Freustié (Jean), Prix   *see* Prix Jean Freustié

Friedenspreis des Deutschen Buchhandels 101

Friedrich-Glauser-Preis—Krimipreis der Autoren 105

Fujin Kôron Literary Prize 101

Gallegos (Romulo) Premio Internacional de Novela
     see Premio Internacional de Novela Rómulo Gallegos

Gay, Lesbian, Bisexual and Transgendered Book Awards.. 102

Gelsted (Otto) prisen   *see* Otto Gelstedprisen

Gemmell (David) Short Story Competition   *see* David Gemmell Cup Short Story Competition

Genevoix (Maurice) Prix   *see* Prix Maurice-Genevoix

Gerard Bonniers Pris.. 42

Giller Award 104

Gironde, Prix Littéraire   *see* Prix Littéraire de la Gironde

Glauser (Friedrich) Preis –Krimipreis der Autoren
     see Friedrich-Glauser-Preis—Krimipreis der Autoren

Glimmer Train Literary Awards 107

Godage Literary Awards 107

Golden Bike Awards   *see* Iranian Book of the Year Awards

Governor General's Literary Awards.. 110

Gradam Litrochta Cló Iar-Chonnachta... 111

Grand Prix de Biographie de l'Académie Française
     see Prix Littéraires de l'Académie Française

Grand Prix de Littérature Française hors de France/Prix Fondation Nessim Habif........................ 113

Grand prix du livre de Montréal 114

Grand Prix National des Arts et des Lettres (GPNAL).. 114

Grand Prix National des Lettres... 115

Grand Prix de Poésie de l'Académie Française   *see* Prix Littéraires de l'Académie Française

Grand Prix du Roman de l'Académie Française   *see* Prix Littéraires de l'Académie Française

Grand Prix RTL-Lire 115

Grand Prix de la Science-Fiction et du Fantastique Québécois 116
Grand Prix Thyde Monnier.. 114
Grandbois (Alain) Prix   *see* Prix Alain-Grandbois
Grigoryev (Apollon) Prize   *see* Apollon Grigoryev Prize
Grosser Literaturpreis der Bayerischen Akademie der Schönen Kunste.. 118
Grosser Preis der Schweizerische Schillerstiftung.. 119
Guardian First Book Award 120
Gyldendal (Soren) Prize   *see* Soren Gyldendal Prize
Gyldendal-prisen 121
Habif (Nessim), Prix Fondation
     see Grand Prix de Littérature Française hors de France/Prix Fondation Nessim Habif
Halldor Laxness Literary Prize.. 122
Hammett Awards.. 122
Harbourfront Reading Series' short stories award   *see* Journey Prize
Havmannprisen 123
Hawthornden Prize.. 124
Head Raddall (Thomas) Fiction Prize   *see* Thomas Head Raddall Fiction Prize
Heinemann (W. H.) Award   *see* W. H. Heinemann Award
Heinrich-Böll-Preis der Stadt Köln 41
Helsingin Sanomat Literary Award... 126
Hemingway (Ernest) Foundation/PEN Award
     see Ernest Hemingway Foundation/PEN Award for First Fiction
Henriette Roland Holst-prijs... 317
Henry (O.) Award   *see* Texas Institute of Letters Awards
Hertzogprys.. 127
Heywood Hill Literary Prize... 128
Hiemstra (Louis) prys vir nie-fiksie   *see* Louis Hiemstraprys vir nie-fiksie
Honchar (Oles) Ukrainian-German Prize   *see* Oles Honchar Prizes
Hooft (P. C.) prijs voor Letterkunde   *see* P. C. Hooft-prijs voor Letterkunde
Hugo Award.. 132
Icelandic Literary Prize... 134
Independent Foreign Fiction Prize 136
Ingeborg Bachmann Preis 26
International Imitation Hemingway Competition.. 138
International IMPAC Dublin Literary Award 138
Internationella Eeva Joenpelto-Litteraturpriset 140
Iranian Book of the Year Awards 141
Irish American Cultural Institute (IACI) Literary Awards 141
Irish Times International Fiction Prize 141
Irish Times Irish Literature Prizes... 142
Itô Sei Bungaku Shô.. 142
Izumi Kyôka Bungaku Shô 143
James A. Michener Memorial Prize.. 181
James Tait Black Memorial Prizes 37
Jaroslav Seifert Award... 332
Jefferson Cup Awards... 144
Jewish Quarterly-Wingate Prizes.. 145
Joenpelto (Eeva), Internationella Litteraturpriset
     see Internationella Eeva Joenpelto-Litteraturpriset
John Newbery Medal.. 203
John W. Campbell Memorial Award for the Best New Writer... 57
Jolson (Leon) Award   *see* National Jewish Book Awards
Jones (Jesse H.) Award   *see* Texas Institute of Letters Awards
Journey Prize.. 146

Jubilee Award for Short Stories   *see* Canadian Authors Association Literary Awards

Kafka (Franz) Prize   *see* Franz Kafka Prize

Kaikô Takeshi Shô 147

Katapultpriset 147

Katharine Briggs Folklore Award 47

Kathleen Mitchell Award 182

Kaufman (Sue) Prize for First Fiction
      see American Academy of Arts and Letters Annual Awards

Kawabata Yasunari Bungaku Shô 148

Kellendonk (Frans)-prijs   *see* Frans Kellendonk-prijs

Kerala Sahitya Akademi Awards 151

Kerry Ingredients Irish Fiction Award.. 151

Khattak (Khushhall Khan) Award   *see* Khushhall Khan Khattak Award

Khatulistiwa Literary Award 152

Khushhall Khan Khattak Award 152

Khwaja Ghulam Farid Award 93

King Fahd bin Abdulaziz Award for Initiative 153

Kiriyama Pacific Rim Book Prize... 153

Kirsch (Robert) Award   *see* Los Angeles Times Book Prizes

Konstantinov (Aleko) Literary Prize   *see* Aleko Konstantinov Literary Prize

Kreisel (Henry) Award for Best First Book   *see* Alberta Book Awards

Kristal Vilenica Award   *see* Vilenica International Literary Awards

Kumar (C. B.) Award   *see* Kerala Sahitya Akademi Awards

Kuttippuzha Award   *see* Kerala Sahitya Akademi Awards

Lakeland Book of the Year Awards 158

Lambda Literary Awards—Lammys.. 158

Lannan Literary Awards.. 159

Lao She Literary Prize 160

Lar Cassidy Award 60

Lara (Fernando) Premio   *see* Premio de Novela Fernando Lara

Larbaud (Valéry), Prix   *see* Prix Valéry Larbaud

Le Heurteur (Claude) Prix   *see* Prix Claude Le Heurteur

Leacock (Stephen) Memorial Medal for Humour
      see Stephen Leacock Memorial Medal for Humour

Libris Awards 162

Lilian Ida Smith Awards.. 338

Lima (José Lezama) Prize   *see* Premio Casa de las Americas

Literárna sútaz Poviedka... 163

Literaturpreis der Landeshauptstadt Stuttgart 164

Literaturpreis der Stadt Solothurn... 164

Little Booker Prize... 164

London Writers Competition 166

Lontar Literary Award... 167

Los Angeles Times Book Prizes.. 167

Louis Hiemstraprys vir nie-fiksie... 128

Lu Xun Literature Awards 168

Lucy B. & C. W. van der Hoogt Prize.. 360

M-Net Book Prize.. 169

Macallan Gold/Silver Dagger   *see* CWA Awards

Macallan/Scotland on Sunday Story Competition 170

MacMahon (Bryan) Short Story Award   *see* Bryan MacMahon Short Story Award

Macmillan PEN Awards... 170

Macmillan Prize   *see* Macmillan PEN Awards

Macmillan Silver PEN   *see* Macmillan PEN Awards

Macmillan Writer's Prize for Africa 171
Mads Wiel Nygaards Legat 173
Magnesia Litera Awards 173
Mail on Sunday/John Llewellyn Rhys Prize 174
Malheiros (Ricardo), Prêmio   *see* Prêmio Ricardo Malheiros
Man Booker Prize 174
Manila Critics Circle National Book Awards 175
Manitoba Literary Awards 175
Mansfield (Katherine) Award
      see Bank of New Zealand Katherine Mansfield Memorial Awards
Manès Sperber-Preis für Literatur 341
Mao Dun Literary Prize 176
Marais (Eugene) prys   *see* Eugène Maraisprys
Mares (José Fuentes), Premio de Literatura   *see* Premio de Literatura José Fuentes Mares
Marian Engel Award 89
Mark Twain Award for Short Fiction 358
Marlowe Award for Best International Crime Novel
      see Raymond Chandler Society's 'Marlowe' Award for Best International Crime Novel
Marten Toonder Award 178
Martinus Nijhoff Prijs voor Vertalingen 205
Mary McCarthy Prize in Short Fiction 172
Mathew Prichard Award for Short Story Writing 264
Maulvi Abdul Haq (Babai-e-Urdu) Award   *see* Babai-e-Urdu Maulvi Abdul Haq Award
McCarthy (Mary) Prize in Short Fiction   *see* Mary McCarthy Prize in Short Fiction
McKitterick Prize 172
McNally Robinson Book of the Year Award   *see* Manitoba Literary Awards
McNamara (Peter) Convenors' Award for Excellence   *see* Aurealis Awards
McTavish Sykes (Eileen) Award for Best First Book   *see* Manitoba Literary Awards
Melbourne University Literature Award
      see Fellowship of Australian Writers Literature Awards
Melsom-prisen 180
Michael L. Printz Award for Excellence in Young Adult Literature 265
Michener (James A.) Memorial Prize   *see* James A. Michener Memorial Prize
Miles Franklin Award 100
Mishima Yukio Shô 182
Mitchell (Kathleen) Award   *see* Kathleen Mitchell Award
Mitchell (W. O.) Prize   *see* W. O. Mitchell Prize
Monnet (Jean), Prix   *see* Prix Jean Monnet de littérature européenne
Monnier (Thyde), Grand Prix   *see* Grand Prix Thyde Monnier
Monsudar Book Awards 185
Montana New Zealand Book Awards 185
Montana New Zealand Book Awards/Best First Book of Fiction Award 186
Montana New Zealand Book Awards/Deutz Medal 188
Mordechai Bernstein Literary Prizes 33
Morton Dauwen Zabel Award   *see* American Academy of Arts and Letters Annual Awards
Multatuli Prize 190
Myanmar Annual National Literary Awards 191
Mythopoeic Awards 191
Mythopoeic Fantasy Award for Adult Literature   *see* Mythopoeic Awards
Mythopoeic Fantasy Award for Children's Literature   *see* Mythopoeic Awards
Mythopoeic Scholarship Award in General Myth   *see* Mythopoeic Scholarship Awards
Mythopoeic Scholarship Award in Inklings Studies   *see* Mythopoeic Scholarship Awards
Mythopoeic Scholarship Awards 192
Namboodiri (K. R.) Award   *see* Kerala Sahitya Akademi Awards

Naoki Sanjûgo Shô 193
National Book Awards 194
National Book Contest 194
National Book Critics Circle Awards 195
National Jewish Book Awards 195
National Outdoor Book Awards 196
Nebula Awards 199
Nelly-Sachs-Preis/Kulturpreis der Stadt Dortmund 321
Neuer deutscher Literaturpreis 200
Neustadt International Prize for Literature 200
New Letters Literary Awards 201
New Millennium Writing Awards 202
New Writer Prose and Poetry Prizes 202
Newbery (John) Medal   see John Newbery Medal
Nibbies   see British Book Awards
Nihon Horâ Shôsetsu Taishô 204
Nihon SF Taishô 205
Nijhoff (Martinus) Prijs voor Vertalingen   see Martinus Nijhoff Prijs voor Vertalingen
NIKE Literary Award 205
NOMA Award for Publishing in Africa 206
Noma Bungei Shô 206
Noma Literature Prize for New Writers 207
Nordic Council Literature Prize 208
Norsk Kritikerlags Pris 209
Norsk Sprakpris 209
Norske Akademis Pris til Minne om Thorleif Dahl 209
North American Native Authors First Book Awards 210
Northern Rock Foundation Writer Award 210
Northern Writers' Awards 211
NSW Writer's Fellowship 212
O'Connor (Flannery) Award for Short Fiction
      see Flannery O'Connor Award for Short Fiction
O'Shaughnessy Poetry Award   see Irish American Cultural Institute (IACI) Literary Awards
Oda Sakunosuke Shô 213
Okigbo (Christopher) Prize   see Association of Nigerian Authors Literature Prizes
Oles Honchar Prizes 130
Olive Schreiner Prize 331
Orange Prize for Fiction 214
Orange Prize for Translation   see Orange Prize for Fiction
Ornish (Natalie) Poetry Award   see Texas Institute of Letters Awards
Oro (Timón de), Concurso   see Concurso de Prosa y Poesia Timón de Oro
Osaragi Jirô Shô 217
Östersundsposten prize 217
Otto Gelstedprisen 102
Otto Stoessl-Preis 343
P. C. Hooft-prijs voor Letterkunde 131
P2-Lyttaranes Romanpris 218
Pakokku U Ohn Pe Literary and Education Awards 219
Palanca (Don Carlos) Memorial Awards   see Don Carlos Palanca Memorial Awards
Palmer (Nettie) Prize for Non-fiction   see Victorian Premier's Literary Awards
Palmer (Vance) Prize for Fiction   see Victorian Premier's Literary Awards
Parker Romantic Novel of the Year 221
Paz Castillo (Fernando), Premio   see Premio Fernándo Paz Castillo
Pegasus Prize for Literature 222

PEN Center USA West Annual Literary Awards 224
PEN/Faulkner Award for Fiction 225
PEN/Robert Bingham Fellowships for Writers.. 228
Peters (Ellis) Historical Dagger   *see* CWA Awards
Pilgrim Award 231
Pitras Bukhari Award 53
Pla, (Josep) Premi   *see* Premi Josep Pla
Poe (Edgar Allen) Awards   *see* Edgar Allan Poe Awards
Portico Prize for Literature.. 232
Posner (Louis) Memorial Award   *see* National Jewish Book Awards
Premi Josep Pla.. 234
Premi Sèrie Negra 234
Premio Alfaguara de Novela 236
Premio Andalucía de Novela 236
Premio Antonio Feltrinelli 241
Premio Azorín 237
Premio Biblioteca Breve 238
Premio Campiello... 238
Premio Casa de las Americas 239
Premio Destino-Guion.. 240
Prêmio D. Diniz 240
Premio Fastenrath 241
Premio Fernándo Paz Castillo.. 257
Premio Grinzane Cavour... 241
Premio Grinzane Editoria   *see* Premio Grinzane Cavour
Premio Internacional de Novela Rómulo Gallegos... 243
Premio Internacional de Novela Yolanda Vargas Dulché 243
Premio Internazionale di Letteratura La Cultura del Mare... 244
Prêmio Jabuti 245
Premio La Sonrisa Vertical 262
Prêmio Ler 245
Premio Letterario Giuseppe Berto 237
Premio Letterario Isola d'Elba – Rafaello Brignetti 246
Premio Letterario Mondello Città di Palermo 246
Premio del Libro... 246
Premio Literario Editorial Costa Rica 247
Prêmio Literário José Saramago... 247
Premio Literario Joven Creación.. 247
Premio de Literatura José Fuentes Mares.. 249
Premio de Literatura Latinoamericana y del Caribe Juan Rulfo................................... 249
Premio de Literatura Ricardo Mimenza Castillo 248
Premio de Literatura Sor Juana Inés de la Cruz.. 250
Premio Nacional de Literatura... 251
Premio Nacional de Literatura El Búho.. 253
Premio Nacional de Narrativa Ignacio Manuel Altamirano 254
Premio Nacional de Novela José Rubén Romero.. 255
Premio Nadal.. 255
Premio Napoli di Narrativa 256
Premio de Narrativa Colima... 256
Premio de Novela Fernando Lara 257
Premio Planeta de Novela... 258
Premio Primavera de Novela 259
Premio Strega 262
Premio UPC de ciencia ficción... 263

Premio Viareggio 263
Prêmio Ricardo Malheiros 251
Premios Literarios Fundación ARCIEN 263
Premju Letterarju 263
Prichard (Mathew) Award for Short Story Writing
    see Mathew Prichard Award for Short Story Writing
Prijs der Nederlandse Letteren 264
Prime Minister's Hebrew Literature Prize 265
Pringle (Thomas) Award   *see* Thomas Pringle Award
Printz (Michael L.) Award
    see Michael L. Printz Award for Excellence
Pritchett (V. S.) Memorial Prize   *see* V. S. Pritchett Memorial Prize
Private Eye Writers of America/SMP Contest 266
Prix Alain-Grandbois 285
Prix d'Ambronay 267
Prix des Amis du Scribe 267
Prix Athanase-David 276
Prix Auguste Teirlinck 305
Prix Bloc-Notes 272
Prix BPT 272
Prix Cazes Brasserie Lipp 273
Prix Champlain 274
Prix Ciné Roman Carte Noire 275
Prix des Cinq Continents de la francophonie 275
Prix Claude Le Heurteur 289
Prix Décembre 277
Prix des Deux-Magots 277
Prix Erckmann-Chatrian 279
Prix Fémina 280
Prix Fémina Etranger 280
Prix de Flore 281
Prix France Culture Français 282
Prix France Télévision 282
Prix Goncourt 285
Prix Goncourt des Lycéens 285
Prix Infini 286
Prix Interallié 287
Prix International Kadima 287
Prix Internet du Livre 288
Prix Jean Freustié 283
Prix Jean Monnet de littérature européenne 298
Prix du Jeune Ecrivain 288
Prix de la Langue de France 289
Prix des Lectrices de Elle 290
Prix des Libraires 290
Prix des Librairies de Création 291
Prix Littéraire de l'ENS Cachan 291
Prix Littéraire de la Gironde 292
Prix Littéraire Henri Deschamps 291
Prix Littéraire des Mouettes 292
Prix Littéraire du Parlement de la Communauté Française de Belgique 300
Prix Littéraire de la Vocation 292
Prix Littéraires de l'Académie Française 293
Prix Littéraires de la Société des Gens de Lettres 294

Prix de littérature Émile Bernheim 294
Prix du Livre Europe 1 295
Prix du Livre Inter 295
Prix du Livre de Picardie 295
Prix du Livre en Poitou-Charentes 296
Prix des Maisons de la Presse 296
Prix Marcel-Couture 276
Prix Marguerite Audoux 269
Prix Maurice-Genevoix 284
Prix Médicis 296
Prix Médicis Etranger 297
Prix Méditerranée 297
Prix Méditerranée étranger 297
Prix Michel Dentan 277
Prix National des Bibliothécaires 298
Prix Polar 301
Prix René Fallet 280
Prix RFI–témoin du monde 302
Prix Roman Historique de Blois 303
Prix Rosny-Aîné 303
Prix Saint Valentin 304
Prix Tour-Eiffel de Science-Fiction 306
Prix Tropiques de l'Agence Française de Développement 306
Prix Valéry Larbaud 289
Prix Victor-Rossel 303
Prix Wepler–Fondation La Poste 308
Promise Prize   *see* London Writers Competition
Pulitzer Prizes in Journalism, Letters, Drama and Music 309
Pushcart Prize: Best of the Small Presses 309
Queensland Premier's Literary Awards 310
Rajasthan Urdu Academy Awards 311
Rancage Literary Award 312
Rauriser Literaturpreis 312
Raymond Chandler Society's 'Marlowe' Award for Best International Crime Novel 62
Rea Award for the Short Story 313
Real Writers/Book Pl@ce Short Story Awards 313
Reed (A. W.) Lifetime Achievement Award   *see* Montana New Zealand Book Awards
Rhys Davies Short Story Competition 314
Rivertonprisen 'Den gylden revolver' 316
Roderick (Colin) Prize for Australian Literature
      see Colin Roderick Prize for Australian Literature
Roland Holst (Henriette) prijs   *see* Henriette Roland Holst-prijs
Romantic Novelists Association New Writers Award 317
Romero (José Rubén), Premio Nacional de Novela
      see Premio Nacional de Novela José Rubén Romero
Rooney Prize for Irish Literature 317
Rosenthal (Richard and Hinda) Foundation Award
      see American Academy of Arts and Letters Annual Awards
Rossel (Victor) Prix   *see* Prix Victor-Rossel
Rulfo (Juan) Premio   *see* Premio de Literatura Latinoamericana y del Caribe Juan Rulfo
Runciman Award 318
Russian Booker Prize   *see* Booker/Open Russia Prize
Sachs (Nelly) Preis   *see* Nelly-Sachs-Preis/Kulturpreis der Stadt Dortmund
Sagittarius Prize 321

Sahitya Akademi Award 321

Saidi (Bismil) Prize   *see* Rajasthan Urdu Academy Awards

Saltire Society Literary Awards 322

Samlagsprisen 323

Sandrof (Ivan) Award   *see* The National Book Critics Circle Awards

Sands (Ron) Prize   *see* Lakeland Book of the Year Awards

Sapphire Awards 323

Saramago (José) Prêmio Literário   *see* Prêmio Literário José Saramago

Saskatchewan Book Awards 324

Schiller, Grosser Preis   *see* Grosser Preis der Schweizerische Schillerstiftung

Scholz (Hugo) Prize   *see* Broumovska literarni cena

Schreiner (Olive) Prize   *see* Olive Schreiner Prize

Science Fiction Achievement Award   *see* Hugo Award

Scorer (Mary) Award   *see* Manitoba Literary Awards

Scottish Arts Council Book of the Year Award 332

Scottish Book of the Year   *see* Saltire Society Literary Awards

Scottish First Book of the Year   *see* Saltire Society Literary Awards

Scottish History Book of the Year   *see* Saltire Society Literary Awards

Seidenbaum (Art) Award   *see* Los Angeles Times Book Prizes

Seifert (Jaroslav) Award   *see* Jaroslav Seifert Award

Shagil (Ahteramuddin) Prize   *see* Rajasthan Urdu Academy Awards

Shah (Syed Waris) Award   *see* Syed Waris Shah Award

Shah Abdul Latif Bhitaee Award 34

Shamus Awards 333

Shirani (Mehmood) Prize   *see* Rajasthan Urdu Academy Awards

Shûgorô (Yamamoto) Shô   *see* Yamamoto Shûgorô Shô

Sidewise Awards for Alternate History 336

Singapore National Book Awards 337

Smirnoff-Booker Prize   *see* Booker/Open Russia Prize

Smith (Lilian Ida) Awards   *see* Lilian Ida Smith Awards

Sofola (Zulu) Prize   *see* Zulu Sofola Prize

Solzhenitsyn Prize for Russian Writing 340

Somerset Maugham Awards 179

Soren Gyldendal Prize 121

Spectrum Prize   *see* Association of Nigerian Authors Literature Prizes

Sperber (Manès) Preis für Literatur   *see* Manès Sperber-Preis für Literatur

Språklig Samlings Litteraturpris 341

St John Thomas (David) Charitable Trust Awards
      see David St John Thomas Charitable Trust Awards

St Martin's Press/Malice Domestic Contest 341

Staatliche Förderungspreise für junge Schriftstellerinnen und Schriftsteller 341

State Prizes for Literature 342

Stead (Christina) Award   *see* Fellowship of Australian Writers Literature Awards

Stephen Leacock Memorial Medal for Humour 161

Stern Silver PEN Prize   *see* Macmillan PEN Awards

Stoessl (Otto) Preis   *see* Otto Stoessl-Preis

Stryjova (Marie) Prize   *see* Broumovska literarni cena

Sturgeon (Theodore) Memorial Award   *see* Theodore Sturgeon Memorial Award

Sunday Times Award for Literary Excellence 344

Sunday Times Young Writer of the Year Award 344

Svenska Dagbladets Litteraturpris 345

Sveriges Radios Lyrikpris/Sveriges Radio P1:s Romanpris 346

SWPA Audiobooks of the Year 346

Syed Waris Shah Award 333

Tanizaki Jun'ichirô Shô 347
Tarjei Vesaas Debutanpris 348
TDK Australian Audio Book Awards 349
TDK Literary Award 350
Teirlinck (Auguste), Prix   see Prix Auguste Teirlinck
Texas Institute of Letters Awards 351
Theodore Sturgeon Memorial Award 344
Thomas Dunne Books Award for the Novel 84
Thomas Head Raddall Fiction Prize 124
Thomas Pringle Award 265
Tidens Skjonnlitteraere Pris 353
Toonder (Martin) Award   see Marten Toonder Award
Toronto Book Awards 355
Trask (Betty) Awards   see Betty Trask Prize
Trask (Betty) Prize   see Betty Trask Prize
Travelling Scholarship Fund 357
Trillium Book Award/Prix Trillium 357
Trinick (Trish) Prize   see TDK Australian Audio Book Awards
Tullie House Prize   see Lakeland Book of the Year Awards
Turner (Steven) Award   see Texas Institute of Letters Awards
Twain (Mark) Award for Short Fiction   see Mark Twain Award for Short Fiction
V. S. Pritchett Memorial Prize 266
Valentin (Saint), Prix   see Prix Saint Valentin
Victorian Premier's Literary Awards 362
Vilenica International Literary Award   see Vilenica International Literary Awards
Vilenica International Literary Awards 363
Virgin Books Newcomer of the Year Award   see British Book Awards
Vursell (Harold D.) Memorial Award
      see American Academy of Arts and Letters Annual Awards
Výrocní ceny Nadace 365
Vysehrad Publishers Awards 365
W. H. Heinemann Award 125
W. H. Smith Children's Book of the Year   see British Book Awards
W. H. Smith Literary Award 366
W. H. Smith Thumping Good Read Award 366
W. O. Mitchell Prize 183
Western Australian Premier's Book Awards 369
Whitbread Book of the Year and Literary Awards 371
Whiting Writers' Awards 372
Wijewardene (D. R.) Memorial Award   see D. R. Wijewardene Memorial Award
Willner (Ernst) Prize   see Ingeborg Bachmann Preis
Wilson (Ethel) Fiction Priz   see British Columbia Book Prizes
Wilson (Titus) Prize   see Lakeland Book of the Year Awards
Winifred Holtby Memorial Prize 130
Wittig (Joseph) Prize   see Broumovska literarni cena
Wong (David T.K) Prize for Short Fiction   see David T.K. Wong Prize for Short Fiction
Writer's Digest Annual Writing Competition 378
Writer's Journal Annual Short Story Contest 378
Writers' Alliance of Newfoundland and Labrador Provincial Book Awards 379
Yamamoto Shûgorô Shô 335
Yokomizo Seishi Shô 380
Yomiuri Bungaku Shô 380
Yorkshire Post Awards 381
Yoshikawa Eiji Bungaku Shinjin Shô 381

Yoshikawa Eiji Bungaku Shô 381
Yukio (Mishima) Shô   *see* Mishima Yukio Shô
Zimbabwean Publishers' Literary Awards 382
Zulu Sofola Prize 339

Biography

Ackerley (J. R.) Prize for Autobiography   *see* J. R. Ackerley Prize for Autobiography
Agatha Awards 5
Ambassador Book Awards... 10
Andersen (H. C.) Prize   *see* H. C. Andersen Prize
Arts Council of England Writers' Awards 15
Arts Council of Wales Book of the Year Awards 15
Augustin-Thierry, Prix   *see* Prix Augustin-Thierry
Balakian (Nona) Citation   *see* The National Book Critics Circle Awards
Bancroft Prizes 26
Beaufort (Henriëtte de) prijs   *see* Henriëtte de Beaufort-prijs
Billetdoux (François) Prix   *see* Prix François Billetdoux
Biographers' Club Prize... 37
Black (James Tait) Memorial Prizes   *see* James Tait Black Memorial Prizes
Boardman Tasker Award 40
Bolt (Carol) Drama Award   *see* Canadian Authors Association Literary Awards
Border Television Prize   *see* Lakeland Book of the Year Awards
Brageprisen.. 45
British Book Awards.. 48
Busken Huetprijs 132
Calvin and Rose G. Hoffmann Prize for a Distinguished Publication on Christopher Marlowe 129
Canadian Authors Association Literary Awards 57
Carême (Maurice), Prix de Poésie
        see Prix de Poésie et Prix d'Etudes Littéraires Maurice Carême
Chalmers (Jack) Poetry Award   *see* Canadian Authors Association Literary Awards
Christopher Awards.. 67
CNA Letterkkunde Toekenning 70
Cooper (Duff) Prize   *see* Duff Cooper Prize
Davies (Hunter) Prize   *see* Lakeland Book of the Year Awards
Deutscher (Isaac and Tamara) Memorial Prize   *see* Isaac and Tamara Deutscher Memorial Prize
Dixon Ryan Fox Manuscript Prize.. 98
Duff Cooper Prize.. 74
Edgar Allan Poe Awards 231
Edgars   *see* Edgar Allan Poe Awards
Enid McLeod Literary Prize 172
European Jewish Publication Society Grant to Publishers... 89
Fletcher (Sir Banister) Prize of the Authors' Club
        see Sir Banister Fletcher Prize of the Authors' Club
Fox (Dixon Ryan) Manuscript Prize   *see* Dixon Ryan Fox Manuscript Prize
Frans Kellendonk-prijs... 149
Franz Kafka Prize... 146
Freustié (Jean), Prix   *see* Prix Jean Freustié
Genevoix (Maurice) Prix   *see* Prix Maurice-Genevoix
Grand Prix de Biographie de l'Académie Française   *see* Prix Littéraires de l'Académie Française
Grand Prix de Poésie de l'Académie Française   *see* Prix Littéraires de l'Académie Française
Grand Prix du Roman de l'Académie Française   *see* Prix Littéraires de l'Académie Française
H. C. Andersen Prize 12

Hawthornden Prize 124

Heinemann (W. H.) Award   *see* W. H. Heinemann Award

Henriëtte de Beaufort-prijs 31

Heywood Hill Literary Prize 128

Hoffmann (Calvin and Rose G.) Prize   *see* Calvin and Rose G. Hoffmann Prize
   for a Distinguished Publication on Christopher Marlowe

Huetprijs (Busken)   *see* Busken Huetprijs

International Einhard Prize 137

Isaac and Tamara Deutscher Memorial Prize 81

J. R. Ackerley Prize for Autobiography 3

James Russell Lowell Prize 319

James Tait Black Memorial Prizes 37

Jefferson Cup Awards 144

Jubilee Award for Short Stories   *see* Canadian Authors Association Literary Awards

Kafka (Franz) Prize   *see* Franz Kafka Prize

Katherine Singer Kovacs Prize 155

Keats–Shelley Prize 149

Kellendonk (Frans)-prijs   *see* Frans Kellendonk-prijs

Kerala Sahitya Akademi Awards 151

Kessel (Joseph) Prix   *see* Prix Joseph Kessel

Kiriyama Pacific Rim Book Prize 153

Kirsch (Robert) Award   *see* Los Angeles Times Book Prizes

Kovacs (Katherine Singer) Prize   *see* Katherine Singer Kovacs Prize

Kumar (C. B.) Award   *see* Kerala Sahitya Akademi Awards

Kuttippuzha Award   *see* Kerala Sahitya Akademi Awards

Lakeland Book of the Year Awards 158

Lambda Literary Awards—Lammys 158

Los Angeles Times Book Prizes 167

Marsh Biography Award 178

McLeod (Enid) Literary Prize   *see* Enid McLeod Literary Prize

Modern Language Association Prize for a First Book 184

Montana New Zealand Book Awards 185

Namboodiri (K. R.) Award   *see* Kerala Sahitya Akademi Awards

National Book Critics Circle Awards 195

National Outdoor Book Awards 196

Nibbies   *see* British Book Awards

NIKE Literary Award 205

NSW Writer's Fellowship 212

Ocho Venado (Rey), Premio   *see* Premio Demac

Pla, (Josep) Premi   *see* Premi Josep Pla

Poe (Edgar Allen) Awards   *see* Edgar Allan Poe Awards

Portico Prize for Literature 232

Premi Josep Pla 234

Premio Demac 240

Prêmio Jabuti 245

Prix Augustin-Thierry 269

Prix François Billetdoux 271

Prix Goncourt 285

Prix Jean Freustié 283

Prix Joseph Kessel 289

Prix Littéraire de l'Age d'Or de France 291

Prix Littéraires de l'Académie Française 293

Prix Maurice-Genevoix 284

Prix de Poésie et Prix d'Etudes Littéraires Maurice Carême 273

Pulitzer Prizes in Journalism, Letters, Drama and Music 309
Reed (A. W.) Lifetime Achievement Award   *see* Montana New Zealand Book Awards
Runciman Award.. 318
Russell Lowell (James) Prize   *see* James Russell Lowell Prize
Saltire Society Literary Awards 322
Sandrof (Ivan) Award   *see* The National Book Critics Circle Awards
Sands (Ron) Prize   *see* Lakeland Book of the Year Awards
Scottish Book of the Year   *see* Saltire Society Literary Awards
Scottish First Book of the Year   *see* Saltire Society Literary Awards
Scottish History Book of the Year   *see* Saltire Society Literary Awards
Seidenbaum (Art) Award   *see* Los Angeles Times Book Prizes
Sir Banister Fletcher Prize of the Authors' Club 96
State Prizes for Literature... 342
SWPA Audiobooks of the Year 346
Toronto Book Awards 355
Tullie House Prize   *see* Lakeland Book of the Year Awards
UBC Medal for Canadian Biography/UBC President's Medal in Biography 359
Virgin Books Newcomer of the Year Award   *see* British Book Awards
Výrocní ceny Nadace... 365
W. H. Heinemann Award... 125
W. H. Smith Children's Book of the Year   *see* British Book Awards
W. H. Smith Thumping Good Read Award... 366
Whitbread Book of the Year and Literary Awards 371
William Hill Sports Book of the Year... 375
Wilson (Titus) Prize   *see* Lakeland Book of the Year Awards

Children's Literature

Academia Brasileira de Letras Children's Literature Prize 1
Adikarya Book Awards... 4
Aesop Prize 4
Africa's 100 Best Books of the Twentieth Century 4
Agatha Awards... 5
Alba Bouwerprys vir Kinderliteratuur 44
Alberta Book Awards... 8
Andersen (Hans Christian) Awards   *see* Hans Christian Andersen Awards
Annett (R. Ross) Award for Children's Literature   *see* Alberta Book Awards
Anzilotti (Rolando) Premio   *see* Premio Rolando Anzilotti
Arts Council of England Writers' Awards... 15
Augustpriset 20
Aurealis Awards... 20
Australian Christian Book of the Year... 21
Australian Christian Children's Book of the Year   *see* Australian Christian Book of the Year
Austrian National Award for Poetry for Children 24
Austrian National Children's and Juvenile Book Awards 24
Aventis Prize 25
Bank of New Zealand Young Writer's Award... 28
Batchelder (Mildred L.) Award   *see* Mildred L. Batchelder Award
Belpré (Pura) Award   *see* Pura Belpré Award
BILBY—Books I Love Best Yearly—Award 36
Biletsky (Oleksander) Prize   *see* National Writers Union of Ukraine Awards
Bilson (Geoffrey) Award   *see* Geoffrey Bilson Award for Historical Fiction for Young People

Blagovist Prize.. 38
Blue Peter Children's Book Awards... 38
Boardman Tasker Award 40
Bokhandlerprisen 41
Bologna New Media Prize (BNMP)... 41
Bologna Ragazzi Award.. 42
Bolt (Carol) Drama Award   *see* Canadian Authors Association Literary Awards
Border Television Prize   *see* Lakeland Book of the Year Awards
Boston Globe–Horn Book Award... 44
Bouwer (Alba) prys vir Kinderliteratuur   *see* Alba Bouwerprys vir Kinderliteratuur
Brageprisen.. 45
Brand (Sarah) and Weinstein (Arik) Award   *see* National Jewish Book Awards
Branford Boase Award 46
British Book Awards.. 48
British Columbia Book Prizes 49
Brüder-Grimm-Preis des Landes Berlin zur Förderung des Kinder- und Jugendtheaters 118
Buxtehuder Bulle 54
C. P. Hoogenhout Award.. 131
California Young Reader Medal 56
Canadian Authors Association Literary Awards 57
Carnegie Medal 60
Castillo (Ricardo Mimenza), Premio de Literatura
          see Premio de Literatura Ricardo Mimenza Castillo
Chalmers (Jack) Poetry Award   *see* Canadian Authors Association Literary Awards
Charlotte Zolotow Award 382
Children's Book Award 63
Children's Book Awards.. 63
Children's Book Guild Award for Non-fiction 64
Children's Book of the Year Awards.. 64
Children's eBook Award   *see* Bologna New Media Prize (BNMP)
Children's Laureate 65
Chrichton Award for Book Illustration.. 66
Christie's (Mr) Book Awards   *see* Mr Christie's Book Awards
City of Vancouver Book Award.. 68
Concurso Annual de Literatura... 72
Cool Awards.. 74
Coretta Scott King Award... 152
CYBER—Children's Yearly Best-Ever Reads—Award 77
Danish Ministry of Culture Children's Book Prize 77
David St John Thomas Charitable Trust Awards... 353
Davies (Hunter) Prize   *see* Lakeland Book of the Year Awards
De Troyes (Chrétien), Prix   *see* Prix Chrétien-de-Troyes
Deutscher Jugendliteraturpreis.. 79
Deutscher Jugendliteraturpreis Sonderpreis 80
Don Carlos Palanca Memorial Awards.. 219
Downey (Violet) Book Award   *see* IODE Violet Downey Book Award
Dymocks Children's Choice Awards.. 85
Edgar Allan Poe Awards 231
Edgars   *see* Edgar Allan Poe Awards
Eggleston (Wilfred) Award for Non-Fiction   *see* Alberta Book Awards
Elder (Ann) Poetry Award   *see* Fellowship of Australian Writers Literature Awards
Eleanor Farjeon Award 93
Elsie Locke Award 165
Esther Glen Award 106

Evans (Hubert) Non-Fiction Prize   *see* British Columbia Book Prizes

Ezra Jack Keats New Writer's and New Illustrator's Award for Children's Books 149

Fellowship of Australian Writers Literature Awards 93

Finlandia Award 94

Firecracker Alternative Book Awards 94

Fitzpatrick (Percy) Medal   *see* Percy Fitzpatrick Medal

Fleck (Norma) Award for Children's Non-Fiction
   see Norma Fleck Award for Children's Non-Fiction

Förderungspreis für Literatur 97

Frans Kellendonk-prijs 149

Geoffrey Bilson Award for Historical Fiction for Young People 36

Gleebooks Prize for Literary or Cultural Criticism   *see* NSW Premier's Literary Awards

Glen (Esther) Award   *see* Esther Glen Award

Golden Bike Awards   *see* Iranian Book of the Year Awards

Golden Kite Award 108

Gouden Griffel/Gouden Zoen 109

Gouden Zoen   *see* Gouden Griffel/Gouden Zoen

Governor General's Literary Awards 110

Grande Prémio Calouste Gulbenkian de Literatura para Crianças e Jovens 116

Greenaway (Kate) Medal   *see* Kate Greenaway Medal

Guardian Children's Fiction Award 119

Gulbenkian (Calouste), Grande Prémio de Literatura
   see Grande Prémio Calouste Gulbenkian de Literatura para Crianças e Jovens

Gustav-Heinemann-Friedenspreis für Kinder- und Jugendbücher 125

Hans Christian Andersen Awards 11

Heywood Hill Literary Prize 128

Hlibov (Leonid) Prize   *see* National Writers Union of Ukraine Awards

Holgersson (Nils) Plaque   *see* Nils Holgersson Plaque

Holloway (Tienie) Medal   *see* Tienie Hollowaymedalje vir kleuterliteratuur

Hopkins (Lee Bennett) Promising Poet Award   *see* Lee Bennett Hopkins Promising Poet Award

Hunapuh e Ixbalamqué, Premio de Literatura
   see Premio de Literatura para Niños Hunapuh e Ixbalamqué

Icelandic Children's Book Prize 134

Icelandic Literary Prize 134

IODE Violet Downey Book Award 140

Iranian Book of the Year Awards 141

Jane Addams Children's Book Award 3

Jenny Smelik IBBY Prijs 338

Jolson (Leon) Award   *see* National Jewish Book Awards

Jubilee Award for Short Stories   *see* Canadian Authors Association Literary Awards

Kate Greenaway Medal 116

Kathleen Fidler Award 94

Keats (Ezra Jack) Awards
   see Ezra Jack Keats New Writer's and New Illustrator's Award for Children's Books

Kellendonk (Frans)-prijs   *see* Frans Kellendonk-prijs

King (Coretta Scott) Award   *see* Coretta Scott King Award

Klein (Norma) Award   *see* PEN/Norma Klein Award

KOALA—Kids Own Australian Literature Awards 154

Korolenko (Volodymyr) Prize   *see* National Writers Union of Ukraine Awards

Kotlyarevsky (Ivan) Prize   *see* National Writers Union of Ukraine Awards

Kreisel (Henry) Award for Best First Book   *see* Alberta Book Awards

KROC—Kids Reading Oz Choice—Award 156

Kulturdepartementets Premiering av Barne- og Ungdomslitteratur 157

Lakeland Book of the Year Awards 158

Laura Ingalls Wilder Award 374
Lazarillo Prize 160
Lee Bennett Hopkins Promising Poet Award 131
Lesya Ukrainka Prize 359
LIANZA Young People's Non-fiction Award   see Elsie Locke Award
Lilian Ida Smith Awards.. 338
Locke (Elsie) Award   see Elsie Locke Award
London Writers Competition 166
Lydecken (Arvid) Prize   see Suomen Nuorisokirjailijat Ry Awards
Lyra (Carmen), Premio   see Premio Literario Carmen Lyra
Macmillan Writer's Prize for Africa 171
Manila Critics Circle National Book Awards.. 175
Mary Vaughan Jones Award 360
Mathew Prichard Award for Short Story Writing... 264
McNamara (Peter) Convenors' Award for Excellence   see Aurealis Awards
Mears (Colin) Award   see Kate Greenaway Medal
Melbourne University Literature Award   see Fellowship of Australian Writers Literature Awards
MER Prize.. 180
Michael L. Printz Award for Excellence in Young Adult Literature.................................... 265
Mildred L. Batchelder Award 29
Mishima Yukio Shô 182
Monteiro Lobato Award... 189
Mr Christie's Book Awards 67
Myanmar Annual National Literary Awards 191
Mythopoeic Awards... 191
Mythopoeic Fantasy Award for Adult Literature   see Mythopoeic Awards
Mythopoeic Fantasy Award for Children's Literature   see Mythopoeic Awards
National Book Contest... 194
National Jewish Book Awards... 195
National Outdoor Book Awards.. 196
National Writers Union of Ukraine Awards 198
Naylor (Phyllis) Working Writer Fellowship   see PEN/Phyllis Naylor Working Writer Fellowship
Nestlé Smarties Book Prize 199
New Zealand Post Children's Book Awards.. 203
Nibbies   see British Book Awards
Nienke van Hichtum Prize.. 360
Nils Holgersson Plaque 129
NOMA Award for Publishing in Africa... 206
Nordisk Skolebibliotekarforenings Barnebokpris... 208
Norma Fleck Award for Children's Non-Fiction 95
Norsk Kritikerlags Barnebokpris 209
NSW Premier's Literary Awards... 211
NSW Writer's Fellowship.. 212
O'Dell (Scott) Historical Fiction Award   see Scott O'Dell Historical Fiction Award
Orbis Pictus Award for Outstanding Non-fiction for Children 215
Orvieto (Laura), Premio letterario   see Premio letterario Laura Orvieto
Pääskynen   see Suomen Nuorisokirjailijat Ry Awards
Palanca (Don Carlos) Memorial Awards   see Don Carlos Palanca Memorial Awards
Paul A. Witty Short Story Award 376
PEN Center USA West Annual Literary Awards 224
PEN/Norma Klein Award... 227
PEN/Phyllis Naylor Working Writer Fellowship.. 227
Percy Fitzpatrick Medal 95
Phoenix Award 230

Poe (Edgar Allen) Awards   *see* Edgar Allan Poe Awards

Posner (Louis) Memorial Award   *see* National Jewish Book Awards

Pownall (Eve) Award for Information Books   *see* Children's Book of the Year Awards

Premio Apel les Mestres 237

Prêmio Jabuti 245

Premio Latinoamericano de Literatura Infantil y Juvenil Norma-Fundalectura 245

Premio letterario Laura Orvieto 216

Premio Literario Carmen Lyra 250

Premio de Literatura Infantil El Barco de Vapor 248

Premio de Literatura Juvenil Gran Angular 248

Premio de Literatura para Niños Hunapuh e Ixbalamqué 249

Premio de Literatura Ricardo Mimenza Castillo 248

Premio Nacional de Literatura 251

Premio Nacional de Literatura Infantil y Juvenil 253

Premio Nacional de Literatura Infantil y Juvenil Castillo de la Lectura 254

Premio Rolando Anzilotti 237

Prichard (Mathew) Award for Short Story Writing
    see Mathew Prichard Award for Short Story Writing

Printz (Michael L.) Award
    see Michael L. Printz Award for Excellence

Prix de l'Assemblée Nationale 268

Prix Baobab de l'album 270

Prix Bernard Versele 307

Prix Chrétien-de-Troyes 274

Prix Chronos de Littérature pour la Jeunesse 275

Prix des Enfants 279

Prix Européen du Roman pour Enfant de la Ville de Poitiers 279

Prix France Télévision 282

Prix Goncourt 285

Prix Littéraires du Ministère de la Jeunesse et des Sports 293

Prix Littéraires de la Société des Gens de Lettres 294

Prix Nautile de Cristal 299

Prix Octogone du livre de jeunesse 300

Prix Sorcières 304

Prix Tibet 305

Promise Prize   *see* London Writers Competition

Pura Belpré Award 32

Queensland Premier's Literary Awards 310

Rhône-Poulenc Prize   *see* Aventis Prize

Riksmalsprisen – Oslo og Baerum riksmalsforenings litteraturpris 315

Rimbaud (Arthur), Prix   *see* Prix Littéraires du Ministère de la Jeunesse et des Sports

Ruth Schwartz Children's Book Award 331

Saltire Society/Times Educational Supplement Scotland Prize for Educational Publications 322

Samlagsprisen 323

Sands (Ron) Prize   *see* Lakeland Book of the Year Awards

Sanlam Literary Award 323

Saskatchewan Book Awards 324

Scheepersprys vir jeugliteratuur 330

Schwartz (Ruth) Children's Book Award   *see* Ruth Schwartz Children's Book Award

Schweizer Jugendbuchpreis 331

Scott O'Dell Historical Fiction Award 213

Scottish Arts Council Book of the Year Award 332

Silas Prisen 337

Singapore National Book Awards 337

Skolebibliotekarforeningens Litteraturpris 338

Slessor (Kenneth) Prize for Poetry   *see* NSW Premier's Literary Awards

Smith (Lilian Ida) Awards   *see* Lilian Ida Smith Awards

Soong Ching Ling Children's Literature Prize 340

St John Thomas (David) Charitable Trust Awards
    see David St John Thomas Charitable Trust Awards

Staatliche Förderungspreise für junge Schriftstellerinnen und Schriftsteller 341

Stead (Christina) Award   *see* Fellowship of Australian Writers Literature Awards

Stewart (Douglas) Prize for Non-fiction   *see* NSW Premier's Literary Awards

Suomen Nuorisokirjailijat Ry Awards 345

SWPA Audiobooks of the Year 346

Sydney Taylor Book Awards (STBA) 349

Taylor (Sydney) Book Awards   *see* Sydney Taylor Book Awards (STBA)

Te Kura Pounamu Award 350

Theo Thijssen Prize for Children's and Youth Literature 352

Tienie Hollowaymedalje vir kleuterliteratuur 354

Tir Na N-og Awards 354

Topelius Prize   *see* Suomen Nuorisokirjailijat Ry Awards

Toronto Book Awards 355

Toyota/Children's Literature Foundation Award 355

Tullie House Prize   *see* Lakeland Book of the Year Awards

Turner (Ethel) Prize for Young People's Literature   *see* NSW Premier's Literary Awards

Ukrainka (Lesya) Prize   *see* Lesya Ukrainka Prize

UNESCO Prize for Children's and Young People's Literature in the Service of Tolerance 359

Ushakov (Mykola) Prize   *see* National Writers Union of Ukraine Awards

Vaka-Helgafell Children's Book Award 360

van Hichtum (Nienke) Prize   *see* Nienke van Hichtum Prize

Vaughan Jones (Mary) Award   *see* Mary Vaughan Jones Award

Versele, Prix Bernard   *see* Prix Bernard Versele

Virgin Books Newcomer of the Year Award   *see* British Book Awards

Výrocní ceny Nadace 365

W. H. Smith Children's Book of the Year   *see* British Book Awards

W. H. Smith Thumping Good Read Award 366

WAYRBA—West Australian Young Readers' Book Award 368

Western Australian Premier's Book Awards 369

Whitbread Book of the Year and Literary Awards 371

White Ravens 371

Wilder (Laura Ingalls) Award   *see* Laura Ingalls Wilder Award

Wilson (Ethel) Fiction Priz   *see* British Columbia Book Prizes

Wilson (Titus) Prize   *see* Lakeland Book of the Year Awards

Witty (Paul A.) Short Story Award   *see* Paul A. Witty Short Story Award

Wrightson (Patricia) Prize   *see* NSW Premier's Literary Awards

Writer's Digest Annual Writing Competition 378

Writers' Alliance of Newfoundland and Labrador Provincial Book Awards 379

YARA—Young Australian Readers' Awards 380

Yukio (Mishima) Shô   *see* Mishima Yukio Shô

Zimbabwean Publishers' Literary Awards 382

Zolotow (Charlotte) Award   *see* Charlotte Zolotow Award

Drama

Abell (Kjeld) Prisen   *see* Kjeld Abell Prisen

Academia Brasileira de Letras Fiction Prize 2

Africa's 100 Best Books of the Twentieth Century 4
Alberta Book Awards.. 8
Alfred Fagon Award.. 91
American Academy of Arts and Letters Gold Medal 11
ANA/Cadbury Prize for Poetry   *see* Association of Nigerian Authors Literature Prizes
Annett (R. Ross) Award for Children's Literature   *see* Alberta Book Awards
Anti-Booker Prize... 13
Arguedas (José Maria) Prize   *see* Premio Casa de las Americas
Arts Council Bursaries and Commissions.. 14
Arts Council of England Children's Award 14
Arts Council of England Writers' Awards 15
Association of Nigerian Authors Literature Prizes 18
Awgie Awards... 25
Bargate (Verity) Award   *see* Verity Bargate Award
Bernstein (Mordechai) Literary Prizes   *see* Mordechai Bernstein Literary Prizes
Biletsky (Oleksander) Prize   *see* National Writers Union of Ukraine Awards
Boardman Tasker Award 40
Bolt (Carol) Drama Award   *see* Canadian Authors Association Literary Awards
Brüder-Grimm-Preis des Landes Berlin zur Förderung des Kinder- und Jugendtheaters................. 118
Bucharest Writers' Association Prizes.. 52
Butler Literary Awards   *see* Irish American Cultural Institute (IACI) Literary Awards
Canada-Switzerland Literary Prize 57
Canadian Authors Association Literary Awards... 57
Cao Yu Drama Literature Prize 59
Čapek (Karel) Award for Literary Achievement
     see Karel Čapek Award for Literary Achievement
Chalmers (Floyd S.) Canadian Play Awards
     see Chalmers Awards for Creativity and Excellence in the Arts
Chalmers (Jack) Poetry Award   *see* Canadian Authors Association Literary Awards
Chalmers Awards for Creativity and Excellence in the Arts.. 61
Chicano/Latino Literary Prize 63
Children's Award (Arts Council of England)   *see* Arts Council of England Children's Award
City of Vancouver Book Award... 68
CNA Letterkkunde Toekenning 70
Concurso Annual de Literatura.. 72
Concurso Nacional de Dramaturgia Teatro Nuevo 74
Dennis (C. J.) Prize for Poetry   *see* Victorian Premier's Literary Awards
Deutscher Kinder- und Jugendtheaterpreis.. 80
Don Carlos Palanca Memorial Awards... 219
Eamon Keane Full Length Play Award 148
Eggleston (Wilfred) Award for Non-Fiction   *see* Alberta Book Awards
Estrada (Ezequiel Martinez) Prize   *see* Premio Casa de las Americas
Fagon (Alfred) Prize   *see* Alfred Fagon Award
Franklin (Miles) Award   *see* Miles Franklin Award
Frans Kellendonk-prijs... 149
Franz Kafka Prize.. 146
Gleebooks Prize for Literary or Cultural Criticism   *see* NSW Premier's Literary Awards
Governor General's Literary Awards... 110
Gradam Litrochta Cló Iar-Chonnachta.. 111
Hawthornden Prize 124
Henriette Roland Holst-prijs... 317
Herman Voaden National Playwriting Competition 364
Hertzogprys.. 127
Heywood Hill Literary Prize.. 128

Hlibov (Leonid) Prize   *see* National Writers Union of Ukraine Awards

Imison (Richard) Memorial Award   *see* Richard Imison Memorial Award

International Playwriting Festival.. 139

Irish American Cultural Institute (IACI) Literary Awards 141

John Whiting Award... 372

Jubilee Award for Short Stories   *see* Canadian Authors Association Literary Awards

Kafka (Franz) Prize   *see* Franz Kafka Prize

Karel Čapek Award for Literary Achievement... 59

Keane (Eamon) Full Length Play Award   *see* Eamon Keane Full Length Play Award

Kellendonk (Frans)-prijs   *see* Frans Kellendonk-prijs

Kerala Sahitya Akademi Awards.. 151

Kjeld Abell Prisen 1

Korolenko (Volodymyr) Prize   *see* National Writers Union of Ukraine Awards

Kotlyarevsky (Ivan) Prize   *see* National Writers Union of Ukraine Awards

Kreisel (Henry) Award for Best First Book   *see* Alberta Book Awards

Kristal Vilenica Award   *see* Vilenica International Literary Awards

Kumar (C. B.) Award   *see* Kerala Sahitya Akademi Awards

Kuttippuzha Award   *see* Kerala Sahitya Akademi Awards

Lao She Literary Prize 160

Lazarillo Prize 160

Lima (José Lezama) Prize   *see* Premio Casa de las Americas

Literaturpreis der Landeshauptstadt Stuttgart 164

London Writers Competition 166

Manila Critics Circle National Book Awards... 175

Meyer-Whitworth Award.. 180

Miles Franklin Award 100

Mishima Yukio Shô.. 182

Moore (Oscar) Screenwriting Prize   *see* Oscar Moore Screenwriting Prize

Mordechai Bernstein Literary Prizes.. 33

Mühlheimer Dramatikerpreis.. 190

Namboodiri (K. R.) Award   *see* Kerala Sahitya Akademi Awards

National Writers Union of Ukraine Awards... 198

Neustadt International Prize for Literature 200

NIKE Literary Award... 205

NOMA Award for Publishing in Africa.. 206

Northern Rock Foundation Writer Award 210

NSW Premier's Literary Awards... 211

NSW Writer's Fellowship 212

O'Shaughnessy Poetry Award   *see* Irish American Cultural Institute (IACI) Literary Awards

Okigbo (Christopher) Prize   *see* Association of Nigerian Authors Literature Prizes

Olive Schreiner Prize... 331

Onassis Cultural Competition Prize 214

Oscar Moore Screenwriting Prize... 189

Palanca (Don Carlos) Memorial Awards   *see* Don Carlos Palanca Memorial Awards

Palmer (Nettie) Prize for Non-fiction   *see* Victorian Premier's Literary Awards

Palmer (Vance) Prize for Fiction   *see* Victorian Premier's Literary Awards

Pels (Laura) Awards for Drama   *see* PEN/Laura Pels Awards for Drama

PEN Center USA West Annual Literary Awards 224

PEN/Laura Pels Awards for Drama.. 226

Premio Alvarez Quintero... 260

Premio Casa de las Americas 239

Premio Letterario Mondello Città di Palermo 246

Premio Nacional de Literatura.. 252

Premio Nezahualcóyotl de Literatura en Lenguas Indígenas.. 257

Prijs der Nederlandse Letteren 264

Pringle (Thomas) Award   *see* Thomas Pringle Award

Prix du Livre en Poitou-Charentes 296

Promise Prize   *see* London Writers Competition

Pulitzer Prizes in Journalism, Letters, Drama and Music 309

Queensland Premier's Literary Awards 310

Quintero (Alvarez) Premio   *see* Premio Alvarez Quintero

Richard Imison Memorial Award 135

Roland Holst (Henriette) prijs   *see* Henriette Roland Holst-prijs

Runciman Award 318

Saltire Society Literary Awards 322

Schreiner (Olive) Prize   *see* Olive Schreiner Prize

Scottish Book of the Year   *see* Saltire Society Literary Awards

Scottish First Book of the Year   *see* Saltire Society Literary Awards

Scottish History Book of the Year   *see* Saltire Society Literary Awards

Slessor (Kenneth) Prize for Poetry   *see* NSW Premier's Literary Awards

Sofola (Zulu) Prize   *see* Zulu Sofola Prize

Soong Ching Ling Children's Literature Prize 340

Spectrum Prize   *see* Association of Nigerian Authors Literature Prizes

Språklig Samlings Litteraturpris 341

Staatliche Förderungspreise für junge Schriftstellerinnen und Schriftsteller 341

Stewart (Douglas) Prize for Non-fiction   *see* NSW Premier's Literary Awards

Tanizaki Jun'ichirô Shô 347

TDK Literary Award 350

Theatre Book Prize 352

Thomas Pringle Award 265

Tsubouchi Shôyô Taishô 358

Turner (Ethel) Prize for Young People's Literature   *see* NSW Premier's Literary Awards

Ushakov (Mykola) Prize   *see* National Writers Union of Ukraine Awards

Verity Bargate Award 28

Victorian Premier's Literary Awards 362

Vilenica International Literary Award   *see* Vilenica International Literary Awards

Vilenica International Literary Awards 363

Voaden (Herman) National Playwriting Competition
      see Herman Voaden National Playwriting Competition

Western Australian Premier's Book Awards 369

Westminster Prize 370

Whiting (John) Award   *see* John Whiting Award

Whiting Writers' Awards 372

Wrightson (Patricia) Prize   *see* NSW Premier's Literary Awards

Writer's Digest Annual Writing Competition 378

Yomiuri Bungaku Shô 380

Yoshikawa Eiji Bungaku Shô 381

Yukio (Mishima) Shô   *see* Mishima Yukio Shô

Zulu Sofola Prize 339

History

AAAS/Orbis Books Prize for Polish Studies 1

Albert J. Beveridge Award 34

Aldo and Jeanne Scaglione Prize for Studies in Slavic Languages and Literatures 328

Aldo and Jeanne Scaglione Publication Award for a Manuscript in Italian Literary Studies 329

Alexander Prize 9
Ambassador Book Awards 10
Atlantic History Prize 19
Augustin-Thierry, Prix   *see* Prix Augustin-Thierry
Auschwitz Foundation Prize 21
Australian/Vogel Literary Award 23
Bancroft Prizes 26
Barbara Jelavich Book Prize 144
Baxter Adams (Herbert) Prize   *see* Herbert Baxter Adams Prize
Beer (George Louis) Prize   *see* George Louis Beer Prize
Bergmann (Anton) Prix   *see* Prix Anton Bergmann
Berry (David) Prize   *see* David Berry Prize
Beveridge (Albert J.) Award   *see* Albert J. Beveridge Award
Bilson (Geoffrey) Award   *see* Geoffrey Bilson Award for Historical Fiction for Young People
Binkley–Stephenson Award 36
Birdsall (Paul) Prize   *see* Paul Birdsall Prize in European Military and Strategic History
Bolt (Carol) Drama Award   *see* Canadian Authors Association Literary Awards
Breasted (James H.) Prize   *see* James H. Breasted Prize
C. H. Currey Memorial Fellowship 75
Calvin and Rose G. Hoffmann Prize for a Distinguished Publication on Christopher Marlowe 129
Canadian Authors Association Literary Awards 57
Castex (Louis) Prix   *see* Prix Louis Castex
Cena Josefa Hlavky 128
Chalmers (Jack) Poetry Award   *see* Canadian Authors Association Literary Awards
Christy Awards 68
City of Vancouver Book Award 68
Clarence H. Haring Prize 123
CNA Letterkkunde Toekenning 70
Cooper (Duff) Prize   *see* Duff Cooper Prize
Cumont (Franz), Prix   *see* Prix Franz Cumont
Currey (C. H.) Memorial Fellowship   *see* C. H. Currey Memorial Fellowship
Darton (Harvey) Award   *see* Harvey Darton Award
David Berry Prize 33
David Thelen Prize 352
Deutscher (Isaac and Tamara) Memorial Prize   *see* Isaac and Tamara Deutscher Memorial Prize
Discailles (Ernest), Prix   *see* Prix Ernest Discailles
Dixon Ryan Fox Manuscript Prize 98
Dobloug Priset 83
Dr Wijnaendts Francken-prijs 99
Duculot (Jules) Prix   *see* Prix Jules Duculot
Duff Cooper Prize 74
Dunning (Jonh H.) Prize   *see* John H. Dunning Prize
Duvivie (Charles), Prix   *see* Prix Charles Duvivie
Enid McLeod Literary Prize 172
Fagg (John E.) Prize   *see* John E. Fagg Prize
Fairbank (John K.) Prize   *see* John K. Fairbank Prize
Feis (Herbert) Prize   *see* Herbert Feis Prize
Foreign-Language Article Prize   *see* David Thelen Prize
Forkosch (Morris D.) Prize   *see* Morris D. Forkosch Prize
Fox (Dixon Ryan) Manuscript Prize   *see* Dixon Ryan Fox Manuscript Prize
Fraenkel Prize in Contemporary History 98
Francis Parkman Prize 221
Francken-prijs (Dr Wijnaendts)   *see* Dr Wijnaendts Francken-prijs
Frans Kellendonk-prijs 149

Geoffrey Bilson Award for Historical Fiction for Young People 36
George L. Mosse Prize 190
George Louis Beer Prize 31
Gershoy (Leo) Prize   *see* Leo Gershoy Prize
Gladstone History Book Prize 105
Grand Prix de Biographie de l'Académie Française   *see* Prix Littéraires de l'Académie Française
Grand prix du livre de Montréal 114
Grand Prix de Poésie de l'Académie Française   *see* Prix Littéraires de l'Académie Française
Grand Prix du Roman de l'Académie Française   *see* Prix Littéraires de l'Académie Française
Haring (Clarence H.) Prize   *see* Clarence H. Haring Prize
Harvey Darton Award 78
Hawthornden Prize 124
Heinemann (W. H.) Award   *see* W. H. Heinemann Award
Herbert Baxter Adams Prize 30
Herbert Feis Prize 93
Hlavky (Josef) Prize   *see* Cena Josefa Hlavky
Hoffmann (Calvin and Rose G.) Prize   *see* Calvin and Rose G. Hoffmann Prize
    for a Distinguished Publication on Christopher Marlowe
Howard R. Marraro Prize in Italian History 177
Institute of Historical Research Prize 137
Isaac and Tamara Deutscher Memorial Prize 81
J. Russell Major Prize 320
James H. Breasted Prize 46
Jefferson Cup Awards 144
Jelavich (Barbara) Book Prize   *see* Barbara Jelavich Book Prize
Joan Kelly Memorial Prize 150
John E. Fagg Prize 91
John H. Dunning Prize 85
John K. Fairbank Prize 91
Jubilee Award for Short Stories   *see* Canadian Authors Association Literary Awards
Katherine Singer Kovacs Prize 155
Kellendonk (Frans)-prijs   *see* Frans Kellendonk-prijs
Kelly (Joan) Memorial Prize   *see* Joan Kelly Memorial Prize
Kirsch (Robert) Award   *see* Los Angeles Times Book Prizes
Kovacs (Katherine Singer) Prize   *see* Katherine Singer Kovacs Prize
Leclère (Léon), Prix   *see* Prix Léon Leclère
Leland (Walso G.) Prize   *see* Waldo G. Leland Prize
Leo Gershoy Prize 103
Littleton-Griswold Prize 165
Longman–History Today Book of the Year Award 166
Los Angeles Times Book Prizes 167
Lynton (Mark) History Prize   *see* Mark Lynton History Prize
Mark Lynton History Prize 169
Marraro (Howard R.) Prize   *see* Howard R. Marraro Prize in Italian History
Marshall Shulman Book Prize 335
McLeod (Enid) Literary Prize   *see* Enid McLeod Literary Prize
Merghelynck (Arthur), Prix   *see* Prix Arthur Merghelynck
Montana New Zealand Book Awards 185
Morris D. Forkosch Prize 97
Mosse (George L.) Prize   *see* George L. Mosse Prize
O'Dell (Scott) Historical Fiction Award   *see* Scott O'Dell Historical Fiction Award
Organization of American Historians Foreign Language Book Prize 215
Parkman (Francis) Prize   *see* Francis Parkman Prize
Paul Birdsall Prize in European Military and Strategic History 37

Premio Academia Nacional de la Historia 235
Premio Del Rey Prize 261
Prijs voor Meesterschap 264
Privat (Edouard), Prix   see Prix Edouard Privat
Prix Anton Bergmann 271
Prix Arthur Merghelynck 298
Prix Augustin-Thierry 269
Prix Baron de Saint-Genois 304
Prix Charles Duvivie 278
Prix Edouard Privat 301
Prix Ernest Discailles 278
Prix Franz Cumont 276
Prix Goblet d'Alviella 284
Prix Jules Duculot 278
Prix Léon Leclère 290
Prix Littéraires de l'Académie Française 293
Prix Littéraires de la Société des Gens de Lettres 294
Prix Louis Castex 273
Prix Roman Historique de Blois 303
Pulitzer Prizes in Journalism, Letters, Drama and Music 309
Queensland Premier's Literary Awards 310
Reed (A. W.) Lifetime Achievement Award   see Montana New Zealand Book Awards
Reese (Trevor) Memorial Prize   see Trevor Reese Memorial Prize
Robert F. Sibert Informational Book Award 336
Runciman Award 318
Russell Major (J.) Prize   see J. Russell Major Prize
Saint-Genois (Baron de) Prix   see Prix Baron de Saint-Genois
Saltire Society Literary Awards 322
Scaglione (Aldo and Jeanne) Prize
        see Aldo and Jeanne Scaglione Prize for Studies in Slavic Languages and Literatures
Scaglione (Aldo and Jeanne) Prize
        see Aldo and Jeanne Scaglione Publication Award for a Manuscript in Italian Literary Studies
Scott O'Dell Historical Fiction Award 213
Scottish Book of the Year   see Saltire Society Literary Awards
Scottish First Book of the Year   see Saltire Society Literary Awards
Scottish History Book of the Year   see Saltire Society Literary Awards
Seidenbaum (Art) Award   see Los Angeles Times Book Prizes
Shulman (Marshall) Book Prize   see Marshall Shulman Book Prize
Sibert (Robert F.) Informational Book Award   see Robert F. Sibert Informational Book Award
Thelen (David) Prize   see David Thelen Prize
Toronto Book Awards 355
Trevor Reese Memorial Prize 313
W. H. Heinemann Award 125
W. H. Smith Thumping Good Read Award 366
Wadsworth Prize for Business History 367
Waldo G. Leland Prize 161
Wesley-Logan Prize 368
Whitfield Prize 372
Wolfson History Prize 376

Illustration

Adikarya Book Awards 4
Amelia Frances Howard-Gibbon Illustrator's Award 131

Andersen (Hans Christian) Awards   *see* Hans Christian Andersen Awards

Belpré (Pura) Award   *see* Pura Belpré Award

Biennial of Illustrations Bratislava (BIB) 35

Border Television Prize   *see* Lakeland Book of the Year Awards

British Book Awards 48

Caldecott (Randolph) Medal   *see* Randolph Caldecott Medal

Charlotte Zolotow Award 382

Chrichton Award for Book Illustration 66

Clark (Russell) Award   *see* Russell Clark Award

Davies (Hunter) Prize   *see* Lakeland Book of the Year Awards

Deutscher Jugendliteraturpreis Sonderpreis 80

Ezra Jack Keats New Writer's and New Illustrator's Award for Children's Books 149

Firecracker Alternative Book Awards 94

Förderungspreis für Literatur 97

Golden Kite Award 108

Governor General's Literary Awards 110

Grand Prix de la Ville de Sierre   *see* Prix du Festival de la Bande Dessinée de Sierre

Grande Prémio Calouste Gulbenkian de Literatura para Crianças e Jovens 116

Greenaway (Kate) Medal   *see* Kate Greenaway Medal

Gulbenkian (Calouste), Grande Prémio de Literatura
     see Grande Prémio Calouste Gulbenkian de Literatura para Crianças e Jovens

Hans Christian Andersen Awards 11

Harries (Katrine) Award   *see* Katrine Harries Award

Howard-Gibbon (Amelia Frances) Illustrator's Award
     see Amelia Frances Howard-Gibbon Illustrator's Award

Kate Greenaway Medal 116

Katrine Harries Award 148

Keats (Ezra Jack) Awards
     see Ezra Jack Keats New Writer's and New Illustrator's Award for Children's Books

Koivu (Rudolf) Prize   *see* Rudolf Koivu Prize

Kulturdepartementets Premiering av Barne- og Ungdomslitteratur 157

Lakeland Book of the Year Awards 158

Laura Ingalls Wilder Award 374

Lazarillo Prize 160

Macmillan Prize for Children's Picture Book Illustration 171

Mears (Colin) Award   *see* Kate Greenaway Medal

Monteiro Lobato Award 189

National Art Library Illustration Awards 193

New Zealand Post Children's Book Awards 203

Nibbies   *see* British Book Awards

Noma Concours for Picture Book Illustrations 207

Premio Apel les Mestres 237

Premio Nacional de Literatura 252

Prix Baobab de l'album 270

Prix du Festival de la Bande Dessinée de Sierre 280

Prix Octogone du livre de jeunesse 300

Prix Sorcières 304

Pura Belpré Award 32

Randolph Caldecott Medal 55

Rudolf Koivu Prize 154

Russell Clark Award 69

Sands (Ron) Prize   *see* Lakeland Book of the Year Awards

Sydney Taylor Book Awards (STBA) 349

Taylor (Sydney) Book Awards   *see* Sydney Taylor Book Awards (STBA)

Toyota/Children's Literature Foundation Award 355
Tullie House Prize   *see* Lakeland Book of the Year Awards
Virgin Books Newcomer of the Year Award   *see* British Book Awards
W. H. Smith Children's Book of the Year   *see* British Book Awards
Wilder (Laura Ingalls) Award   *see* Laura Ingalls Wilder Award
Wilson (Titus) Prize   *see* Lakeland Book of the Year Awards
Zolotow (Charlotte) Award   *see* Charlotte Zolotow Award

Lifetime Achievement

A. A. Phillips Prize 229
Academy of American Poets Fellowship 2
Addison Metcalf Award   *see* American Academy of Arts and Letters Annual Awards
Adelbert-von-Chamisso-Preis der Robert-Bosch-Stiftung 62
Agatha Awards 5
Ali (Mast Tauq) Award   *see* Mast Tauq Ali Award
American Academy of Arts and Letters Annual Awards 11
American Academy of Arts and Letters Gold Medal 11
Andersen (Hans Christian) Awards   *see* Hans Christian Andersen Awards
Anisfield-Wolf Book Awards 12
Astrid Lindgren Translation Prize 163
Asturias (Príncipe de), Premio   *see* Premio Príncipe de Asturias
Attila (Jozsef) Prize   *see* József Attila Prize
Australia Council Literature Board Emeritus Awards 21
Austrian Award of Merit for Children's Literature 23
Balzan Prize for Culture 26
Benson Medal 32
Berliner Preis für deutschsprachige Gegenwartsliteratur 32
Bhakta (Bhanu) Memorial Award   *see* Bhanu Bhakta Memorial Award
Bhanu Bhakta Memorial Award 34
Bialik Prize for Literature 35
Bienek (Horst) Preis fur Lyrik   *see* Horst Bienek Preis für Lyrik
Blixen (Karen) Medaljen   *see* Karen Blixen Medaljen
Brageprisen 45
Brand (Sarah) and Weinstein (Arik) Award   *see* National Jewish Book Awards
British Book Awards 48
Broumovska literarni cena 51
Büchner (Georg) Preis   *see* Georg-Büchner-Preis
Čapek (Karel) Award for Literary Achievement   *see* Karel Čapek Award for Literary Achievement
Cartier Diamond Dagger   *see* CWA Awards
Cavour (Grinzane) Premio   *see* Premio Grinzane Cavour
Chamisso (Adelbert von) Preis   *see* Adelbert-von-Chamisso-Preis der Robert-Bosch-Stiftung
Children's Book Guild Award for Non-fiction 64
Children's Laureate 65
China Literature Foundation Awards 65
Cholmondeley Awards 66
Chuang (C. W.) Literary Prize   *see* China Literature Foundation Awards
Cohen (David) British Literature Prize   *see* David Cohen British Literature Prize
Constantijn Huygens Prize 133
Creasey (John) Memorial Dagger   *see* CWA Awards
Cultural Center of the Philippines Literary Awards 75
CWA Awards 76

David Cohen British Literature Prize 71
Den Store Pris 343
Deutscher Jugendliteraturpreis Sonderpreis 80
DV Cultural Award 85
Echeverría (Esteban), Premio   see Premio Esteban Echeverría
Edgar Allan Poe Awards 231
Edgars   see Edgar Allan Poe Awards
Edwards (Margaret) Award   see Margaret A. Edwards Award
Egyptian Literary Award 87
Emerson-Thoreau Medal 88
Erich-Fried-Preis 100
Faisal (King) International Prize   see King Faisal International Prize for Arabic Literature
Féval (Paul), Grand Prix   see Grand Prix Paul Féval de Littérature Populaire
Fleming (Ian) Steel Dagger   see CWA Awards
Franz Kafka Prize 146
Fried (Erich) Preis   see Erich-Fried-Preis
Friedrich Gundolf Preis für die Vermittlung deutscher Kultur im Ausland 121
Friedrich-Glauser-Preis —Krimipreis der Autoren... 105
Frost Medal... 101
G H s'Gravesande Prize 320
Gal (Henri), Grand Prix de Littérature   see Grand Prix de Littérature Henri Gal
Georg-Büchner-Preis... 52
Glauser (Friedrich) Preis—Krimipreis der Autoren
        see Friedrich-Glauser-Preis—Krimipreis der Autoren
Goldsmith (Barbara) Award   see PEN/Barbara Goldsmith Freedom to Write Awards
Gottfried Keller Prize 150
Grand Prix de Biographie de l'Académie Française   see Prix Littéraires de l'Académie Française
Grand Prix de la Francophonie 112
Grand Prix Halperine-Kaminsky 112
Grand Prix Littéraire Poncetton 112
Grand Prix de Littérature Henri Gal 113
Grand Prix de Littérature Paul Morand 113
Grand Prix Paul Féval de Littérature Populaire 281
Grand Prix de Poésie de l'Académie Française   see Prix Littéraires de l'Académie Française
Grand Prix Ramuz... 115
Grand Prix du Roman de l'Académie Française   see Prix Littéraires de l'Académie Française
Grosser Literaturpreis der Bayerischen Akademie der Schönen Kunste.. 118
Grosser Österreichischer Staatspreis für Literatur 119
Grosser Preis der Schweizerische Schillerstiftung.. 119
Gundolf (Fiedrich) Preis
        see Friedrich Gundolf Preis für die Vermittlung deutscher Kultur im Ausland
Hans Christian Andersen Awards 11
Haryana Sahitya Akademi Awards.. 123
Heine (Heinrich) Medaille   see Heinrich-Heine-Preis der Landeshauptstadt Düsseldorf
Heinrich-Heine-Preis der Landeshauptstadt Düsseldorf.. 124
Herder Prize 127
Heywood Hill Literary Prize.. 128
Horst Bienek Preis für Lyrik.. 35
Huygens (Constantijn) Prize   see Constantijn Huygens Prize
IBBY-Asahi Reading Promotion Award.. 133
IBC International Book Award.. 133
Innis-Gérin Medal... 136
International Lotus Prize for Poetry.. 139
International Vaptsarov Prize 139

Ireland Fund of Monaco Literary Award 141
Ivanov (Miroslav) Award for Non-Fiction   *see* Miroslav Ivanov Award for Non-Fiction
Jacinto Prado Coelho Award.. 70
Jnanpith Award.. 145
John Steinbeck Award... 342
Jolson (Leon) Award   *see* National Jewish Book Awards
Jozsef Attila Prize 19
Kafka (Franz) Prize   *see* Franz Kafka Prize
Karel Čapek Award for Literary Achievement... 59
Karen Blixen Medaljen.. 38
Kaufman (Sue) Prize for First Fiction   *see* American Academy of Arts and Letters Annual Awards
Keller (Gottfried) Prize   *see* Gottfried Keller Prize
Kellgrenpriset.. 150
Kerala Sahitya Akademi Awards... 151
Kikuchi Hiroshi Shô... 147
King Faisal International Prize for Arabic Literature 92
Kirsch (Robert) Award   *see* Los Angeles Times Book Prizes
Kossuth Prize 155
Kumar (C. B.) Award   *see* Kerala Sahitya Akademi Awards
Kuttippuzha Award   *see* Kerala Sahitya Akademi Awards
Lannan Literary Awards... 159
Lewis Thomas Prize... 353
Lilly (Ruth) Poetry Prize   *see* Ruth Lilly Poetry Prize
Lindgren (Astrid) Translation Prize   *see* Astrid Lindgren Translation Prize
Lorne Pierce Medal... 230
Los Angeles Times Book Prizes... 167
Macallan Gold/Silver Dagger   *see* CWA Awards
Magsaysay (Ramon) Award   *see* Ramon Magsaysay Award
Mahendra Pragya Puraskar   *see* Royal Nepal Academy Awards
Mann (Thomas) Preis   *see* Thomas-Mann-Preis
Margaret A. Edwards Award... 86
Margit Pahlson Prize... 219
Mast Tauq Ali Award 10
Miroslav Ivanov Award for Non-Fiction 142
MLA Award for Lifetime Scholarly Achievement.. 183
Montalte (Louis) Prix de Poésie   *see* Prix de Poésie Louis Montalte
Montana New Zealand Book Awards... 185
Morand (Paul), Grand Prix   *see* Grand Prix de Littérature Paul Morand
Morton Dauwen Zabel Award   *see* American Academy of Arts and Letters Annual Awards
Nabokov Award   *see* PEN/Nabokov Award
Namboodiri (K. R.) Award   *see* Kerala Sahitya Akademi Awards
National Artists Award 193
National Jewish Book Awards.. 195
National Kamal-E-Fun Award.. 196
Native Writers Circle of the Americas Lifetime Achievement Award for Literature 198
NCTE Award for Excellence in Poetry for Children 199
Neustadt International Prize for Literature.. 200
New Brunswick Excellence in the Arts Awards 201
Nibbies   *see* British Book Awards
Nobel Prize in Literature 205
Noma Literacy Prize 207
Nordiska Priset 208
Nowlan (Alden) Award   *see* New Brunswick Excellence in the Arts Awards
Oktober-Prisen... 213

Österreichischer Staatspreis für Europäische Literatur 217
Pahlson (Margit) Prize   *see* Margit Pahlson Prize
Pakokku U Ohn Pe Literary and Education Awards 219
Pels (Laura) Awards for Drama   *see* PEN/Laura Pels Awards for Drama
PEN/Barbara Goldsmith Freedom to Write Awards.. 223
PEN/Laura Pels Awards for Drama.. 226
PEN/Nabokov Award 227
Peters (Ellis) Historical Dagger   *see* CWA Awards
Phillips (A. A.) Prize   *see* A. A. Phillips Prize
Pierce (Lorne) Medal   *see* Lorne Pierce Medal
Poe (Edgar Allen) Awards   *see* Edgar Allan Poe Awards
Poirier (Pascal) Award   *see* New Brunswick Excellence in the Arts Awards
Posner (Louis) Memorial Award   *see* National Jewish Book Awards
Premi d'Honor de les Lletres Catalanes.. 233
Premi Nacional de Literatura de la Generalitat de Catalunya.. 234
Premio Camões.. 238
Premio Cervantes.. 239
Premio Esteban Echeverría.. 241
Premio Grinzane Cavour 241
Premio Grinzane Editoria   *see* Premio Grinzane Cavour
Premio Internacional Alfonso Reyes 243
Premio Internazionale Fregene 244
Prêmio Machado de Assis 250
Premio Nacional de las Letras Españolas.. 251
Premio Nacional de Literatura.. 252
Premio Nacional de Literatura.. 253
Premio Nacional de Literatura.. 253
Premio Nacional a la obra de un traductor.. 255
Premio Pessoa.. 258
Premio Príncipe de Asturias 260
Premio Reina Sofía de Poesía Iberoamericana 260
President's Award for Pride of Performance.. 264
Prijs der Nederlandse Letteren 264
Prijs voor Meesterschap 264
Prithvi Pragya Puraskar   *see* Royal Nepal Academy Awards
Prix Gouverneur de la Rosée du Livre et de la Littérature.. 285
Prix Littéraire Prince Pierre-de-Monaco 292
Prix Littéraires de l'Académie Française 293
Prix Littéraires de la Société des Gens de Lettres 294
Prix du Meilleur Livre Etranger 298
Prix de Poésie Louis Montalte.. 301
Pushkin Poetry Prize.. 310
Rajasthan Urdu Academy Awards.. 311
Ramon Magsaysay Award.. 173
Ramuz (C. F.), Grand Prix   *see* Grand Prix Ramuz
Reed (A. W.) Lifetime Achievement Award   *see* Montana New Zealand Book Awards
Reyes (Alfonso) Premio Internacional   *see* Premio Internacional Alfonso Reyes
Rosenthal (Richard and Hinda) Foundation Award
        see American Academy of Arts and Letters Annual Awards
Royal Nepal Academy Awards.. 318
Ruth Lilly Poetry Prize 162
RÚV (Icelandic State Radio) Literary Award 320
s'Gravesande (G H) Prize   *see* G H s'Gravesande Prize
Saidi (Bismil) Prize   *see* Rajasthan Urdu Academy Awards

Schiller, Grosser Preis   *see* Grosser Preis der Schweizerische Schillerstiftung

Scholz (Hugo) Prize   *see* Broumovska literarni cena

Seidenbaum (Art) Award   *see* Los Angeles Times Book Prizes

Shagil (Ahteramuddin) Prize   *see* Rajasthan Urdu Academy Awards

Shevchenko (Taras) Award   *see* Taras Shevchenko Award

Shirani (Mehmood) Prize   *see* Rajasthan Urdu Academy Awards

Sidewise Awards for Alternate History 336

Singh (Bhai Santokh) Award   *see* Haryana Sahitya Akademi Awards

Sino-American Literary Exchange Prize   *see* China Literature Foundation Awards

Southeast Asia (SEA) Write Award 340

State Prize of the Russian Federation in Arts and Letters 342

State Prizes for Literature 342

Stora Priset 343

Stryjova (Marie) Prize   *see* Broumovska literarni cena

Sur Award   *see* Haryana Sahitya Akademi Awards

Taras Shevchenko Award 335

Tarlan Independent Prize 348

Thomas (Lewis) Prize   *see* Lewis Thomas Prize

Thomas-Mann-Preis 176

Triumph Prize 357

Tun Seri Lanang Award 358

Vaptsarov (International) Prize   *see* International Vaptsarov Prize

Vedvyasa (Maharshi) Award   *see* Haryana Sahitya Akademi Awards

Virgin Books Newcomer of the Year Award   *see* British Book Awards

Vursell (Harold D.) Memorial Award
       see American Academy of Arts and Letters Annual Awards

Vysehrad Publishers Awards 365

W. H. Smith Children's Book of the Year   *see* British Book Awards

Wittig (Joseph) Prize   *see* Broumovska literarni cena

Wolfson History Prize 376

Würdigungspreis für Literatur 380

Yomiuri Bungaku Shô 380

Non-fiction

AAAS/Orbis Books Prize for Polish Studies 1

Academia Brasileira de Letras Essay Prize 2

Africa's 100 Best Books of the Twentieth Century 4

Agatha Awards 5

AIP Science Writing Awards in Physics and Astronomy 6

Alberta Book Awards 8

Albrand (Martha) Award for First Non-fiction
       see PEN/Martha Albrand Award for First Non-fiction

Albrand (Martha) Award for the Art of the Memoir
       see PEN/Martha Albrand Award for the Art of the Memoir

Aldo and Jeanne Scaglione Prize for Comparative Literary Studies 326

Aldo and Jeanne Scaglione Prize for French and Francophone Studies 326

Aldo and Jeanne Scaglione Prize for Germanic Languages and Literatures 327

Aldo and Jeanne Scaglione Prize for Italian Studies 327

Aldo and Jeanne Scaglione Prize for Studies in Slavic Languages and Literatures 328

Aldo and Jeanne Scaglione Publication Award for a Manuscript in Italian Literary Studies 329

Alex Awards 9

Alexander Prize 9

Altron Literary Award   *see* Bill Venter/Altron Literary Award

Ambassador Book Awards 10

American Academy of Arts and Letters Gold Medal 11

Anisfield-Wolf Book Awards 12

Annett (R. Ross) Award for Children's Literature   *see* Alberta Book Awards

Anthony Awards 13

Anti-Booker Prize 13

Anugerah Persuratan (Bidang Esei Sastera) 13

Arguedas (José Maria) Prize   *see* Premio Casa de las Americas

Asher Prize   *see* Society of Authors Medical Book Awards

Associated Writing Programs (AWP) Award Series in Poetry, Fiction and Creative Non-fiction 17

Audiffred (François-Joseph), Prix   *see* Prix François-Joseph Audiffred

Augustpriset 20

Auschwitz Foundation Prize 21

Australian/Vogel Literary Award 23

Aventis Prize 25

Balakian (Nona) Citation   *see* The National Book Critics Circle Awards

Balzan Prize for Culture 26

Bank of New Zealand Essay Award 27

Barbara Jelavich Book Prize 144

Bayon (Daniel), Prix   *see* Prix Daniel Bayon

BBC Wildlife Magazine Literary Awards 30

BBC Wildlife Magazine Nature Writing Award   *see* BBC Wildlife Magazine Literary Awards

BBC Wildlife Magazine Poet of the Year Award   *see* BBC Wildlife Magazine Literary Awards

BBC4 Samuel Johnson Prize for Non-Fiction 145

Bernheim (Emile) Prix de littérature   *see* Prix de littérature Émile Bernheim

Bernstein (Mordechai) Literary Prizes   *see* Mordechai Bernstein Literary Prizes

Berry (David) Prize   *see* David Berry Prize

Best First Book of Non-Fiction Award
      see Montana New Zealand Book Awards/Best First Book of Non-Fiction Award

Besterman/McColvin Medals 33

Biletsky (Oleksander) Prize   *see* National Writers Union of Ukraine Awards

Bill Venter/Altron Literary Award 361

Billetdoux (François) Prix   *see* Prix François Billetdoux

Blagovist Prize 38

BMA (British Medical Association) Medical Book Competition 39

Boardman Tasker Award 40

Bolt (Carol) Drama Award   *see* Canadian Authors Association Literary Awards

Border Television Prize   *see* Lakeland Book of the Year Awards

BP Natural World Book Prize 45

Bradt Travel Writing Award   *see* BBC Wildlife Magazine Literary Awards

Brageprisen 45

British Academy Book Prize 48

British Book Awards 48

British Columbia Book Prizes 49

Busken Huetprijs 132

CAA Air Canada Award 54

Canada-Switzerland Literary Prize 57

Canadian Authors Association Literary Awards 57

Canadian Literary Awards 59

Čapek (Karel) Award for Literary Achievement   *see* Karel Čapek Award for Literary Achievement

Cappon (Alexander Patterson) Fiction Prize   *see* New Letters Literary Awards

Cappon (Dorothy Churchill) Prize   *see* New Letters Literary Awards

Cartier Diamond Dagger   *see* CWA Awards

Castillo (Ricardo Mimenza), Premio de Literatura
    see Premio de Literatura Ricardo Mimenza Castillo
Cena Josefa Hlavky 128
Chalmers (Jack) Poetry Award   *see* Canadian Authors Association Literary Awards
Charles Veillon European Essay Prize 361
Children's Literature Association Book Awards 65
China Literature Foundation Awards 65
Christopher Awards 67
Christopher Ewart-Biggs Memorial Prize 90
Christy Awards 68
Chuang (C. W.) Literary Prize   *see* China Literature Foundation Awards
City of Vancouver Book Award 68
Clarence L. Holt Literary Prize 130
Cohen (Morton N.) Award   *see* Morton N. Cohen Award for a Distinguished Edition of Letters
Colin Roderick Prize for Australian Literature 316
Concurso de Prosa y Poesía Timón de Oro 73
Cooper (Derek) Award   *see* Guild of Food Writers Awards
Cooper (Duff) Prize   *see* Duff Cooper Prize
Crawshay (Rose Mary) Prize   *see* Rose Mary Crawshay Prize
Creasey (John) Memorial Dagger   *see* CWA Awards
Curtius (Ernst-Robert) Preise für Essayistik   *see* Ernst-Robert-Curtius-Preise für Essayistik
CWA Awards 76
Dahl (Thorlief), Norske Akademis Pris   *see* Norske Akademis Pris til Minne om Thorleif Dahl
Dartmouth Medal 77
David Berry Prize 33
David St John Thomas Charitable Trust Awards 353
David Watt Prize 367
Davies (Hunter) Prize   *see* Lakeland Book of the Year Awards
Dennis (C. J.) Prize for Poetry   *see* Victorian Premier's Literary Awards
Deutscher (Isaac and Tamara) Memorial Prize   *see* Isaac and Tamara Deutscher Memorial Prize
Diniz (D.) Prêmio   *see* Prêmio D. Diniz
Don Carlos Palanca Memorial Awards 219
Donner Prize 83
Dr Wijnaendts Francken-prijs 99
Duff Cooper Prize 74
Dupont (S. T.) Gold PEN   *see* Macmillan PEN Awards
Ed A. Hewett Book Prize 127
Eggleston (Wilfred) Award for Non-Fiction   *see* Alberta Book Awards
Ehrenpreis des Österreichischen Buchhandels für Toleranz in Denken und Handeln 87
Elder (Ann) Poetry Award   *see* Fellowship of Australian Writers Literature Awards
Elie Wiesel Prize in Ethics Essay Contest 374
Enid McLeod Literary Prize 172
Ernst-Robert-Curtius-Preise für Essayistik 76
Estrada (Ezequiel Martinez) Prize   *see* Premio Casa de las Americas
European Jewish Publication Society Grant to Publishers 89
European Online Journalism (EOJ) Award 90
Evans (Hubert) Non-Fiction Prize   *see* British Columbia Book Prizes
Evelyn Richardson Non-fiction Award 314
Evens Foundation European Prize for Literature 90
Ewart-Biggs (Christopher) Memorial Prize   *see* Christopher Ewart-Biggs Memorial Prize
Faber (Geoffrey) Memorial Prize   *see* Geoffrey Faber Memorial Prize
Fairlight Talking Book Award of New South Wales 92
Fellowship of Australian Writers Literature Awards 93
Feltrinelli (Antonio) Premio   *see* Premio Antonio Feltrinelli

Fenia and Yaakov Leviant Memorial Prize 162
Firecracker Alternative Book Awards 94
Fleming (Ian) Steel Dagger   see CWA Awards
Fletcher (Sir Banister) Prize of the Authors' Club
    see Sir Banister Fletcher Prize of the Authors' Club
Fraenkel Prize in Contemporary History.. 98
Francken-prijs (Dr Wijnaendts)   see Dr Wijnaendts Francken-prijs
Frans Kellendonk-prijs.. 149
Franz Kafka Prize... 146
Freud (Sigmund) Preis   see Sigmund-Freud-Preis für wissenschaftliche Prosa
Freustié (Jean), Prix   see Prix Jean Freustié
Friedenspreis des Deutschen Buchhandels... 101
Gantrelle (Joseph), Prix   see Prix Joseph Gantrelle
Gay, Lesbian, Bisexual and Transgendered Book Awards.. 102
Gelsted (Otto) prisen   see Otto Gelstedprisen
Geoffrey Faber Memorial Prize 90
George Polk Awards... 232
Geschwister-Scholl-Preis 103
Gladstone History Book Prize... 105
Gleebooks Prize for Literary or Cultural Criticism   see NSW Premier's Literary Awards
Glenfiddich Food & Drink Awards.. 106
Gold Medallion Book Awards 108
Golden Bike Awards   see Iranian Book of the Year Awards
Gourmand World Cookbook Awards.. 110
Governor General's Literary Awards... 110
Grand Prix de Biographie de l'Académie Française   see Prix Littéraires de l'Académie Française
Grand prix du livre de Montréal 114
Grand Prix National des Arts et des Lettres (GPNAL).. 114
Grand Prix de Poésie de l'Académie Française   see Prix Littéraires de l'Académie Française
Grand Prix du Roman de l'Académie Française   see Prix Littéraires de l'Académie Française
Guardian First Book Award 120
Guild of Food Writers Awards... 120
Gustav Prellerprys vir literatuurwetenskap en letterkundige kritiek.. 233
Gustav-Heinemann-Friedenspreis für Kinder- und Jugendbücher 125
Hawthornden Prize.. 124
Heinemann (W. H.) Award   see W. H. Heinemann Award
Henriette Roland Holst-prijs.. 317
Hewett (Ed A.) Book Prize   see Ed A. Hewett Book Prize
Heywood Hill Literary Prize.. 128
Hlavky (Josef) Prize   see Cena Josefa Hlavky
Hlibov (Leonid) Prize   see National Writers Union of Ukraine Awards
Holt (Clarence L.) Literary Prize   see Clarence L. Holt Literary Prize
Honchar (Oles) Ukrainian-German Prize   see Oles Honchar Prizes
Hooft (P. C.) prijs voor Letterkunde   see P. C. Hooft-prijs voor Letterkunde
Houziaux (Joseph), Prix   see Prix Joseph Houziaux
Howard R. Marraro Prize... 177
Huetprijs (Busken)   see Busken Huetprijs
Icelandic Literary Prize.. 134
Idunn-prisen   see Tano Aschehoug-Prisen/Idunn-Prisen
ILAB-LILA Bibliography Prize.. 134
International Langhe Ceretto Prize for Food and Wine Culture 138
Iranian Book of the Year Awards 141
Irish Times Irish Literature Prizes.. 142
Isaac and Tamara Deutscher Memorial Prize 81

Itô Sei Bungaku Shô 142
Ivanov (Miroslav) Award for Non-Fiction   *see* Miroslav Ivanov Award for Non-Fiction
J. Greshoff Prijs 117
Jacob's Creek World Food Media Awards 143
James Russell Lowell Prize 319
Jan Strzelecki Prize 343
Jefferson Cup Awards 144
Jelavich (Barbara) Book Prize   *see* Barbara Jelavich Book Prize
Jewish Quarterly-Wingate Prizes 145
Joan Kelly Memorial Prize 150
Johann-Heinrich-Merck-Preis für literarische Kritik und Essay 180
John Newbery Medal 203
Johnson (Samuel) Prize   *see* BBC4 Samuel Johnson Prize for Non-Fiction
Jubilee Award for Short Stories   *see* Canadian Authors Association Literary Awards
Julien (Stanislas), Prix   *see* Prix Stanislas Julien
Kafka (Franz) Prize   *see* Franz Kafka Prize
Kaikô Takeshi Shô 147
Kalinga Prize 147
Karel Čapek Award for Literary Achievement 59
Katherine Singer Kovacs Prize 155
Keats–Shelley Prize 149
Kellendonk (Frans)-prijs   *see* Frans Kellendonk-prijs
Kelly (Joan) Memorial Prize   *see* Joan Kelly Memorial Prize
Kenneth W. Mildenberger Prize 181
Kerala Sahitya Akademi Awards 151
Kessel (Joseph) Prix   *see* Prix Joseph Kessel
King Fahd bin Abdulaziz Award for Initiative 153
Kiriyama Pacific Rim Book Prize 153
Kirsch (Robert) Award   *see* Los Angeles Times Book Prizes
Korolenko (Volodymyr) Prize   *see* National Writers Union of Ukraine Awards
Kostakowsky (Lya), Premio Anual
         see Premio Anual de Ensayo Literario Hispanoamericano Lya Kostakowsky
Kotlyarevsky (Ivan) Prize   *see* National Writers Union of Ukraine Awards
Kovacs (Katherine Singer) Prize   *see* Katherine Singer Kovacs Prize
Kraszna-Krausz Book Awards 156
Kreisel (Henry) Award for Best First Book   *see* Alberta Book Awards
Kruyskamp-prijs 157
Kumar (C. B.) Award   *see* Kerala Sahitya Akademi Awards
Kuttippuzha Award   *see* Kerala Sahitya Akademi Awards
Ladles   *see* Jacob's Creek World Food Media Awards
Lakeland Book of the Year Awards 158
Lambda Literary Awards—Lammys 158
Lannan Literary Awards 159
Lanson (Champagne) Prix   *see* Prix du Champagne Lanson
Lazarillo Prize 160
Leacock (Stephen) Memorial Medal for Humour
         see Stephen Leacock Memorial Medal for Humour
Leviant (Fenia and Yaakov) Memorial Prize
         see Fenia and Yaakov Leviant Memorial Prize
Libris Awards 162
Lilian Ida Smith Awards 338
Lima (José Lezama) Prize   *see* Premio Casa de las Americas
Literary Achievement Award 164
Llull (Ramon) Premi   *see* Premi de les Lletres Catalanes Ramon Llull

Los Angeles Times Book Prizes 167

Lukas (J. Anthony) Prize   *see* Lukas Prize Project

Lukas Prize Project 168

Macallan Gold/Silver Dagger   *see* CWA Awards

Macmillan PEN Awards 170

Macmillan Prize   *see* Macmillan PEN Awards

Macmillan Silver PEN   *see* Macmillan PEN Awards

Magnesia Litera Awards 173

Manila Critics Circle National Book Awards 175

Manitoba Literary Awards 175

Marraro (Howard R.) Prize   *see* Howard R. Marraro Prize

Marshall Shulman Book Prize 335

McColvin Medal   *see* Besterman/McColvin Medals

McCormick (E. H.) Non-Fiction Award
    see Montana New Zealand Book Awards/Best First Book of Non-Fiction Award

McLeod (Enid) Literary Prize   *see* Enid McLeod Literary Prize

McNally Robinson Book of the Year Award   *see* Manitoba Literary Awards

McTavish Sykes (Eileen) Award for Best First Book   *see* Manitoba Literary Awards

Melbourne University Literature Award   *see* Fellowship of Australian Writers Literature Awards

Merck (Johann-Heinrich) Preis
    see Johann-Heinrich-Merck-Preis für literarische Kritik und Essay

Michael L. Printz Award for Excellence in Young Adult Literature 265

Michael Smith Award   *see* Guild of Food Writers Awards

Mildenberger (Kenneth W.) Prize   *see* Kenneth W. Mildenberger Prize

Mina P. Shaughnessy Prize 334

Miroslav Ivanov Award for Non-Fiction 142

Mitchell (Eric) Prize   *see* Mitchell Prize for Art History/Eric Mitchell Prize

Mitchell Prize for Art History/Eric Mitchell Prize 183

Modern Language Association Prize for a Distinguished Bibliography 184

Modern Language Association Prize for a First Book 184

Modern Language Association Prize for Independent Scholars 185

Montana Medal   *see* Montana New Zealand Book Awards/Montana Medal

Montana New Zealand Book Awards 185

Montana New Zealand Book Awards/Best First Book of Non-Fiction Award 187

Montana New Zealand Book Awards/Montana Medal 188

Mordechai Bernstein Literary Prizes 33

Morton N. Cohen Award for a Distinguished Edition of Letters 70

Myanmar Annual National Literary Awards 191

Naipaul (Shiva) Memorial Prize   *see* Shiva Naipaul Memorial Prize

Namboodiri (K. R.) Award   *see* Kerala Sahitya Akademi Awards

National Book Awards 194

National Book Contest 194

National Book Critics Circle Awards 195

National Outdoor Book Awards 196

National Writers Union of Ukraine Awards 198

New Letters Literary Awards 201

New Millennium Writing Awards 202

New Writer Prose and Poetry Prizes 202

Newbery (John) Medal   *see* John Newbery Medal

Nibbies   *see* British Book Awards

NIKE Literary Award 205

NOMA Award for Publishing in Africa 206

Noma Bungei Shô 206

Norske Akademis Pris til Minne om Thorleif Dahl 209

Northern Palmira Prize.. 210
Northern Rock Foundation Writer Award 210
NSW Premier's Literary Awards.. 211
NSW Writer's Fellowship.. 212
Oles Honchar Prizes 130
Oro (Timón de), Concurso   *see* Concurso de Prosa y Poesía Timón de Oro
Orwell Prize 216
Otto Gelstedprisen 102
Ôya Sôichi Nonfikushon Shô 218
P. C. Hooft-prijs voor Letterkunde... 131
Palanca (Don Carlos) Memorial Awards   *see* Don Carlos Palanca Memorial Awards
Palmer (Nettie) Prize for Non-fiction   *see* Victorian Premier's Literary Awards
Palmer (Vance) Prize for Fiction   *see* Victorian Premier's Literary Awards
Pandora Award.. 220
Parker (William Riley) Prize   *see* William Riley Parker Prize
Paz (Octavio), Premio de Poesía y Ensayo   *see* Premio Octavio Paz de Poesía y Ensayo
Paz Castillo (Fernando), Premio   *see* Premio Fernándo Paz Castillo
Pemenang Anugerah MAPIM-Fuji Xerox... 222
PEN Center USA West Annual Literary Awards 224
PEN/Architectural Digest Award for Literary Writing on the Visual Arts............... 223
PEN/Jerard Fund Award 225
PEN/Martha Albrand Award for the Art of the Memoir 226
PEN/Martha Albrand Award for First Non-fiction 226
PEN/Spielvogel-Diamonstein Award for the Art of the Essay................................... 228
Peters (Ellis) Historical Dagger   *see* CWA Awards
Pla, (Josep) Premi   *see* Premi Josep Pla
Polk (George) Awards   *see* George Polk Awards
Portico Prize for Literature.. 232
Preller (Gustav) Prize   *see* Gustav Prellerprys vir literatuurwetenskap en letterkundige kritiek
Premi Josep Pla... 234
Premi de les Lletres Catalanes Ramon Llull... 233
Premio Antonio Feltrinelli 241
Premio Anual de Ensayo Literario Hispanoamericano Lya Kostakowsky 236
Premio Casa de las Americas 239
Prêmio D. Diniz... 240
Premio Fastenrath 241
Premio Fernándo Paz Castillo.. 257
Premio Internacional de Ensayo Mariano Picón Salas... 242
Premio Internazionale di Letteratura La Cultura del Mare....................................... 244
Prêmio Jabuti 245
Premio de Literatura Ricardo Mimenza Castillo 248
Premio Nacional de Literatura... 252
Premio Nezahualcóyotl de Literatura en Lenguas Indígenas..................................... 257
Premio Octavio Paz de Poesía y Ensayo.. 258
Premio Rivadeneira 261
Premio Viareggio... 263
Premios Literarios Fundación ARCIEN 263
Prijs der Nederlandse Letteren 264
Pringle (Thomas) Award   *see* Thomas Pringle Award
Printz (Michael L.) Award
        see Michael L. Printz Award for Excellence
Prix de l'Académie des Sciences, Arts et Belles Lettres de Dijon 267
Prix Amerigo Vespucci.. 307
Prix des Amis du Monde diplomatique... 267

Prix Astrolabe–Etonnants Voyageurs 269
Prix Bordin 272
Prix Bourbonnais.. 272
Prix du Champagne Lanson 273
Prix Champlain 274
Prix Daniel Bayon.. 271
Prix Erckmann-Chatrian.. 279
Prix Fnac–Andersen du livre d'entreprise 282
Prix France Télévision.. 282
Prix François 1er: prix Cognac de la critique littéraire.. 283
Prix François Billetdoux... 271
Prix François-Joseph Audiffred 269
Prix International Kadima... 287
Prix Jean Freustié 283
Prix Joseph Gantrelle... 283
Prix Joseph Houziaux... 286
Prix Joseph Kessel 289
Prix La Mazille   *see* Gourmand World Cookbook Awards
Prix des Lectrices de Elle.. 290
Prix Littéraire des Mouettes.. 292
Prix Littéraire du Parlement de la Communauté Française de Belgique............................. 300
Prix Littéraires de l'Académie Française 293
Prix Littéraires de la Société des Gens de Lettres 294
Prix de littérature Émile Bernheim 294
Prix du Livre Numérique NewsFam.com.. 295
Prix du Livre de Picardie 295
Prix des Maisons de la Presse 296
Prix Médicis de l'Essai... 296
Prix Pelléas 301
Prix Polar 301
Prix RFI–témoin du monde... 302
Prix Roberval.. 302
Prix Stanislas Julien 288
Prix Théophraste Renaudot 302
Pulitzer Prizes in Journalism, Letters, Drama and Music 309
Pushcart Prize: Best of the Small Presses 309
Queensland Premier's Literary Awards 310
Rauriser Förderungspreis 312
Raymond Williams Community Publishing Prize 375
Reed (A. W.) Lifetime Achievement Award   *see* Montana New Zealand Book Awards
Renaudot (Théophraste) Prix   *see* Prix Théophraste Renaudot
Rennyo Shô 314
Rhône-Poulenc Prize   *see* Aventis Prize
Richardson (Evelyn) Non-fiction Award   *see* Evelyn Richardson Non-fiction Award
Robert F. Sibert Informational Book Award... 336
Roderick (Colin) Prize for Australian Literature
        see Colin Roderick Prize for Australian Literature
Roland Holst (Henriette) prijs   *see* Henriette Roland Holst-prijs
Rose Mary Crawshay Prize... 75
Round (Jeremy) Award   *see* Guild of Food Writers Awards
RSM Library Prize   *see* Society of Authors Medical Book Awards
Runciman Award.. 318
Russell (Walter McRae) Award   *see* Walter McRae Russell Award
Russell Lowell (James) Prize   *see* James Russell Lowell Prize

Salas (Mariano Picón), Premio   *see* Premio Internacional de Ensayo Mariano Picón Salas

Saltire Society Literary Awards 322

Saltire Society/Times Educational Supplement Scotland Prize for Educational Publications 322

Sandrof (Ivan) Award   *see* The National Book Critics Circle Awards

Sands (Ron) Prize   *see* Lakeland Book of the Year Awards

Saskatchewan Book Awards 324

Scaglione (Aldo and Jeanne) Prize
    see Aldo and Jeanne Scaglione Prize for Comparative Literary Studies

Scaglione (Aldo and Jeanne) Prize
    see Aldo and Jeanne Scaglione Prize for French and Francophone Studies

Scaglione (Aldo and Jeanne) Prize
    see Aldo and Jeanne Scaglione Prize for Germanic Languages and Literatures

Scaglione (Aldo and Jeanne) Prize   *see* Aldo and Jeanne Scaglione Prize for Italian Studies

Scaglione (Aldo and Jeanne) Prize
    see Aldo and Jeanne Scaglione Prize for Studies in Slavic Languages and Literatures

Scaglione (Aldo and Jeanne) Prize
    see Aldo and Jeanne Scaglione Publication Award for a Manuscript in Italian Literary Studies

Scarborough (William Sanders) Prize   *see* William Sanders Scarborough Prize

Scorer (Mary) Award   *see* Manitoba Literary Awards

Scottish Book of the Year   *see* Saltire Society Literary Awards

Scottish First Book of the Year   *see* Saltire Society Literary Awards

Scottish History Book of the Year   *see* Saltire Society Literary Awards

Seidenbaum (Art) Award   *see* Los Angeles Times Book Prizes

Selskabets Pris 333

Shaughnessy (Mina P.) Prize   *see* Mina P. Shaughnessy Prize

Shiva Naipaul Memorial Prize 192

Shulman (Marshall) Book Prize   *see* Marshall Shulman Book Prize

Sibert (Robert F.) Informational Book Award   *see* Robert F. Sibert Informational Book Award

Sigmund-Freud-Preis für wissenschaftliche Prosa 100

Singapore National Book Awards 337

Sino-American Literary Exchange Prize   *see* China Literature Foundation Awards

Sir Banister Fletcher Prize of the Authors' Club 96

Slessor (Kenneth) Prize for Poetry   *see* NSW Premier's Literary Awards

Smith (Lilian Ida) Awards   *see* Lilian Ida Smith Awards

Society of Authors Medical Book Awards 339

Society of School Librarians International Book Awards 339

Spielvogel-Diamonstein Award
    see PEN/Spielvogel-Diamonstein Award

Språklig Samlings Litteraturpris 341

St John Thomas (David) Charitable Trust Awards
    see David St John Thomas Charitable Trust Awards

Stead (Christina) Award   *see* Fellowship of Australian Writers Literature Awards

Stephen Leacock Memorial Medal for Humour 161

Stern Silver PEN Prize   *see* Macmillan PEN Awards

Stewart (Douglas) Prize for Non-fiction   *see* NSW Premier's Literary Awards

Strzelecki (Jan) Prize   *see* Jan Strzelecki Prize

Sunday Telegraph Catherine Pakenham Memorial Award 344

Sunday Times Award for Literary Excellence 344

Sunday Times Young Writer of the Year Award 344

SWPA Audiobooks of the Year 346

Tano Aschehoug-Prisen/Idunn-Prisen 348

TDK Australian Audio Book Awards 349

TDK Literary Award 350

Thomas Cook/Daily Telegraph Travel Book Award 353

Thomas Pringle Award 265
Toronto Book Awards 355
Trinick (Trish) Prize   *see* TDK Australian Audio Book Awards
Tullie House Prize   *see* Lakeland Book of the Year Awards
Turner (Ethel) Prize for Young People's Literature   *see* NSW Premier's Literary Awards
Ushakov (Mykola) Prize   *see* National Writers Union of Ukraine Awards
Veillon (Charles) European Essay Prize   *see* Charles Veillon European Essay Prize
Venter (Bill) Literary Award   *see* Bill Venter/Altron Literary Award
Vespucci (Amerigo), Prix   *see* Prix Amerigo Vespucci
Victorian Premier's Literary Awards 362
Virgin Books Newcomer of the Year Award   *see* British Book Awards
Vucinich (Wayne S.)Book Prize   *see* Wayne S. Vucinich Book Prize
Výrocní ceny Nadace 365
Vysehrad Publishers Awards 365
W. H. Heinemann Award 125
W. H. Smith Children's Book of the Year   *see* British Book Awards
W. H. Smith Thumping Good Read Award 366
Walford Award for Contributions to Bibliography 367
Walter McRae Russell Award 319
Watt (David) Prize   *see* David Watt Prize
Wayne S. Vucinich Book Prize 365
Wellcome Trust Prize 368
Western Australian Premier's Book Awards 369
Wheatley Medal for an Outstanding Index 370
Whitfield Prize 372
Whiting Writers' Awards 372
Wiesel (Elie) Prize in Ethics Essay Contest   *see* Elie Wiesel Prize in Ethics Essay Contest
William Hill Sports Book of the Year 375
William Riley Parker Prize 220
William Sanders Scarborough Prize 330
Williams (Raymond) Community Publishing Prize
      see Raymond Williams Community Publishing Prize
Wilson (Ethel) Fiction Priz   *see* British Columbia Book Prizes
Wilson (Titus) Prize   *see* Lakeland Book of the Year Awards
Wine Book of the Year Gold Label Award   *see* Prix du Champagne Lanson
Wolfson History Prize 376
World Book of the Year Prize 377
Wrightson (Patricia) Prize   *see* NSW Premier's Literary Awards
Writer's Digest Annual Writing Competition 378
Writers' Alliance of Newfoundland and Labrador Provincial Book Awards 379
Yomiuri Bungaku Shô 380
Yorkshire Post Awards 381
Young Wine Writer Award 382
Zimbabwean Publishers' Literary Awards 382

Poetry

Academy of American Poets Fellowship 2
Addison Metcalf Award   *see* American Academy of Arts and Letters Annual Awards
Africa's 100 Best Books of the Twentieth Century 4
Akron Poetry Prize 7
Al-Uweis Literary Award 8

Alberta Book Awards.. 8
Aldeburgh Poetry Festival First Collection Prize.. 8
Alice Fay di Castagnola Award 61
Ambassador Book Awards.. 10
American Academy of Arts and Letters Annual Awards 11
American Academy of Arts and Letters Gold Medal 11
An duais don bhfiliocht as Gaeilge... 83
ANA/Cadbury Prize for Poetry   *see* Association of Nigerian Authors Literature Prizes
Andrei Malyshko Prize 174
Annett (R. Ross) Award for Children's Literature   *see* Alberta Book Awards
Anti-Booker Prize 13
Arar Literary Award.. 13
Arguedas (José Maria) Prize   *see* Premio Casa de las Americas
Artaud (Antonin) Prix   *see* Prix Antonin Artaud
Arts Council of England Writers' Awards... 15
Arts Council of Wales Book of the Year Awards 15
Arvon Poetry Competition... 15
Associated Writing Programs (AWP) Award Series in Poetry, Fiction and Creative Non-fiction 17
Association of Nigerian Authors Literature Prizes 18
Atlanta Review Poetry Competition 18
Atlantic Poetry Prize 19
Austrian National Award for Poetry for Children 24
Balakian (Nona) Citation   *see* The National Book Critics Circle Awards
BBC Wildlife Magazine Literary Awards... 30
BBC Wildlife Magazine Nature Writing Award   *see* BBC Wildlife Magazine Literary Awards
BBC Wildlife Magazine Poet of the Year Award   *see* BBC Wildlife Magazine Literary Awards
Beatriceprisen... 30
Bellmanpriset 31
Bernheim (Emile) Prix de littérature   *see* Prix de littérature Émile Bernheim
Bernstein (Mordechai) Literary Prizes   *see* Mordechai Bernstein Literary Prizes
Best First Book of Poetry Award
      see Montana New Zealand Book Awards
Bienek (Horst) Preis fur Lyrik   *see* Horst Bienek Preis für Lyrik
Biletsky (Oleksander) Prize   *see* National Writers Union of Ukraine Awards
Blagovist Prize.. 38
Bloom (John) Humor Award   *see* Texas Institute of Letters Awards
Blyth (R. H.) Award   *see* R. H. Blyth Award
Boardman Tasker Award 40
Bogin (George) Memorial Award   *see* George Bogin Memorial Award
Bollingen Prize in Poetry 41
Bolt (Carol) Drama Award   *see* Canadian Authors Association Literary Awards
Border Television Prize   *see* Lakeland Book of the Year Awards
Bourne (Louise Louis/Emily) Student Poetry Award
      see Louise Louis/Emily F. Bourne Student Poetry Award
Bradt Travel Writing Award   *see* BBC Wildlife Magazine Literary Awards
Brageprisen.. 45
Bridport Prize... 47
Brignetti (Rafaello), Premio   *see* Premio Letterario Isola d'Elba – Rafaello Brignetti
British Columbia Book Prizes 49
Broumovska literarni cena 51
Bucharest Writers' Association Prizes 52
Canada-Switzerland Literary Prize 57
Canadian Authors Association Literary Awards 57
Canadian Library Association Book of the Year for Children Award... 58

Canadian Literary Awards 59
Carducci (Giosue), Premio Nazionale di Poesia   *see* Premio Nazionale di Poesia Giosuè Carducci
Carême (Maurice), Prix de Poésie   *see* Prix de Poésie et Prix d'Etudes Littéraires Maurice Carême
Castagnola (Alice Fay di) Award   *see* Alice Fay di Castagnola Award
Cecil Hemley Memorial Award.. 126
Chalmers (Jack) Poetry Award   *see* Canadian Authors Association Literary Awards
Chicano/Latino Literary Prize 63
Chôkû Shô.. 66
Cholmondeley Awards 66
City of Vancouver Book Award.. 68
CNA Letterkkunde Toekenning 70
Colorado Prize 71
Concurso Annual de Literatura.. 72
Concurso de Prosa y Poesia Timón de Oro 73
Cooper (Duff) Prize   *see* Duff Cooper Prize
County of Cardiff International Poetry Competition 75
David St John Thomas Charitable Trust Awards.. 353
Davies (Hunter) Prize   *see* Lakeland Book of the Year Awards
Denis Devlin Memorial Award for Poetry.. 81
Dennis (C. J.) Prize for Poetry   *see* Victorian Premier's Literary Awards
Devlin (Denis) Memorial Award for Poetry   *see* Denis Devlin Memorial Award for Poetry
Dickinson (Emily) Award   *see* Writer Magazine/Emily Dickinson Award
Diniz (D.) Prêmio   *see* Prêmio D. Diniz
Discovery/The Nation Joan Leiman Jacobson Poetry Prizes 82
Don Carlos Palanca Memorial Awards.. 219
Dr Allama Muhammad Iqbal Award 140
Duff Cooper Prize.. 74
Eggleston (Wilfred) Award for Non-Fiction   *see* Alberta Book Awards
Elder (Ann) Poetry Award   *see* Fellowship of Australian Writers Literature Awards
Eliot (T. S.) Prize   *see* T. S. Eliot Prize
Eric Gregory Trust Fund Award 117
Estrada (Ezequiel Martinez) Prize   *see* Premio Casa de las Americas
European Jewish Publication Society Grant to Publishers.................................... 89
Evans (Hubert) Non-Fiction Prize   *see* British Columbia Book Prizes
Faber (Geoffrey) Memorial Prize   *see* Geoffrey Faber Memorial Prize
Farber (Norma) First Book Award   *see* Norma Farber First Book Award
Fellowship of Australian Writers Literature Awards 93
Feltrinelli (Antonio) Premio   *see* Premio Antonio Feltrinelli
Fernando Rielo World Mystical Poetry Prize 315
Firecracker Alternative Book Awards 94
FNB VITA Poetry Award.. 96
Forward Prizes for Poetry.. 97
Frans Kellendonk-prijs.. 149
Franz Kafka Prize.. 146
Frogmore Poetry Prize.. 101
Frost Medal.. 101
Gautier (Théophile) Prix   *see* Prix Théophile Gautier
Geoffrey Faber Memorial Prize 90
Georg Trakl Preis für Lyrik.. 355
George Bogin Memorial Award 40
Gerald Lampert Award 159
Gleebooks Prize for Literary or Cultural Criticism   *see* NSW Premier's Literary Awards
Glimmer Train Literary Awards.. 107
Golden Bike Awards   *see* Iranian Book of the Year Awards

Governor General's Literary Awards 110
Grace Leven Prize for Poetry 161
Gradam Litrochta Cló Iar-Chonnachta 111
Grand Prix de Biographie de l'Académie Française   *see* Prix Littéraires de l'Académie Française
Grand Prix de Poésie de l'Académie Française   *see* Prix Littéraires de l'Académie Française
Grand Prix Ramuz 115
Grand Prix du Roman de l'Académie Française   *see* Prix Littéraires de l'Académie Française
Gregory (Eric) Trust Fund Award   *see* Eric Gregory Trust Fund Award
Griffin Poetry Prize 117
Guardian First Book Award 120
H-shi Shô 121
Haidan Shô 122
Halldis Moren Vesaas-Prisen 122
Hemley (Cecil) Memorial Award   *see* Cecil Hemley Memorial Award
Henriette Roland Holst-prijs 317
Henry (O.) Award   *see* Texas Institute of Letters Awards
Herb Barrett Award 29
Herman Gorterprijs 109
Hertzogprys 127
Heywood Hill Literary Prize 128
Hlibov (Leonid) Prize   *see* National Writers Union of Ukraine Awards
Hooft (P. C.) prijs voor Letterkunde   *see* P. C. Hooft-prijs voor Letterkunde
Hopkins (Lee Bennett) Promising Poet Award   *see* Lee Bennett Hopkins Promising Poet Award
Horst Bienek Preis für Lyrik 35
Huchel (Peter) Preis   *see* Peter-Huchel-Preis
Icelandic Literary Prize 134
Iqbal (Dr Allama Muhammad) Award   *see* Dr Allama Muhammad Iqbal Award
Iranian Book of the Year Awards 141
Irish Times Irish Literature Prizes 142
Jacobson (Joan Leiman) Poetry Prizes
    see Discovery/The Nation Joan Leiman Jacobson Poetry Prizes
James Laughlin Award 160
Jan Campert Prize 57
Jaroslav Seifert Award 332
John Newbery Medal 203
Jones (Jesse H.) Award   *see* Texas Institute of Letters Awards
Jubilee Award for Short Stories   *see* Canadian Authors Association Literary Awards
Kadan Shô 146
Kafka (Franz) Prize   *see* Franz Kafka Prize
Kathryn A. Morton Prize in Poetry 189
Kaufman (Sue) Prize for First Fiction
    see American Academy of Arts and Letters Annual Awards
Keats–Shelley Prize 149
Kellendonk (Frans)-prijs   *see* Frans Kellendonk-prijs
Kerala Sahitya Akademi Awards 151
Khatulistiwa Literary Award 152
Kick Start Poets Open Poetry Competition 152
King Fahd bin Abdulaziz Award for Initiative 153
Kingsley Tufts Poetry Prize 358
Kirsch (Robert) Award   *see* Los Angeles Times Book Prizes
Klaus Rifbjergs Debutantpris for Lyrik 315
Korolenko (Volodymyr) Prize   *see* National Writers Union of Ukraine Awards
Kotlyarevsky (Ivan) Prize   *see* National Writers Union of Ukraine Awards
Kreisel (Henry) Award for Best First Book   *see* Alberta Book Awards

Kristal Vilenice Award   *see* Vilenica International Literary Awards
Kumar (C. B.) Award   *see* Kerala Sahitya Akademi Awards
Kuttippuzha Award   *see* Kerala Sahitya Akademi Awards
Lakeland Book of the Year Awards 158
Lambda Literary Awards—Lammys... 158
Lampert (Gerald) Award   *see* Gerald Lampert Award
Lannan Literary Awards... 159
Laughlin (James) Award   *see* James Laughlin Award
Lazarillo Prize 160
Lee Bennett Hopkins Promising Poet Award 131
Lenore Marshall Poetry Prize.. 178
Leven (Grace) Prize for Poetry   *see* Grace Leven Prize for Poetry
Lilian Ida Smith Awards... 338
Lilly (Ruth) Poetry Prize   *see* Ruth Lilly Poetry Prize
Lima (José Lezama) Prize   *see* Premio Casa de las Americas
Literary Achievement Award... 164
Literaturpreis der Landeshauptstadt Stuttgart 164
Long Madgett (Naomi) Poetry Award   *see* Naomi Long Madgett Poetry Award
Lontar Literary Award 167
Los Angeles Times Book Prizes.. 167
Louise Louis/Emily F. Bourne Student Poetry Award 44
Lucille Medwick Memorial Award 179
Lucy B. & C. W. van der Hoogt Prize.. 360
Lyric Poetry Award.. 169
Mackay (Jessie) Poetry Award
    see Montana New Zealand Book Awards
Malyshko (Andrei) Prize   *see* Andrei Malyshko Prize
Manila Critics Circle National Book Awards... 175
Marshall (Lenore) Poetry Prize   *see* Lenore Marshall Poetry Prize
Marten Toonder Award 178
Mary Gilmore Award... 104
Medwick (Lucille) Memorial Award   *see* Lucille Medwick Memorial Award
Melbourne University Literature Award   *see* Fellowship of Australian Writers Literature Awards
Michael L. Printz Award for Excellence in Young Adult Literature... 265
Mitchell (W. O.) Prize   *see* W. O. Mitchell Prize
Montalte (Louis) Prix de Poésie   *see* Prix de Poésie Louis Montalte
Montana New Zealand Book Awards... 185
Montana New Zealand Book Awards/Best First Book of Poetry Award 187
Mordechai Bernstein Literary Prizes.. 33
Morton (Kathryn A.) Prize in Poetry   *see* Kathryn A. Morton Prize in Poetry
Morton Dauwen Zabel Award   *see* American Academy of Arts and Letters Annual Awards
Mr H Prize   *see* H-shi Shô
Myanmar Annual National Literary Awards 191
Nakahara Chûya Prize.. 192
Namboodiri (K. R.)Award   *see* Kerala Sahitya Akademi Awards
Naomi Long Madgett Poetry Award 166
National Book Awards... 194
National Book Contest.. 194
National Book Critics Circle Awards.. 195
National Outdoor Book Awards.. 196
National Poetry Competition.. 198
National Writers Union of Ukraine Awards 198
NCTE Award for Excellence in Poetry for Children 199
Nelligan (Émile) Prix   *see* Prix Émile-Nelligan

Nestlé Smarties Book Prize 199
Neustadt International Prize for Literature 200
New Millennium Writing Awards 202
New Writer Prose and Poetry Prizes 202
Newbery (John) Medal   see John Newbery Medal
Newcastle Poetry Prize 204
NIKE Literary Award 205
NOMA Award for Publishing in Africa 206
Norma Farber First Book Award 92
Norske Lyrikklubbens Pris 210
Northern Palmira Prize 210
Northern Rock Foundation Writer Award 210
Northern Writers' Awards 211
NSW Premier's Literary Awards 211
NSW Writer's Fellowship 212
Okigbo (Christopher) Prize   see Association of Nigerian Authors Literature Prizes
Olive Schreiner Prize 331
Ornish (Natalie) Poetry Award   see Texas Institute of Letters Awards
Oro (Timón de), Concurso   see Concurso de Prosa y Poesía Timón de Oro
Osterweil (Joyce) Award for Poetry   see PEN/Joyce Osterweil Award for Poetry
Ottakar's Faber National Poetry Competition 218
P. C. Hooft-prijs voor Letterkunde 131
Pakokku U Ohn Pe Literary and Education Awards 219
Palanca (Don Carlos) Memorial Awards   see Don Carlos Palanca Memorial Awards
Palmer (Nettie) Prize for Non-fiction   see Victorian Premier's Literary Awards
Palmer (Vance) Prize for Fiction   see Victorian Premier's Literary Awards
Paz (Octavio), Premio de Poesía y Ensayo   see Premio Octavio Paz de Poesía y Ensayo
Peer Poetry International Competition 221
PEN Center USA West Annual Literary Awards 224
PEN/Joyce Osterweil Award for Poetry 225
PEN/Voelcker Award for Poetry 229
Peter-Huchel-Preis 132
Peterloo Poets Open Poetry Competition 229
Poetry Life Open Poetry Competition 231
Poetry London Competition 232
Portico Prize for Literature 232
Prêmio Academia Brasileira de Letras de Poesia 235
Premio Adonais de Poesía 235
Premio Antonio Feltrinelli 241
Premio Casa de las Americas 239
Premio del Rey Ocho Venado 261
Prêmio D. Diniz 240
Premio Fastenrath 241
Premio Hispanoamericano de Poesía Sor Juana Inés de la Cruz 242
Prêmio Jabuti 245
Premio Letterario Isola d'Elba – Rafaello Brignetti 246
Premio Nacional de Literatura 252
Premio Nacional de Literatura El Búho 253
Premio Nacional de Poesía Tintanueva 255
Premio Nazionale di Poesia Giosue Carducci 257
Premio Nezahualcóyotl de Literatura en Lenguas Indigenas 257
Premio Octavio Paz de Poesía y Ensayo 258
Premio de Poesía Ciudad de Medellín 259
Premio de Poesía Mensajero 259

Premio Reina Sofía de Poesía Iberoamericana 260
Premio Viareggio 263
Premios Literarios Fundación ARCIEN 263
Prijs der Nederlandse Letteren 264
Pringle (Thomas) Award   *see* Thomas Pringle Award
Printz (Michael L.) Award   *see* Michael L. Printz Award for Excellence
Prix Antonin Artaud 268
Prix Apollinaire 268
Prix Charles Vildrac de la Poésie 308
Prix Claude Sernet 304
Prix Émile-Nelligan 299
Prix Goncourt 285
Prix Heredia 286
Prix de littérature Émile Bernheim 294
Prix Littéraires de l'Académie Française 293
Prix Littéraires du Ministère de la Jeunesse et des Sports 293
Prix Littéraires de la Société des Gens de Lettres 294
Prix du Livre en Poitou-Charentes 296
Prix Paul Verlaine 307
Prix de Poésie Louis Montalte 301
Prix de Poésie et Prix d'Etudes Littéraires Maurice Carême 273
Prix Théophile Gautier 284
Prix Voronca 308
Pulitzer Prizes in Journalism, Letters, Drama and Music 309
Pushcart Prize: Best of the Small Presses 309
Queen's Gold Medal for Poetry 310
R. H. Blyth Award 39
Raiziss/de Palchi Translation Award 311
Rajasthan Urdu Academy Awards 311
Ramuz (C. F.), Grand Prix   *see* Grand Prix Ramuz
Reed (A. W.) Lifetime Achievement Award   *see* Montana New Zealand Book Awards
Rielo (Fernando) World Mystical Poetry Prize   *see* Fernando Rielo World Mystical Poetry Prize
Rifbjergs (Klaus) Debutantpris for Lyrik   *see* Klaus Rifbjergs Debutantpris for Lyrik
Rimbaud (Arthur), Prix   *see* Prix Littéraires du Ministère de la Jeunesse et des Sports
River Styx International Poetry Contest 316
Robert H. Winner Memorial Award 376
Roland Holst (Henriette) prijs   *see* Henriette Roland Holst-prijs
Rosenthal (Richard and Hinda) Foundation Award
        see American Academy of Arts and Letters Annual Awards
Ruth Lilly Poetry Prize 162
Saidi (Bismil) Prize   *see* Rajasthan Urdu Academy Awards
Saltire Society Literary Awards 322
Sandrof (Ivan) Award   *see* The National Book Critics Circle Awards
Sands (Ron) Prize   *see* Lakeland Book of the Year Awards
Sasakawa Haiku Prize 324
Saskatchewan Book Awards 324
Scholz (Hugo) Prize   *see* Broumovska literarni cena
Schreiner (Olive) Prize   *see* Olive Schreiner Prize
Scottish Book of the Year   *see* Saltire Society Literary Awards
Scottish First Book of the Year   *see* Saltire Society Literary Awards
Scottish History Book of the Year   *see* Saltire Society Literary Awards
Seidenbaum (Art) Award   *see* Los Angeles Times Book Prizes
Seifert (Jaroslav) Award   *see* Jaroslav Seifert Award
Sernet (Claude) Prix   *see* Prix Claude Sernet

Shagil (Ahteramuddin) Prize   *see* Rajasthan Urdu Academy Awards

Shelley Memorial Award 334

Shirani (Mehmood) Prize   *see* Rajasthan Urdu Academy Awards

Simonenko (Vasyl) Prize   *see* Vasyl Simonenko Prize

Singapore National Book Awards 337

Slessor (Kenneth) Prize for Poetry   *see* NSW Premier's Literary Awards

Smith (Lilian Ida) Awards   *see* Lilian Ida Smith Awards

Sofola (Zulu) Prize   *see* Zulu Sofola Prize

Spectrum Prize   *see* Association of Nigerian Authors Literature Prizes

Språklig Samlings Litteraturpris 341

St John Thomas (David) Charitable Trust Awards
        see David St John Thomas Charitable Trust Awards

Staatliche Förderungspreise für junge Schriftstellerinnen und Schriftsteller 341

State Prizes for Literature 342

Stead (Christina) Award   *see* Fellowship of Australian Writers Literature Awards

Stevens (Wallace) Award   *see* Wallace Stevens Award

Stewart (Douglas) Prize for Non-fiction   *see* NSW Premier's Literary Awards

Stryjova (Marie) Prize   *see* Broumovska literarni cena

Sunday Times Young Writer of the Year Award 344

Sveriges Radios Lyrikpris/Sveriges Radio P1:s Romanpris 346

T. S. Eliot Prize 87

T. S. Eliot Prize for Poetry 88

Tabla Poetry Competition 347

Takami Jun Shô 347

Tanning Prize 347

Texas Institute of Letters Awards 351

Tezuka Osamu Bunka Shô 351

Thomas Pringle Award 265

Tolman Cunard Prize   *see* Forward Prizes for Poetry

Toonder (Martin) Award   *see* Marten Toonder Award

Trakl (Georg) Preis für Lyrik   *see* Georg Trakl Preis für Lyrik

Tufts (Kate) Discovery Award   *see* Kingsley Tufts Poetry Prize

Tufts (Kingsley) Poetry Prize   *see* Kingsley Tufts Poetry Prize

Tullie House Prize   *see* Lakeland Book of the Year Awards

Turner (Ethel) Prize for Young People's Literature   *see* NSW Premier's Literary Awards

Turner (Steven) Award   *see* Texas Institute of Letters Awards

Ushakov (Mykola) Prize   *see* National Writers Union of Ukraine Awards

Vasyl Simonenko Prize 337

Ver Poets Open Competition 362

Verb Writing Competition BBC 362

Verlaine (Paul) Prix   *see* Prix Paul Verlaine

Victorian Premier's Literary Awards 362

Vildrac (Charles), Prix de la Poésie   *see* Prix Charles Vildrac de la Poésie

Vilenica International Literary Award   *see* Vilenica International Literary Awards

Vilenica International Literary Awards 363

Vursell (Harold D.) Memorial Award
        see American Academy of Arts and Letters Annual Awards

Výrocní ceny Nadace 365

W. O. Mitchell Prize 183

Wallace Stevens Award 342

Walt Whitman Award 373

Waterstone's Prize   *see* Forward Prizes for Poetry

Western Australian Premier's Book Awards 369

Whitbread Book of the Year and Literary Awards 371

Whiting Writers' Awards.. 372
Whitman (Walt) Award   *see* Walt Whitman Award
William Carlos Williams Award... 375
Williams (William Carlos) Award   *see* William Carlos Williams Award
Wilson (Ethel) Fiction Priz   *see* British Columbia Book Prizes
Wilson (Titus) Prize   *see* Lakeland Book of the Year Awards
Winner (Robert H.) Memorial Award   *see* Robert H. Winner Memorial Award
Wittig (Joseph) Prize   *see* Broumovska literarni cena
World Wide Writers Competition.. 377
Wrightson (Patricia) Prize   *see* NSW Premier's Literary Awards
Writer Magazine/Emily Dickinson Award... 378
Writer's Digest Annual Writing Competition 378
Writer's Journal Annual Short Story Contest 378
Writers' Alliance of Newfoundland and Labrador Provincial Book Awards 379
Writers' Week Poetry Competition.. 379
Yomiuri Bungaku Shô 380
Yoshikawa Eiji Bungaku Shô 381
Zulu Sofola Prize 339

Translation

Akademieprys vir Vertaalde Werk.. 6
Akademiets Oversætterpris 6
Aldo and Jeanne Scaglione Prize for a Translation of a Literary Work.. 328
Aldo and Jeanne Scaglione Prize for a Translation of a Scholarly Study of Literature..................... 329
André-Gide-Preis für deutsch-französische Literaturübersetzungen 104
ASF Translation Prize.. 16
Astrid Lindgren Translation Prize.. 163
Bastian Prize 29
Bataillon (Laure) Prix   *see* Prix Laure Bataillon
Bernard Shaw Prize.. 334
Biletsky (Oleksander) Prize   *see* National Writers Union of Ukraine Awards
Braem (Helmut M.) Preis   *see* Helmut M. Braem Preis
British Comparative Literature Association Translation Prize.. 50
Bucharest Writers' Association Prizes... 52
Calwer Hermann-Hesse-Preis.. 56
Canada-Switzerland Literary Prize 57
Cavour (Grinzane) Premio   *see* Premio Grinzane Cavour
Celan (Paul) Preis   *see* Paul-Celan-Preis
Christoph-Martin-Wieland-Preis 373
Coindreau (Maurice-Edgar) Prix   *see* Prix Maurice-Edgar Coindreau
Dahl (Thorlief), Norske Akademis Pris   *see* Norske Akademis Pris til Minne om Thorleif Dahl
de Nerval (Gérard), Prix   *see* Prix Gérard de Nerval
Eesti Kirjanduse Aastapreemia.. 86
European Jewish Publication Society Grant to Publishers... 89
Fenia and Yaakov Leviant Memorial Prize 162
Florio (John) Prize   *see* John Florio Prize
Förderungspreis für Literatur 97
Franko (Ivan) Prize   *see* Ivan Franko Prize
Gide (André) Preis   *see* André-Gide-Preis
Glassco (John) Prize for Literary Translation
     see John Glassco Prize for Literary Translation

Governor General's Literary Awards 110
Grand Prix Halperine-Kaminsky 112
Gregory Kolovakos Award 154
Gyula Illyes Prize 135
Harold Morton Landon Translation Award 159
Hellenic Foundation for Culture Translation Award 125
Helmut M. Braem Preis 45
Heywood Hill Literary Prize 128
Hlibov (Leonid) Prize   *see* National Writers Union of Ukraine Awards
Icelandic Children's Book Prize 134
Illyes (Gyula) Prize   *see* Gyula Illyes Prize
Independent Foreign Fiction Prize 136
Institutció de les Lletres Catalanes Translation Prize 137
Ivan Franko Prize 100
Jan Parandowski Prize 220
Johann-Heinrich-Voss-Preis für Übersetzung 364
John Florio Prize 96
John Glassco Prize for Literary Translation/Prix de Traduction John-Glassco 105
Josef Jungmann Prize 146
Jungmann (Josef) Prize   *see* Josef Jungmann Prize
Kerala Sahitya Akademi Awards 151
Kolovakos (Gregory) Award   *see* Gregory Kolovakos Award
Korean Literature Translation Award 155
Korolenko (Volodymyr) Prize   *see* National Writers Union of Ukraine Awards
Kotlyarevsky (Ivan) Prize   *see* National Writers Union of Ukraine Awards
Kulturdepartementets Premiering av Barne- og Ungdomslitteratur 157
Kumar (C. B.) Award   *see* Kerala Sahitya Akademi Awards
Kuttippuzha Award   *see* Kerala Sahitya Akademi Awards
Landon (Harold Morton) Translation Award   *see* Harold Morton Landon Translation Award
Leviant (Fenia and Yaakov) Memorial Prize   *see* Fenia and Yaakov Leviant Memorial Prize
Lindgren (Astrid) Translation Prize   *see* Astrid Lindgren Translation Prize
Literaturpreis der Landeshauptstadt Stuttgart 164
Lois Roth Award for a Translation of a Literary Work 318
Lu Xun Literature Awards 168
Magnesia Litera Awards 173
Manheim (Ralph) Medal for Translation   *see* PEN/Ralph Manheim Medal for Translation
Marsh Award for Children's Literature in Translation 177
Ministry of Culture National Translation Prize 182
Mishima Yukio Shô 182
Monteiro Lobato Award 189
Namboodiri (K. R.) Award   *see* Kerala Sahitya Akademi Awards
National Writers Union of Ukraine Awards 198
Norske Akademis Pris til Minne om Thorleif Dahl 209
Österreichischer Staatspreis für Europäische Literatur 217
Österreichischer Staatspreis für Literarische Übersetzer 217
Parandowski (Jan) Prize   *see* Jan Parandowski Prize
Paul-Celan-Preis 61
PEN Award for Poetry in Translation 223
PEN/Book-of-the-Month Club Translation Prize 223
PEN/Ralph Manheim Medal for Translation 228
Petrarca-Prize for Translation 229
Poggioli (Renato) Translation Award   *see* Renato Poggioli Translation Award
Premia Bohemica 235
Premio Grinzane Cavour 241

Premio Grinzane Editoria   *see* Premio Grinzane Cavour

Prêmio Jabuti 245

Premio Letterario Mondello Città di Palermo 246

Premio Nacional a la mejor traducción 254

Premio Nacional a la obra de un traductor.. 255

Prêmio Paulo Rónai 262

Premio Valle Inclán 263

Prix Baudelaire 270

Prix FIT Aurore Boréale de la traduction 281

Prix Gérard de Nerval 299

Prix International Kadima... 287

Prix Laure Bataillon.. 270

Prix Maurice-Edgar Coindreau... 276

Prix Tristan Tzara de Traduction 306

Raiziss/de Palchi Translation Award.. 311

Renato Poggioli Translation Award 232

Rónai (Paulo), Premio   *see* Prêmio Paulo Rónai

Roth (Lois) Award   *see* Lois Roth Award for a Translation of a Literary Work

Sasakawa Prize for Translation 324

SATI Award For Outstanding Translation 325

Scaglione (Aldo and Jeanne) Prize
     see Aldo and Jeanne Scaglione Prize for a Translation of a Literary Work

Scaglione (Aldo and Jeanne) Prize
     see Aldo and Jeanne Scaglione Prize for a Translation of a Scholarly Study of Literature

Schlegel-Tieck Prize.. 330

Scott Moncrieff Prize 332

Shaw (Bernard) Prize   *see* Bernard Shaw Prize

Sjöberg (Leif and Inger) Prize   *see* ASF Translation Prize

Staatliche Förderungspreise für junge Schriftstellerinnen und Schriftsteller...................................... 341

Suomalaisen kirjallisuuden tiedotuskeskus.. 345

Teixeira-Gomes Prize.. 350

Tibor-Déry-Preis.. 78

Translated Book Contest... 356

Tzara (Tristan), Prix de Traduction   *see* Prix Tristan Tzara de Traduction

Ushakov (Mykola) Prize   *see* National Writers Union of Ukraine Awards

Vondel Translation Prize 364

Voss (Johann Heinrich)-Preis für Übersetzung
     see Johann-Heinrich-Voss-Preis für Übersetzung

Vysehrad Publishers Awards... 365

Wieland (Christoph-Martin) Preis   *see* Christoph-Martin-Wieland-Preis

Yomiuri Bungaku Shô 380

Yukio (Mishima) Shô   *see* Mishima Yukio Shô